'80s Chart-Toppers

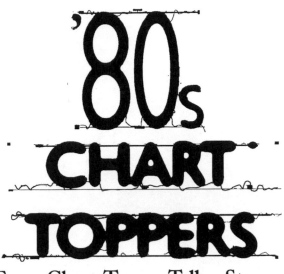

'80s CHART TOPPERS

Every Chart-Topper Tells a Story

Sharon Davis

MAINSTREAM
PUBLISHING

EDINBURGH AND LONDON

First published in Great Britain in 1999 by
MAINSTREAM PUBLISHING COMPANY (EDINBURGH) LTD
7 Albany Street
Edinburgh EH1 3UG

ISBN 1 85158 838 8

A catalogue record for this book is available from the British Library

Typeset in Plantin
Printed and bound in Great Britain by Creative Print Design Ltd

*This book is dedicated to the memory of
Graham 'Fatman' Canter and our
fun life together*

BRITISH NO.1 SINGLES

1980–89

CONTENTS

Introduction   13

1980
January   THE PRETENDERS   Brass In Pocket   17
February   KENNY ROGERS   Coward Of The County   21
March   BLONDIE   Atomic   24
April   THE DETROIT SPINNERS   30
               Working My Way Back To You/Forgive Me Girl
May   DEXY'S MIDNIGHT RUNNERS   Geno   35
June   DON McLEAN   Crying   37
July   OLIVIA NEWTON-JOHN   Xanadu   40
August   ODYSSEY   Use It Up And Wear It Out   45
September   THE POLICE   Don't Stand So Close To Me   49
October   BARBRA STREISAND   Woman In Love   53
November   ABBA   Super Trouper   60
December   JOHN LENNON   (Just Like) Starting Over   78

1981
January   JOHN LENNON   Imagine   87
February   JOHN LENNON   Woman   88
March   SHAKIN' STEVENS   This Ole House   94
April   BUCKS FIZZ   Making Your Mind Up   96
May   ADAM AND THE ANTS   Stand And Deliver   98
June   SMOKEY ROBINSON   Being With You   101
July   MICHAEL JACKSON   One Day In Your Life   107
August   SHAKIN' STEVENS   Green Door   112
September   SOFT CELL   Tainted Love   115
October   ADAM AND THE ANTS   Prince Charming   119
November   QUEEN AND DAVID BOWIE   Under Pressure   122
December   HUMAN LEAGUE   Don't You Want Me?   132

1982

January	BUCKS FIZZ The Land Of Make Believe	136
February	THE JAM A Town Called Malice/Precious	137
March	KRAFTWERK The Model/Computer Love	142
April	BUCKS FIZZ My Camera Never Lies	145
May	PAUL MCCARTNEY AND STEVIE WONDER	147
	Ebony And Ivory	
June	MADNESS House Of Fun	155
July	IRENE CARA Fame	159
August	DEXY'S MIDNIGHT RUNNERS	162
	Come On Eileen	
September	SURVIVOR Eye Of The Tiger	164
October	CULTURE CLUB	167
	Do You Really Want To Hurt Me?	
November	EDDY GRANT I Don't Wanna Dance	170
December	THE JAM Beat Survivor	173

1983

January	PHIL COLLINS You Can't Hurry Love	175
February	MEN AT WORK Down Under	180
March	MICHAEL JACKSON Billie Jean	182
April	DURAN DURAN	188
	Is There Something I Should Know?	
May	SPANDAU BALLET True	191
June	THE POLICE Every Breath You Take	194
July	ROD STEWART Baby Jane	196
August	PAUL YOUNG	205
	Wherever I Lay My Hat (That's My Home)	
September	UB40 Red Red Wine	209
October	CULTURE CLUB Karma Chameleon	212
November	BILLY JOEL Uptown Girl	215
December	FLYING PICKETS Only You	220

1984

January	PAUL MCCARTNEY Pipes Of Peace	220
February	FRANKIE GOES TO HOLLYWOOD Relax	225
March/April	LIONEL RICHIE Hello	227
May	DURAN DURAN The Reflex	235
June	WHAM! Wake Me Up Before You Go Go	239
July/August	FRANKIE GOES TO HOLLYWOOD	242
	Two Tribes	
September	GEORGE MICHAEL Careless Whisper	245
October	STEVIE WONDER	247
	I Just Called To Say I Love You	

November   CHAKA KHAN   I Feel For You   256
December   BAND AID   Do They Know It's Christmas?   260

1985
January   FOREIGNER   I Want To Know What Love Is   263
February   DEAD OR ALIVE   266
                You Spin Me Round (Like A Record)
March   PHIL COLLINS AND PHILIP BAILEY   268
                Easy Lover
April   USA FOR AFRICA We Are The World   271
May   THE CROWD   You'll Never Walk Alone   274
June   SISTER SLEDGE   Frankie   276
July   EURYTHMICS   There Must Be An Angel   279
                (Playing With My Heart)
August   MADONNA   Into The Groove   285
September   DAVID BOWIE AND MICK JAGGER   288
                Dancing In The Street
October   MIDGE URE   If I Was   290
November   WHAM!   I'm Your Man   293
December   WHITNEY HOUSTON   295
                Saving All My Love For You

1986
January   PET SHOP BOYS West End Girls   299
February   BILLY OCEAN   When The Going Gets Tough,   301
                The Tough Get Going
March   DIANA ROSS   Chain Reaction   304
April   CLIFF RICHARD AND THE YOUNG ONES   317
                Living Doll
May   GEORGE MICHAEL A Different Corner   318
June   WHAM!   The Edge Of Heaven   319
July   MADONNA   Papa Don't Preach   321
August   CHRIS DE BURGH   The Lady In Red   322
September   COMMUNARDS   Don't Leave Me This Way   325
October   MADONNA   True Blue   328
November   BERLIN   Take My Breath Away   329
December   EUROPE   The Final Countdown   331

1987
January   JACKIE WILSON   332
                Reet Petite (The Sweetest Girl In Town)
February   GEORGE MICHAEL AND ARETHA FRANKLIN   337
                I Knew You Were Waiting (For Me)

March	BEN E. KING Stand By Me	345
April	BOY GEORGE Everything I Own	348
May	STARSHIP Nothing's Gonna Stop Us Now	350
June	MADONNA La Isla Bonita	352
July	WHITNEY HOUSTON I Wanna Dance With Somebody (Who Loves Me)	355
August	PET SHOP BOYS It's A Sin	358
September	MICHAEL JACKSON AND SIEDAH GARRETT I Just Can't Stop Loving You	359
October	RICK ASTLEY Never Gonna Give You Up	370
November	BEE GEES You Win Again	373
December	PET SHOP BOYS Always On My Mind	381

1988

January	BELINDA CARLISLE Heaven Is A Place On Earth	382
February	KYLIE MINOGUE I Should Be So Lucky	385
March	ASWAD Don't Turn Around	391
April	PET SHOP BOYS Heart	393
May	S EXPRESS Theme From S Express	396
June	WET WET WET With A Little Help From My Friends	397
July	BROS I Owe You Nothing	400
August	YAZZ AND THE PLASTIC POPULATION The Only Way Is Up	403
September	PHIL COLLINS A Groovy Kind Of Love	404
October	THE HOLLIES He Ain't Heavy, He's My Brother	407
November	WHITNEY HOUSTON One Moment In Time	411
December	CLIFF RICHARD Mistletoe And Wine	416

1989

January	KYLIE MINOGUE AND JASON DONOVAN Especially For You	430
February	SIMPLE MINDS Belfast Child	432
March	JASON DONOVAN Too Many Broken Hearts	436
April	MADONNA Like A Prayer	438
May	BANGLES Eternal Flame	443
June	THE CHRISTIANS Ferry 'Cross The Mersey	445
July	SOUL II SOUL FEATURING CARON WHEELER Back To Life (However Do You Want Me)	448

August/   BLACK BOX   Ride On Time   452
September
October   LISA STANSFIELD   All Around The World   453
November   NEW KIDS ON THE BLOCK   You Got It   456
               (The Right Stuff)
December   BAND AID II   Do They Know It's Christmas?   461

INTRODUCTION

The '80s were a decade of rock music, glam music, charity music, gay music, pop music and so much more, although many would suggest it was a decade which should be remembered with some indifference, perhaps even disinterest, following as it did the wild and disco-dominated '70s. But let's think positively and wander through some of the musical highlights because the '80s were far from dull.

Only a handful of acts crossed over from the '70s into the new decade: Abba, the Police, Blondie, Queen, David Bowie and, of course, Rod Stewart, the Bee Gees and the evergreen Cliff Richard. To a certain extent, and in their own inimitable style, these guys are still with us a decade later. That's some staying power!

The '80s were determined to abandon the '70s' disco stranglehold. Now known as 'dance', it failed to totally escape the pull of the beat. Not too many acts reached the pole position, but the American trio Odyssey, Irene Cara and Chaka Khan and the male outfit the Detroit Spinners did! Sister Sledge, Eddy Grant and Madonna followed, flying the varying degrees of the dance flag as nightclubs were packed with dancers. However, the '80s belonged to Michael Jackson, who switched from beat to ballad, as a soloist and duettist with old and new. The rise of Jackson into international stardom was expected but the magnitude of that spiralling success took everyone by surprise – except, possibly, the artist himself. With world power, though, came disaster in the form of allegations of child abuse, which, even into the '90s, remain prevalent in his public life, despite attempts to curb the accusing fingers.

Along with Jackson, the American élite included Barbra Streisand, Diana Ross, Ben E. King, Lionel Richie, Smokey Robinson and Stevie Wonder. Unfortunately they could muster only one chart-topper each. Nonetheless, pure class!

The '80s were also a decade of glamour thanks to the commercial birth of the stylish New Romantic movement spearheaded by Duran Duran, Spandau Ballet and Human League. The music was delicately presented, with a sharp image to match. As an offshoot, the glamour of the costume and the pull of the greasepaint were highlighted by Boy George and Culture Club and by Soft Cell, while Dexy's Midnight Runners' image was more, how shall I say, earthy. Then, as if to blow that statement into obscurity, Adam Ant dressed as his music dictated – pirates on vinyl indeed! It sounds dreadful, doesn't it? But believe me, the whole scenario was immense fun.

Dance music Brit-style was at its peak during the '80s thanks to the dangerously innovative Frankie Goes To Hollywood, Pet Shop Boys and Communards, among others. However, two young men, Andrew Ridgeley and George Michael, were responsible for the most unexpected of British explosions. Wham! was quickly born and disbanded, leaving a somewhat sombre Michael to hit the soloist trail to peak as a megastar, although, like Jackson before him, he too would fall foul of the law. Eurovision Song Contest contestants and subsequent hit makers Bucks Fizz also enjoyed a lengthy success story despite their critics, and with the bouncy European sound came rock'n'roll courtesy of Shakin' Stevens and reggae courtesy of Aswad. Dull? Not a chance in hell!

And in this decade crammed with musical change, the British music scene had never been stronger. Stock, Aitken and Waterman, music makers of extraordinary proportions, nurtured artists into stars. Their successes were too numerous to list but a mention of Kylie Minogue and Jason Donovan, late of Neighbours, will bring back memories, as will, I hope, the soulful drawl of Rick Astley. The SAW trio also spearheaded the recording of the benefit single 'Do They Know It's Christmas?' by Band Aid II, another offshoot of the most adventurous and biggest money spinner of all time. Bob Geldof's dream of helping the starving nation of Ethiopia had spawned the first version of 'Do They Know It's Christmas?'. Recorded by a host of British acts, the single gave birth to the Live Aid charity gala and later inspired the USA For Africa project. It was a joining of musical forces that spanned countries to give financial aid to those dying of hunger.

Unfortunately this tragedy wasn't isolated, as during the decade football disasters stunned the nation, prompting artists to once more band as one to record a pair of benefit singles under the names the Crowd and, later, the Christians. And, of course, this was the decade when a Beatle died. John Lennon was shot dead; this time, the world grieved openly.

Oh, there's so much more to tell, but if I carry on much longer there'll be no need to read through the following pages. Suffice to say, the '80s were a decade of fun music, romance, political protest, computerised whizzy things, funk/soul and controversy. Like the '60s and '70s, this decade catered for all musical preferences and was a challenge to write about and a joy to listen to.

I had believed that having completed the first two decades of this chart-topping trilogy, the '80s would be a doddle by comparison. How could I have been so misled! This book took on a life of its own, running into hundreds of manuscript pages with a seemingly never-ending supply of clippings, fanzines, articles, interviews and so on. As before, the numerous artists' biographies were an absolute delight to read and are, with pleasure, credited at the close of each chart-topper section. Thank you for sharing your knowledge. Reference books – where would we be without them? – were also consulted, none more so than my copy of British Hit Singles, published by Guinness and compiled by Paul Gambaccini, Jonathan Rice and Tim Rice. Thank you, guys!

The '80s project was an awesome but satisfying task from start to finish, kept under control by my head researcher Gerry Constable who, as the trilogy progressed, recruited an equally dedicated (is that the right word?!) team. So, folks, my thanks to Phil Symes, Andy Hill, Julie Rough, Ivan Constable (late of the Punk and New Romantic movements), Chris Williams, the staff in the music section at Eastbourne's library in East Sussex (long may you stay ladies!), Gail Nixon and everyone who supported us during these three long, and often tetchy, years. We have achieved our goal. See, I said it could be done!

As always, my greatest thanks to (a now relieved) Bill Campbell at Mainstream Publishing, for keeping the musical faith. We made it happen!

That's all for now, except to say a big thank you to the many artists whose talent made this book possible and to you, the readers, for your continued loyalty. It's been just great. See you in the '50s!

Sharon Davis
September 1999

January 1980

THE PRETENDERS

Brass In Pocket

Through compilations and reissues, the sound of the Pretenders lives on. The group's achievements during its life were second to none; in fact, their music has stood the test of time, particularly this chart-topper, thanks to the outstanding vocal quality of Ms Hynde.

Chrissie Hynde, born in Akron, Ohio, on 7 September 1951, was raised on American R&B before becoming the guitarist with a group called Saturday Sunday Matinee during the mid-'60s. Following three years as a student attending Kent State University, Hynde relocated to London, where she became a model at St Martin's School of Art during 1973. The young girl later befriended Nick Kent, journalist for the weekly music paper NME; through him Hynde joined the ranks as a writer.

Late in 1974 and following a short spell working in Sex, a clothes store owned by Malcolm McLaren, Hynde moved to Paris to pursue her growing music ambitions. Once there, she joined the Frenchies, taking the role of lead singer. From France, Hynde returned to America and drifted through the group named Jack Rabbit before making London her home to perform with the Berk Brothers.

In 1977 Hynde appeared on vinyl for the first time, as support vocalist on Chris Spedding's 'Hurt' and on a demo tape for Dave Hill, late of Anchor Records, soon to be signed to Real Records. With her ambitions now starting to be realised, Hynde decided she needed her own group of musicians to further her career. To this end she recruited James Honeyman-Scott, born in Hereford on 4 November 1956, Pete Farndon, also born in Hereford on 12 June 1952, and Martin Chambers, born, you've guessed it, in Hereford on 4 September 1951. Together they recorded the title 'Stop Your Sobbing' via a relationship with Real Records and swiped the name 'the Pretenders' from the single 'The Great Pretender' recorded by the Platters and, of course, Queen's Freddie Mercury.

'Stop Your Sobbing', the Pretenders' debut single, presented them with their first hit by peaking in the British Top 40 during February 1979. Five months on, the follow-up 'Kid' likewise became a Top 40 hit. Prior to and following these releases, the Pretenders embarked upon a series of concert dates, taking in several London nightspots including The Marquee. The word was growing and the Pretenders made important inroads with audiences, but nobody could have expected the group's career to peak so quickly. As 1979 ended, their third single, titled 'Brass In Pocket', was issued. Penned by Hynde and Honeyman-Scott, the title slowly gathered momentum to top the British chart in January 1980, the perfect welcome to the new decade that now promised so much. 'Brass In Pocket', with Hynde's sultry, soulful vocals, held the top position for two weeks, during which time the Pretenders issued their debut eponymous album, which entered the chart at No.1, and once more embarked upon a nationwide tour. Hynde told NME that she viewed the British chart-topper as a responsibility: 'I didn't want to be a responsible adult. There's always something to do – TV interviews, photos, rehearsals, recording. We're always busy.' On the other hand, Honeyman-Scott was grateful for the new status, claiming that 'staying in nice hotels makes it a lot easier when you're 25 dates into a tour and you're edgy and very tired'. Typical male!

From Britain, the Pretenders' music crossed the Atlantic when Real Records was purchased by Sire Records. The group suddenly became more than a name on a recording contract. Indeed, the Pretenders album soared into the American Top 10 the same month as it dominated the British listing. As 'Talk Of The Town', the follow-up to 'Brass In Pocket', was issued and peaked in the Top 10, the Pretenders landed on American soil to embark upon a short promotional tour that included a sell-out concert in Santa Monica. The result was that 'Brass In Pocket' shot into the American Top 20, followed by 'Stop Your Sobbing', a Top 70 falterer. While touring, Hynde met and dated the Kinks' leader Ray Davies, who had, in fact, composed 'Stop Your Sobbing' some years earlier. However, romance was put on hold as work beckoned and before 1980 ended the Pretenders had performed Canadian dates and fulfilled further British dates. Busy indeed!

Hynde's composition 'Message Of Love' was the Pretenders' first single of 1981 and became a No.11 British hit, while the group's next album, imaginatively titled *Pretenders II*, soared into the Top 10 in Britain and America. Once more America called, this time for a three-month tour where again packed houses greeted the British band. In the Pretenders' absence, two singles – 'Day After Day' and 'I Go To Sleep' – were released in Britain, Top 50 and Top 10 hits respectively. Incidentally, both were staggering examples of a confident music outfit whose excellent musicianship was further highlighted by Hynde's white R&B vocals.

The American trip was shortened when Chambers badly cut his hand. Then, before 1981 had closed, he'd also injured the other one, forcing more postponed dates for the group. All was not lost, though;

those dates were picked up early in 1982, with further concerts through Japan and Australia following. The Pretenders' overwhelming success suffered a downside when Farndon was sacked from the membership following the group's Australian trek. Sadly, he would die from a drugs overdose in April 1983, although his post mortem insisted he had drowned in his bath.

On the personal front, Hynde's planned marriage to Davies was aborted, a traumatic enough decision for them – but not as tragic as Honeyman-Scott's sudden death on 16 June 1982 from drug misuse. The effect on Hynde was devastating, so much so that she flew to America 'to get away from it all', although she returned for her musician's funeral. For a group to suffer two tragic deaths within such a short time was incomprehensible.

When Hynde's grieving was manageable, she recruited two replacements, Billy Bremner and Tony Butler, whose first public appearance was via the 'Back On The Chain Gang' single, a Top 20 British hit, later Top 5 in America thanks to its inclusion in the movie titled *King of Comedy*.

The solitary 1983 single titled '2000 Miles' was issued to cash in on the Christmas market and became a Top 20 British hit, while Hynde gave birth to a daughter, Natalie. However, the Pretender's relationship with Davies would end, and she married Jim Kerr from Simple Minds in May 1984. This marriage suffered from, yet survived, the demands of the music business. For instance, when Simple Minds rested, invariably the Pretenders were touring. Kerr would fly across the world to be with his wife, often combining his trip with Simple Minds' business. More often than not, Hynde would hire nannies to enable her to take her children (she also had a second daughter named Jasmin) on the road with her.

Through the mid-'80s, the Pretenders sustained a high-ranking public profile both in the charts and on the concert circuit. The group's most notable singles were 'Learning To Crawl' early in 1984; a version of the Persuaders' 1971 R&B chart-topper 'Thin Line Between Love And Hate'; the novelty release of 'I Got You Babe' with UB40, their remake of the Sonny and Cher classic which soared to No.1 in the British chart (please see UB40, 'Red Red Wine'); and 'Don't Get Me Wrong', which, like its predecessors, was a good-selling title. Touring-wise, the Pretenders kicked in their world tour before appearing at the Live Aid benefit gala at the JFK Stadium in Philadelphia.

Into 1987, the Pretenders strode out once more on a world tour, leaving behind a Top 6 album titled *Get Close* and a Top 10 single 'Hymn To Her'. In the September the group recorded the title 'If There Was A Man' for inclusion in the soundtrack to the James Bond movie *The Living Daylights*. Yes, remember now? The title was issued as a single under the name 'Pretenders For 007' and reached the British Top 50.

Following a further duet between Hynde and UB40 titled 'Breakfast In Bed', Hynde, a lifetime vegetarian and devoted campaigner for animal rights, announced she had firebombed a McDonald's restaurant. It's unclear whether she was prosecuted or not. Returning to music, in 1990 the Pretenders issued the poor-selling *Packed* album; as Hynde's recording career showed signs of crumbling, so her marriage to Jim Kerr ended.

Now a recognised and respected contributor to PETA (People for the Ethical Treatment of Animals), Hynde performed at the organisation's 1993 Animals Ball staged in Washington, DC, while on the recording front the Pretenders' career took an unexpected turn with the Top 10 British hit titled 'I'll Stand By You' in April 1994. Quickly following was the album *Last Of The Independents*, which easily soared to No.8 in the British chart and entered the Top 40 in America. It was treated as the group's 'comeback' album and the Pretenders, with a revamped membership, returned to British concerts during September 1994 in support of their recent success and forthcoming single 'Night In My Veins', a Top 30 British hit. A month later, the band returned to America where the *Last Of The Independents* passed gold status as the superb 'I'll Stand By You' shot into the Top 20.

Although it was probably the last thing on Hynde's mind at this juncture, she was destined to perform with three diverse artists on disc. In March 1995 she joined Neneh Cherry, Cher and Eric Clapton to record 'Love Can Build A Bridge' to benefit the Comic Relief project. The single shot to the top of the British chart as the public swarmed to support one of Britain's best-loved charities.

Through to the close of 1995, Hynde, with and without the Pretenders, performed several high-profile performances, notably at the Cleveland Stadium in Ohio and in New York, where the concerts were sell-outs. Recording-wise, the Pretenders' final British hit (to date), titled 'Kid', faltered in the Top 40.

It goes without saying that the Pretenders were one of the most outstanding groups of the '80s. But it's also true to say that without Chrissie Hynde's smoky, sensitive vocal stylings, the group would have fallen into the 'average' category.

KENNY ROGERS

Coward Of The County

He was one of a selected few from the country world to become a consistent chart name in mainstream music. With his warm voice and cuddly appearance, he was every inch the gentleman, or perhaps the country squire!

Born Kenneth Donald Rogers in Houston, Texas, on 21 August 1938, Rogers was a student at the Jefferson Davis High School when he joined the membership of the doo-wop group the Scholars. The unit won a recording contract with the Cue label, where numerous singles were issued including the noted title 'Poor Little Doggie'. From Cue, the Scholars switched to Imperial Records to release 'Kangewah', among other tracks, before recording the title 'That Crazy Feeling', penned by Ray Doggett for Carlton Records. This release led to the group performing selected dates in the locality plus a television spot on ABC TV's American Bandstand, a high-ranking entertainment programme.

During 1959, now married to Janice, Rogers recorded for a pair of record companies simultaneously: for Carlton (as a soloist) and for Ken-Lee Records, owned by the singer and his brother Lelan (as a member of the Bobby Doyle Trio). In time, though, the Bobby Doyle Trio recorded the *In A Most Unusual Way* album for the CBS Records subsidiary Columbia.

Into the mid-'60s, Rogers switched to Mercury Records. He became a performing and recording member of the New Christy Minstrels, until the First Edition group was born from the Minstrels' membership to release its eponymous album via Reprise Records. The album's swiped single titled 'Just Dropped In (To See What Condition My Condition Was In)' soared into the American Top 5 in March 1968. A year on, Kenny Rogers and the First Edition enjoyed their British debut single 'Ruby, Don't Take Your Love To Town', a big-selling title which peaked at No.2 in the October. With Rogers' soft growl telling the sad tale of a severely injured Korean War veteran's fight to prevent his woman from straying, the single also shot into the American Top 10. Needless to say, an album bearing the single's name followed late in the year.

Into the '70s, the soundalike single 'Something's Burning' returned Kenny Rogers and the First Edition to the British Top 10, reaching the Top 20 in America. Once more, an album bearing the hit's title followed, capitalising on the success. 'Something's Burning' heralded the group's final British hit, and Kenny Rogers' last until 1977, although the group continued to notch up American charters until 1972. Rogers told author Joe Smith, 'We'd put out songs and, boom, they'd go right up the charts. I thought, "This is easy. We've stumbled on to a magic formula. Amazing how stupid everyone else is."' It was a little premature on the singer's part, because in 1972 New Edition disbanded, leaving Rogers $65,000 in debt – 'and I'm thinking, "What happened to that magic formula I was so sure I had?"'

Kenny Rogers had little choice but to revert to solo work within the country and western environment. To this end he secured a recording deal with United Artists, where his debut album and single, both titled 'Love Lifted Me', were issued early in 1975. Both were dismal sellers. It took a further two years before Rogers regained his selling power, when he released the single titled 'Lucille'. It became his first British chart-topper and reached the Top 5 in America, passing gold status. The accompanying album *Kenny Rogers* peaked in the British Top 20, American Top 30. In retrospect, Rogers believed this period of his career to be his favourite. With a chart-topper to his credit, he was obviously in demand. Whereas previously he would grab anything offered to promote his music, now he could afford to be choosy, setting aside time to plan his future – 'In this business, once it happens for you, you become an order taker. You take the best orders that come in, the best requests.'

'Daytime Friends' was the title of the chart-topper's follow-up single; remarkably, it struggled into the British Top 40 and the American Top 30. An album carrying the single's title followed, heavily promoted via the singer's first major British tour at the close of 1977.

Through to the '80s, Rogers, now married for a third time, established himself as America's premier country entertainer. His widespread popularity shocked him, particularly when the music industry honoured him with awards that included a 1978 Grammy for Best Country Vocal Performance, Male, for 'Lucille' and a year on the American Music Award for the Favourite Male Artist, Country.

Albums, including the titles *Love Or Something Like It* (1978), *The Gambler, Kenny* and *The Kenny Rogers Singles Album* (1979), were all big American sellers, all passing gold status, while his duet album with Dottie West titled *Classics* stalled in the Top 90. While his recording career soared, the singer diversified by debuting as an actor in the television movie titled *The Gambler*, inspired by his single and album of the same name.

To start 1980, and following a further handful of awards, Rogers soared into the American Top 3 with the single 'Coward Of The

County'. However, he took the title higher in Britain, where it topped the chart for two weeks. Like 'The Gambler' before it, 'Coward Of The County' went on to become a television movie starring Rogers. During this period, the singer felt he had peaked as an entertainer, although he still failed to appreciate the public accolades, saying he wasn't an exceptional singer by any means. The media comparison to Elvis Presley particularly annoyed him. 'He was a very special man. He changed the course of music. I didn't. All I did was have some hit records.'

Returning to duets, Rogers teamed up with Kim Carnes, this time to record 'Don't Fall In Love With A Dreamer', a single swiped from the *Gideon* album. Both titles were American Top 10 hits. From Carnes, Rogers turned to Lionel Richie when he recorded his composition 'Lady' as a single, a song which many felt was earmarked for Richie's group the Commodores. The endearing ballad, typical of Richie's sensitive writing talent, shot to the top of the American charts during November 1980. When released in Britain, 'Lady' soared into the Top 20. In actuality, Rogers recorded the track, he said, because he felt his material had become stagnant, he needed new input and therefore had approached Richie's publishing house, Jobete, owned by Motown Records, for guidance. Mixing country and R&B was Rogers' intention, as he cited Ray Charles as a prime innovator – 'What he did was he took country tracks and he sang them R&B. Country music is the white man's R&B.' Richie went on to produce the album *Share Your Love* for Rogers, while he in turn introduced Richie to his manager Ken Kragen, who went on to represent Richie when he departed from the Commodores. Indeed, it was also Kragen who partly instigated the 'We Are The World' charity project in 1985.

Into the '80s, Rogers' star continued to shine via his film appearances in *Six Pack* and the television movie *The Gambler II*, his duets with Sheena Easton and Dolly Parton, his hit mainstream material and country chart-toppers, and his lengthy touring schedules.

During 1983 Rogers switched record companies from Liberty to sign an expensive deal, reputedly in the region of $20 million, with the major company RCA Records. The move strengthened his selling power, or perhaps Dolly Parton did, because together they topped the American chart during October with the single 'Islands In The Stream', penned by (of all people) the Bee Gees. Taken from the album *Eyes That See In The Dark*, the single went on to chart in the British Top 10, while its mother, co-written and produced by Barry Gibb, soared into the American Top 10, Top 60 in Britain. Predictably, both titles collected various music-industry awards and honours, adding to the singer's already vast collection. The unexpected success of Rogers and Parton led to them recording the festive

23

album titled *Once Upon A Christmas* during 1984, following the American television special *A Christmas to Remember*.

Through to the next decade, Rogers' high profile as a singer and entertainer failed to wane, while on the personal front he married for the fourth time. His new wife was actress Marianne Gordon, with whom he became a driving force to fight world hunger and poverty.

By the start of 1990, and with his third seasonal album titled *Christmas In America* and *Something Inside So Strong* passing gold status, Rogers performed selected prestigious concerts, including his first in Florida. He then joined his musical contemporaries to record the charity disc 'Voices That Care', with proceeds earmarked for the American Red Cross Gulf Crisis Fund. Returning to film work briefly, the singer appeared in the television one-off titled *The Gambler Returns: The Luck of the Draw* during 1991, before participating in a series of documentaries like *The Real West* a year later.

Rogers' status as America's highest-paid country star, with no serious competition waiting in the wings, ensured the continuation of his huge popularity, despite adverse publicity during 1992. Following allegations from several women that he had encouraged them to participate in lurid sex antics over the telephone, Rogers replied that he was dismayed that the consenting women had allowed the information to become public knowledge. The mind boggles.

On the business front, the singer divided much of his entertaining life between television and concerts. He switched record companies once more, this time to Giant Records, where the *If Only My Heart Had A Voice* album was his debut release. From Giant he moved to Magnatone Records, a Nashville company, during 1996, but on this side of the Atlantic at least, his public profile today appears to be confined to regurgitated CD releases.

(Quotes: *Off the Record: An Oral History of Popular Music* by Joe Smith)

March 1980

BLONDIE

Atomic

It's not 'Automatic', 'Automic' or even 'Automobile', but 'Atomic' – my, how this single's title has caused problems over the years. A minor point, granted, but how many people can, almost two decades later, actually remember the chorus? Thought not!

Born Deborah Harry in Miami, Florida, on 1 July 1945, she was adopted as a toddler by Catherine and Richard and was relocated to Hawthorne in New Jersey. Harry's first taste of show-business proper came when she joined the membership of the flower-power group Wind In The Willows, who recorded an eponymous album during 1968 for Capitol Records.

From that group Harry shifted career direction to become a Playboy bunny at Max's Kansas City Club in New York, where apart from waiting on tables she was able to socialise with visiting musicians. From here she joined an all-female trio known as the Stilettos, who specialised in the new-wave music movement. Chris Stein, born in Brooklyn, New York, on 5 January 1950, was a student at New York City's School of Visual Art. Upon graduation, he too joined the membership of the Stilettos.

In time, the Stilettos disbanded, whereupon Harry and Stein, now lovers, formed a new musical unit called Angel and the Snake, the nucleus of the future Blondie. However, prior to the creation of the hit-making group of the '70s, several musicians drifted though, including Billy O'Connor on drums, Fred Smith, bass guitarist, and several female support singers. None, however, hampered the group's success on the punk circuit.

During 1976, and known as Blondie, the group – with the permanent line-up of Harry and Stein, drummer Clem Burke, born in New York on 24 November 1955, keyboardist Jimmy Destri, born in Brooklyn on 13 April 1954, and Gary Valentine – secured a recording contract with Private Stock Records. Late in 1976, the group's debut single titled 'X Offender' was issued, extracted from the *Blondie* album. Both were slow sellers. However, on the strength of these releases, Blondie toured America before visiting Britain. Then more upheaval hit the membership. Valentine departed to concentrate on his own group called Know. His replacement, Frank Infante, late of World War II, joined in time to move with Blondie to Chrysalis Records, where they recorded and released the *Plastic Letters* album.

Into 1978, Blondie cracked the pop system when their single 'Denis', a revamped, updated version of the Randy and the Rainbows 1963 American hit, soared into the British Top 2. Clem Burke told John Palmer, 'We were touring clubs like Barbarella's in Birmingham and we could see the record slowly moving up the chart week by week, and as it got higher more people were locked outside of the clubs than those who had managed to get in. You could see the momentum . . . building up.'

The *Plastic Letters* album followed, another money spinner proving the relationship between Blondie and Chrysalis Records was a positive one. Blondie's second outing, '(I'm Always Touched By Your) Presence Dear', likewise swiped from the album, reached the British Top 10. It was an excellent start for an American group in an overseas territory; a pity home support wasn't as strong!

Following these releases, Blondie teamed up with British record producer Mike Chapman, who had first seen the group perform in 1977 at The Whiskey Club, where Tom Petty was support act. In fact, so smitten was Chapman that he watched the show four times. Incidentally, Chapman had been in partnership with Nicky Chinn, known as Chinnichap, whose success had been prolific via groups like the glitter and glitz unit Sweet. The bonding with Blondie, though, was instant and profitable for both.

The group's next single, titled 'Picture This', followed hot on the heels of a British tour and reached the Top 20, while 'Hanging On The Telephone' soared into the British Top 5 before 1978 ended. In between releases, Harry had sidestepped into the movie world to appear in *The Foreigner*. As it was abundantly clear she was now Blondie's figurehead, she was cultivated and exploited to glow in the image of a blonde sex kitten. Eventually she would openly criticise the 'cheesecake' image; for the time being, though, she was content saying that 'sex sells and I do exploit my sexuality'.

With Britain and Europe securely in Blondie's grasp, they concentrated on their home country, where, to date, their success had been embarrassingly negligible. The wait for home acceptance was thankfully over when their next single, titled 'Heart Of Glass', lifted from their forthcoming *Parallel Lines* album, earned them the recognition they deserved. Released in February 1979 and aimed squarely at the powerful dance scene and not inspired by the new-wave/punk demands, 'Heart Of Glass' first shot to the top of the British chart, where it stayed for four weeks, and two months on stormed up the American charts to the top, taking both group and record company by surprise. Said Stein, 'We didn't expect the song to be that big. We did it as a novelty item.' The single's climb to the American top may have been boosted by a threatened radio station ban, due to the opening lyrics including the word 'ass'. A further version was recorded and serviced to those stations who were mild in attitude. Blondie, however, refused to be concerned, as Harry clearly summed up the situation: 'Any kind of controversy causes excitement and more interest in the long run.'

Following their long-awaited American success, Blondie repaid the public support by touring. Their performances were to cross-section audiences. According to Burke, 'People thought we were a mellow band, but when they came to see us they found something quite different, yet we appealed to people at different levels.'

Meanwhile *Parallel Lines*, the result of their studio sessions with Mike Chapman, likewise soared to the top of the British chart during 1979 before selling in excess of 19 million copies worldwide. Chapman's enthusiasm for the group, particularly Harry, ensured they had a lucrative future together, as he told Joe Smith: 'Debbie Harry was, and probably still is, one of the most extraordinary and unusual artists that you could hope to come across.'

That aside, when she was given the title of the decade's most exciting sex kitten, Debbie Harry was less than amused. 'In America they put girls into two categories. Either you're a sweet, clean-cut girl or you're a real nasty bitch. And I know which one they've figured me out to be.' There was also another problem to overcome: Blondie was the name given to the whole group, not merely Harry. They blamed themselves for the public confusion. Said Burke, 'It's not that we mind if people want to speak to Debbie, but I don't like it when people speak to me but don't really know who they are talking to. We all want to be recognised for what we are and what we are doing.'

Following their British and American chart-topper 'Heart Of Glass', Blondie enjoyed their second British No.1 single in June 1979. Titled 'Sunday Girl' and composed by Stein, the single dominated the British chart for three weeks. Two months on, the group's next album, *Eat To The Beat*, a further result of the group's sessions with Mike Chapman, likewise shot to the top of the chart. The album peaked in the American Top 20. Said Burke, '[The album was] a development of the Blondie sound. We feel that we have our own style, but we never consciously set out to write hit records.'

In the October, the single 'Dreaming' soared into the British Top 2, reaching the Top 30 in America. According to Burke, 'When you get to the point of having your singles getting regularly to No.1, you start to take things for granted. "Dreaming" didn't reach No.1 in Britain, and I think that was good for us, because it shook us up a little.'

Before the decade ended, the 'Union City Blue' single likewise bypassed No.1 to become a Top 20 hit. This title was inspired by the movie *Union City* starring Harry, although not included in its soundtrack.

In the '80s came a further British chart-topper in the March with the Harry- and Destri-penned 'Atomic'. It was a position the title held for two weeks, although it only made the Top 40 in America. It was another lifted from the *Eat To The Beat* album. And there was more. 'Call Me', the follow-up to 'Atomic', likewise hit the top in both Britain and America. Written and produced by Giorgio Moroder for the Paul Schrader *American Gigolo* movie starring Richard Gere, the title dominated the American chart for six long weeks. Harry had attended a rough screening of the movie which included the musical track of the song before writing the lyrics herself.

Her next movie involvement was in June when *Roadie* was premièred in America; Meatloaf was her co-star. Said Burke, 'We enjoyed making that one and now that we have our Screen Actors' Guild cards we may be doing a Blondie film . . . based around the story of Blondie.' Meanwhile, the year ended on a further high note when Blondie's version of the Jamaican group the Paragons' single titled 'The Tide Is High' became a British chart-topper for two weeks; it would reach the same position in America early in 1981. Blondie had first heard the track, written by John Holt, on a cassette given to them during a visit to London. Said Harry, 'Chris fell madly in love with the song, as did I, and we just decided to do it. We thought it was a potential hit song.' The title was swiped from their *Autoamerican* album, which marked the group's return to the producing talents of Mike Chapman and became a Top 3 British hit (Top 10 in America).

As 'Rapture', the follow-up single to 'The Tide Is High', soared into the British Top 5, Harry recorded a solo album titled *Koo Koo* with Chic members Nile Rodgers and Bernard Edwards, cementing rumours of her intention to leave the group. The first single lifted, 'Backfired', stalled in the British Top 40, while the album itself soared into the Top 10.

Moving into 1982 and the inescapable record company marketing ploy, Blondie released their *Best Of Blondie* album. This release held back the group's next album proper, featuring all group members, titled *The Hunter*, which peaked in the British Top 10. A pair of singles lifted from this Chapman-produced project, namely 'Island Of Lost Souls' and 'War Child', floundered in the Top 40 on both sides of the Atlantic, as did the group's touring plans. During September 1982, Blondie's British tour was cancelled. According to *NME*, the tour promoter had said, 'Ticket sales have not been as good as we hoped,' and Blondie's future as a performing unit looked uncertain. The music paper also reported that Destri had left the group and that Infante was seeking legal advice to prevent Blondie performing without him. Incredible as it seems, these incidents heralded the decline of Blondie, much to the regret of the music industry who believed there remained much mileage in the group.

Through to 1986, Debbie Harry concentrated on her film career, appearing in *Hairspray* and as a stage actress in the off-Broadway comedy *Teaneck Tanzi*. Chris Stein, on the other hand, opened his own record outlet, Animal, distributed by Chrysalis Records in Britain, before suffering from pemphigus, a genetic disorder which forced him to be hospitalised and in need of care for several long months. When Stein was sufficiently recovered, he and Harry composed together once more. According to Chapman, '[Debbie] had this intense relationship with Chris Stein, and the two of them were unbelievably talented. They did some incredible things . . . drugs and what-have-you destroyed all that.'

Late in 1986, Harry's single 'French Kissin' In The USA' re-established her as a charting act, reaching the Top 10 in Britain and the Top 60 in America. This title, and its follow-up 'Free To Fall', a poor-selling item, were lifted from her *Rockbird* album, itself a good seller. During 1989, Harry's solo career crawled on with the *Once More Into The Bleach* album and a performance at London's Borderline Club, followed by further dates during June 1990 at the Brixton Academy. The venues were pint-sized by comparison with Blondie's heyday; nonetheless, Harry performed a group and solo repertoire before loyal and enthusiastic audiences.

Before the '80s closed, the singer was earmarked to star in the Disney movie *Mother Goose Rock 'N' Rhyme* and issued her *Def, Dumb And Blonde* album, which reunited her with producer Mike Chapman. A couple of lifted singles were issued and became British hits, namely 'I Want That Man' at the end of 1989 and 'Sweet And Low' at the start of 1990.

In the '90s, following the release of two further albums titled *Dead City Radio* and *Red Hot + Blue*, a compilation titled *The Complete Picture: The Very Best Of Deborah Harry And Blondie*, featuring group and solo material, soared into the British Top 3. Once more, Harry performed in Britain, the highlight a concert at Wembley Stadium, before returning to the film world to appear in *The Killbillies* and *Intimate Stranger*.

Switching from Chrysalis Records to Sire Records during 1993, Harry issued her first album in at least four years, titled *Debravation*, which became a Top 30 hit. Into 1994, a further Blondie compilation hit the streets, titled *Blonde And Beyond*, while during the September a reworked version of 'Atomic' peaked in the British Top 20. Inspired by this unexpected bonus, *The Platinum Collection* was issued before the close of the year. During 1995 Harry performed on a New York stage with a new Blondie line-up, the 'Heart Of Glass (Remix)' single soared into the British Top 20, and was followed by a revamped mix of 'Union City Blue'.

Through to 1997, Harry, now 51 years old, continued to tour selected dates until Blondie, including Chris Stein, performed their first reunion concert in Washington during August. A month earlier, Harry and the Jazz Passengers had performed a trio of dates at London's Jazz Café, while back in America the finishing touches were being added to Sylvester Stallone's *Copland* movie, which co-starred Robert De Niro, Harvey Keitel and Harry.

Reforming Blondie was a permanent move, encouraged by the

discovery of the group's dance tracks like 'Atomic' by nightclub DJs and punters. Then, with sufficient material to record a new album, Blondie returned to the recording studio in early 1998, and following a breakdown in negotiations to release the completed project titled *No Exit* via EMI Records, the group signed a distribution deal with the independent American label Beyond Music, distributed via BMG Records. *No Exit*, an album geared towards the future and not past fans, spawned the single 'Maria' which, against strong competition, shot to the top of the British chart in February 1999. When asked by reporter Neil McCormick what her motivation was in returning to the music business, Harry replied, 'This is a business. We've been successful and we have this legacy that we can cash in on. We'd be stupid if we didn't.' She then added, 'We're just getting going. Who knows where we'll end up with this?'

Watch this space.

(Quotes: *Off the Record: An Oral History of Popular Music* by Joe Smith; *Underground Girl: The Deborah Harry Fanzine* by Sarah Conley)

April 1980

THE DETROIT SPINNERS

Working My Way Back To You/Forgive Me Girl

'[When the single first] came out in 1974, anyone born in, say, 1960, who would have been twenty this year, would only have been four when it first became a hit for the Four Seasons. So, knowing that most of our record buyers continue to be teenagers, there was still a lot going on for the song itself' – Pervis Jackson

Bobby Smith, born on 10 April 1936 in Detroit, Michigan; Billy Henderson, born on 9 August 1939 in Detroit; Henry Fambrough, born on 10 May 1938, also in Detroit; Pervis Jackson, born on 16 May 1939 in that city as well; and C.P. Spencer were all raised in the rough quarter of Michigan's city.

During World War II their families, like so many others, had relocated to the city to work in the munitions factories and, also like other ghetto children, the boys were shunted into the Lincoln High School. While studying they actually formed their first group, called the Domingos, a name inspired by the Flamingos, whom they greatly admired. However, before they could set off on their ambitious course to become a recording act, Smith was drafted into the US

Army, whereupon his replacement was George Dixon, who himself was later replaced by Chico Edwards. When Smith eventually returned to the membership, the group settled down to establish themselves as a vocal unit. Jackson told journalist Roger St Pierre, 'At first we didn't know anything about a band. We'd go out, buy the records, learn them by heart and sing the songs a cappella style.'

The group worked with Bob Collins and The Esquire Of Rhythm, the resident outfit at the Glen Lodge Show Bar in Royal Oak, Michigan. In an interview with author Tony Cummings, Jackson said, 'It was tough recording-wise in the '50s because they didn't have any major record companies in Detroit. In '57 we became the Spinners and were considered like an amateur group. We didn't know nothing.' That is until they met producer/singer Harvey Fuqua, who signed the membership as the first act to his Tri Phi record label during 1961. Fuqua also insisted on being the group's lead singer as well as their composer and manager, a formula which was relatively successful for the short period the Spinners were signed to the label. The group's stay spawned the solitary hit titled 'That's What Girls Are Made For', issued during June 1961; it became a Top 90 American hit. The title, featuring a young Marvin Gaye on drums, was, Bobby Smith thought, destined to reach the sky. When it stopped short, the group ploughed on.

The Spinners switched to Motown Records during 1963 when Fuqua's brother-in-law Berry Gordy Jr purchased the label and its signed acts. Minus Fuqua in the membership, the group was relegated to session-singer status for artists who included Marvin Gaye! Eventually, though, the Spinners were given access to the recording studio to record their debut single, the Mickey Stevenson composition titled 'Sweet Thing'. However, for reasons known only to Motown Records, the title was not issued for a year following the recording session in October 1964. 'Sweet Thing' sold in sufficient quantities for the Spinners to be added to the Motown Revues (touring across America) and later on the Marvin Gaye Revue, where they became an audience attraction not for their music but for their impersonations. One performance prompted the *Detroit Courier* to print, 'The Spinners' take-off of the Beatles, complete with long-haired wigs and instruments, will fracture you. Even in the take-off they are better than the Beatles.' Oh yeah? It was performances such as these that sustained the Spinners financially until hit material took over.

Although their recording career started shakily with Motown Records, they released 'I'll Always Love You' and 'Truly Yours', a pair of the company's finest soul singles, during 1965 and 1966 respectively, although only the former title was released in Britain. A quiet year then passed until the group's next single, titled 'For All We Know', and their debut album, *The Original Spinners*, were issued in

1967. In Britain the album was retitled *The Detroit Spinners*, as there was already an established Liverpool folk group calling themselves the Spinners.

The American group's final single via the Motown label, titled 'Bad Bad Weather (Till You Come Home)', was issued in October 1968, although the title 'In My Diary' was scheduled for release the following year. 'In My Diary' was not lost altogether; the track heralded the Spinners' first release on Motown's VIP subsidiary, followed by the then highly controversial 'Message From A Black Man' single in 1970, bypassed for British release.

By this time, member Chico Edwards had left the group to be replaced by G.C. Cameron, who sang lead vocals on the Lee Garrett/ Stevie Wonder/Syreeta composition titled 'It's A Shame' which marked the Spinners' debut British and American hit, peaking at No.20 during 1970. Flushed with this success, Wonder went on to pen the follow-up single 'We'll Have It Made', which a year on sadly failed to repeat its predecessor's success.

When Cameron left the Spinners to embark upon a solo Motown career, he was replaced by Phillipe Wynne, born in Cincinnati, Ohio, on 3 April 1941, and the group, disillusioned by their seven-year relationship with Motown Records, packed their microphones for pastures new. Jackson said at the time, 'We're not bitter, but we hoped for a little more than we got. It was an experience and one that we will not forget lightly. We had some hits with Motown but I think it was the fact that they had so many groups. The Temptations and groups with the big hits got in first and we got the material nobody else wanted.'

At the instigation of Aretha Franklin, the Spinners secured a recording contract with her record company Atlantic, where, with Wynne's attractive falsetto vocals and the craftsmanship of producer/composer Thom Bell, the group went on to reach the stardom they had craved and which had previously been denied them. Said Jackson, 'We played Atlantic some tapes we'd made in Detroit with Jimmy Roach. They seemed to like them but in the same breath they asked us whether we would mind cutting some tracks with a producer of their choice. We agreed 'cause it was obvious they were trying to do something for us.'

Said Bell, 'I went to Atlantic and they said, "Here's a list of every artist we have. We'd like you to produce any one you want." So I looked down the list and right at the bottom was the Spinners. Atlantic was kinda surprised that I wanted the Spinners but it worked out real fine. I wrote some songs, got some other things together and then went into Sigma [Studios] and put the tracks down. The voiceovers by the group were done in Detroit.' One of the several tracks recorded was 'I'll Be Around', released as the Spinners' debut single for Atlantic Records. It marked the first in a series of hit singles to highlight the delicate vocal styling against an uptempo, warm, thudding beat that was to become the group's trademark. 'I'll Be Around', composed by Bell and Phil Hurtt, started its life as the B-side to 'How Could I Let You Get Away?' but when radio stations flipped the disc 'I'll Be Around' soared into the American Top 3, selling in excess of two million copies on the way.

During 1973 the group's career spiralled with a pair of gold American Top 10 titles, namely 'Could It Be I'm Falling In Love?' and 'One Of A Kind (Love Affair)'; the former single peaked at No.11 in the British chart during April 1973. The final single of 1973 was Linda Creed's composition 'Ghetto Child', a hard-hitting swipe at America's lowest, a Top 10 British hit (Top 20 in America). It was also during this year that the Spinners toured America with soul icon Dionne Warwick, who, at the time, was suffering from poor record sales. According to Wynne, 'We loved her music and she dug us. Finally we talked over the idea of recording together. There was a big hassle over contracts – she was with Warners and we were with Atlantic – but eventually some arrangement was worked out.' Thankfully so, as the collaboration 'Then Came You' shot to the top of the American chart in October 1974, reaching the Top 30 in Britain. Unhappily, the title was a one-off duet.

From 1975 to 1978 the Spinners maintained extremely high placings in the American chart with hit singles that included 'They Just Can't Stop It (The Games People Play)', 'The Rubberband Man', 'Wake Up Susan', 'You're Throwing A Good Love Away' and 'Me And My Music'. Of these titles, only two, namely 'The Rubberband Man' and 'Wake Up Susan', became British hits, reaching No.16 and No.29 respectively. Also during this period, albums titled *Mighty Love, Pick Of The Litter* and *Labour Of Love*, among others, were issued.

Into the new decade, John Edwards replaced Wynne as lead singer. Wynne departed following a concert in California and launched a solo career with his *Starting All Over Again* album via the Cotillion label. Behind the public spotlight, he became a practising minister. Both careers were successful. By 1984 Wynne had issued a further pair of albums titled *Wynne Jammin'* and *Phillipe Wynne*.

Meanwhile, the group he had left behind during 1980 peaked in Britain when they recorded a cover version of the Four Seasons' 1966 British Top 50 hit 'Working My Way Back To You'/'Forgive Me Girl'. The reworking marked the Spinners' last with Bell at the helm but first with the new team of Michael Zager and Jerry Love, and topped the British chart in April 1980 for two weeks. At first the group was wary of recording a tried and tested song, as Jackson told David Nathan in 1980. 'It was Michael Zager's idea for us to do the tune and, to be very truthful, we really had to sit down and talk about it and think whether it would work for us. We hadn't ever covered anyone else's material, so there was definitely some scepticism within the group about doing it . . . after we'd recorded it, we were happy with it . . . in the studios we played around with it and I guess the result justifies our decision.'

To close the year, the group struggled into the British Top 40 with 'Body Language' and the further medley 'Cupid'/'I've Loved You For A Long Time', a runaway Top 4 hit, sadly marking the group's final British showing.

Through the '80s, the group continued to record and several singles charted in America, including the titles 'Long Live Soul Music' (1981), 'Magic In The Moonlight' (1982) and 'Right Or Wrong' (1994). With producer Leon Sylvers at the helm, the Spinners issued the *Cross Fire* album and contributed to the *Twins* movie soundtrack. A year on, they released the *Lovin' Feelings* album, a return to their musical heritage which included a reworking of 'That's What Girls Are Made For' with Fuqua also producing the new version. Also during 1983, the single titled 'Funny How Time Slips Away', a further revamped original, this time from Willie Nelson, represented the Spinners' last American hit. As the Spinners struggled on, former group member Phillipe Wynne died from a heart attack on 14 July 1984.

Towards the end of the decade, the Spinners left Atlantic Records to join Fantasy Records, the home of disco stars Sylvester and Fat Larry's Band, to release the *Down To Business* album on the company's Volt subsidiary. Nothing worked; the group's former glory did not return. However, their music did. Into the '90s, Atlantic Records dug deep into their treasured group catalogue to issue a remixed version of the group's 1973 British hit 'Ghetto Child', as the group itself joined the Rappin' 4-Tay on the title 'I'll Be Around', a Top 30 British hit.

To date, with their recording career exhausted, Rhino Records issued the compilation *A One Of A Kind Love Affair* in tribute to the Spinners' wealth of talent. Still a major contributor to both black and mainstream music, the group continues to dominate the American nostalgia touring circuit, with the occasional British visit.

(Quotes: *Blues and Soul* magazine, 1980, interview by Roger St Pierre; *The Sound of Philadelphia* by Tony Cummings; *Motown: The History* by Sharon Davis)

May 1980

DEXY'S MIDNIGHT RUNNERS

Geno

'I think [the single] is one of the nicest things that someone has ever said about me' – Geno Washington

It took a fusion of Stax Records' influence and, perhaps, Van Morrison's stylings to elevate the struggling Dexy's Midnight Runners to the top of the British chart. The single responsible was a tribute to soul singer Geno Washington, who enjoyed a series of hit singles in 1966 and 1967 including his most popular, 'Hi Hi Hazel', backed by the Ram Jam Band.

Kevin Rowland, born in Wolverhampton, West Midlands, on 17 August 1953 to Irish Catholic parents, abandoned plans to become a priest when he first brushed with music as a member of the Lucy and the Lovers group. From this outfit he switched to the punk unit The Killjoys. With Rowland as guitarist, the band secured a recording contract with Raw Records and issued the 'Johnny Won't Get To Heaven' single late in 1977. In time, Rowland and fellow guitarist Al Archer left the group to pursue a career with their own band. In 1978 they formed Dexy's Midnight Runners, the name taken from the drug Dexedrine. It was a strange choice, as Rowland at the time condemned the use of both drugs and alcohol. Next came the image, which was reputedly swiped from the cast of the *Mean Street* movie starring Robert De Niro. Said Rowland, 'It was a very spiffy look, very Italian. I felt it was a very smoky image.' With a membership of Babyface Junior, Pete Saunders, Jimmy Patterson, Steve Spooner, Pete Williams, Jeff Blythe and, of course, Archer and Rowland, Dexy's Midnight Runners hit the nightclub circuit where, during one performance, they were signed to a management deal by Bernie Rhodes. He went on to negotiate a recording deal with Oddball Productions, whose product was distributed by EMI Records.

Under this arrangement the group issued their first single, titled 'Dance Stance', which peaked in the British Top 40 early in 1980. Two months on, in the May, their second single, 'Geno', was released on the Late Night Feeling label. It soared to the top of the British chart, where it stayed for two weeks. The raw yet brassy musical dedication was penned by Rowland, despite the fact he had never met the soul singer. As the single was issued, Washington was involved in self-confidence and motivation hypnotherapy training: '[The song] forced me to get myself together quick because if people started to point me out . . . and if I got on stage and sounded like shit . . . they'd go, "He's no fuckin' legend, listen to that load of shit!"'

'Geno' elevated Dexy's Midnight Runners from the second league into hit makers, although sustaining that success proved to be difficult. Perhaps alienating the media, particularly the press, contributed to their future struggle, following statements like those printed in the *NME* when the music paper announced that the group had decided not to conduct interviews. The paper further stated, 'With full-page ads in the publications they profess to detest, Dexy's Midnight Runners announced an embargo on any publicity other than their own. "We won't compromise by talking to the dishonest hippy press," they claim, adding that they will use advertising space to "accommodate our own essays, which still state our point of view".' Ouch!

Before Dexy's Midnight Runners' next single could hit the stores, the story broke that they had stolen the tapes of their first album, titled *Searching For The Young Soul Rebels*, from EMI Records by luring their producer, Pete Wingate, from the studio, enabling the tapes to be snatched. The group refused to return them until the record company had renegotiated their recording contract. When finally issued, the album shot into the British Top 10 during July 1980.

The follow-up to 'Geno', titled 'There There My Dear', peaked at No.7 during August 1980, whereupon the group embarked upon a lengthy European tour. Before the year ended, the third single, 'Keep It Part Two', issued without the approval of the group, bombed. Ironic as it seems, it was this clash of opinion that led to the chart-topping group disbanding. Rowland formed a new group with Patterson and six newcomers, including Brian Maurice, while the remaining original members formed the group Bureau.

Early in 1981, EMI Records issued the single 'Plan B' by the new Dexy's Midnight Runners. It was a half-hearted move by the company, as the relationship with Rowland was apparently at its lowest. Paul Burton, Runners' manager, told an *NME* journalist, 'We didn't want . . . "Plan B" released. They went ahead against our wishes.' On the other hand, an EMI Records spokesman said, 'It was released with the full co-operation and active support of the band and their management.' All that fuss for a Top 60 single! Burton further told *NME* that EMI's failure to take up a contractual option had left the Runners free agents and confirmed that they had already recorded tracks independently with Tony Visconti.

With their recording career uncertain and without EMI's financial support, Dexy's Midnight Runners had no choice but to cancel their proposed British tour. Rowland later conceded, 'I did loads of stupid things, like the way I used to argue with EMI Records. I just look back to the time now and wonder how I would have reacted to some prick coming into my office shouting and kicking things.'

Before 1981 ended, Dexy's Midnight Runners did switch record companies to sign with Phonogram, where their debut single 'Show Me', produced by Visconti, was issued on the Mercury subsidiary. The title soared to No.16 in the chart. Not so its follow-up, 'Liars A To E'. It bombed, heralding the departure of bass guitarist Steve Wynne and the arrival of Giorgio Kilkenny.

Taking a sidestep in their careers, Dexy's Midnight Runners performed in *The Projected Passion Review* staged at London's Old Vic. The critics were kind.

With a history of discontent and frustration, the high-wired Dexy's Midnight Runners would replace their volatile image with a positive, attitude-free future, leaving the music to speak for itself. A good move, too.

Also see: 'Come On Eileen', August 1982

(Quotes: *Keep On Running* magazine, 1997, published by Neil Warburton)

June 1980

DON McLEAN

Crying

I bet there aren't too many people who will remember this version of Roy Orbison's immortal weepy. I also bet that when Don McLean's name is mentioned, the single 'American Pie' springs to mind. Ah, that's the way of the world!

Born on 2 October 1945 in New Rochelle, New York, McLean suffered from asthma from a young age, thereby precluding him from the usual childhood rough and tumble and, of course, any sports activities. Instead, he ploughed his energies into music, notably that recorded by Buddy Holly and Frank Sinatra.

McLean was 15 years old when his father died, prompting him to embark upon a musical career. To this end, and while still attending Iona College, later Villanova University, he played guitar and banjo at friends' parties. This amateur groundwork paid dividends when he became a regular entertainer on the local club network.

As early as 1967 McLean began composing songs and, encouraged by his new manager Herb Gart, moved further afield, performing university gigs and finally taking up a residency at the Saratoga Springs-based Caffe Lena during 1968. Also this year he was named 'Hudson River Troubadour' by the New York State Council of the Arts, which entailed performing before communities situated along the Hudson River. By the time he had completed his lengthy touring schedule, the singer was intimately familiar with all the townships alongside that stretch of water. McLean's unusual jaunt then took a giant step when Pete Seeger requested that he join him on a trip down the Hudson on the boat *Clearwater*. It was to be an environmental education journey for the benefit of the river's folk which saw McLean as a member of the crew and of the group called the Sloop Singers. The six-week trip was also televised for American viewers.

Into the '70s, McLean recorded for the first time. While composing suitable tracks for his forthcoming album, he chanced to read a biography of the artist Vincent Van Gogh. This inspired McLean to pen 'Vincent', a song of considerable quality but one which would shine at a later date. Produced by Jerry Corbitt, known for his work with the Youngbloods, McLean's debut album titled *Tapestry* was testament to his enthusiasm and youth which, unfortunately, wasn't shared by the music industry. Indeed, 34 record companies rejected the project until the Mediarts label took the chance. *Tapestry* bombed.

In 1971 United Artists Records purchased the Mediarts label and its artist roster, whereupon McLean found his name splashed across a new record label, and issued a taster from his second album. Titled 'American Pie', devoted in the main to his musical hero Buddy Holly and his tragic death in 1959 – 'the day the music died' – the track was too long to issue as a three-minute single. United Artists therefore split the song in two, not intending to deprive record-buyers of what McLean described as his masterpiece. 'American Pie' jumped to the top of the American chart in January 1972, a position it held for four weeks, and reached No.2 in Britain. The singer told author Joe Smith, 'When the record started selling, it caused me to deal with a very boring subject which was people asking me what the song was about . . . When the song turned into an anthem, some of the fun was taken out of it.' The title also, he said, prevented him from enjoying the natural progression so important to an artist. In other words, 'American Pie' plagued the life out of him in much the same way perhaps as David Bowie and 'The Laughing Gnome'.

As was expected, the *American Pie* album likewise shot to No.1 in America, highlighting McLean's talent to write sympathetically about the subjects that interested him.

During March the singer's chart-topper follow-up peaked in the

American Top 12. Not wishing to overlook 'Vincent', United Artists set the title free, along with its mother, *Tapestry*. Ironically, 'Vincent' fared much better in Britain, catapulting to No.1 during June 1972, a position it held for two weeks. *Tapestry* likewise notched up healthy sales, peaking in the Top 20. Perhaps the Americans didn't recognise the painter's work?

In between releases, the singer performed regularly in America before crossing the ocean into Europe. At a concert in Los Angeles, Lori Lieberman was a member of the audience. She was so impressed by McLean that she asked two composers, Fox and Gimbel, to write a track for her devoted to McLean. The result was the aptly titled 'Killing Me Softly With His Song', a track Lieberman recorded for her eponymous album. Most people, however, know the song by soul artist Roberta Flack, who enjoyed an American chart-topper and a British No.6 hit with the song in 1973.

McLean toured on; through the bulk of the next year he trekked the world, releasing two albums in between countries, namely *Don McLean* and *Playin' Favourites*. Both titles sold extremely well in Britain and America.

Albums also dominated his recording output through 1974 into the '80s, with titles that included *Homeless Brother*. The years also saw the artist perform in Britain twice, first in 1975, where the lengthy haul included prestigious performances at the Royal Albert Hall, London, and at a free concert staged in Hyde Park before over 80,000 people.

Shortly before 1980 arrived, McLean switched record companies from United Artists, who had launched him as a top-selling name, to Millennium Records, issued via EMI Records in Britain. McLean's first hit single under this new arrangement was, for some reason, a cover version of the Roy Orbison classic 'Crying', which he had taken to No.2 in America and No.25 in Britain during 1961. McLean's sensitive interpretation, however, outsold Orbison's original by racing to the top of the British chart during June 1980, a position it dominated for three weeks. Issued in America during March 1981, the single faltered in the Top 5. Again British buyers rose to the call. Hot on the heels of the chart-topper, EMI Records released the *Chain Lightning* album, which peaked in the Top 20 in Britain and Top 30 in America, and to further capitalise on the success and the singer's touring presence in Britain, the compilation *The Very Best Of Don McLean* earned the singer a Top 4 hit.

While McLean continued to weave his musical web in America with singles titled 'Since I Don't Have You', 'It's Just The Sun' and 'Castles In The Air', it took a further two years for him to appear once again in the British listing with the latter title. His next significant release was during 1987, when the further compilation *Don McLean's*

Greatest Hits: Then And Now, containing both released and new tracks, was issued. Once more the release coincided with the singer's annual British touring schedule.

Now into the '90s, and following another record-company switch to Capitol Records, where his *Love Tracks* was issued, and later to Gold Castle Records, with whom a live album and compilation set were issued, the singer returned to the British Top 20 with 'American Pie' during 1991. The title was his final charting single to date, although Curb Records issued his *River Of Love* album, which sold poorly.

It does now appear that Don McLean prefers to spend time with his family, with touring schedules booked at a slower pace. He continues to compose, although many believe his most creative period was during the '70s and '80s; well, they would say that, wouldn't they? He'll be back.

(Quotes: *Off the Record: An Oral History of Popular Music* by Joe Smith)

July 1980

OLIVIA NEWTON-JOHN

Xanadu

'I hope that seeing *Xanadu* will provide pleasure and a chance for people to get away from their problems' – Olivia Newton-John

Born in Cambridge on 26 September 1948, Olivia Newton-John moved with her family to Melbourne, Australia. As a teenager, she sang in a folk group and duetted with Pat Carroll on regular television spots. In 1964, the duo won the Johnny O'Keefe talent contest, where the first prize was a trip to Britain. Newton-John told author Joe Smith, 'I didn't really want to go, but my mother . . . said, "We need to broaden your horizons. You should go to Europe." . . . I didn't want to leave my boyfriend. I was very young and I thought Australia was everything.' Once Newton-John had reached 18 years of age and had completed her education, she and Carroll hit British soil, where they performed on the folk circuit until Carroll's visa expired, forcing her to return to Australia.

Newton-John remained in Britain, working as a soloist. She secured a recording contract with Decca Records to issue her version of Jackie De Shannon's 'Till You Say You'll Be Mine' in 1966. At this juncture, she befriended and began dating Bruce Welch, member of the Shadows, Cliff Richard's backing group. Welch offered her a role in

Richard's forthcoming *Cinderella* pantomime; she declined, prefer-ring to return to Australia. Her stay there was short-lived; she returned to live with Welch in London.

Following a spell with the quartet Toomorrow, also the name of a science-fiction musical, Newton-John duetted with Cliff Richard on 'Don't Move Away' early in 1971. In the April, she recorded her second single, titled 'If Not For You'. It was another cover version, this time of the Bob Dylan classic, leased to Pye Records by the Australian-based Festival Records. Produced by John Farrar, married to her one-time duettist Pat Carroll and one third of the breakaway Shadows trio Marvin, Welch and Farrar, 'If Not For You' soared to No.7 in the British chart, reaching No.25 in America. Before the year was out, 'Banks Of The Ohio' hit the British Top 6 and American Top 100.

During 1972 Newton-John released two singles, namely 'What Is Life', which was a Top 20 British hit, and 'Just A Little Too Much', which wasn't. She guested weekly on Cliff Richard's long-running BBC TV shows, while on the personal front her relationship with Bruce Welch finished. For the next two years, Newton-John was a regular charting name with titles like 'Take Me Home Country Roads' and 'Let Me Be There', her first American million-seller and winner of the Grammy Award in 1974 for the Best Country Vocal Performance, Female. In the April, Newton-John represented Britain in the Eurovision Song Contest staged in Brighton, East Sussex, with the track 'Long Live Love'; Abba won the competition with 'Waterloo'. Two months on, the singer switched to EMI Records based in London, where the October-released 'I Honestly Love You' peaked at No.22 in the British chart, No.1 in America.

Early in 1975, Newton-John, with her new manager and partner Lee Kramer, and John Farrar, her regular composer/producer, relocated to California, where she was enjoying the bulk of her recorded success. Said Newton-John, 'Helen Reddy and Jeff Wald took me under their wing. They said, "If you want to have a big hit in America, you have to be here. You have to concentrate on this country." I decided they were right [and] moved into the Sunset Marquis Hotel in West Hollywood.'

For the following three years she became one of the country's most successful acts, recording a succession of million-selling titles like 'Have You Ever Been Mellow?' and 'Please Mr Please' and collecting awards and trophies by the armful. On the personal front, her relation-ship with Kramer ended; he subsequently resigned as her manager.

In May 1977, following her debut at the Metropolitan Opera House, New York, Newton-John was dining with Reddy and Wald when she met Allan Carr. 'He was goofing about at the table and started talking about me doing *Grease*. I had seen the show in London and Richard Gere as the lead. When Allan asked me to do it, I got very nervous, but I did it.'

As *Saturday Night Fever* had been such an unexpected success, Robert Stigwood injected further cash into the *Grease* movie, raising the budget to $6 million. Originally, John Travolta had informed Stigwood he was unhappy with the script and with being typecast in the role of Danny, a working-class punk. The script was subsequently rewritten, and when Newton-John, with her distinct Australian accent, accepted the role of Sandy, her character was amended from an American to an Australian import! However, she was concerned that her fans would not accept the raunchier image towards the close of the film, namely as a leather-clad, gum-chewing biker's tart. A lengthy telephone conversation with her co-star calmed her anxiety. 'My image had been so white bread, so milkshake, and *Grease* was a chance to do something different. I didn't want to be 40 years old and still be the girl next door.'

Filming together naturally instigated media rumours that Travolta and Newton-John were romantically involved off-set. She said at the time, 'The hand-holding and kissing are for the cameras only. We've just become very good friends. And that friendship is working to capture the love we must have for the cameras.' But still the rumourmongers persisted!

Grease was premièred amidst a mammoth publicity campaign during June 1978, eventually grossing $150 million in box-office receipts. It went on to become the 11th highest earner (1987) behind movies directed by Steven Spielberg and George Lucas, while the soundtrack album sold in excess of 24 million copies, topping both the American and the British charts and earning the distinction of being the second-best-selling film soundtrack behind *Saturday Night Fever*.

John Farrar composed the film's biggest hits, the first being 'You're The One That I Want', a duet between Travolta and Newton-John. The title soared to the top of the American chart in June 1978, selling in excess of two million copies, while in Britain it shot to the top for an incredible nine-week stay, becoming at the time Britain's third-biggest-selling single ever.

Frankie Valli, late of the Four Seasons, also joined the *Grease* merry-go-round by recording the film's title song. It shot to the top of the American chart in August 1978, presenting the singer with his first American chart-topper in 16 years. 'Grease' was the second single lifted from the soundtrack to reach the top of the American chart. In Britain, the disc became a Top 3 hit.

Grease-mania was everywhere. Dress styles changed to match those of Danny and Sandy, while the stars behind the characters were musical sensations. Newton-John told author Joe Smith, 'When

Grease hit, I was accepted . . . It meant I could have a hit movie with hit songs and a new image.' And further, '*Grease* was the biggest single event of my whole life. It affected everything . . . It was fun to do and it's harmless, but it was a little raunchy in places.'

The couple's second duet was likewise swiped from the *Grease* soundtrack album as a follow-up to the international chart-topper 'You're The One That I Want'. Titled 'Summer Nights', the track was once again a mega-seller, although it faltered at No.5 in America. *Grease*-mania was still rife in Britain and 'Summer Nights' shot to the top of the chart in October 1978, a position it held for a remarkable seven weeks, with sales of one million plus. Meanwhile, the movie's soundtrack became Britain's top-selling album for a staggering 12 weeks; it went on to sell in excess of 20 million copies, earning it sixth position in the world's biggest-selling soundtrack race. The film became the biggest-grossing musical of all time. Travolta and Newton-John became record-breakers with their second consecutive British chart-topper. They were the only mixed-sex duo to enjoy two No.1 singles, and they hit the top with their first and last single.

Following the release of the 'Summer Nights' single, Travolta released his solo 'Greased Lightnin'' and 'Sandy' singles before eventually returning to the movie world. (Following a sticky start, he had by 1997 regained his mega-star status thanks to films like *Pulp Fiction*, *Michael* and *Face Off*.) In 1978 Olivia Newton-John issued her solo track from *Grease* titled 'Hopelessly Devoted To You'. The ballad soared to No.3 in America in the September; three months on, it fared better in Britain at No.2.

Through to the next decade, Newton-John was a sought-after woman, but with acting still in her veins she returned to the movie world to co-star with Gene Kelly in the musical *Xanadu*. Newton-John told *After Dark* magazine, 'I had great fear and trepidation at the thought of dancing with him, but on the first day of rehearsals he put me at ease completely.' The film was a multi-million-pound wild musical fantasy with special effects of exaggerated proportions, as the singer appeared as one of nine nurses courted by a punk rocker played by Michael Beck and a rich merchant, Gene Kelly's role. As revolutionary as *Xanadu* was, it failed to attract the public. Said Newton-John, 'I don't regret it or anything I've done. I learned a lot and the music was successful. I'd have been upset if the music flopped.' Yes, the soundtrack saved the movie from slipping into total oblivion, due to the involvement of the Electric Light Orchestra. This ensured the soundtrack sold in excess of one million copies, spawning five American Top 20 singles.

The first was Newton-John's 'Magic', composed and produced by John Farrar, in August 1980, which shot to the top of the American chart, becoming her third chart-topper in ten weeks. The single reached the Top 40 in Britain during the September. 'Xanadu' was issued as a single by Newton-John with the ELO and soared to the top of the British chart in July 1980. Described as musically whizzy, as it pounded at breakneck speed across the grooves, the title dominated the chart for three weeks, leaving exhausted dancers on the dance floor. Meanwhile, the film's soundtrack peaked at No.2, topping the American listing. As her chart-topper's follow-up, Newton-John's duet with Cliff Richard titled 'Suddenly' was issued but faltered in the British and American Top 20 while a pair of ELO singles, namely 'I'm Alive' and 'All Over The World', concluded the film's musical chart run.

Aside from the experience she had gained with *Xanadu*, Newton-John had befriended dancer/actor Matt Lattanzi, whom she married in 1985.

In the '80s, Newton-John's image further changed, and quite dramatically, as she swopped her 'milkshake' persona for that of an independent woman of the new decade. It was a risky strategy, but one that worked for her. With the release of the fiery 'Physical' single late in 1981, she shot to the top of the American chart in the November, a position she dominated for ten long weeks. 'I wasn't in the mood for tender ballads. I wanted peppy stuff because that's how I was feeling. We thought it was a great title because of the [then current] keep-fit craze.' Despite its innocence as an aerobics class track, 'Physical' was actually banned by selected radio stations due to its sexual innuendo. Newton-John was flabbergasted. 'I think the song has a *double entendre* . . . but it's meant to be fun.' Suggestive or not, the single sold in excess of two million copies in America before soaring to No.7 in Britain, indicating, perhaps, a less body-conscious nation! In the December, the *Physical* album followed; it was another million-seller and Top 10 album on both sides of the Atlantic. By the way, the so-called controversial single remained linked to aerobics classes and work-outs a decade later! Sad, eh?

Remaining an immensely high-profile singer, Newton-John returned to acting to co-star with John Travolta in the poorly received *Two of a Kind* movie. Early in 1984, the film's soundtrack album was issued. 'Twist Of Fate' was the first title to be lifted as a single by Newton-John and reached the American Top 5 and British Top 60. It was followed by 'Livin' In Desperate Times', which bombed.

Newton-John maintained her recording career through to 1988, when the album *The Rumour* faltered in the American Top 70. A year on, she turned her back on music to be elected Goodwill Ambassador for the United Nations Environment Programme. Now also a mother to daughter Chloe, she switched record companies to Geffen Records and issued an album of children's songs and 'standards' under the title *Warm And Tender* in 1990. In 1991 her past caught up with her when a pair of remixed compilations, 'The Grease Megamix' and '*Grease* – The Dream Mix' became British hits. Newton-John capitalised on the success by releasing the album titled *Back To Basics: The Essential Collection 1971–1992*, which included a handful of new titles, including her poor-selling single 'I Need Love'. Outside music, her chain of stores called Koala Blue went bankrupt and the singer was in danger of losing her £1.5 million Malibu beach home.

Following her appearance on *A Call to Action in the War against AIDS*, an American television special screened in 1992, the singer announced she had breast cancer. 'I made a decision that I was going to be OK and that I would look at everything positively.' Following intense treatment, she was in remission by 1993. 'Now I wake up and I'm so grateful for each and every morning.' However, her life was further blighted when in 1994 her marriage to Lattanzi was reported to be on shaky ground. This was confirmed when the couple separated before later divorcing in secret.

Back to the music, and after starring in the American television movie *A Christmas Romance* during 1994, she once again duetted with Cliff Richard on the single 'Had To Be', lifted from the stage show *Heathcliff*, in which Richard had the starring role. From this she returned to the studio to record *Gaia (One Woman's Journey)*, a Top 40 British album.

Into 1997 and on the personal front, Newton-John, now 50 years old, reported that she was romantically involved with Vince Gill, a country and western singer ten years her junior. She then dated television cameraman Patrick McDermott following a chance meeting at one of her concerts. The couple plan a 1999 wedding.

(Quotes: *Off the Record: An Oral History of Popular Music* by Joe Smith)

August 1980

ODYSSEY

Use It Up And Wear It Out

'We sang in French, Spanish, Italian, Swahili and Yoruban . . . we were very international' – Louise Lopez

Born in Stamford, Connecticut, of parents from the Virgin Islands, the three Lopez sisters, Louise, Lillian and Carmen, launched themselves as the Lopez Sisters on their neighbourhood circuit. The line-up became relatively successful and they peaked by performing at Carnegie Hall in New York as headliners of the New Faces of 1968 concert. According to Louise, 'An agent heard us there and asked if we would like to go to Europe. We played a lot of clubs throughout Europe and the Scandinavian countries.' Their 'playing' spanned five months! Upon their return to familiar territory, Carmen left the group to marry and raise a family; her replacement was Manila-born Tony Reynolds.

The trio became an in-demand item on the New York club circuit until 1976, when Louise and Lillian became affiliated as composers with Chappel Music. There they befriended Sandy Linzer, then producer of the Savannah Band, whose membership included August Darnell, later to become Kid Creole. The sisters went on to work with Linzer, and from the sessions the title 'Native New Yorker' was earmarked for single release. Odyssey was born as a recording unit.

'Native New Yorker' became the trio's debut via a recording deal with RCA Records. The title shot to No.21 in America during October 1977 but soared higher in Britain, reaching No.5 two months on. This track was included on Odyssey's eponymous album, likewise a big seller. Record-buyers believed the singers were indeed New Yorkers; certainly for the Lopez sisters this was untrue, but as Lillian told journalist John Abbey, 'We have been living in New York for so long now that we consider ourselves "native". We certainly think of it as home . . . I like living there because there's always something happening . . . The only thing I don't care for are the winters.'

At this juncture the trio's line-up altered. Reynolds left and was replaced by ex-We The People group member Bill McEachern, although, to be fair, the public was hard-pushed to notice the switch. 'Weekend Lover' followed 'Native New Yorker' early in 1978; failing to repeat its predecessor's success, the title floundered in the American Top 60. It was a worrying setback as Odyssey appeared to lose their way – disastrous in the early stages of a recording career. The single's fate obviously marked a lull in their career, and it would be during the next decade that Odyssey would ascend to stardom.

The single that elevated them to the top of the British chart in August 1980 was 'Use It Up And Wear It Out', composed by Linzer and L. Russell Brown. The dubiously titled song was a slice of dance music emulating the sound of 'Native New Yorker' without its sharpness. The Lopez sisters had intentionally swiped Odyssey's initial hit style and worked it into R&B and mainstream dance. The formula had worked. Said Lillian, 'The first album was a good R&B-type album, but we didn't want to be classified just as an R&B group.

We prefer to be somewhere between R&B and pop, because it's all too easy for people to categorise you. We always aim for that crossover, because that is the way to get through to more people. And that's good business!'

She conceded that with Odyssey's second album, titled *Hollywood Party Tonight*, they had departed too much from the 'Native New Yorker' mould and had suffered in sales for the error. However, with the third album, *Hang Together*, with its religiously styled packaging, which spawned the British chart-topper, they had returned to the comfortable groove. Said Lillian, 'With "Use It Up And Wear It Out" and Sandy Linzer, [we've] got the closest to the real Odyssey so far.'

Hang Together housed a further gem, this time a weaving ballad cloaked in beauty, both in lyric and in melody. Titled 'If You're Looking For A Way Out' and written by Ralph Kotkov and Sandy Linzer, it peaked at No.6 in the British chart during September 1980. According to Lillian, 'When we were in the studio, Sandy said he felt it was too country and western in its flavour, but by the time we had it finished it had a distinctly R&B taste to it too.' When the track was performed on stage, the spotlight fell on Lillian, sitting at her piano, singing note-perfect before a silent audience. 'You know, there were a lot of husbands walking out on a lot of wives when that song came out. It meant a lot of things to a lot of people . . . I guess it also broke up a lot of relationships . . . but when I hear it, I feel good.'

In between releases, Odyssey, with Al Jackson replacing McEachern, capitalised on their British success by touring the country, meeting the public's demand and cementing their following. A further trek was scheduled to coincide with the release of their next album, *I've Got The Melody*, and their Top 5 single titled 'Going Back To My Roots', also affectionately known as 'Zipping Up My Boots'. This title was the follow-up to the album title track 'Hang Together', a staller in the British Top 40 early in 1981. The trio's reworking of the Lamont Dozier classic 'Going Back To My Roots' also shot to the top of the then British dance chart, yet, quite remarkably, bypassed the American mainstream listing.

Steve Tyrell was drafted in to produce the *I've Got The Melody* album, replacing Linzer, who had been responsible for Odyssey's previous three. According to Lillian, 'We needed a change . . . simply for the sake of having a new injection, a new approach. The only thing that we considered was wrong with our previous albums was that we felt we were missing out a little on the R&B market, and getting too closely associated with disco.'

The follow-up to 'Going Back To My Roots', 'It Will Be Alright', struggled into the British Top 50 during September 1981. It would be a further year before Odyssey re-entered the British chart.

Meanwhile, though, RCA Records released the *Best Of Odyssey* compilation, an immediate big-selling item during the 1981 Christmas period. Louise said about this album, 'I suppose it's a tribute to the act and a measure of their success, and we all feel that it's particularly nice that the UK has released it first, since the fans have given us so much support.'

Through their career with Odyssey, the Lopez sisters have always given their composing talents priority. Louise, for instance, had recently co-penned the Grammy-winning title of the Broadway show *Bubbling Brown Sugar.* 'Songwriting is something that I personally have been doing for about 15 years . . . We fully realise that a self-contained unit is a much better proposition in terms of longevity . . . It's a kind of insurance, I guess.'

During September 1982, Odyssey returned to the British Top 10 with 'Inside Out', another title to bypass the American chart. The single's ascent was boosted by the trio's hands-on promotion organised by Eyes and Ears, the top British-based press and promotions company. Typical of the '80s dance style, 'Inside Out' climbed to top the disco chart. 'Magic Touch' followed to stall in the Top 50 and marked the end of Odyssey's recording association with RCA Records. The move was fated; the trio switched to Priority Records, where '(Joy) I Know It' was their final British hit during August 1985.

Unable to revive their career, Odyssey disbanded until the '90s when Lillian Lopez resurrected the name for the British nightclub circuit. Typical of Odyssey's touring schedule was their 1996 performance at Butlin's Holiday Camp in Bognor Regis, Sussex, playing before a young audience. Astonishingly, the reception resembled their charting period, particularly when Lillian, Odyssey's voice, sang 'If You're Looking For A Way Out'. Although the lavish gowns, borrowed from Indian and Spanish designs, long, flowing and vividly colourful, have matured into classic suits, the voice that was Odyssey is as sublime as ever, fiery yet true in depth and range.

Following a lengthy absence, Lillian Lopez and Al Jackson returned to the recording studio to rework their biggest-selling items. Erwin Keites and John Thirkell oversaw the project issued early in 1998 under the title *The Very Best Of Odyssey* via Tabasco Entertainment.

The Odyssey story could begin again!

(Quotes: *Blues and Soul* magazine, 1980, interviews by John Abbey; 1981, interview by Bob Killbourn; 1982, interview by Sharon Davis)

September 1980

THE POLICE

Don't Stand So Close To Me

'We were energetic, loud and noisy, and as the punk bands fell by the wayside, for various reasons we stayed and survived' – Sting

Stewart Copeland, born in Alexandria, Virginia, on 16 July 1952, was the son of an American CIA agent and spent much of his younger life in the Middle East. He attended college in California before relocating to Britain and perfecting his art as a drummer to perform with the group Curved Air. The group's manager was Miles, Stewart's brother.

Sting was born Gordon Matthew Sumner in Wallsend, Tyne and Wear, on 2 October 1951. He told author Joe Smith that he ended up at the age of 15 or 16 playing with guys who had been playing since the '50s. He would play jazz standards rather than learn Led Zeppelin riffs, a move that would stand him in good stead later in his career. Whilst employed in various jobs that included a ditch digger, a civil servant and a primary school teacher, he worked his way through groups that included Earthrise, the River City Jazz Band and the Ronnie Pierson Trio. In fact, the nickname 'Sting' was given to him by Gordon Soloman, a local jazz player, because he wore yellow and black striped jumpers.

Copeland and Sting first met when Sting was in the group Last Exit and they performed at a Newcastle venue. They met again in London during 1977, when they decided to form their own group of musicians. Recruiting guitarist Henri Padovani, they began rehearsing in earnest, usually at Copeland's own studio in Mayfair. The first results of this musical liaison included the title 'Fall Out' which was, during May 1977, issued on Copeland's own Illegal label. Sales pushed the title into the then indie chart. Meanwhile, the group linked up with the American singer Cherry Vanilla, touring Britain's low-key clubs with her and Johnny Thunders and the Heartbreakers. A European tour with Wayne County's Electric Chairs followed.

During this period, Copeland and Sting befriended guitarist Andy Summers, born in Poulton-le-Fylde, Lancashire, on 31 December 1942. In the June he officially joined the group, now known as the Police, by performing at The Marquee Club and The Music Machine in London. Before 1977 closed, Padovani left the line-up, leaving the trio to appear for the first time without him at Rebecca's Club,

Birmingham, before supporting Eberhard Schoener on his album titled *Video Flashback*, recorded in Munich.

Early in 1978, the Police began recording their first album until touring commitments in Britain as support act to the American group Spirit took precedence. While the trio was on the road, Miles Copeland secured a one-off recording deal for their single 'Roxanne'. Said Sting, 'Being brought up on jazz, I was locked out when I started going around record companies. I went to every major record company with my songs, and they all said it wasn't commercial enough.'

The Police needed an identity, and as the punk movement was prolific at the time, Sting opted to steer the group at that market, in much the same way as Bob Geldof had reluctantly guided his Boomtown Rats. Indeed, the Police went on to appear in an American television advertisement for Wrigley's Chewing Gum because of their reputed association with the punk fraternity. Sting believed the Police's music to be mellow, yet it contained the anger and sense of wanting needed to revolutionise the music industry – 'So [we] flew that banner for a while'.

During March 1978, Miles Copeland strode one giant step forward when he secured a recording contract with A&M Records, where the title 'Roxanne' was the trio's debut single. Although the track was later immortalised by comedian actor Eddie Murphy, he was too late to prevent it from bombing. Seven months on, the Police issued their second single, 'Can't Stand Losing You', a Top 50 British hit. The title would probably have charted higher if the trio had been on hand for promotion purposes, but instead they had embarked upon an American tour. A further month on, the Police's *Outlandos D'Amour* album, recorded for the princely sum of £3,000, eventually rose into the British Top 10. The 'So Lonely' track had already been swiped from the album for single release.

Early in 1979, the Police returned to America for a further lengthy tour. In their absence from home ground, 'Roxanne' was reissued. This time it soared into the British Top 12, reaching the Top 40 in America. Persistence had paid off; the public had finally succumbed. Hot on the heels of the single's success, the trio embarked upon their first fully fledged British tour, which included appearing at the Reading Rock Festival. Said Sting, 'I didn't plan to be a pop star. My real ambition was to be a respected musician.'

With no titles suitable for single release, the Police's second single, 'Can't Stand Losing You', was reissued during the August and shot into the British Top 2. At this juncture Sting exercised his acting muscle when he starred in the movie *Quadrophenia*, playing the role of Ace. This short diversion fuelled rumours of further acting roles;

however, any that might have been in the pipeline were shelved to enable Sting to concentrate on his music career and, more immediately, the Police's next single.

Using a pending British tour to publicise the title, 'Message In A Bottle' soared to the top of the British chart during October 1979, a position it dominated for two weeks. When issued in America in the December, the track faltered in the Top 80. The British chart-topper and its follow-up, another Sting composition, 'Walking On The Moon', were both swiped from the group's second album, *Reggatta De Blanc*, released in the October. It crashed through the chart to peak at the top, where it stayed for four weeks; it reached the Top 30 in America. Incidentally, the album went on to win the Grammy Award for Best Rock Instrumental Performance.

Meanwhile, the second lifted single, 'Walking On The Moon', likewise topped the British chart, thanks to the innovative promotional video filmed at Houston's Kennedy Space Centre. The Police, like Queen, were dedicated video masters, believing visuals were as important as the music itself. Yet nothing matched the hands-on promotion touring provided, when group and audience gelled. Indeed, the Police's audiences were becoming uncontrollable, to say the least, as the trio was elevated to a teenybop sensation – a strange position to be in, considering their previous struggles to win any kind of acceptance. Indeed, fan hysteria instigated riot situations during their concerts, prompting Summers to tell the music weekly NME, 'I never thought we'd get that kind of teenage audience . . . but we haven't compromised at all. Some of our music is definitely not teenage-orientated, but I don't mind. You get a tremendous amount of enthusiasm with kids of that age.' Following tradition, Sting, as prime singer and focal point, became the teenybop pin-up. 'To a lot of people, teenyboppers are a sub-species not even to be entertained. I don't agree. If you can transcend the screaming, you can take a generation with you into something else. It's a real challenge . . . I never visualised myself as a pin-up. I realise it's not just my music that I'm selling, it's the whole thing, and I can probably accept total responsibility for it.'

In the '80s came the Police's first world tour, covering 19 countries, including a concert in Bombay which earned them the distinction of being the first Western group to play there. So important was the Indian visit that a film crew accompanied them. Said Sting, 'We are doing this for a charity, and we're actually raising money for people in Bombay. We can sort of salve our conscience with that.'

Following the tour and the release of 'Six Pack', a collection of singles pressed in blue vinyl which reached the British Top 20, the Police returned to the recording studio to work on their third album.

They also performed at a pair of significant concerts: a benefit concert in Milton Keynes, Buckinghamshire, and the Dublin-staged Dalymount Festival. Then, following a lengthy European tour, the trio released their next single, 'Don't Stand So Close To Me'. The title became a British chart-topper in September 1980, a position it held for four weeks; it reached the Top 10 in America in April 1981. The accompanying video returned Sting to a school classroom as a teacher. The track survived the test of time, not so the promotional tool.

Before 1980 ended, as the *Zenyatta Mondatta* album soared to the top of the chart, they embarked upon a North American and Canadian tour and they issued the 'De Do Do Do, De Da Da Da' single during a fit of the stutters. It hit the British Top 5 and became a Top 10 American hit.

Into 1981, the Police kicked off their American tour with a standing-room-only concert in New York before crossing over to Japan and Australia, among other countries. With the Police then relegated to the back burner, Sting turned to the film world once more to do the preliminary work on BBC TV's drama *Artemis W*, written by David Redken, in which the singer played an angel, before winning an Ivor Novello Award for Songwriter of the Year. His two careers seemed to run easily together, and this would stay true when the Police disbanded.

Moving to Montserrat, the trio began recording their next album, *Ghost In The Machine*, from which the title 'Invisible Sun' was swiped for single release. The track soared into the British Top 2 amidst public outrage because the accompanying promotional video was shot in war-torn Belfast. Every care was taken during filming to ensure the result was non-partisan, but still the public heaved in dismay. Needless to say, the Police need not have bothered putting visuals to tape; the video was banned. Said Sting, 'The video . . . could be misinterpreted and said to convey meanings which are not present in the lyrics.' Meanwhile, the album *Ghost In The Machine* shot to the top of the British chart.

In complete contrast to the serious statement within the lyrics of 'Invisible Sun', the trio released 'Every Little Thing She Does Is Magic', a title which nobody could object to. So popular was this perky slice of pop music that it became a British chart-topper in 1981 and reached the Top 3 in America, while the follow-up, 'Spirits In The Material World', peaked in the British Top 20, reaching No.11 Stateside a year on.

Early in 1982, the Police took the unusual step of performing at San Francisco's Filmore Stadium to raise funds for Freddie Laker's innovative but doomed airline, then went on to win the Best British

Group award at the Brit ceremony held in London, one of several awards the group received this year.

As Sting, recently the proud recipient of the Ivor Novello Award for Songwriter of the Year, continued to expand his movie career, he also took the initiative to record and release his debut solo single titled 'Spread A Little Happiness', lifted from the movie soundtrack *Brimstone And Treacle*. The track reached the British Top 20, and heralded the start of his future lucrative career. The remaining members of the group had also pursued their own projects: Copeland had written the film score for *Rumble Fish* and was engrossed in the music for an American ballet version of *King Lear*, while Summers went on to issue his own instrumental album *I Advance Masked*.

Nonetheless, the Police joined forces once more, again with a multisales result.

Also see: 'Every Breath You Take', June 1983

(Quotes: *Off the Record: An Oral History of Popular Music* by Joe Smith)

October 1980

BARBRA STREISAND

Woman In Love

'I am a mass of contradictions. I am simple, complex. Generous, selfish. Unattractive and beautiful. Lazy and driven . . . I'm simply complex' – Barbra Streisand

Born Barbara Joan Streisand in Brooklyn, New York, on 24 April 1942, the future star was one of three children. Their father died when Streisand was 15 months old, leaving the family to struggle through life. From an early age Streisand showed signs of becoming an entertainer; indeed, she could sing before she could walk. Listening to the radio, the child memorised the melodies and lyrics of the current material, and so obsessed was she with Joni James that at the age of ten she journeyed on the subway to MGM Records, James's company, where she demanded an audition, only to be rejected. This rejection was received badly, and from then on Streisand confined her entertaining activities to school functions.

From high school the youngster moved to Manhatten, where she took acting lessons. With failed auditions and her employment insurance exhausted, Streisand had little option but to turn to singing to pay the rent. 'I thought to be called a singer was demeaning, that it was a second-class profession,' she once said. Joining fellow acts of an opera singer and a comic, Streisand's first performance was at The Lion, where she performed 'A Sleepin' Bee' from the *House of Flowers* musical to a standing ovation. From The Lion, Streisand switched to The Bon Soir in Greenwich Village. Once more, the reluctant singer attracted great attention from the audiences and later from newspaper reviewers. Due to her popularity, Streisand's initial two-week engagement was extended to three months, whereupon she secured club dates in and around Detroit and St Louis and appeared on television before turning tail to return to The Bon Soir.

In June 1961, with no future bookings in her diary, Streisand met and befriended Marty Erlichman, who went on to become her personal manager. He said, 'She was the most incredible performer I had ever seen, the wonder of my generation.' According to Streisand, 'He told me I didn't have to change my name, my nose, nothing. I would become a big star just the way I was.' The combination was perfect.

Two months on, Streisand auditioned for the revue *Another Evening with Harry Stoones*. Sadly, the musical opened and closed on the same night. Further auditions led to Streisand joining the musical *I Can Get It For You Wholesale*; despite being an also-ran in the cast, Streisand attracted glowing reviews. While performing in the musical, the singer recorded her vinyl debut, a track on the cast album of *I Can Get It For You Wholesale* at Columbia's Thirtieth Street recording studio. So impressed were executives at Columbia that they secured her to a recording contract. Streisand was due to earn 5 per cent royalties on 98 per cent of records sold over a five-year period, one year guaranteed, four options. All recording costs were to be recouped, naturally.

Throughout mid-1962 Streisand remained in her Broadway musical, earning $200 a week. She was bored with the show but her one escape was her co-star Elliott Gould, signed to the cast when Gene Kelly rejected the role. In time the two artists became lovers, he moving into Streisand's apartment situated above a fish restaurant on Third Avenue. Needless to say, the flat was cheap and stank!

During October 1962 the young singer recorded four tracks as a soloist. Two sides comprised her first single, namely 'Happy Days Are Here Again' and 'When The Sun Comes Out'. Both titles bombed, while her next, titled 'My Coloring Book', recorded in less than one hour, was one of several versions released to sell poorly. However, by the close of 1962 Streisand was free; her stay in *I Can Get It For You Wholesale* was over. It was reported that the singer raced in glee to the wings as the final curtain hit the stage!

Recording for three days during January 1963 at Studio A in

Seventh Avenue, Streisand completed her first album, titled – after much deliberation by her record company – *The Barbra Streisand Album*. With no immediate commitments, the singer promoted its release with a three-week engagement at Miami Beach, the kick-off venue for a lengthy trek that also included radio and television guest spots. With this concentrated promotion, *The Barbra Streisand Album* climbed up the American chart into the Top 5.

Now an artist of note, Streisand's image required an overhaul. Her wardrobe was redesigned and refined, whereupon the glamorous Streisand look was born. The fishy apartment was also dumped for a Central Park West duplex. Through to 1972 the singer established herself as a successful artist, enjoying 18 American singles in the Top 100 chart; the content varied from novelty songs through to mainstream and musical show tunes. The biggest titles, incidentally, were Laura Nyro's classic 'Stoney End' in 1971 and the previous hit, 'People', lifted from the *Funny Girl* musical based on the life of Fanny Brice, a teenage headliner in the Ziegfield Follies and comedienne extraordinaire. Streisand had played the leading role on the Broadway stage. Following the success of 'People', the cast soundtrack album shot into the 100,000 sales bracket, while the single itself went on to win a Grammy Award for Best Single Performance. Streisand personally collected the Best Female Vocalist Grammy and recorded her own *People* album, a two million seller.

As her star rose professionally, so did Streisand's personal life. She married actor Elliott Gould during September 1963 in Carson City and the couple honeymooned in Los Angeles, where Streisand was performing.

With such an overwhelming presence in the *Funny Girl* project, it was inevitable that Streisand would play her stage role in the movie version. Prior to the film's shooting, the singer gave birth to her first son, Jason, in December 1966 and completed her third American television special titled *The Belle of 14th Street*, based on a vaudevillian troupe, in which Streisand played seven different characters.

It became apparent during the filming of *Funny Girl* that Streisand's marriage to Gould was finished. She turned to Omar Sharif, who said at the time, 'I fell madly in love with her. The feeling was mutual for four months, the time it took to shoot the picture.' When the filming ended in the December, so did the romance. The $12 million musical was premièred at the Criterion Theatre, off Times Square, and Streisand, hailed as 'magnificent, sublime, radiant', won an Oscar for her role.

While she was busy with the film's schedules, Streisand's recording contract with Columbia Records expired. With several third-party companies hovering, Streisand negotiated a sweet deal with

Columbia and stayed where she had started. It was reputed that the singer was guaranteed $850,000, with a royalty rate of 10 cents per single, 40 cents per album, while Columbia celebrated her return by issuing a pair of albums, namely *Simply Streisand* and *A Christmas Album*.

When Streisand had agreed to perform in the *Funny Girl* movie, produced by Ray Stark, she had also sealed her name for three further films. However, she rejected the scripts Stark gave her, preferring to appear in a pair of MGM films. In turn, Stark claimed the actress was in breach of her agreement with him by working for a third party. She ignored him and started rehearsing her role of Dolly Levi in *Hello Dolly*, a film that endured daily chaos that worsened when she argued with her leading man Walter Matthau. Due to constant verbal altercations, the media were barred from the film set. *Hello Dolly* was premièred in December 1969 in New York City; once again, reviews were ecstatic, but public response was poor. The movie nosedived.

From *Hello Dolly* Streisand moved to Paramount Pictures' *On A Clear Day You Can See Forever*. Principally shot in New York, the film moved to Britain's East Sussex town of Brighton, where 12 days were spent on location in the Royal Pavilion. With the unexpected bombing of *Hello Dolly* and the struggling *Paint Your Wagon*, Paramount Pictures decided to cut the length of *On A Clear Day You Can See Forever* to two hours, causing Streisand to comment, 'What the public saw was not the picture we envisioned and I learned a very important lesson about final control.'

During July 1970 Streisand returned to her music to record the aforementioned *Stoney End* project in Los Angeles. Once again she agreed to participate in the album's promotional schedules, a move, quite frankly, her record company didn't anticipate. Subsequently, when the 'Stoney End' single was issued in September 1970, it attracted media criticism claiming Nyro's styling was alien to Streisand's vocals. Nonetheless, 'Stoney End' soared to No.6 in the American chart, while in Britain the single marked her second chart hit by peaking in the Top 50 during January 1971. Upon re-entry a month later, the title soared into the Top 30. (As an aside, Streisand's first British hit, 'Second Hand Rose', had reached No.14 early in 1966.) Flushed with high-profile success, Columbia Records happily issued the *Stoney End* album. Once again, reviewers were confused; thankfully sales were positive enough to pass gold status. *Stoney End* really was a brilliantly conceived album.

It took three years for Streisand to dominate the American chart, although, of course, many believed that most of her singles warranted chart-topping status. In February, with a Marvin Hamlisch co-penned track, Streisand enjoyed her No.1 single 'The Way We Were' for three weeks. Sales were naturally boosted because the single was the theme from the movie of the same name in which the singer co-starred with Robert Redford. It was a wonderful, weepy film that captured romantics' imaginations the world over. When released in Britain, 'The Way We Were' peaked in the Top 30.

Once again, with Streisand's career on the up, so too was her personal life, thanks to her romance with Ryan O'Neal, who was married to Leigh Taylor-Young. The couple were discreet at first, wary that the adverse publicity would damage both their careers, before bathing in the media glare for their film *What's Up Doc?*, premièred during March and going on to gross in excess of $50 million. Streisand would move on to have affairs with the former Canadian Prime Minister Pierre Trudeau, Jon Peters and Andre Agassi.

On the chart-topping front, Streisand's next American hit was another theme from a movie in which she starred. This time, she co-starred with Kris Kristofferson in *A Star Is Born*, while its title song 'Love Theme From *A Star Is Born* (Evergreen)' dominated the American singles sales for two weeks during March 1977. It was a satisfying result, particularly as the singer had co-written the song with Paul Williams. 'I was going through a period of feeling very inadequate because so many of our songstresses today write their own songs,' she remarked at the time. Her frustration turned into determination and as she 'fooled around' on her guitar, 'a song was born. It just came out of absolute impatience.' Unfortunately, the film failed to run as smoothly as the song's melodies. Arguments during shooting, scripts being rewritten and so on all went into making the final product that, once more, romantics applauded. Shame the critics slated the slush.

It was thanks to the ingenuity and obvious creative mind of a Kentucky radio DJ that Streisand enjoyed her next American chart-topper. Gary Guthrie had received new albums from Streisand and Neil Diamond. Included on both albums was the track 'You Don't Bring Me Flowers' and each artist sang it in the same key. Guthrie interspliced the two tracks, creating a duet, which he played on air. Telephone calls to the station from members of the public wanting to purchase the duet forced Columbia Records to contact both Streisand and Diamond to ask them to record the song. Both agreed; 'You Don't Bring Me Flowers' was issued and soared to the top of the American chart in December 1978, reaching the Top 5 in Britain. Later, when the single was nominated as Record of the Year at the annual Grammy Awards ceremony, Streisand performed the song live, the first time she had done so. However, the success of 'You Don't Bring Me Flowers' had a downside: the agreement drawn between Guthrie and Columbia Records to utilise his initial idea wasn't honoured. The DJ filed a breach of contract against the company estimated at $5 million, whereupon Columbia settled.

In the lead-up to the '80s, Streisand returned to the top of the American chart, again with a duet. This time it was with the most unlikely of partners, disco diva Donna Summer. When Streisand began session work on her *Wet* album, she visualised it as a concept project based on water. Composers Paul Jabara and Bruce Roberts desperately wanted Streisand to record their 'No More Tears (Enough Is Enough)', but the track didn't hold water. (Yes, pun intended!) So the composers wrote an introduction along the lines 'It's raining, it's pouring'. Clever lads! 'No More Tears (Enough Is Enough)' topped the American listing in November 1979 and reached No.3 in Britain.

Following the duets, Streisand sought a new musical challenge. The Bee Gees were likewise searching for an artist to work with. Through contacts, the two met with the intention of Streisand recording five Bee Gees tracks for inclusion on her next album. Once the acts agreed to work jointly, the arrangement needed to be approved by the trio's manager, Robert Stigwood. Originally, all three Bee Gees were to sing with Streisand, but when Stigwood asked for three-quarters of Columbia Records' advance and royalties, the three brothers were reduced to one – Barry. Despite an attack of nerves, Barry said Streisand was 'mellow, laid back, a pussy cat'. Eventually, she requested an album's worth of Bee Gees material, produced by Barry, whereupon *Guilty* was born. She also duetted with the Bee Gee on the track titled 'Woman In Love', the obvious choice for single release. However, Columbia Records were unsure, eventually conceding to issue 'Woman In Love' five weeks prior to the mother album's release. The company believed that if the title bombed, it wouldn't affect album sales. 'Woman In Love' soared to the top of the American chart during October 1980, the same month as Streisand scooped her first and only (to date) British chart-topper. Barry Gibb told *Billboard* magazine, 'I'd have to say at least 80 per cent of the success of that record belongs to her.' He also admitted that Streisand had hesitated before recording 'Woman In Love' due to the track's sentiments: 'She felt it was a little liberationist; that it might be a little too strong for a pop song.' She was proven wrong; the public flocked to own every sentimental note.

Meanwhile, the *Guilty* album topped the charts in 15 countries and sold in excess of 20 million copies around the world, becoming the artist's biggest-earning album in 19 years. Two further Streisand/Gibb duets followed the chart-topper, namely the album's title and 'What Kind Of Fool'; both peaked in the American Top 10, while 'Guilty' faltered in the British Top 40. Barry Gibb wanted to repeat the musical triumph but Streisand refused, saying she needed to concentrate on her acting career.

Through to the close of the '80s, the star enjoyed three further British hit singles: 'Comin' In And Out Of Your Life' and 'Memory', Top 70 and Top 40 titles respectively during 1982, and 'Till I Loved You (Love Theme From *Goya*)', a duet with Don Johnson, a Top 20 hit in 1988.

From music to movies and Streisand's next major project, *Yentl*, the story of a rabbi's daughter who possessed the body of a woman and the soul of a man. Not only did Streisand play the lead role, she also undertook the roles of film director, author, co-producer and singer of the movie's soundtrack, earning her the distinction of becoming the first woman in the film business to work in all capacities. Streisand approached several companies to part-finance the project; most rejected her proposals until early 1981, when United Artists rose to the challenge with $14.5 million. A year on, *Yentl* was in production and Streisand relocated to Britain, Prague and California for shooting. When the budget rose, the media tagged the film 'Barbra's folly'. The doubters were to eat their printed words when, after *Yentl* was simultaneously premièred in New York and Los Angeles, the critics were united in wild enthusiasm. Within a short time, the film was America's third top title, winning a handful of industry awards before being nominated for six Academy Awards.

Into the '90s and reverting to music, Streisand's second love, she charted four times in Britain with 'Places That Belong To You', Top 20 in 1992, 'With One Look', Top 30 a year on, and a pair during 1994, namely 'The Music Of The Night' and 'As If We Never Said Goodbye (From *Sunset Boulevard*)', Top 60 and Top 20 respectively.

In March 1998 Streisand released her strongest of albums for some time, titled *Higher Ground*, which entered the American chart at No.1. To promote the release, the star agreed to meet the media, a part of her career she had always treated with trepidation. The first single swiped from the album was her duet with Celine Dion titled 'Tell Him'. Streisand told Marc Freden in *GMTV Magazine* that her album was inspired by the hymn 'On Holy Ground' sung at President Clinton's mother's funeral: 'I felt it was the connective tissue among souls. Songs like that elevate the spirit. It connects us to a force that is higher than all of us.' *Higher Ground* sold over five million copies and became her 12th multi-platinum title and her 37th gold, a feat, Columbia Records boasted, no other female act had achieved. And, once more, with her career peaking, Streisand's personal life also shone with love when she met actor/film director James Brolin at a dinner party during the shooting of *The Mirror Has Two Faces*. Brolin's most recent successes at the time were the television series *Pensacola:*

Wings Of Gold and his director debut film *My Brother's War*. The couple managed to keep their romance a secret until they confirmed they were engaged to be married. The ceremony took place in 1998.

Professionally speaking, Streisand received the 1998 Academy Awards nomination for Best Composer for 'I've Finally Found Someone', the theme from *The Mirror Has Two Faces*.

So, one of Hollywood's most ambitious women, Barbra Streisand is a perfectionist in every project she tackles. Outside the entertainment business she's an active campaigner for AIDS awareness and a supporter of Bill Clinton, like others of her ilk, and as such she was a guest at the White House early in 1998 to greet Tony Blair during his much-hyped visit. Without question, the artist is either loved or loathed, but she is undeniably one of the most successful stars of the twentieth century. She really is respected equally as a singer, an actress and a businesswoman. Her talent is awesome, her vision international. She really is a jewel among jewels.

(Quotes: *Barbra Streisand: The Woman, the Myth, the Music* by Shaun Considine; *Barbra Streisand: The Woman and the Legend* by James Spadd)

November 1980

ABBA

Super Trouper

'Coming from Sweden, the [Eurovision] contest was the only way of promoting ourselves in other countries. We knew that nobody would really listen to us otherwise . . . We decided to take a chance' – Bjorn Ulvaeus

Bjorn Ulvaeus, born in Gothenburg, Sweden, on 25 April 1945, was introduced to music from an early age. When he was 11 years old his family relocated to Västervik, where he purchased an acoustic guitar and joined his first skiffle group. With school friends from Västervik High, and with the encouragement of their art teacher, Ulvaeus pursued Dixieland Jazz, building up a solid local following.

Upon graduation during 1963, it was intended Ulvaeus would progress to law college. But music pulled. Taking a few months' detour, Ulvaeus and his group travelled around Europe, busking and performing to cover their daily expenses that included the upkeep of their travel-weary Volvo. During their absence, Ulvaeus's mother entered them in a national talent contest sponsored by Swedish radio. Using the name the West Bay Singers, the group lost the contest but won the attention of Stig Anderson and his business partner Benjt Bernhag, owners of the newly formed publishing house and record label titled Polar Music.

Following lengthy discussions, including those about whether Ulvaeus should resume his education, the group, with a membership of Hansi Schwarz, Tony Roth, Johan Karlberg and Ulvaeus, were contracted as Polar Music's first act. With a name change from the West Bay Singers to the Hootenanny Singers, their debut single, titled 'Jag Vantar Vid Min Milla', released in 1964, was the track they had performed in the talent contest. The title became a Swedish hit, whereupon the group turned professional, although Ulvaeus took a hiatus in 1965 to study economics and law at the University of Stockholm before being called, with the other group membership, to do national service. During their lifetime, the Hootenanny Singers recorded in excess of 20 hit singles and nine albums and became a top touring name in Europe.

With encouragement from Stig Anderson, Ulvaeus embarked upon a solo career in 1968, his singles including 'Honey', a cover version of Bobby Goldsboro's 1968 hit. Ulvaeus may have shrugged off the confines of a group for the immediate future, but he was soon to join another when he met the Hep Stars, fronted by Benny Andersson.

Born Goran Bror Benny Andersson in Stockholm, Sweden, on 16 December 1946, he, like Ulvaeus, was born into a musical household. His father and grandfather, both accomplished musicians, had taught Andersson to play the accordion and piano by the time he was ten years old. But it was his later awareness of the Beatles that persuaded him his ambitions were musically based. Meanwhile, on the personal front, Andersson became engaged to his school sweetheart Christina; both were 15 years old. They never married but had two children. As much as Andersson was devoted to his family, the pull of music was stronger. Subsequently, when he was offered the keyboardist vacancy in the Hep Stars, he didn't hesitate. With vocalist Svenne Hedlund, the group quickly became forerunners in Swedish music. The first track to feature Andersson was 'Tribute To Buddy Holly', released as a single during 1964.

By the next year, Andersson had begun composing for the group. His first track, titled 'No Response', was included on the Hep Stars' album *We And Our Cadillac*. The title was later lifted as a single to become their biggest European hit. Encouraged by this success, Andersson wrote further songs for the unit, notably 'Sunny Girl', 'Wedding', 'It's Nice To Be Back' and 'Consolation'; all titles helped the Hep Stars grow in status to become Sweden's biggest-selling group. Their success was instant; the group had little time to consider business dealings that included the Hep House production company, originally opened by the group for their use only. Following a series of failed business ventures, including the costly movie titled *Habari Safari* which was ultimately shelved, Hep House faced the bankruptcy court in 1968. In turn, the Hep Stars owed the Inland Revenue a fortune in back taxes. Andersson's personal debt totalled in excess of £100,000. It took him four years to clear.

During 1969, the Hep Stars split up. A trio from the membership, namely Christer Petterson, Janne Frisk and Lennart Hegland, continued using the group name, while Svenne Hedlund and Andersson joined Charlotte Walker.

Benny Andersson and Bjorn Ulvaeus had met occasionally while each was a member of his respective band. Yet it was to be 1969 before the two actually collaborated as songwriters. Their first composition was titled 'Isn't It Easy'.

The third member of the future Abba was born Anni-Frid Lyngstad in Bjorkasen, Norway, on 15 November 1945 following a love affair between her mother Synni and a German officer, Alfred Haase. Mother, daughter and grandmother were subsequently outcasts in their small community, and when Norway was liberated in 1945, Haase was reported lost at sea. Devastated, Synni Lyngstad sank into a deep depression which ultimately killed her. She was 21 years old. Actually Haase was very much alive; he had returned to Germany at the end of the war, where he was married with two children.

Unable to live among her fellow men, Anni-Frid and her grandmother crossed the border into Sweden. Desperate and with no money, Mrs Lyngstad worked her way through a series of low-paid jobs before securing a regular sewing position in a factory based in Eskilstuna. Anni-Frid's early life, therefore, was poverty-stricken and insecure, yet she was educated and cared for by her devoted grandmother. During the evenings, the pair listened to their battered gramophone scratch its way through the grooves on 78rpm jazz records. Anni-Frid was smitten. She performed as a singer for the first time at the age of 11; two years later, looking older than her years, she sang professionally as part of the Ewaldek Jazz Group. At 16, now streetwise and ambitious, she switched jazz outfits to the Bengt Sandlund Band. In time she befriended the band's bass player, Ragner Frederickson, and they eventually left the line-up to form, with two others, The Anni-Frid Four. Frederickson and Lyngstad went on to marry; they had two children.

Careers began to drift until Lyngstad returned to the spotlight via the occasional nightclub appearance. In 1967 she won first prize in

Sweden's famed talent contest singing 'A Day Off', whereupon she instantly resang the title on national television, joining a gala of Scandinavian stars. Such was her subsequent popularity that she was offered a recording contract with EMI Records. Embarking on a solo career meant relocating to Stockholm, leaving her husband and family.

Her debut single in 1967, titled 'En Ledit Dag', was quickly followed by 'Din'; neither was a big-selling title but they were sufficient to launch Lyngstad as a popular Swedish performer. From EMI Records she switched to Columbia Records, where, from 1968, she enjoyed a handful of minor-selling singles including the titles 'Simsalabim' and 'Mycket Kar'. However, her destiny was set when, in 1969, she chanced to appear in the same Malmö nightclub as the Hep Stars and befriended Benny Andersson. Within weeks of that meeting the two were lovers and in August 1969 they became engaged to be married.

Agnetha Ase Faltskog, born in Jönköping, southern Sweden, on 5 April 1950, debuted on stage at the age of 15 in a Christmas pantomime. The performance had been encouraged by her father, Ingvar, an enthusiastic member of his local amateur society. However, all did not go according to plan; as the youngster recited 'Billy Boy', her pants fell down! However, this incident failed to end her ambitions of singing as a career; indeed, two years on she was a proficient pianist and a regular stage performer. She left school at 15, whereupon she became a telephonist in a local car showroom, pursuing her first love at the weekends, singing with the Bengt Enghardt Orchestra. This association led Enghardt to oversee a handful of demo recordings with his vocalist, the most notable being 'Folj Med Min' and 'Jag Var Sa Kar'. In turn, these tracks were given to a talent scout, with the unlikely name of Little Gerhard, for the CBS Records subsidiary Cupol Records. So impressed was this little fella that he offered Faltskog a recording contract that did not include the orchestra. Like any ambitious young singer in her position, Faltskog signed the contract.

Her debut Cupol single, titled 'I Was So In Love', topped the Swedish chart during 1968, the same year as her self-penned eponymous album. By 1969 she was a top-selling artist across Scandinavia, thanks to her second album, *Agnetha Faltskog Vol 2*, and a series of hit singles that included the titles 'En Gang Fannsbara Vi Tvo' and 'Zigenarvan'.

Following the failure of a German career instigated by composer Dieter Zimmerman, Faltskog returned to her home country to re-launch herself. She was initially rejected but it was a short-lived situation, thanks to singles like 'Ta Det Bara Med Ro' and a duet with

Jorgen Edman titled 'Sjung Denna Sang'. Unwittingly, Faltskog had often appeared on the same bill as the Hootenanny Singers, but it was on a television show in Stockholm that they first met. That meeting led to a relationship with Bjorn Ulvaeus.

During 1969, both the Hep Stars and the Hootenanny Singers disbanded, whereupon Benny Andersson and Bjorn Ulvaeus joined forces as composers and producers. A year on, both Faltskog and Lyngstad continued their respective solo careers, having become friends via their partners. Or had they? Years on, they admitted theirs was hardly the perfect working relationship. Nonetheless, they socialised and holidayed together. After stockpiling compositions, Andersson and Ulvaeus decided to record as a unit. Their debut album, titled *Lycka*, was completed in Stockholm's Metronome Studios and featured the uncredited Lyngstad and Faltskog on the solitary track 'Hej Gamle Man'. This title was the first to contain all four members of the future Abba. Released during 1970, *Lycka* soared into Sweden's album chart; in turn, Andersson and Ulvaeus embarked upon a tour of selected dates until November 1970, when they were joined on stage by Lyngstad and Faltskog, using the name the Festfolk Quartet (the 'Engaged Couples Quartet').

Early in 1971, Andersson and Ulvaeus entered their composition 'Livet Gar Sin Gang' in the Malago Melody Festival. Although it faltered at sixth place, the track was widely sold to other countries, including France, where it was recorded by Françoise Hardy. Meanwhile, Faltskog secured a starring role in the Swedish production of *Jesus Christ Superstar*, written by Tim Rice and Andrew Lloyd Webber, subsequently enjoying a Swedish hit single with 'I Don't Know How To Love Him', taken from the musical's sound-track. Lyngstad, on the other hand, having failed an audition to represent her country in the 1971 Eurovision Song Contest, recorded her second solo album, titled *Frida*, with her partner, Andersson, producing.

On the personal front, Bjorn Ulvaeus and Agnetha Faltskog married on 7 July 1971 in the village of Verum, southern Sweden. The occasion was marred when, the following day, Stig Anderson informed them that his business partner, Benjt Bernhag, had committed suicide and asked Andersson and Ulvaeus if they would replace him at Polar Music. Before the year closed, both became the company's in-house producers, where their first project was to work with the Hootenanny Singers on their *Our Loveliest Tunes: Part Two* album, before producing the debut release by new Swedish soloist Ted Gardestad.

A year on, Andersson, Ulvaeus, Faltskog and Lyngstad recorded in English together at the Metronome Studios. The result was a handful of titles that included 'People Need Love', 'She's My Kinda Girl' and 'Santa Rosa'. 'People Need Love' was the first single to be released in Sweden in June 1972, using the credit Bjorn, Benny, Agnetha and Anni-Frid. The title peaked at No.2 in the Swedish charts and was issued in America by Playboy Records, although it faltered outside the Top 100. 'She's My Kinda Girl' was issued in Japan only, using only Andersson's and Ulvaeus's names, and sold half a million copies, while 'Santa Rosa' was entered in the 1972 Japanese Song Festival, requiring all four to perform. The single bombed.

Following the chart success of the 'People Need Love' single, a second title was issued featuring the quartet. Titled 'He Is Your Brother', it again shot up their home chart before doing likewise in France and Germany. It was at this juncture that the decision was made to record as a group.

Late in 1972, Andersson and Ulvaeus were requested by the Swedish Broadcasting Corporation to compose an entry for the 1973 Swedish heat of the Eurovision Song Contest. In January 1973 their composition, 'Ring Ring', with lyrics by Stig Anderson, was recorded in Swedish, French, German and English; for the English version, the partnership of Neil Sedaka and Phil Cody provided the lyrics. 'Ring Ring' stalled at third position in the Swedish heat but went on to soar into countless European charts. At the same time, Agnetha Faltskog gave birth to Linda on 23 February 1973.

Following the unexpected failure and subsequent success of 'Ring Ring', the four recorded their debut album using the single's name as its title. Upon its release, the group entered the Swedish music history book – 'Ring Ring' the single was No.1 and No.2 in the Swedish chart! The first version was sung in Swedish, the second in English. The *Ring Ring* album had peaked at No.3 in its chart. To take advantage of this unusual success, the four toured Europe, promoting themselves as a serious, full-time group, creating maximum media attention. Stig Anderson, now the group's official manager, likewise conducted his equal share of press interviews. However, quickly tiring of constantly using the members' individual names, he decided to lift the first initial from each first name. Abba was born – it was as easy as that.

In October 1973, Abba began recording in earnest for a new album before realising that entries for the Swedish heat of the 1974 Eurovision Song Contest were due. Following historical research, Abba's manager believed 'Waterloo' to be an ideal song title. He wrote lyrics befitting the famous battle, omitting the glaring fact that 40,000 men had died there, whereupon Andersson and Ulvaeus composed the melody. However, before 'Waterloo' was completed, Anderson had composed a second possible entrant titled 'Hasta

Mañana'. Both tracks were equally strong; 'Waterloo' was finally chosen because it featured both female vocalists instead of just one.

In February 1974, Abba performed 'Waterloo' before the Swedish nation and won. This in turn led to the group representing their country in the Eurovision Song Contest proper. However, prior to the event, Stig Anderson spearheaded a mammoth advertising campaign to promote the group and title; he saturated European record companies with Abba promotional packs and generally whipped up an enthusiastic hype. Subsequently, when Abba arrived in Britain, they were guests at a party hosted by their new music publishing house, United Artists, and held interviews to boost media interest.

Staged at the newly renovated Dome Theatre, situated in the heart of Brighton on the East Sussex coastline, the 1974 Eurovision Song Contest, held on 5 April, got under way. Abba were the seventh act to appear. Dressed in skin-tight trouser suits of the Napoleonic style with high boots and hanging braids, the group sang and smiled their way through the track, despite looking ridiculous and feeling extremely uncomfortable in their second-skin clothing, before an estimated five hundred million viewers. Their jaunty song won the contest by a clear 24 points, pushing Italy into second place.

When the champagne had run dry, Abba were guests of honour at the obligatory party hosted by BBC TV, who had televised the contest. The following day, the group were besieged by the media – interviews were naturally stilted, due to their limited use of the English language – as they transferred to the Bedford Hotel, where their new British record company, CBS Records, celebrated the success with a champagne breakfast. The afternoon was spent on Brighton beach for an unofficial photo shoot. Unlike many future winners of the Eurovision Song Contest, when British interest became practically non-existent due to the low calibre of musical entrants, Abba were swamped by television guest spots, international interviews and record-company offers. However, Stig Anderson, confident the group was a winner, had already secured most record-company deals and had further arranged an extended stay in London to cement the demand for his act. No one in Britain could escape the Abba hype!

Returning to Sweden via Holland to appear on selected television shows, Abba spent the Easter weekend together, away from the public spotlight, deliberating the fate of 'Waterloo' now that the Eurovision Song Contest was over. They didn't wait long.

In May 1974, the winning song, released via CBS Records' subsidiary Epic, soared to the top of the British chart, a position it held for two weeks. 'Waterloo' repeated its British success across

Europe, while in America it peaked at No.6. Regrettably, it spear-headed a run of soundalike Eurovision Song Contest entries for years to come. The chirpy, happy-go-lucky, smiley sound with short, sharp lyrics would eventually drive the voters to distraction. It was hardly a fitting memorial for the 40,000 lost lives – but then that's show-business!

Prior to winning the 1974 Eurovision Song Contest, Abba had agreed to tour Sweden's 'folk parks' in the July. All future schedules now had to be reorganised and as the 'folk park' project would involve a month to prepare and a further month to undertake, Abba had little choice but to cancel the tour. At once, the quartet was publicly attacked by the media and organisers, who issued statements like, 'This is, without question, the ugliest betrayal I have experienced in my many years in this business . . . and now I am ridiculed by a group of Swedish amateurs, assuredly forgotten within one year' and 'Abba's decision is terribly immoral. Abba have won an important international music competition with the support of the Swedish people. Now they abandon their home audience completely to con-centrate on the foreign markets.' To placate fiery tempers, the group hastily announced details of their debut European tour, which included dates in Sweden!

Hot on the heels of the 'Waterloo' single, the group's album bearing the single's name was issued, whereupon they embarked upon a further British promotional trip. The single 'Honey Honey' was released as the chart-topper's follow-up single became a European hit. The title bypassed Britain, much to the dismay of their record company.

However, the hiccup was quickly passed over when, during June 1974, a remixed version of 'Ring Ring' was released in Britain. The single's chart progress, however, was severely hampered by industrial action at BBC TV which involved the non-screening of the music show *Top of the Pops* and Abba's subsequent performance of the single. Eventually, 'Ring Ring' moved slowly and stalled in the Top 40, leaving the group fair game for the media, who spared no punches in predicting their immediate downfall as 'one-hit wonders'. Indeed, at the time, this scenario was likely.

Next Abba visited America for the first time, again as a promotional ploy. The general consensus appeared to be that predicted by their British counterparts – 'one-hit wonders'. Upon their return to Sweden, Faltskog and Lyngstad attended vocal and dance lessons to tighten their stage routines, leaving Ulvaeus and Andersson to produce a pair of albums for Polar Music acts.

With the 1974 European tour looming, Abba recruited tried and tested musicians to support them on stage; the Abba sound had to be recreated if the tour was to be successful. The group then chose their costumes, vividly coloured or sparkling skin-tight suits of varying styles. Let's face it, Abba would never win any awards for stage clothes!

The tour opened in Denmark and passed through West Germany, Austria and Switzerland on its way to Britain. However, the final stage of the tour was cancelled; Britain did not consider Abba to be a musical force of any longevity and promoters were dubious as to whether to chance financing a week's trek. Instead, the quartet moved the dates to Norway, finishing in Sweden. The entire tour was an unequalled success, inspiring Andersson and Ulvaeus to prepare for their next album. Meanwhile, Faltskog recorded her sixth and last solo album, titled *Elva Kninnor I Ett Has*, which included her version of the future Abba track titled 'SOS'; and Lyngstad completed her *Ensam* album, featuring the track 'Fernando', another future Abba single.

The group's eponymous album was issued first in their home country, where advance orders were in excess of 100,000. Future sales passed the 450,000 mark, earning Abba the distinction of being Sweden's biggest-selling unit ever. Prior to the album's British release, the 'I Do I Do I Do I Do I Do' single struggled for life as CBS Records' promotion budget remained unimpressive compared to other chart-topping acts. Perhaps the record company needed assurance that Abba were worth further investment. Whatever the reason, 'I Do I Do I Do I Do I Do' was afforded only relatively low-key promotion that included record-company personnel, dressed in the wedding attire of top hat and tails, delivering the singles to radio stations. It was rather passé for the '70s!

Like 'Ring Ring' a year before, the title floundered in the Top 40 during July 1975. Elsewhere, though, the disc topped charts. According to Andersson, 'In England, we didn't get the image we deserved. Because we won Eurovision, we got the image that goes with Eurovision, and it's not really correct . . . I think we'd prefer the sort of reputation that the Mamas and Papas had.'

Despite Abba nursing further blows, the poor-selling album received excellent media reviews. Indeed, this project was stylishly presented and produced, although one critic felt otherwise, stating, 'Stick to singles, Abba, you are just a mediocre album band.'

By now, Abba's popularity in Europe had catapulted beyond Stig Anderson's expectations, particularly when a massive interest was noted in Eastern Europe, where record companies were government-owned, each having a yearly budget to pay for Western music imports. In 1975, Poland's entire import budget was spent on Abba albums, while Russia imported 25,000 albums, a figure way below public demand. Hence the albums became costly purchases on both countries' black markets.

Then there was Britain. During September 1975, the group issued the 'SOS' single. Thankfully the title dispelled any fears of a jinx by soaring to No.6 in the chart. Ulvaeus said, 'We thought "SOS" would make a very good single . . . would give our fans some sort of clue as to what musical direction we're heading for.' Correct. The single topped most European charts and reached No.10 in America, prompting a further promotional visit by the group. During their stay, they appeared on seven television shows including *The Mike Douglas Show*, *The Merv Griffin Show* and *The Dinah Shore Show*, when the hostess asked if Andersson and Lyngstad would like to get married on her show. The response was short: 'We'll get married when we have the time and in a place we want to!'

Touring, however, took its toll on Faltskog, who openly admitted she pined for her home life and was not a champagne partygoer like the other group members, preferring to return to the seclusion of her hotel room when a day's work was completed. The blonde singer also detested flying, and this would get worse, instead of better, the more the group had to travel. Ulvaeus said, 'When we go on the road we need about 40 people plus a whole mass of equipment to ensure that we get the results on stage that we want. We've relied on videos to boost our record sales rather than undertake the high cost and problems involved in doing a tour.'

To capitalise on the British success of 'SOS', its follow-up single was hastily issued and soared to the top of the chart during February 1976. Titled 'Mamma Mia', it dominated the British chart for two weeks. One-hit wonders no more! Once again, the group and the British media clashed. Ulvaeus, in particular, felt the press remained uncertain of their ability as musicians and somewhat negative, but it was Andersson who said, 'We thought that it was extremely difficult to reach the English but we believe so much in ourselves, we have so much self-confidence, that we agreed sooner or later it was bound to happen in England.' It must have been Andersson's modesty that appealed to the British journalists!

With two British chart-toppers to their credit, Abba had finally broken down the barrier erected by a nation last in the queue to fall for the group's magic. Europe, Australia and, to a certain extent, America had supported their music since 1974. Britain had been more cautious.

During the start of 1976, Abba were recording tracks for a further album, but to placate worldwide demand, they lifted their version of the Lyngstad solo track 'Fernando' from the sessions for single release. While the title climbed the international charts, the quartet visited Australia, where Abbamania had taken hold. Indeed, when they arrived at Melbourne Airport, it was crammed with thousands of hysterical fans, prompting Faltskog to say, 'The Australian tour was the most incredible of all the things that I experienced with Abba. There was fever, hysteria, ovations; there were sweaty, obsessed crowds.' It was also, she added, very scary, so much so that she was afraid the crowds would crush her 'and I'd never get away again'.

Upon their return to Sweden, 'Fernando' topped most European charts, including Britain's, a position it dominated for four weeks from May 1976. The single was hotly chased by the inevitable big seller, the *Greatest Hits* album. In Britain the release was advertised on television and advance orders in excess of 100,000 copies catapulted it to No.1 in the album chart, a position it held for a remarkable nine weeks.

By now the British press seemed to be mellowing, but like all those involved in creating headlines, they remained keen to knock Abba's success. This time they dissected the group's members, especially Faltskog and Lyngstad: 'the beautiful and the ugly'. 'The beautiful' was obviously Faltskog. Lyngstad (who had shortened her first name to Frida) was, naturally, furious at her media label. And it was surely remarks like this that added to the personal rift between the singers. In retrospect, the two personalities were totally opposite. Faltskog was introvert, moody and insecure, yet silently delighted she was the favoured one; Lyngstad was vivacious and outgoing, with a wild attitude to life. Her jealousy of Faltskog possibly led to her over-enthusiastic approach to performing. Whatever their personal attitudes, however, the two ladies acted the true professionals before their public; indeed, their closeness on stage, their eye contact and their general body language prompted many a journalist to report that they were gay. When this avenue proved to be without foundation, the scribes moved on to unearth further scandals. Abba just could not win! Said Lyngstad, 'Unlike some groups, we all like being together. Despite the fact that we're all paired off romantically, we all genuinely like each other.'

What of Benny Andersson and Bjorn Ulvaeus? They never argued, they said. In actual fact, they could not afford to; without their composing partnership there would be no Abba.

During June 1976, Abba were the only entertainers invited to the wedding gala of King Carl Gustaf to Silvia Sommerlath in Sweden, where the new Queen was introduced to the world. Many believed that Abba's next single, which they performed at the gala, was composed for her. Not so – the track, titled 'Dancing Queen', had been composed several months prior to its release. Nonetheless, the title fitted the occasion, so no one was any the wiser!

The majestically presented slice of Abba brilliance 'Dancing Queen' was quietly aimed at the decade's flourishing disco scene. The subtle dance beat, disguising the group's usual stilted lyrics, was Abba's finest production to date. The selling pattern of previous releases was repeated across Europe and Australia (the track went on to top the charts in 15 countries) and this time Britain bowed down to the quartet's musical expertise. 'Dancing Queen' shot to the top of the chart during September 1976, where it stayed for six long weeks, selling in excess of 800,000 copies. The single likewise topped the American chart during April 1977.

Before 1976 ended, the group starred in their first television documentary titled *Abba D'Abba Doo*, filmed during recording sessions, press interviews and at their homes in Stockholm. Due to international interest, the programme was retitled *Abba: From the Beginning* and rerecorded in English. The group visited Poland for the first time, America for the third, and released the *Arrival* album, with advance orders in Britain totalling 400,000. It may have taken a while, but Abbamania now had the British in its grasp. *Arrival* was an absolute Abba gem. Said Andersson, 'It's the best album we've made up until now, but it hasn't been easy and that's the reason [it's] six months late . . .You have to make yourself happy before you can make other people appreciate it. Each song on the album should be strong enough to stand up on its own.' Critics agreed (for once). The weekly music newspaper *NME* glowed, '[It] is their most accomplished set to date . . . they deliver their material with such gusto that if you try to turn a deaf ear, they'll just pummel your brain into submission.' The album soared to No.1 in the chart in January 1977.

British Abba-fever was further confirmed when, following the announcement of their debut concert date at the Royal Albert Hall during February 1977, the booking office received three million applications for 11,000 seats! The London date was one of a series of concerts around Britain. Faltskog said, 'The concerts at the Albert Hall were unforgettable. The English were crazy about us.'

The group's final single of the year, titled 'Money Money Money', lifted from the chart-topping *Greatest Hits* album, rocketed into the British Top 3, breaking the consecutive run of No.1 singles.

Abba were now under the harsh glare of the world's spotlight but they defiantly refused to let slip any mention of their private lives or, indeed, any disharmony within the group. If they had, the public would have been aware of the growing gap between 'the beautiful and the ugly'. Not a good way to sell records!

As *Arrival* climbed to the top of the international charts, the quartet visited London for yet another promotional trip, which included a press reception on the *Mayflower Queen*, moored on the

River Thames. The group travelled from Heathrow to the Thames via helicopter, in keeping with the *Arrival* album's artwork. During the reception, they received 30 silver, gold and platinum discs representing varying British record sales – the shipping cost to Sweden must have been astronomical, but now CBS Records could easily afford it! The group also taped a BBC1 Radio special to be aired across the pending Christmas season and conducted exhaustive press interviews, with Ulvaeus invariably nominated as the group's spokesman.

The remainder of 1976 was spent locked in rehearsals for the following year's world tour – the make-or-break disaster/ spectacular. Meanwhile, Abbamania continued, showing no signs of abating. Once the concerts were announced, the hype got under way. Tickets were sold out in one day, as fans throughout Europe fought to secure a seat. It was a phenomenal slice of music history in the making, the likes of which had not been experienced since the Beatles. With this whirlwind came the (usual) killjoy aspect, with rumours circulating in the media that the quartet had been killed in a plane crash in West Berlin. Such was the strength of the story that Abba were forced to issue a forceful denial with Ulvaeus appearing on Swedish television.

With a touring entourage of approximately 100 people, including a 12-piece backing group, costing £9,000 a day, Abba opened their world tour in January 1977 in Sweden. The British dates were during February, following which the group flew to Australia for 11 dates in Sydney, Melbourne, Adelaide and Perth. It was decided that the Australian leg would be filmed for the big screen, an awesome task in itself. The resultant film, titled *Abba: The Movie*, included onstage and behind-the-scenes footage, loosely held together by a storyline of a radio DJ's attempts to interview the group within a week's deadline. By the time the tour was completed, Abba had performed 28 concerts.

The British performance was faultless. Comprising the obligatory hit singles, the show began with a simulated helicopter landing and featured the mini-musical *The Girl with the Golden Hair*, where Faltskog and Lyngstad, wearing similar blonde wigs and costumes, sang a selection of songs from the *Arrival* album. While the remainder of Europe showered unprecedented accolades upon the group, British critics were reticent: 'a clinical disappointment', 'glib and contrived'. Statements like 'they are the greatest thing since the Beatles' were, regrettably, few and far between.

The British performance was also the launching pad for Abba's next single, titled 'Knowing Me Knowing You', which, thanks to the promotion, shot to the top of the chart during April 1977, a position it dominated for five weeks. The single was autobiographical; if listeners cared to dissect the lyrics, the future break-up of the two couples could have been detected.

The world tour took its toll. According to Ulvaeus, 'It's a bit of an unsocial life . . . you just eat, sleep, go on stage and nothing more. It kills creativity in a way that I don't like.' Faltskog said, 'One day when I woke up . . . I started to think – where am I? And it's terrible.'

Faltskog was also the centre of attraction for a reason not of her own making. The media's (rather distasteful) attention surrounded her bum, and when headlines glared 'The sexiest rear in show-business', she replied she didn't know if it was true or not, as she hadn't seen it! This unwanted attention followed the singer for several years.

With the tour behind them, a press statement was issued saying that Abba would not be available for interviews or performances until October 1977, giving them a break of six months. Ulvaeus said, 'We are not toys, we have a desperate need to have peace and quiet.' Besides, Faltskog was pregnant with her second child. It was a carefully planned pregnancy, calculated with her husband Ulvaeus not to clash with professional commitments. Sadly, the second child failed to save their marriage.

By the close of 1977, Abba had sold in excess of 20 million singles and 30 million albums worldwide. Not bad for a group many believed would be destined for the 'also-ran' heap following their 1974 Eurovision Song Contest winner which, in all honesty, *was* tailor-made for the garbage bin.

During their six-month break, Abba issued their sixth British chart-topper. Titled 'The Name Of The Game', it dominated the chart in November 1977, staying at No. 1 for four weeks. Most music critics claimed the title was a bomber; once again they were proved wrong. The beat was lazy, the lyrics a little more complex than previous singles, but it was the Abba production that sold the song. As the quartet was engrossed in recording their next album, they did not personally promote 'The Name Of The Game'. Instead they used a promotional video directed by Lasse Hallstrom, who was responsible for filming *Abba: The Movie*, yet to be premièred, and the group's previous promotional film for 'Knowing Me Knowing You'.

Needless to say, 'The Name Of The Game' topped charts in Europe, where still the group could do little wrong. The title was to be included in the next album, originally planned to be issued alongside the now completed *Abba: The Movie*. However, as advance orders for the album were exorbitant, Abba's several record companies were unable to press sufficient copies for the scheduled December 1977 release date. The same applied to the movie: could enough copies be available to meet cinema demand?

Before either project could be released, Faltskog gave birth to her second child, a son, on 4 December, 13 days before *Abba: The Movie* was premièred in Amsterdam's City Theatre. Meanwhile, it was decided that the album now titled *Abba: The Album* be released only in Sweden to coincide with the film's première there.

When *Abba: The Album* was issued in Britain during February 1978, critics were mixed in their reaction. 'Abba's least satisfactory album' tended to be the general reaction. Once again, though, the record-buying public thought otherwise; the album entered the chart at No. 1, thanks to advance orders in excess of a million. The title would eventually pass triple-platinum status in Britain alone, and gold status in America.

Also in the February, *Abba: The Movie* was premièred at the Warner Cinema, London. The group attended as part of a four-day promotional tour. Following the première, guests were invited to attend a reception held at Regent Street's Café Royal. Some critics were generous: 'This movie will stun you.' Others were less so. 'This full-blown epic is shockingly bad!' Meanwhile, back home in Sweden, the finishing touches were being made to Abba's own Polar Music record studio in Stockholm, built to Andersson's and Ulvaeus's specifications. Said Andersson, 'It has many facilities that you cannot find in any other studio anywhere else.'

By releasing both the movie and the album at the start of 1978, Abba would be able to use the remainder of the year for other projects and, of course, their valued home life. Both projects would sustain the group's high public profile until new material was available. As promoters from across the world clamoured to request concert dates, Abba holidayed in the Caribbean.

In their absence, the Abba empire jogged on. No one glanced ahead to peek at the slow descent of both their professional and their personal lives.

As a recording group, Abba had achieved more than any other musical unit. What more could this Swedish quartet desire? A stable personal life, perhaps, because for some time tempers had been frayed. By 1978, their behind-the-scenes story was bitter-sweet: when Andersson and Lyngstad finally married in the October, Ulvaeus and Faltskog filed for divorce. The latter wrote in her autobiography, 'When [we] separated, we always told the media it was a "happy" divorce, which, of course was a front . . . It has always felt like a failure that Bjorn and I couldn't keep our family together. You never get it back, but to this day I don't regret splitting up.'

Early in 1979, the group sang the plaintive ballad 'Chiquitita' at the 'Music for UNICEF' concert staged in New York as part of the celebrations for the International Year of the Child. All proceeds from the subsequent sale of the 'Chiquitita' single went to UNICEF. The title shot to No.2 in the British chart during the February and reached the Top 30 in America in 1980. In May 1979 the unlikely choice of the mid-rocker 'Does Your Mother Know?' was issued as a single and soared to No.4, making the American Top 20. This single was the lead-in to the group's first album to be recorded in Polar Music's state-of-the-art studio, titled *Voulez-Vous*. The album entered the British chart at the top, selling one million copies in doing so. As it slowly descended, two titles were swiped as a double-A-sided single, namely 'Angeleyes' and 'Voulez-Vous' (an unusual move for Abba, who generally earmarked specific titles for single release). Whatever the reason, the single peaked at No.3 in Britain; 'Voulez-Vous' staggered into the Top 80 in America during September 1979, the month the group toured there. A month on, the title 'Angeleyes' fared marginally better, reaching the Top 70.

In October 1979, Abba toured Britain once more, where the inevitable mayhem and fan hysteria shadowed their every move. Among the handful of dates, they performed six concerts at Wembley Arena (all were, naturally, sold out). During the shows they previewed their next single, 'Gimme Gimme Gimme (A Man After Midnight)', which rose into the British Top 3 during the November. Also during this month, Abba entered the *Guinness Book of Records* under the heading 'Biggest-Selling Group in Music History'. With the voices of the International School of Stockholm as support, Abba's final single of the year was 'I Have A Dream', a Top 2 British hit.

To start the new year and the new decade, the compilation *Greatest Hits Volume 2* peaked in the American Top 50, while the single 'The Winner Takes It All' returned the quartet to the top of the British chart during August 1980. It was the group's first chart-topper since 'Take A Chance On Me' in 1978. Before the year ended, the *Super Trouper* album followed its predecessors to top the British chart. Advance orders for the album passed one million copies; once on sale, it sold 160,000 copies in one day! The album went on to sell seven million copies worldwide. As *Super Trouper* dominated British album sales, 'Super Trouper' the single shot up the chart to the top during November 1980. It was an incredibe achievement.

Following this record-breaking slice of history, Andersson publicly announced that his marriage had ended; he cited his girlfriend Mona Norklit as the reason. The statement said: 'The decision has been taken after considerable consideration and mutual agreement . . . This step won't affect our partnership in Abba. It is of a completely private nature.'

Abba suffered further when an anonymous note was delivered to

Polar Music claiming the safety of the group and their children was in jeopardy. Faltskog said, 'Whoever's writing the notes said that if we went on tour they'd hurt our children.' Swedish police treated the threat seriously, while the quartet cancelled touring plans to remain in Stockholm.

During the next year, Abba released a pair of British singles, namely 'Lay All Your Love On Me', a dance track pressed as a 12-inch single which reached the Top 10, and the slower-paced 'One Of Us', a Top 3 hit. Their solitary album, with advance orders of 700,000 in Britain, titled *The Visitors*, shot to No.1 in the December, ironically marking the disintegration of the group, beginning with their last concert, staged in Stockholm, and the 'Head Over Heels' single which stalled in the British Top 30 in March 1982.

As Abba celebrated their tenth anniversary in the music business, they issued the title 'The Day Before You Came', which struggled into the Top 40 in the British singles chart, while Lyngstad went to London to release her big-selling solo album, titled *Something's Going On*, from which the Top 20 single 'I Know There's Something Going On' was lifted.

On the personal front, Andersson and his new wife Mona became parents to a son, while Ulvaeus and his wife, Lena, celebrated the birth of their daughter. They too later relocated to Britain to live in Henley-on-Thames. According to Ulvaeus, 'In Sweden I felt the lack of freedom and that so many decisions were taken away from me by politicians. For example, they take more than 80 per cent of income in tax. It wasn't that the remaining 20 per cent wouldn't have been enough, it was the fact that I couldn't make my own decisions about what to do with my own money.'

On the professional front, Abba and Russia were at loggerheads. Russian authorities banned the group and its recorded work when the promotional video for 'When All Is Said And Done' was used in an American television documentary where artists protested against the Russian foray into Poland. Andersson admitted the group would suffer financially but added, 'We are worried about our fans being denied the chance to hear our music.'

History books were finally closed in November 1982 when Abba issued the double compilation *The Singles: The First Ten Years*, their final British chart-topping album. The title 'Under Attack' was swiped for single release and faltered in the British Top 30 a month later.

Although no statement was issued regarding the group's demise, it became apparent when Agnetha Faltskog followed in Lyngstad's footsteps and recorded the solo album *The Heat Is On*, while Andersson and Ulvaeus collaborated with Tim Rice to compose the 1985 musical *Chess*. Said Andersson, 'For a long time Bjorn and I have been talking about how great it would be if there was a chance for us to move into the music theatre. So when Tim came to us in Stockholm and asked if we wanted to collaborate with him, we seized the chance.' Two British hit singles were lifted from the musical's soundtrack, namely 'I Know Him So Well', a duet between Elaine Page and Barbara Dickson, and 'One Night In Bangkok' by Murray Head.

With Lyngstad and Faltskog concentrating on solo careers, the final Abba single to chart in Britain was released. Titled 'Thank You For The Music', the title reached the Top 40 in 1983. With the group having disbanded, their manager, Stig Anderson, sold Polar Music, building a bigger gulf between him and the membership. When the Swedish Inland Revenue investigated the group's financial affairs, it was estimated that Faltskog and Ulvaeus owed £1 million each in back taxes. This figure was in addition to their plummeting share prices. Stigwood was blamed for crippling their various financial investments; Abba sued Polar Music for loss of earnings reputed to be worth £16 million. Eventually the group and Polar reached a private settlement, but publicly reputations had been smeared, even to the extent that the media suggested Abba should be jailed for tax evasion!

Into the '90s, Faltskog remarried and appeared to retire from the music business. Lyngstad went on to marry a German architect; she also abandoned her music to concentrate on environmental issues. Only Andersson and Ulvaeus remained active in music. In 1992, when the bulk of Abba's recording contracts around the world had expired, including that with CBS Records in Britain, Polydor Records purchased the rights to the group's back catalogue and issued 'Dancing Queen', the first Abba single in ten years. While the title climbed the European charts, the compilation *Abba Gold* passed platinum status in 20 countries, selling approximately five million copies. With this remarkable achievement, rumours obviously abounded that Abba would re-form. Not so. According to Ulvaeus, 'When we split up in 1982, that was it . . . I don't believe in making any half-assed comebacks. I think it is so pathetic when old bands who have broken up go back on the road again.'

In 1993, the further compilation *More Abba Gold* was released and repeated the success of its sister record. Who on earth was buying these discs? Surely everyone who wanted an Abba title had purchased it first time round? True, the introduction of CDs obviously helped sales, but even so! Polydor Records, who in actual fact took a tremendous risk buying Abba's tried and tested material, must have been hysterical with delight. Two years on, the four-CD boxed set titled *Thank You For The Music* and *Gold – Greatest Hits* were multi-million sellers. Ulvaeus, though, remained unimpressed. 'I realise that millions of records are being sold out there, and that it has something to do with me . . . It was another time and I was another person.'

The Swedish quartet also lives on through tributes from third parties and musical clones. In June 1992 Erasure released the 'Abbaesque EP', while Abba's worst nightmare turned into reality when Bjorn Again, Australian impersonators, toured the world earning an extremely good living!

However, the real thing refused to lie down. Indeed, Andersson and Ulvaeus actually took their music one step further by presenting a selection on stage. *Mamma Mia*, hailed as 'the first great musical hit of the new millennium', opened in London to enthusiastic audiences and looks set to run for years to come.

'I don't know if there is anything more to achieve. How could there be?' – Benny Andersson

'I really don't miss all the fame and success of Abba' – Agnetha Faltskog

(Quotes: *Abba: The Music Still Goes On: The Complete Story* by Paul Snaith; *As I Am: Abba Before and Beyond* by Agnetha Faltskog with Brita Ahman)

December 1980

JOHN LENNON

(Just Like) Starting Over

'I like being rich and famous, but I sometimes think it would be nicer to be rich and famous and invisible . . . to get all the credit and the fun' – John Lennon

Born on 9 October 1940 to Julia and Fred in Woolton, Liverpool, John Winston Lennon worked his way through musical trends before forming the Quarry Men. When he befriended Paul McCartney, a fellow Liverpudlian, and later George Harrison and Ringo Starr, the Beatles were born. They would go on to conquer and rule the musical world until the late '60s. Although the comradeship, support and, yes, love that bound the quartet had by the end of the decade cracked, their music somehow managed to survive. Nonetheless, the fairytale ended in a nightmare, yet no one was prepared to make the first move to disband the unit known as the Fab Four. In time, it was McCartney who made the move, but Lennon was the first to record outside the group. The couple who had launched a million sales again and again were, like the Beatles, destined to be a recent memory.

Lennon's life had changed in a way he could never have envisaged when he met Yoko Ono, born on 18 February 1933 in Tokyo, a Japanese artist with a bizarre outlook on life. In October 1967, Yoko Ono opened her art exhibition at London's Lisson Gallery. Using the overall title of 'Yoko Plus Me', the 'me' was later identified as John Lennon, who had agreed to sponsor Ono financially on the understanding he remained anonymous. A year on Ono and Lennon, married to Cynthia with one son, Julian, were lovers, and professionally speaking the Fab Four became Five. Lennon and Ono were inseparable, and that included her presence during recording sessions which had previously barred wives, girlfriends and hangers-on. Dismayed at his friends' inability to understand how important Ono was to him, Lennon retreated further into his new life.

During May 1968 the couple appeared in public for the first time, attending the launch party for the opening of Apple's second boutique. The handful of Apple companies, including a record label, had recently been opened by the Beatles, with Lennon and McCartney being the prime instigators of the new set-up. The organisation protected the group's financial business in a deal which included their future material carrying the Apple logo but continuing to be distributed by EMI Records, with whom the group had signed in 1962.

During August 1968 Lennon's wife Cynthia filed for divorce, citing his adultery with Ono. Lennon did not contest; Cynthia was later granted a decree nisi. Two months on, and following a drugs raid by police at 34 Montague Square, London, and Lennon and Ono's subsequent remand on bail, Lennon announced Ono was expecting their child. She later miscarried.

At the close of November, Lennon and Ono's first recorded work, titled *Two Virgins*, was issued. To be frank, the music was garbage, but the packaging proved popular – the couple posed nude. Yes, folks, purchasers could see Lennon's tackle for the price of an album! The more sensitive of record stores sold the albums covered in plain paper; others proudly displayed their wares. Said Ono, 'The album was actually John's idea . . . We decided that we should both be naked. He took the picture himself with an automatic camera. The picture isn't lewd or anything like that. Basically we are both very shy and square people.' Lennon retaliated to the public outcry, saying, 'The trouble is I've spoiled my image. People wanted me to stay in their own bag. They want me to be lovable, but I was never that.'

Two Virgins followed hot on the heels of the Beatles' first double album, titled *White Album*, which, in comparison, offered nothing in the way of packaging but magnificent music.

The following year represented the Beatles' last together as a creative musical unit. They recorded material for their final pair of albums and performed in their last movie, titled *Let It Be*. Meanwhile, behind the scenes, when the American businessman Allen Klein was engaged by Lennon to untangle the group's business affairs, the move wedged a split between Lennon, Harrison and Starr on the one hand and McCartney on the other, who had hired his own financial advisers, Eastman and Eastman, father and brother of Linda, whom McCartney married on 12 March 1969. Lennon and Ono likewise married in the March. The couple flew to Gibraltar, to be married in the British Consulate, before travelling to Paris. From there they relocated to Amsterdam, where they held a bed-in for peace in a room at the Hilton hotel. The Lennons spent seven days in bed where they met the world's media, some of whom laughed at their stupidity. When the seven days ended, the couple flew to Vienna, Austria, where they conducted a press conference at the Hotel Sacher from inside a large white bag.

As the Beatles' single 'Get Back' was issued in April 1969, Lennon changed his name by deed poll to John Winston Ono Lennon and purchased Tittenhurst Park in Berkshire. He and his wife then travelled to Montreal to start an eight-day bed-in for peace at the Queen Elizabeth Hotel. Following this, the single credited to the Beatles but in fact featuring only Lennon and McCartney was released. Titled 'The Ballad Of John And Yoko', the track told of the couple's life so far. It was banned by numerous American radio stations for the liberal use of the word 'Christ'. British stations, on the other hand, afforded the single maximum airplay to push it to the top of the British chart.

During July 1969 the Plastic Ono Band issued their debut single, titled 'Give Peace A Chance'. It became a Top 2 British hit, Top 20 in America. The anthem-like track went on to become the international peace title. A hastily assembled Plastic Ono Band, including Eric Clapton and Klaus Voormann, later performed at a rock'n'roll gala staged at Toronto's Varsity Stadium. The group played on a bill that included Chuck Berry and Bo Diddley among others. Lennon said at the time, 'I don't care who I have to play with but I'm going back to playing rock on stage. I can't remember when I had such a good time.'

Following her second miscarriage at King's College Hospital in London, Ono and the Plastic Ono Band's single 'Cold Turkey' was issued. As the title suggested, the song told of drug withdrawal, and it reached the British Top 20. This single was later namechecked in a letter written by Lennon to the Queen when he returned his MBE in protest at Britain's involvement in the war in Nigeria and in support of the war raging in Vietnam. Hot on the heels of this single, the Lennons issued *The Wedding Album*. The title bombed. In December 1969 the Plastic Ono Band's album *Live Peace In Toronto* was another slow seller.

Into the '70s, a selection of Lennon's lithographs were displayed at the London Arts Gallery. Within 24 hours police raided the exhibition and confiscated eight lithographs. They claimed them to be indecent, portraying as they did the Lennons in numerous lovemaking positions, with Ono masturbating and the two of them in the act of cunnilingus. Lennon signed each lithograph, saying, 'Sex is the only exercise I get!' The case was subsequently dropped.

From pictures to music, the Plastic Ono Band's next single 'Instant Karma' soared into the British Top 5. Produced by Phil Spector and recorded with club punters at Hatchetts in London, the title also went on to peak in the American Top 3. The Beatles' own 'Let It Be' single and album followed, paving the way for the movie of the same name. Meanwhile, before 1970 ended, Lennon's first solo album, *John Lennon/Plastic Ono Band*, was issued, making the Top 11 in Britain and Top 6 in America, and McCartney filed a lawsuit in the London High Court for the dissolution of the Beatles and Co, heralding the first official move to end the group's working relationship.

By now the remaining Beatles had either recorded their own work or intended to do so, leaving Lennon to release his next single, the chanting 'Power To The People', again credited to the Plastic Ono Band. It became a Top 10 British hit, Top 20 in America. Alongside their music, the Lennons' love affair with celluloid continued. None of their films were, to be blunt, taken that seriously, but they persevered. Probably the most controversial to date was *Self Portrait*, a 15-minute film showing Lennon's erect penis. Many rose above the temptation to watch this! The latest batch, however, included *Fly*, which was world-premièred at the Cannes Film Festival in May 1971 and preceded the publication of Ono's book titled *Grapefruit*, which she heavily promoted with Lennon at her side.

Days prior to the release of the *Imagine* album in August 1971, Lennon and Ono flew from Heathrow to New York. Lennon never returned to Britain. The album's title track was swiped as a single and shot into the American Top 3 (the single's British release was in 1975), while the album topped the chart on both sides of the Atlantic. This was Lennon's finest hour; musically he was at his solo peak. Before 1971 ended, however, 'Happy Xmas (War Is Over)' was issued in America and bombed. When released in Britain to capture the Christmas market in 1972, the title catapulted to No.4, and to this day remains a festive favourite.

Midway through 1972, Lennon issued his double album *Some Time In New York City*, which was somewhat controversial, thanks to tracks like 'Woman Is A Nigger Of The World'. It was a poor seller, probably due to its sombre, rather intense theme.

Into 1973, and following a deportation notice issued the previous year for his drugs conviction in 1968, Lennon's long battle began against the American immigration authorities to stay in his adopted country. Pressure was applied from President Nixon and the FBI to deport the Lennons because of their radical views, which in turn encouraged the couple to embark upon a high-profile political campaign. During 1972 and 1973 the FBI compiled a lengthy dossier on what they considered to be a 'highly controversial and dangerous man'; Lennon was followed and his telephones were tapped. Eventually, the Beatle 'snapped'; his marriage disintegrated and he fell headlong into what he later called his 'lost weekend'. It was hardly a two-day binge – Lennon's drunken stint in Los Angeles spanned a whole year! The media followed his every drunken move until he returned to his wife. Said Lennon, 'The separation didn't work out. I feel as though I've been on Sinbad's voyage and I've battled all those monsters and I've got back.'

Lennon's music continued. In 1973 he issued his next album, *Mind Games*, which was a Top 20 British hit, Top 10 in America. The album's title track was extracted for single release but faltered in the British Top 30 and American Top 20 during the November. This was followed by *Walls And Bridges* a year on, from which 'Whatever Gets You Through The Night' was swiped as a single. It struggled into the British Top 40, but American sales pushed the unexciting single to No.1. Its mother album was a similar success in the States, but in Britain the album floundered.

Into 1975, the *Rock'n'Roll* album returned Lennon to his first musical love. Originally a joint project with Phil Spector in 1973, the two disagreed with the result, whereupon Lennon reworked the entire album. It was a Top 10 hit on both sides of the Atlantic. Eight months after the album's release, Ono gave birth to Sean Taro on 9 October 1975, Lennon's 35th birthday. Lennon abandoned his career to adopt the role of househusband, a role that spanned five years. While enjoying his domesticity, his application for a green card was approved, permitting him to take up American residency. Meanwhile, to close 1975, his 'Imagine' single was issued in Britain for the first time and hit the Top 6, while the compilation *Shaved Fish* soared into the Top 10 in both Britain and America.

The '80s were destined to be a decade Beatles fans would never forget or forgive. In January, while McCartney was arrested upon his arrival in Japan for carrying marijuana, Lennon and Ono were on vacation in Palm Beach. Lennon used this break to recharge his creative batteries following his lengthy period of domestic bliss. Upon his return to New York he worked on unfinished material, backlogged from several years.

During March 1980, Lennon and Ono celebrated their 11th wedding anniversary, while the Beatles' *Rarities* album was issued in an attempt to rekindle interest in their music. A month on, Lennon shaved off his beard before embarking upon a further vacation alone, this time a sailing trip to Bermuda on the yacht *Megan Jaye*. It was at Ono's request he travelled solo; she wanted him to explore his creative mind and regain his independence. This separation added credibility to the speculation surrounding the divorce said to be planned by Ono at this time. It's unclear, however, whether Lennon was aware of her intention.

While in Bermuda, Lennon visited the Botanical Gardens, where he noticed a family of freesia called Double Fantasy. He memorised the name, intending to use it on his next album, earmarked for release during 1980. While he was dabbling with his own compositions like 'Watching The Wheels' and 'Beautiful Boy', Ono was working on her solo musical projects. During their separation they played their respective music to each other via the telephone, prompting Lennon to view his pending album as a conversation piece. The last song Lennon composed in Bermuda was 'Woman'.

At the start of August, with producer Jack Douglas, Lennon and Ono were reunited in the recording studio at New York's Hit Factory. The initial sessions were volatile, as Lennon smoked dope throughout. Nonetheless, the optimism was such that a joint (no pun intended) press release was issued, claiming, among other things, that the comeback project would include 'sexual fantasies between men and women'. The couple were filmed working with the footage earmarked for '(Just Like) Starting Over'. So intense were these sessions, with Lennon's determination to return to music's fast lane, that one track was completed daily. During September, as the sessions were switched from the Hit Factory to the Record Plant East, Lennon and Ono signed a recording deal with David Geffen, owner of Geffen Records. By the end of the month, '(Just Like) Starting Over' was remixed for single release.

From the day that the Lennons moved into the Dakota building in New York, they were plagued by fans who loitered or camped outside their home. Most were content to stand and watch; others waited for a glimpse of or a chat with Lennon. The singer was happy with this situation; Ono, on the other hand, was increasingly worried at possible security flaws, and to this end regularly discussed the problem with their immediate personal bodyguards, who, in the main, protected their son Sean.

On 9 October 1980 Lennon celebrated his 40th birthday, an occasion highlighted by visiting fans, while eight days on his first single in five years was issued in America. The aforementioned '(Just

Like) Starting Over', released in Britain before the month closed, received a mixed reception and sold poorly. This disappointment did not deter the release of the *Double Fantasy* album, whose sales were much healthier, representing as it did Lennon's first serious return to music in months. Containing a handful of his finest work, the album recharged Lennon's creative flow, encouraging him to work passionately on ideas for his next project.

During November, Lennon and Ono returned to the film world, this time simulating the sex act. Around this time they also promised their support to striking Japanese workers who planned to march through the streets of San Francisco during mid December.

Early in December, Lennon met the media, particularly *Rolling Stone* magazine's Jonathan Cott and Britain's DJ Andy Peebles, who interviewed both Lennon and Ono for a future Radio One programme. The text of this series of interviews was later published under the title *The Lennon Tapes*.

On 8 December 1980, following an early breakfast, Lennon was engaged in a photo shoot with Annie Leibovitz from *Rolling Stone* magazine to accompany the interview. Early in the afternoon, Lennon and Ono returned to the Dakota building for a further series of interviews before leaving to journey to the Record Plant East. Outside the Dakota, Lennon autographed a copy of the *Double Fantasy* album for a waiting fan named Mark Chapman. He wrote, 'John Lennon, 1980.' The recording sessions devoted to 'Walking On Thin Ice', a track to be included on his next album, *Milk And Honey*, finished at 10.30 p.m. At 10.50 p.m. the couple arrived at the Dakota.

Born in Texas in 1955, Mark Chapman was obsessed by the Beatles, and later by Lennon. He drifted through various jobs, including one as a security guard, where he learned to use a gun. Relocating to Hawaii and following two suicide attempts, Chapman emulated Lennon by marrying a Japanese-American named Gloria Abe. During September 1980 he was in Honolulu, where he read a Lennon interview in *Newsweek* magazine which, he later said, left him with the impression that the singer was a hypocrite about his music and his talent. The next month Chapman read the book *John Lennon: One Day At A Time*, written by Anthony Fawcett, which further convinced him of Lennon's hypocrisy. A long-time psychologically disturbed young man, Chapman convinced himself that Lennon-the-hypocrite must die.

At the close of October, Chapman, with an empty Charter Arms .38 special handgun in his possession, relocated to New York. Once in the city he purchased bullets before keeping a low profile outside the Dakota building, where he was told by security guards that the Lennons were away for a few days. Frustrated at their absence, Chapman contacted his wife, telling her of his intention to kill

Lennon. He then travelled to Honolulu, returning to New York on 7 December 1980. Early on 8 December 1980 Chapman left the Sheraton hotel, where he had booked a room, to return to the Dakota. He was told the Lennons had already left the building. Instead of staying, Chapman spent time in nearby Central Park, returning to the Dakota, where he saw the Lennons, at 10.50 p.m.

Having returned by limousine, Lennon and Ono had walked to the entrance of their home when Chapman shouted Lennon's name. The singer turned to see who had called him. Chapman adopted the combat stance he had been taught during his time as a security guard – dropping to one knee, holding his weapon with two hands – and pumped two shots at Lennon's back. The impact swung Lennon around. Three further shots were fired; two bullets caught the singer in the shoulder. Instead of then falling to the ground, Lennon staggered up the six steps into the security office, where the guard was relaxing, reading a newspaper. There Lennon collapsed, crying, 'I've been shot!' The cassettes and recorder he'd been holding crashed to the stone floor.

The guard immediately pressed the alarm button, alerting police from the nearby 20th Precinct. Applying the rudimentaries of first aid, the guard made Lennon comfortable as blood gushed from his chest and mouth. Throughout the singer was conscious; Ono was screaming. Within seconds a patrol car driven by Officer James Moran pulled up, into which the bleeding Lennon was carried. In an attempt to keep the singer conscious, the officer asked him questions. It was futile: Lennon had no pulse by the time he reached the Roosevelt Hospital, where every effort was made to save his life. It was useless. Two bullets had shattered his left shoulder. One had exited, while the other had severed his windpipe and aorta. The two bullets that had hit his back had pierced his lung. Lennon had also lost six pints of blood. At 11.15 p.m. on 8 December 1980, John Lennon was officially pronounced dead. His wife was by his side.

Meanwhile, Mark Chapman was arrested without a struggle outside the Dakota building. He had dropped his gun but clutched a copy of *The Catcher in the Rye*, a novel by J.D. Salinger.

'Do you know what you just did?' he was asked.

'Yes, I just shot John Lennon.'

The perpetrator of a mindless and violent murder which robbed the world of a Beatle would become one of the most famous names in music history thanks to his gun firing lethal bullets. In his police statement, Chapman said that as Lennon walked past him, his wife was ahead of him: 'There was a dead silence in my brain . . . I aimed at his back. I pulled the trigger five times. The explosions were deafening. After the first shot, Yoko crouched down and ran around the corner into the courtyard. Then the gun was empty and John Lennon had disappeared.'

Chapman was later taken to Bellevue Hospital for psychiatric sessions, or perhaps, as many fans felt later, to be mollycoddled thanks to the mental-health law sympathetic to murderers. Ignoring his lawyer's advice, he would on 21 June 1981 plead guilty to the charge of murder. Files relating to Lennon's death were secreted in the vaults of one of New York's police departments where they reputedly remain unseen to this day. Yoko Ono included in her statement, 'I heard shots . . . He walked to the door upstairs. Said, "I'm shot." I followed him. He was standing but staggering. I told him to lie down.' She added that she saw Chapman standing nearby and he made no attempt to escape.

The morning of 9 December 1980, Britain rose to the news that John Lennon had been murdered. Throughout the day tributes were placed and vigils held outside the Dakota building and the Beatles' repertoire was played on radio stations throughout the world. Newspapers and magazines prepared obituaries as fans collapsed in grief.

Following an autopsy, the official cause of death was given as shock resulting from massive haemorrhaging. However, it was also intimated that if Lennon had not been moved and attempts had been made to resuscitate him at the scene of the crime, he might well have lived. His body was taken to the Frank J. Campbell funeral chapel before being cremated at the Ferncliff Mortuary on 10 December. His ashes were given to his widow. In time it was discovered that Lennon's body had been secretly photographed by a mortuary assistant. The photographs were sold for $10,000.

On 14 December 1980 Ono requested a ten-minute silence throughout the world at 2.00 p.m. EST in her husband's memory. Radio stations blanked airwaves and the general public halted in memory. Fans remained in disbelief. Ono said, 'Bless you for your tears and prayers.'

Such was the united feeling of grief over Lennon's murder that his current single '(Just Like) Starting Over' spiralled from its chart downturn to the top of the British chart in December 1980; before the month closed, the single also dominated the American chart. There was more to come.

'If you stay in this business long enough it will get you in the end' – John Lennon

Also see: 'Imagine', January 1981; 'Woman', February 1981

(Quotes: *Lennon* by John Robertson; *1940–1980: A Biography* by Ray Connolly)

January 1981

JOHN LENNON

Imagine

'You may say I'm a dreamer, but I'm not the only one' – John Lennon

Following the senseless murder of John Lennon on 8 December 1980, the remaining three Beatles became more aware of their own mortality. To this end, all doubled their security, practically isolating themselves from the world. Lennon's death also bonded Ringo Starr, George Harrison and Paul McCartney together in grief. The Fab Four was no more – Mark Chapman had seen to that. Starr and his wife Barbara had, in actual fact, travelled to New York to comfort Ono. Due to the Dakota building being under siege by mourning fans, the Starrs' stay was short; McCartney and Harrison telephoned through their condolences.

Before the second single could be lifted from Lennon's *Double Fantasy* album, his much-revered title 'Imagine' soared to the top of the British chart in January 1981. It had been expected, seeing as it had been backed by advance orders of over 300,000. One of Lennon's more fragile of tracks, 'Imagine' outlived the majority of his solo work because it clearly represented his talent in the eyes of the British public, who transformed it into his memorial. It remains as popular today as it was when first issued in November 1975.

Joining 'Imagine' in the 1980 chart were the Plastic Ono Band's 'Happy Xmas (War Is Over)' at No.2, the track's second re-entry since its original release in December 1972, and 'Give Peace A Chance' in the Top 40, this single's first re-entry since its original release during July 1969. The irony of this renewed success did not pass unnoticed. A man of peace had been killed by a weapon of war, something he had protested against so loudly in life.

Lennon's albums likewise recharted. Fans continued to mourn their loss and the media, for once, joined them, with barely a derogatory article about Lennon.

While 'Imagine' dominated the British chart, Ono's open letter to the world in the form of advertisements was published in newspapers and magazines. In the text she expressed her thanks for the millions of messages of condolences which, she wrote, 'were a consolation to me, since both John and I believed in brother and sisterhood that goes beyond race, colour and creed . . . I thank you for your feeling of anger for John's death. I share your anger.'

Ono then went on to explain his murder in some detail, including the following: 'I am angry at myself for not being able to protect John . . . When John fell beside me, I felt like we were in a guerrilla war, not knowing who or where the enemy was . . . I saw the death photo. John looked peaceful, like on the back of the "Imagine" cover . . . I saw the photo where he signed the autograph [for Mark Chapman]. Somehow that photo was harder for me to look at than the death photo. John's head was bent forward, obviously to sign his name . . . then I realised he was signing for the gate of heaven.' In conclusion, Ono wrote that this letter to the world was the best she could do at this time in response to the communications received by her. However, she did not know the answer to the question – why had John Lennon been shot?

Also see: '(Just Like) Starting Over', December 1980; 'Woman', February 1981

(Quotes: *Lennon* by John Robertson)

February 1981

JOHN LENNON

Woman

'It's for your mother or your sister, anyone of the female race' – John Lennon

In the aftermath of John Lennon's murder, his recorded work was much in demand. Catalogue items that had remained static for some time were now selling by the thousand, while his singles were shifting in and out of the British chart.

While Lennon lived, he had issued his *Double Fantasy* album from which '(Just Like) Starting Over' had been swiped as the first single. The plan was then to lift 'Woman' as its follow-up. However, before that could happen, Lennon died and the British public showed their respect by purchasing 'Imagine', pushing that to No.1 in January 1981. Now back on course, 'Woman' was released as a single and topped the British chart a month on, reaching No.2 in America. In actual fact, the song had been recorded during his August/September sessions at the Hit Factory, which he considered to be his 'Beatles/early Motown' period. As Lennon had planned this title for single release, he'd also completed its accompanying promotional video. As heartbreaking as it was to watch, it made the senselessness of his murder really strike home. Chapman remains incarcerated to this day.

While 'Woman' was on release, Yoko Ono was ensconced in the recording studio working on her husband's unfinished track titled 'Walking On Thin Ice'. Indeed, it was this tape that Lennon had grasped tightly as he was shot.

Although none of the material released so far was considered to be cashing in on to the tragedy, Andy Peebles' interviews were. Taped during December 1980, they were broadcast in a series of six programmes by Radio One during the following month. The listening figures were astronomical.

A month on from these broadcasts, Ono agreed to release 'Walking On Thin Ice' with a flipside titled 'It Happened'. The double-A-sided disc was tragically spooky: Lennon had completed the topside himself, with the exception of a slight reworking from Ono, bringing a strikingly vivid recollection of his recent death, while the flipside included a conversation between the Lennons during the video shoot for the 'Woman' single. Chillingly realistic was Lennon's comment at a person's expression which was instantly recognised by listeners as a reference to his own death.

During March 1981, 'Watching The Wheels' was the third single taken from *Double Fantasy*, which itself went on to win the Grammy Award for Album of the Year. Like 'Walking On Thin Ice', the title seemed to reflect Lennon's pending death. Also this month, his home city, Liverpool, paid tribute to its hero with a memorial service held at the Anglican Cathedral, while New York renamed the section of Central Park nearest to the Dakota building 'Strawberry Fields' in Lennon's memory. The couple had often walked this particular area of the park. Said Ono, 'John would have been very proud that this was given to him . . . rather than a statue or a monument.'

George Harrison, with contributions from Ringo Starr and Paul McCartney, released *All Those Years Ago* in May 1981 as a tribute to Lennon and the Beatles. Meanwhile, across the Atlantic, Ono, having followed Japanese protocol by shearing her hair to mark the pending first anniversary of her husband's death, accepted New York's highest honour, the Handel Medallion, on his behalf. She also retrieved Lennon's bloodstained clothes from New York's Coroner's Office. She then turned to music by issuing her *Season Of Glass* album, her first since Lennon's death; the project was treated with some trepidation, particularly as her husband's bloodstained glasses dominated the album's front cover.

Before 1981 ended, Mark Chapman was sentenced to life, despite strong feelings from some that he should face the death penalty. Imprisoned by a New York court, Chapman was to serve his time in

Attica state. Of course by now he had been elevated to the status of a semi-hero by some sick people, receiving fan mail by the sackful. It was probably this that prompted him to contact Ono to request her help with a book he planned to write. All proceeds, he said, would go to charity.

Through 1982 a flurry of Beatles material was issued, including an album of the group's Decca Records audition dating back to 1962, while EMI Records set up plans to release celebratory tracks for the group's 20th anniversary since their debut single. 'Love Me Do' was the first to soar to No.4 in the British chart. *The John Lennon Collection* followed in the November, alongside Ono's own 'My Man' single, which was accompanied by *It's Alright*, her second album since Lennon's murder.

Into 1984, the *Milk And Honey* album which Lennon had begun working on shortly before his death was ready for release. The first lifted single was 'Nobody Told Me', a Top 10 hit in both Britain and America. *Milk And Honey*, meanwhile, containing six Lennon tracks and six Ono tracks, soared into the British Top 3 and the American Top 20.

'Borrowed Time' was issued as the British follow-up, while the title 'I'm Stepping Out' was released in America during March 1984. Eventually the releases were switched, ensuring neither country missed out on potential sales. Meanwhile, Lennon's son Julian embarked upon a short-lived but successful recording career, and Sean, his son with Ono, contributed to her *Every Man Has A Woman* album, which she had intended as a gift for Lennon's 50th birthday. Included alongside Ono's material on the album was Lennon's version of 'Every Man Has A Woman', later destined for single release.

Following Lennon's death, several tributes were issued. Some, of course, were the inevitable 'cash-ins', while others were considered more sincere, like Elton John's 'Empty Garden (Hey Hey Johnny)' and 'The Man Who Never Died', Pink Floyd's 'Not Now John', Paul McCartney's 'Here Today' and Queen's 'Life Is Real (Song For Lennon)'.

Through to the next decade Lennon's memory maintained a high profile due to his widow's diligence and business acumen, which was both criticised and praised. For example, his *Live In New York City* album and video were issued, remixed by Ono, who omitted her tracks to allow Lennon's public to enjoy his work without distraction; his drawings, lithographs and sketches were re-exhibited in California, and his poems and articles were published under the title *Skywriting By Word Of Mouth*. Music-wise, his album titled *Menlove Avenue*, featuring canned tracks from his *Rock'n'Roll* and *Walls And Bridges* albums, was released. Publications were numerous and tracks were repackaged and reissued by the handful. Documentaries and short films were collated and released, including *Imagine: John Lennon*, an authorised biography that included the artist's interviews and a previously unheard track, 'Real Love', from 1980, premièred in New York during October 1988.

The first major event of the '90s was the John Lennon Tribute Concert staged at the Pier Head Arena, Merseyside, during May 1990. The gala included performances by Joe Cocker, Natalie Cole, Ray Charles, Roberta Flack and Ringo Starr. Ono organised and later hosted the entire concert. Proceeds went to the Lennons' Spirit Foundation.

On 9 October 1990, the immortal 'Imagine' was simultaneously aired by 1,500 radio stations in 150 countries to celebrate what would have been Lennon's 50th birthday. Ono said, 'I wanted to provide a way for John's fans to do something together.'

Through 1991 and 1992 Lennon's catalogue continued to notch up healthy sales, while Ono issued a six-CD boxed set titled *Onobox* containing a number of unissued items. However, Lennon's fans began to despair at her recorded work, even more so when she hosted an exhibition in Los Angeles during 1993. Using the title 'Family Album (Blood Objects)', the exhibits included a bronze bullet-riddled shirt representing the one her husband wore and his bloodstained glasses.

A year on, in 1994, McCartney inducted his late friend into the Rock'n'Roll Hall of Fame during a New York ceremony. He read an open letter to the audience that included the words 'I'm the number one John Lennon fan. I love him to this day and I always did love him.' Following the ceremony Ono presented him with a trio of unissued Lennon tapes, namely 'Free As A Bird', 'Grow Old With Me' and 'Real Love'. With George Harrison and Ringo Starr, McCartney reworked the titles to release the 'Free As A Bird' title as a Beatles single in 1995, the group's first new song for 25 years.

The New York attendees and media devoured the news of the tapes being available but, as Beatles fans knew, 'Real Love' and 'Free As A Bird', the so-called 'lost' tapes, had been played in Lennon's demo form by Ono to anyone who cared to listen. On the other hand, 'Grow Old With Me' was included on Lennon's *Milk And Honey* album, recorded with Ono. Following Lennon's death, his widow gave McCartney and Apple executive Neil Aspinall permission to rework the tracks; indeed, the titles were more or less completed when Ono publicly handed the tapes to McCartney at the Rock'n'Roll Hall of Fame ceremony. Just a slight deviation from the truth, but never mind; the act had the right media reaction and kicked in the Beatles hype needed to promote the forthcoming group project.

Film producer Chip Chipperfield finally completed the film *The*

Beatles Anthology, assisted by a support team of ten and using approx-imately 10,000 pieces of music and footage. Screened by ITV in Britain, the six-part series began in November 1995 and was followed by the three double-CD package housing unreleased tracks, obscure items, recordings and narrations. Videos and sundry publications followed. Beatles hype was at full strength to promote both the singles and the television series. Needless to say, the three remaining group members were prominent on the promotional roundabout which the bulk of the British public gratefully received. McCartney told Chris Hutchins that the three Beatles had been planning a television docuseries for some time but nothing had been concrete until 1989 when 'we'd solved all our business problems and decided to go ahead and start making *The Beatles Anthology*'. Chip Chipperfield located taped interviews with Lennon, then arranged for McCartney, Starr and Harrison to record their own contributions to turn the docuseries into the complete Beatles story, finally correcting any misconceptions the public might have harboured about the famous four.

It was thought that the Beatles would gross at least £200 million from the music project and spin-offs, with the television docuseries alone grossing £48 million!

And the music just kept on comin' . . . In May 1997 a tape of Lennon and McCartney material was unearthed. As the story unfolded, it became clear that Lennon had been working on Nilsson's album titled *Pussycats* in a Los Angeles studio during March 1974 when McCartney and his wife Linda joined the session that stretched to two hours. The tape that finally surfaced in 1997 spanned 35 minutes and was obviously a bootleg version of the master tape from those sessions which, incidentally, marked the last time Lennon and McCartney worked together.

Mingled with the high-wire verbal activities, the bootleg tape contained three versions of 'Stand By Me' and one of 'Cupid', among others. Lennon later spoke about the session on BBC TV's music show *Old Grey Whistle Test* in 1975. With the passing of time, McCartney believed the tape to be lost, while a Liverpool salesman knew this wasn't so. He had in fact purchased a copy of the bootleg in 1985 from a Californian Beatles collector, intending to sell it for £2 million.

As an aside to the Beatles' music, legal or not, let's take a look at Lennon's financial position following his death. Yoko Ono naturally took control of his estate (worth $200 million in 1998) that included various music interests like his 25 per cent share of Apple Corps with its regular payments to each Beatle. In 1994 the company paid £1.5 million four times, while prior to that, covering a ten-year period, each Beatle was paid £4.5 million in dividends. MacLen, the company set up during 1965 to cater for Lennon and McCartney's composing income, was said to have an annual turnover of £1.1 million, while other non-music concerns like a dairy cattle breeding farm, property speculations and other investments were overseen by Ono.

Lennon's dependants were his sons Julian and Sean, the former by his first marriage to Cynthia, who was left $100 a week together with a £50,000 trust fund that paid out when Julian reached 25 years old. When Julian contested his inheritance there followed a costly and lengthy legal battle, with him accepting settlement of a percentage ownership in several of his father's compositions. On the other hand, Lennon's son Sean, by Ono, was more fortunate, living in the £2 million apartment next to his mother's home in New York and enjoying the lifestyle of a multi-millionaire's son.

Following a successful stab at a recording career, marred by the media's constant reference to him being Lennon's son, Julian retired from music for seven years until 1998, when he released another album on his own label, Music From Another Room. Titled *Photograph Smile*, the album was issued on the same day as Sean Lennon's *Into The Sun* album. Coincidence or what! During a series of interviews, Julian said his relationship with Ono was as strained today as it had been when his father was alive – 'I feel that she thinks I'm a thorn in her side,' he said. As well as concentrating on his renewed recording career, Julian was avidly purchasing his father's priceless memorabilia – 'A lot of Dad's things were sold off at auction without my even being asked.' Apparently, Ono, despite her wealth, had decided to take this course because the American death duties were so high, leaving Julian to dig deep in his pockets to provide a heritage for his children.

And still John Lennon's name remains headline news, both professionally and personally. For example, during September 1998, his American record company Capitol announced that 100 previously unheard Lennon songs had been found in the company's vaults. It was planned to release the tracks for the 1998 Christmas period in a boxed set containing four CDs. Lennon's selling power had been proved the previous year with the multi-million sales attributed to the compilation *Lennon Legends*, and it was forecast that this boxed set would sell in even greater quantities. The unheard material, said to include half-completed tracks, out-takes and cover versions, had been recorded between 1970 and 1975. A huge marketing campaign was expected to promote the new project to the world.

On a personal level, following a lifetime of searching by Lennon and 18 years after his death, the ex-Beatle's sister contacted the media. In 1964, when Lennon had discovered he had a sister, Victoria, he had launched an appeal to find her. His failure to do so haunted him until he died. When Lennon's parents separated, his mother Julia had had an affair with a young soldier, become pregnant and given birth to Victoria in Liverpool's Salvation Army nursing home in 1945. Lennon was four years old. Victoria was adopted by the Pedersens, who changed her name to Lillian Ingrid Maria. She was unaware of her beginnings until 1966, when she needed her birth certificate to marry David Dennis. It's ironic, but at one time the two families lived within a few miles of each other in Liverpool, yet Lennon was still unable to find her! Maybe if Lillian had known, she would have contacted her brother. However, as it was, she did not contact the media until her adoptive mother's death in 1998, following a promise between mother and daughter.

Before the newspaper print had dried on this revelation, Kristina Hagel claimed that she was Lennon's daughter following a brief encounter between the star and her mother in an Austrian hotel in March 1965 which coincided with the Beatles filming *Help!* there. Hagel's birth certificate carries Lennon's name as father.

Presumably both women can claim a percentage in Lennon's estate, a thought that can't have escaped Yoko Ono's mind. Indeed, she must dread reading the morning newspapers!

And so Lennon lives on . . .

'John was a great man and I loved him dearly . . . I'm one of his biggest fans because I worked so closely with him . . . He was really strong and I feel very lucky to have worked with him' – Paul McCartney

Also see: '(Just Like) Starting Over', December 1980; 'Imagine', January 1981

(Quotes: *Lennon* by John Robertson; *Today* newspaper, October 1995, interview by Chris Hutchins; *The Look*, August 1998, interview by Helen Weathers)

March 1981

SHAKIN' STEVENS

This Ole House

With his greased hair, curling lip and gyrating 'naughty bits', our Shaky was every inch the rock singer. He was a good-looking guy as well!

Born Michael Barratt in Ely, Wales, on 4 March 1948, Stevens was one of 12 children raised in an environment devoted to '50s rock'n'roll thanks to his brothers' unusual musical tastes. With rock fever in his blood, Stevens joined his first serious group the Sunsets in 1968, who played, well, rock'n'roll! The group rocked its way across the club circuit until early in 1970, when, known as Shakin' Stevens and the Sunsets, they secured a recording contract with the EMI Records' subsidiary Parlophone.

With Dave Edmunds controlling the production, Shakin' Stevens and the Sunsets recorded the album titled *A Legend* at the producer's own studio, Rockfield, in Wales. The album, which carried a '50s flavour, bombed, as did the lifted single 'Down On The Farm'. The group was subsequently dropped by Parlophone. A year on, they switched to CBS Records and released the *I'm No JD* album. That too bombed.

Two years on, Shakin' Stevens and the Sunsets had carved a lucrative career as a touring unit in Europe, and it was through this they secured a recording contract with Dureco Records, based in Holland. From there, they drifted through further recording outlets including the dubiously titled Pink Elephant label. Midway through 1976, the group issued its final single together. Titled 'Jungle Rock', it repeated its predecessors' fate.

With no group and no record company, Stevens turned to the stage, where he was one of a trio of singers playing Elvis Presley in London's West End. The musical *Elvis*, written by Jack Good, ran for approximately two years and elevated Stevens to a high public profile as a soloist. In 1977 his stage success reaped rewards when he signed a recording deal with Track Records, although remarkably his one-year stay there was unsuccessful. This time, and again with no record company supporting him, Stevens turned to television. Under Jack Good's influence, he joined fellow rocker Alvin Stardust on the '50s-inspired music show *Oh Boy*, screened during 1978. Before the year closed, Stevens returned to recording by signing a contract with CBS Records' Epic label. With Mike Hurst as producer, Stevens' first single, titled 'Treat Her Right', bombed.

During the following year, nothing the singer recorded worked. Then, early in 1980, his patience and determination paid off when his single titled 'Hot Dog' entered the British Top 30. Stevens was finally a charting act. With the single's semi-success, its mother album *Shakin' Stevens Take One* likewise charted, albeit in the Top 70.

The single's follow-up was a reworking of the Blasters' rock track 'Marie Marie', which fared better in the British Top 20 during the September. In fact, most of Stevens' future work was non-original, including his next outing. With a version of the Stuart Hamblen track, also a 1954 No.1 single by Rosemary Clooney, titled 'This Ole House', Stevens shot to the top of the British chart in March 1981.

The track may have been a hit of the '50s but Stevens had heard it for the first time in 1980 as he told journalist Robin Katz. 'A pal of mine in Los Angeles . . . has an incredible record collection. He invited me along to his place to hear some records and that is how I heard [it]. What's really amazing is that nobody thought to cover it before.' His version dominated the British top spot for three weeks, while an album bearing the same name soared into the Top 2 one month on.

Finally the rocker had found his niche in the British marketplace. More importantly, Stevens, now based in Surrey, probably spearheaded a rock'n'roll revival, albeit with diluted versions of the real American sound. Said Stevens, 'I prefer to dig up obscure original songs from the '50s. There's no point in doing a classic like Elvis's "Don't Be Cruel" or things by Jerry Lee Lewis or Eddie Cochran. There's no way you can stand up to the original version . . . it alienates people. But to rearrange something in a new way or introduce a lost song, then people of all ages enjoy it.'

Indeed, this was a musical trend that would transform Stevens into a British household name.

Also see: 'Green Door', August 1981

(Quotes: *Smash Hits*, 1981, interview with Robin Katz)

April 1981

BUCKS FIZZ

Making Your Mind Up

Say 'Bucks Fizz' to some people and they'll reply, 'Make mine a large one.' Say 'Bucks Fizz' to others and the reply will be something like, 'Oh, them, they won Eurovision with, er, that song.' As this is a music book, not the local wine bar, the subject is 'that song'.

Comprising two female vocalists – Cheryl Baker, born Rita Crudgington in London on 8 March 1954, and Jay Aston, also born in London on 4 May 1961 – and two male vocalists – Mike Nolan, born in Dublin on 7 December 1954, and Bobby G, born Robert Gubby in London on 23 August 1953 – the Bucks Fizz membership was handpicked by composer Andy Hill and music publisher Nicola Martin for the sole purpose of representing Britain in the 1981 Eurovision Song Contest. Martin then went on to become the group's manager.

An aside here: prior to joining Bucks Fizz, Gubby was a builder with ambitions to become a professional singer, while Baker was already that as a member of the group named Co-Co, who, ironically, had represented Britain in the 1978 Eurovision Song Contest with the title 'Bad Old Days'. It had lost, but it soared to No.13 in the British chart via the Ariola Hansa label during the April.

Once the public vote had been counted, Hill and Martin's composition, penned with the European market in mind and titled 'Making Your Mind Up', was chosen as the British entry. Appearing confident and dressed in bright colours, Bucks Fizz energetically harmonised, danced and smiled their way through the song. Quite rightly, 'Making Your Mind Up' won the 1981 Eurovision Song Contest staged in Dublin at the Royal Dublin Society Hall. Said Nolan, 'It was a wonderful night and the excitement didn't stop for the next two or three years.' Following a recording deal with RCA Records in Britain, the track was issued as a single and became a chart-topper in April 1981, a position it held for three weeks.

Unlike Eurovision Song Contests in later years, when contestants refused to stay within past musical confines, Bucks Fizz typified the lightweight, bouncy, perhaps musically spontaneous style of British entries that had dominated the '70s until the Contest had started to be regarded with a certain amount of ridicule. By the '90s, the Contest's role in world music was again taken more seriously. Incidentally, the Contest was first staged in 1956 as a means of linking European countries through music, media and live television. Britain has competed every year bar 1956 through to the present. The winning song is always decided by a panel of judges sited in each contributing country.

Returning to 1981, the overwhelming success of 'Making Your Mind Up' in Britain and across Europe saved Bucks Fizz from relative obscurity as unseen voices in a recording studio. Now they had a career to honour.

Publicly speaking, many suspect that the group's Eurovision success was remembered not just for the song but as much for the moment midway through their act when G and Nolan whipped off the girls' skirts to reveal shorter ones underneath.

Also see: 'The Land Of Make Believe', January 1982; 'My Camera Never Lies', March 1982

(Quotes: *Daily Mail*, March 1998, interview by Lina Das)

ADAM AND THE ANTS

Stand And Deliver

Antmusic didn't start with face make-up and fancy, brightly coloured costumes, as most people believed. It was, in actual fact, a commercial derivation of punk music. That's what music historians say, anyway. Well, it was fun, wasn't it?

Adam Ant, born Stuart Leslie Goddard in London on 3 November 1954, drifted through a pair of groups, including Bazooka Joe, while at grammar school. Transferring to the Hornsey School of Art in 1976, he advertised in the weekly music paper *Melody Maker* for musicians to form his new band.

Through the replies, Ant met Andy Warren; together they formed the group the B-Sides, rehearsing with and later recruiting musicians that included drummer David Tampin and guitarist Lester Square (no kidding!). With Warren on bass guitar and Ant on guitar and vocals, the unit was drawn into the rising punk market. The move (and their success) was short-lived, however. When Ant was hospitalised with nervous exhaustion – and had married fellow student Carol Mills – the B-Sides disbanded, leaving as a testimony to their existence a punk interpretation of Nancy Sinatra's 1966 British chart-topper 'These Boots Are Made For Walkin''.

However, the group refused to die entirely, because within a short time Ant, Warren, Square and drummer Paul Flanagan had formed the Ants, prefixed by 'Adam' with the 'd' reversed, although it's not clear from where the name originated, despite many a suggestion being forthcoming. From early 1977 they performed as support act to the punk outfit Siouxsie and the Banshees, among other groups. Following the Banshees' dates Square left the Ants, to be replaced by Mark Ryan, whereupon the group continued their punk trek by touring with X-Ray Spex, primarily on the London circuit.

Through 1977 the Ants supported the punk movement with a passion before performing in Derek Jarman's film *Jubilee*, based around, er, punk. Ant said at the time, 'I wasn't really acting, I was just having a good laugh. I was myself. *Jubilee* is very good but it's going to be years before people begin to realise how good it really is.'

Into 1978, and following their first BBC Radio One spot via the compulsive John Peel show, the Ants recorded a handful of demo tapes which included the title 'Catch A Falling Star'. Mid-year, a further personnel change occurred before they secured a recording contract with Decca Records. Needless to say, success was not immediate. During January 1979, the record company issued the 'Young Parisians' single, which, of course, bombed. Undeterred, the Ants moved to Do It Records before embarking upon their debut British tour. Said Ant, 'We want to create an electrifying atmosphere, one that leaves the kids soaked in sweat, exhausted, but elated. Without the kids there would be no artists, and because of that we're loyal to them . . . We're not aiming at a specific group – anyone can be seduced by our music. At our shows, I've seen punks dancing with skins, trendies and rock and rollers.'

Two tracks recorded at the Roundhouse Studios in London, titled 'Zerox' and 'Whip In My Valise', a play on bondage punk-style, were released by Do It Records. The single bombed.

In between concert dates, the Ants recorded their first album, titled *Dirk Wears White Sox*, which was issued during October 1979. Ant admits, 'Looking back at it, the biggest fault for me is that it tried to do too much, it had too many ideas, got too diverse. When I listen to *Dirk* and think of what it could have been, it kills me.' Nonetheless, the album topped the newly formed British indie album chart, a position which did not require huge sales but which would hopefully be reflected in the mainstream listing at some point. But still the group struggled, and still it suffered from membership upheaval. Warren left as the album charted, to be replaced by Lee Gorman, while Malcolm McLaren became the Ants' manager, adding a female vocalist to the line-up, thereby 'padding' the sound. All was not well; nothing appeared to work.

To start the new decade, McLaren formed the new unit called Bow Wow Wow from the membership of the Ants, leaving Adam Ant to his own devices. He met guitarist Marco Pirroni, born in London on 27 April 1959, late of Siouxsie and the Banshees, among other groups. Together they formed a composing partnership before recruiting drummer Chris Merrick, born in London on 3 March 1954, to form the new Ants. The trio recorded a pair of tracks – 'Kick!' and 'Cartrouble' – which completed the Ants' commitment to Do It Records. Now they were free to pursue their changing career, which included the transition from punk to Ant music.

By May 1980, with the additions of Kevin Mooney and Terry Miall, who was born in London on 8 November 1958, the Ants had recorded material primarily composed by Ant and Pirroni. The group was also partway through a British tour, introducing audiences to their new music and new image of flamboyant, vividly coloured costumes more befitting a pantomime than a serious music stage. Before the year ended, the Ants had once again secured a recording contract, this time with CBS Records, where their first single, 'Kings Of The Wild Frontier', was issued during August. When the record company refused to finance a promotional video, the group produced one themselves for a paltry £300, comprising clips shot for their previous releases. The title became a British Top 50 hit and Adam Ant was on his way to stardom following a frustrating period of time when a lesser mortal would have retired.

The follow-up single was quickly released. Titled 'Dog Eat Dog', it raced into the British Top 5, proving that Antmusic was gaining public acceptance, but there were still many hurdles to jump in order to achieve chart-topper status.

Into 1981, when everyone appeared to want a slice of Adam and the Ants' success, Do It Records rereleased the single 'Zerox', while Decca Records reissued 'Young Parisians.' The latter title hit the Top 10; the former, the Top 50.

However, in between these singles, CBS Records issued the *Kings Of The Wild Frontier* album which left its competitors gasping by shooting to the top of the British chart. Said Ant, [When the] album sold a quarter of a million copies I went out for a curry . . . I like food, any sort of food really. I'll eat anything . . . But I don't drink alcohol, I don't smoke and I don't take drugs. I've never taken drugs. I keep pretty clean.' Meanwhile, the group's 'Antmusic' single narrowly missed the No.1 position.

That was soon to change when Adam Ant further diversified his image by introducing the pirates – well, their costumes, then, – to the public. He said, 'It's mainly frilly shirts, waistcoats, jackets, trousers. Not that big. Make-up is the main thing. It takes about an hour to do.' So, with the reissued 'Kings Of The Wild Frontier' and the album *Dirk Wears White Sox* enjoying considerable sales, Adam and the Ants capitalised on the mature material to issue the single which would become their debut British No.1. Titled 'Stand And Deliver', the single shot to the top during May 1981. As the title suggested, the band members presented themselves as swashbucklers in make-up through a video produced by the imaginative Mike Mansfield from the 'Supersonic' team. Record-buyers did not know what had hit them but, my, did Adam Ant the pirate start a new trend! Sales of body paint had never been so high. Ant said, 'My mum and dad are very proud of me, which is nice. I'm very pleased that everything is going so well at the moment. I've had too many failures. I don't want to have any more misses.'

Happily, this wave of colourful foolery went from strength to strength with future singles. The public really gelled with the group, whose members were determined to enjoy the success while it lasted. Who can blame them?

Also see: 'Prince Charming', October 1981

(Quotes: Flexipop magazine, 1980; *Adam and the Ants Annual*, 1983)

June 1981

SMOKEY ROBINSON

Being With You

'I believe in God and I believe He sent me a message to do this – the melody and the words . . . There are a lot of songs I write which I never record but I don't necessarily feel I am recording the cream of my compositions' – Smokey Robinson

Born William Robinson on 19 February 1940 in Detroit, Michigan, he lived in the north end of the city with his mother. Naturally, he lived in a musical environment, ranging from jazz to gospel, and at the age of three years he performed for the first time. Emulating (as best he could) Billy Eckstein, Robinson sang for a trainload of soldiers destined for Europe and the Second World War. Three years on, the youngster sang 'Ragtime Cowboy Joe' at the Michigan State Fair.

By listening to the radio and by fooling around on his mother's piano, Robinson developed a growing interest in music. However, his contented childhood was tragically shattered when his mother died from a brain haemorrhage at the age of 43, whereupon his sister Geraldine became his legal guardian.

From the age of 11 and while still at school, Robinson worked, delivering packages for a grocery store before becoming a cleaner for the Two Sisters Unique store. With encouragement from one of his schoolteachers who formed a Young Writers' Club, Robinson experimented with verse. He told author David Ritz, 'I had me a Big Ten notebook where I'd . . . be jotting down songs. Mrs Harris was one of the first to make me see the value of writing.'

His jotting at Northern High School led to him forming a group called the Five Chimes, comprising Warren 'Pete' Moore, born on 19 November 1939 in Detroit, James Grice, Donald Wicker and Clarence Dawson. When Wicker and Dawson later departed the line-up, they were replaced by Ronnie White, born on 5 April 1939 in Detroit, and Sonny Rogers, and as such they won the local but prestigious Ed McKenzie television talent contest. James Grice was the next to leave the group, whereupon Bobby Rogers, born on 19 February 1940 in, yep, Detroit, replaced him. With Robinson the lead vocalist, the Five Chimes became the Matadors.

In June 1957, Robinson graduated from Northern High School; instead of continuing his education at the Highland Park College, he opted to plough his energies into the Matadors. College could wait a year. Sonny Rogers was then drafted into the Army and was replaced by Bobby's sister, Claudette Rogers, born on 20 June 1942. The group's new membership then auditioned for Jackie Wilson's manager Nat Tarnopol, singing a selection of Robinson's compositions. They were told, 'You're not bad, but you got the same set-up as the Platters, and who needs another Platters?' However, before leaving the audition room Robinson met Berry Gordy Jr, who, unbeknown to the young singer, had also heard the audition. (At this juncture, Gordy was Jackie Wilson's songwriter; Robinson told Gordy he had stockpiled 100 songs, which would later all be discarded by Gordy.) Gordy asked the Matadors to sing a current track, believing any true potential had been lost in singing Robinson's material. Impressed with what he heard, Gordy agreed to work with the group.

As Gordy's success with Wilson had been limited, he had kept his day job, working on the assembly line in the Ford Motors factory, but was able to secure local dates for the Matadors, before negotiating a recording contract for them with End Records. What to record? Robinson's first composition of note, titled 'Got A Job', was his 'answer' to the Silhouettes' single 'Get A Job'. Gordy assisted Robinson in the song's completion and the Matadors recorded it and its flipside 'Mama Done Tole Me' at the United Sound Studio during November 1957. The group now had a single and a new name – the Miracles.

'Got A Job' was a local Detroit hit during 1958, which encouraged End Records to release a second single, titled 'Money' – not to be confused with the later Motown hit, recorded by Barrett Strong, 'Money (That's What I Want)' – with the B-side 'I Cry'. Said Robinson, 'For these first four sides – and this includes producer's fee, publishing income, writers' and artists' royalties – Berry got a cheque for $3.19. And keep in mind "Got A Job" was something of a hit.' Gordy framed the cheque rather than cashing it, claiming it was the first and last he'd receive because he intended to open his own record company, Motown.

With $800 borrowed from his family and royalties received from Jackie Wilson's recordings, Gordy still did not have sufficient finances to totally control the recording and distribution of records, so he was forced to lease his material to major record companies who had the expertise – and the funds. In time, of course, he ran the entire operation himself, from song conception to record store. In the meantime, the Miracles' next pair of singles were issued via Chess Records, namely 'Bad Girl', the group's debut mainstream American hit, albeit in the Top 90, followed by 'I Need A Change'. On the personal front, Robinson married Claudette Rogers in November 1959.

All future Miracles singles would be released on the Tamla label, starting with 'Way Over There'. The group's wait for American success was short. The single 'Shop Around', composed by Robinson and Gordy and released during February 1961, earned Motown its first million-selling disc by soaring to No.2 in the chart. While Robinson headed the Miracles, the group enjoyed a remarkable recording career in America. But it was 1966 before the group cracked the British chart with 'Going To A Go-Go', the first of nine hits that included a pair of reissued titles, namely '(Come 'Round Here) I'm The One You Need' in 1966 and 1971 and 'Tears Of A Clown' in 1970 and 1976. Indeed, it was with this latter title that the Miracles shot to the top of the British chart during August 1970, a position it held for two weeks, before repeating the success in America.

Although he spearheaded the Miracles' recordings, Robinson also became a valued composer/producer with Berry Gordy in the growing Motown company. Indeed, Robinson went on to become responsible for countless hits by third-party Motown artists including Mary Wells, the Temptations and the Marvelettes, prompting Gordy to give him a vice-presidency position within the company. During 1964, the Miracles' membership was reduced to a quartet when Robinson's wife Claudette retired from live performances, preferring to remain a full-time wife. (In 1968 their son Berry was born, followed two years later by their daughter, Tamla.) She did, however, continue to record with the Miracles for a time.

With the arrival of the '70s, Smokey Robinson and the Miracles struggled for their American hits, as their lead singer spent his time elsewhere within Motown's operation. The situation changed at Robinson's instigation when, following a lengthy American farewell tour, he left the group during July 1972, citing his intention to retire from the music business to concentrate on his family life. In actuality, he had been planning the departure for some time, but since the group's financial situation was unstable, he agreed to stay until their standing was more positive. William Griffin, born on 15 August 1950 in Detroit, Michigan, replaced the departing Robinson, who said, 'I felt like a prisoner in a cage of my own making. My Miracle thing had been dead for years, yet here I was, still performing, still trying to act like my heart was in it.' Robinson turned his back not only on the Miracles but also on Detroit, relocating to Beverly Hills, California, where Berry Gordy had also moved to concentrate on Diana Ross's film career.

'I Can't Stand To See You Cry', released early in 1973 and faltering in the American Top 50, marked Robinson's final single with the Miracles, while a double album tracing their career titled *1957–1972* struggled into the Top 80. It was not an ideal epitaph for one of Motown's premier groups.

The 'new' Miracles' debut single in September 1973, titled 'Don't Let It End ('Til You Let It Begin)' failed abysmally in the American Top 60. The group went on to struggle recording-wise until March 1976, when their single 'Love Machine' topped the American chart, the same month as it soared into the British Top 3. The title marked the Miracles' final hit. When their recording contract with Motown expired, they switched to CBS Records and plummeted to further commercial depths. Eventually the group disbanded, to retire from the music business until the '90s, when the London-based Motorcity Records, headed by Ian Levine, signed them to his artist roster. The new liaison proved fruitless for the Miracles, whereupon they returned to their daily lives. On 26 August 1996, Ronnie White died from leukaemia at the Henry Ford Hospital in Detroit.

Returning to 1973, Smokey Robinson's retirement was short-lived. He tired of being the company talent scout and financial admin-istrator. He wanted to sing. To this end he released his debut single, 'Sweet Harmony', during the September; it was a Top 50 American entrant. He also returned to live performances, following his debut at a Florida nightclub. Early the next year, he enjoyed his first Top 30 hit with 'Baby Come Close', while 'Just My Soul Responding' marked his debut solo British hit in the Top 40 during the February. Robinson told *Black Music* magazine, 'The initial music for "Just My Soul Responding" was done by a guy who has been with me since my time with the Miracles . . . he's still with me, in fact – Marv Tarplin. We've done many tracks together . . . "Just My Soul Responding" was inspired by his music. Those lyrics deal with the problem of the country I live in . . . the huge injustice in the treatment of the Red Indian. The Sioux medicine chant is done by Tom Bee, a Navajho Indian' (formerly of the Motown group XIT).

The next time the soloist appeared in the British chart, he was joined by fellow artists Marvin Gaye, Stevie Wonder and Diana Ross on the tribute single for Berry Gordy's father, titled 'Pops We Love You'. The title reached the Top 70 in Britain, the Top 60 in America, during February 1979.

Like the majority of Motown acts, Robinson was by now a regular visitor to Britain; indeed, the staff at Motown's London office treated him as 'one of the gang'. During 1976, he embarked upon a lengthy British tour, where his performances comprised material requested by his audiences. Remarkably, Robinson was rarely caught out with a song he didn't know! Two years on, he toured once more, closing the trek with a concert at London's Royal Albert Hall.

As the new decade loomed, Robinson's recorded work became more commercial; his style had altered due to him working with outside influences. He broadened his musicianship by composing the soundtrack for the movie *Big Time*, which he also financed, and issued a series of albums, all critically acclaimed, notably *A Quiet Storm*, *Deep In My Soul* and *Where There's Smoke*. And with the '80s, Robinson's career upturned. 'Cruisin'', his first single lifted from the mother album *Where There's Smoke*, shot to No.4 in America, but despite a mammoth amount of hype by Motown's British office, all attempts to repeat the American success failed.

Mid-1980, Robinson released the *Warm Thoughts* album, from which the track 'Let Me Be The Clock' was swiped to reach the American Top 40. The next year, as Robinson celebrated his 25th anniversary in the music business, he struck gold. He released 'Being With You', originally written by Robinson for Kim Carnes, as a single. In May 1981 the title shot into the American Top 2, while a month on it catapulted to the top of the British chart, a position it held for two weeks. The *Being With You* album followed soon after, earning the distinction of becoming the singer's debut British charter in the Top 20. Before the year closed, 'You Are Forever' peaked in the American Top 60 singles chart, while Robinson hosted the ABC TV special *Smokey Robinson – 25th Anniversary Special* and issued the *Yes It's You Lady* album.

During March 1983, when Motown itself celebrated its 25th anniversary by way of a musical gala staged at Los Angeles' Pasadena Civic Auditorium, Robinson and the Miracles reunited to perform alongside numerous other company acts, past and present. In the August, the singer duetted with High Inergy member Barbara Mitchell on the 'Blame It On Love' single, a Top 50 American hit, before duetting with Motown funk master Rick James on the 'Ebony Eyes' single.

On the personal front, Robinson's life was in turmoil. Following two affairs during his marriage to Claudette, and the birth of his son, Trey, in 1984 from his second lover, it was decision time. His marriage had been troubled for several years but he chose to stay with his wife and family. Now with a third child, he was unable either to sever his family ties or to disclaim Trey. So he chose drugs, preferring rock cocaine cigarettes to his family home. He moved to live alone in

1985, where his self-destruction spanned two miserable years. 'I had no stomach lining left. I had no hope. I heard things that weren't there. I saw things that weren't there.' He was unable to work, and touched death's door more than once. 'My recording career was going down the toilet. I hadn't had a hit since "Being With You". I was too fucked up to run, too fried to play golf, too frazzled to do concerts.' The artist refused both medical and friendly help; his dealer was his only guest. Through a friend, however, Robinson became involved with the Ablaze Ministry and attended their meetings, with the eventual result that he cleaned his system, saving his life. With his nightmare behind him, Robinson and his wife Claudette divorced, allowing him to concentrate fully on reforming his life and hopefully his career.

It took Robinson until 1986 to hit the headlines once more, this time as a contributor to the 'We Are The World' project recorded by USA For Africa, a conglomeration of artists, following Bob Geldof's Band Aid success. A year on he re-entered the British chart with the single 'Just To See Her', which reached No.52, while in America the title soared into the Top 10. The track went on to win a 1988 Grammy Award for the Best R&B Vocal Performance – Male.

To start the '90s, and following his unexpected departure from Motown Records, Robinson released his debut album *Double Good Everything* for SBK Records. The album's title track was swiped for single release in November 1991; it bombed.

Regarded as one of music's foremost composers, Smokey Robinson was constantly in demand. Sure, his recording career had fizzled out, but his compositions and presence helped and encouraged others. He continued to tour Britain, although in America his performances were restricted to special occasions or charity earners, such as performing with Aretha Franklin (his life-long friend) to help the Gay Men's Health Crisis or joining the 1993 celebrations of 'An American Reunion' staged at the Lincoln Memorial, Washington. As recently as 1996, Robinson supported a tribute concert for the late Ella Fitzgerald and was the recipient of yet further honours for his vast contribution to music as composer, producer and singer during the past three decades.

For an artist to survive over three decades in the music business is indeed a tremendous feat. His contribution to mainstream music made an indelible mark, so much so that most people in the Western world will have a Smokey Robinson composition in their household. To his loyal fans who kicked in with the Miracles during the '50s, well, he's simply 'Smoke, the man'.

'I try to stay simple. If I meet my fans on the street, I'm glad they recognise me. I'm glad they want my autograph. I don't forget that they got me here, made my life comfortable, allowed me to sing' – Smokey Robinson

(Quotes: *Smokey: Inside My Life* by Smokey Robinson with David Ritz; *Black Music*, Gavin Petrie; *Motown: The History* by Sharon Davis)

See *Every Chart-Topper Tells a Story: The Seventies* regarding Smokey Robinson and the Miracles

July 1981

MICHAEL JACKSON

One Day In Your Life

It seems ironic that it was a discontented Michael Jackson who left Motown with his brothers to join CBS Records, yet it was Motown who was responsible for his first solo British chart-topper following the defection.

Michael Joseph Jackson, born on 29 August 1958 in Gary, Indiana, was encouraged to perform with his elder brothers from the time he could walk. Jackie, born Sigmund Esco, on 4 May 1951; Tito, born Toriano Adaryll, on 15 October 1953, and Jermaine La Juane, born on 11 December 1954, likewise in Gary, were the eldest children of Joe and Katharine Jackson. While youngsters, and with their parents' encouragement, the brothers performed locally under the name the Jackson Family. Marlon David, born on 12 March 1957, was next to join the singing group, then came Michael.

Their father was guitarist with the Falcons, a Chicago-based blues band in the '50s. He married young, and while his wife mothered nine children, Joe decided to transfer his interest in music to his offspring. 'In Gary, with all the steel mills, the kids didn't have anything to do except go to school and come home,' he said. 'So I had them learn to sing or play some kind of instrument and they worked for four hours every day. My goal was to get them on stage where they could perform with other amateurs at talent shows.' It took a year for the brothers' act, based on the Miracles and the Temptations, from whom they pinched stage routines and songs, to be perfected. Eight-year-old Michael was lead singer; his brothers played instruments and provided backing vocals. Michael wrote in his autobiography, 'If you messed up you got hit . . . my father was real strict with us . . . I remember my childhood as mostly work, even though I loved to sing.

I wasn't forced into this business by stage parents the way Judy Garland was. I did it because I enjoyed it.'

As their local reputation grew, and following their first single, titled 'I'm A Big Boy Now', produced by Gordon Keith and issued by Steeltown Records during 1968, followed by 'Some Girls Want Me For Their Love', the brothers joined Motown Records. Now known as the Jackson Five, their first single 'I Want You Back', soared to the top of the American chart, reaching the Top 2 in Britain in February 1970. The title represented the first in a succession of million-selling singles and albums under the Motown banner.

Together with the five performing brothers, younger brother Randy, born Stephen Randall Jackson on 29 October 1962, sisters Rebbie, born Maureen Jackson on 29 May 1950, Latoya, born on 29 May 1956, and Janet, born on 16 May 1966, all in Gary, and their parents would occasionally join the group on stage.

During the heady days of Jackson Five mania, a white Mormon group named the Osmonds gave chase. When Donny Osmond issued his debut solo single 'Sweet And Innocent' in June 1971, Michael released 'Got To Be There'. His title shot into the American Top 4 and the British Top 5. Osmond's single peaked in the American Top 7. 'Got To Be There' was the starting point of Michael's solo career, although he continued to record with his brothers. In time, though, as Michael ascended, the Jackson Five's popularity declined.

In September 1972, Motown/EMI Records in Britain issued Michael's version of the Bill Withers classic track 'Ain't No Sunshine', which shot into the Top 10. As this single rose, his solo album *Ben* shot into the Top 5 in America and the Top 20 in Britain. A month on, the album's title track was swiped for single release and gave the young singer his first solo American chart-topper. The track, written by Don Black and Walter Scharf, was also the title song to the movie *Ben*, the follow-up film to *Willard*, and had originally been intended for Donny Osmond. When 'Ben' was issued in Britain, it soared to No.7. Two Jackson careers ran simultaneously, although the group suffered falling sales which, in turn, led to animosity between them and their record company.

A year on, when arguments had reached boiling point, the unthinkable occurred. Following an unsuccessful meeting between Michael Jackson and Berry Gordy, coupled with the increasing ambitions of Joe Jackson, who had, it appeared, been secretly scouting third-party record companies, the Jackson Five announced to the world that they, minus Jermaine, were leaving Motown for CBS Records' Epic subsidiary. Jermaine, who by this time had married Hazel, Berry Gordy's daughter, wasn't told of his father's intention to move the group and had no intention of leaving Motown, the record company who had invested so heavily in his future. Meanwhile, the financial details of the brothers' new agreement were publicised: a signing fee of $750,000, plus a guaranteed payment of $350,000 per album. All monies were to be recouped from royalties, said to be 27 per cent of the gross record price. When compared to Motown's 2.7 per cent, the new deal was a godsend. As the brothers were unable to record for CBS Records for eight months, Motown issued the first of several albums. Titled *Moving Violation*, it peaked in the American Top 40, while the lifted single, a cover version of the Supremes' 1968 hit 'Forever Came Today', stalled in the Top 60. Meanwhile, unable to use the name the Jackson Five, the brothers became known as the Jacksons and as such agreed to host a series of four variety programmes screened by ABC TV during June 1976. Despite Michael's earlier reservations, the series was a success and subsequently launched their new career.

Early the next year, and following their second television series, the Jacksons released their debut eponymous album, produced by Gamble and Huff. The title reached the American and British Top 40, while the extracted track 'Enjoy Yourself' soared to No.6 in America, reaching the Top 50 in Britain. Midway through the year, the brothers toured Britain, their first visit for at least five years. With the group's success under way once more, Michael, against his father's wishes, accepted the role of Scarecrow in *The Wiz*, the movie version of *The Wizard Of Oz*. His co-star, in a cast of notable artists, was Diana Ross, who had publicly launched the young brothers as a Motown recording act.

Before 1977 closed, the further track 'Show You The Way To Go' shot to the top of the British chart, while 'Dreamer', also swiped from the mother album, became a Top 30 British hit. The title track from their pending album *Goin' Places* likewise reached the Top 30 in Britain and Top 60 in America; the album went on to reach the British Top 50 and American Top 70. These were healthy enough chart positions, but worrying for a group like the Jacksons, whose heritage was glittered with million-sellers and in whom, of course, much had been invested. The tide was to change.

Before the '70s closed, the Jacksons once again proved their selling power with a pair of Top 5 British singles, namely 'Blame It On The Boogie' in 1978 and 'Shake Your Body (Down To The Ground)', which went on to pass platinum status in America. Both titles were lifted from the magnificent *Destiny* album, itself a Top 40 British hit, Top 10 in America, selling in excess of one million copies *en route*. The 'Destiny' tour of America followed but was riddled with problems, the most serious of which concerned Michael's loss of voice. Eventually the tour was abandoned.

It was also during 1979 that Michael departed from the restrictive confines of the group to record as a soloist once again, releasing his debut for the Epic label. Titled 'You Can't Win', the single was a poor seller, faltering in the American top 100 in the March. Born as *Girlfriend* but released as *Off The Wall*, produced by Quincy Jones and issued during the October, Michael's debut album spawned its first single 'Don't Stop 'Til You Get Enough', which soared into the British Top 3 and topped the American chart. Earmarked for the dance floor, the song had been composed by Jackson at his home 24-track studio after enlisting the help of brother Randy on piano. The track's most endearing features were his spoken-word introduction and the high-pitched 'WHHOO!' leading into the sharp funk beat. The title went on to win a Grammy Award for the Best R&B Vocal Performance – Male, among many other honours.

This runaway success pushed *Off The Wall* into the Top 5 on both sides of the Atlantic, eventually selling in excess of ten million copies, while its title track was released and reached the British Top 10. Journalists have often reported that while recording *Off The Wall*, which, by the way, introduced the singer's new nose to the public on its packaging, Jackson decided not to wash or change his clothes, much to the obvious disgust of his fellow studio musicians. Quincy Jones nicknamed the artist 'Smelly', although this was later said not to have anything to do with the singer's personal habits. Nonetheless, Latoya persuaded Jackson to clean up.

With his first major success, Michael had taken the first step to free himself from his father's stranglehold. 'In 1979 I turned 21 years old and began to take full control of my career. My father's personal management contract with me ran out around this time, and although it was a hard decision, the contract was not renewed.'

Two further tracks were lifted from *Off The Wall*, namely the low-keyed 'Rock With You' and the smoochie 'She's Out Of My Life'. Jackson said, 'The words . . . had such a strong effect on me. I was 21 years old and I was so rich in some experiences while being poor in moments of true joy.' Both titles were Top 10 British hits, No.1 and No.10 American hits respectively. These astonishing chart successes earned Jackson the distinction of being the first soloist to achieve four hit singles from one album. Yep, the Michael Jackson story was gradually unfolding. 'Girlfriend', penned by Paul McCartney for the singer, was issued as the follow-up single to 'She's Out Of My Life' in August 1980. It stalled in the British Top 50, much to the surprise of Jackson and his record company. Shortly after this release, he joined his brothers to release the *Triumph* album during August.

Into 1981, Motown rose to the challenge of reaping a percentage of Jackson's current record-sales potential by issuing the *One Day In*

Your Life album. Comprising tracks that had previously been canned during his stay with the company, the album crawled around the American top 100 while shooting into the British Top 30 during the August. Mind you, these sales were heavily boosted when the album's title track was rereleased in Britain during April on the much-loved old Tamla Motown label. Originally a track on the *Forever Michael* album, Motown/UK's then product manager John Marshall had lifted it for British release in 1975; it had bombed. During 1981 the story was quite different. A remixed version of the song was released in America and it was this mix that soared to the top of the British chart in July 1981. Ironically, 'One Day In Your Life' replaced Smokey Robinson's 'Being With You' at the top of the British chart, the first time in Motown/UK's history that one company artist had followed another to the top.

The Motown follow-up titled 'We're Almost There', another mellow sound, failed to dent the British chart, crawling into the Top 50. The Motown hit run was all but over, but the company had proved a point. Michael Jackson was a sellable item irrespective of the age of his recordings.

Let's change tack here. When Jackson first saw the movie *ET*, he, like so many, melted and cried at the fate of the little creature. The film's producer Steven Spielberg had engaged Quincy Jones to produce the soundtrack album, then together they had approached Jackson to narrate the storybook. It transpired that Jackson actually worked on the ET project and the follow-up album to *Off The Wall* at the same time. The pressure worked this time: the *ET – The Extra Terrestrial* record was issued by MCA Records during February 1983, with a lavish booklet and an unissued Jackson song, and reached the British Top 40. The cute photo of the singer and the little creature was alone worth the price of the package. Jackson went on to win a Grammy Award in the Best Children's Recording category.

Prior to the release of Jackson and friend's project, the singer's mentor and one-time guardian Diana Ross released his composition titled 'Muscles', which was the name of his pet snake (although the subject was the rippling kind in Diana's song). The title reached the British Top 20 and the American Top 10. By now, of course, artists were begging for Jackson material, but he tended to compose only for those he knew personally or for a special project. He rarely composed just for the sake of it. Realistically, Jackson needed all the tracks he might have stockpiled for himself, particularly at this juncture in his career, because he was setting his sights high. He told CBS Records that his forthcoming album had to outsell *Off The Wall* by several million copies, and that in itself meant he had to guarantee the completed project was perfect in every way. The initial tracks, though, fell short of his expectations. 'We sat there in . . . Westlake Studio in Hollywood and listened to the whole album. I felt devastated.' He told his record company the album wouldn't be released. 'I knew it was wrong. If we hadn't stopped the process and examined what we were doing, the record would have been terrible . . . It's like taking a great movie and ruining it in the editing. You simply have to take your time.'

With new directives, Jackson and his studio team drew short breaths before remixing the project. The result was, of course, *Thriller*, which broke through every music-industry barrier and surpassed several milestones on the way to becoming the best-selling album ever.

Also see: 'Billie Jean', March 1983; 'I Just Can't Stop Loving You' with Siedah Garrett, September 1987

(Quotes: *Moonwalk* by Michael Jackson)

August 1981

SHAKIN' STEVENS

Green Door

Now rapidly earning the reputation of Britain's leading rock'n'roll revivalist, Shakin' Stevens, every inch the artist gyrating the Presley way, with knee bends, crotch swivels, hand flicks and lip curls, watched his career leap by great strides.

With one British chart-topper – 'This Ole House' in March 1981 – to his credit following a lengthy period of vinyl disappointments, Stevens needed to raise his and the public's adrenalin once more. The chart-topper's follow-up titled 'You Drive Me Crazy', not a cover version but penned by Ronnie Harwood, narrowly missed the British top spot in the May, peaking at No.2. No one complained, though!

Returning to non-original material, the rocker chose a track previously associated with the suave singer and entertainer Frankie Vaughan, titled 'Green Door'. (Jim Lowe had also recorded the track, itself a Top 10 British hit, in 1956.) Incidentally, when Vaughan performed the title, which shot to No.2 during November 1956, his audiences screamed when he kicked high with top hat in hand. Doubtless many recalled those suggestive antics when Stevens released his version of the song, which topped the British chart in

August 1981. Based more or less on the previous versions, Stevens' tamer interpretation dominated the top spot for four weeks. What the true rockers felt about Stevens' song remains to be seen; nonetheless, his formula continued to work.

Bravely, Stevens changed musical direction with the chart-topper's follow-up. Titled 'It's Raining', he ventured from rock'n'roll to choose one of Irma Thomas's better soul tracks and enjoyed a Top 10 hit during October 1981. His album *Shaky* followed, predictably topping its chart at the end of the year.

Into 1982, the denim-clad rocker abandoned cover versions to record and release his own composition 'Oh Julie'. The title became his third British No.1 during the January, his first and last of the year. Nevertheless, he did excellent business with four further singles, namely a trio of reworkings: 'Shirley', swiped from John Fred and His Playboy Band, 'I'll Be Satisfied', borrowed from Jackie Wilson, and 'Blue Christmas', from Elvis Presley. Stevens' versions were Top 10 hits. The outsider of the year, 'Give Me Your Heart Tonight', penned by Billy Livsey, stalled at No.11 in the chart. Two singles charted during 1983, both non-originals, namely Rick Nelson's 'It's Late' and Bob Heatlie's 'Cry Just A Little Bit', while the year's solitary album *The Bop Won't Stop* peaked in the Top 20. Although Shakin' Stevens was having great fun reviving those rock sounds from the past to enjoy an extremely desirable and wealthy career, he would wait a further two years before securing his third and final chart-topper.

To start 1984, he was joined on disc by Bonnie Tyler (herself a raunchy rocker of note with a voice that would gravel any front path) to release 'A Rockin' Good Way (To Mess Around And Fall In Love)'. The song, previously a one-off 1960 hit for Dinah Washington and Brook Benton, soared into the British Top 5, much to the despair of music connoisseurs. Tyler went on to capture the No.2 position in August 1985 with her breakneck single 'Holding Out For A Hero' and would enjoy a relatively successful recording career until 1991.

The single's follow-up, titled 'A Love Worth Waiting For', returned solo Stevens to the Top 5 during the April. Certainly the frequency of his releases was meeting his fans' appetites which, at this time, showed no signs of letting up. Through to the end of the year, Shaky returned to the Top 10 with 'A Letter To You', while 'Teardrops' shot into the Top 5, leaving the long-awaited *Greatest Hits* compilation to shoot into the Top 20. His only American hit, 'Try Just A Little Bit', faltered in the Top 80. I guess the listening public across the Atlantic preferred their own true sound and not a British rock soundalike.

Starting 1985 with the Top 20 British entrant 'Breaking Up My Heart', Shaky turned to the blues to issue the dated 'Lipstick, Powder And Paint', extracted from his album of the same name. With fellow rocker Dave Edmunds on production credits, the non-original single peaked in the Top 20, while the album staggered into the Top 40. However, Shaky closed 1985 in higher spirits than he had started it when he recorded the Bob Heatlie composition 'Merry Christmas Everyone'. The title was gift-wrapped for the festive-season revellers, who purchased sufficient copies to present Shaky with a chart-topper in December 1985. When reissued a year on, the title peaked in the Top 60. This evergreen track has, of course, been included on countless Christmas compilations and is played across the nation by radio stations hell-bent on joining in the celebrations.

With a pair of Top 20 titles – 'Turning Away' and 'Because I Love You' – in 1986, Shaky swiped Gary Glitter's 1977 Top 40 hit titled 'A Little Boogie Woogie (In The Back Of My Mind)' to record. The rocker's version reached the Top 20 during August 1987. Then, for some reason, he chose a further recently popular track, 'Come See About Me', previously a Top 30 hit in 1965 for the Supremes. Shaky's version likewise stalled in the Top 30. Turning the music clock back further, the rocker returned to the '50s to release a version of Emile Ford and the Checkmates' 1959 chart-topper 'What Do You Want To Make Those Eyes At Me For?'. This time the single managed a Top 5 placing, while an overdue album titled *Let's Boogie* crept into the Top 60.

Heading towards the '90s, Shaky's recording career showed signs of crumbling. Of his singles, only two reached the Top 30, namely 'Feel The Need In Me', yet another non-original, this time a version of the Detroit Emeralds' 1973 British hit, and 'Love Attack'. In between these releases he abandoned the beat to record the smoochie 'True Love', one of those songs most performers feel compelled to record at some point in their career. For Shaky, though, the single could only manage a Top 40 entrant. Up to 1991, Shakin' Stevens' recorded output included 'The Best Christmas Of Them All' during 1990 and a return to the Top 40 in 1991 with 'I'll Be Home This Christmas'. The rocker's final British hit (to date) was 'Radio', another Top 40 struggler in 1992.

As he was one of the '70s most successful British entertainers and charters, Shaky's annual tours are as popular today as they always were. Whether he can swivel his hips and curl his lip with the same flexibility as he did in 1970 remains to be seen!

Also see: 'This Ole House', March 1981

SOFT CELL

Tainted Love

'When we did "Tainted Love" I wanted to take that sound and make it ours' – Marc Almond

Peter Marc Almond was born in Southport, Lancashire, on 9 July 1959, and met David Ball, born in Blackpool, Lancashire, on 3 May 1959, during 1979. Almond wore make-up and nail varnish and was regularly sent home from school. He claimed he was the class weed because he entertained people. 'I only liked art and English because they let me use my imagination. I hated maths and subjects that reminded me of Formica . . . I was really into Syd Barrett and I had my hair backcombed and shaggy over my eyes. The teachers were convinced I was a drug addict. It's amazing I was never expelled.'

The troublesome shaggy-haired youth relocated from Southport College, where he studied design and general art on a foundation course, to Leeds Polytechnic to study for a BA in Fine Art. Ball shared his enthusiasm for the purest of American R&B known in Britain as Northern Soul, a name conceived by Britain's leading music historian Dave Godin.

'I was doing performances, drawing and painting,' Almond said of his time attending Leeds Polytechnic. 'I made super-8 films and did slide shows.' However, he admitted college bored him until he noticed the sound room there and was able to experiment with what he called 'noises' – 'That's how we started writing actual songs, because before my pieces were like verbal diarrhoea.'

By mid-1980, Almond and Ball, now known as Soft Cell, recorded a four-track disc titled 'Mutant Moments'. Issued via their own label, Big Frock, the single sold sufficiently well to boost the attendance at their live show during the Futurama 2 Science Fiction Music Festival staged in the West Yorkshire area. More importantly, though, the tracks came to the attention of Stevo, owner of Some Bizzare Records, who invited the duo to contribute to the forthcoming album titled *The Girl With The Patent Leather Face* featuring synthesised futuristic artists.

Into 1981, Soft Cell eventually secured a recording contract with Phonogram Records as part of a two-way deal with Some Bizzare Records. The first release to fall within the contract was the *Some Bizzare Album*, while Soft Cell's debut, titled 'Memorabilia', was issued during the March. The single bombed. It was a minor setback; Soft Cell's second outing elevated them to the status of Britain's top-selling duo!

Returning to Northern Soul, whose followers loyally promoted and supported American acts usually confined to the R&B and soul charts, Soft Cell searched for inspiration. The idea to record a cover version of 'Tainted Love' came to them both, although it was Ball who credited the track as his most memorable Northern Soul track. Almond, on the other hand, had only heard it on the radio. Recorded by Gloria Jones, who went on to rise to international fame not through her music but by being the mother of Marc Bolan's son Rolan, 'Tainted Love' was transformed into a synthesised soul track. Said Almond, 'We were in the studio and Dave said, "Let's do it." I liked the lyrics because they were very androgynous. It was just the perfect song to do. I wouldn't sing anything unless I was into the lyrics.' Soft Cell issued their version and enjoyed their first British chart-topper in September 1981, a position the title held for two weeks. 'Tainted Love' then repeated this success in most European countries before earning the distinction of becoming Britain's best-selling single of 1981. Incidentally, the title was to chart again in Britain: Top 50 in January and July 1982, Top 50 in 1985, and in 1991, when it soared into the Top 5.

The new-wave duo had finally left their indelible mark on the decade's music, although the hype and image surrounding the release accounted for a large proportion of the track's success. Before 1981 closed, the chart-topper's follow-up titled 'Bedsitter' soared into the British Top 5.

Into 1982, the duo maintained chart status by enjoying a pair of Top 3 singles, namely 'Say Hello, Wave Goodbye' and 'Torch'. Soft Cell's album, *Non-Stop Erotic Cabaret*, likewise became a top seller, its sales boosted by the run of singles. Almond said of the album, 'We've been moving into a more sad song direction and a more listening sound rather than a sound people can dance to.' It was at this point that, despite the success enjoyed, Ball announced his decision to retire from the public spotlight to devote time to composing, leaving Almond to concentrate on varying musical projects. However, Soft Cell lived on. At the start of 1983, the duo's next album titled *The Art Of Falling Apart*, with a free single containing a trio of Jimi Hendrix cover versions ('Purple Haze', 'Voodoo Child' and 'Hey Joe'), soared into the British Top 5 reaching the Top 20 in America. When the single 'Numbers', coupled with 'Barriers', was likewise sold with a free disc, this time containing the title 'Tainted Love', Almond was furious. He was told by Phonogram Records that the marketing ploy had been executed to increase sales; in fact the ploy led to Soft Cell and record company parting company, but not before Almond and Stevo, owner of Some Bizzare Records, trashed the Phonogram's lawyers' office, smashing discs on the walls and using a fire extinguisher to spray the debris. Stevo told *NME* that the marketing strategy had shown Phonogram's lack of confidence in the track, before insisting it was 'degrading to give away a two-year-old record with it without anybody's knowledge or consent'. Almond also told the media, 'The record company had no faith in us even after [the success of] "Tainted Love". They should have no right to cheapen and slag us . . . What is a record company anyway? Nothing but a glorified bank. I'd like to walk in there and just laugh at them.'

Also during 1983, Ball's penned stage show titled *Suddenly Last Summer* and Marc and the Mambas' album *Torment And Toreros* were fried by critics. Almond had formed the group when he realised Soft Cell was progressing into other musical areas. He wanted to expand further. 'I wanted to do things a little bit more personal . . . so I went into the studio to record "Fun City" and "Sleaze", which stem from my performance days and are all about the Piccadilly meatrack scene.' Unsure of what name to adopt, the singer drew on his love of snakes to give birth to Marc and the Mambas.

Almond once more stunned his public with unacceptable antics. He was attacked outside his home by a passer-by as he raced after fans who constantly rang his doorbell, then he threatened a music journalist with a whip. In the light of these incidents, the singer prepared an open letter to the media, which cited he was 'confused and unhappy . . . I no longer wish to sing on records, in fact I no longer wish to sing. If there are any future recordings they will be extremely few, which will come as a great relief to those who find my singing a pain to the ears.' Despite this statement, Soft Cell embarked upon an American tour at the end of the year, before performing their last concert together in London during January 1984. Almond's future was mapped as a soloist, while Ball formed the group Other People and in 1988 joined English Boy And The Love Ranch. Two years on he duetted with Richard Norris as Grid to release the British Top 60 single titled 'Floatation' via East West Records, while a compilation album of Soft Cell and Marc Almond material was issued under the title *Memorabilia: The Singles* to peak in the Top 10 during June 1991.

Meanwhile, back to the plot and March 1984. Soft Cell issued their final album titled *This Last Night In Sodom* and Almond released his debut solo single, appropriately titled 'The Boy Who Came Back'; it was a Top 60 hit. This release, albeit poor selling, heralded a lucrative recording career for the young man, supported loyally by the gay community. Through 1985 he issued three singles, kicking off with his version of the Donna Summer hit 'I Feel Love (Medley)' with Bronski Beat, 'Stories Of Johnny' and 'Love Letters', where he was joined on disc by the Westminster City School Choir. Before the year closed, Almond's first album, *Stories Of Johnny*, was issued via his new recording association with Phonogram Records.

For the next two years, the singer regularly frequented the British chart as a soloist and with others, including a guest spot on Sally Timms's 'This House Is A House Of Tears' single. During 1986, though, with the release of the 'Ruby Red' single, Almond ran into conflict once more. Some Bizzare Records was now distributed through Virgin Records and it was with this company that Almond and Stevo clashed regarding the promotional video for 'Ruby Red'. Virgin Records decided that certain parts of the video, which contained scenes of nudity and Satanism, were extremely offensive and insisted it be re-edited for television screening. In fact, a spokesman for the record company said that although he personally enjoyed the video, it was 'too camp' for television, adding it was also 'not the sort of thing that Saturday morning children's BBC TV show *Saturday Superstore* would show'. In retaliation, Stevo told the media, 'Who are Virgin to make moral statements? They have a large roster of transient garbage they can manipulate without trying it on with Marc.' No comment, except that the published stills from the video were, er, revealing. In between releases, Almond boosted his career with selected performances which included Christmas concerts in London.

During 1988 Almond secured a new deal with EMI Records' Parlophone label to release *The Stars We Are* album, from which two singles were extracted, namely 'Tears Run Rings' and 'Bitter Sweet'; both were Top 40 British hits. One year on, under his new recording relationship, Almond duetted with Gene Pitney on a version of the latter's 1967 Top 5 British hit titled 'Something's Gotten Hold Of My Heart'. The unlikely duo, grey-haired Pitney with his unmistakable deep, gravelly voice, and petite, ultra-glam Almond, captured the public's imagination sufficiently for the title to become Britain's top-selling single in January 1989, a position it held for four weeks. Pitney enjoyed a welcome interest in his career.

While Almond's single 'Tears Run Rings' was released in America and faltered in the Top 70, his 'Only The Moment' title sneaked into the British Top 50. The mother album titled *The Stars We Are* faltered outside both countries' listings.

Into the '90s, Almond ploughed on by issuing the *Enchanted* album, from which a pair of Top 40 British hits were taken, 'A Lover Spurned' and 'The Desperate Hours'. The next year saw the release of the singer's version of Scott Walker's 'Jacky', a Top 30 British single, before Almond rejoined Ball in the October to recreate Soft

Cell and record several tracks on the *Tenement Symphony* album, a Top 40 chart entrant. To capitalise on Soft Cell's rebirth, a remixed version of 'Say Hello, Wave Goodbye' was issued but sales were poor. During this period, Almond maintained a high profile as a performer by appearing in benefit galas for AIDS charities in both Britain and America, while of his many television spots, perhaps starring in *Rapido*, screened by BBC TV, was the most notable.

Through 1992 and 1993 the singer was a chart regular via titles like 'The Days Of Pearly Spencer' and 'What Makes A Man A Man', swiped from his recorded performance at London's Royal Albert Hall during September 1992. The full show was issued as an album during mid-1993 under the apt title *12 Years Of Tears: Live At The Royal Albert Hall*.

Maintaining a relatively low public profile through the following two years, the singer continued to record. His most interesting singles both became Top 40 British entrants, namely 'Adored And Explored' and 'Child Star'.

Always one to provide excellent copy, Marc Almond is also a talented and extrovert entertainer. He never disguised his sexuality, either; as he once said, 'I've never gone out to capture that market [but] if you want me in your living-room you have me on my terms . . . why pretend?'

He'll be back!

(Quotes: *ZigZag* magazine, August 1982, interview by Paul Barney)

October 1981

ADAM AND THE ANTS

Prince Charming

'Antmusic isn't just English music. It's been ignored by the English press for three years. It's only now that it's successful that it's been acclaimed by the press' – Adam Ant

With his squeaky voice that appeared to be caught in his throat, Adam Ant, if nothing else, introduced a fun element to music. He pranced and danced and dressed to kill in costumes that reflected his singles, and those singles came alive in promotional videos. It was fantasy world: the complete entertainment package. With one British chart-topper to their credit – 'Stand And Deliver' in May 1981 – Adam and the Ants returned to the top in October 1981 with 'Prince

Charming'. My, how the guys could dress up! To complement his costume, Ant wore a weave in his hair, often with tiny coloured bows attached, and each sideburn was exaggerated to reach a point across each cheekbone. A thick white stripe stretched across the bridge of his nose and under each eye, with pale pink lipstick, black eyeliner and blue eyeshadow completing the warpaint, er, make-up. The casting of Britain's favourite actress Diana Dors as the good fairy and the choreographed ballroom sequence added the usual touch of humour to the video accompanying 'Prince Charming'. An album bearing the chart-topper's title soon followed, capturing the No.2 position; it also marked the group's debut American placing, albeit just inside the Top 100.

Back in Britain, Antmusic strode on. The single 'Ant Rap' catapulted into the Top 3 early in 1982; it was compulsive and fun, and bankable. So it came as a shock when Adam announced his intention to pursue a solo career. Many believed he had lost his senses, turning his back on a hit music formula. However, he proved the critics wrong by swiping that money-spinning sound with his first solo outing, titled 'Goody Two Shoes'; it shot to No.1 in the British chart and entered the American Top 20. Before 1982 ended, he issued a further pair of singles, 'Friend Or Foe' and 'Desperate But Not Serious', which made the Top 10 and Top 40 respectively.

These were the poorest sales figures since his hit run began. While the titles appeared to struggle, however, the album *Friend Or Foe* soared into the Top 5 during October 1982 and, happily, was a big-selling American item too, reaching the Top 20. It was these placings that encouraged Ant to visit America. 'I've never been before so I was very excited when I arrived, knackered but excited,' he said. 'It's like a Woody Allen film, everybody's so neat, they all look like their shirts have been taken out of the box about an hour before.'

His chart profile broadened his market appeal, this time into the black music sector, when he was invited to appear in Motown Records' 25th anniversary gala titled 'Motown 25: Yesterday, Today, Forever'. He was an odd choice, particularly when the show featured past and current company acts. Indeed, when Ant performed a version of the Supremes' 'Where Did Our Love Go?', Diana Ross joined him on stage, although her presence was totally unrehearsed. Said Ant, 'Being on the show was like Hollywood, with people like Jack Nicholson in the front row. I thought I was doing all right when suddenly everybody cheered. I thought, great, I've cracked it. I turned around and ten yards away was Diana dancing. I didn't know she was coming on. I go over to her, dance a bit, and as I turn round she's gone. What can you do to follow that?'

Back on safer soil, during November 1983 Phil Collins teamed with

Adam Ant to produce the 'Puss 'N' Boots' single – with costumes to match, of course; it was a Top 5 British hit. To capitalise on its success, Ant issued the *Strip* album, which reached the Top 20. The magic appeared to be intact, yet late in the year, when the 'Strip' single was issued, the title faltered in the Top 40. Reasons given for the slow sales included the record company's limited promotion due to Ant's refusal to alter the single's accompanying video, which, naturally, was based around the track's title! A year on, the solitary single 'Apollo 9' peaked in the British Top 20 while mid-1985 he issued 'Vive Le Rock', a staller in the Top 50. In between these singles, Adam Ant and a revamped support group performed at Bob Geldof's Live Aid spectacular staged at Wembley Stadium alongside the finest in British rock.

Ant's final serious stab at the British chart occurred during the September with the *Vive Le Rock* album. When that struggled, he turned his back on music to move into the theatre, where he performed in *Entertaining Mr Sloane* before relocating to America permanently, where his ambition was to crack the movie market. To this end, the singer appeared in numerous television programmes including *The Equaliser*, but unfortunately his acting star failed to rise.

Into the '90s, Adam Ant returned to his first love, music, by signing a recording contract with MCA Records. His first release, 'Room At The Top', returned him to the British and American Top 20 singles charts during March 1990. The title was extracted from the album titled *Manners And Physique* which, incidentally, reunited him with Marco Pirroni. It was a Top 20 British hit, Top 60 in America. Ant admitted he was extremely impatient working in the recording studio but that Pirroni acted as a relaxant: 'We work as a team. We decided it was either going to be a Rodgers and Hammerstein set-up or forget it!' The final outing of the year, 'Can't Set Rules About Love', stalled in the British Top 50.

After joining others to contribute to the reworking of the John Lennon classic 'Give Peace A Chance', recorded with the Peace Choir in 1993, Ant turned to the stage once again to perform dates across America, while planning recording sessions for his second album via MCA Records. All the while, his acting career continued, albeit on a low-key level, with performances in television movies including the well-received *Northern Exposure*.

In his absence, Ant's music lived on in Britain with *Antmusic: The Very Best Of Adam Ant*, a Top 10 compilation late in 1993. A year on, the film world beckoned as the singer performed a variety of roles, including his most distinguished in *Drop Dead Rock* and *A Sailor's Tattoo*. However, mayhem prevailed on the recording front; when MCA Records shelved his second album titled *Persuasion*, the singer managed to secure a new deal with EMI Records, where his first release was 'Wonderful'. It presented him with a British Top 40 hit during February 1995. This success was sufficient for Ant to grab his new audience by performing selected British dates through the next month, which, in turn, paved the way for the *Wonderful* album, a Top 30 entrant. During the June, Ant's British follow-up single 'Gotta Be A Sin' struggled into the Top 50, marking the end of his charting recording career. Ant said he was prepared for the day when his high profile as an artist crashed around him: 'You can do what Sinatra did, or what Bowie did. If you're good enough, if you show that you're willing enough to make more effort than anyone else, then you won't stand still. It's always useful and comforting to look at what has happened in the past.'

In retrospect, Adam Ant's music and image were treated with some ridicule, often from people who were afraid of change. He'd probably be the first to admit that he opened himself to ridicule with the pantomime costumes and such like, but most people agree that the music spoke for itself. Public support sustained the singer until 1995, so he can't have been that bad! It was a sad day when the fun ran out.

Also see: 'Stand And Deliver', May 1981

(Quotes: *Flexipop* magazine, 1981; *Adam and the Ants Annual*, 1983)

November 1981

QUEEN AND DAVID BOWIE

Under Pressure

It came about by accident. The fusing of two of Britain's most innovative and creative forces. The flamboyance that formed so much of their professional lives was set aside to record one of the decade's most memorable singles.

Despite public belief, Queen did not start out with lead singer Freddie Mercury but with Brian May. Born in Twickenham, Surrey, on 19 July 1947, May used a section from a nineteenth-century fireplace to carve his first guitar. It was on this instrument that he perfected the art that would form the basis of Queen's musical trademark.

He formed his first group, Smile, and recruited guitarist Tim Staffell, a fellow student at the Imperial College, and drummer Roger

Taylor, born Roger Meddows-Taylor in King's Lynn, Norfolk, on 26 July 1949. During 1969, Smile recorded and released the Staffell composition 'Earth' for Mercury Records in America (there was no British release). When it bombed, Staffell left the group to join the membership in Humpy Bong, recommending his friend as his replacement. Freddie Mercury, born Frederick Bulsara in Zanzibar, Tanzania, on 5 September 1946, joined May and Taylor to form Queen. Musically speaking, Mercury had passed through groups like Sour Milk Sea and Wreckage as a vocalist.

The three Queen members and a succession of bass players began securing regular local gigs, but the group could not develop musically without a permanent guitarist. John Deacon, born in Leicester on 19 August 1951, was the final Queen member to be recruited during February 1971.

Early in 1972, the group demonstrated new recording equipment at De Lane Lea Studios in return for free recording time. Working with engineers/producers John Anthony and Roy Thomas Baker, Queen recorded a series of demo tracks which, when played to the owners of the recording studio, Trident Audio Productions, led to a three-pronged contract covering management, publishing and production. Now contracted, Queen began experimenting with tracks for a debut album, while Trident secured a recording deal for them with EMI Records.

During July 1973, the 'Keep Yourself Alive' single and *Queen* album were released. The short-sighted Radio One banned the single, claiming it was the subject of an industry hype. The title subsequently bombed. In April 1974, their *Queen II* album was issued and soared to No.5 in the British chart, while, following the release of their debut album in America, the quartet toured there, as support act to Mott The Hoople. For their second single, the group decided to remix a track from their first album. Titled 'Seven Seas Of Rhye', it captured the public's imagination and peaked in the British Top 10 during April 1974.

A return tour of America, this time as headliners, followed. Midway through the tour, however, Brian May developed hepatitis, which in turn led to a duodenal ulcer, forcing the group to postpone the remainder of the tour. They returned to the recording studio to work on their third album, to be titled *Sheer Heart Attack*. The blinding 'Killer Queen' was lifted as the first single and reached No.2 in the British chart during November 1974, the same position as the album.

Queen fulfilled their American commitments early in 1975, again as headliners. Fate struck once more, though, when Mercury developed a throat virus which led to the dates being cancelled. While in America, Queen instructed Jim Beach, a music-business lawyer, to negotiate the expiry of their Trident agreements due to waning interest on the company's part. Meanwhile, 'Now I'm Here' was issued as the follow-up single to 'Killer Queen' in February 1975; it was a British Top 20 hit.

Not a group to be idle, Queen began recording tracks for their new album titled *A Night At The Opera*. Having purchased the Mountain Studios in Montreux, Switzerland, they used these and, reputedly, five others to complete the album, which included their most innovative slice of sheer brilliance, titled 'Bohemian Rhapsody'. Highlighting Mercury's passion for opera and Roy Thomas Baker's adeptness at full-blown productions, the single, seven minutes of Queen's innovative rock/opera, was dealt a blow by EMI Records when the decision was taken to edit the track to the acceptable three minutes-plus befitting a 45rpm single. When Capital Radio's Kenny Everett played the full-length version 14 times in two days, however, listener calls swamped the station's switchboard to such an extent that EMI Records were forced to issue the single in its full glory. 'Bohemian Rhapsody' shot to the top of the British chart in December 1975, where it stayed for a remarkable nine weeks, while the album *A Night At The Opera* dominated its chart, remaining on the listing for a year and passing platinum status.

The group's next album, *A Day At The Races*, was issued upon their return from the Australian trek during 1976. To promote its release, the group fêted the media at Kempton Park, where EMI Records sponsored a special race titled 'A Day At The Races Stakes'.

Once more the group embarked upon an American trek, where Mercury exaggerated his passion for theatrical costumes, much to the delight of the audiences. The tour pushed the single 'Somebody To Love' into the Top 20. Queen continued to tour outside Britain until the end of March 1977, when the track 'Tie Your Mother Down' was issued. It stalled in the British Top 40, the American Top 50.

During October 1977, Queen fan-club members were invited to appear in the promotional video for their next single, titled 'We Are The Champions', filmed at the New London Theatre. The group remained on stage following the video shoot to perform an impromptu concert for their loyal audience. The heavy chanting of 'We Are The Champions' was teamed with 'We Will Rock You' for a double-A-sided single, which shot to No.2 in the British chart. Both titles were swiped from the *News Of The World* album, also issued during October 1977. It reached No.4 in Britain, No.3 in America.

Prior to the release of their seventh album, *Jazz*, the tracks 'Bicycle Race'/'Fat Bottomed Girls' were lifted for single release. Issued during the November, the single reached No.11 in the British chart. As a publicity stunt to help the disc's ascent, the group hired 50 naked girls to race around a Wimbledon track, with the intention of using a picture of the naked girls' bums as the single's front cover. Such was the public outcry that certain countries insisted the bare bums were covered by superimposed knickers! The album launch party was held, appropriately enough, in New Orleans. While on American soil, Queen performed at New York's Madison Square Garden, where the audience was treated to semi-naked lady cyclists riding on stage during 'Fat Bottomed Girls' and where the group earned the prestigious Gold Ticket for an audience numbering in excess of 100,000 people!

To start the next decade, *The Game* album spawned the singles 'Play The Game' and 'Another One Bites The Dust'. Both reached the British Top 20 while the album topped its chart. At the close of 1980, the quartet's *Flash Gordon* soundtrack album from the science-fiction movie of the same name was finally issued, contributing to Queen's 45,000,000 album sales registered worldwide.

Throughout the '80s, the quartet continued their high profile on record and on stage. The ambitious project of *Greatest Hits* (the album), *Greatest Pix* (the book) and *Greatest Flix* (the video) paved the way for their 12th album, titled *Hot Space*. While the group was experimenting in their Montreux studio, David Bowie arrived unexpectedly.

The future star was born David Robert Jones in Brixton, London, on 8 January 1947, to Peggy and John. John had previously been married to an Irish singer, with whom he had a daughter, Bowie's half-sister. Peggy too gave birth to a son before her marriage. Named Terry, he was born during 1937 and would in later years play a significant role in the singer's life. When Terry showed schizophrenic tendencies, he lived with various members of the family, including Bowie's parents; it was during these stays that Terry and Bowie bonded.

The young Bowie developed an interest in music by listening to his father's records. He attended one of the first art-orientated high schools in Britain, later attending the Bromley Technical High School, Kent, where he studied with future musician Peter Frampton, whose father was the tutor. Bowie, using the name David Jones, played his way through the groups the Kon-Rads, the Underwood, and the King Bees, who issued the poor-selling single titled 'Liza Jane' for the Vocalion label, a subsidiary of Decca Records. Bowie then switched to the Manish Boys to record the title 'I Pity The Fool', issued by EMI Records' Parlophone label during March 1965. Three months on the Manish Boys disbanded, whereupon Bowie created the Lower Third, who also recorded for Parlophone.

Early in 1966, the Lower Third secured a recording contract with

Pye Records and Davy Jones became David Bowie because he felt confusion would arise with the Monkees' member of the same name. David Bowie and the Lower Third released the 'Can't Help Thinking About Me' single; it bombed. The group subsequently folded, leaving Bowie to pursue a solo career with his single 'Do Anything You Say' in April 1966. Following the release of 'I Dig Everything' and still with no success, singer and record company parted. Undeterred, Bowie returned to Decca Records, this time its subsidiary Deram, where his debut outing 'Rubber Band' was issued late in 1966.

Into the new year, Bowie, now experimenting with face make-up, strode into an obscure musical direction by recording 'The Laughing Gnome' as a single. Despite the title meaning little in 1967, Bowie issued his eponymous album during the June, from which the poor-selling title 'Love You Till Tuesday' was extracted for single release. Developing an interest in dance and mime technique, Bowie studied under Lindsay Kemp, a theatrical artist of considerable note. On the musical front, his career bombed, and with no further solo releases in the offing, Bowie formed Feathers, a trio comprising John Hutchinson and Hermione Farthingale.

Before the '60s closed, Bowie repromoted his first album, with the additional track 'Space Oddity'. On the strength of the new title, the singer signed a recording deal with Mercury Records. Then a reworked version of 'Space Oddity' was released as a single to coincide with the recent Apollo landing, whereupon the title fired itself into the British Top 5 in September 1969. With this success to his credit, Bowie signed a lucrative recording contract with Philips Records, and it was under this new relationship that his *David Bowie* album was issued late in 1969.

Into the new decade, the singer formed his first support group called Hype, recorded the single 'Memory Of A Free Festival' and issued the *The Man Who Sold The World* album. The release raised eyebrows – the packaging showed Bowie wearing a dress.

America beckoned at the start of 1971. He had just completed a short promotional trip there and was working on material for a future album when an RCA Records executive, excited at Bowie's demo album tapes, signed the singer to the company, whereupon the *Hunky Dory* album was issued at the end of the year. To start 1972 Bowie was trapped in a lengthy British tour during which he introduced his alter egos, Ziggy Stardust and the Spiders, to the audiences. From Britain, Bowie and his friends switched to the American circuit, promoting on the way their new album titled *The Rise And Fall Of Ziggy Stardust And The Spiders From Mars*, which, despite the length of its title, marked Bowie's British chart debut in the Top 5. In America it faltered in the Top 70.

An extremely successful 1972 for the artistic singer was signified by a further British and American trek, the release of the hit single titled 'John I'm Only Dancing', the reissued album *The Man Who Sold The World* and a further British hit (and American bomber) titled 'The Jean Genie'.

Into 1973 and on a world tour, Bowie hit the American circuit once again on the strength of his debut Top 20 hit there, the rereleased 'Space Oddity'. By the April, and while Bowie was in Japan, his *Aladdin Sane* album dominated the British chart, reaching the Top 20 in America. During the May he closed his world tour at London's Earls Court before an estimated 18,000 fans and a sell-out concert at Hammersmith Odeon. Coinciding with these final dates, the 'Live On Mars' single shot into the British Top 3, to all intents and purposes burying his musical obsession with space-orientated material. Indeed, following the Hammersmith Odeon date, he stunned his band by announcing to his audience that it marked the end of his career as a live performer.

Meanwhile, like a recurring nightmare, 'The Laughing Gnome', reissued by Deram, shot into the British Top 10, while *Pin Ups*, an album containing Bowie's favourite '60s' titles, shot to the top. The extracted single 'Sorrow' soared into the Top 3.

While 1974 saw the release of the *Diamond Dogs* album, the following year was devoted to the 'Young Americans' album and single, Bowie's musical exercise in what he called 'plastic soul', his viewpoint of American music at the time. 'Young Americans', co-written by Luther Vandross, reached the British Top 20; the album soared into the Top 2. American sales were also high, Bowie's best to date. Then, for some reason, the 1969 track 'Space Oddity' was once again issued, topping the British chart in November 1975. This single, along with 'The Laughing Gnome', plagued Bowie through-out his career. He did so want to forget they existed!

A year on, the artist undertook his 1976 world tour, when audiences saw him dropping his theatrical costumes and elaborate stage props to return to the basics of rock'n'roll. His single 'Golden Years', swiped from the British Top 5 album *Station To Station*, set the pace.

Through to the '80s, Bowie's career encompassed recording and touring. Now living in Montreux, Switzerland, he had recorded the theme for the *Cat People* movie before paying a visit to Queen's recording studio. That unexpected visit gelled two of the world's most famous of music forces and the title 'Under Pressure' was the result. Penned by Queen and Bowie and featuring vocal interplay by Mercury and his visitor, the sharp, direct song with an introduction that sounded off-key on first listening was one of the decade's catchiest of tracks. According to Mercury, 'That record came about by pure chance. We began to dabble in something together. It happened very spontaneously . . . and we were both overjoyed by the result.' So, indeed, were Queen's record company, who insisted it be issued as a single. As there was no flipside available, Queen's 'Soul Brother' was hastily included. 'Under Pressure', the bonding of the giants, shot to the top of the British chart in November 1981, making the Top 30 in America during January 1982, and represented their first and last recording liaison. Interestingly, the song's recognisable musical riff became the subject of a legal wrangle in 1990. American rapper Vanilla Ice sampled it without permission in his American chart-topper 'Ice Ice Baby'. The British acts, naturally, felt they should have been asked and should benefit from Vanilla Ice's record sales. A mutually acceptable deal was reached.

In 1984 the British Top 2 title 'Radio Gaga', swiped from Queen's *The Works* album, was promoted by one of the group's most exciting of videos, directed by David Mallett. 'I Want To Break Free', again swiped from *The Works*, followed, peaking at No.3, and was later used in Shell television commercials.

Following solo projects by Roger Taylor and Freddie Mercury, Queen's next release of note was the *A Kind Of Magic* album which shot straight to the top of the British chart, later remaining in the Top 5 for 13 consecutive weeks. The album's title track was lifted and soared into the British Top 3 during April 1986, thanks, once again, to an ingenious video.

To close the decade, and despite his failing health, Mercury satisfied a personal ambition by recording his composition 'Barcelona' with his musical heroine, the opera star Montserrat Caballe. During October 1988, Mercury and Caballe performed the single at a star-studded concert to launch the city's bid for the 1992 Olympic Games at the Avinguda De Maria Cristina Stadium. Unbeknown to the audience, Mercury was suffering from a throat infection and was forced to lipsynch. It was at this point that concern escalated regarding his health; rumours began to grow within the music industry that he was an extremely sick man. Only his close friends knew the truth: he had AIDS.

Early in 1991, Queen issued the six-and-a-half-minute single 'Innuendo', followed by the album of the same name. Both discs became British chart-toppers. Shortly after this success, Mercury appeared in what was to be his last promotional video, for a future single titled 'These Are The Days Of Our Lives.' Shot in black and white, the film portrayed a desperately ill lead singer and was the group's most moving video of all.

On 23 November 1991, in a personally written statement, Freddie

Mercury announced to the world that he had AIDS. He died the next day, aged 45 years, at his Kensington home. Following Mercury's death, Queen announced he had donated all rights to 'Bohemian Rhapsody' to the Terrence Higgins Trust. EMI Records honoured his wish that the title, with 'These Are The Days Of Our Lives' as the flipside, should be issued almost immediately. In December 1991, 'Bohemian Rhapsody' once more dominated the British chart, where it stayed for five weeks.

Prior to Mercury's death, Brian May had been commissioned by a London advertising agency to compose music for a forthcoming campaign for Ford cars. 'Driven By You' was the result, and when released as a single during December 1991 the title peaked at No.6 in the British chart, with 'Bohemian Rhapsody' sitting five places higher. 'Driven By You' went on to win an Ivor Novello Award for the Best Theme from a TV/Radio Commercial.

May and Roger Taylor attended the Novello ceremony held at the Grosvenor House, London, and announced plans for an open-air concert to be held at Wembley Stadium as a celebration of Mercury's life, with all the proceeds going to AIDS Awareness. It was intended that some participating artists would perform Queen material: the response was overwhelming. Elizabeth Taylor, undaunted by the musical mayhem around her, pleaded for AIDS tolerance. Liza Minnelli led an all-star choir for 'We Are The Champions'; David Bowie and Annie Lennox sang 'Under Pressure'; Elton John chose 'Bohemian Rhapsody', while George Michael duetted with Lisa Stansfield before singing 'Somebody To Love', backed by the London Community Gospel Choir. In 1993, this last performance would be released as part of Queen's 'Five Live' EP, with proceeds going to Mercury's Trust. Michael's version of 'Somebody To Love' entered the British chart at No.1 in the May, where it stayed for three weeks before becoming a Top 10 hit in over 30 countries.

Titled 'A Concert for Life', the gala was watched by an audience of 72,000 at Wembley Stadium on 20 April 1992 and broadcast to 70 countries. Midway through 1992, the Mercury Phoenix Trust was founded to represent and distribute the money raised by the concert.

Freddie Mercury's high recording profile was sustained after his death. *The Freddie Mercury* album was reissued in November 1992; 'In My Defence' was lifted as the first single, followed by 'The Great Pretender' two months later, while 'Living On My Own' soared to the top of the British chart in the spring of 1993. It was estimated that following Mercury's death, Queen albums sold in excess of 20 million copies in Britain, while in America it was one quarter of that figure.

During November 1995, after four years in the making, Queen's 20th album was issued. Titled *Made In Heaven*, it featured the last material to be recorded by Mercury and the group. The title 'Mother Love' was the very last vocal track to be recorded, while 'A Winter's Tale', a British No.6 single in December 1995, was Mercury's final composition. Prior to the release of this single, the first title swiped from *Made In Heaven* was 'Heaven For Everyone', a Top 2 British hit. In March 1996, a further track was lifted, titled 'Too Much Love Will Kill You'. It reached the British Top 20. A large proportion of the album was recorded in the studio in Montreux, where Mercury owned property. The artwork of *Made In Heaven* was drawn from the breathtaking view across the lake which Mercury's house overlooked, with the darkened backs of Taylor, May and Deacon on one side and the statue of Mercury with arm raised in the opposite corner. The project was 'Dedicated to the immortal spirit of Freddie Mercury', and was considered by many to be their finest work ever. Meanwhile, Mercury danced and pouted for visitors to London's Museum of Moving Image, captured forever within a fully animated, full-colour hologram called a holomovie.

In November 1996 the commercial video *Made In Heaven: The Films* was released by Wienerworld. Instead of relying on dated Queen footage or computer-generated imagery, May and Taylor approached the British Film Institute, who in turn contacted producers Hot Property, to commission new young film directors to demonstrate their skills on the individual tracks. Said May, 'Freddie loved film, and we've no doubt that he would definitely have approved.' The evolution of *Made In Heaven: The Films* was another notable chapter in the history of Queen.

A year on, following a solitary appearance with Elton John at the Théâtre National de Chaillot in Paris, the group recorded their first new song in six years, titled 'No One But You (Only The Good Die Young)'. This track was included in the new compilation *Queen Rocks*, released during November 1997. Into 1998, Brian May released his solo album *Another World* in June, from which 'The Business', dedicated to May's friend Cozy Powell, who had been tragically killed in a car accident in the April, was extracted for single release.

In 1982, following David Bowie's joint chart-topper with 'Under Pressure', the album titled *Changestwobowie* peaked in the British Top 30 and American Top 70, with the *Christiane F* soundtrack album and 'Cat People (Putting Out Fire)' single hot on its heels.

From music to acting, Bowie began location shooting in the Pacific for the *Merry Christmas Mr Lawrence* film with co-star Tom Conti. And before 1982 closed, he took the unusual step of releasing the title 'Peace On Earth' – 'The Little Drummer Boy', his duet with Bing Crosby which they had actually recorded during 1977. It was a Top 3 hit.

With a switch of record companies to EMI America Records,

following a reputed $10 million incentive, Bowie recorded and released his most exciting single since 'Under Pressure.' With the pulsating disco boom prevalent, the singer aimed his 'Let's Dance' at the dance floor. The track, swiped from the album of the same name, was produced primarily by Chic mentors Nile Rodgers and Bernard Edwards. Both titles topped their respective British charts, while in America the single became a chart-topper during the May, leaving the album to peak in the Top 4. Not one to rest on his laurels, during June Bowie embarked upon the 'Serious Moonlight '83' tour, with London concerts as the opening dates. Meanwhile, the single titled 'China Girl' soared into the British Top 2, reaching the Top 10 in America. The world tour finally ended in December 1983 in Thailand.

A series of singles – including 'Blue Jean' and 'Tonight' – and albums – *Fame And Fashion* and *Tonight* – during the next two years ensured Bowie's continued high chart profile until he duetted with Mick Jagger as part of the Live Aid fundraising project, instigated by Bob Geldof and supported by British and American rock acts. The Bowie/Jagger duet, confined to a video, was their version of Martha and the Vandellas' Motown classic 'Dancing In The Street'. (Please see 'Dancing In The Street', September 1985.)

Into the '90s, Bowie's acting interests escalated to include roles in the films *Absolute Beginners* and *The Last Temptation of Christ*, while his recording career ticked over with albums like *Never Let Me Down* during 1987. Two years on, the artist formed the new group Tin Machine, who made their debut at the International Music Awards ceremony staged in New York and released their eponymous album in June 1989.

With the new decade came the new world tour, 'The Sound and Vision World Tour 1990', which kicked in with Canadian dates and went through to Britain and America. Used to promote Bowie's album *Sound + Vision*, the tour boosted the album's sales sufficiently for it to win the 1990 Grammy Award for Best Album Package. In the March, *Changesbowie*, unrelated to the previous album series, shot to the top of the British chart, as the *Pretty Woman* movie soundtrack carried a revamped version of his 'Fame 90'.

During 1992, Bowie's public profile was higher than ever before. He attended Elizabeth Taylor's 60th birthday party, appeared in the AIDS fundraising gala 'A Concert for Life – Freddie Mercury Tribute' and attended Bill Clinton's presidential rally in New Jersey. The following year on the music front, the much-awaited Bowie album titled *Black Tie White Noise* crashed into its chart at No.1 via a deal with Savage Records in the April. Three months on from the release, the record company fell into liquidation, leaving Bowie and the album to flounder.

With no record company to release his material, the artist secured a worldwide recording deal with Virgin Records midway through 1995. His debut album *Outside* soared into the British Top 10 (Top 30 in America) during the October. Hot on the heels of this release, Bowie returned to the British touring stage with the 'The Outsiders' tour. Then in 1996, following his induction into the Rock'n'Roll Hall of Fame during a ceremony held in New York, Bowie was honoured by Britain when he received a Brit Award for his Outstanding Contribution to British Music. During the gala evening, the artist performed his current single titled 'Hello Spaceboy' with the Pet Shop Boys, swiped from the *Outside* album. The single went on to become a Top 20 hit, while Bowie's performance was quite possibly remembered more for his dangling earring and stiletto shoes worn with a men's designer suit than for its musical content.

Into 1997, Bowie celebrated his 50th birthday, released his 21st studio album, titled *Earthling*, an international seller, and sold himself on the stock market. Via the Bowie Bond issue scheme, shares were reputedly worth £50 million in total, thus giving the phrase 'selling your soul' a whole new meaning!

Well, that's David Bowie, the man and artist who scratched his way into British music. The ever-unpredictable Bowie, who began his career by the slow transformation from the straight singer to the periphery of transvestism in the form of Ziggy Stardust, which, many believe, was the escape mechanism needed to protect the shy, everyday young man. Yep, that's him.

(Quotes: *Queen Biography* by Jacky Smith; *The Show Must Go On: The Life Of Freddie Mercury* by Rick Sky; *Off the Record: An Oral History of Popular Music* by Joe Smith; *Rock'n'Roll Babylon* by Gary Herman)

See *Every Chart-Topper Tells a Story: The Seventies* regarding Queen and David Bowie

December 1981

HUMAN LEAGUE

Don't You Want Me?

Sharp dressers, designer suits, tasteful make-up. Certainly nothing trashy here. The group's image was complemented by a sophisticated yet conscious sound, which was an ideal combination to launch a new musical movement that, sadly, didn't last as long as it should have done.

Ian Craig Marsh, born in Sheffield on 11 November 1956, and Martyn Ware, also Sheffield-born on 19 May 1956, played together in the Dead Daughters. Hooked on computer games and being computer operators by trade, they, naturally, performed preprogrammed, synthesised music, emulating their peers Kraftwerk, the electronic wizards from Germany.

During 1977 Philip Oakey, born in Sheffield on 2 October 1955, and Adi Newton joined Marsh and Ware, whereupon Oakey took on the role of composer and lead vocalist. Changing his public image regularly, Oakey's appearance at one stage was described as 'half man, half woman' by author Peter Nash, which was 'a crafted touch directly influenced by a Michael Moorcock science-fiction character called Jerry Cornelius, who combined both sexes.' Be that as it may, Oakey was, to say the least, an interesting addition to the group, who now called themselves the Future. They continued along the road of electronic-styled music before changing their name once more to the Human League, swiped from a science-fiction board game called Starforce. Before the close of 1977, Newton left the band to join Clock DVA, another Sheffield group. His replacement was Adrian Wright, born in Sheffield on 30 June 1956.

During the next year, the Human League secured a recording contract with the Scottish record company Fast Product Records. The first single, composed by the group members, titled 'Being Boiled', was released in April 1978. The title bombed but made sufficient sales impact to entice Virgin Records into offering the group a recording deal. Following a British tour, the Human League's next single, via Fast Product, was the EP titled 'Dignity Of Labour Parts I–IV', which the group called a 'drab and miserable release' and which coincided with their across-Europe tour with Iggy Pop. In October 1979, the Human League's debut album was issued. Titled *Reproduction*, it faltered in the British Top 30, while its extracted single 'I Don't Depend On You' bombed.

To start the '80s, the Human League cracked the British singles chart for the first time, reaching the Top 60 with the May-released title 'Holiday '80'. On the strength of this success they embarked upon a short British tour, introducing audiences to their fast-moving synthesised art and accompanying light and slide show. During the tour, the group's second album *Travelogue* was issued and soared into the British Top 20. Oakey was unhappy with the album: 'The songs are half decent but the production is outrageous. I think it's disgusting that anyone should pay six quid for it.' He added that the Human League had discussed disbanding at this juncture, particularly when Virgin Records refused to issue the singles the group dictated. 'We'd lots of arguments . . . but that was because Virgin were in big trouble themselves. They'd made some wrong moves, they were selling property like mad . . . they got to the stage where they wouldn't even dare to release singles.' Be that as it may, the public, unaware of the behind-the-scenes traumas, was finally latching on to the growing popularity of synthesised music, or new-wave music, as it became known, and with this increased interest came more groups expressing their computer-influenced art.

'Empire State Human' was the Human League's next single released by Virgin Records. Like its predecessor, the title was a poor seller. There was a change in the group's personnel when Marsh and Ware departed to form the British Electric Foundation, later Heaven 17, selling the rights to the name 'Human League' to the remaining Oakey. In return, Marsh and Ware would be entitled to a percentage of the Human League's future earnings. Into the group came Ian Burden, born in Sheffield on 24 December 1957, late of the group Graph, and as Oakey wanted the Human League to smack of 'showbiz', he hired a pair of former female nightclub entertainers, Susanne Sulley, born on 22 March 1963, and Joanne Catherall, born on 18 September 1962, both Sheffielders. The girls' first introduction to the Human League's stage shows was the imminent trek across Europe. Oakey had assured the girls' parents they would be well cared for, while admitting he had little idea of how to integrate their vocals into the group's material.

Into 1981, the revamped Human League issued the 'Boys and Girls' single, a Top 50 entrant. Two months on, the group enjoyed its biggest-selling single to date, 'The Sound Of The Crowd', which soared to No.12 in the chart. Its follow-up titles sold in much healthier quantities: the first, 'Love Action (I Believe In Love)', shot into the Top 3 during August, while 'Open Your Heart', with the record label reading 'Human League Blue', hit No.6 in the October, the same month as the group's album *Dare* crashed up the chart to No.1. The album made the Top 3 in America and later sold in excess of 5.5 million copies on the international market.

It was this album that gave birth to the Human League's first and only British chart-topper in December 1981. Titled 'Don't You Want Me?', it was composed by Callis Wright and Oakey. The title became Britain's top selling single of 1981, with sales over the one million mark. 'Don't You Want Me?' also represented all that was good about synthesised music at the time. More importantly, the single represented the Human League's debut American chart-topper during July 1982, a position it held for three weeks. This surprise success opened the American doors for further British new-wave groups like Culture Club to have a stab at chart success.

As always happens, the Human League's previous record company capitalised on the group's current high status by rereleasing 'Being Boiled'; remarkably, the single soared into the Top 10, despite its dated sound. 'Holiday '80', a further reissue, faltered in the British Top 50 in 1982.

Into 1983, the Human League returned to the higher reaches of the chart with '(Keep Feeling) Fascination'. As this title settled at No.2, it peaked in the American Top 10. One further single was released in America this year, namely 'Mirror Man', a Top 30 hit. (The title was a British release in 1982, when it peaked at No.2.) As the Human League's members then concentrated on individual projects, it was a year before the group returned to the British chart with 'The Lebanon' single and the *Hysteria* album during May 1984. Both titles sold badly because, the group insisted, their record company refused to promote them properly; nonetheless, chart positions of No.11 and No.3 respectively aren't that bad! The single and album were also mediocre American sellers, which, of course, wasn't expected.

Giorgio Moroder, disco composer/producer of considerable note, having been responsible for some of the finest dance tracks during the '70s, teamed up with the Human League. The result of this unusual collaboration was the theme track from the *Electric Dreams* movie titled 'Together In Electric Dreams'. The Human League released this as a single and it raced into the British Top 3 in October. 'Goodbye Bad Times', their second Moroder working, failed to repeat its predecessor's success, stalling in the British Top 50, while the album *Philip Oakey And Giorgio Moroder* peaked in the Top 60 in Britain.

After recording with the top producers of commercial R&B, Jimmy Jam and Terry Lewis, at the Flyte Studios in Minneapolis, the Human League returned to the British Top 10 and the position of America's top-selling group. With the ballad 'Human' the first release, swiped from the *Crash* album, the Human League enjoyed their second and final American chart-topper. Oakey admitted, 'Jimmy and Terry brought us down to earth. That had been our problem on the previous album. We were doing a lot of talking instead of getting on with it . . . They tried to fit a record to us, which I think they did very well as an outsider hearing the song.' As well as presenting the Human League with their second American No.1 title, 'Human' also represented Jam and Lewis's second, their first being 'When I Think Of You', recorded by Janet Jackson.

The Human League had peaked, but could they cling on to international success? Time would tell.

Into the '90s, and with a reduced membership of Oakey and the female vocalists, plus a keyboardist and a guitarist, the Human League issued the *Romantic?* album. The project, an attempt to

135

retrace the glorious electronic dance movement, faltered in the British Top 30 in the September, while the extracted single 'Heart Like A Wheel' suffered the same charting fate.

The Human League's name faded from the British singles chart until 1995, when, following a switch of record companies from Virgin to East West Records, and with the group reduced to a trio comprising Oakey, Catherall and Sulley, they debuted with the 'Tell Me When' single. The title re-established the group as Top 10 artists and was quickly followed by the album *Octopus*, another Top 10 hit. A further Top 20 entrant, 'One Man In My Heart', was issued in March 1995, and before the year closed the Human League enjoyed two more hits, namely 'Filling Up With Heaven' and a remixed version of 'Don't You Want Me?'. The single 'Stay With Me Tonight' in 1996 represented the Human League's final charter in the British Top 40.

In retrospect, the Human League were lucky to have been given a second lease of life by Jam and Lewis. Without their input, the group could easily have died in 1990. Oakey was quick to credit the American duo as their saviours: 'For a couple of years we [hadn't] been writing . . . good songs, and we'd have been silly to turn down good songs, especially when they were written for us by a couple of guys that we like very much.' That second lease of life led to a third, but it took until 1995 to do so. The lack of chart presence, however, did not deter audiences packing British concert halls to see the Human League perform during 1999. Indeed, along with those of like-minded Romantic groups, the Human League's career as a performing unit has risen again. Good for them!

(Quotes: *Human League* by Peter Nash)

January 1982

BUCKS FIZZ

The Land Of Make Believe

Except for the most innovative of acts, it was a rare feat indeed for a winner of the Eurovision Song Contest to enjoy further charting success once the excitement of the occasion had passed. Indeed, even Abba initially discovered this although, of course, their composing talents finally enabled them to enjoy a remarkable career.

Bucks Fizz capitalised on their 1981 Eurovision success and British chart-topper 'Making Your Mind Up' with the hasty follow-up single

'Piece Of The Action'. The title, as impulsive as its predecessor, shot into the Top 12 during June 1981. Lest the impetus should waver, it was only three months before Bucks Fizz issued their next single, titled 'One Of Those Nights'. Surprisingly, the title marked a change of style from bounce to tepid, a chancy business for any successful singing unit but even more so for a Eurovision winner with no previous track record. The public expressed their feelings by stalling 'One Of Those Nights' at No.20 in the chart. Nonetheless, the placing was healthy.

These titles paved the way for the group's debut eponymous album, which was issued during September 1981. Appealing more to the mature audience, the album soared into the British Top 20, its sales boosted by regular television appearances and live performances.

Into 1982, Bucks Fizz re-established their selling power when their first single of the year shot to the top of the British chart. Titled 'The Land Of Make Believe', it dominated singles sales for two weeks. Considered to be all-round entertainers, the group could do little wrong, and this was to continue for some time despite the fact that their behind-the-scenes relationships were so stormy.

Also see: 'Making Your Mind Up', April 1981; 'My Camera Never Lies', April 1982

February 1982

THE JAM

A Town Called Malice/Precious

Relying on hard-hitting topical issues to move themselves away from the punk movement into mainstream music, the group's mentor Paul Weller soon earned respect for his liberal, aggressive, yet sincere attitude to life as he saw it. He captured the times he lived in through his music, rebelling and condoning, thereby transforming his group into one of the most successful British bands of the '70s and '80s.

Paul Weller, born John Weller in Woking, Surrey, on 25 May 1958, was the son of a featherweight boxer. When he was a child, Weller's mother took him to see an Elvis Presley movie, thereby introducing her son to music. When one Christmas he was given a guitar, Weller's future was sealed.

School bored the youngster, but when Steve Brookes arrived at Woking's Sheerwater Secondary Modern School during 1971, the two became close chums, with the common bond of music. Weller's father supported his son's enthusiasm and arranged for the duo to perform at the Woking Working-Men's Club during November 1972. Styling their act on Simon and Garfunkel but using original material, the duo were a successful addition to a drinking evening. Weller and Brookes were inseparable: they rehearsed in each other's homes and composed where they could. In addition to his family's loyalty, Weller's music teacher supported the youngster's musical passion by allowing him the use of the school's music room.

The duo of Weller and Brookes expanded with the addition of Dave Waller and Neil Harris in 1972. A further personnel change at a later stage saw Harris and Brookes depart to be replaced by Bruce Foxton, born in Woking on 1 September 1955, and Rick Buckler, born Paul Richard Buckler, also in Woking, on 6 December 1955. Now known as the Jam, the new line-up became an established name on the local club circuit including Michael's in Woking, where they became the resident group, Chelsea Football Club during 1975, and other working-men's clubs.

During October 1976 the Jam performed in London's Soho market, their act sponsored by Rock On Records, the intention being to introduce the group to the passing public. The result was a poor review in *Melody Maker*. From the Soho market, the Jam switched to the Soho nightclub Ronnie Scott's before performing as support act to the Sex Pistols for a single date in Dunstable.

And so it went on until the Jam performed at The Red Cow in Hammersmith, when their act was seen by Polydor Records' A&R scout Chris Parry. Island Records and Chiswick Records also had their music spies in Hammersmith, but the Jam chose Polydor. The company financed demo sessions for the group in a local studio, with an advance of £6,000, before the ink was dry on the recording contract. Polydor Records were afraid the Jam would sign elsewhere in much the same way as the Sex Pistols and the Clash had some months earlier. However, the Jam were unable to cash the £6,000 cheque because their manager, Paul's father John, didn't have a bank account! One was opened rapidly.

The arrangement spanned one single, plus an option for an album. Yep, all that fuss for one 45rpm slice of vinyl! In June 1977 Polydor Records issued the Jam's debut single, titled 'In The City'. Heavy sales pushed the title into the British Top 40. Naturally, the Jam were hastily offered an extended deal by Polydor Records, whereupon the group strode on into their first album, titled after the hit single. Composed by 19-year-old Weller during an 11-day brainstorming session, the project soared into the Top 20 album chart. Said Weller, 'It was all done really quickly but . . . we really felt things were happening.' Indeed they were; the *In The City* album was favourably compared to those most recent releases by their punk peers the Clash and the Damned.

To promote the album, the Jam kicked off a lengthy British tour in Birmingham, followed by an across-Europe stint. The schedule spanned 40 dates but was cut to three-quarters when the group were too exhausted to lift their guitars. Foxton and Buckler wrote in their autobiography that the Jam had dispensed with their Union Jack stage backdrop by the time of their last date at London's Hammersmith Odeon due to the growing numbers of National Front followers, plus the fact that 'the overtones of violence and tension were running high throughout a year given over to rabid media patriotism.' When describing themselves on stage, they wrote: 'The Jam represented one of the most authentic adrenalin buzzes on the circuit. The spectre of violence, much exaggerated by the media for its own purposes, crept in only occasionally.' One incident that warranted particular mention was a Jam date in Hastings, East Sussex, where the violence was particularly excessive. It seemed the provincial town believed that violence represented the group's audience reactions in London, encouraged by the media when it gleefully gloated that punk and aggression went together. Police were also called to calm an uncontrollable audience when the Jam cancelled their performance at Stamford Bridge, London.

Before 1977 closed, the Jam issued two further singles: 'All Around The World', a Top 20 hit performed first on Marc Bolan's final television show before he died in a car accident during September 1977, and 'The Modern World', a Top 40 hit. In the December, their *This Is The Modern World* album peaked in the Top 30. To boost record sales, the Jam embarked upon 'The Modern World Tour' through the latter part of 1977. The media followed avidly and, indeed, the group hit the headlines, due not to their performances but rather a brawl between the group and members of an entire Australian rugby team! The brawl resulted from a lack of alcohol in a Leeds hotel. A fight developed and Weller punched the rugby team's manager. He was arrested and spent the night in prison. He was acquitted the next day and decided that life in London with his girlfriend Gill Price was much quieter.

Into 1978, the Jam's first single of the year titled 'News Of The World' hit the British Top 30 and, following a management deal with Eric Gardner in America, the group toured the country as one of several support acts to Blue Oyster Cult. However, the tour throughout March and April was disastrous for the British group, who, for the first time in their career, performed at venues which held audiences of 20,000, with groups joining and exiting the tour as they pleased, to the extent that the Jam had no idea from one date to another who shared their bill. Foxton and Buckler noted, 'It didn't really work [with the] sort of music that those bands were playing . . . and we'd go on there without suits and play this sort of punk stuff at them. It just went right over their heads.'

Throughout the year, as the Jam once again hit the British touring trail, they managed to record and release material that included the high-profile single titled 'Down In The Tube Station' and their next album *All Mod Cons*. A year on, a pair of Top 20 hits, namely 'Strange Town' and 'When You're Young', and the Top 3 title 'The Eton Rifles' sustained the group's growing popularity. The album *Setting Sons* peaked at No.4 in the chart during the November.

As the new decade dawned, the Jam finally enjoyed their first taste of American success when the *Setting Sons* album scraped into the Top 100. Originally intended by Weller to be a conceptual project based on the knowledge he had gained from reading classic literature, his idea was later confined to five tracks. As the album's lifted single 'Going Underground'/'Dreams Of Children' was issued in Britain, the group embarked upon their fourth American tour. Indeed, as the Jam were on their way from Houston to Austin in February 1982, they celebrated the news that 'Going Underground' had topped the British chart, a position it held for three weeks. The American trek was shortened to enable the group to return to Britain to 'enjoy some of the adulation while it lasted', and to celebrate with their fans with a concert at London's Rainbow Theatre. So excited was the audience that during the show they ripped out much of the theatre's seating!

Polydor Records naturally capitalised on the Jam's chart-topping status by rereleasing the group's earlier work, including the title 'In The City' through to 'Strange Town'. All titles charted. While the public gorged itself on these items, the Jam sustained their high touring profile by visiting Scandinavia, Japan and Turkey, among other countries, before returning to the studio to record their next album, titled *Sound Affects*, due for British release in December 1980. In between these concentrated sessions, the Jam shot to the top of the British chart for the second time in a year with the title 'Start'. As the single peaked, Weller was accused of 'borrowing' a riff from the Beatles track 'Taxman'. In his defence, Weller insisted the title had actually been inspired by the Beatles. To close the year, *Sound Affects* soared into the British Top 2, boosted by a further British tour. It was said to reflect Weller's indecisive period, although he later cited the album as his favourite.

At this juncture in the Jam's career, their reputation of being hellraisers and attracting public attention meant they were often not able to reside in certain hotels or, indeed, eat at particular restaurants. In addition, sometimes the very mention of the group's name evoked adverse and often violent reactions. Eventually, the Jam had no option but to hire a trio of bodyguards to protect them. Not the move of a streetwise group! It's fair to say, though, that a proportion of the group's blemished reputation was media-conceived. As expected, the public believed the printed word.

Into the '80s, the Jam's single 'That's Entertainment', swiped from the *Sound Affects* album, peaked in the British Top 20, marking their first hit of 1981. Throughout the year, the group's chart profile was high and their touring schedules exhausting. An early 1981 trek took in Japan, one of the group's most receptive of countries, before they kicked in a British tour, where fans and alcohol were in excessive quantities. As an aside, Weller's alcohol abuse had ultimately caused him complicated stomach problems, prompting his abstinence for a time. Doctors and the other group members feared for his health. Foxton and Buckler remarked, 'It had got to the stage where his heavy drinking continually resulted in him having total blackouts. He would just get drunk and pass out.' On the business side, though, Weller was in total control. He had opened his own record label, Respond, and financed the opening of a magazine titled *Jamming*.

Into 1982, and following recording sessions to complete their sixth album, the Jam issued the 12-inch single titled 'Town Called Malice'/'Precious', which returned the group to the top of the British chart during February 1982. The double-header attracted dance-floor support with its beaty Motown influence, although Weller believed the track relied on a Madness riff. Whatever, the single was hailed as a first-rate mainstream dancer, while the second title, 'Precious', was Weller's attempt at 'white funk'. Hot on the single's heels, Polydor Records issued the album *The Gift*, incorporating a musical change. It was more slanted towards black soul and, if anyone but realised it, represented the foundation of Weller's new group, the Style Council. However, that aside, *The Gift* was considered by stalwart fans as the Jam's finest musical hour, spearheaded by an adventurous Weller working with producer Pete Wilson for the first time.

While the album topped the British chart but reached only the Top 90 in America, the Jam kicked in their 'Trans Global Unity Express' tour covering Britain, America and, of course, Japan. By July 1982, Weller, bursting with revolutionary ideas of how he wanted his music to progress, announced he was disbanding the Jam but would honour outstanding group commitments. Meanwhile, 'Just Who Is The Five O'Clock Hero?' peaked in the British Top 10.

With Weller's guidance, the Jam reaped further British success, but it was clear his mind was elsewhere.

Also see: 'Beat Survivor', December 1982

(Quotes: *The Jam: Our Story* by Bruce Foxton and Rick Buckler with Alex Ogg)

March 1982

KRAFTWERK

The Model/Computer Love

'I think our music has to do with emotions. Technology and emotion can join hands' – Ralf Hutter

However, many an uneducated ear believed the music was no more than a mishmash of electronic mumbo-jumbo. Still, that's life.

Ralf Hutter, born in Krefeld, Germany, in 1946, and Florian Schneider-Esleben, born in Düsseldorf in 1947, met at the Düsseldorf Conservatory during 1968 while studying jazz improvisation. With Hutter playing electric organ and Schneider a woodwind unit, they performed at selected venues in the Ruhr region.

The pair went on to meet fellow musicians Fred Monicks, Basil Hammoudi and Butch Hauf, and together they formed the outfit called Organisation. Under this name they released the album titled *Tone Float* during 1970 via a recording contract with RCA Records. It bombed, probably due to the fact that the group emulated Pink Floyd and were believed by critics to be a poor imitation of the original, despite the project being produced by future Ultravox associate Konrad Plank. With no hit, RCA Records dropped Organisation.

Schneider and Hutter, more experienced following failure, moved on to team with Thomas Homann and Klaus Dinger to form Kraftwerk and released their first eponymous album through Philips Records based in Germany. The musicians decided on the group name, meaning 'power plant', as they said it ideally described their music, and this was highlighted by a picture of a power generator within the album's packaging. *Kraftwerk* sold considerably more copies than *Tone Float,* but not enough to chart. Eventually the two albums were released in Britain as one package by Vertigo Records.

At this juncture in their career, Kraftwerk's membership disbanded. Schneider and Hutter remained together, taking the group name, while the remaining musicians formed Neu, a German rock outfit. With poor-selling material to their credit, Kraftwerk had little option but to return to the concert circuit to lay the groundwork for future recordings, the most significant of which was the *Var* album in 1971, released in Germany only. Two years on, Schneider and Hutter released *Ralf And Florian*, produced by themselves and Plank, and by the close of 1973 the main men had recruited Wolfgang Flur and Klaus Roeder to work on their next album, due to be called *Autobahn*.

Vertigo Records issued the album late during 1974, and due to concentrated radio play the record company decided to swipe an edited version of 'Autobahn' for single release. Despite being musically repetitive, portraying as it did the monotony of German motorways, the single soared to No.11 in Britain in May 1975, reaching the Top 30 in America. This unexpected success took both record company and group totally by surprise, simply because neither had expected a synthesised Eurodisco sound to appeal outside their cult-following perimeter. In reality, the disc heralded the breakthrough for future Eurodisco musical conglomerations which few record-buyers understood – or wanted to.

Naturally enough, the single's success boosted sales of the *Autobahn* album, which peaked in the Top 5 in both Britain and America, but Kraftwerk's success was tinged with anger: Vertigo Records owned the full rights to the album due to what the group called an irregular contractual condition.

The follow-up single, 'Kometmelodie 2', bombed, giving all indications that Kraftwerk had fallen into the dreaded one-hit-wonder category. Not so, disbelievers, there was more to come. But first a change in group personnel and a record company switch were effected. Klaus Roeder departed the line-up late in 1975 to be replaced by Karl Bartos, while Kraftwerk launched Kling Klang, their own record label, distributed by Capitol Records. This latter move ensured all future product would be owned by the group.

Away from the public eye, Schneider and Hutter had developed their own instruments to reproduce the electronic styles their music now demanded. Their combined passion for percussion was particularly evident in their pending project titled *Radioactivity*, issued early in 1976. The title bombed in Britain and America (despite it being the first to feature English lyrics), although poor sales did not deter Kraftwerk from performing a London date during the year. Staged before a backdrop of lights and slide shows used to exaggerate certain musical high spots, Kraftwerk met with an enthusiastic British response. As for *Radioactivity*, critics were glowing in their praise, including *Record Collector* magazine's Steve Roberts, who believed the group's vision of an all-electronic sound was taking shape: 'Clever use of electronic percussion, with electric pads hit with batons which completed a circuit, and the group's by-now familiar minimalist lyrics and melodies made it an important step forward.'

Into 1977, and following the release of the poor-selling *Trans-Europe Express* album, Kraftwerk toured Britain once again. A year on, the six-track *The Man-Machine* album transformed Kraftwerk into a Top 10 British act, although American sales faltered. While the album was around, the single titled 'Neon Lights' peaked in the British Top 60 during November 1978.

With the new decade came a changing musical trend of New Romantic or Futurist music, which encompassed acts like OMD and Ultravox, who were now beginning to stamp their own identity on vinyl after emulating their peers Kraftwerk. It was probably this break-through and regular nightclub exposure that boosted the sales of the repromoted 'The Model'/'Computer Love' to the extent that it reached the top of the British chart during February 1982. The double-headed single had been issued the previous year following the release of the *Pocket Calculator* album, when it had stalled in the Top 40. It was unclear who was more surprised with this 1982 chart-topper, EMI Records (Capitol's British mother company) or Kraftwerk. But it gave both the inspiration they needed, and within a month the single 'Showroom Dummies' had been issued as a follow-up. There was no high chart placing this time, though; the title stalled in the British Top 30. It was back to square one and back to the keyboard.

During 1983, not only did the group abandon a British tour but EMI Records scheduled then cancelled the album titled *Techno Pop*. Whatever the reason, it didn't prevent Kraftwerk from returning to the British Top 30 with 'Tour De France', the theme to the European cycle race. Upon reissue in August 1984, the single returned Kraftwerk to No.24 in the chart. This title was their last charting single until 1991, when EMI Records issued the album *Electric Café*, a Top 60 entrant. Once again, though, Kraftwerk found American sales sluggish, despite switching record companies to Warner Bros.

Into the '90s, with Kraftwerk performing sporadically, their 'The Robots' single peaked in the British Top 20 during 1991 and a compilation of reworked tracks titled *The Mix* was issued. Also in 1991 the group split up, with Wolfgang Flur and Karl Bartos forming the splinter outfit Elektric while the remaining members recruited a pair of instrumentalists to tour Britain late in the year in the wake of 'Radioactivity' charting in the Top 50. This was to be their final hit in Britain. Within four years, Kraftwerk appeared to be no more, although a group using the name appeared occasionally on selected German and British dates.

Most certainly, Kraftwerk's use of the unusual had been vital to their success. Using Karlheinz Stockhausen, one of several electronic experimentalists, the group's precise yet explorative use of drum machine, synthesiser, and various forms of technological wizardry, against an often compelling repetitive beat, was refreshing. On the other hand, though, some believed it was a cacophony of machine-made noises bereft of emotion and sensitivity.

April 1982

BUCKS FIZZ

My Camera Never Lies

One of the most exciting success stories of the decade continued, despite media criticism aimed at Bucks Fizz for being too twee. They couldn't win.

With two British chart-toppers safely achieved, Bucks Fizz followed their second British No.1, titled 'The Land Of Make Believe', early in 1982 with a zingy, high-pitched track titled 'My Camera Never Lies'. The single shot to the top of the British chart during April 1982, heralding their third but last No.1. Plagued by comparisons to Abba, Bucks Fizz attempted time and again to break away from the musical sameness. This chart-topper was one such attempt.

Two months on the group issued their second album, titled *Are You Ready?*. It was a Top 10 hit, while their final single of 1982 highlighted their tight harmonising talent. Titled 'Now Those Days Are Gone', the ballad, promoted by a wartime themed video, was a Top 10 entry. Sadly, the group's sales would waver during 1983, although their popularity maintained its high level.

To start the year the single 'If You Can't Stand The Heat' returned Bucks Fizz to the musical fast lane, peaking in the Top 10, while its follow-up, 'Run For Your Life', despite borrowing some of the frenetic rhythm, faltered in the Top 20. The next, 'When We Were Young', returned Bucks Fizz to the Top 10, probably thanks to its Abba-soundalike appearance and the group's performance at the Royal Variety Show; however, the single deserved its high placing. By the close of 1983, though, the quartet felt the pinch when the single 'London Town' struggled into the Top 40. In between these releases, the group issued their third album, titled *Hand Cut*, a Top 20 hit, while at the close of the year RCA Records compiled a *Greatest Hits* package to capitalise on the Christmas market, which, remarkably, stalled in the Top 30.

The following year was dismal for the thrice-chart-topping group. Of the trio of singles issued, one, namely the group's version of the Romantics' hit 'Talking In Your Sleep', reached the Top 15. The remaining pair – 'Rules Of The Game' and 'Golden Days' – struggled into the Top 60. The solitary album, *I Hear Talk*, likewise suffered, stalling in the Top 70.

At this juncture Bobby G issued his solo, self-composed single titled 'Big Deal', the theme from the BBC TV series of the same name. This temporary departure from the group indicated that relationships were still at boiling point. However, personal problems were pushed aside in December 1984 when on the homeward trek from a performance in Newcastle the group's £250,000 travelling coach collided with an articulated lorry. The members of Bucks Fizz suffered varying degrees of injury. Nolan, who had been thrown backwards through the windscreen, was in a coma for four days with possible brain damage. His recovery was torturously slow and resulted in a personality change, as he told journalist Lina Das: 'I went from being a real extrovert to being a terribly introverted character.'

During the group's lengthy convalescence, RCA Records swiped the title track from their *I Hear Talk* album as a single. It reached the Top 40 early in 1985 and was followed by two Top 50 titles, 'You And Your Heart So Blue' and 'Magical'.

As the group struggled to keep Bucks Fizz's body and soul together, Aston departed, offering stories to the media that included her attempted suicide and her affair with Andy Hill. Her replacement, Shelley Preston, born in Wiltshire on 14 May 1960, slotted perfectly into the vacancy.

Into 1986, Bucks Fizz switched record companies from RCA to Polydor Records, where their aptly titled single 'New Beginning (Mamba Seyra)' soared to No.8 in the British chart. Sung in English and Swahili, the title looked set to rejuvenate the group's career, but it was not to be. With their cover version of Stephen Stills's magnificent 'Love The One You're With', which stalled in the Top 50, and its follow-up, titled 'Keep Each Other Warm', Bucks Fizz walked the road to decline.

Using the next two years to concentrate on live performances in order to sustain their career, Bucks Fizz's chart profile demanded attention. To this end they returned to RCA Records to release the 'Heart Of Stone' single, which was a Top 50 hit in November 1988. But this and other titles could not save the group's flagging career. By 1989 Bucks Fizz were no more. Baker switched careers into television, starring on children's shows and later as a guest presenter during the evenings on programmes like *Record Breakers* with (the late) Roy Castle, while the remaining members dabbled in music away from the public spotlight.

Into the '90s, Bucks Fizz once more grabbed newspaper headlines – but this time there were two groups. Mike Nolan, tired of constant arguments, departed from the membership of the original group in March 1995. He cited one particular incident to journalist Lina Das: 'I [was] on stage one night trying to introduce the group. The others were all chatting behind me.' As a joke he said, 'Will you three just stand still while I introduce you.' Once the performance was finished, he and G argued, whereupon Nolan retired for 15 months, leaving David Van Dey, one half of Dollar, to replace him.

Eventually, G and Van Dey parted company, whereupon Van Dey formed his own Bucks Fizz with Nolan, working under the title 'Bucks Fizz: Starring Mike Nolan and Co-starring David Van Dey'. After advertising for two female vocalists in *The Stage*, the couple chose Sally Jacks and Lianna Lea from 500 replies. The revamped membership not only attracted concert bookings but recorded a version of 'Making Your Mind Up'. Meanwhile, Bobby G headed *his* Bucks Fizz group with members Graham Crisp, Heidi Manton and Louise Hart; they too are regular attractions on the nightclub circuit. Says Bobby G, 'There is room for us both to work . . . I'm the one who kept Bucks Fizz going. The original four of us became very close over the years, but my friendship with Mike has fallen apart over this.' According to Nolan, 'I was in Bucks Fizz for 15 years, so I'm not going to throw my career away for nothing.'

Whether there is room for Bucks Fizz by two remains to be seen, but isn't it sad that the group who carried home the Eurovision trophy and enjoyed so much recorded success should end up in a quandary like this? Spin your discs and remember the happy days!

Also see: 'Making Your Mind Up', April 1981; 'The Land Of Make Believe', January 1982

(Quotes: *Daily Mail*, March 1998, interview by Lina Das)

May 1982

PAUL McCARTNEY AND STEVIE WONDER

Ebony And Ivory

'As we had mutual respect for each other throughout the years, it was a good time and a good song to get that message across, about ebony and ivory' – Stevie Wonder

As the Beatles finished their last album, *Let It Be*, as a group, Paul McCartney, born in Liverpool on 18 June 1942, had completed his first solo album. For some time, relationships had been strained, particularly when John Lennon introduced Yoko Ono into the group's inner sanctum. When the situation became irreversible in 1970 – George Harrison, for example, was frustrated at not having his compositions recorded, while Ringo Starr attempted to control and/or override the disagreements which dogged recording sessions and filming schedules – the Beatles publicly disbanded. Despite Lennon having already recorded with the Plastic Ono Band, McCartney was blamed for the breakdown of the world's most famous group because of the growing rift between him and the remaining three.

Although the Beatles had earned in excess of £50 million since 1963, the members weren't millionaires. No one person controlled the business side of the group's Apple operation, and eventually Lennon, Starr and Harrison hired New York accountant Allen Klein, while McCartney turned to his future father-in-law Lee Eastman, who assigned his son John to straighten out Apple's tangled web. Klein adopted the role of Apple's chief, while Eastman acted in an advisory capacity. Arguments naturally flared, money changed hands, conflict raged and Klein negotiated a more lucrative recording arrangement between EMI Records and the Beatles with higher royalty rates and so on.

While the media concerned itself with the complex business issues during 1970, Ringo Starr issued the *Sentimental Journey* album, while McCartney released his eponymous solo album which, not surprisingly, soared to No.2 in the British chart in May 1970. It reached No.1 in America, a position it held for three weeks. The swiped track 'Another Day' was released early in 1971 and again reached No.2 in Britain, No.5 in America. Many felt *McCartney* was the work of a desperate man, with material that was inferior to that he had produced while in the Beatles. Was Lennon's absence to blame? Alongside critical acclaim for the cosy-sleeved project, McCartney was hurting too, his confidence damaged: 'I've been accused of walking out on the Beatles, but I never did . . . One day John left and that was the last straw. It was a signal for the others to leave.' He further told journalist Hunter Davies, 'Suddenly I didn't have a career anymore.' He had also lost his livelihood; his money was tied up in the group's 37 Apple companies, due to the contracts he and the others had so freely signed.

Midway through 1971, McCartney issued the *Ram* album bearing his wife, Linda's name. Born Linda Louise Eastman in Scarsdale, New York, on 24 September 1942, she met McCartney at the London club, Bag O'Nails, where she was photographing the performing group, Traffic. They married in 1969. McCartney needed a co-composer, and Linda filled Lennon's vacant place. *Ram* was greeted with some trepidation by the media, with its attack on Lennon via tracks 'Too Many People' and 'Dear Boy'. Many believed the public wanted McCartney in his group mode, not as a soloist, and the comments regarding his lacklustre material infuriated him. Meanwhile, Lennon's own 'How Do You Sleep?' and 'Crippled Inside' on the *Imagine* album were aimed squarely at McCartney, who told a *Melody Maker* journalist that his ambition was for the four Beatles to sign the necessary documentation, divide the money and finally dissolve the partnership. 'But John won't do it. Everybody thinks I am the aggressor, but I'm not . . . I just want out.' Lennon retaliated, once again in *Melody Maker*: 'If you're not the aggressor, as you claim, who the hell took us to court and shat all over us in public?' This was not what Beatles fans wanted; if the group was indeed no more, at least let the members call a truce.

However, as the dust finally settled, McCartney formed a new group, Wings, comprising Denny Laine, late of the Moody Blues, Denny Seiwell, Linda and himself. Henry McCullough, late of the Grease Band, completed the membership early in 1972. The group's name came as a flash of inspiration to McCartney when he was waiting in London's King College Hospital for his daughter Stella to be born. It was a difficult birth and McCartney slept in his wife's hospital room on a camp bed. When discussing the name of the child, the phrase 'wings of an angel' came to mind.

Through to the end of 1971, Wings released the single 'Back Seat Of My Car', which stalled in the British Top 40, while the American-released 'Uncle Albert'/'Admiral Halsey' became a chart-topper. Uncle Albert was, in fact, based on a member of McCartney's family who used to read the Bible when he was drunk – the only time he did! The title was also the second American chart-topper from a solo Beatle: George Harrison's 'My Sweet Lord' was first in December 1970. The *Wings Wildlife* album followed, reaching the Top 20 in Britain and Top 10 in America. It was McCartney's first album not to carry his name but that of a group; even the project's packaging showed an unrecognisable shot of the ex-Beatle with his wife, Laine and Seiwell. Although *Wings Wildlife* reached a respectable chart position, it was a poor seller, so much so that the planned single titled 'Love Is Strange' was canned. Also included in the track listing was a peace offering to Lennon titled 'Dear Friend', replacing a letter he couldn't actually write to him.

Despite the relative failure of *Wings Wildlife*, McCartney was determined to hit the comeback circuit. His first British tour was a low-key affair early in 1972, with performances confined to the college circuit including universities in Hull, York and Nottingham. During July and August Wings toured through France, West Germany and Denmark. However, Linda McCartney's presence on stage was criticised by fans and media alike, and this would worsen when Wings progressed into larger venues.

McCartney's new music was alien to the material he had composed for the Beatles. In time, though, his musical flair became more adventurous, albeit often smacking of middle-of-the-road influences. Horrified at the carnage associated with the bloody conflict in Northern Ireland, particularly the recent Bloody Sunday massacre, the ex-Beatle wrote and released 'Give Ireland Back To The Irish', a strongly worded single publicly airing the views of so many. Needless to say, Radio One failed to share his stand by banning the single outright. The ban subsequently spanned other entertainment areas. In retaliation, the singer reverted to his childhood by releasing the nursery rhyme 'Mary Had A Little Lamb' set to music. No one found offence with this, enabling the inane track to peak in the British Top 10 during June 1972 and the Top 30 in America. McCartney had vented his anger!

Before the year closed, though, he was banned once more, this time for the innocuously titled single 'Hi Hi Hi', his farewell to the drug haze of the '60s. With a Radio One blackout, the furious singer flipped the disc to allow 'C Moon' to soar into the British Top 5, while in America, with no such restrictions on airplay, the topside shot into the Top 10!

As a member of the Beatles, McCartney was hounded by the police, particularly when drugs were suspected. One imagines that when he televised the fact that he and the other members had used LSD to record *Sgt Pepper's Lonely Hearts Club Band* – the album that transformed the music business into a more exciting world – he opened the gates for future surveillance. Police attention was at its most diligent at the close of 1972, when he and Linda were arrested twice, once in Sweden, and then again in their Scottish home, for growing cannabis. They were fined £100 and ordered to pay legal costs. Indeed, McCartney's British drugs record went on to cause immense problems when he applied for an American visa.

Into the '80s, McCartney and the law clashed once again, this time in Japan. He was arrested for possession of one half-pound of marijuana at the Narita International Airport and subsequently jailed for nine days in Tokyo. The Japanese customs officers originally believed the marijuana to be Linda's, before McCartney confirmed it was indeed his: 'We got some good grass in America and no one could face putting it down the toilet. It was an absolutely crazy move. I was very frightened.' The intended Japanese tour was cancelled and

McCartney was extradited from the country, with all charges dropped, following the intervention of the British Consulate. It cost the singer in excess of £300,000 in promoter and legal fees.

During 1973, and following the ATV special titled *James Paul McCartney* filmed at Boreham Wood studios, Wings released the album *Red Rose Speedway*. It became a Top 5 British hit and was No.1 in America. A year on, their finest to date, recorded in Nigeria and titled *Band On The Run*, was issued. This magnificent release with star-studded packaging went on to sell in excess of six million copies internationally, and rightly topped both the British and American charts.

Singles-wise, Wings released the haunting 'My Love', one of the most endearing ballads of the decade. The title peaked in the British Top 10, but soared to the top in America. Hot on its heels was the complete musical contrast, as McCartney was asked to compose and record the theme to the forthcoming James Bond movie *Live And Let Die*. He read the book in a day, composed the track during the next day and recorded it a week later. One of the Bond producers had suggested American soulster Thelma Houston record it, but George Martin had persuaded him to keep the track as McCartney had recorded it. A thundering track befitting the Bond musical formula and sung by Brenda Arnau on the film's soundtrack, it was issued by McCartney as a single and peaked in the British Top 10 during June 1973, making the Top 2 Stateside.

With the year end looming, the hell-on-wheels single, properly titled 'Helen Wheels', reached the British Top 20. Following American release early the next year, it fared better, making the Top 10. McCartney's jeep had been the inspiration, while his black Labrador pup, who escaped from the McCartneys' garden to return pregnant, was the subject of the follow-up single 'Jet'. The title was a Top 10 hit on both sides of the Atlantic, despite the singer's indifference to the title being issued.

Mid-1974, Wings, with the addition of drummer Geoff Britton, issued a pair of charting singles, namely 'Band On The Run', swiped from the album of the same name – a Top 3 British hit, American chart-topper and winner of the Grammy Award for Best Pop Vocal Performance by a Duo, Group or Chorus – and 'Junior's Farm', a Top 20 British and Top 3 American hit. The 'Band On The Run' project concerned McCartney's views on groups who had combined music and drugs in the '60s and who were now, a decade on, regularly busted. Yes, band on the run indeed! The album went on to sell six million copies during 1974; Lennon believed it was 'great' and that, no matter who played on it, 'It's Paul McCartney's music and it's good stuff.'

Through the next year, when Geoff Britton was replaced by Joe

English, McCartney released the *Venus And Mars* album, another crammed with blinding material. One track in particular attracted special attention: as unlikely as it seemed, the track was the theme to the television soap *Crossroads*. Meanwhile, *Venus And Mars* and the lifted single, the first not to appear on the Apple label, 'Listen To What The Man Said', topped the respective American charts simultaneously, while the single contented itself with a British Top 10 placing as the album became Britain's No.1 seller.

To capitalise on this success and that throughout the world, Wings embarked upon the long-overdue year's tour, starting in Britain and including approximately ten countries, with the 'Wings Over America' leg proving the most arduous. The trek finally ended during October 1976 in the vast Wembley Stadium; Wings had performed before two million people, which surely cemented their international popularity. Incidentally, in their absence, the music played on, notably 'Letting Go', 'Silly Love Songs' and 'Let 'Em In' as singles, and the *Wings At The Speed Of Sound* album. All were big sellers.

On the home front, the McCartney family moved from their St John's Wood home to a cottage situated in the harbour town of Rye in Sussex. In time they would purchase 160 acres known as East Gate Farm, build a five-bedroomed house on the land and rename it Waterfalls.

It was also during this year of 1976 that McCartney purchased the Edwin H. Morris Music company, responsible for Buddy Holly's music catalogue. To celebrate, the late singer's 40th birthday was honoured by McCartney with the first of future annual Buddy Holly Weeks in the September. McCartney told Paul Gambaccini during a *Rolling Stone* interview, 'You've got to invest . . . in something . . . I love Buddy Holly, I've been crazy about him since I was a kid.' The purchase of this music catalogue meant that Buddy Holly was protected by someone who cared; this would not be the case in a later buy-out of the Beatles' own material.

The next year, with McCulloch and English having departed from Wings, McCartney composed and recorded the biggest-selling single in Britain with sales surpassing the three million mark. He would probably have held this distinction for longer but for 'Do They Know It's Christmas?', recorded by Band Aid and issued in 1984. Nonetheless, the ex-Beatle's single 'Mull Of Kintyre', a Scottish anthem, lazy and relaxing, was inspired by a tip of the Kintyre peninsula, situated 11 miles from the singer's Campbeltown family farmhouse. 'Mull Of Kintyre' topped the British chart for a remarkable nine weeks yet bombed in America, probably due to the Americans' disinterest in Scottish melodies. Instead they settled for 'Girls' School', McCartney's thoughts about pornographic film advertising, hidden away on the B-side. The title faltered in the Top 40. But the artist had created a monstrous sound with the topside, which sold beyond his wildest ambitions – and rightly so. From the vinyl came the honours, including the Ivor Novello Award for the Best-Selling A-Side Single. With the intention of composing a modern-day Scottish song, McCartney rewrote the track to utilise 21 bagpipers, following instruction from the local Campbeltown pipers.

Following such a monumental single was impossible, so it was no surprise when the sprightly 'With A Little Luck' was issued without a bagpipe in sight! The title soared into the British Top 5, selling in excess of two and a half million copies, and became No.1 in America, the ex-Beatle's sixth single to reach that position. With the band once more flushed with success, the album *London Town* (originally titled *Water Wings* – it was largely recorded on a yacht moored in the Virgin Islands) followed and was another big seller.

Through to the new decade and with Wings reduced to a trio, McCartney continued his consistent chart run with singles like 'I've Had Enough', 'Goodnight Tonight' and 'Old Siam Sir'. Also issued were a pair of albums, namely *Wings Greatest*, with its front cover showing an art deco statuette purchased by Linda and transported to Switzerland, where a crew spent a week photographing it in the right setting, and *Back To The Egg*, recorded in a replica studio of Abbey Road's Studio No 2. This had been built in the basement of McCartney's Soho Square MPL offices because on occasion when he wanted to book the original Studio 2 another act was recording in it. This way he could come and go as his inspiration dictated.

At this juncture the artist signed a recording deal with the Columbia label in America for a reputed $2 million per album. This arrangement was said to stipulate a trio of albums in as many years. CBS Records, the mother company, on the other hand, loudly boasted it had purchased a Beatle! The deal also included McCartney gaining the Frank Loesser publishing catalogue, Loesser being owner of the score for *Guys And Dolls*. Soon afterwards McCartney performed with the Crickets at Hammersmith Odeon as part of the celebrations for the 1979 Buddy Holly Week. Finally, touring-wise, Wings took to the British circuit during the closing months of the year, culminating with a performance at the 'Concert for the People of Kampuchea' staged in London.

Now the recipient of a rhodium-cast medallion, presented during a *Guinness Book of Records* awards ceremony, in recognition of his composing career that had spanned 43 songs from 1962 to 1978, and recognised as the most successful composer of all time, McCartney started the '80s with his first solo single in nine years, titled 'Wonderful Christmastime'. It became a Top 10 British hit.

Throughout his remarkable career as a soloist, the artist never once fell into the easy trap of acting the star. His behaviour was always that of a quiet-mannered musician who, despite having instigated the mayhem known as Beatlemania, avoided any public outcry. His fame and, indeed, fortune have afforded him a luxurious lifestyle beyond anyone's expectations, yet he remains modest by multi-millionaire status. His family too lead as normal a life as possible, despite knowing he is the 30th richest man in Britain with an estimated bank balance of £420 million.

In 1980 McCartney returned to the top of the British chart with his *McCartney II* album and worked with the Beatles' mentor George Martin to record the 'We All Stand Together' track. Instead of using the Abbey Road Studios where Martin oversaw the bulk of the Beatles' recordings, they worked in Martin's studio, AIR in London. 'We All Stand Together', bearing the label credit 'Paul McCartney and the Frog Chorus', became a Top 3 British hit late in 1984. Accompanied by an animated video based on the *Daily Express*'s Rupert Bear cartoon series, which McCartney owned, the song remained a children's favourite through to the next decade. The short film titled *Rupert and the Frog Song* went on to support the singer's future feature film when released on the cinema circuit.

Of his other singles during 1980, 'Coming Up' was the biggest seller of all, peaking at No.2 in Britain. Yes, McCartney could do little wrong. His star was shining brightly just as one was burned out: John Lennon was murdered on 8 December 1980 outside the Dakota Building in New York. McCartney said, 'I feel shattered, and very, very sad . . . There was no question that we weren't friends. I really loved the guy.'

During the next two years Wings disbanded, leaving its founder to duet with Stevie Wonder on the chart-topping title 'Ebony and Ivory'. (See also Stevie Wonder, 'I Just Called To Say I Love You', October 1984.) During February 1981, Wonder and his girlfriend flew to Montserrat, a tiny volcanic island in the West Indies, to record 'Ebony and Ivory' with McCartney, a track destined for the ex-Beatle's forthcoming *Tug Of War* album. The plea for racial harmony inherent in the track was disguised by a strong commercial melody. According to Wonder, 'Even though I didn't write the song, I am in total agreement with what the lyric was saying and because of that I felt it would be right for Paul and me to do the song together. I felt that whatever significance we both have in a multi-racial society – we're all many different colours and cultures – it would be good for us to sing something like that. And so when I was approached to do it, I said it would be really good . . . It was my pleasure, outside of being a fan of his, the fact that we had mutual respect for each other throughout the years. It was a good time and a good song to get that message across about ebony and ivory.'

The single's subsequent sales were boosted by one of the then most expensive videos ever shot. Wonder's part was filmed in America and was superimposed on McCartney's final copy to show the two artists singing together on a piano keyboard, black on white, white on black, among other sequences. It was an imaginative visual without doubt, although observant viewers could spot the 'joins'. 'Ebony and Ivory' shot to the top of the British chart in May 1982 before becoming an American chart-topper for seven long weeks. The single represented Wonder's first British No.1 title, with sales in excess of one million.

As an aside, when McCartney issued his *Red Rose Speedway* album, he had had the words 'We love you' inscribed for Wonder in braille on the upper left-hand corner of the disc's packaging. Wonder received the message, and years later he learned that McCartney had composed a track for him. The rest was history.

As the unique duet topped the American chart, McCartney issued his *Tug Of War* album, which became No.1 in both Britain and America.

Also see: 'Pipes Of Peace', January 1984

(Quotes: *McCartney: The Biography* by Chet Flippo)

For further information regarding the Beatles and Paul McCartney, please see *Every Chart-Topper Tells a Story: The Sixties; Every Chart-Topper Tells a Story: The Seventies*

June 1982

MADNESS

House Of Fun

'Our original idea of nuttiness has gone a bit coy, a bit Walt Disney, which was never the intention' – Chris Foreman

It may be hard to believe now but Madness rode the chart for a wonderful eight years, enjoying a run that included 20 hit titles, the majority of which were Top 20 entrants. The lovable group, whose act was highlighted by 'funny dances' and weird clothes, appealed to all ages. 'Welcome to the house of fun, da di dada da . . .'

Lee Thompson, born 5 October 1957 in London, Christopher

Foreman, born 8 August 1958 in London, and Mike Barson, born 21 May 1958 in, er, London, friends at Camden's Gospel Oak School, formed the group the Invaders during the mid-'70s. With a trio of casual members including a vocalist, the group specialised in blue beat and ska, which, by any stretch of the imagination, were specialist sounds. Nonetheless, a public following was built. By the end of 1977, though, a personnel change had led to the permanent additions of Daniel Woodgate, born 19 October 1960 in London, Cathal Smyth, born 14 January 1959 in (where else?) London, Mark Bedford, born 24 August 1961 in, um, London, and Graham McPherson, born 13 January 1961 in . . . no, he's not a Londoner, but Sussex born and raised. As the group's principal vocalist, he became affectionately known as 'Suggs'.

Early in 1979 the Invaders became Madness, and via their concerts with the Coventry-born the Specials, the group signed to the Specials' 2-Tone label, a record company specialising in ska and blue beat. The label was financed and distributed by Chrysalis Records. 'Gangsters' was the label's debut single recorded by the Specials; it reached the British Top 10 in September 1976. The second release introduced Madness to the record market. Titled 'The Prince', a tribute single to Prince Buster, originator of ska, it peaked at No.16 in the chart during the October; its sales increased when Madness toured Britain with the Specials and Selector.

The success of 'The Prince' prompted Madness to switch record outlets from 2-Tone to Stiff Records before the end of 1979, and under the new commitment the group issued their second single, titled 'One Step Beyond', which soared into the British Top 10. This title also graced their first album, with Alan Winstantley and Clive Langer credited as producers. It romped up the chart, peaking at No.2.

Into the new decade, 'My Girl' was Madness's first single. As the title climbed into the Top 10, the group embarked upon a tour spanning Europe. By this time the band's appeal was twofold. On the downside, they attracted support from the National Front; in time this situation was publicly condemned by the band on a track included on the 'Work, Rest And Play EP', a Top 10 entrant in April 1980. On the brighter side, Madness attracted youngsters by the thousand, and to encourage this teenage adoration the group performed concerts geared towards their fans' age.

The solitary album of 1980, *Absolutely*, hit the Top 2 in Britain, while the swiped single 'Baggy Trousers' peaked a position lower during the October. With a large dose of humour combined with a zany stage act usually instigated by Suggs strutting his stuff, the group's popularity expanded further. A lengthy tour of Britain confirmed this, and their teenage audiences were treated to matinee performances at each date with ticket prices restricted to £1 each. The trek closed at the Hammersmith Odeon in London, and the final single of 1980, titled 'Embarrassment', returned Madness to the British Top 5.

The next year, the group issued a trio of excellent singles, namely 'Return Of The Los Palmas Seven', 'Grey Day' and 'Shut Up'; all were Top 10 titles. Around the same time, the *Seven* album became a hefty British seller and once again the group, who had been touring constantly since October 1979, were on the road. From Britain they trekked across Australia and America; it was a long haul. According to Suggs, 'When I come back off the road I'm a bit disorientated for a few days while I wind down because all of a sudden there's no one telling you what to do and there's no routine.'

Madness music was now well established and during the next year their career peaked. Following the release of the titles 'It Must Be Love', a version of Labi Siffre's 1972 Top 20 hit which peaked in the Top 4, and 'Cardiac Arrest', which didn't, Madness finally topped the British chart during May 1982 with 'House Of Fun' – and it was! The happy-go-lucky single danced away at the top of the chart for two weeks and, as remarkable as it seems, represented their only chart-topper during their distinguished career. A pair of further singles followed, namely 'Driving In My Car' and 'Our House'. Both were Top 5 sellers and oh so typical of the wonderful off-beat Madness sound.

Midway between these two releases, the album *The Rise And Fall* peaked in the Top 10. Foreman composed six of the 13 tracks, compared to three on the previous album, and was obviously an influential factor in the group's success. However, he was now keen to discard much of their wacky, nutty, often ridiculous musical antics to concentrate on music of a more serious nature. Conceived as a concept album, *The Rise And Fall* changed direction when the group members realised the tracks would require links between each other. Foreman told journalist Peter Silverton, 'People get a bit bloody bored with that sort of thing . . . We had a concept that linked four or five songs lyrically. The idea was an average bloke going mad. Madness in its various shapes and forms. But then we found we'd have had to have all these monologues to explain what was going on. And if you don't do it properly, it can sound dreadful.' At this juncture Foreman also stressed that he was more aware of the world's injustices than he was, say, three years previously: 'I intend to write more serious lyrics, about what I'm involved in, like CND, for instance . . . You can't stay naïve forever.'

Naïve or not, through 1983 Madness sustained their run of hit singles and their status as a high-earning touring act. Into 1984, their single 'Michael Caine', actually featuring the actor's voice, reached the Top 20, soon followed by 'One Better Day', their final single via Stiff Records. Madness decided they wanted to be totally self-contained so they formed their own label, titled Zarjazz (from a science-fiction cartoon), and used the mighty Virgin Records as distributor. Under this new arrangement, the single 'Mutants In Mega City', under the name the Fink Brothers (namely Suggs and Smash aka Smyth), was the first release, while Madness's debut proper was 'Yesterday's Men', a British Top 20 entrant during September 1985. The album *Mad Not Mad* also made it into the Top 20. These sales were not considered great, bearing in mind the group's previous pulling power; when the single 'Uncle Sam' faltered outside the Top 20, their first title to do so, the group's disappointment turned to despair. It would have been unfair to blame the situation on new record-company bosses; in fact, it was due to changing public taste, as fickle as that now sounds.

Towards the '90s Madness struggled on, with one single selling in sufficient numbers to reach the Top 20. Titled '(Waiting For) The Ghost Train', it peaked and died during November 1986, the same year the compilation *Utter Madness* struggled into the Top 30.

Two years on, the group, now reduced to the quartet of Suggs, Smyth, Foreman and Thompson, linked properly with Virgin Records, where their first release, 'I Pronounce', stalled in the Top 50. Despite the new recording deal and obvious marketing support, it was apparent that Madness was a name of the past, and by June 1988, when the 'What's That?' single bombed, the group had no choice but to disband. Each member embarked upon solo projects, with Suggs remaining most in the public spotlight.

However, it was the group's past material that continued to chart, namely 'It Must Be Love', 'House Of Fun' and 'My Girl'. In the autumn of 1992 the group actually performed a pair of open-air concerts at London's Finsbury Park alongside a host of acts that included Ian Dury and the Blockheads and the main man himself, Prince Buster. In the November, an album, *Madstock*, recorded at those concerts, was issued and reached the British Top 30, while a movie of the same was screened by Channel 4 one month on. The remainder of the year was spent touring Britain; yeah, some things never change!

The single that sealed the fate of Madness, though, was 'Night Boat To Cairo'. Issued early in 1993, it crept into the British Top 60. With the group now in limbo, Suggs embarked upon a solo career as an East West Records artist. As such he enjoyed a trio of charting titles including the heavyweight 'I'm Only Sleeping'/'Off On Holiday' during August 1995. A year on, his 'Cecilia' single became his best-selling single as a soloist to date by soaring into the Top 5, later re-entering the chart twice. Its follow-up, titled 'No More Alcohol', peaked in the Top 30 during the September.

Let's face it, there will always be a place for groups of the Madness ilk in British music. They had fun and enjoyed performing, generating a warmth and respect towards their audiences. In comparison, isn't '90s music far too serious?

(Quotes: *Smash Hits* magazine, January 1983)

July 1982

IRENE CARA

Fame

'Fame! I'm gonna live forever!' So boasted the chart-topper. It didn't, but never mind. Even those healthy young things couldn't have performed those eye-watering acrobatic routines that pulled muscles and distorted smiling faces in later life. Or could they?

Born in the Bronx, New York City, on 18 March 1959, Cara was playing piano by ear by the age of five and later, encouraged by her parents, studied dance and music: 'I didn't have to go to school, graduate and then go, "What am I going to do?" I knew from the beginning.' While still a seven-year-old she appeared on local Spanish television and radio in the New York area, while a year on she played an orphan in the Broadway show titled *Maggie Flynn*, also starring Shirley Jones and Jack Cassidy. She then appeared in a television music documentary titled *Over 7*.

At ten years of age, Cara was invited to perform in a tribute gala for Duke Ellington, staged at Madison Square Garden, alongside Sammy Davis Jr and Roberta Flack, among others. Further performances included a role in the Broadway musical *The Me Nobody Knows* and a year-long stay with *The Electric Company*, an educational series for children. With her earnings Cara financed her way through school in New York, while during 1972 she was lured back to acting, starring in *Via Galactica*, and co-hosted the NBC talk programme *The Everything Show*. By now the young girl had also developed her composing talent, citing her influences as Ashford and Simpson and Carole King.

From composing, Cara returned to the public platform and at the age of 16 debuted as an actress in the movie titled *Aaran Loves Angela*, before securing the lead role in the Warner Bros-financed *Sparkle* movie a year later. From the big screen, she switched to the Broadway stage once more during 1978 to appear in *Ain't Misbehavin'*, a musical tribute to Fats Waller. Once more television beckoned, this time for guest spots on *Kojak* and talk programmes that included the *Merv Griffin*, *Johnny Carson* and *Dinah Shore Shows*. These appearances led to her major breakthrough on the small screen with the role of the young Bertha Palmer in the *Roots* mini series. This was followed by starring roles in the docu-drama *The Guyana Tragedy*, the story of Jim Jones, and with Diahann Carroll and Rosalind Cash in *Sisters*. Most certainly, Irene Cara wasn't one to drag her heels.

Into the '80s, Cara's star rose more sharply when she was cast as Coco Hernandez, a talented teenager from the South Bronx, in the Alan Parker dance film *Fame*, for which she also composed the title music. Centred around the lives of eight dance students attending a High School of Performing Arts in New York, *Fame* became a surprising overnight sensation. Cara's song 'Fame' went on to win an Oscar for Best Film Theme before soaring to the top of the British chart in July 1982. Dance mania had once again gripped Britain; *Fame* was this decade's equivalent to the *'70s' Saturday Night Fever*. Only the dance steps had changed – being more frenetically complex.

To sustain the impetus, *Fame* was adapted for a television series. By and large the storylines were believable, but it was the cast of young, talented dancers and actors who captured the viewers' support. Main characters like Valerie Landsburg, who was originally rejected for the film role of Doris Schwartz but won the part in the small-screen spin-off, said, 'I'm lucky to be paid for doing something I would do for free.' Carlo Imperto was cast as Danny Amatullo, Morgan Stevens as drama coach David Peardon, Cindy Gibb as Holly Laird, Lee Curreri as Bruno Martelli and Billy Hufsey as Christopher Donlan. Gene Anthony Ray, despite his lack of formal dance training, won the role of Leroy Johnson, and Erica Gimpel won the role of Coco Hernandez, Cara's character in the movie version. Debbie Allen, who had masterminded the *Fame* stage show which had toured Europe, became a tireless contributor to the television series. From *Fame* Allen went on to appear on numerous television shows before embarking upon a recording career. According to her, '*Fame* is a good, realistic show, with good production values. I think it's been such an international success because it deals with young people growing up. And that's universal, whatever language is spoken.'

Back to Irene Cara. Her chart-topper's follow-up single 'Out Here On My Own', likewise extracted from *Fame* and issued by RSO Records, stalled in the British Top 60, reaching the Top 20 in

America. 'Out Here On My Own' and its predecessor 'Fame' went on to make Academy Award history when both were nominated for the Best Original Song Oscar in 1981. 'Fame' won the Oscar, and Cara went on to receive two Grammy nominations early in 1981 in the Best New Female Artist and Best New Pop Artist categories. She then secured a nomination for the Best Motion Picture Actress in a Musical Golden Globe Award. She received industry acclaim for her most recent work by winning *Billboard* magazine's 1980 Top Singles Artist award, while its sister magazine *Cashbox* honoured her as Most Promising Female Vocalist and Top New Female Vocalist.

Glowing with deserved pride and success, the young artist released her debut solo album in January 1982. Titled *Anyone Can See*, Cara wrote or co-penned five of its tracks, but despite her immense popularity the album and lifted single sold poorly. So from music Cara returned to the big screen to play the role of a singer in a band involved with a murderer, co-starring with George Segal in *The Man in Apartment 5A*, then appeared with Lee Majors in the television special *A Face of the Eighties*.

However, it wasn't all bad news for Cara's singing career. She returned with the title 'Flashdance . . . What A Feeling', released by Casablanca Records. The artist had co-penned the track with Giorgio Moroder as the title song to the dance movie *Flashdance* and had recorded it despite not appearing in the film. It shot to the top of the American chart during May 1983 and reached the Top 2 in Britain a month later. Although *Flashdance* paled by comparison with the international success of *Fame*, the film sparked the British disco-dancing championship with the final staged in London. 'Flashdance . . . What A Feeling' marked Cara's final British hit, and her second solo album, *What A Feeling*, issued in the December, was a musical showcase for her respected talent.

From Casablanca Records the artist switched companies to Geffen and enjoyed the 1983 American hit titles 'Why Me?' and 'The Dream (Hold On To Your Dream)' from the film *D C Cab*. A year on, she returned to the American Top 10 with the 'Breakdance' single. However, despite this sporadic success, her relationship with Geffen Records soured, and following a period of inactivity she issued the *Carasmatic* album via a new recording deal with Elektra Records during 1987.

The entire *Fame* explosion was great fun, and although the film has not been revered in the same manner as *Saturday Night Fever*, it has returned to the stage. In 1998 *Fame: The Musical* hit London's Prince of Wales Theatre.

(Quotes: *Fame Annual*, 1985)

DEXY'S MIDNIGHT RUNNERS

Come on Eileen

'I promised myself that if "Come On Eileen" didn't do well I'd find another way of making money' – Kevin Rowland

With one British No.1 single to their credit – 'Geno' in May 1980 – Dexy's Midnight Runners looked set to enjoy a profitable recording career. Ironically, that was not to be. Within months of their success, the group and EMI Records parted company – and not amicably, either.

In 1982 came fresh ideas, a clear outlook and new members; it was the year of change. With the addition of a trio of violinists known as the Emerald Express, their music took on an Irish folk flavour, with accompanying stage clothes of scruffy sandals or trainers, bandanas, well-worn overalls or baggy jeans and, more often than not, hats perched at a jaunty angle. Said Rowland, '[The] look was put together from loads of different elements . . . it was a contrived image intended to convey a wild feeling, not necessarily a gypsy look.' During the March, the change was reflected on record with 'The Celtic Soul Brothers' single, a Top 50 British hit. It was a healthy enough placing, but it would be the next single that would elevate them to the top.

Following the departure of original member Jimmy Patterson, the chanting 'Come On Eileen' single, penned by him, Rowland and Adams, topped the British chart in August 1982. It stayed at No.1 for four weeks, selling in excess of one million copies *en route*. These sales also sent the mother album *Too-Rye-Ay* into the Top 2, while the single went on to win the Brit Award for Best British Single and an Ivor Novello Award for Best-Selling A-Side. Rowland explained the meaning behind the single to *Melody Maker*: 'It is about . . . a girl I grew up with basically, and it's absolutely true all the way along.' Being raised within the Catholic faith, the singer was taught that sex was for married partners only. He said 'Come On Eileen' retold the guilty feeling he had experienced as a 15-year-old when having sex with his girlfriend: 'It was a funny thing. Sex came into it and our relationship had always been so clean. It seemed at that time to get dirty and that's what [the single] is about. I was really trying to capture that atmosphere. I don't honestly think that sex is dirty now.' 'Come on Eileen' also topped the American chart in April 1983.

The chart-topper's follow-up, a cover version of Van Morrison's 'Jackie Wilson Said', carried the record-label credit of Kevin Rowland and Dexy's Midnight Runners. The title peaked in the British Top 5 during the October. Jackie Wilson was, incidentally, one of soul music's foremost artists, yet when Dexy's Midnight Runners performed the single on BBC TV's music programme *Top of the Pops*, a backdrop of Jocky Wilson, the darts player, hung behind the performing band! Reputedly, it was not an intentional error, more the show's production crew being musically ignorant! Before 1982 closed, the group returned to the Top 20 with the single 'Let's Get This Straight (From The Start)'.

The first outing of the new year was a reworking of 'The Celtic Soul Brothers' which, this time, shot into the Top 20, reaching the Top 90 in America. A full-blown tour across Britain ensured chart success yet it wasn't enough; for the second time, Dexy's Midnight Runners disbanded.

Following a hiatus of two years, the album *Don't Stand Me Down* returned the group to the Top 30 during the September. When it was reissued on CD with additional tracks during 1997, Rowland admitted in the sleeve notes that he had been terrified to release the original project: 'I felt that I didn't have a friend in the world . . . at that time. All the media seemed to desperately want me to fail and I was consumed with self-loathing . . . In the end I sabotaged the record's chances of success by disallowing the record company to promote it effectively. Just as well – I couldn't have dealt with its success at the time.' Nonetheless, the 1985 release was supported by a British tour, closing in London. The mild audience reception received led to Dexy's Midnight Runners disbanding once again.

A year on, the group issued the Top 20 single titled 'Because Of You', the theme to BBC TV's comedy series *Brush Strokes*. Three years later, Kevin Rowland's solo single 'Walk Away', swiped from *The Wanderer* album, was issued. Both the single and the album bombed.

Into the '90s, Rowland was declared bankrupt and lost his London house as a result. In an attempt to recapture his past glory, he partnered Jimmy Patterson to record the *Manhood* album, promoted by selected television spots. In turn, this prompted the release during 1991 of the inevitable 'greatest hits' compilation under the title *The Very Best Of Dexy's Midnight Runners*, featuring tracks from both the EMI Records and the Mercury Records catalogues. The album soared to No.12 in the British chart. Attempts to re-establish the group's career were futile, though; Dexy's Midnight Runners once more slipped into obscurity.

By 1994 Rowland's name was headline news again – not through his music, rather his reliance on state benefits and drugs. And a year on Dexy's Midnight Runners were once more prominent in record stores with the Nighttracks label release *The Radio One Sessions*, while a trio of CDs were issued in 1996, namely *Too-Rye-Ay* and *Dexy's Midnight Runners* via Mercury Records and *It Was Like This* from EMI Records' EMI Premier subsidiary. Also during this year, Rowland secured a recording contract with Creation Records, who were responsible for Oasis, among others. In a written press release which announced the signing to the media, Rowland confirmed that he planned to record a collection of songs that had touched him throughout his life before commencing a new Dexy's Midnight Runners album. He also fed the media's appetite for scandal by saying, 'I experienced hollow success with "Come On Eileen" and *Too-Rye-Ay*, the music sound of which, folky fiddle and texture, mixed with Tamla-type soul, came from Archer and not me, as I claimed. The idea and sound was his. I stole it from him, hurting Archer deeply in the process.' Needless to say, the statement, bravely presented, was splashed across the tabloids, but in truth only stalwart fans of Dexy's Midnight Runners would have taken notice.

'I don't want to be in a loser group, touring around everywhere, suffering for my art' – Kevin Rowland

Also see: 'Geno', May 1980

(Selected information: *Keep On Running* magazine, 1997, published by Neil Warburton)

(Quotes: *The Face*, 1982, interview by Lesley White)

September 1982

SURVIVOR

Eye Of The Tiger

'It's a great feeling to watch Stallone . . . working out to "Eye Of The Tiger". Just like the character he performs, Survivor is still hungry for success' – Jim Peterik

Jim Peterik, born on 11 November 1950, studied at the University of Illinois, where between classes he joined a group called the Ides of March – a Blood, Sweat and Tears soundalike, he reckoned. As a member of this group, Peterik recorded and released the single titled

'Vehicle', which surprised all concerned by shooting to No.2 in the American chart during May 1970.

From the Ides of March, Peterik moved on to record a solo album, which bombed, before singing on radio and television commercials. In 1978 he met David Bicker and Frank Sullivan and formed Survivor. Peterik said, 'We called ourselves [that] because we're all survivors of different bands and rock'n'roll situations.' Bursting with ideas and enthusiasm, Survivor hit the touring circuit, particularly nightspots in the Mid West, before coming to the attention of the Scotti Brothers recording outlet. Early in 1980 the group issued its first album, titled *Survivor*; it bombed. The lifted track 'Somewhere In America', though, reaped some financial rewards by peaking in the Top 70.

The membership of Survivor increased with the addition of newcomers Marc Dronbay and Stephen Ellis during February 1981. They released the single titled 'Poor Man's Son', an American Top 40 hit during December 1981, lifted from their second album *Premonition*, issued in January 1982. This time, the group's album reached the American Top 100. It was not a money-spinning position but not a bomber either. The second single was likewise lifted from the album, namely 'Summer Nights', a falterer in the Top 70. No matter how disappointing these chart positions were, though, at least Survivor were making their presence felt.

While they were planning their next musical project, Sylvester Stallone was considering his most impressive of fights in his pending *Rocky III* movie, where Rocky was to pit his fists in the ring against Clubber Land, whom movie buffs recognised as the infamous 'Mr T'. Stallone's first music choice was Queen's 'Another One Bites The Dust' (appropriate enough, one suspects), but then he chanced to hear Survivor's 'Poor Man's Son'. Peterik told the *Los Angeles Times* that Tony Scotti, part-owner of the group's record company, had previously issued a single by Stallone's brother Frank and 'Tony knew about Sylvester wanting a title song for *Rocky III*, so he played him our last album, *Premonition*. Sylvester liked the beat and the drive of our music so he let us have a shot at writing the theme.' Peterik and Sullivan were then given a rough cut of the film with the instruction that the star wanted a strong, semi-rock track. Said Peterik, 'He wanted a contemporary theme, something that would appeal to the rock crowd.'

While viewing the film's rough cut, Peterik became aware of the regular use of the phrase 'eye of the tiger' by Rocky's trainer. Ultimately, two versions of 'Eye Of The Tiger' were recorded. On the movie soundtrack, tiger roars were included alongside the music, while the group refused their addition on the single version, claiming, 'If the song doesn't roar itself, a little tiger roaring ain't gonna help.'

In July 1982, the single 'Eye Of The Tiger' topped the American chart, a position it held for six weeks on its way to passing platinum status. A month on, Survivor's album, bearing the single's name, shot to No.2 in the American chart, leaving the *Rocky III* soundtrack to peak in the Top 20. The single's American success crossed the Atlantic in September 1982 when it likewise topped the British chart, this time for four consecutive weeks. The group's album roared into the British Top 20, the soundtrack making only the Top 50. Remarkably, Survivor's British chart-topping single was their last entry in the listing until 1986.

The title 'American Heartbeat' was also extracted from the *Eye Of The Tiger* album as the chart-topper's follow-up. The single peaked in the American Top 20 at the close of 1982.

Until their next British hit, Survivor struggled on in their home country, supporting releases with across-state tours. During 1983 and 1984, the singles 'The One That Really Matters' and 'Caught In The Game' faltered in the Top 80, while 'The Moment Of Truth', lifted from *The Karate Kid* movie soundtrack, stalled in the Top 70. However, before 1984 ended, the doom and gloom lifted when Survivor returned to the American Top 20 with 'I Can't Hold Back', followed early in 1985 with the bigger seller titled 'High On You', a deserved Top 10 entrant. Album-wise, Survivor issued two, namely *Caught In The Game* in 1983 and *Vital Signs* in 1985, both high sellers. A pair of singles were also issued this year: the first, 'The Search Is Over', re-established Survivor as Top 5 artists; the second, 'First Night', didn't, faltering in the Top 50.

With 1986 came Stallone once more, this time with the *Rocky IV* movie. Again Peterik and Sullivan were approached to compose a track. 'Burning Heart' was the result, a shattering musical explosion which presented Survivor with their second British hit at No.5 in the March, following its American success at No.2 a month earlier. Obviously Stallone and Survivor gelled well together!

During the next two years Survivor sustained their American profile with both heavy and poor singles sales. On the upside, titles like 'Is This Love?' soared into the Top 10, while on the downside 'Man Against The World' stalled in the Top 90. Two albums were also issued, namely *When Seconds Count* and *Too Hot To Sleep*, a Top 50 hit and a bombing title respectively. As the '90s began, the band disbanded, but when their *Greatest Hits* package was issued in 1993, the group re-formed to promote the release in person, trekking across Canada and America in an attempt to remind audiences of their musical past.

Regrettably, Survivor were unable to live up to their name. Happily, the tiger lives on.

(Quotes: *The Billboard Book of Number One Hits* by Fred Bronson)

CULTURE CLUB

Do You Really Want To Hurt Me?

With reviews that included 'weak, watered-down fourth-division reggae' and 'the group's only asset is the ludicrously unphotogenic Boy George', it really is a wonder this single left the record plant! Thankfully, George took on the task of promoting the single to the top.

Born George O'Dowd in Eltham, Kent, on 14 June 1961, he was one of six children born to Dinah and Jerry. First educated at Middle Park Primary School, where he excelled in English and art, George won awards for swimming as a member of the school team. From Middle Park he switched to Eltham Green School. Throughout his teenage years, George idolised Britain's finest like T Rex's Marc Bolan and David Bowie, as he wrote in his autobiography *Take It Like A Man* – 'I put Mum's lipstick on and pranced about singing into a hairbrush, "Metal Guru is it you?" . . . I found an all-in-one silver lurex catsuit and wore it around the house. I wanted to waltz into the street looking like a lurex legend. Dad wouldn't have it . . .'

With his young, flamboyant behaviour and unconventional outlook on life which was a contributory factor to his 'bunking off' from school, George was finally expelled with no prospects of getting a secure job. He first took the position of part-time shelf-filler at Tesco in Eltham, before moving to a weekend job at a Chislehurst public house. However, he came alive at night when he and friends frequented nightspots that included the Black Prince public house in Bexleyheath.

Thanks to Oxfam stores, George and his group dressed cheaply, creating new designs to parade along London's King's Road in at the weekends and to dance in during the week. By now in his teens, George was open about his gayness, but for being so public with his sexuality he suffered greatly at others' hands.

Following his first serious position at the Red Tape Printers in London's West End as a messenger and office boy, George moved through numerous jobs including one at Chingford Fruit Packers. His nightclub travels led him to the Blitz Club in Covent Garden, where Steve Strange and Rusty Egan were the hosts, the first in a new breed of club entrepreneurs. George became the cloakroom attendant at the Blitz until it closed in 1980, whereupon Strange hosted nights at other London venues. Through these night travels George saw Malcolm McLaren's group Bow Wow Wow, featuring Annabella Lu Win. McLaren and Lu Win did not enjoy a mutually satisfying relationship, and in February 1981 George replaced her onstage as a member of the group. Further musical dalliances followed until George formed his own group, Praise of Lemmings, later the Sex Gang Children, featuring Mikey Craig, born in London on 15 February 1960.

In 1981, now with further members Jon Moss, born in London on 11 September 1957, and Roy Hay, born in Essex on 12 August 1961, Culture Club was born. Said George, 'We all agreed Sex Gang Children was the wrong name. We toyed with new ones.' He took a step back to study the actual line-up of the group, namely an Irish transvestite, a Jew, a black man and an Ango-Saxon, and 'That's how I came up with the name Culture Club. Nightclubbing, roots and culture.' He chose 'Boy George' for its reggae vibe, in tune with nightclub DJs using names like Prince Jammy and King Tubby. 'I also liked the idea of playing with sexual ambiguity. Is it a bird? Is it a plane? No, it's Boy George!'

Producer Steve Levine worked with Culture Club on their first demo recordings, including the title 'White Boy' recorded at EMI Records' studio. The record company rejected the group's music, leaving them to concentrate on the London circuit, beginning with their debut show in October 1981 at the Crocs nightclub in Rayleigh, known as the 'premier freak club'. It was during these performances that Culture Club were spotted by Danny Goodwin from Virgin Music, who in turn persuaded Richard Griffiths, a company music executive, to invest £500 in further demo recordings with the group. This time the sessions were recorded on the Virgin studio barge, with three titles being completed, including the track 'Kissing To Be Clever'.

Within weeks of these sessions, Culture Club secured a recording contract with Virgin Records. During May 1982, the group's first single, titled 'White Boy', bombed, as did its follow-up, 'I'm Afraid Of Me', issued one month on. However, it wasn't all bad news, with George attracting a high media profile particularly in the weekly music papers, trendy magazines and fanzines.

Mid-1982, Radio One DJ Peter Powell offered Culture Club the opportunity to perform a handful of new tracks for his programme. The group decided to compose new material for the occasion, with the track 'Do You Really Want To Hurt Me?' shining above the other titles. Virgin saw potential in the hastily composed track and issued it as a single; Culture Club, on the other hand, were fearful the song would bomb like its predecessors. Said George, '[The song] was too personal, and it wasn't a dancy record.'

No man was happier than Boy George to see 'Do You Really Want To Hurt Me?' soar to the top of the British chart during October 1982, a position it held for three weeks. The accompanying video was filmed in a '30s nightclub, a '50s health club and a courtroom, with the group dressed in '40s clothes. Their guests were dressed in all manner of outrageous designs. The result was great fun! However, despite being Britain's biggest-selling artist, George discovered he had other problems to overcome: radio stations were unsure he was suitable for interviews. 'We don't interview transvestites' was one response, while Nina Myskow, then writing for the *News of the World*, called him 'Wally of the Week'.

'Do You Really Want To Hurt Me?' also cracked the American market by charting at No.2 during March 1983. Glowing with success, Culture Club issued their *Kissing To Be Clever* album in December; it reached the Top 5 in Britain. As the album left the pressing plant, the chart-topper's follow-up titled 'Time (Clock Of The Heart)', not included on the album, soared into the British Top 3 and American Top 2.

With Helen Terry as back-up singer, Culture Club then released 'Church Of The Poison Mind'. The single became a further No.2 hit during April 1983, reaching the American Top 10 in the December.

With this much-craved success to his credit, George was awash in unexpected pressures ranging from record promotion to fan worship. He also became more aware of his image, which, in turn, made him self-conscious: 'The pretty face adorning bedroom walls and projected on to a million TV screens was carefully constructed . . . I quickly became trapped in my image.' Being imprisoned by his fame was definitely not part of his game plan, whereupon Culture Club temporarily escaped to tour across Europe and to eat, because food was, George said, his reliable friend.

It has to be said that Boy George's outspoken, fashionable image sustained Culture Club. He certainly cared little for the middle lane, leaving his public to wonder what his next creation, musically and otherwise, would be. Culture Club never failed to please!

Also see: 'Karma Chameleon', October 1983

(Quotes: *Take It Like a Man: The Autobiography of Boy George* by Boy George and Spencer Bright)

November 1982

EDDY GRANT

I Don't Wanna Dance

Grant worked his apprenticeship with the Equals, and as his dreadlocks grew, so did his determination to embark upon a solo career. The move was a struggle at first, but it later paid off without him selling his soul.

Born Edmond Montague Grant on 5 March 1948 in Plaisance, Guyana, Grant emigrated to Britain during 1960 with his parents. Residing in London, Grant was educated in Camden and mastered various musical instruments including guitar and piano. With music as his ambition, Grant nurtured a group of musicians – twin brothers Lincoln and Derv Gordon, Patrick Lloyd and John Hall – and formed the Equals. Their music was a combination of rock and soul mixed with R&B, and from 1965 the Equals played in and around north London, before recording for President Records two years later. Following limited success with the company, the group left Britain to tour Europe for six months, where they commanded a loyal following. In July 1968 the Equals topped the British chart with the Grant composition 'Baby Come Back', followed by the title 'Laurel And Hardy'. Other chart material ensured the Equals earned a living.

During 1969 Grant was hospitalised following a car accident in West Germany. This in turn affected the Equals' live performances, and without Grant's distinctive input the group's touring schedules were abandoned. However, when Grant decided to leave the group entirely to concentrate on his newly formed production company, he was replaced by Jimmy Haynes, later Dave Martin. Further personnel changes occurred during the early '70s, but this failed to deter the Equals from performing as a unit throughout Britain and Europe. As a recording band, though, they bombed. They would, however, return to the club circuit during the '90s, with the public once again dancing and clapping to the immortal 'Baby Come Back'.

With his financial situation sound thanks to his royalties from the Equals as a composer and performer, Grant opened his own label, Ice Records, based in both London and Guyana. His intention was to pursue a solo career and to this end he issued his first album, titled *Message Man*, in 1977. The unique aspect of this project, however, was the fact he played all the instruments himself as well as singing all vocal tracks. The project, however, received a disappointing public response.

As the '80s neared, the musician's fate changed for the better when he secured a licensing deal for Ice Records with Ensign Records. The debut release here was his self-contained *Walking On Sunshine* album in July 1979. The track 'Living On The Front Line' was released and soared to No.11 in the British chart, re-establishing Grant as a selling name. Assisted by heavy dance sales, Grant's success spread through Europe into America, where the single, released by CBS Records' subsidiary Epic, positioned itself in the lower portion of the R&B chart.

Into 1980, his second album, titled *Love In Exile*, was issued, while the next year Grant charted once again with 'Do You Feel My Love?'. The commercial yet hard reggae feel appealed to the record-buyers, who sent it to No.8 in the British singles chart in the May. The title 'Can't Get Enough Of You' followed, but faltered in the Top 20. The album *Can't Get Enough*, released mid-1981, earned the musician his first hit in the Top 40 and spawned the single 'I Love You, Yes I Love You'. It stalled at No.37 in the British chart, indicating that perhaps Grant needed a musical rethink.

Grant did more than rethink. In 1982 he relocated to Barbados and switched his label from Ensign Records to the major RCA Records (later known as BMG Records). The result of Grant's rebirth was 'I Don't Wanna Dance', which, with the mighty marketing arm of RCA Records and concentrated disco promotion on the nightclub circuit, shot to the top of the British chart in November 1982, a position it dominated for three weeks. A light-flavoured reggae sound with a distinctive dance beat, 'I Don't Wanna Dance' charted in most countries including America, where it peaked in the mainstream Top 60.

A year on, Grant's *Killer On The Rampage* album notched up magnificent sales to hit the British Top 10, whereupon the 'Electric Avenue' track was swiped for single release and flashed to No.2 in the British chart. As often happens when an act switches from one company to another, Mercury Records, owner of Ensign Records' repertoire, reissued 'Living On The Front Line'/'Do You Feel My Love?'. The title reached the British Top 50.

Thanks to his British chart presence, Grant was hitched to the American company Portrait Records, where 'Electric Avenue' was issued. It shot to No.2 in the singles chart, selling in excess of one million copies. Meanwhile, *Killer On The Rampage* passed gold status to reach the Top 10. Just shows what concentrated promotion can do! A satisfied Grant closed the year in Britain with the Top 50 single titled 'Till I Can't Take Love No More'.

Actors Michael Douglas and Kathleen Turner were inadvertently responsible for the singer/musician's next release, a Top 50 hit during

1984. As the couple starred in the *Romancing the Stone* movie, so Grant composed its title track, subsequently garnering worldwide acceptance as a composer. In retrospect, it was a rather strange state of affairs as the single wasn't actually included in the film! The 'Romancing The Stone' single peaked in the British Top 60 and American Top 30.

For the next four years Grant kept a relatively low profile. When he decided to return to the spotlight, he re-established himself with a Top 10 hit titled 'Gimme Hope Jo'anna', dripping with lyrics regarding the South African anti-apartheid laws. Grant's hiatus also prompted him to switch the licensing of Ice Records once again, this time to EMI Records. Under the new arrangement, the album *File Under Rock* was a poor seller.

Into 1989, Grant bounded back with a stunning single. It was not an original release but a reissue of the track 'Walking On Sunshine'; it became a Top 70 British hit. Soon after came a compilation carrying the single's name, featuring Grant's best-selling singles.

Early into the '90s the musician entered a battle of a different nature. He stood against MCA Records, Island Records and Rita Marley to purchase the late Bob Marley's publishing and recording rights. The bidding stakes were, naturally, in the multi-million-dollar bracket. Eventually Grant lost to Island and Rita Marley's joint bid, but on the upside he secured a further licensing deal for Ice Records with Pinnacle Records and released his first album in three years in February 1992. Titled *Paintings Of The Soul*, it was the musician's first since *File Under Rock* in 1988 and marked a significant phase in the re-establishment of his career. The album was preceded by the single 'Paco And Ramone', and at around the same time Grant prepared for his acting debut in the movie *The Mustard Bath*. The start of his career as an actor was somewhat fiery. While filming a 500-strong procession in his native Guyana, Grant's one-metre dreadlocks burst into flames when he accidentally knocked into a huge oil-burning torch. The musician, who played a Rastafarian priest, was rushed to a local hospital, where he was treated for minor burns, while his dreadlocks were reported to be in a sorry state.

As Eddy Grant, who was last seen on Channel 4's 'Soul Night' screened in 1998, still toils with his music behind the scenes, he will be remembered for being in the handful of reggae artists to spread the Jamaican word across the world. Naturally, Grant added touches of commerciality to ensure the music was played to wider audiences, but he did so without severing his roots.

See *Every Chart-Topper Tells A Story: The Sixties* for further information regarding the Equals

December 1982

THE JAM

Beat Survivor

According to music historians, the Jam were the most consistently successful British singles group since the Beatles. However, what the historians don't say is that when the group disbanded, so did the friendships.

Prior to the announcement that the Jam were to disband, they issued the single 'The Bitterest Pill (I Ever Had To Swallow)', featuring Jenny McKeowen on vocals. It soared to the British Top 2, and following Weller's press statement about the group spliting up, the Jam headed off on a further British tour during November 1982. This farewell trek was more explosive than others as fans reached uncontrollable levels of hysteria.

The tour, which also introduced additional back-up vocalists Caron Wheeler and Afrodiziac plus keyboardist Jimmy Telford, ended at Wembley Arena. In retrospect it was not a happy trek, particularly as the group were aware of their audiences' anger at the split. When fans asked Rick Buckler and Bruce Foxton why the Jam was to end, they had no answer. The couple wrote in their autobiography that they were bitter at Weller's decision: 'Having worked for so many years to achieve this level of popularity, we didn't really want to throw in the towel at the height of our careers.'

That level of popularity was once again proved when the Jam returned to the top of the British chart with the title 'Beat Survivor' during December 1982. In fact, the single entered the chart at No.1. Then, as if to seal the fate of the Jam, a 14-track live album spanning 1977 to 1982, titled *Dig The New Breed*, soared to No.2 in the British chart, a fitting tribute to the group committed to hard-hitting musical messages.

The group still owed Polydor Records one further album. Weller was, apparently, in no mood to record new material, so to start 1983 the Jam's 16 singles were rereleased. He then folded the *Jamming* magazine and watched as his group's recorded work enjoyed further marginal American success. His association with the Jam had been truly severed.

Via a recording contract with Arista Records, Bruce Foxton was the first to release a solo project in July 1983. Titled 'Freak', the single peaked in the Top 30. Two months on, the Jam's repertoire was further rifled and a double album featuring their best-selling hits was issued. Under the title *Snap!*, the albums were first issued with an accompanying four-track disc and a complementary music video. The temptation was too great to resist; the Jam enjoyed a No.2 album, while the video soared to the top in its chart.

Paul Weller, lead vocalist and guitarist of the Jam and responsible for at least 13 British Top 20 singles, formed the Style Council with Mick Talbot. Signed to Polydor Records, the Style Council concentrated on Weller's love of soul music and debuted with the 'Speak Like A Child' single. The title re-established Weller as a high-profile seller, peaking at No.4 during March 1983. The group then went on to enjoy a remarkably successful career through to the new decade, when they disbanded following Polydor Records' rejection of their *Decades Of Modernism* album.

Weller moved on, this time to form the Paul Weller Movement for recording and performing purposes. By 1992, with a recording contract with Go! Discs hot in his hand, Weller issued his debut solo single titled 'Uh Huh Oh Yeh'. Swiped from his eponymous album, it became a Top 20 British hit. As a soloist, Weller embarked upon a high-rating career, with charting material that included his *Wild Wood* and *Stanley Road* albums, and singles like 'Sunflower' and 'Out Of The Sinking'. Aside from his recording commitments, the singer toured extensively. The size of the venue was not an issue, ranging as they did from the Town and Country Club in London and the huge Japanese theatres through to festivals and benefit functions. Weller's attraction spread across the media, as he was the subject of radio and television documentaries, and through the music industry, with awards and honours that included the Brit Award for Best Male Vocalist, which he won twice in consecutive years.

During 1996 and 1997, to support his recorded work, Weller took to the touring stage once more, appearing at London's Victoria Park during August 1997 alongside Carleen Anderson. As recently as 1998, Weller announced his plans to tour Britain again. The Jam may be a name of the past, but Paul Weller seems determined that nobody will forget him.

'We worked as a real unit. There was a genuine spirit to the band when it was going and I think that depended on all three of us' – Rick Buckler

Also see: 'A Town Called Malice'/'Precious', February 1982

(Quotes: *The Jam: Our Story* by Bruce Foxton and Rick Buckler with Alex Ogg)

January 1983

PHIL COLLINS

You Can't Hurry Love

'I prefer being on my own because it means I can be more personal'
– Phil Collins

Born Philip David Collins on 30 January 1951 in Chiswick, London, to June and Greville, he was raised in a musical household and at the age of five was given his first toy drum. When he showed interest in playing this (constantly, by all accounts!), his uncles Len and Reg constructed a proper drum kit for him which, apparently, neatly fitted into a suitcase. Collins told author Johnny Waller, 'I remember sitting in the front room playing along to the television.'

Collins was educated at Chiswick County Grammer School, where he excelled at soccer. This soon took second place, however, when he discovered music. His first public appearance as a drummer was at the Richmond Yacht Club, of which his family were members. In fact, the youngster remembered he was constantly asked to contribute to the club's entertainment. In time, he swapped his train set for a proper drum kit until his parents relented, giving him a full-sized kit. Collins was all of 12 years old!

Playing along to the radio, the young boy soon mastered the riffs of the then current songs, like those from the Shadows. Aside from his music, Collins also showed an uncanny aptitude for acting which later led to him joining his mother's talent agency, where he won auditions for bit radio and television roles. Alongside hundreds of hysterical youngsters, Collins appeared in the Beatles' movie *A Hard Day's Night*, though he's hard to spot, as he explained: 'You can't actually see me in it . . . I just happen to like the fact that I was in a Beatles film!'

At the age of 14 Collins played the role of the Artful Dodger in the West End production of *Oliver!*; the part included him singing 'You've Got To Pick A Pocket Or Two'. The role ended after nine months when his voice broke, whereupon Collins left school to attend the Barbara Speake Stage School. Through his mother's various connections the teenager became a popular face and voice on television and radio and could easily have earned a lucrative living in this area. But no, he wanted to be a drummer. To this end he joined his first group, called the Real Thing, who emulated American R&B acts and the Who. Said Collins, 'We all took it very seriously . . . I used to sing and drum at the same time because no one else could sing . . . It was a good group.'

From the Real Thing Collins moved through various units to Flaming Youth, managed by Ken Howard and Alan Blaikely, also proficient composers. The enterprising couple financed the group to record the album titled *Ark II*, released during November 1969 by Fontana Records. To promote the project, Flaming Youth performed at the Lyceum in London, but even this prestigious gig and others failed to chart the album. Nonetheless, one single, titled 'Guide Me Orion', was issued – but it followed the fate of its mother, whereupon Fontana Records had little choice but to drop Flaming Youth from its artist roster. Collins left the group at this point.

After auditioning for several further units including Manfred Mann's Earth Band, Collins was asked to audition for a new band called Genesis. Formed at Charterhouse, the public school based in Surrey, with members Tony Banks and Peter Gabriel, the outfit played the immortal Stax Records' material. A second Charterhouse group, the Anon, featuring among others Anthony Phillips and Mike Rutherford, was gaining popularity at a speedy rate and following an end-of-term concert decided to join forces with the Genesis membership.

As the new Anon, the group sent a demo tape of several tracks to Jonathan King, himself an ex-Charterhouse pupil and now a growing name in the music business, working at Decca Records. King, highly impressed with the tracks, renamed the group Genesis and secured them a five-year publishing deal, later reduced to a one-year arrangement with yearly options. Financing further recording sessions to find material suitable for the band, Gabriel and Banks composed the title 'The Silent Sun', which was later issued as a single, followed by 'A Winter's Tale'. Both were issued by Decca Records and both bombed.

Early in 1969 the *From Genesis To Revelation* album sold less than a thousand copies, yet Decca took a chance to release the further single 'Where The Sour Turns To Sweet'. That too bombed, whereupon record company and group parted. The members of Genesis decided to retire from music temporarily to pursue educational activities before returning to the recording studio to try again. The new demo tape that resulted was hawked around numerous record companies; the group was back to square one.

Meanwhile, live work beckoned when Genesis secured a residency at Ronnie Scott's Club in Soho, which naturally attracted music-business A&R executives enjoying an evening's entertainment. One such executive from Charisma Records saw Genesis perform and spread the word to Tony Stratton-Smith, owner of Charisma, who not only went on to sign the group to his company but also took over their management. Genesis had their first serious break.

Under the new arrangement the group recorded and released the *Trespass* album in October 1970, from which the track 'The Knife' was extracted for single release. At this juncture, Phillips left the group, whereupon Mick Barnard was recruited as guitarist for a time until Steve Hackett joined the group. Now with a permanent workable line-up, Genesis recorded their third album, *Nursery Cryme*, featuring Collins on vocals for the first time.

Once again live performances beckoned and following a concert in Belgium, Genesis's 'Happy The Man' single was issued in May 1972. Before the close of the year their *Foxtrot* album soared into the British Top 20: the tide was turning. While the album climbed, the group debuted on the American stage. They performed twice: the first occasion at the University in Boston and the second a charity concert in New York's Philharmonic Hall. According to Collins, the latter was a living nightmare: 'It was full of mistakes. We were very nervous and terribly tired, physically and mentally.' The audience failed to notice.

By August 1973 the group had successfully toured both Britain and America. As a reminder of the trek, the *Genesis Live* album, recorded during the British leg, was released and entered the Top 10. By this time Gabriel was, naturally enough, the prime group member. Being lead singer he attracted the bulk of public attention, and this encouraged him to exaggerate his appearance and, of course, his performances, leaving the remaining group members in his shadow in much the same way as, for instance, Diana Ross did with the Supremes. Said Collins: 'Pete became the obvious focus of attention, but eventually that started backfiring internally. I know I felt frustrated.'

At the close of 1973, Collins was again a featured vocalist on the group's *Selling England By The Pound* album. This time Genesis cracked the British Top 5; the album also became their debut charting album in America, albeit in the lower regions of the Top 100. Their fortunes were changing for the better, yet despite this the group earned £35 a week!

Hot on the heels of *Selling England By The Pound*, the title 'I Know What I Like (In Your Wardrobe)' debuted in the British Top 30 singles chart during April 1974. This long-awaited hit boosted sales of the group's previous albums, in particular *Nursery Cryme*, which peaked in the Top 40, preparing the way for the adventurous double-album set titled *The Lamb Lies Down On Broadway*, which shot into the British Top 10 and American Top 50. The release went on to lend its name to an equally ambitious world tour.

In May 1975 Genesis suffered a further membership upheaval when Gabriel departed, leaving Collins to replace him as lead singer and drummer. On the personal front, Collins had married Andrea Bertorelli, whom he had met at the Barbara Speake Stage School. The couple went on to have two children, Simon and Joely. The marriage was doomed, though. Long periods away from home either touring or producing other acts including Brand X was the cause of its breakdown; returning from an American tour, Collins learned his wife was having an affair: 'I just couldn't believe that this bloke I'd got in to decorate my house had actually gone off with my wife.' The couple attempted a reconciliation, later relocating to Vancouver, but it was Collins who returned to Britain to live in Guildford.

Back to the music. Continuing as a quartet, with and without additional musicians, Genesis enjoyed a handful of hit singles through to the '80s, including the 'Spot The Pigeon' EP, a Top 20 entrant, and 'Follow You Follow Me', which made the Top 10. The first hit of 1980, 'Turn It On Again', was followed by a pair of poor-selling singles, 'Duchess' and 'Misunderstanding', the latter becoming the group's first American Top 10 entrant which encouraged them to return to America for an across-state tour. During this trip Collins met teacher Jill Tavelman.

Album-wise, Genesis continued to chart, particularly with titles *And Then There Were Three* and *Duke*, No.3 and No.1 hits in Britain respectively.

Since the nucleus of Genesis had been formed, members had drifted through frequently, so it came as no surprise when Collins signed a solo recording contract with Virgin Records during 1981, maintaining he would support both careers. Not an easy task, for sure, but he coped. Collins said, 'I signed to Virgin to get away from the nest . . . I thought that anybody who would see an album by me out after I'd been with Genesis for ten years and Brand X for five would think, oh, another Genesis album.' He admitted he felt comfortable with the Virgin Records set-up, although another deal offered by CBS Records was a highly attractive proposition, but 'I liked the idea of going to a company and people knowing my name and me knowing their names.'

During February 1981 the drumming singer debuted as a soloist with the 'In The Air Tonight' single (a song rejected by Genesis) swiped from his pending *Face Value* album. The single soared to No.2 in the British chart, later winning the Ivor Novello Award for the International Hit of the Year, while the album became his first solo British chart-topper, selling in excess of one million copies. In America the project soared into the Top 10, passing gold status. Hot on the heels of this unexpected success, a second single was issued, titled 'I Missed Again', a Top 20 hit on both sides of the Atlantic. The final British single of 1981, 'If Leaving Me Is Easy', returned Collins to the Top 20.

Into 1982, Collins's second album, *Hello, I Must Be Going*, shot into the Top 2 in the November to spend approximately 200 weeks on the listing, while the extracted single 'You Can't Hurry Love', an upbeat version of Diana Ross and the Supremes' 1966 hit, presented Collins with his first solo British chart-topper in January 1983. The accompanying video portrayed Phil Collins as a trio of singers – 'It was meant to be a replica of the song' - reminding the public of dated promotional films when singers wore their pants too short and their jackets too tight! Fans of the Motown trio, meanwhile, bemoaned his version. A month on, both the album and the single became Top 10 entrants in their respective American charts.

The British follow-up titled 'Don't Let Him Steal Your Heart Away' faltered in the Top 50, while a further track 'I Don't Care Anymore' reached the American Top 40. In between these releases, Collins produced third party acts including recordings by Abba's Frida (the redhead) and Adam and the Ants.

During the next two years, singles like 'Against All Odds (Take A Look At Me Now)' became a British Top 2 seller and Collins's first American chart-topper. The track was a revamped version of the *Face Value* album track 'How Can You Sit There?'. The singer then joined his music colleagues to record the 'Do They Know It's Christmas?' charity single, proceeds of which went to the starving people of Ethiopia.

'Sussudio', a word dreamt up by Collins after hearing the drum roll he played on the track, was the title of his first British single of 1985, a Top 20 hit. Originally 'Sussudio' was considered to be too similar to Prince's '1999', sharing as it did the same rhythm. When Collins's keyboardist convinced him the two tracks were different, he recorded the song. In retrospect, though, he believed recording the track was probably the worst move he could have made, as he told *Rolling Stone* magazine: 'I could never write a song like Prince because I'm not from that environment . . . I have never been under any misconception of who I am or where I come from.' The title was extracted from Collins's third solo album, *No Jacket Required*, which shot into the British chart at No.1. Meanwhile, 'Sussudio' became his third American chart-topper in July 1985, the same month as Collins carved music history by achieving a feat no other artist had even attempted – he was televised performing live in one day in two different countries. Following on from 'Do They Know It's Christmas?', Bob Geldof organised an impressive charity gala 'Live Aid', staged at Wembley Arena, with the American gala during the evening. On the afternoon of 13 July 1985, Collins performed on the British stage, then flew by Concorde across the Atlantic to the JFK Stadium in Philadelphia, where the American event, that included performances by Tina Turner and Mick Jagger, was in full swing. Arriving at the stadium at 7 p.m., Collins was on stage ten minutes later, performing with Eric Clapton and others. When questioned as to why he did it, Collins replied, 'Because I was asked to!'

What a nice man!

Also see: 'Easy Lover' (with Philip Bailey), March 1985; 'A Groovy Kind Of Love', September 1988

(Quotes: *The Phil Collins Story* by Johnny Waller)

February 1983

MEN AT WORK

Down Under

'They're melodic, contemporary and humorous, and they're effectively telling the world that there are more good things coming from down under' – Glenn Baker

Colin Hay, born in Scotland on 29 June 1953 and who emigrated as a teenager with his parents to Australia, and Ron Strykert, born in Australia on 18 August 1957, first met as students at Melbourne's La Troube University. As they were both interested in music they became close friends and in time decided to form their own group, first recruiting fellow student and Australian Greg Ham, born 27 September 1953. Drummer Jerry Speiser and bass guitarist John Rees completed the membership. Swiping the name Men At Work from a road sign, the group became the resident act at the Cricketer's Arms Hotel in Melbourne and spent a year playing the amateur circuit, experimenting with various musical styles before finding their niche of rock/pop.

During one of their many performances Men At Work were seen by a representative from CBS Records who eventually persuaded the company chief to sign his discovery to the Columbia subsidiary in America, Epic in Britain, during 1979.

It then took a further two years for Men At Work to release their first single, titled 'Who Can It Be Now?'. The wait was worth it: the title shot to the top of the American chart in October 1982, its sales boosted by the group touring the country as support act to Fleetwood Mac. By the end of the trek, Men At Work were considered to be in the same league as, say, the Cars. 'Who Can It Be Now?'

also marked the group's British chart debut, sadly not in such a high position, faltering as it did in the Top 50. Nonetheless, the title was considered a hit. Lifted from the group's first album, *Business As Usual*, which likewise topped the American listing for a staggering 15 weeks, the titles naturally became Australian chart-toppers.

Now established as a prime act, Men At Work headlined their own tour across America, cementing the way for future releases as they familiarised their audiences with music not previously released. The concentrated series of dates paid off: Men At Work returned to the top of the American chart with their second single, titled 'Down Under'. The unashamed tribute to their home country, where it was naturally a chart-topper – 'We're proud to be Australians and we keep pushing that angle' – went on to become the group's first and only No.1 British single in February 1983. The impact Men At Work made on American music led to their receiving the Grammy Award for Best New Artist shortly prior to the release of their second album, *Cargo*, and its extracted single titled 'Overkill', which peaked at No.21 in the British chart and reached the American Top 3. Its mother album, meanwhile, became a Top 10 hit on both sides of the Atlantic.

The follow-up single to 'Overkill', a further album track titled 'It's A Mistake', struggled into the British Top 30 during the July, marking the beginning of the group's decline. In America, though, the title climbed into the Top 10. The last outing of the year sold badly; titled 'Dr Heckyll And Mr Jive', it floundered around the Top 40 in both America and Britain, heralding their final hit in the latter country.

During the next two years, Men At Work maintained a relatively low profile and switched personnel before finally re-emerging with their third album, titled *Two Hearts*, from which the track 'Everything I Need' was the first to be lifted as a single in June 1985. Despite critical acclaim, both titles failed to restore Men At Work to their former glory.

As the '90s approached, the group was all but a memory. In mid-1996, with no recording company for support, Colin Hay opened his own label, Lazy Eye, based in Australia, to release his *Topanga* album, while the group he left behind lived on through compilations and radio airplay.

Men At Work rose and fell within two years. This probably means that it's unlikely British record-buyers can now recall their name, let alone the title of the chart-topping single. Still, at least Glenn Baker from *BAM* magazine flew the flag to the end: 'What Men At Work have done is [give] the whole scene a focus and possibly a rock respectability that appeals to both radio programmers and the public.'

MICHAEL JACKSON

Billie Jean

'["Billie Jean" is] a case of a girl who says that I'm the father of her child and I'm pleading my innocence because "the kid is not my son"' – Michael Jackson

From the start of 1983, Michael Jackson's recording career rocketed to such unimaginable heights that not even he could have dreamed of such wealth and success. Sure, he demanded the follow-up album to *Off The Wall* surpassed every frontier, but did he realise that in order to do that his life would be changed beyond all recognition?

Conceived as *Starlight* and originally recorded in his home studio, *Thriller* became a living challenge to Jackson, particularly when he instructed his studio musicians, Quincy Jones and Rod Temperton, to change to high gear in creating the biggest-selling album in music's history. How did they respond? Apparently, they laughed! Jackson wrote in his autobiography, 'There were times during the *Thriller* project when I would get emotional or upset because I couldn't get the people working with me to see what I saw.' His craving for perfection also meant the project was delayed, but when CBS Records executives finally heard the remixed album, it became immediately obvious that it had, if marketed correctly, multi-million sales potential.

Released in December 1982, *Thriller* immediately topped the British and American album charts (in America the album held the top spot for an incredible 37 weeks) before becoming the No.1 album throughout Europe, Australasia and just about everywhere else. During its life, *Thriller* sold in excess of 40 million copies worldwide, giving birth to seven Top 10 American singles, winning a staggering 12 Grammy Awards and seven American Music Awards, and earning an entry in the *Guinness Book of Records*. With his royalty rate of 42 per cent, the album earned Jackson a reputed $130 million from worldwide sales.

The first track lifted as a single was the duet between Jackson and Paul McCartney titled 'The Girl Is Mine': 'I wanted to repay the favour he had done me in contributing "Girlfriend" to *Off The Wall*. I wrote "The Girl Is Mine", which I knew would be right for his voice and mine working together.' The result was a somewhat shabby track, but it sold in vast quantities and reached the Top 10 on both sides of the Atlantic due to its uniqueness. Certainly it misled the public; it wasn't an honest reflection of *Thriller*. The further Jackson/ McCartney duet 'Say Say Say' came from that same recording session.

During March 1983, *Thriller* spawned its second single, titled 'Billie Jean'. Originally called 'Not My Lover' (listen to the lyrics), the track was, Jackson explained, part-inspired by Theresa Gonsalves, who had reputedly plagued him with letters before issuing an ultimatum that she'd kill herself and her baby if the singer refused to admit he was her child's father. The second inspiration was the cheerleader for the LA Lakers basketball team, later the in-vogue choreographer Paula Abdul, who was at the time romantically linked with Jackson's brother Jackie to the point that his marriage ended.

With Jackson recording his vocals in one take (an almost unheard-of occurrence years later), 'Billie Jean' was a magnificent heavy dance track which propelled Jackson into a different musical area, as Quincy Jones told *Time* magazine: 'Black music had to play second fiddle for a long time, but its spirit is the whole motor of pop. Michael has connected with every soul in the world.' The single's promotional video, funded by CBS Records at a cost of $250,000 and directed by Steve Baron, likewise crossed the visual barrier. Against the sharp music, Jackson's brash choreography defined by a drum machine and heavy bass line showed the beginnings of the intricate, fast-paced routines he would later utilise. He said, 'It was great to dance for the video. That freeze-frame where I go on my toes was spontaneous, so were many of the other moves.' Indeed, when he danced, paving slabs lit up. Magic, eh? Claimed at the time to be the most innovative of dance videos ever, Jackson would overshadow it time and again in the future.

During the high-profile publicity associated with 'Billie Jean', Motown Records celebrated its 25th anniversary with a spectacular gala staged at Los Angeles's Civic Center. Under the banner 'Motown: Yesterday, Today and Forever', Jackson and his brothers were reunited on stage before a packed theatre and approximately 50 million viewers worldwide. Having watched company acts past and present, including Marvin Gaye, Diana Ross, Mary Wells, the Supremes and Lionel Richie, the audience gasped as the Jackson brothers sang and danced as one. When first asked to contribute to the show, Michael had declined; he was now a soloist, he argued, several light years on from his brothers. However, he changed his mind when granted permission by Berry Gordy to perform as a soloist as well as a group member. The track he selected was 'Billie Jean', which he lipsynched. He also moonwalked while debuting his one white sequinned glove. Following his electrifying performance, the singer was contacted by his dancing hero Fred Astaire; 'You're a hell of a mover,' he told Jackson during their brief conversation.

In April, another single from *Thriller* shot into the British Top 3 and to the top in America. Titled 'Beat It', it was actually issued while 'Billie Jean' dominated the American listing. CBS Records believed the move was suicidal, claiming the sales for 'Billie Jean' would suffer. Jackson's manager at the time, Frank Dileo, thought otherwise – both singles would hit the top and would be in the Top 10 simultaneously. He was right.

The accompanying video this time was directed by Bob Giraldi and financed by the singer at a cost of $160,000. As Jackson was inspired to compose the song by street gangs, streetwise youngsters who were a part of the Los Angeles gang fraternity were asked to work on the video. Said Jackson: 'We had some rough kids on that set . . . those guys in the pool room in the first scene were serious, they were not actors. That stuff was real.' The video's storyline was that two gangs met, clashed and bitterly fought; Jackson's role was to come between them, demanding they turn the other cheek with the words, 'Hey, these guys are your brothers.' The street bullies responded to his squeaky request. Oh yeah? That's realistic! In all honesty, the choreography was priceless – vital, frenetic, precise, almost menacing. Jackson said, 'I came to realise that the whole thing about being bad and tough is that it's done for recognition . . . They're rebels, but rebels who want attention and respect . . . For a few days at least, they were stars.'

Before 1983 cranked to a close, 'Wanna Be Startin' Something' notched up Top 10 sales on both sides of the Atlantic, 'Human Nature' reached the Top 10 in America, 'Say Say Say' was No.2 in Britain, No.1 in America, and the album's title track 'Thriller' made the Top 10 in Britain. When issued in America early in 1984, it stalled at No.4. The 'Thriller' video was on a higher plane altogether. From the song's opening quotes from Vincent Price, the undisputed king of horror, the public realised it wasn't a film to take home to mother. Directed by Jon Landis, the visuals were inspired by his *An American Werewolf in London* movie, to which Jackson was addicted. The cost of the video was awesome; to cover the cost it was decided to shoot two videos, the first to promote the single, the second showing the making of the first. Vestron, MTV and Showtime, the cable network corporation, financed the projects. During February 1984 the *Thriller* movie debuted on MTV and sales of the single rocketed, which in turn added a further 14 million sales to the album within six months of the movie's official release. It was said that one million albums were sold during one week's trading. By the way, prior to the release of both videos and with heavy pressure from the Jehovah's Witnesses, Jackson ensured a disclaimer appeared on the video packaging confirming that the film did not endorse a belief in the occult. That said, the films were classed as 'soft horror', with decaying corpses rising from graves, zombies shuffling about wide eyed and the transformation of Jackson into a hideous werewolf. Yes, good clean viewing for the youngsters!

Reeling from the uncontrollable public hysteria generated by *Thriller* and its commercial spin-offs, Jackson was fighting his conscience. His brothers wanted to tour, particularly following the success of their performance at Motown's 25th anniversary gala upon which his family was desperate to capitalise. Michael was reluctant but once again relented. Their father Joe had recruited the services of boxing promoter Don King to negotiate a 40-city American tour which would, they believed, net $24 million, broken down as $3.4 million to each brother and an estimated $1 million to each parent and King himself. Pepsi Cola were keen to sponsor the project for a further $5 million, despite the fact that Michael never touched the soft drink. From the outset Michael made it clear to King and his brothers that he intended to ostracise himself from backstage negotiations and to this end directed King that in no way did he have permission to act on Michael's behalf. Somehow, the two muddled through.

Part of the Pepsi Cola arrangement was for the brothers to endorse the drink in television advertising. Reluctantly Michael participated, with the proviso that his face was shown on screen for no more than four seconds at any one time, that he chose the music and that he oversaw the choreography. Three thousand fans crammed into the Shrine Auditorium, Los Angeles, to watch the commercial being filmed on 27 January 1984. Amid the plethora of lights on stage, Michael appeared at the top of a staircase to descend. Partway down, a magnesium flash bomb ignited and set his hair alight. 'He looked like a walking inferno,' one witness later said. The singer was flung to the floor and sprayed with a fire extinguisher and cold water before being carried to a waiting ambulance. Following Jackson's short stay at Cedars-Sinai Medical Center and the burns department at Brotman Medical Center, Culver City, the accident cost Pepsi Cola $1.5 million – which Jackson promptly gave to the Brotman Medical Center for a new burns unit in his name.

A week following his release from hospital, CBS Records hosted a party in his honour at the Museum of National History in New York to celebrate the success of *Thriller*. Norris McWhirter from Guinness Publishing presented the singer with one of the early copies of the *Guinness Book of World Records* which listed him as the best-selling solo artist of all time with *Thriller*, replacing *Saturday Night Fever*. To date, *Thriller* had spawned 40 gold and platinum discs, prompting Jackson to say, 'I've only just begun.'

In February 1984, wearing one of his favourite Sgt Pepper jackets and one white jewelled glove, Jackson returned to the Shrine

Auditorium to scoop eight Grammy Awards for *Thriller*, his story-telling disc book for children *ET: The Extra Terrestrial* and related singles. His star was its brightest yet!

A month on, looking for diversion, Jackson met Mick Jagger to try to persuade him to record a duet with him. Jagger was hesitant, to say the least, but relented. The result, 'State Of Shock', issued during June, peaked in the British Top 20 and American Top 3. A month earlier, Jackson had been invited to meet President Reagan and his wife at the White House. This meeting was reputedly arranged after the Department of Transportation had sought permission to use 'Beat It' across an anti-drink/drive television commercial. The singer agreed on the condition he be invited to the White House. Before a flock of media, President Reagan presented Jackson with a hastily prepared public safety award. These things really do happen!

During this period, Michael rejoined his brothers on tour to fulfil the Pepsi Cola commitment. To coincide with the American dates, the Jacksons recorded and released the *Victory* album during June 1984. Tickets for the concerts were priced at $30 each and sold in blocks of four, total $120, to be posted to a post-office box number in New York. As there were only one million tickets available and public response was expected to be at least twelve times that figure, money banked would be in excess of $1 billion, plus interest, until unsuccessful ticket applicants' money was returned. A furious Michael, disgusted at the way their fans had been treated, donated his earnings to charity.

The tour kicked in during July at the Arrowhead Stadium, Kansas City. The act was a combination of fireworks, lasers, video screens and pyrotechnics which were themselves quite out of this world. Michael took advantage of the situation he was in to boost his popularity during a solo spot. Jermaine likewise enjoyed solo status. Twenty-two trailers were used to transport the magnificent stage sets across America. Fan hysteria greeted the brothers at each concert, with police and concert security being stretched beyond their means, while behind the scenes the brothers seethed as Michael attracted the bulk of the media attention. When finished, the Victory tour was listed in the *Guinness Book of Records* as the biggest tour of all time.

While the brothers were on the American trail, Motown Records issued Michael's solo album, *Farewell My Summer Love*, plus the *Michael Jackson and the Jackson 5: 14 Greatest Hits* compilation. The title track from Michael's album was released as a single and reached the British Top 10 and the American Top 40.

For some time now, Michael Jackson had been attracting the odd 'garbage' story in the tabloid press on subjects such as his appearance, his eccentric lifestyle and so on. A certain number of the stories had emanated from Michael himself, but others tended to cross the barrier of privacy. Jackson attempted to quash these rumours by calling a press conference during September 1984 – which he, as it turned out, failed to attend! His manager therefore held court to read a statement from Michael that included the following: 'I have been searching my conscience as to whether or not I should publicly react to the many falsehoods that have been spread about me . . . Performers should always serve as role models who set an example for young people. It saddens me that many may actually believe the present flurry of false accusations.' He concluded that he had never undergone cosmetic eye surgery, nor had his cheekbones altered, and that should any further stories be printed he would 'prosecute all guilty to the fullest extent of the law'. As time progressed, the media ignored Jackson's statement and continued to pursue him.

However, the media failed to be alerted to negotiations that had begun in September 1984 and went through to March 1985 when Jackson and his lawyers beavered away to purchase the 4,000 titles in the ATV Music Publishing catalogue, which included the Beatles' compositions dating 1964–71, plus tracks by Little Richard among others. Paul McCartney was also unaware of these negotiations. Three years earlier he had wanted to buy the catalogue himself for an estimated $20 million but had been unable to convince Lennon's widow, Yoko Ono, to help finance the deal. Jackson paid twice the original purchase price. Up to this time, strict control had been exercised over leasing the Beatles' material, but once in Jackson's camp the group's tracks were licensed for commercial use, notably for advertising. McCartney and Beatles fans alike were shocked at Jackson's insensitivity.

Early in 1985, inspired by Bob Geldof's Band Aid project resulting in 'Do They Know It's Christmas?', Jackson and Lionel Richie composed the track 'We Are The World', which would be recorded by America's finest rock musicians and singers under the name USA For Africa. Proceeds from the record's sales would go to the USA For Africa Fund. Released during April 1985, 'We Are The World' shot to the top of the British and American charts.

British police faced Jackson mania during the March, when the singer visited Madame Tussaud's Waxwork Museum in London to view his wax likeness. To enable the hundreds of excited fans to gain visual access to him, the singer jumped on to the roof of his waiting limousine to thank them for their constant support. Back in America, he turned to the big screen. Conceived as 'The Intergalactic Music Man', the 17-minute, 3-D *Captain E0* epic movie cost $20 million and took one year to shoot. Jackson played the role of an intergalactic entertainer against a backdrop of special effects that reputedly cost

$1 million a minute! The film also featured a pair of songs, namely 'Another Part Of Me' and 'We Are Here To Change The World'. For exclusive use by Disney, *Captain EO* was screened in two cinemas, Disneyworld, Orlando, and Disneyland, and needless to say, visitors flocked to see Jackson and his space fantasy.

During this time, and following the press coverage of his London visit, the singer's name glared from newspaper headlines once again. This time the story was that he was so obsessed with hygiene that he had taken to wearing a surgical mask in public. True or not, in June 1986 he underwent surgery on his face. Obviously the press had the proverbial field day on both sides of the Atlantic. In retrospect, the mask stories were considered inconsequential when compared to the exclusive but unlikely picture of the singer lying inside a hyperbaric chamber, a life-sized contraption designed to prevent divers from suffering the bends. The headlines led to column inches informing readers that Jackson planned to live until he was 150 years old and intended to sleep in this oxygen-filled tube to halt his ageing process. The story was a sham. Jackson later confirmed the picture was of him lying in a burns victim's chamber which he had donated to the Brotman Medical Center.

But Michael Jackson had proved himself to be a star beyond any other, with a talent that outshone that of his contemporaries. He had vaulted musical barriers to bring his brand of soul music into a mainstream audience and he had delighted the media with all manner of stories. All this was to continue through to the '90s, but he suffered a downside that very nearly destroyed him – his living nightmare which refused to die.

Also see: 'One Day In Your Life', July 1981; 'I Just Can't Stop Loving You' (with Siedah Garrett), September 1987

(Quotes: *Moonwalk* by Michael Jackson; *Michael Jackson Unauthorised: The Shocking Inside Story* by Christopher Anderson)

April 1983

DURAN DURAN

Is There Something I Should Know?

It was one of those singles that slipped the memory from a group that worked with twenty guitarists and ten singers before settling on a permanent line-up. Duran Duran developed the New Romantic image with toned-down funk and coiffeured hairstyles.

John Taylor, born in Birmingham on 20 June 1960, Nick Rhodes, born Nicholas Bates in Birmingham on 8 June 1962, Stephen Duffy and Simon Colley formed the school group Duran Duran during 1978, the group name borrowed from the movie *Barbarella* starring Jane Fonda.

The group became a regular act in the upmarket chain of Barbarella nightclubs but its membership was to be short-lived. Duffy and Colley departed, to be replaced by Roger Taylor, born in Castle Bromwich, Warwickshire, on 26 April 1960, and Andy Wickett. Still the line-up failed to gell. After an advert was placed in *Melody Maker*, Andy Taylor, born in Tyne and Wear on 16 February 1961, joined the group, completing a line-up that also included a pair of temporary vocalists.

Into 1980, Duran Duran were still without a permanent lead vocalist. As they despaired at the thought of more rehearsals with possible candidates, a nightclub waitress came to the rescue by suggesting Simon Le Bon. Born in Bushey, Hertfordshire, on 27 October 1958, a drama student at Birmingham University and previous child actor in a Persil television advertisement, Le Bon brought flair and enthusiasm to the group during mid-1980. With the line-up finally completed, Duran Duran signed a management deal with Michael and Paul Berrow, owners of the Rum Runner nightclub.

Following a lengthy tour as support act to Hazel O'Connor, the group secured a recording contract with EMI Records, thanks to the enthusiasm of Dave Ambrose, then company head of A&R. From the start of their recording career, Duran Duran threw themselves into the growing New Romantic sound, born as the pacifist alternative to the violent punk movement. New Romantics were usually extremely good-looking, clean, slickly presented and dressed in designer clothes, and their songs comprised intimate melodies, confused lyrics and sweeping rhythms. The punk movement, on the other hand, was devoted to staples and safety pins, unclean appearance and foul mouths and charged by brash, political lyrics and jerky musical rhythms. While hardcore punk stalled on the periphery of mainstream success, the New Romantics glided in thanks to the smooth shuffles of acts like Visage and Spandau Ballet, themselves wearers of identical make-up and silk suits.

During March 1981 Duran Duran's debut single was issued. Titled 'Planet Earth', it marked the band's first Top 20 British hit. 'Careless Memories' was issued as the follow-up single and peaked in the Top 40 while the catchy 'Girls On Film' became their biggest-selling title of 1981, soaring into the Top 5. Still a classic today, the title helped Duran Duran develop a career that would span several years, proving as it did that there was more to the membership than eye-liner and designer casuals. To close the musical year, the title 'My Own Way' returned the group to the Top 20.

By this time the group had issued their eponymous album, a Top 3 entrant, and embarked upon their first international tour, including numerous dates in Britain.

Through 1982 Duran Duran toured on, while their second album, titled *Rio*, soared to No.2 and a trio of singles sustained their continued chart profile: 'Hungry Like The Wolf', which, when issued in America, climbed quickly into the Top 3, 'Save A Prayer' and the album's title 'Rio', Top 2 and Top 9 hits respectively. These successes were boosted by imaginative and highly visual promotional videos, first directed by Russell Mulcahy, later by Godley and Creme, who were responsible for the video accompanying the single 'Girls On Film' which, due to its debatable content, was banned by BBC TV. However, across the Atlantic, MTV had no such qualms. The video channel screened the group's videos regularly and probably because of this promotion Duran Duran cracked the lucrative American market. Rhodes admitted, 'Before [MTV] radio wouldn't touch us, but the reaction was so good on MTV that we got picked up by radio stations. We always knew that all we needed was major exposure there.'

The band's popularity was elevated to amazing proportions: female-fan hysteria caused the usual mayhem on tour and concerts were swamped by screaming, uncontrollable audiences who heard not a note being sung on stage! Such was Duran Duran's pulling power, their next single couldn't fail. Titled 'Is There Something I Should Know?', it entered the British chart at the top during April 1983, thereby earning the group the distinction of being one of the country's top-selling units. When the single was released in America in the August, it peaked in the Top 4, passing the one million sales mark.

As 'Is There Something I Should Know?' enjoyed its British accolades, Duran Duran were struggling with over-enthusiastic fans in New York. Nothing changes, does it? Duran Duran mania was spreading quickly; within a short time the group would have America firmly in its grip.

Also see: 'The Reflex', May 1984

SPANDAU BALLET

True

The term 'New Romantics' was one dreamt up by the media, who have always felt comfortable putting new trends into neat compartments. Easier for headlines, one suspects. Many believed that the media, particularly the press, missed the point entirely; the changing music and fashion of the early '80s was individualism. More importantly, though, the look of the New Romantics wasn't entirely unique; didn't, say, the Gatsby look with its sleek, tailored, colour co-ordinated style come first? According to Gary Kemp, 'It's not hard to look smart anymore. Oh, sure, you can go on about how kids have got nothing and come from deprived backgrounds. But surely if you've got nothing, then you've got to look smart, 'cos that's all you've got.'

With this so-called new movement, group followers chose their own venues to patronise. These included London clubs like Le Beat Route but, of course, there were several others. Spandau Ballet championed the New Romantics with a straight image, said to be inspired by Hollywood icons like Valentino, until the movement died a natural death.

Gary Kemp, born in London on 16 October 1960, learned to play the guitar as a youngster. His brother Martin was born on 10 October 1961, also in London. Both attended the Owens Grammar School and studied acting at Anna Scher's Children's Theatre. Tony Hadley, born on 2 June 1959, likewise in London, started his entertainment career at an early age when he won a talent show with his version of Gary Puckett and the Union Gap's 1968 British chart-topper 'Young Girl'.

The nucleus of Spandau Ballet was established during 1976 when Gary Kemp formed the group the Makers, whose membership included fellow schoolers Steve Norman, another Londoner, born on 25 March 1960, and John Keeble, yet another, born on 6 July 1959. While the Makers endeavoured to perfect a stage act, Hadley had forged a career for himself as a character in love stories featured in girls' magazines.

By the close of the '70s, the Makers had been renamed Spandau Ballet by journalist Robert Elms following a trip he made to nightspots in Berlin, and former Makers member Steve Dagger adopted the role of group manager. Dagger organised serious rehearsal sessions during a six-month period, then debuted the group at an Islington studio before a small invited audience. Further selected dates followed at venues the group felt were 'comfortable', like Heaven in London, HMS *Belfast* moored on the Thames and Cardiff's Casablanca Club.

Here was a group commanding its own loyal following but with no recording deal. That was until Spandau Ballet were invited to the opening night of Steve Strange's Blitz nightclub. While there the group met Chris Blackwell, founder of Island Records, who was eager to secure them to an exclusive contract. Dagger was hesitant; he preferred to launch Spandau Ballet's own label. When the group later featured in its own London Weekend Television documentary, Dagger was able to play one record company off against the other before opting to sign to Chrysalis Records, with its influential presence in the music market in both Britain and America.

To welcome the '80s, Spandau Ballet recorded for their own label Reformation, licensed through Chrysalis, and worked to present themselves to the general public. Before 1980 ended, the group spearheaded the expanding New Romantic movement with their first single. Titled 'To Cut A Long Story Short', it shot into the British Top 5 and went on to be treated as the movement's anthem, while the group itself surprisingly attracted criticism from the press. Curiosity forced some tabloid journalists into venues crammed with New Romantics, while others continued to slam what they failed to understand. Writer Steve Sutherland noted, 'The movement was accused of everything from glam-rock revivalism to overt fascism.' Spandau Ballet ignored the headlines, claiming the media were dated and totally out of touch with reality. 'To Cut A Long Story Short' and its follow-up, 'The Freeze', issued early in 1981 and peaking in the Top 20, were both lifted from Spandau Ballet's debut album, titled *Journey To Glory*, produced by Richard James Burgess, known for his work with Landscape. Released in the wake of 'The Freeze', the album soared into the British Top 5. The group's dress sense obviously contributed enormously to the success. Interestingly, in the early '80s, one of Gary Kemp's stage outfits cost approximately £30, John Keeble spent £50 on his, and Tony Hadley's was £13.44, without his favourite classic British military shoes. 'It's not hard or really expensive to take pride in your appearance,' they said.

With support in their home country secured, Spandau Ballet performed in New York, spreading the new musical word, before issuing the Top 10 single titled 'Musclebound' in May 1981. However, quite possibly the group's most diverse of releases was the soul/funk injection from Beggar and Co on the title 'Chant No.1 (I Don't Need This Pressure On)'. The pulsating disco mood, still with

Spandau Ballet's distinctive styling, was an electric release which shot into the British Top 3. The final single of the year was, by comparison, disappointing; 'Paint Me Down' crawled into the British Top 30.

Following a musical collaboration with Pamela Stephenson, Spandau Ballet's second album, *Diamond*, stalled at No.15 in the British chart in March 1982. Of the handful of singles issued during the year, the most successful was the stunning 'Lifeline', which soared to No.7 during the October. Early into the next year, as follow-up to the single titled 'Communication', a Top 20 hit, Spandau Ballet issued the unexpected ballad 'True'. Composed by Gary Kemp, the title became a British chart-topper during May 1983, a position it dominated for four weeks. 'True' likewise marked Spandau Ballet's first American charter by soaring into the Top 5. An album of the same name followed in the wake of a series of selected prestigious performances in Britain, including one at London's Royal Albert Hall, and the release of a second extracted track titled 'Gold', a British Top 2 but a staller in the American Top 30.

Through 1984 Spandau Ballet issued four charting singles in Britain including the biggest-selling title 'Only When You Leave', which peaked at No.3. Their solitary album, *Parade*, soared to No.4 in the July. Like so many other British acts, Spandau Ballet then rose to Bob Geldof's call to record 'Do They Know It's Christmas?', before performing at the Live Aid gala in July 1985. To close the year, the group, now basking in the glory of being one of Britain's foremost selling units, played further selected dates, including a long-awaited sell-out concert at Wembley Arena.

With such a powerful British and European presence and a strong, secure following that showed no signs of faltering, it appeared strange that the American market was so difficult to crack. Sure, Spandau Ballet had enjoyed a brief taste of success there, but that didn't appear to have been fully exploited by their record company. It was a situation for which Spandau Ballet blamed Chrysalis Records. The group issued a writ alleging negligence on the part of the label and stating their desire to be released from their recording contract, which had one further year to run. Spandau Ballet's lawyer told *NME*, 'The recent writ . . . is a direct result of the group's dissatisfaction over their company's failure to honour its contract and support and promote the group as agreed. Overall, they feel they have not enjoyed the support to which a band of their proven stature and success is entitled.' The lawyer further insisted, '[The group] is estimated to be currently responsible for 25 per cent of Chrysalis sales.'

The negotiations took time to resolve. During May 1986, however, when freed from Chrysalis, Spandau Ballet negotiated a recording deal with CBS Records, where the debut single 'Fight For Ourselves' peaked in the Top 20. The album *Through The Barricades*, from which a further pair of singles including the album's title track were swiped, peaked in the British Top 10.

Two years on, in 1988, Gary and Martin Kemp switched careers from music to acting to appear in the movie *The Krays*, playing the roles of the Kray twins Ronnie and Reggie. A year later Spandau Ballet released their second album via CBS Records, titled *Heart Like A Sky*, but, like the single before it, titled 'Be Free With Your Love', poor sales resulted in low chart placings. It was this position that forced CBS Records to drop plans to issue the album in America; the group was gutted and the association between them and the record company ended.

Into the '90s, Spandau Ballet disbanded, with the members embarking upon solo careers. Hadley signed a recording contract with EMI Records and enjoyed three singles, all semi-British hits, including 'For Your Blue Eyes Only' in 1992. Martin and Gary Kemp returned to the film world: Martin moved into television, using *Growing Rich* as his kick-off point, while his brother starred with Whitney Houston and Kevin Costner in the movie *The Bodyguard*.

Martin's promising acting career was halted suddenly when, in 1995, he was diagnosed with a brain tumour. He had felt the lump on his skull while filming in America and was told it could have been growing for ten years. Four operations saved his life. He recuperated in his London home with his wife Shirlie, one half of the singing duo Pepsi and Shirlie, and their family. Happily he returned to acting in September 1998, playing DI Eddie McEwan in the Lynda La Plante television drama *Supply And Demand* before landing a major role in *Eastenders* as nightclub owner and murderer Steve Owen.

It's sad, though. The clean image and music have gone. It's not the same just playing the songs at home; one had to be there to soak up the atmosphere of a performance, drink the Martini and smoke with a cigarette holder. Or was that the Gatsby era?

June 1983

THE POLICE

Every Breath You Take

'I am certainly not the archetypal, couldn't-care-less, drug-taking, degenerate, rebellious rock star because I'm not that type of person' – Sting

As the members of the Police followed individual careers, with Sting enjoying the bulk of the solo spotlight, the trio recorded his composition titled 'Every Breath You Take'. Released midway through 1983, the title topped the British chart in June and stayed there for four weeks, during which time the success was repeated in America, where it stayed at the top spot for a staggering eight weeks. Influenced by Bob Marley's warm reggae backbeat against an emotive lyric, the intention wasn't to release a love song; it was quite the contrary, as Sting said at the time. 'I consider it a fairly nasty song. It's about surveillance, ownership and jealousy.' The mother album, *Synchronicity*, likewise roared to chart-topping status in both countries. Through to the close of the year, the trio entered the chart twice, first with 'Wrapped Around Your Finger', then with 'Synchronicity II'; both were Top 20 British and American hits.

From 1984 through to 1986, the trio continued to pursue individual careers. Summers released his second album, titled *Bewitched*, while Copeland issued *The Rhythmatist* album. Sting, on the other hand, went from strength to strength as songwriter, actor and solo performer. And he longed to tour. To this end he formed a new line-up of musicians, the Blue Turtles Band, released *The Dream Of The Blue Turtles* with them, then took the project and group on a world tour.

On the personal front, Sting married Trudie Styler, the mother of his three children, during August 1992. The entertainment at the wedding was a brief set from a reunited Police during the reception held at Sting's Wiltshire mansion.

Professionally speaking, the trio were reunited on record two months later, when the *Greatest Hits* compilation soared into the British Top 10. A year on, a specially compiled four-CD box set which featured in-demand tracks and their five albums, titled *Message In A Box: The Complete Recordings*, was issued. A *Live* album followed in 1995 and reached the British Top 30. Also during 1995, the live version of 'Can't Stand Losing You' was the first Police single of the year, a Top 30 hit in May.

However, it would be Sting who would dedicate his future career to high-profile entertainment. Alongside the Police issues, and with the release of *Fields Of Gold: The Best Of Sting 1984–1994*, a Top 10 British and American charter, the singer issued the 'This Cowboy Song' single, which peaked at No.15 early in 1995. He then lent his name and talent to a pair of prestigious concerts, the first the Rainforest Foundation Benefit Concert held at Carnegie Hall, New York; the second at the Fleadh Festival in Finsbury Park, London. Doesn't have the same ring, somehow, does it! Nonetheless, if the galas related to the singer's beliefs, he gave his support willingly, and that remains true today.

So, with the Police behind him, Sting has emerged the most dedicated and perhaps adventurous group member. Maybe his constant high media profile has secured his status. Whatever, he is an active supporter of human-rights campaigns and environmental issues. His music is as far reaching as his political views, while on his tours, always a major provider of funds for his beliefs, he plays before packed houses. Suffice to say, Sting is a wealthy man in terms of talent and convictions; he's certainly classed as a figurehead of the decade.

'At the beginning . . . Police was all fantasy. We fantasised about having a No.1 hit . . . I did not imagine we would become as mega as we did' – Sting

Also see: 'Don't Stand So Close To Me', September 1980

(Quotes: *Off the Record: An Oral History of Popular Music* by Joe Smith)

July 1983

ROD STEWART

Baby Jane

'I fancied myself as a singer, and I would be at a railway station singing with a bunch of guys, playing harmonica and singing while waiting for the train' – Rod Stewart

Roderick Stewart was born in Highgate, London on 10 January 1945 to Scottish parents, Robert and Elsie, who already had two daughters, Mary and Peggy, and two sons Bob and Don. The family lived at 507 Archway Road, Highgate, and Stewart's father had retired from the building trade to run a newsagent's store. Said Stewart, 'I came from a very poor family but I was extremely well fed and happy. I was incredibly spoilt as the youngest of five kids.' The Stewart males were football addicts, following the Scottish teams, while Stewart senior ran the Highgate Redwings club in his spare time.

Attending the Highgate Primary School, Stewart failed the 11-plus examination but excelled in sports, before moving to the William Grimshaw Secondary Modern School in Hornsey. There he befriended fellow sports enthusiasts Ray and Dave Davies and Pete Quaife (who went on to form the Kinks). His introduction to music proper came as a 14-year-old when his father gave him a guitar: 'I didn't ask for it and I hardly used it . . . I hated music at school.'

Eventually, though, that line of thinking changed. He began to show an interest in guitar playing, which led to him joining his first school group, the Kool Kats, during 1960. The group comprised eight guitarists, their repertoire a cross between rock'n'roll and skiffle, and somehow they managed to produce semi-decent music.

At 15 years old, Stewart and school parted company. He worked as a silk-screen printer, but his obsession with football led to him becoming an apprentice at Brentford Football Club. The position was short-lived, though; the teenager was physically incapable of coping with the training sessions. With funds from his father, Stewart then sailed to France to earn a living but returned home within days to work in the family newsagent's, perform with his group and join CND marches. When he outgrew the latter he befriended the Mods, his long beatnik-styled hair shorn in favour of his spiky style that later became his trademark.

Music-wise, Stewart moved on to play harmonica and sing with the Five Dimensions, an R&B outfit from Birmingham. They then backed singer Jimmy Powell before joining the Hoochie Coochie Men, support group for Long John Baldry, who had signed a recording contract with United Artists Records. Stewart's association with Baldry led to Mike Vernon, record producer with Decca Records, signing Stewart as a soloist to record 'Good Morning Little Schoolgirl' in 1964. (The Yardbirds likewise recorded the track to enjoy a No.44 British hit during November 1964.) Also the same year, and with Long John Baldry and the Hoochie Coochie Men, Stewart recorded the title 'You'll Be Mine' for United Artists, before appearing briefly on the *Long John's Blues* album. However, with no success the Hoochie Coochie Men disbanded, leaving Stewart to pass through the Soul Agents before teaming up with Steampacket in 1965. The membership here was Baldry, Brian Auger and Julie Driscoll, among others, managed by Giorgio Gomelski.

Steampacket were extremely popular with north of England audiences, particularly in clubs like the Twisted Wheel, itself the heart of Northern Soul, a particular style of American music that attracted a loyal cult following. While still a member of Steampacket, Stewart flexed his solo muscle to record for the EMI Records label Columbia, where his debut was titled 'The Day Will Come'. It bombed.

Early in 1966 Stewart joined the Jeff Beck Group, whose line-up included Ronnie Wood (future member of the Faces). Stewart debuted on stage with the group during March 1967 at the Finsbury Park Astoria, before touring across America with them a year on. In time, though, the rivalry between Stewart and Beck became apparent. Stewart told authors Tim Ewbank and Stafford Hildred, 'Beck's was a miserable fucking band, horrible. Beck is a miserable old sod, but I do love him as a guitar player.' When Beck refused to perform at Woodstock, the rock festival staged in August 1969, Stewart and the others played alone. This inevitably led to the disintegration of the group, which was, ironically, the turning point in Stewart's career – Mercury Records offered him a contract. His first album, with the Faces as support musicians, was titled *An Old Raincoat Won't Ever Let You Down*, released in February 1970. The project bombed in Britain but was a minor American hit. Stewart also signed a recording deal with Phonogram Records and would from now on run two careers – as lead singer with the Faces and as a solo artist – simultaneously.

The Faces, with the line-up of Ron Wood, Ronnie Lane, Kenny Jones and Ian McLagan, were a wild bunch of musicians to put it mildly, as Stewart recalled. 'Me and Woody had a lot of fun . . . It was the ultimate heavy-drinking band. Not because we had a mission in life to be a load of boozers. We were scared shit, and we didn't think we were very good.' Nonetheless, the outfit built up a solid following, although Stewart could not understand why. 'We never had the musicianship. Individually we were good, but we did not come together as a band . . . People must hear something I can't.'

Meanwhile, the title *Gasoline Alley* in June 1970 was Stewart's second solo album, but it was the *Every Picture Tells A Story* album (released in October 1971) that launched him as a soloist of note thanks to the lifted track 'Maggie May'. Penned by the singer and Martin Quittenton, telling the tale of a schoolboy's first sexual encounters, the single shot to No.1 in Britain and America in November 1971. Quittenton said of the chart-topper, 'I couldn't see what all the fuss was about. It took me a long while to realise it was actually a very good popular song.' 'Maggie May' helped its mother album to the top of both the British and American charts.

The single's runaway success pushed the Faces to the back line. In reality they became Stewart's support group, prompting the future billing of Rod Stewart and the Faces. This was not, of course, what the group had intended, and disagreements inevitably resulted. In between altercations, the unit recorded and released their next album, appropriately titled *Never A Dull Moment*, which likewise soared to the top on both sides of the Atlantic. The swiped single, another rock ballad penned by Stewart and Quittenton titled 'You Wear It Well', became the singer's second consecutive chart-topper in September 1972. The Faces, meantime, maintained their position as backing group, letting Stewart bask in the glory. The chart-topper's follow-up was the double-A-sided 'Angel'/'What Made Milwaukee Famous (Has Made A Fool Out Of Me)', which peaked in the British Top 5 during December 1972.

With Stewart promoting two careers, it was inevitable that a split of loyalties would eventually show. This situation was highlighted when the Faces were due to record what would be their last studio album, titled *Ooh-La-La*. While the group was ensconced in the studio, Stewart was absent for two weeks, saying he was disinterested in the project. When the album was finally issued, the singer told the media it was a 'bloody mess'. McLagan said, 'He slagged the album off. There was no reason for him to do that . . . he had everything to gain from it being a success.' Their private disagreements were now public and the media bayed for more.

Following the release of the Faces' Top 2 single 'Cindy Incidentally' in February 1973, a track recorded while Stewart was a member of the Jeff Beck group was issued by RAK Records, namely 'I've Been Drinking'; it was a Top 30 British hit. Meanwhile, Stewart's own official single 'Oh No Not My Baby', a reworking of the Maxine Brown 1964 classic released via Wand Records, peaked at No.6 in the British chart during the September, making the Top 60 in America. The last charting title of the year was the Faces' own 'Pool Hall Richard'/'I Wish It Would Rain'.

Whatever means were tried, nothing could remove the animosity which had developed between Ronnie Lane and Stewart. Lane wanted Stewart to leave the group, which would in turn elevate him to leader. The other Faces disagreed. However, it was Lane who left during June 1973. Said McLagan, 'I didn't speak to him for some years, and of course it turned out that around that time he realised he had MS . . . It was very sad that we kicked him out but he never told us.'

During May 1974 Stewart duetted with Denis Law on the Scotland World Cup squad's album, and in the October the single titled 'Farewell'/'Bring It On Home To Me'/'You Send Me' (his tribute to the late black singer Sam Cooke) peaked at No.7 in the British chart. Behind the scenes the atmosphere was far from happy. Stewart's dispute with his existing record companies had reached boiling point. For some time neither had been satisfied with the recording arrangement afforded them by the singer, nor the arrangement over who chose what material went to which. Instead of negotiating new contracts, Stewart signed a solo recording deal with Warner Bros, which, in turn, sealed the fate of his career with the Faces.

Apart from their recording achievements together, Stewart and the Faces were money-spinning performing artists. Their concert dates were sold out as audiences were treated to both the group's material and Stewart's solo repertoire, and by 1974 they were the biggest-grossing working band in Britain. However, it was clear the public flocked to see the lead singer, a fact even the Faces couldn't dispute. But following an extended American tour in 1975 on which relationships were far from amicable, the group realised Stewart's departure was imminent. According to Stewart, 'The friction came when promoters started putting up signs saying "Rod Stewart and the Faces".' In fact, he admitted Billy Gaff, their manager, used to travel to a town early to ensure he could remove the signs advertising concerts before the group arrived. One night, however, Gaff failed, whereupon the atmosphere on stage was fractious, to say the least.

Behind the performances, Stewart had other, more pressing matters on his mind, namely romance. During March 1975 in Los Angeles he met Britt Ekland, a Swedish actress mourning a loveless marriage to Peter Sellers which had produced a daughter, Victoria. This meeting was the start of a well-documented relationship, despite the fact that the singer already had a partner, Dee Harrington, tucked away in Britain. Stewart said at the time, 'I'm a changed man. I just don't fancy other birds any more. Britt's everything I want.' When not with women, Stewart could be seen in the company of Elton John. The friendship the two built up over the years was sincere, solid and humorous, and both personal and professional. Who can have missed their appearances as 'Phyllis' (Stewart) and 'Sharon' (John) usually dressed in drag!

After meeting Ekland and owing British taxes in excess of £700,000, the singer applied for American citizenship. He said at the time, 'I left Britain because I was paying 83 per cent of everything I was earning to the taxman. I was in a position to move and I fell in love with the place.' The relocation to America had a remarkable effect on his music and he produced his finest album to date, the aptly titled *Atlantic Crossing*, produced by Tom Dowd and recorded with the Muscle Shoals Rhythm Section in Alabama. The album went on to spawn Stewart's next international chart-topper, titled 'Sailing'. Written by Gavin Sutherland and originally recorded as an album track by the Sutherland Brothers, the title soared to the top of the British chart during September 1975, a position it held for four weeks. Earning the distinction of being the longest-running chart single of the year, 'Sailing' was adopted as an anthem by football fans and was the theme music to the BBC TV series *HMS Ark Royal*. This latter exposure during 1976 returned the single to the British chart in the October, when it peaked in the Top 3. Ten years on the single reappeared, with all royalties earmarked for the survivors and families of the Zeebrugge ferry disaster.

Backtracking to the first release of 'Sailing', Stewart was still working with the Faces and to this end was committed to an American tour with them. It was an abysmal trek but was nonetheless completed because the concerts were sold out and the group refused to disappoint their public. Said McLagan, 'Each of us was feeling insecure because everything was different to how it usually was.' In their absence, 'This Old Heart Of Mine', a cover version of the Isley Brothers' 1966 and 1969 Motown hit, was issued by Stewart in Britain as the follow-up to the chart-topping 'Sailing'. The title reached the Top 4 and represented the debut release on Riva Records, a company owned by Billy Gaff.

Following months of dalliance, Stewart announced to the media his intention to leave the Faces to concentrate on his solo career. It was a move he didn't want to make: 'Woody went with the Stones, then we lost Ronnie Lane. For me, Lanie was the Faces. He was to the Faces what Keith Richards is to the Stones. Once Lanie left, it took the ass out of it for me.'

'Tonight's The Night', swiped from his next album titled *A Night On The Town*, followed in June 1976 and reached the British Top 5, while the mother album easily secured the No.1 position, No.2 in America. The single's lyrical content, however, caused controversy Stateside because it told of a 'virgin's deflowering'. Radio airplay was subsequently restricted. It was not so in Britain, where BBC Radio One turned an unusually deaf ear, yet its weekly television music show *Top of the Pops* banned it, claiming the single unfit for family viewing! 'The Killing Of Georgie (Parts I and II)' likewise attracted media controversy, telling as it did of the murder of a young gay man in New York. The single was a Top 2 British hit.

Into 1977 Stewart toured Britain, following a lengthy Norwegian hike. The British trek debuted the singer's new backing group, comprising guitarists Phil Chen, Jim Cregan, Billy Peek and Gary Grainger and drummer Carmine Appice. All concerts were sold out.

Two further singles became British hits during the year, namely another double header titled 'I Don't Want To Talk About It'/'The First Cut Is The Deepest', which topped the chart for four weeks, his fourth title to do so, and 'You're In My Heart', which didn't, but which soared into the Top 3 during the October.

On the personal front, the singer's relationship with Ekland deteriorated; she said his womanising proved too difficult to accept. At the time of their separation Ekland claimed she and Stewart had had a verbal agreement to pool their financial resources. She now wanted recompense. Author Gary Herman reported, 'Everything, she said, should have been split down the middle and, considering how she had sacrificed her acting career to help Rod, she felt she deserved £6 million – especially since Rod was about to sign a £13 million deal when he left her. As an interim award, Britt asked for £2,750 a month while her claim was being assessed.' No matter how strong the actress believed her case was, however, the judge rejected it, leaving Stewart free to pursue his future wife.

Back to the music, and following two recent Top 5 British hits, namely 'Hotlegs' and 'Ole Ola (Mulher Brasileira)' featuring the Scottish World Cup squad, Stewart released the title 'Da Ya Think I'm Sexy?', lifted from the *Blondes Have More Fun* album. The single was directly aimed at the lucrative disco market of the decade. It was not an unusual move for artists of his calibre, but as such he found it difficult to return to his tried and tested formula of rock/pop. More worryingly, though, his credibility was disintegrating as his then manager Arnold Stiefel told Ewbank and Hildred. 'He had this terrible image problem. His image became this glitzy guy with Britt Ekland and beautiful blonde girls who wore fabulous things and drove fabulous cars. I told him that we had to take four to six years to . . . rebuild him without ever admitting to the world that there was any rebuilding to be done.' Stiefel also felt that 'Da Ya Think I'm Sexy?', penned by the singer and Carmine Appice, 'offended and eroded his core male audience'. He was probably right; indeed, when impersonators played Stewart, it was usually that song they chose – using, of course, highly exaggerated movements.

Following the rise of the 'offending and eroding' single to the top of the American chart in February 1979, Stewart married Alana Hamilton, ex-wife of actor George, in Beverly Hills. The marriage produced two children but spanned only five years despite the singer saying, 'I have always had a weakness for long-legged blondes, but since I'm married to the best I'm not going to be interested any more in testing for any other fish in the sea.'

During the first three years of the '80s, Stewart's British chart success wavered. (His last hits were 'Ain't Love A Bitch' and 'Blondes (Have More Fun)' at the close of 1979.) By 1983, though, he re-established himself as a chart-topping artist when 'Baby Jane' soared to the top of the British chart in the July, reaching the Top 20 in America. Reminiscent of his earlier work like 'You Wear It Well', this was obviously the formula his buying public wanted.

While his career had been rejuvenated, his marriage to Alana had ended. Proving he still had selling power, he issued the *Camouflage* album in 1984, from which the Top 30 British hit 'Infatuation' featuring Jeff Beck was lifted. 'Some Guys Have All The Luck' followed and reached the Top 20. Two years on, Stewart recorded the title 'Love Touch' for the movie *Legal Eagles* starring Robert Redford and Debra Winger. Later issued as a single, the title peaked in the Top 30. The follow-up in July 1986, titled 'Every Beat Of My Heart', however, soared to No.2 in the British chart. Through to the end of the decade, the singer maintained regular chart appearances, embarked upon extensive world tours, thereby maintaining his super-star status, and enjoyed gossip pieces in the tabloids.

During 1990, Stewart was prime newspaper fodder when he was subjected to two lawsuits, both the result of his practice of kicking footballs into the audience during performances – a splendid idea until the ball actually lands! On the recording front, and following a guest appearance at the Brit Awards ceremony in February 1990, he enjoyed a Top 10 hit with the memorable 'Downtown Train'. Singing with Tina Turner was next, when they recorded the Marvin Gaye and Kim Weston classic 'It Takes Two'. The novelty element of the two giant voices and Pepsi Cola, who used it to advertise their soft drink on television, pushed the single into the British Top 5. The single's title bore relevance to Stewart's personal life, because before 1990 closed he remarried. His new wife Rachel Hunter was a New Zealand model; meanwhile, his former live-in girlfriend Kelly Emberg filed a multi-million-dollar palimony suit against him. Life was never dull for Stewart! Then his best friend Elton John took Stewart's recent marriage one step further when he dressed up as a bride to join him on stage during a London concert.

Rod Stewart was back in vogue. His British tours guaranteed sell-out shows, while his American treks ensured multi-million-dollar pay cheques. During 1991 his British chart presence was his most impressive for some time. 'Rhythm Of My Heart' and 'The Motown Song', featuring the Temptations on vocals, were both Top 10 singles. The latter title boasted an animated promotion video featuring selected Motown acts – Michael Jackson's appearance was particularly biting.

In 1992, Stewart's next Top 10 title was the unlikely 'Tom Traubert's Blues (Waltzing Matilda)', while a year on he issued his version of the Rolling Stones' Top 3 1967 British hit 'Ruby Tuesday', which peaked in the Top 20 during the February. Hot on its heels came the album *Rod Stewart: Lead Vocalist*, the compilation *The Best Of Rod Stewart* and a further cover version, this time 'Shotgun Wedding', first recorded by Roy C. It had reached the Top 10 in Britain in 1966 and 1972; Stewart's update stalled just outside the Top 20 in the April.

When the undisputed queen of soul hosted her own television show titled *Aretha Franklin: Duets*, she invited Stewart to sing 'People Get Ready' with her. He then went on to perform at the World Music Awards ceremony staged in Monte Carlo. During this gala, he was presented with a unique award in recognition of his contribution to the music industry. The song he chose to perform, 'Have I Told You Lately?', was later issued as a single and peaked in the British and American Top 5. As the title sold, his *Unplugged And Seated* album hit the stores. To close 1993, a pair of singles faltered in the British Top 50, namely 'Reason To Believe' and 'People Get Ready'.

The singer started the new year on an industry high by being inducted into the Rock'n'Roll Hall of Fame during a New York ceremony, while the single titled 'All For Love' featuring Stewart, Sting and Bryan Adams topped the American chart, reaching the Top 2 in Britain. Inspired by this success, Stewart hit the American concert circuit, followed by one of the most prestigious performances of his career, staged at the Copacabana Beach, Rio de Janeiro, where he performed before an audience of three million via the Brazilian television network.

'You're The Star' was the artist's first 1995 outing and became a Top 20 British hit, while the 'Leave Virginia Alone' single flopped in the American Top 60. While trekking across the British concert trail, the album *A Spanner In The Works* flew into the Top 4 in the June. His final single of the year, 'Lady Luck', was a staller in the Top 60. Indeed, touring, particularly through America, dominated much of the next year, when his recorded success in Britain was restricted to a pair of singles, namely 'Purple Heather' and 'If We Fall In Love Tonight', Top 20 and Top 60 hits respectively.

Record-buyers once again flocked to the stores in May 1998 when Stewart released his strongest project for some years. Titled *When We Were The New Boys*, it was his first self-produced album since *Never A Dull Moment*. Tracks included 'Cigarettes And Alcohol', penned by Noel Gallagher, and Graham Parker's 'Hotel Chambermaid'. To launch the CD's release Stewart hosted a Saturday night showcase on British television, where before a specially invited audience he strutted through old and new material, soaking his green silk shirt as he did so. This compulsive-viewing show encouraged the audience to purchase expensive tickets for his British tour later in the year.

One of Britain's more colourful artists, Rod Stewart now appears to be the respectable voice of pop/rock. When his name becomes newspaper fodder, the stories range from the occasional drunken binges to, more often, a new release, a new baby and so on. Imagine the public's surprise when headlines in 1999 revealed the pending divorce of Stewart and Rachel Hunter. Stewart's calmer and mature lifestyle was cited as the cause, because he is now as comfortable sitting on Des O'Connor's television sofa as he is prancing around on a *Top of the Pops* set. My, age has certainly mellowed the rebel of sex, drugs and rock'n'roll. Or has it?

(Quotes: *Rod Stewart: The Best-Selling Biography* by Tim Ewbank and Stafford Hildred)

PAUL YOUNG

Wherever I Lay My Hat (That's My Home)

'People think I'm old fashioned by covering other people's tunes, but it's really the other way around. People have been writing and covering tunes for 20 years now and it's about time they changed' – Paul Young

Born Paul Anthony Young in Luton, Bedfordshire, on 17 January 1956 to Tony and Doris, he learned to play the piano and bass guitar while at school. His musical ambitions spurred him into action through local groups including Kat Kool and the Kool Kats. Alongside his music Young needed to earn a living, so he became an apprentice at a Vauxhall factory.

From the Kool Kats, Young formed Streetband, his first serious outfit, who impressed Logo Records executives sufficiently for them to record and release the 'Toast' single during November 1978. Produced by Chaz Jankel, the title soared into the British Top 20, the group's only charting success. However, before disbanding, Streetband went on to release a pair of albums, *Dilemma* being one. Young told *Newsweek*. 'I was trying to hang on to my English accent, although I'd been listening to a lot of soul. It came out quite weird.'

From Streetband, the singer switched to the Q-Tips, an eight-piece outfit specialising in performing American R&B, with, of course, a blue-eyed soul slant. The group performed regularly during a three-year period when, Young said, he 'found his voice' because 'there's nothing that improves your voice more than hearing it coming back at you night after night over the feedback on a live stage.'

Into the '80s the Q-Tips had built a solid reputation and had a loyal following, often performing as support act for touring artists. This flow of work came to the attention of Chrysalis Records, with whom the group later released a handful of singles. None sold in sufficient quantities to chart, but the Q-Tips' eponymous album did, peaking in the British Top 50.

During 1981 Muff Winwood, A&R executive for CBS Records, believed Young showed potential as a soloist. The move took until September 1982 when the Q-Tips disbanded, leaving Young free to secure a recording contract with CBS Records. Early in his relationship with the record giant, Young admitted the company was unsure how to promote him – 'They had in mind to push me in a poppy, lightweight-soul direction' – and his debut proved this. Titled 'Iron Out The Rough Spots', it bombed, as did its follow-up early in 1983, 'Love Of The Common People', a rerecording of Nicky Thomas's Top 10 British hit in June 1970.

Disappointed but not deterred, Young, with ex-Q-Tips member Ian Kewley, formed the Royal Family as his support group. Together they recorded a version of a Marvin Gaye B-side (to 'Too Busy Thinking About My Baby', issued in 1969) titled 'Wherever I Lay My Hat (That's My Home)'. Remarkably, the British public loved Young's worthy version and sent the title to No.1 in August 1983, where it stayed for three weeks. When released in America, the single faltered in the Top 70 in the October, much to the dismay of the singer but maybe not that of the Americans, who obviously preferred their homegrown Motown original. However, Young had finally found his own niche in the British market with a cover version which would sustain his career for several years yet.

Hot on the chart-topper's success, the singer issued his debut album *No Parlez* which likewise shot to the top of its chart. Containing cover versions of several soul classics, the album attempted to portray Young's R&B styling. According to Young, 'I don't think I write singles, which is why so many of our singles are covers. I want to search out and find great songs . . . quality songs.' When released in America, the album sold poorly, prompting Young to tell *Rolling Stone* magazine, 'When that didn't happen, I was left up in the air. It began to get to me. It's important . . . America knows what I'm doing is good, because 90 per cent of my influences are American.' That situation was destined to change.

A further track from *No Parlez* was issued as the chart-topper's follow-up in October 1983. This time Young's version of Jack Lee's 'Come Back And Stay' soared into the British Top 4. Meanwhile, plans were afoot to reissue 'Love Of The Common People' to capitalise on the Christmas market. Its second outing gave Young and the Royal Family a Top 2 single. To promote this pair of singles, Young and his group kicked in a lengthy British tour.

To start 1984 Young and the Royal Family toured America in the hope of generating additional album sales and to pave the way for the pending single 'Come Back And Stay'. The ploy worked; the single peaked inside the Top 30, followed by 'Love Of The Common People', a Top 50 hit. Upon their return, the singer joined others of his ilk to appear at the Prince's Trust gala staged at the Royal Albert Hall. During June 1984, the singer and company toured further afield to Australasia and Japan, boosting sales of *No Parlez* beyond seven million, while home sales passed platinum status three times!

Then Young was hit by illness. From August to October he was ordered to rest by doctors as he suffered from voice problems. In his absence, a new male vocalist was recruited into the Royal Family. Once recovered, Young returned with a vengeance to promote his version of Ann Peebles' soul masterpiece 'I'm Gonna Tear Your Playhouse Down', a Top 10 hit, by touring Britain. When issued across the Atlantic, the single peaked in the Top 20.

Following his contribution to the Live Aid single 'Do They Know It's Christmas?', the singer issued his own title, the full-blooded 'Everything Must Change', a composition he co-penned with Ian Kewley. Subsequently, Young closed the year with a British Top 10 single.

'Every Time You Go Away' started 1985 in fine style for Young, peaking in the British Top 4. A cover version of the Hall and Oates original, the single went on to top the American chart in the July, Young's first and only chart-topper there. Hall told the *Music Connection* magazine that he had intended the song to be a gospel track, never thinking of it being interpreted otherwise. He then heard Young's version: 'I was really surprised to hear the production they did because it kept the elements but commercialised [the sound].'

Shortly prior to his American chart-topper, Young issued his *The Secret Of Association* album, his second British No.1 title and a Top 20 hit in America. Meanwhile, on the singles front, his 'Tomb Of Memories' peaked in the British Top 20.

Mid-1986, and following his appearance at the Prince's Trust rock gala staged at Wembley Arena with other high-ranking acts like Tina Turner and Paul McCartney, Young's next single, titled 'Wonderland', was his first since 1983 to falter in the British Top 30. Was this the start of Young's decline? Many believed it was. However, in November 1986, the singer proved his critics wrong when his album *Between Two Fires* peaked in the British Top 4, although by comparison American sales were poor, resulting in the project stalling in the Top 80. To boost flagging sales, a further single was extracted, titled 'Some People'. The ploy failed; the title struggled into the British Top 60 and American Top 70.

As his selling power was obviously on the downward turn, Young lifted the third track from the *Between The Fires* album for single release. 'Why Does A Man Have To Be Strong?' sold badly in 1987, marking the singer's imposed retirement when he relocated to Jersey, claiming he needed to escape from the British tax system and wanted to spend quality time with his wife and daughter.

With the advent of the '90s, and following Young's absence from the public spotlight when the music press decreed the singer's talent had burned itself out, he returned to enjoy a British Top 21 single with 'Softly Whispering I Love You', a gem of a song and a sweeping version of the Congregation's 1971 Top 4 British hit. Now encouraged, Young released his fourth solo album in the June titled *Other Voices*, comprising his versions of third-party originals. The title peaked at No.4 in Britain but bombed in America. From that album, Young swiped the track 'Oh Girl', previously a 1972 British No.14 hit for the American soul group the Chi-Lites. Young's updated version peaked at No.25 but made the Top 10 in America, re-establishing him as a selling act of note. With this in mind, the singer toured Canada and North America before closing 1990 with a British trek, reclaiming his audiences who had probably remained loyal but just didn't shout about it until Young was in vogue again!

Four more singles ensured Young's name remained in the British chart, although a couple featured him with other singers. The first outing, 'Calling You', solo Young, stalled in the Top 60; while 'Senza Una Donna' with Zucchero soared into the Top 4 and 'Both Sides Now' with Clannad peaked in the Top 80. The final release, solo Young, 'Don't Dream It's Over', peaked in the Top 20. In between these singles, CBS Records compiled and issued the album *From Time To Time: The Singles Collection*, which, despite the singer's falling chart positions, shot to No.1.

Young's version of Jimmy Ruffin's 1966 Top 10 British hit 'What Becomes Of The Brokenhearted?' peaked in the American Top 30 in 1992, and his next British hit a year on was a further stroke of genius. Titled 'Now I Know What Made Otis Blue', the single peaked in the British Top 20, and was a timely hit as it boosted the advance orders on his pending album *The Crossing*. With help from several high-profile American musicians, the album peaked at No.23 in the British chart. To end 1993, the single 'Hope In A Hopeless World' stalled in the British Top 50, while its follow-up fared marginally better. 'It Will Be You' peaked at No.32 during April 1994, the same year as Young recorded a collection of soul tracks to be marketed under the title *Reflections*. The album stalled in the Top 70.

Following a further hiatus, Young returned in 1997 with his eponymous album issued on the East West label, distributed through Warner Music. From this album a trio of singles were issued during 1997, namely 'Ball And Chain', 'I Wish You Love' and 'Tularosa'; all were poor-selling titles, as was the final single of 1997, titled 'Make Someone Happy'. Alongside *Paul Young*, two further albums were also issued, *Tracks Of My Tears* via Hallmark Records and *Some Kind Of Wonderful* by A-Play Collection, both being credited to Paul Young and the Q-Tips.

It goes without saying that, like Dusty Springfield and perhaps Tom Jones before him, Paul Young will forever be associated with British soul – not necessarily the outmoded term of blue-eyed soul (that's far too twee), but more as a stylist of commercial R&B. It is a title few deserve.

(Quotes: *The Billboard Book of Number One Singles* by Fred Bronson)

September 1983

UB40

Red Red Wine

'We'd never heard of the Neil Diamond version. We had no idea [he] had anything to do with it. The only version we were aware of was the Tony Tribe version' – Robin Campbell

Alastair Campbell, born in Birmingham on 15 February 1959, and his brother Robin, also Birmingham-born on 25 December 1954, two of four sons born to a Scottish singer, cut their professional teeth in the family's barber-shop group. The brothers later recruited other Birmingham-born members Mickey Virtue, born on 19 January 1957, Astro, born on 24 June 1957, Earl Falconer, born on 23 January 1959, Norman Hassan, born on 26 January 1957, and Jim Brown, born on 20 November 1957.

Calling themselves UB40, the name of the unemployment benefit form ('it made a lot of sense to us, as we were all unemployed'), the group teamed up with Bob Lamb, late of the reggae unit Locomotive and now record producer with his own local recording studio. Thanks to Alastair's misfortune, UB40 were workable, as Robin explained. 'He got injured in a bar fight, where he had a pint glass smashed into his face. He had 90 stitches on the left side of his face and a corneal implant and was awarded Criminal Injuries Compensation . . . When he got the money, he bought a set of drums and a couple of guitars, and we went from there.'

Within a short time UB40 built up a solid following through Birmingham and surrounding areas. The Pretenders' lead vocalist Chrissie Hynde attended one of their performances and invited the boys to join her 1980 British tour. A recording deal followed with the Graduate label, operating from a Dudley-based record store.

In April 1980 UB40 released their debut single, a tribute to the late Martin Luther King Jr, titled 'King'. However, it was the disc's flipside 'Food For Thought' that attracted radio airplay to push the title to the top of the then British independent chart before it crossed over to No.4 in the mainstream listing. A month on, UB40 and the

Pretenders kicked in their British tour, with record companies dangling cheques at every venue hoping UB40 would sign up with them.

Returning to the chart at No.6 during the July with the single 'My Way Of Thinking' and later, in November, with 'The Earth Dies Screaming' in the Top 10, UB40 then issued their first album titled *Signing Off*, a Top 2 hit. It was inevitable that with such staggering selling power UB40 and Graduate Records would part, although the group's move wasn't directly to a major company, but rather to open their own record label, DEP International, licensed to Virgin Records. The group's debut under their new logo was the *Present Arms* album, which repeated its predecessor's success at No.2 in June 1981, its sales initially boosted by the giveaway disc attached to the record. Two singles were extracted from the mother album, namely 'Don't Let It Pass You By' and 'One In Ten', Top 20 and Top 10 hits respectively. Performing-wise, UB40 combined paying-audience concerts with benefit shows, including one staged for the arrested perpetrators of the summer's inner-city riots.

Into 1982 the group issued a trio of singles: 'I Won't Close My Eyes', 'Love Is All Is Alright' and 'So Here I Am' – none, however, made it higher than the Top 30. This situation, though, failed to prevent Graduate Records from capitalising on UB40's recent success by releasing *The Singles Album*, a Top 20 hit. Hot on its heels UB40 issued their official project titled *UB44*, the first to be packaged in a hologram sleeve; it was a Top 4 hit.

Early in 1983, the single 'I've Got Mine' faltered in the British Top 50, as did the album *UB40 Live*. With the negative, however, came the positive. UB40 topped the British chart during September 1983 with their version of the Neil Diamond track 'Red Red Wine', although one would be hard-pushed to recognise it as the same song! The single also peaked in the American Top 40, the group's first taste of an American hit. As 'Red Red Wine' dominated British sales for three weeks, UB40 were adamant they had not heard Neil Diamond's original version, citing the Jamaican artist Tony Tribe's interpretation as their inspiration. Tribe's single, incidentally, had peaked in the British Top 50 during 1969.

As UB40's soft reggae blended easily into the Diamond melody, it wasn't surprising when the group issued the *Labour Of Love* album crammed with non-original tracks, all 'UB40-ised'. The album topped the British chart. At this point, as the group expanded their membership with Brian Travers, Birmingham-born on 7 February 1959, two further cover versions were swiped from *Labour Of Love* as singles, namely 'Please Don't Make Me Cry' and 'Many Rivers To Cross', Top 10 and Top 20 British hits.

An attack on the Conservative Party was prevalent through the group's 1984 album titled *Geffrey Morgan*, a Top 3 hit, while its extracted singles 'If It Happens Again', a swipe at Margaret Thatcher, and 'Riddle Me' notched up Top 10 and a struggling Top 60 placings for the group. From politics, UB40 joined others, like Special AKA and Madness, to record the title 'Starvation', their contribution to the Ethiopian famine appeal. Remarkably, the title sold poorly, but the next did not. UB40 pulled the groove from the studio to release their version of the Sonny and Cher 1965 British chart-topper 'I Got You Babe', with Chrissie Hynde sharing lead vocals. The single rightly topped the British chart in August 1985, reaching the Top 30 in America. *Baggariddim*, UB40's next album, failed to reach the top, faltering in the Top 20.

With thoughts of South African activists foremost in their minds, UB40's biggest-selling single of 1986, titled 'Sing Our Own Song', was followed by the album *Rat In The Kitchen*, which peaked in the Top 10. The record's title track was the group's first 1987 single, peaking at No.12, while its follow-up, 'Watchdogs', faltered in the Top 40. As the vinyl struggled, Virgin Records took the initiative by releasing the group's video *UB40 CCCP*, a visual record of their successful Russian visit, together with *The Best Of UB40: Volume 1*, crammed with video hit material, before issuing a 'greatest hits' audio package.

Mid-1988, UB40 teamed up for the second time with Chrissie Hynde to release the No.6 British hit titled 'Breakfast In Bed'. As the single climbed, the group embarked upon a world tour, with a temporary group member replacing Earl Falconer who, whilst over the legal alcohol limit, had been involved in a car accident which had killed his brother Ray. Falconer was jailed for six months. Meanwhile, UB40's touring schedule stretched to America, where in October 1988 the September 1983 chart-topper 'Red Red Wine' topped the American chart. It only took five years! The title's release was instigated when a programme director for a Phoenix, Arizona, radio station listened to *Labour Of Love*. He subsequently aired 'Red Red Wine' constantly, whereupon other radio stations followed his lead. Public demand for single release encouraged UB40's American record company, A&R Records, to reissue the track, even though their promotional budget was earmarked for the group's current single 'Breakfast In Bed'.

Into the '90s, as the poor-selling single 'Here I Am (Come And Take Me)' sank, the Top 4 hit 'Kingston Town' and the Top 3 album *Labour Of Love II* restored UB40's high-profile selling status. Four singles charted, namely 'Wear You To The Ball', 'I'll Be Your Baby Tonight', recorded with Robert Palmer, 'Impossible Love' and a reworking of the Temptations' 1964 American hit 'The Way You Do

The Things You Do', which also peaked in the American Top 10, further cementing their successful career in the States.

During 1992 the group's selling power rose once again. Following their joint release with 808 State, the reworking of UB40's 'One In Ten', a Top 20 charter, UB40 recorded a version of Elvis Presley's 1962 British No.1 'Can't Help Falling In Love', which likewise shot to the British top during the June and a month on reached the pole position in America. The *Promises And Lies* album rounded off the trio of chart-toppers. Two further singles, 'Higher Ground' and 'Bring Me Your Cup', went on to become British hits before 1993 closed.

In 1995, when Campbell temporarily departed from the group to release his own album, *Big Love*, and a string of extracted singles, released via his own Kuff label, licensed through Virgin Records, UB40 charted for the last time with 'Until My Dying Day', a Top 20 hit. However, as recently as August 1998 the group was seen on British television screens when their video of 'Live in the New South Africa' concert was shown to viewers.

October 1983

CULTURE CLUB

Karma Chameleon

'"Karma Chameleon" was the kind of song everyone bought and no one liked. It had a niggling quality that provoked renditions everywhere I went' – Boy George

With his immaculately made-up face adorning most magazines aimed at the young and fashionable, Boy George's private life likewise attracted media interest. The most regular name linked with the singer's was Marilyn, a young man who shared the love of the greasepaint but whom, George maintained, he didn't fancy – 'I was addicted to him.' However, George conceded he overexposed himself during the early stages of Culture Club's career, jumping on the interview bandwagon with Jon Moss, being fêted by record-company personnel and media, maintaining his love of nightclubbing (when he could) and generally basking in his newly found fame. He wanted to be regarded as an artist or pop singer whom parents loathed, but because 'I was such a polite, friendly boy and I wanted everyone to love me', he reluctantly shrugged off the 'bad boy' image to be himself.

America was the next on Culture Club's touring agenda. The group visited New York as 'Do You Really Want To Hurt Me?' climbed the chart via a recording contract with Epic Records. The group's debut performance was staged at the Ritz Theatre, New York, during December 1983, where the audience was both straight and gay, and they were a sensational hit. In between the tight promotional schedules and personal appearances, Culture Club, which more often than not now featured Helen Terry and Alison Moyet, recorded and released their second British chart-topper. Titled 'Karma Chameleon', the single shot to the top in October 1983, a position it dominated for six wonderful weeks, having entered the listing at No.3. 'Karma Chameleon' went on to sell 1.3 million copies in Britain alone, earning it the distinction of becoming the 11th best-selling single ever. It also won the Best British Single award and Culture Club the Best British Group category at the Brit Awards ceremony held in London.

The chart-topper's promotional video, shot along the banks of the River Thames on a dull, grey day, was an attempt to recreate the Southern American theme with a paddle steamer and over a hundred extras. The group dressed as slave traders, with George as himself. Culture Club loathed the result.

When released in America in February 1984, 'Karma Chameleon' likewise topped the chart, a position it held for three weeks, selling in excess of one million copies. In Canada Culture Club became the first group ever to sell one million copies of a single.

As 'Karma Chameleon' dominated British sales, Culture Club hit the home touring route once more. Within three days, though, the trek was postponed after Jon Moss broke a finger in a fight with George on their touring coach. The driver was silenced with cash. Also during October 1983, the title *Colour By Numbers* was issued, the group's second album and first to enter the British chart at No.1. The album later scored similar success across Europe into Japan, Australia and America, where it peaked at No.2 for approximately six weeks.

To close this incredible year, Culture Club issued the 'Victims' single, which peaked in the British Top 3. It was an alien sound to the group, being a ballad without a dance bounce. Perhaps this was the reason why the title stalled outside the top spot.

'It's A Miracle' was Culture Club's first British hit at No.4 in 1984. It reached the Top 13 in America in June, a month after the group scooped a Grammy Award for the Best New Artist of 1983. During October 1984, with George switching his image and now appearing slicked-up and with a black wig, Culture Club's 'The War Song' single soared to No.2 in Britain and made the Top 20 in America. The group's album *Waking Up With The House On Fire* quickly capitalised on the success to likewise peak at No.2 in the British chart, making the Top 30 in America. The album release coincided with Culture Club's American tour, which itself followed the group's sell-out Canadian trek, when they had been greeted by 3,000 fans at the Mirable Airport in Montreal. It was a nightmare. Said George, '[Fans] would hide in cupboards, under tables, bent in two for hours, holding their breath. Those with cars would follow us everywhere. It made me so angry.' This was the trend throughout the Canadian tour; it was the price of fame.

Before 1984 closed, George was a lead vocalist on the charity single 'Do They Know It's Christmas?', recorded in the November to become a British chart-topper, and Culture Club's single 'The Medal Song' struggled into the Top 40.

Through the next year, George and Culture Club took a break, in theory to catch their breath and to rethink their future career. In actual fact, George binged on a creative session for the group's next album and on nightclubbing and drugs, usually heroin or Ecstasy. He travelled extensively, often collecting industry awards for Culture Club's musical achievements *en route*.

Culture Club returned in 1986. The single 'Move Away' peaked in the British Top 10 in the April, the Top 20 in America. A month on, 'God Thank You Woman' was the follow-up title, faltering in the Top 40. The mother album, *From Luxury To Heartache*, co-produced by Arif Mardin, peaked in the British Top 10 and American Top 40. As sad as it was at the time, these releases marked the end of Culture Club; the in-group arguing and creative fighting had won out. Roy Hay formed the outfit This Way Up, while Moss conceived Promised Land, leaving George to return to his beloved night-time activities – dance and dope. In time he would embark upon a serious solo career, but to close the book on Culture Club, during 1987 the *This Time* album peaked in the Top 10, while in the early '90s both the group's and George's material were issued under the one title *At Worst: The Best Of* . . .

Now back to Boy George; backtrack to 1986. Now slimline, having deliberately shed pounds, George was publicly exposed by his brother David to the tabloid newspapers as being a regular heroin user. George's parents had often tried unsuccessfully to wean their son off drugs and as a last, desperate resort had persuaded David, then a freelance photographer, to break the news. Said George, 'My use of heroin became more and more regular . . . I was taking far too much. In my mind I had it all under control, I didn't consider that I would ever become an addict.' *The Sun* newspaper carried the headline in July 1986 'Junkie George Has Eight Weeks To Live'; other newspapers carried spin-off stories in the days that followed. Richard

Branson, founder of Virgin Records, took the singer under his wing and introduced him to Dr Meg Patterson, who agreed to treat the ailing singer with her 'black box' method. George described it in his autobiography as 'a battery-operated metal box attached to an elastic waistband with an electrode that clipped on to your ear. It worked by sending out subtle electrical impulses to stimulate the endorphins.' As the singer underwent the painful treatment, his friends and acquaintances were being rounded up by the police on varying drugs charges.

On 29 July 1986, George had been fined £250 for heroin possession at Marylebone Magistrates Court, and while he was staying with his parents, Michael Rudetski, the American keyboardist who contributed to Culture Club's last album, had been found dead from a drugs overdose in George's home. Yet the singer somehow survived the doom and gloom of his most recent past to rise as a stronger person. This strength crossed into his professional life where, once more, he rose to the dizzy heights of Britain's best-selling act.

Also see: 'Do You Really Want To Hurt Me?', October 1982; 'Everything I Own', April 1987

(Quotes: *Take It Like a Man: The Autobiography of Boy George* by Boy George and Spencer Bright)

November 1983

BILLY JOEL

Uptown Girl

'I like [it] when other people do my songs. That was my original intention, to be a songwriter. I've gotten criticism over the years for not being enough of a stylist' – Billy Joel

Born William Martin Joel in Hicksville, Long Island, New York, on 9 May 1949, his parents encouraged him at four years old to play the piano. However, the young boy's classical keyboard training soon took second place with the advent of rock'n'roll's popularity in mainstream music.

Now with ambitions to join the rising artists like Elvis Presley, the 14-year-old Joel formed his first group called the Echoes, performing nights on the local club circuit. By now Joel's parents had separated, his father returning to Germany, his home country, leaving the youngster to support his family, which he did by becoming a boxer until his nose got broken!

Joel moved on in his music career to join the Hassles, who later recorded unsuccessfully for United Artists Records. From the Hassles, the youngster switched to the Attila trio, signed to CBS Records' Epic subsidiary. Once again, there was to be no success. It was at this juncture that the young man decided to switch rock'n'roll for songwriting: 'I had been in bands for years, and to get up on stage, to want to be a star, you have to have a tremendous self-centred thing.' Joel didn't, nor did he want to become a slave of the public spotlight.

That ambition was to change. By 1972 Joel had embarked upon a solo career and issued his debut album, titled *Cold Spring Harbour*, following an arrangement with Family Productions and Records. His appearance at a Puerto Rico festival excited an A&R scout from Columbia Records, who tried to get his signature on a recording contract. However, Joel was unable to join the company due to a legal problem with the Family organisation, whereupon he relocated to Los Angeles to work as a nightclub pianist using the name Bill Martin.

His anonymous lifestyle lasted until 1974, when Clive Davis, then working for Columbia Records, discovered him, this time securing his signature. He went on to record the *Piano Man* album. The project's title track was swiped for single release and presented Joel with a Top 30 American hit. It was from this starting block that the artist recorded a further pair of albums, namely *Streetlife Serenade* and *Turnstiles*, which went on to spawn a handful of hit titles. Joel told Joe Smith that his previous record company 'still [got] a piece of me, but I came to grips with it. I used to get mad, but I honoured an agreement, however dishonourable it was.'

Despite enjoying a good career so far, Joel was unable to cross the one-million-sales barrier. However, this situation was to end when he began working with producer Phil Ramone, notably on the album titled *The Stranger* during 1977. In 1978 the singer enjoyed the Top 3 American hit 'Just The Way You Are', 'Movin' Out (Anthony's Song)' (Top 20), 'Only The Good Die Young' (Top 30) and 'She's Always A Woman' (Top 20). He was well and truly carving a successful future from a granite beginning.

Columbia Records' parent company, CBS Records, likewise issued Joel's recorded work in Britain, from his debut hit 'Just The Way You Are', which achieved a Top 20 placing in February 1978, to 'Movin' Out (Anthony's Song)', a struggler in the Top 40, four months on. With this British success to his credit, Joel performed in Britain for the first time, choosing the stylish Theatre Royal in London's Drury Lane to present his art.

In the lead-up to the '80s, Joel returned to the top section of the American chart with the title 'My Life', extracted from the chart-topping *52nd Street* album issued at the close of 1978. The album went on to sell in excess of two million copies and peaked at No.10 in Britain. 'My Life' likewise returned the singer to the British chart, reaching No.12 in January 1979. Two additional tracks were then swiped from *52nd Street* to chart in Britain, namely 'Big Shot' and 'Until The Night'.

Joel greeted the new decade in fine style with the rock album titled *Glass Houses*, once more with Phil Ramone at the production board. From this project, and following the release of the 'You May Be Right' single, Joel finally topped the American chart with 'It's Still Rock And Roll To Me' during July 1980; the title reached No.14 in Britain. It should be noted that the *Glass Houses* album moved Joel away from the so-called crooner market slap bang into the rock one, much to the dismay of his fans and critics who believed he could master other musical avenues far better artistically. But the project transformed its creator into an extremely rich man and an artist of worth. In total, four hit singles were lifted from *Glass Houses*, ending with the track 'Sometimes A Fantasy' during November 1980, while the album went on to scoop the Grammy Award for Best Rock Vocal Performance, Male, among the many high-profile awards honouring its release.

In 1981 Joel issued one album, *Songs In The Attic*, a live release of early material, from which the title 'Say Goodbye To Hollywood' was extracted. It was a poor-selling single. These releases were classed as 'stand-ins' as the artist prepared material for his next studio album titled *The Nylon Curtain*. However, it was during this time that Joel was involved in an accident, when his motorcycle collided with a car on a Long Island highway. Joel said, 'Right before I hit, I had a flood of images, jumbled-up thoughts. I thought I was going to die and I thought, "You can't do this to me, I'm not ready."' Happily, Dr Death agreed. As Joel underwent extensive surgery to mend his broken body, he continued to work on his musical project that ultimately dealt with what he called his generation's 'American experience – guilt, pressures, relationships and the Vietnam syndrome'. *The Nylon Curtain* hit the American Top 10 and British Top 30 during October 1982.

While promoting the album across America, Joel met model Christie Brinkley (his marriage to his first wife had ended in divorce). The two became inseparable, attracting high-profile media coverage.

Returning to the music, in September 1983 Joel topped the American chart for the second time. With a track swiped from his pending *An Innocent Man* album, 'Tell Her About It' dominated

American sales for a week. Meanwhile, the mother album soared to No.4 on its way to 2.5 million sales; in Britain, the project fared even better at No.2 during October 1983. Joel said the character behind the album was a sweet person 'who is in love and feeling good. It's a guy enjoying the courtship rituals, the gamut of passions that come with romance.' However, the best was to come when a further album track was extracted for single release. 'Uptown Girl', a love poem to his fiancée Brinkley set to a Four Seasons musical soundalike, topped the British chart in November 1983 at the start of a five-week stay, selling in excess of one million copies. Needless to say, *An Innocent Man* was rifled for singles, including its title track, 'The Longest Time' and 'Keeping The Faith', all high-selling items during 1984 and 1985. On the personal front, Joel married his Uptown Girl in March 1985 during a lavish ceremony held aboard a yacht moored in New York Harbour. Their daughter, Alexa, was born in 1986.

For the next two years the artist combined his recorded output with touring the world. He enjoyed across-Atlantic hits with singles like 'A Matter Of Trust' and his material was also included in an episode of the *Moonlighting* television series starring Bruce Willis and Cybill Shepherd and the movie *Ruthless People* with a cast headed by Bette Midler. Album-wise, and following the obligatory 'greatest hits' compilation, Joel charted with the studio project titled *The Bridge* and the live set *Kohyept*, taped from a series of concerts in the then-named Leningrad.

Joel enjoyed his third American chart-topper in December 1989. Titled 'We Didn't Start The Fire', the single topped the chart for two weeks and when issued in Britain peaked in the Top 10. It was the artist's love of history and a conversation with a colleage despairing at the world's dilemma that inspired the chart-topper: 'This was '89, before the whole Iron Curtain came down. He was worried about AIDS, pollution, the situation in Red China.' Joel counteracted this inspiration with his knowledge of Dien Bien Phu, the Suez Canal crisis and the Hungarian freedom fighters.

While basking in the glory of another No.1 title, Joel suffered behind the scenes; he underwent an operation for the removal of kidney stones and fired his manager/former brother-in-law Frank Weber, later filing a charge of fraud against him. A New York judge finally awarded Joel $2 million in damages.

Hot on the heels of 'We Didn't Start The Fire', the artist issued his *Stormfront* album, promoted by an across-America tour using the album's name. Into 1990, and inspired by the list of names and events from 1949 included in his 'We Didn't Start The Fire' single, Joel recorded cassettes of the track with a short speech to be included in the *Junior Scholastic* magazine after being informed that fifth-grade students were consulting the single's lyrics during history lessons. The magazine also published the song's lyrics because, Joel explained, 'Some people thought "trouble in the Suez" was "trouble in the sewers".'

Throughout 1990, the artist's American concerts were high-grossing affairs that included a pair in Atlanta earning $800,000 and one in Minneapolis grossing in excess of $1 million. A year on, Joel hit the Australian touring trail, where Sony Music Australia (previously CBS Records) presented him with a crystal award for being the company's top-earning artist. Performing at charity functions also dominated 1991, ranging from a benefit concert to assist Montauk's Indian Field Ranch to supporting an Atlanta radio station threatened with closure. Into 1992, Paul Simon inducted Joel into the New York Songwriters Hall of Fame, while on the recording front Joel enjoyed one hit single, 'All Shook Up', on both sides of the Atlantic before contributing to the *Honeymoon In Vegas* film soundtrack. Once again he was obliged to call upon America's legal system, this time to file a lawsuit against his former lawyers, the Grubman law firm, alleging fraud and malpractice among other breaches.

From 1993 onwards, when Joel wasn't thrashing the legal network he was touring, notably with his 'River Of Dreams' trek, so named after his 1993 album which was an American No.1 title and made the British Top 3. The tour kicked off in Britain at London's Earl's Court on its way into Europe. In the summer of 1994, Joel toured with Elton John through America. On the personal front, meanwhile, Joel and his second wife were divorced during August 1994, the same year as the artist announced his intention to retire from lengthy touring schedules. As the media revelled in the divorce, Joel enjoyed his final British hit, titled 'No Man's Land', in the Top 50.

Now more selective with his public appearances, Billy Joel tends to take a more leisurely approach to his career. His contribution to date has been remarkable, his talent imaginative and popular thanks to his ability to cross from R&B through rock'n'roll into mainstream music. The spotlight won't stay off forever.

'I don't think I'm much of a singer. I always wanted to sing like Ray Charles or Sam Cooke or Wilson Pickett. I am a white kid from Levittown, but I always wanted to do that' – Billy Joel

(Quotes: *Off the Record: An Oral History of Popular Music* by Joe Smith; *The Billboard Book of Number One Hits* by Fred Bronson)

December 1983

FLYING PICKETS

Only You

This was one of those singles you either loved or hated. Whatever the feeling, the title was a chart-topper, earning the Flying Pickets well deserved public recognition which upped their earning power for a while.

With a membership that included Gareth Williams and Rick Lloyd, the Flying Pickets captured the British public's attention – and money – during the unpredictable Christmas period. The single 'Only You' dominated the singles chart in December 1983, its novelty element boosting sales as parties were planned and singalongs encouraged.

Formed during 1980, the Flying Pickets specialised in a cappella delivery which delighted audiences at the Edinburgh Festival in 1982 and a host of nightclub punters who liked that sort of act. The group's popularity eventually came to the attention of executives at 10 Records, who during 1983 issued the British chart-topper solely for the festive market. By the very nature of their act, many predicted the Flying Pickets would be one-hit wonders, but no. The group returned to enjoy a Top 10 hit with 'When You're Young And In Love' during April 1984. The Marvelettes, one-time premier female group with Motown Records, had enjoyed their only British hit with this title in 1967. To close 1984, the Flying Pickets charted for the last time with the Top 8 hit titled 'Who's That Girl?'.

A trio of albums was issued during the group's recording careers, including the 1982 item *Live At The Albany Empire* and *Lost Boys* two years later. But a cappella became passé and the Flying Pickets lost their selling power. However, the group sustained themselves financially by rejoining the nightclub and holiday-camp circuits.

January 1984

PAUL McCARTNEY

Pipes Of Peace

The success of the 1982 duet 'Ebony and Ivory', recorded with Stevie Wonder, Motown's top-selling male soloist, encouraged Paul

McCartney to record with another company-related artist, Michael Jackson. Following lengthy deliberations, the two singers recorded 'The Girl Is Mine', swiped from Jackson's *Thriller* album, which reached the British Top 10 and American Top 2. Then, during November 1983, the second title 'Say Say Say' peaked just one position from the British top, while in America it went all the way, where it stayed for six weeks.

To start 1984, McCartney's 'Pipes Of Peace' became a British chart-topper, his second as a soloist. The title was supported by an expensive, thoughtful video depicting the Christmas Day truce during the First World War. The title track from McCartney's next album, the chart-topper boosted the *Pipes Of Peace* album into the British Top 4 and Top 20 in America, while the follow-up single, 'No More Lonely Nights', soared into the British Top 2. It was the theme from McCartney's debut feature film in which he starred with his wife Linda, Tracey Ullman, Sir Ralph Richardson and Ringo Starr. Titled *Give My Regards To Broad Street*, the film premièred in New York, Los Angeles, London and Liverpool late in 1984. With promotion advertising the $9 million drama/musical fantasy as something it was not, McCartney suffered a box-office bomb. In fact, this return to the film world had surprised many, bearing in mind McCartney's past failure with the Beatles' *Magical Mystery Tour*. The movie's fate shook its creator during a period when Wings had disbanded and when he was mourning John Lennon's death.

The next year was one of mixed emotions. In the July, McCartney was in control as he performed 'Let It Be' during his contribution to the Live Aid charity gala staged at Wembley. Out of his control was his inability to purchase ATV Music, owner of Northern Songs, responsible for 263 Beatles tracks. McCartney was outbid by Michael Jackson, whom he had previously held in high esteem as a friend and artist; McCartney viewed Jackson's move as a betrayal of that position. Jackson reputedly paid $53 million for the music catalogues. Before the Jackson acquisition, the titles had been guarded and permission was rarely granted for commercial use, particularly in television advertisements. Jackson appeared not to share that same respect, another aspect that annoyed McCartney and, needless to say, the remaining Beatles and their stalwart fans, who believed such compositions were sacred. Years on, McCartney tried desperately to buy back the catalogue, but Jackson refused to acknowledge his offers, saying the matter was controlled by his managers.

Through to the '90s, McCartney accepted further industry awards and other honours, including the Special Award of Merit from the American Music Awards board; an honorary doctorate from the University of Sussex; a statuette for his Outstanding Services to

British Music at the Ivor Novello Awards ceremony held in London; and a PRS award for his Unique Achievement in Popular Music. Album-wise, he issued his obligatory 'greatest hits' compilation *All The Best!* and the new *Flowers In The Dirt*, while singles included 'Once Upon A Long Ago', 'This One' and 'Figure Of Eight'. All were charting titles. He also contributed to the chart-topping charity single 'Ferry 'Cross The Mersey' with fellow Liverpudlians the Christians, Holly Johnson and Gerry Marsden. All royalties from the single's sales went to the Hillsborough Disaster Fund.

However, it was McCartney's world tour, his first trek for approximately 13 years, that excited the public the most. The tour started in Sweden during September 1989. It included North America, when during one show Stevie Wonder joined him on stage to sing 'Ebony And Ivory'. His concert in Rio de Janeiro won him an entry in the *Guinness Book of Records* for playing before a staggering 184,000-strong audience, the biggest attendance since 1980 when Frank Sinatra had performed at the same venue. When the trek ended in Chicago, McCartney had performed in 46 cities and presented approximately 100 concerts, several of which had been recorded. The result was the *Tripping The Live Fantastic* album during December 1990, a Top 20 British hit, Top 30 in America. The entire road trip earned the singer a fortune, a proportion of which he donated to charity, including $100,000 to Friends of the Earth.

Into the new decade, McCartney contributed his version of the Presley classic 'It's Now Or Never' to *The Last Temptation Of Elvis* compilation; all proceeds went to Nordoff Robbins Music Therapy. With his own music, he began the '90s with the 'Put It There' single, a falterer in the British Top 40. A year on, he diversified musically when, following a low-key concert at the Mean Fiddler, London, he composed the classical piece 'Liverpool Oratorio', performed by the Royal Liverpool Philharmonic Orchestra at the city's cathedral during June 1991. The work was later premièred in America during the November, under the conductorship of Carl Davis, while a month on the *Paul McCartney's Liverpool Oratorio Conducted by Carl Davis* album was issued.

In 1992, with his home city still foremost in his mind, McCartney donated £500,000 to the Liverpool Institute for the Performing Arts, designed to teach young people to dance. The total sum eventually donated by the singer was said to be twice the original figure and included £110,000 he received from King Carl Gustaf of Sweden during a ceremony staged in Sweden by the Royal Swedish Academy for his imaginative contribution to music during 30 years. Into 1993, the *Off The Ground* album, recorded at his home studio at Rye, East Sussex, where the McCartney family now spent much of their time, was issued. The swiped track 'Hope Of Deliverance' peaked in the British Top 20 during the January, reaching the Top 90 in America. As the album peaked in the British Top 5, the singer embarked upon a further world tour, opening in Perth, Australia. In the April, the show landed at Las Vegas, before spanning America, closing in Detroit, Michigan. During this stint, McCartney contributed to the Earth Day concert staged at the Hollywood Bowl, joining artists like k d lang and Steve Miller. All proceeds went to Greenpeace, PETA (People for the Ethical Treatment of Animals) and Friends of the Earth.

Early in 1994, McCartney inducted the late John Lennon into the Rock'n'Roll Hall of Fame during a ceremony staged at the Waldorf Astoria Hotel, New York. His speech was full of emotion for his lost friend: 'I love him to this day and I always did love him.'

A year on, McCartney shifted musical gear once more when he performed at a charity dinner to benefit the London Royal College of Music. His set included excerpts from his 'Liverpool Oratorio' and the Beatles' 'Lady Madonna', with Brodsky Quartet as support. In the May, he directed *Oobu Joobu*, a 13-part radio series aired in America via Westwood One Radio, which included previously unheard Beatles interviews and recordings. However, behind the scenes for over a year McCartney had been mulling over a television project called *The Beatles Anthology*, covering the life and times of the group. The original plan was for him to collaborate with Ringo Starr and George Harrison to provide incidental music for the proposed series. Once the trio began experimenting in the recording studio, however, the plan changed. McCartney told journalist Nick Bradshaw, 'Even if we hit something really great it would still be George, Ringo and myself, and that's not quite as much fun as if, somehow, John could be in on it.' To this end, he contacted Lennon's widow, Yoko Ono, who played him a tape of demo tracks which included 'Free As A Bird', 'Real Love' and 'Grow Old With Me'. McCartney believed the first title was workable. 'I took the tapes back to England, got copies made for the guys. They liked it, so we decided to do it.' What Lennon would have felt when a demo track that he obviously had considered unsuitable for release was finally issued as a new Beatles track is probably unthinkable. Nonetheless, the pure historical element of 'Free As A Bird' was overwhelming, although it failed to reach the top of the British chart, peaking at No.2. The title 'Real Love' followed.

Meanwhile, Chip Chipperfield had completed the film *The Beatles Anthology*, assisted by a support team of ten and using approximately 10,000 pieces of music and footage. Screened by ITV in Britain, the six-part series began in November 1995, soon followed by the three double-CD packages, housing unreleased tracks, obscure items, rerecordings and narration, as well as videos and sundry publications.

Obviously Beatles hype was at full strength to promote both the singles and the television series. The three remaining group members were at the forefront of the promotional roundabout which the bulk of the British public gratefully digested. The Beatles were back!

While McCartney was publicly turning dreams into reality, behind the scenes his family suffered anguish when Linda was diagnosed with breast cancer during 1995. After an emergency operation following her routine check-up, Linda spent most of the next year undergoing chemotherapy. The diagnosis of his wife's cancer was a poignant and stark reminder for her husband, whose mother had died of cancer during 1956. Linda was treated privately in America with her husband by her side. In 1996, after withdrawing from the public spotlight, she joined McCartney to be filmed at a Los Angeles animal-rights function to accept an award from PETA.

From then on the ex-Beatle's life appeared to be one of husband and father first, with musician and singer a close second. He remained level-headed throughout his career, despite selling 150 million singles during the past 30 years, and, unlike some, has always been seen as approachable by media and public alike. His family are vegetarians – Linda spearheaded her own range of vegetarian dishes with Ross Foods – while their daughters' upbringing did not reflect McCartney's vast wealth. He claimed, 'People find it hard to accept that I am an ordinary bloke because I have a lot of money.' His many tireless contributions to charity were finally recognised in March 1997 when he was knighted by the Queen at Buckingham Palace. He said he accepted the second honour (he had already been awarded the MBE) on behalf of the Beatles and all the people living in Liverpool, while stressing he would remain 'Paul' and not 'Sir Paul McCartney'! Linda was prevented from attending the ceremony but she displayed great courage to attend her daughter Stella's fashion debut in Paris.

Also in 1997, on the recording front, McCartney issued his first collection of new tracks since 1993 under the title *Flaming Pie*. The title 'Young Boy' was the first to be swiped for single release in the May. Naturally, both titles were international sellers.

Lady Linda McCartney lost her battle against cancer, which had spread to her liver, in April 1998. She died with her husband by her side at their Californian home. She was 56 years old. Following her cremation her ashes returned to Britain, where some were scattered on their Peasmarsh farm in East Sussex. In his sad and reluctant press statement, McCartney said, 'Linda was, and still is, the love of my life and the past two years we spent battling her disease have been a nightmare . . . She was the kindest woman I have met, the most innocent.' Apart from being the ex-Beatle's wife and a successful photographer, Lady McCartney will be remembered both for her dedicated and utterly tireless courage in fighting for animal welfare and for her culinary skills with her successful range of vegetarian meals and recipe books.

Six months after his wife's death McCartney issued her CD, titled *Wide Prairie*, from material recorded during her battle against cancer. All profits from the CD were earmarked for Linda's animal charities.

'I don't actually want to be a living legend' – Paul McCartney

Also see: 'Ebony And Ivory' with Stevie Wonder, May 1982

For further information regarding Paul McCartney, please see *Every Chart-Topper Tells a Story: The Sixties*; *Every Chart-Topper Tells a Story: The Seventies*

February 1984

FRANKIE GOES TO HOLLYWOOD

Relax

'I think we quite simply made a classic disco record without being tame' – Holly Johnson

Holly Johnson, born William Johnson in Khartoum, Sudan, on 19 February 1960, excelled at English at school but neglected his academic studies to pursue the fashion world. First he adopted the David Bowie look, followed by a stab at the '40s, before adopting a blond skinhead haircut with his social security number dyed on to the side of his scalp. A mini-Mohican was next. He once said that he was influenced by traditional rock and by the gay culture, hence was into all things decadent.

On the more serious side, Johnson's talent for composing was realised when he was 13 years old and as a performer he drifted through the Big In Japan pre-punk cult group, working with Bill Drummond and Jayne Casey, before embarking upon a solo career to release a pair of singles, 'Yankee Rose' and 'Hobo Joe'. His next move was forming the group Hollycaust.

Mark O'Toole, born in Walton, Liverpool, on 6 January 1964, attended St Matthew's Secondary School but his first love was rock'n'roll. With his cousin, Brian Nash, likewise born in Liverpool on 20 May 1959, they passed through local groups including the Sons Of Egypt, where they befriended Peter Gill, born in Liverpool on 8 March 1964, and, later, Paul Rutherford, born in Liverpool on 8 December 1959.

The five musicians eventually met up and with Johnson's guiding force formed Frankie Goes To Hollywood, a name taken from a newspaper headline announcing the singer Frankie Vaughan's ambition to embark upon an acting career in the heart of movieland.

Among the group's local performances was a successful concert at 'Larks In The Park', an open-air jamboree in Liverpool's Sefton Park. However, Johnson felt that if the group stood a chance in the music industry, it needed to make an impact – 'So we lived out our fantasy, that's the Frankie Goes To Hollywood thing. We had the Leatherpets [two girls dressed, or at least very nearly dressed, in leather] writhing about in a cage, and the rest of the boys were given strap and bondage in leather knickers and half T-shirts.' As lead vocalist, Johnson wore leather chaps and G-string with his bum naked, one cheek painted blue, the other pink.

It was not surprising, then, when Frankie Goes To Hollywood's popularity spread through the cities to London, and when the capital's music papers began printing their obvious 'raunchy' photographs, the media could resist them no longer. The group were invited to perform on Channel 4's *The Tube*, where their act marked the first of the group's national scandals. The outcry might have been instigated by the members' codpieces or by the Leatherpets, dressed in little but a smile, being tied up and dancing erotically to a disco beat. Whatever caused the rumpus, Frankie Goes To Hollywood secured a recording deal with ZTT (Zang Tumb Tumm), an Island Records subsidiary and brainchild of producer Trevor Horn and Paul Morley, ex-music journalist with a talent for imaginative marketing campaigns.

In November 1983 Frankie Goes To Hollywood issued their debut single titled 'Relax' and once again walked headlong into controversy. To accompany the release, the group's video, directed by Bernard Rose, was a mock Roman orgy, with transvestites in cages and men clothed in leather, and was, many thought, a slice of Fellini fantasy. Naturally, the filmed excitement was instantly banned, whereupon a second, tamer version was shot. Early in 1984, BBC Radio One banned the 'Relax' single, spurred on by its DJ Mike Read's condemnation of the lyrics. Ironically, by this time 'Relax' had been aired at least 90 times and the group had appeared on BBC TV's *Top of the Pops*! Among his comments, Read said, 'From the outset the band were very open about what they were and the simulated sex scenes on their video made it clear that "Relax" was about gay sex.' Radio One's controller, Derek Chinnery, said he had no choice but to ban the track, particularly when 'the group seemed to confirm it as referring to fellatio and ejaculation'.

In the end, no airtime was afforded the single; the public had no means of 'officially' hearing what had caused the banishment to the BBC vaults. Realistically, though, the banning by Auntie Beeb led to an increase in sales, as 'Relax' steadily climbed the British chart and reached the top during February 1984, a position it clung to for a remarkable five weeks, selling in excess of one million copies. The position also earned Frankie Goes To Hollywood the distinction of being the first band to reach No.1 with a banned single since the Sex Pistols' 'God Save The Queen'. Now the BBC had a chart-topper which couldn't be promoted on *Top of the Pops*!

To be frank, 'Relax' was a masterpiece of its kind, certainly a hallmark in dance music of the '80s with its thunderous, driving beat that linked mainstream pop with gay disco. The grooves burst alive with music; it was compulsive listening at its very best. However, alongside the group's later explanation of its lyrics, what had provoked instant outrage was the word 'come'. According to Johnson, 'As far as I'm concerned . . . "come" wasn't only meant in a sexual sense. It's a philosophy for the whole of life, but that's what people clicked on to immediately . . . It was controversial, outrageous and dealt with sex . . . We'd like to think "Relax" was subversive in its own way, but not in a blatant way. I wouldn't like to think we shoved it down anybody's throats.'

Frankie Goes To Hollywood were naturally splashed across newspapers, magazines and the like as they conducted their interviews in gay bars irrespective of the journalists' preferences. Needless to say, 'Relax' attracted a fair number of awards, including a Brit Award for Best British Single, while the band won Best British Newcomer and Trevor Horn scooped the Best Producer award in 1985.

There was more excitement to come. Oh dear.

'Because it was our first single and there's no ready market, we just had to have as much fun as we could when we were making it. We just thought "buzz" and then we'll know when it's right' – Johnson

Also see: 'Two Tribes', July/August 1984

(Quotes: *Frankie Goes To Hollywood* by Dean Anthony)

March/April 1984

LIONEL RICHIE

Hello

'Fame is hard to deal with; I confess it is like a double-edged sword most of the time' – Lionel Richie

When Lionel Richie left the Commodores, his career escalated so quickly that many wondered where it would end. No challenge was too great: his composing pen broadened as his music expanded, and, of course, his record sales were staggering. One could be forgiven for thinking the Commodores had done a good job in suppressing this talent that begged to be freed!

While still in the group, Richie, born on 20 June 1949 in Tuskegee, had flexed his solo muscle. In 1980 his first composition not to be recorded by the Commodores, titled 'Lady', gave country and western star Kenny Rogers an American chart-topper for six weeks from November 1980. The collaboration began with Rogers approaching Richie's publishing house for material to record. The two artists met in Las Vegas, whereupon Richie played two tracks – 'Lady' and 'Goin' Back To Alabama' – to Rogers. Rogers recorded both titles during the same night session. 'Lady' went on to sell in excess of 16 million copies, earning Richie $1 million and a share in a cosmetics range bearing the single's name.

Within a year Richie was once again top of the American chart, this time with fellow Motown artist Diana Ross. The duet was 'Endless Love', the title track from the Franco Zeffirelli movie of the same name starring Brooke Shields. 'Endless Love' was an American chart-topper for a staggering nine weeks from August 1981 and a British Top 10 hit during the September. According to Richie, 'Polygram called me and asked did I have a song for their new movie. I didn't have. I really didn't want anything else to do at that time. Then Polygram said all they wanted was an instrumental, and that I could do it on a weekend. Next thing I know, Polygram want lyrics and wanted me to sing them. So I agreed. It was still only a weekend thing. Then I'm told Polygram have got Diana Ross to sing it with me. Now I had a problem! It was turning into a bigger project by the minute, but it turned out to be a wonderful weekend. Diana was in Atlantic City and I was in New York, and neither of us had the time to visit each other. So we met in Nevada.' The couple recorded the track overnight, then returned to their respective states. 'Endless Love' went on to win an Oscar nomination, an American movie award, two American Music Awards and countless other honours.

Richie could not write a bum note at this time and by the close of 1981 he was represented in the American Top 100 with six singles, namely 'Endless Love', the Commodores' 'Oh No' (which he wrote and co-produced) and 'Lady (You Bring Me Up)' (a co-production), Kenny Rogers' 'I Don't Need You' and follow-up 'Share Your Love', and the title 'Still', rerecorded by John Schneider. It was a remarkable feat.

During June 1981 the Commodores released their *In The Pocket* album, which coincided with Richie hiring a public-relations company to handle his image, once more fuelling rumours of his imminent departure from the group. Richie believed the new album afforded Commodores member Clyde Orange the opportunity to express his talent. 'Before the Commodores made it in terms of records, Clyde was the lead vocalist. I was the horn holder and the shoop-shoop guy. For the past few years because I wrote the songs I came to the front as being the lead singer. On this album he's coming to light as the great performer he is.' However, as cynics correctly guessed, Richie was ensuring that when he left the group, it would safely survive without him as lead singer.

With the release of his first solo single, 'Truly', and his eponymous album in September 1982, which later passed platinum status, earning it the distinction of becoming the first album from a black act to pass the one million sales figure in 1982, Richie publicly confirmed his intention to concentrate on a solo career. With the Commodores' hit records on the sharp decline, he was naturally criticised for not recording those tracks planned for his debut solo album with the group. Richie retaliated to such criticism by saying, 'If I was lucky I got two of my compositions on each album. There's six guys with a song each, so there wasn't too much room for me anymore. I was never the writer for the Commodores, it was just that some of my songs became singles and were hits, and everyone assumed the role was mine. A lot of the Commodores' non-success is due to lack of communication and co-ordination.' Despite his feelings, the singer admitted that he had never intended to leave the group, but 'it was stifling . . . I'd been a member of that group, for 15 years or so, and to leave wasn't the easiest of things for me to do, but we knew it wasn't going to work, particularly when the friction started.'

During February 1983, while Marshall Arts promoted a pair of British concerts by the Commodores, minus Richie, at London's Hammersmith Odeon, and while Motown Records released their single titled 'Reach High', lifted from the group's *All The Great Hits* compilation, Richie enjoyed a Top 50 hit with 'You Are', the follow-up single and diluted clone to 'Truly'. The title enjoyed higher sales in America, peaking in the Top 4. During the May his third solo outing, 'My Love', again oh so reminiscent of the Commodores' ballads, soared into the American Top 3 but struggled into the British Top 70.

Four months after his contribution of 'You Mean More To Me' to Motown's 25th anniversary gala celebrations, Richie embarked upon his first solo world tour, spanning 48 concerts in America and introducing to his audiences his next single, 'All Night Long (All

Night)', from the pending *Can't Slow Down* album. His support act was the Pointer Sisters, while his backing musicians carried heavy credentials – Greg Phillinganes, Henry Davis, Carlos Rios and percussionist Sheila Escavedo, among others. Richie said at the time, 'All the musicians are so good to work with. When we all go out on stage, we're all glad to be there and we all enjoy it so much. It's not working, it's a real pleasure.' During his performance, among his and the Commodores' material, Richie sang 'Endless Love', accompanied not by Diana Ross but a life-sized laser projection of her!

In November 1983, the calypso-tinged Jamaican-vocalled 'All Night Long (All Night)' stormed to the top of the American chart, where it stayed for four weeks, peaking at No.2 in Britain. It outsold 'Endless Love' to earn the distinction of becoming Motown Records' biggest single seller. Said Richie, 'It's one thing to have a hit in the US and Britain, but for the record to take off all over the world, well, that's something very hard to believe.' Record buffs noticed an unusual credit on the record's label: that of Dr Lloyd Byron Greig, dialect coach. He was not a church minister or a man of research, rather a gynaecologist! According to Richie, 'He would come by and visit us and I started listening to his accent. We got talking a lot and when I was in the studio working on the single, I kept phoning him up, saying "talk to me". I wanted to do something different with this single, and when I found myself saying some of his phrases, I knew I wanted to use his accent on the record.'

Before 1983 ended, the *Can't Slow Down* album shot to the American top spot for a three-week stay, going on to sell in excess of eight million copies during its chart stay of three years. The album likewise topped the British chart before world sales topped the 15 million sales figure. *Can't Slow Down* won the Album of the Year Grammy Award in 1985, while Richie and his co-producers collected the Producer of the Year honour. The album went on to spawn five consecutive hits, consolidating the singer's place in mainstream music history.

Into 1984, the title 'Running With The Night' peaked in the Top 10 singles charts on both sides of the Atlantic during January, while four months on Richie signed an $8.5 million deal with Pepsi Cola which included sponsorship of two tours, spanning a two-year period, while the singer promoted the drink via television advertising. It was described as the largest and most comprehensive agreement between a corporation and a performer, and followed hot on the heels of a similar one the drinks company had secured with the Jacksons worth $5.5 million. Not to be outdone, Pepsi's biggest competitor Coca-Cola announced a three-year $7 million contract with Spanish heart-throb Julio Iglesias.

As the tour began, with Tina Turner his support act, Richie's next single, lifted from *Can't Slow Down*, topped the American chart. Titled 'Hello', the ballad also became a British chart-topper in April 1984, a position it dominated for a remarkable six weeks, selling in excess of 800,000 copies. To be honest, 'Hello' was dated when released because it had been earmarked for Richie's first album two years previously. For some reason the track had been rejected, despite heavy objections from Richie's wife Brenda. And when it was considered for inclusion on *Can't Slow Down*, it had once again been given the thumbs-down until Brenda took the case on and won.

The 'Hello' video caused a public stir in 1984. Richie played a drama teacher, coaching a class of students in scenes which could well have been swiped from *Fame*, and he fell in love with one student. The Bob Giraldi-directed video showed Richie 'haunting' her, which, some felt, could be interpreted as a trailer for a John Carpenter horror movie, until the close of the video, when he discovered the student was blind and had sculptured a bust of his likeness. Fine – nothing too sinister here. But, as *Melody Maker*'s Dessa Fox wrote, blind people would be deeply offended at the way they were visually portrayed. 'The leading lady has been given a white stick, told to flutter her eyes, look "enigmatic" and in general behave like a sugar-fed Bambi. What she is not doing is acting human like the rest of us. The sleaziest section of "Hello" comes at the end of the bed sequence. The telephone rings and – in an insult to blind people everywhere, who know exactly where familiar noise sources are – this "actress" attempts to squeeze tears from us sentimental record-buyers by groping for the telephone.'

When the single topped the American chart, 1984 became the seventh consecutive year that one of Richie's compositions occupied the position. However, on the downside, as the single peaked, an allegation of plagiarism was made by a New York housekeeper, Marjorie White, who claimed she'd written the song under its original title 'I'm Not Ready To Go'. She lost the claim.

This year was certainly a milestone for the ex-Commodore. In the January he had hosted the 11th American Music Awards ceremony, where he also received the Favourite Soul Single Award for 'All Night Long (All Night)'. His smooth co-ordination throughout the ceremony was an integral part of the show's success, prompting Dick Clark, executive producer of the ABC TV annual broadcast, to ask Richie if he would host the next ceremony in 1985. When the singer agreed, he became the first to fulfil this role two years running.

Also in 1984, Richie was asked by David Wolper, producer of the Los Angeles Olympic Games, to perform the final song at the closing ceremony. Selecting 'All Night Long (All Night)', with additional lyrics suitable for the spectacular occasion, the singer and 200 dancers attracted 2.6 billion television viewers! On the singles front, he also enjoyed a Top 10 American and Top 20 British hit with 'Penny Lover', while Diana Ross hit the American Top 10 with the Richie composition 'Missing You', a tribute to their late friend and fellow artist Marvin Gaye.

To start 1985, Richie's manager Ken Kragen and producer Quincy Jones persuaded the singer to co-compose a track with Michael Jackson to raise funds for the starving African population, reserving a percentage to help the needy and starving in America. An all-star contribution resulted in the 'We Are The World' single, which became an international chart-topper. Midway through 1985, Richie joined a host of American stars at the JFK Stadium in Philadelphia to stage the sister concert to the London leg of the Live Aid project held at Wembley Stadium. To close the year, the title 'Say You, Say Me' soared into the Top 10 in Britain. The track, an Oscar winner from the movie *White Nights* which Richie composed to reflect the interaction between actors Mikhail Barishnakov and Gregory Hines, also became his fourth solo American No.1. With 'Say You, Say Me' dominating the top spot, the singer earned the distinction of being the only composer in music history to achieve nine American chart-toppers in nine consecutive years. The magic that was Richie's showed no signs of faltering.

During August 1986 Richie released his *Dancing On The Ceiling* album; it was an American No.1 and a British No.2. The album's title track had already been swiped as a single, reaching No.2 in America, No.7 in Britain. Said Richie, 'The album has been over one year and four months in the making and there were times when I was actually in doubt that we were going to make it.' As the album's title was odd, he explained his inspiration. 'I was driving at 3 a.m. down Sunset and pulled up after hearing a load of noise coming from people outside a club. Sitting in the car listening to them, I heard a voice say, "What's been going on in there?" The reply was, "Man, we've just been dancing on the ceiling." I wrote the title down with a thank you very much and drove home. The excitement that could be generated with that one line was incredible.' The single's sales were obviously boosted by what the singer described as an outrageous few visual minutes, where viewers saw him dancing up, down and around. 'I worked with Stanley Donen to help me pull it off. It took ten days of rehearsing to get it done properly. But how we danced on the walls and ceilings will remain a secret. All I will say is it was magical.' The video, not surprisingly, went on to win numerous awards, including one for platinum sales across America.

Following, or even matching, such a wild, energetic sound was impossible, so Richie didn't try. Two further titles were lifted from the *Dancing On The Ceiling* album, namely 'Love Will Conquer All' and 'Ballerina Girl', the album's obligatory ballad.

Early in 1987, when the artist had won a further handful of American Music Awards including Favourite Male Artist, Soul/R&B, during a ceremony staged at the Shrine Auditorium, and following a lengthy sell-out American tour, Richie at long last embarked upon his debut solo British trek. 'I want to crank up the show in Birmingham so that by the time we get to London it will be ready.' The standing-room-only Wembley Arena performances during May were electrifying. Using state-of-the-art stage props, Richie captivated his British following during a series of shows that saw his musicians being hoisted in a most ungainly fashion up to the theatre ceiling by wires, where they moved like marionettes during 'Dancing On The Ceiling'. Originally, Richie had intended to join them dangling in the air, but his insurance company forbade him even to think about it!

Before 1987 ended, 'Sela' was the last track to be extracted from the *Dancing On The Ceiling* album. Surprisingly, the title faltered around the American Top 20 and British Top 50. The album was exhausted; so too was the singer.

Having always been ready to praise his wife Brenda for her devotion and support, Richie stunned his public when the media told of his reputed affair with model Diane Alexander. Printing that Brenda had discovered the couple together at the model's apartment, whereupon her ensuing actions led to her being arrested on counts of disturbing the peace, battery, injury to a spouse and resisting arrest, the tabloid press had a field day. Richie and Brenda separated a year later, following 17 years of marriage, before eventually divorcing. He told journalist Sue Russell, 'I was very close to Diane and I found myself coming back and forth into this wonderful relationship. What I liked most was she wanted nothing to do with showbusiness.' The actual divorce frightened him beyond his expectations, particularly as his public had seen it as the perfect marriage – 'I just didn't have any idea the loss was going to come in my house. It was something I had to deal with and it was the best and worst of times.'

Two years into the new decade, Richie returned to the British singles chart with 'Do It To Me'. A struggler in the Top 40, the title fared better in America by peaking at No.21 in the June. His five-year hiatus from recording had naturally prompted his critics to gloat that he was dried up, his talent extinguished. Richie fought back. 'I heard it all. People saying I was afraid to put out a new record and so on. I just thought about all the things I've heard over the years. People saying "You'll never be able to top that" or "You've peaked". I've stopped letting all of that stuff bother me; you can't fear failure in this business, you must risk and constantly challenge yourself. And take it one song at a time . . . I've got a lot of catching up to do.'

While the hatchet job continued, the truth behind the singer's first lengthy break since 1973 was more serious, as he later explained. 'I had been working for 15 years straight and I realised I had missed 12 family reunions in a row. I had to slow down . . . and these past few years have been very important in terms of personal growth. I experienced a lot. My father died a couple of years ago and he was like a rock for me. My marriage ended and although we've survived as friends, the pressure of public life definitely took its toll. And lastly I went through a major problem with my throat that posed a threat to my ability to sing. I learned that I'm definitely very human.' In actual fact, Richie had suffered polyps on his vocal chords and haemorrhaging from his left vocal chord, necessitating surgery.

The single 'Do It To Me' had been the first title swiped from the *Back To Front* album, a collection of the smoothest greatest hits from the Commodores and solo Richie, together with a trio of new Richie tracks. The compilation entered the British chart at No.1 where it stayed for six weeks; it made the Top 20 in America. The remaining pair of new tracks, 'My Destiny' and 'Love Oh Love', were likewise issued as singles and became hits on both sides of the Atlantic during 1992. These tracks, incidentally, also represented Richie's final recordings for Motown Records, where he had started his fruitful career as a member of the Commodores and later worked as a soloist. In August he switched to Mercury Records for a reputed $30 million cheque which would span five albums. On the personal front, the singer's partner, Diane Alexander, gave birth to their son Miles during May 1994 and in 1997 the couple married at the Metropolitan Club in New York, with a small group of friends attending.

Musically speaking, the result from his unexpected move to Mercury Records was eagerly awaited. It took until 1996 for the *Louder Than Words* debut album to be issued, his first for approximately ten years. The title 'Don't Wanna Lose You', a typical Richie composition, was lifted as the first single and reached the British Top 20 and American Top 50 in April 1996. To promote both releases, the singer visited Britain for a short promotional trek that included meeting the press and doing various television spots, including one on the *Des O'Connor Show*. Next he moved into the movie world, joining Whitney Houston and Denzel Washington in the big-grossing film *The Preacher's Wife*. Initially Richie was apprehensive at joining the cast, but once he had acclimatised himself to the new situation, he claimed he enjoyed the experience.

Six years after the release of the compilation *Back To Front*, Richie's previous record company Motown issued the *Truly: The Love Songs* CD containing more or less identical tracks. Now managed by Elton John's manager John Reid, the singer promoted the CD by visiting Britain; it went on to pass gold status.

As the compilation proved that Richie's buying public had remained loyal through the lean times, his record company expected little trouble in selling his second studio CD issued during July 1998. Titled *Time*, the bulk of the project was produced by the artist and James Anthony Carmichael, who had, of course, steered the Commodores through their finest hours. Extracted as the first single, 'Closest Thing To Heaven' was promoted in Britain by the singer, notably with a long-overdue appearance on *Top of the Pops*. By Richie's standards, both single and CD sold badly. However, this hiccup didn't prevent plans for his 1998 British concert dates from going ahead.

In view of his track record, it goes without saying that Lionel Richie will return to those heady heights once more. All he needs is another 'Hello'. Not too much to ask, is it?

'You spend your whole life saying "I want to be famous" and then one day somebody hands it to you . . . It's like being put in a little capsule that isolates you from being a normal human being. So you have to struggle to get back to real human life' – Lionel Richie

(Quotes: *Blues and Soul*, 1986, 1987, interviews by Sharon Davis; *Hello!* magazine, 1997, interview by Sue Russell)

May 1984

DURAN DURAN

The Reflex

With one British chart-topper to their credit ('Is There Something I Should Know?' in April 1983), Duran Duran embarked upon a further world tour, covering Australia, America and, of course, Britain. A handful of concerts were filmed and recorded for the future album titled *Arena* destined for release late in 1984; it was a Top 10 entrant on both sides of the Atlantic. The album's release coincided with the television documentary *Sing Blue Silver* which included footage shot on and off stage.

In the group's absence, 'The Union Of The Snake' was issued as a single and shot into the British and American charts during November 1983. The title was extracted from their album *Seven And The Ragged Tiger* scheduled for release a month later; it would top the British listing and peak in the American Top 10. Nick Rhodes told the *Los Angeles Times*, 'No one was delighted with [the album]. There was a lot of tension in the studio. It was obvious that we were either going to take a break from Duran or make a dreadful album.' It couldn't have been that dreadful!

Duran Duran's first single of 1984 was likewise lifted from *Seven And The Ragged Tiger*. Titled 'New Moon On Monday', it peaked in the British and American Top 10. The follow-up was also originally recorded as an album track, but following a remix by Chic's mentor Nile Rodgers, the group decided it was ideal for single release. Titled 'The Reflex' and written by Duran Duran, the result shot to the top of the British chart during May 1984, where it stayed for four weeks. When released in America a month later, 'The Reflex' also topped the chart there for two weeks, whereupon the success spread across Europe, the single selling in excess of one million copies on the way. Among the honours attracted by the single was the Ivor Novello Award in 1985 for the International Hit of the Year.

As the group's career peaked, so did its members' personal lives. Two married, namely Roger Taylor to Giovanna Cantonne and Nick Rhodes to Julie Anne Friedman, with whom he had a daughter. The marriage limped on until 1992 when the couple agreed to an official separation. Simon Le Bon would marry Yasmin Parvanah at the close of 1985.

The further Nile Rodgers production 'Wild Boys' was issued as the follow-up single to 'The Reflex'. Unable to secure the top spot again, the title settled at No.2 in the British and American charts during November 1984. At this point, the group opted to step back from the spotlight to enable John Taylor and Andy Taylor to expand themselves musically to work with Bernard Edwards and Robert Palmer in New York. The short-lived studio group, known as Power Station, issued the single 'Some Like It Hot' during 1985 on EMI Records' Parlophone label. The title peaked in the British Top 20 and American Top 10, paving the way for the *Power Station* album, itself a No.12 British hit. The group's second charter, 'Get It On', a cover version of T Rex's 1972 hit, reached the British Top 30, while their single 'Communication' was issued late in 1985 but sold badly on both sides of the Atlantic. In 1996, via Chrysalis Records, Power Station issued their final British chart entrant titled 'She Can Rock It'; it peaked in the Top 70.

During this time, the remaining trio of Durans formed the group Arcadia and recorded the *So Red The Rose* album for the Odeon label.

The title 'Election Day' was swiped for single release, reaching both the British and the American Top 10 in 1985. The mother album, however, slumped in the Top 40. Two further singles were issued in 1986, namely 'The Promise' and 'The Flame'; both were poor sellers.

As a reunited group, Duran Duran performed at the Live Aid benefit gala staged in Philadelphia, following their participation in the all-star recording of 'Do They Know It's Christmas?', released under the name Band Aid. The New Romantic group then joined forces with James Bond to compose the movie theme to Roger Moore's final appearance as 007 in *A View To A Kill*. At the time the biggest-grossing Bond themes were Carly Simon's 'Nobody Does It Better' from *The Spy Who Loved Me*, and Paul McCartney's 'Live And Let Die', although Gladys Knight's 'Licence To Kill' and Tina Turner's 'Goldeneye' must surely rank alongside these big sellers. However, 'A View To A Kill' soared to No.2 in Britain in May 1985, and when issued in America two months on, the title became the group's second chart-topper, a position it dominated for two weeks, earning the distinction of becoming the first James Bond theme to become a No.1 seller. The single also marked the disintegration of Duran Duran. Said Rhodes, 'Around the time we did the single we . . . had musical differences. John and Andy wanted to do heavier rock. That's why they did Power Station. Simon and I wanted to do something more experimental and abstract.'

Despite the individual activities of 1986, Duran Duran survived, although the membership was reduced to a trio. First single out was the disbanded Arcadia's 'The Promise', followed by the American Top 40 release 'Goodbye Is Forever'. John Taylor's solo outing was next in the April, the theme from the *9½ Weeks* movie titled 'I Do What I Do'; it was a Top 50 British hit, Top 30 in America. Meanwhile, Roger Taylor retired from the music business for health reasons. Originally he intended simply to take a year's leave of absence, but he never returned. In June 1986 Andy Taylor was the second Duran to depart; he wanted to pursue a solo career in America and would sign a recording contract with MCA Records before relocating to Los Angeles. Taylor's debut single 'When The Rain Comes Down' coincided with Duran Duran's 'Notorious' single, the title track from their new album. The group's release peaked in the British Top 10 in 1986. The album would be issued before the year closed, reaching the British Top 20. The trio was supplemented in the studio by session musicians and singers in order to maintain the Duran Duran sound. When issued in America, the 'Notorious' single soared into the Top 2, while the album settled in the Top 20.

Into the new decade, Duran Duran toured the world and sustained their chart popularity as a bankable act. However, sales from recorded work were not guaranteed; public taste was changing, and Duran Duran were obliged to follow. Singles of note were 'I Don't Want Your Love' in 1988 and 'All She Wants Is' a year on, when they also recorded 'Do You Believe In Shame?', lifted from the *Big Thing* album and included in the *Tequila Sunrise* movie.

The *Decade* compilation marked the start of the '90s, while Duran Duran's studio album *Liberty* closed 1990. In between this pair, the group issued two singles, 'Violence Of Summer (Love's Taking Over)' and 'Serious'; both struggled for life. Throughout the next two years Duran Duran's profile was unhealthily low, although their name regularly appeared in the tabloid press, usually in connection with non-musical items such as Le Bon's involvement in a motorcycle accident, his cheating death when his ship *Drum* capsized off the Cornish coast in stormy seas during the Fastnet Race, or his attending a fashion show or film première with his international-model wife.

It took until 1993 but Duran Duran returned to the British Top 5 and American Top 3 with the single 'Ordinary World'. The group appeared to be in vogue once more, but this time they knew just how quickly they could fall. Flushed with success, the group issued *Duran Duran (The Wedding Album)*, a Top 10 British and American entrant. Not only did they re-establish themselves recording-wise, they also did so as performers, embarking upon a world tour that included countries like South Africa, America (where they received a star on the Walk of Fame in Hollywood) and, naturally, Britain. While on the road, two singles sustained British presence, namely 'Come Undone' and 'Too Much Information', Top 20 and Top 40 hits respectively.

Duran Duran enjoyed two further British hits in 1985, 'Perfect Day' and 'White Lines (Don't Do It)', plus one album, titled *Thank You*.

Not many groups outlive a particular music trend, but Duran Duran did. A forerunner in the New Romantic movement, the group lived longer than the trend they helped create and popularise. Now a new generation can appreciate the group first hand. Duran Duran returned to the British touring trail to perform at venues in Birmingham, Sheffield, Manchester and London on their 'Greatest and Latest: The Greatest Hits Tour' during December 1998.

Also see: 'Is There Something I Should Know?', April 1983

June 1984

WHAM!

Wake Me Up Before You Go Go

'We've become firmly established now, and even though I say it myself, I do feel we're one of the best bands in the country' – Andrew Ridgeley

George Michael was born Georgios Kyriacou Panayiotou on 25 June 1963 in Finchley, London. His father Jack had left Cyprus during the '50s with his best friend Jimmy Georgiou to find work as waiters in a London restaurant. When they met their future wives, the friends split to pursue separate ambitions; nonetheless, their friendship remained intact. In time Jack, his wife and family relocated to Hertfordshire, where Michael began his secondary-school education at Bushey Mead.

Andrew Ridgeley, born on 26 January 1963 in Windlesham, Surrey, likewise attended the Bushey Mead comprehensive school, where in 1975 he met George Michael. According to Michael, 'From the moment we met we really hit it off and all we seemed to talk about was music.' The youngsters were inseparable; socially they danced the nights away in Watford nightspots, where they later befriended Shirlie Holliman, who would play an integral role in the future Wham! membership.

With their education behind them, the friends decided music was their consuming ambition, despite having unsuccessfully formed a group called the Executive in 1979 with Ridgeley's brother in the line-up. Michael said, 'The only thing we had to go on was the records we'd been collecting for years.' They also had no equipment of their own to practise with, and relied on friends' generosity. According to Michael, 'Most of the day was spent writing and trying our own compositions. We knew that if we were to stand any chance of landing a contract with one of the major companies then it would have to be on demos of our own compositions and not cover versions.'

Although Ridgeley was unemployed, Michael worked through a series of jobs mainly in London's nightclubs like Soho's Le Beat Route, where, of course, he was inspired by the electric atmosphere and frenetic disco sounds that hypnotised dancers on the floor.

Early in 1982 the couple recorded a handful of self-composed tracks including 'Wham Rap', 'Club Tropicana' and 'Careless

Whisper' in Ridgeley's parents' home. Record companies failed to share the youngsters' naïve enthusiasm. All wasn't lost, however; the boys, now using the name Wham!, met Mark Dean, who had recently opened the Innervision label specialising in dance music. When negotiations were settled, Wham! signed to the label, although they would rue the day. The contract was hastily drawn up and according to *Bare*, written by Michael and Tony Parsons, was 'tighter than a lobster's ass at 50 fathoms'. For a £500 advance each, to be paid back out of future royalties, the boys from Wham! signed a five-year contract with Innervision. Wham!'s royalty rates were 8 per cent for albums and singles in Britain, 6 per cent elsewhere, while 12-inch singles earned the singers nothing at all. It was a severe oversight, as '70s' sales of disco-mixed 12-inch formats usually meant 5,000 immediate sales, which could chart a title in the British top 75. The Innervision contract also tied the couple to unworkable deadlines which years later proved the label owned Wham! inside and out, due probably to the tight deal between Dean and CBS Records, who, after all, had invested a vast amount of money in the independent company. Once the recording side had been secured, Ridgeley and Michael signed a publishing deal with the Morrison/Leahy Music Group, an operation owned by Dick Leahy, late owner of GTO Records, and Bryan Morrison, ex-manager of the Pretty Things.

In April 1982 Wham! issued their debut single, 'Wham Rap (Enjoy What You Do)'. They recruited Shirlie and Mandy Washburn to dance with them through personal appearances and the audiences loved the fresh new sound – but, regrettably, not sufficiently for the single to chart. Nonetheless, the track and the couple's promotion laid invaluable groundwork for the next single, titled 'Young Guns (Go For It)', which presented Wham! with their first hit, reaching the Top 3 during October 1982. The song just couldn't fail; like its predecessor, 'Young Guns (Go For It)' was crammed with a vital commercial sound mingled with a driving dance backbeat. It was totally compulsive. On stage, Ridgeley and Michael danced and pranced, their love of body movement captivating the fawning youngsters. According to Michael, 'We decided to elaborate on the original kind of routines that we used in the clubs . . . it was always the thing to try and develop your own style so that you'd be a bit different from everyone else.'

To cash in on the Top 3 success, 'Wham Rap (Enjoy What You Do)' was reissued early in 1983 and reached the British Top 10, while in the May Michael's first solo composition, titled 'Bad Boys', was issued. The title danced its way to No.2 and featured Washburn's replacement Dee C Lee and Deon Estus among the session musicians. (Estus went on to work with Marvin Gaye before recording as a soloist.) Hot on the heels of the hard-hitting 'Bad Boys', Wham! unleashed their debut album, titled *Fantastic*, which entered the British chart at the top in the July. To coincide with this achievement, a fourth track was swiped for single release. Titled 'Club Tropicana', it shot into the Top 4, prompting the announcement of the duo's long-expected first British tour. While Ridgeley and Michael basked in public acclaim, behind the scenes something stirred. Unhappy with Innervision, Michael hired manager Simon Napier-Bell to oversee Wham!'s business affairs. This enabled the singer to concentrate on the duo's music and his partner to assume responsibility for their image on stage and video.

Sponsored by Filo sportswear, Wham! hit the road. According to Michael, 'We wanted to put together a show that fans would really remember. We didn't want to just go out on stage and leap about to the music, but put together a good piece of theatre too.' Every move was precision-planned, from the music and the matching choreography through to the costumes and support musicians. Both Shirlie and Dee C Lee contributed to the vocal and visual elements of the shows, which predictably played before packed venues of hysterical, uncontrollable fans. Wham! had definitely arrived.

As an aside, prior to the debut tour, Michael had recorded a solo version of 'Careless Whisper' at the Muscle Shoals Studios, Atlanta, under the supervision of Jerry Wexler, who was responsible for the world's greatest soul innovators like Aretha Franklin. Remarkably, Michael was dissatisfied with the result and reworked 'Careless Whisper' in London.

Back to Wham!, and before 1983 closed, Dee C Lee left the group to join Paul Weller's Style Council; Pepsi filled the vacancy. Backstage, tempers rose. Wham! demanded they be released from their Innervision contract and to this end began legal action against the label. In retaliation, Innervision issued the 12-inch single 'Club Fantastic Megamix', which soared into the Top 20. Naturally, Wham! condemned the release.

Following a tour in Japan early in 1984, the couple, finally free from Innervision, signed a recording contract proper with CBS Records. Their debut single under the new, lucrative deal was 'Wake Me Up Before You Go Go', composed by Michael, who also produced it. The song's title was inspired by a scribbled note left for him by Ridgeley. 'Wake Me Up Before You Go Go' shot to the top of the British chart during June 1984; the title also topped nine European charts. When issued in America in the November, Wham! enjoyed their first American chart-topper.

The single's accompanying video was filmed at the Brixton Academy crammed with fans. George now says he believed the single was 'undoubtedly the most remembered of Wham! songs because it is that much more stupid than anything else'. He also admits that 'I was completely into the idea of being screamed at. I was very young and I can't pretend my ego didn't need that.'

His ego was fuelled further as the years passed, both as a member of Wham! and as a soloist. Wham! were rightly hailed as the pop sensation of the '80s – they were young, nice to look at and ultra-fashionable, while their music reflected that relentless beat that made dancing a priority. However, like most success stories, Ridgeley and Michael would attract more than their fair share of adverse publicity.

Also see: 'I'm Your Man', November 1985; 'The Edge Of Heaven', June 1986

(Quotes: *Wham! Special 1985* by John Kercher; *Bare* by George Michael and Tony Parsons)

July/August 1984

FRANKIE GOES TO HOLLYWOOD

Two Tribes

With slogans reading 'Frankie Goes To Hollywood didn't just come, they exploded' and 'Their music assault on popdom has changed the rules', the group were the talk of Britain. The talk wasn't all good, though!

While the furore over 'Relax' lived on, Frankie Goes To Hollywood issued their second single titled 'Two Tribes', again produced by Trevor Horn and again a pot pourri of controversy. Although sex remained on the back boiler this time, the group instead dealt with the evils of nuclear war over a sharp, dramatic dance beat not too dissimilar to the '70s' disco style. To be honest, it was a magnificent slice of music! 'Two Tribes' entered the British chart at the top during July 1984, where it stayed for a staggering nine weeks. Its remarkable sales pattern resulted in the single passing silver status within two days and gold within a week until it reached platinum level, earning the group the distinction of enjoying platinum singles with their first two releases. Now that's selling power – yet still people scoffed.

Once again 'Two Tribes' was promoted by a startling video, this time directed by Godley and Creme. The theme was a gladiatorial fight between the Soviet leader Chernenko and America's finest,

President Reagan. Said Rutherford, 'It's about any confrontation. To give you the glorious saying "we won" is really shallow. It's far more noble to be able to say we're not offended by you and we don't really want to fight with you . . . But it can mean relationships as well.' On the other hand, Johnson explained that 'Two Tribes' was inspired by a line ('Are we living in a land where sex and horror are the new gods') from a '30s film being shown on television one evening, and that the original concept was heavier than that issued.

For their live performances, Frankie Goes To Hollywood changed image; they dropped the leather for American and Soviet army uniforms. In actual fact, they would continue to change costumes with each future release, probably due to the passion for fashion Johnson had had since he was a young boy. 'I was more interested in dressing up, which led to problems at home. Sexuality wasn't what worried my parents so much as the make-up and the odd teenage problems.'

Returning to 1984, the wonderous success of 'Two Tribes' rubbed off on the 'Relax' single to return it to No.2 in the British chart, while sales of their debut album *Welcome To The Pleasure Dome* catapulted it into the chart at the top. It became Britain's biggest-selling album to date. Before the end of the year, Frankie Goes To Hollywood enjoyed their third consecutive British chart-topper, this time with a dramatic musical epic. Titled 'The Power Of Love' and accompanied by a seasonal video directed by Godley and Creme, the single dominated Christmas singles sales and earned the group the honour of being the first since Gerry and the Pacemakers (with 'How Do You Do It?', 'I Like It' and 'You'll Never Walk Alone' in 1963) to scoop the British top spot with their first three singles. These guys could do no wrong, and the publicity they constantly attracted boosted sales no end. Incidentally, 'The Power Of Love' went on to be used in Britain's first television advertisement for condoms, and when remixed and reissued in 1993, the title reached the British Top 10.

From the chart, Frankie Goes To Hollywood hit the touring trail. As they trekked across Britain in March 1985, 'Two Tribes' won an Ivor Novello Award for the Best Contemporary Song. Indeed, the single lived on; in 1994 it was remixed and released and reached the Top 20. The title cut from the *Welcome To The Pleasure Dome* album was issued as the follow-up single to 'The Power Of Love' and reached No.2. The group then embarked upon a European tour which spanned several months.

The first Frankie Goes To Hollywood single of 1986, titled 'Rage Hard', swiped from their pending double album titled *Liverpool*, stalled at No.4 in the September. The album peaked a position lower. Had the guys' appeal diminished? Critics believed so. Nonetheless, nobody could fault the sheer excitement of the group's work, a feeling that would be prevalent for some time yet, which made the events of 1987 appear incredible to say the least. However, before that situation arose, Frankie Goes To Hollywood issued their final single of 1986, namely 'Warriors Of The Wasteland', a struggler into the Top 20.

Into 1987, and despite being promoted during a lengthy British tour, 'Watching The Wildlife' failed to kickstart their poor singles sales, peaking in the Top 30. Frankie Goes To Hollywood thought long and hard and came to a decision.

For their final appearance the group chose Channel 4's *Saturday Live* programme, following which their record company announced their intention to take a nine-month break. It was, however, a permanent move for Johnson and Rutherford; the remaining trio said they intended to re-form Frankie Goes To Hollywood and record under that name. To this end the unit negotiated a recording contract with Circa Records, but before the ink had dried Johnson legally prevented the reuse of the name. Subsequently, the recording deal was cancelled.

By April 1987, Johnson officially announced Frankie Goes To Hollywood was no more and that he had secured a solo recording deal with MCA Records in the July. The transitional period was fraught with problems. Johnson and MCA Records counter-fought an injunction served by Zang Tumb Tumm (ZTT) to prevent him from embarking upon a solo career under the terms of his contract with the label. The case was heard in London's High Court early in 1988. During the hearing, ZTT claimed that the group members did not actually play on their chart-topping singles; instead, session musicians and Trevor Horn were responsible. Irrespective of this, Johnson won artistic freedom with substantial damages. Interestingly, Frankie Goes To Hollywood was the fifth act to leave ZTT during the last two years due to contractual reasons.

Before 1988 closed, Rutherford issued his debut solo single titled 'Get Real' via the 4th and Broadway label; it was a Top 50 British hit. Johnson's success was more immediate when, in February 1989, his debut solo release 'Love Train' soared into the Top 4. Three months on, his first album, *Blast*, shot to the chart's top position, while the second swiped single, 'Americanos', likewise peaked at No.4. His final outings of the year, 'Atomic City' and 'Heaven's Here', stalled in the Top 20 and Top 70 respectively.

Into the new decade, Johnson struggled to sell the 'Across The Universe' single and *Dreams That Money Can't Buy* album. His reputation was saved when the compilation *Bang!: Greatest Hits Of Frankie Goes To Hollywood* soared to No.4 in the album chart. On a more personal level, the singer published his autobiography titled *A Bone In My Flute* and revealed he was HIV positive.

It seems ironic, or perhaps sad, that although Frankie Goes To Hollywood introduced an abundance of intense creativity, excitement and originality into the world of music, their professional peak only spanned two years. Both gay and straight audiences responded to their music in much the same way as they had done to the Village People in the '70s.

As an aside, 'Two Tribes' was described by *NME* as 'the first genuine protest song for eight years, picking holes in the Official Secrets Act'. Then, in April 1998, the same track was used as the musical backdrop in television commercials for Burger King! Such a classic track deserves more respect, surely?

Also see: 'Relax', February 1984

(Quotes: *Frankie Goes To Hollywood* by Dean Anthony)

September 1984

GEORGE MICHAEL

Careless Whisper

Two-timing as a teenager inspired George Michael to compose 'Careless Whisper' – 'The whole time I thought I was being cool, being this two-timer, but there really wasn't that much emotion involved.'

During 1984, after Wham! had established themselves in the music industry, the duo celebrated their first British chart-topper titled 'Wake Me Up Before You Go Go'. Instead of immediately releasing a Wham! follow-up, George Michael issued his solo title 'Careless Whisper'. This track had in fact been penned by Michael during the pre-Wham! days and had been recorded in 1983 at the Muscle Shoals Studios under the production control of Jerry Wexler. As the sweeping, subtle ballad was, of course, alien to the fun dance sound of Wham!, it was agreed Michael should record the title as a soloist.

Despite Wexler's soul heritage, Michael was disappointed in the finished product, claiming 'Careless Whisper' sounded too much like a middle-of-the-road track and not like an Atlantic Records-produced song. Nonetheless, he had the highest regard for the producer, saying, 'I think [he's] a wonderful man and I loved working with him.'

Rerecording 'Careless Whisper' in London, Michael pulled on his teenage memory of dating two girls simultaneously. 'A two-timing bastard. I thought that was clever . . . the whole idea of "Careless Whisper" was the first girl finding out about the second, which she never did.' The reworked song, dedicated to his parents Jack and Lesley ('Five minutes in return for 21 years'), topped the British chart in September 1984, a position it held for three weeks, selling one million copies. To promote the title, Michael shot a £30,000 video in Miami. However, that figure soon escalated – news broke in Britain of the singer's £17,000 haircut! The humidity of Miami had transformed Michael's hair from slick to frizz and his sister Melanie had been ordered to his side, where she trimmed, styled and dyed his hair. By anyone's standards, it was an expensive trip to the hairdresser!

Michael's success spread across Europe and into America, where 'Careless Whisper' soared to the top during February 1985. For this release, the record label read 'Wham! featuring George Michael'.

Following Michael's solo success, the public believed Wham! to be a duo of the past. But there was still mileage in the group and, besides, Michael lacked the confidence to stride into a solo career at this time.

With the Ivor Novello Award for Songwriter of the Year to his credit, Michael duetted with Stevie Wonder and Smokey Robinson at Motown's first celebration gala held at the Apollo in New York during May 1985, the same month as Wham!'s 'Everything She Wants' dominated the American chart. From this Michael switched to London in the July to perform 'Don't Let The Sun Go Down On Me' at the star-studded Live Aid concert staged at Wembley Stadium. Andrew Ridgeley confined himself to providing support vocals backstage. Michael said, 'I was aware that after Live Aid I was seen in some quarters as a solo act. The interpretation I did of "Don't Let The Sun Go Down On Me" was very close to what Elton [John] had done. I was out of tune for the first couple of verses.' Before 1985 ended, Michael worked once again with John by duetting with him on 'Wrap Her Up' and adding support vocals to 'Nikita', both tracks from John's *Ice On Ice* album.

With the start of the new year, the future of Wham! was decided. The partnership would be dissolved. According to Michael, 'When I split with Andrew I was in the middle of a very heavy depression . . . I was feeling very negative about the whole Wham! thing. I was feeling trapped by a lot of things.'

Also see: 'A Different Corner', May 1986; 'I Knew You Were Waiting For Me' (with Aretha Franklin), February 1987

(Quotes: *Bare* by George Michael and Tony Parsons)

October 1984

STEVIE WONDER

I Just Called To Say I Love You

It's ironic. This single was Wonder's first British chart-topper as a soloist. He managed the No.2 position four times and enjoyed one chart-topping duet with Paul McCartney. And, more remarkable, 'I Just Called To Say I Love You' wasn't a soul classic by any means. It was a pop song in every sense of the word. It's a strange world indeed!

'I was born 13 May 1950 in Saginaw, Michigan, but the life of Stevie Wonder began in 1971. Shortly after my birth my family moved with my two older brothers Calvin and Milton . . . to Detroit until 1971. We lived on Breckinridge Street, which is on the west side with very beautiful people. There was a warm atmosphere and I did all the things that the normal boy did . . . We had enough to get by but I didn't know what being poor was like. We were very appreciative of what we received. Sometimes we would go without eating. I can prove that by the pain I felt in my stomach, but my mother raised us in the early part of that time by herself. She was fortunate enough to meet my second father . . . my mother gave birth to three other children, Timothy, Renee and Larry.'

Wonder's mother, Lulu Mae Hardaway, called him Steveland. His natural father's surname was Judkins, although his birth certificate showed Morris. Wonder was not blind from birth; born prematurely, too much oxygen was pumped into his incubator, thereby destroying his sight for life.

Lulu Mae worked as a cleaner at Motown Records and her eight-year-old son accompanied her. According to Wonder, 'When I first met Berry [Gordy, founder of Motown Records] I didn't know he was the same guy I'd heard a lot about. But I did know he was a black man and someone who was making a good, positive direction in the black community. Anybody who would let me into their studio and let me play drums, piano, guitar, bongos and so many other things had to be a good person.'

During 1960 Wonder's mother signed his five-year recording contract with Motown which stipulated the company would handle all his business affairs and that money earned would be held in trust for the youngster until he reached 21 years old. Meanwhile, Wonder was given an allowance for his upbringing; special schooling was also part of the deal, fitted in where possible. Berry Gordy rapidly became aware of the youngster's special talent as a composer and singer, so Motown writer/producer Clarence Paul was instructed to guide him. Indeed, Paul penned and produced Wonder's first singles and with Hank Cosby wrote 'I Call It Pretty Music But The Old People Call It The Blues (Part I)', Wonder's debut single issued under the name Little Stevie Wonder in August 1962. 'Little Water Boy', a duet with Paul, and 'Contract On Love', with the Temptations on support vocals, followed.

Although Little Stevie attracted special attention because of his youth and his blindness, it was a live recording that won him his first American chart-topper. Gordy had taped the youngster's performance at Chicago's Regal Theatre; the track that caught the imagination was 'Fingertips'. None of the spontaneity and atmosphere of Wonder's performance was lost as the track crossed both sides of the single. However, it was 'Fingertips Part II' that shot to the top of the American chart during 1963, a position it held for three weeks. The accompanying album, *Recorded Live: The 12-Year-Old Genius*, likewise topped its listing. Before 1963 ended, Wonder issued the chart-topper's follow-up, 'Workout Stevie Workout', a falterer in the Top 40, and visited Britain to promote his talent to the media, including a performance on the live-music programme *Ready, Steady, Go*.

By 1964 Little Stevie Wonder was 14 years old and had released five singles and four albums, namely *Tribute To Uncle Ray*, *The Jazz Soul Of Little Stevie*, the aforementioned *Recorded Live: The 12-Year-Old Genius* (not wishing to split hairs, but Wonder was in fact 13 years old) and *With A Song In My Heart*. All were produced by Paul, except *Recorded Live*, which credited Gordy. For these albums Little Stevie adhered to his producers' wishes, although he suggested tracks he preferred and worked on their arrangements. On the singles front, Wonder also issued a trio of mediocre titles during 1964 – 'Castles In The Sand', 'Hey Harmonica Man' and 'Happy Street' – and attended the Fitzgerald School for the Blind, where he learned Braille until Ted Hull was hired by Motown to act as his teacher, manager and chaperon. Wonder's formal education would end in 1969 when he graduated and Hull was dismissed. According to Wonder, 'I had spent two weeks out of the month at the Michigan school, then when I was on the road I would do two hours a night, then I'd spend two weeks at home and I would work four hours a day. I always had homework to do.' Musically speaking, Paul continued to be his mentor, guardian and music director, responsible for the youngster's early career.

With schooling behind him, Little Stevie toured with other Motown acts on the revues which crossed America during the '60s and devoted his time to his career. The album *Stevie At The Beach* was issued in 1964 before Wonder appeared in two films, *Muscle Beach Party* and *Bikini Beach*, although he was unhappy with the choice. Returning to the singles, the enthusiastic 'Uptight (Everything's Alright)' was next in 1966, followed by the album bearing the same name. The single shot to No.3 in America and represented Wonder's debut British hit at No.14 in the March. The single set the selling pace for 'Nothing's Too Good For My Baby' and the semi-ballads 'Blowin' In The Wind' and 'A Place In The Sun'. Both peaked in the American Top 10. The latter track, a Bob Dylan cover version which soared into the British Top 40, was the first of several political statements Wonder would make on vinyl. Meanwhile, the singer's composing expertise flourished as he wrote with his mother or Motowners Hank Cosby or Sylvia Moy. 'I usually had things worked out. Hank would come up with a chord pattern for my melody, then maybe he'd help Sylvia with the lyrics. I would come up with the basic idea, maybe a punchline, and she would write the story.'

When Wonder was planning the title 'I Was Made To Love Her', which told the tale of his first girlfriend, the follow-up to the poor-selling 'Travelin' Man', he was said to be dating Diana Ross's sister. In truth, the singer was dating Rita Wright, later known as Syreeta to mainstream record-buyers. 'I Was Made To Love Her', a belting single, shot into the American Top 2 and British Top 5, prompting requests for the singer to tour. Wonder was no longer a boy. He was now 17 years old, his voice had broken and he was a master on the piano, organ, drums and harmonica; gradually he was realising his full potential as a musician and a vocalist.

As the 'I'm Wondering' single closed 1967, a Top 20 American and Top 30 British hit, Wonder's first album of 1968 was a 'greatest hits' compilation; it was a healthy seller on both sides of the Atlantic. Meanwhile, a trio of singles sustained his chart presence, namely 'Shoo-Be-Doo-Be-Doo-Da-Day', 'You Met Your Match' and 'For Once In My Life', while using the name Eivets Rednow (his name in reverse), Wonder released the instrumental titled 'Alfie'.

Into 1969, Wonder kicked in his fifth British tour during the March, with his support acts of the Flirtations and the Foundations. 'I'm [now] a native of England. I like the people very much, they're so relaxed,' he said. His single 'I Don't Know Why' was issued to coincide with the tour and peaked in the Top 20. However, it was this single's B-side that garnered the sales. Titled 'My Cherie Amour' and fashioned on Paul McCartney's 'Michelle', the track soared to No.4 in both America and Britain. To capitalise on this unexpected turnaround, the prepared album, now with its title hastily changed to *My Cherie Amour*, was issued. It peaked in the British Top 20, but was a surprising staller in the American Top 40 late in 1969. Now locked in the ballad mode, Wonder closed the year with 'Yester-me, Yester-you, Yesterday', a British Top 2 hit.

With the dawn of a new decade, Wonder reached 20 years old and issued his first single of the '70s, titled 'Never Had A Dream Come True', a further shmaltzy slow song, a Top 10 British hit during the March. It was extracted from the *Signed, Sealed And Delivered* album released in August 1970, four months on in Britain. In between these titles the singer married Syreeta Wright on 14 September in Detroit's Burnette Baptist Church. The couple honeymooned in Bermuda; upon their return to Detroit, they collaborated on Wonder's next project, titled *Where I'm Coming From*, destined to be the final album under the terms of the singer's original recording contract with Motown – 'I was in the process of getting my thing together,' he said. It transpired that his 'thing' included controlling his own career and composing and producing for other Motown acts like the Spinners, who benefited from the singles 'It's A Shame' and 'We'll Have It Made'. He aimed other material at acts like Martha Reeves, although Wonder did say at the time, 'I would get the product there and nobody would listen to it and I'd say "fuck it".' However, Wonder did manage to gain creative control over *Where I'm Coming From*, featuring his musical influences of Jimi Hendrix and Sly Stone and his opinions on the world's injustices that included but wasn't limited to black issues. Released in April 1971 in America and two months later in Britain, *Where I'm Coming From* sold badly, barely reaching the American Top 70. As Motown gloated, Wonder was devastated. '[It] was kind of premature to some extent, but I wanted to express myself. I don't think Motown promoted it properly.' Indeed, 'If You Really Love Me' was the only swiped single, hitting the American Top 10 in the October. When released in Britain in February 1972, the title peaked in the Top 20, so Wonder might have had a point.

In May 1971 the singer reached 21 years of age. His childhood contract with Motown expired and money, including record royalties, in the region of $1 million was freed to him. With the money, Wonder relocated from Detroit to New York, booked rooms in the Howard Johnson Motor Inn and secured recording time in Greenwich Village's Electric Lady Studios to start work on his next album. Wonder's recording contract with Motown wasn't immediately re-signed; he wanted time to reflect. 'I talked to just about every company there was . . . I had gone as far as I could go. I just kept repeating "the Stevie Wonder sound" . . . I wanted to see what would happen if I changed.' And change he did with the *Music Of My Mind* album, which cost him a quarter of a million dollars in studio time. With the project completed, Wonder opened negotiations with Motown, finally re-signing with the company who offered him control of his publishing via his own Black Bull Publishing Company, a lucrative royalty rate and creative freedom, which in turn meant Motown were bound to accept the material Wonder gave them. *Music Of My Mind* failed to please Motown, but when issued in March 1972 in America and two months on in Britain critical praise was instant and fans devoured each melody. To pave the way for the album's British release Wonder undertook a month's tour, also promoting his *Greatest Hits Volume 2* package and single titled 'If You Really Love Me', Top 30 and Top 20 hits respectively. In June 1972 the artist hit the American touring road for an eight-week trek as support act to the Rolling Stones. Ironic, really – in 1964 the British group had supported Wonder on tour!

As an aside, the 1972 tour was not a happy one for the Motown artist. He had no management and Motown did nothing to promote him, nor *Music Of My Mind*. Then Wonder's drummer suddenly departed, while Mick Jagger and Keith Richards enjoyed what has been classed as the most decadent of Stones tours, with sex, drugs and alcohol a high priority. The tour was filmed for a documentary aptly titled *Cocksucker Blues*. In retrospect, though, Wonder believed the tour was vital to his growth, citing his love of music as his saviour during the negative moments. 'No matter how many hassles we had, the good vibes more than offset the bad ones,' he said.

A pair of singles were issued to coincide with these tours, namely 'Superwoman (Where Were You When I Needed You?)' and 'Keep On Running'. Behind the public stage, Wonder and his wife Syreeta separated, and although no statement was offered to the media at the time, Wonder later commented, 'She's a Leo and I'm a Taurus. They're two fixed signs and I'm stubborn.' Despite their eventual divorce, the couple continued to work together, with Wonder producing Syreeta's first two albums.

Meanwhile, her ex-husband prepared to issue his next significant project titled *Talking Book*. With contributions from Ray Parker Jr, Deniece Williams and Jeff Beck among others, the album was infectious from the opening track, none more so than the title 'Superstition', which Wonder had in actual fact composed for Beck. To this end, Wonder gave Motown the strict instruction that 'Superstition' should never be issued as a single but should remain an album track. The record company ignored the artist and issued 'Superstition'; it topped the American chart in January 1973 and reached No.11 in Britain. Naturally, Beck was furious, as Wonder blushed. *Talking Book*, meanwhile, soared into the American Top 3 and the Top 20 in Britain.

The single 'You Are The Sunshine Of My Life', written by the artist for Gloria Bartley, his new girlfriend, topped the American chart and reached the Top 10 in Britain during June 1973. The compelling song went on to become an evergreen track, recorded by a host of artists including Liza Minnelli and Perry Como.

Behind his extremely high public profile, a tragedy almost occurred when Wonder was involved in a car accident while journeying from Greenville, South Carolina, where he had performed the previous night. His driver, cousin John Harris, swerved to overtake a truck on Highway 85 *en route* to Durham, North Carolina, where Wonder was due to perform at the Duke University. Harris misjudged his overtake and ploughed into the truck, whereupon a log fell from the load and crashed through the front windscreen, hitting the sleeping singer on the head. Unconscious and bleeding, Wonder was rushed to the Rowan Memorial Hospital, later being transferred to the North Carolina Baptist Hospital. He was diagnosed with a fractured skull and brain contusion, and remained comatose for four days. Wonder initially lost his sense of taste and smell through shock, and at this juncture it was debatable whether he would perform again. The singer said he believed the accident 'was meant to be' and, further, 'I know it made me much more aware of my surroundings, the people around me, the things in life that are important.' Days prior to the accident, Wonder's *Innervisions* album had crashed into the American Top 4 and British Top 10, while he recovered sufficiently to perform for the first time since the accident with Elton John at the Boston Gardens during September 1973. Further performances were, however, ruled out until 1974. On a happier note, the singer met Yolanda Simmons, who would bear his children.

Through to the '80s, the Motown star rose to wear the crown of black music's top-selling name via albums like *Fulfillingness's First Finale* and the infectious *Songs In The Key Of Life*. All were Wonder masterpieces as he stretched his musical muscle from one topic to another in the innovative style befitting a man of his immense talent. Contributing to third-party recordings and touring the world to capacity-filled venues filled the time between recording sessions. Wonder worked anytime, anywhere, irrespective of day or night and what country he chanced to be in, much to the frustration of his entourage, who really had no idea when they would sleep or eat.

In 1980 came Wonder's most commercial album to date, titled *Hotter Than July* and dedicated to Dr Martin Luther King, who was assassinated in Memphis during April 1968. The incredible album spawned several million-selling singles, such as Wonder's tribute to Bob Marley titled 'Masterblaster (Jammin')', 'I Ain't Gonna Stand For It' and the sweeping ballad 'Lately', before he issued the perennial 'Happy Birthday'. All singles charted across the world, while their mother album soared into the Top 3 on both sides of the

Atlantic. Undoubtedly, Wonder's career had peaked commercially; he was in demand everywhere there was a theatre!

Also during 1980 Motown celebrated its 20th anniversary, and to add to the many other special events and releases, Wonder directed his 'Hotter Than July Music Picnic' tour to Britain, where during the September he was joined on the Wembley Arena stage by Marvin Gaye and Diana Ross. Wonder also boosted further fellow Motowner Jermaine Jackson's career by composing and contributing to his multi-million-selling single titled 'Let's Get Serious', re-establishing Jackson as an international top-selling act.

Now knee-deep in awards, honours and silver, gold and platinum discs, Wonder recorded and released a duet with Paul McCartney. Titled 'Ebony And Ivory', the duet topped the British chart in May 1982. (Please see 'Ebony And Ivory', May 1982.) While the duet went on to dominate the American top spot, Wonder's own *Stevie Wonder's Original Musiquarium I* soared into the American Top 4 and reached No.8 in Britain as his singles 'Do I Do' and 'Ribbon In The Sky' sustained his chart presence.

After appearing with fellow acts at Motown's 25th Anniversary Gala before a star-studded audience, Wonder, now the father of two children, Keita and Aisha, co-wrote and sang on Gary Byrd's 'The Crown' 12-inch single, an off-the-wall international hit. During 1984, and as the Motown star toured Britain, his 'I Just Called To Say I Love You', a track extracted from the soundtrack of the Gene Wilder movie *The Woman in Red*, surprised the industry by topping the British chart in October, a position it dominated for six long weeks. Wonder did not initially shoot a video for promotional purposes; instead he allowed a film crew to capture him singing the song during his stage act, where stalwart fans, already fuming at the style of the commercial song, were appalled to see their hero singing into a telephone handset. When released in America, the title repeated its British success for three weeks. Interestingly, 'I Just Called To Say I Love You' re-entered the British Top 70 in 1985.

Dionne Warwick was the instigator behind Wonder becoming involved with *The Woman in Red*, and said that, despite his blindness, he 'saw' the movie, because 'There's no way in the world that you can write the pieces of music that he wrote, for the sequences he wrote for, directly'. With 15 Grammy Awards already in his possession, Wonder went on to win an Oscar for 'I Just Called To Say I Love You', which he accepted on behalf of Nelson Mandela, the then imprisoned leader of the African National Congress. In retaliation, the state-operated South African Broadcasting Corporation issued a ban on Wonder's material, to which the singer replied, 'If my being banned means people will be free, ban me mega times.'

Before 1985 ended, Wonder had contributed to the Beach Boys' track 'I Do Love You' and the Eurythmics' 'There Must Be An Angel (Playing With My Heart)' and composed and supported the title 'She's So Beautiful' for Cliff Richard, from the soundtrack of Dave Clark's stage show *Time*. Of his own work, Wonder issued 'Part-Time Lover', his ninth single to top the American chart (reaching No.3 in Britain), while its mother album, titled *In Square Circle*, hit the Top 5 in both America and Britain.

Following several years of lobbying the American Senate, the Motown singer was finally successful in encouraging the body to vote in favour of a national holiday on the third Monday of January in memory of Dr Martin Luther King. The first holiday was in 1986, with Wonder celebrating the achievement during his perform-ance at the Radio City Music Hall, where, before an audience of 4,000 fans, he said, 'I'm so happy that America has this holiday ... Let's celebrate that we have the first holiday that was demanded by the people. Let's celebrate our democratic process that allows us these opportunities. Let's celebrate our collective effort that brought blacks, whites, reds, browns and yellows together ... I just want to give you a standing ovation and my heartfelt thanks and applause.'

Into the '90s, Wonder issued the solitary album *Characters*, an American Top 20 hit but a British flounderer. However, from the album Wonder released his duet with Michael Jackson titled 'Get It', an American Top 80 and British Top 40 hit issued as the follow-up single to 'Skeletons', an American Top 20 and British Top 60 entrant. Performing was still high on the artist's agenda as audiences packed theatres to witness Wonder's spectacular, albeit lengthy act. His work for and dedication to numerous charities were also highlighted via personal apearances, donations and royalty proceeds.

When Wonder and Spike Lee negotiated a deal for the forthcoming movie *Jungle Fever* early in 1991, the artist became immersed in composing the soundtrack, postponing his own project tentatively titled *Conversation Peace*. In the June, the completed soundtrack *Music From The Movie 'Jungle Fever'* was issued. It peaked in the American Top 30 and British Top 60 while the movie premièred in New York. With the project now public, Wonder returned to the American stage, notably to perform with other acts including Gladys Knight, on the tribute gala for the late Temptation and subsequent soloist David Ruffin, and to perform for the late Motown queen Mary Wells in Los Angeles, where the other participating acts included Natalie Cole. Of his further awards, Wonder was presented with the Honorary Global Award for his recorded contribution to the 'don't drink and drive' campaign via the single 'Don't Drive Drunk' and the Nelson Mandela Courage Award during a ceremony held in Los Angeles.

Into 1992 Wonder toured once more and, using the banner 'European Natural Wonder', dates in Britain were included. Before the year closed, he was the recipient of the prestigious Songwriter's Lifetime Achievement Award from the National Academy and the NAACP (National Association for the Advancement of Coloured People) Image Award for Male Artist. From his performance with Prince on a Minneapolis stage, Wonder hit the touring trail once more early in 1995 with dates across America, before performing in London at Soho's Ronnie Scott's Club during the March. While on the road, the Motown star's recorded work included the singles 'For Your Love' and 'Tomorrow Robins Will Sing', his final British hit in July 1995. Both were sluggish sellers, while his album *Conversation Peace* hit the American Top 20 and British Top 10 during March 1995. It was true to say that the artist's releases had been negligible of late, except, of course, for the ongoing run of compilations, although none contained his material dated from the mid-'70s onwards, a restriction imposed by Wonder himself.

More recently, Wonder's output has been slight. However, his presence at music-related functions has been regular. Indeed, it was during one of these functions that he told the media of his intention to relocate to South Africa. His most recent appearance was to attend a 1998 American media reception for Prince, now known as the Artist, where they spent most of the evening talking. Wonder is also notorious for stopping by selected nightclubs, where he's known to stun the customers with impromptu performances and jam sessions.

Wonder's dedicated and unselfish work has rightly elevated him to the status of a leader of the American black community. An influential voice, he is a mouthpiece for racial pressure groups and ethnic minorities, while his passion for the African nations remains as strong as ever. A spiritual leader to his people, his humane approach to those in need sets him apart from others, whilst as a singer, composer and producer of some of the world's most exciting music he has broken through the barriers of R&B into mainstream music.

Also see: 'Ebony And Ivory' by Stevie Wonder and Paul McCartney, May 1982)

(Quotes: *Motown: The History* by Sharon Davis; *Stevie Wonder* by John Swenson)

CHAKA KHAN

I Feel For You

'Chaka Khan, Chaka Khan, let me rock you . . .' So rapped Grandmaster Melle Mel at the start of the chart-topper that exploded into a funk/dance monster. Remember now?

Born Yvette Marie Stevens in Great Lakes, Illinois, on 23 March 1953, she had one sister, who became known as Taka Boom, and a brother, Mark, who went on to join the Jamaica Boys. With school-friends, the youngster formed a group called the Crystalettes, and she told journalist David Nathan, 'I was very active in school but was very unhappy too about the things I saw around me. So I opted for singing rather than another career which might have involved a more direct chance of bringing about changes.'

As a Crystalette, she performed on the local talent circuit before switching to Chicago's Afro-Arts Theatre. While associated with the Black Panther movement, the youngster adopted the name Chaka Khan. 'My father's a well-travelled man and the name itself has two meanings in two different languages. In one particular African dialect, the word symbolises fire, war, heat and the colour red – all of which are appropriate to me. And in Hawaiian it simply means, "Hi, what's happening?"'

At the age of 16, Khan left home following an argument with her mother; at 17, she married. Despite her personal upheavals, she continued with her career, drifting through the Lock and Chain group and Lyfe before joining the outfit Ask Rufus as replacement for the departing vocalist Paulette McWilliams.

During 1973 the group, now simply known as Rufus, secured a recording contract with ABC Records. In the August, their eponymous album was issued but faltered outside the American chart. A year on, Rufus issued their first American hit, a version of Stevie Wonder's 'Tell Me Something Good'; it reached No.3. At the same time, their *Rags To Rufus* album soared into the Top 4, and before 1974 closed, the 'You Got The Love' single peaked in the American Top 20.

Into 1975, Rufus's American success rubbed off in Britain, when they debuted with the album *Rufusized* in the Top 50. The title 'Once You Get Started' was the first extracted single; it was a further American Top 10 entrant. During the year the group toured Britain before supporting Elton John at a Wembley Arena concert.

Through the next two years Rufus issued a pair of albums, namely *Rufus Featuring Chaka Khan* and *Ask Rufus*, the latter becoming their biggest-selling item, passing platinum status. Singles included 'Sweet Thing', a million-selling hit, 'At Midnight (My Love Will Lift You Up)' and 'Hollywood'. By this time, Khan was naturally the visual point in the otherwise all-male membership. Her stage act was raunchy, her image verging on that of a sex bomb. Indeed, the public identified with this free-thinking woman, so much so that in 1978, following the release of the *Street Player* album, the group's billing was changed to reflect her growing popularity and became known as Rufus and Chaka Khan. The songstress also secured her own recording deal with Warner Bros Records. Her first solo outing, the *Chaka* album, produced by Arif Mardin, during December 1978 soared into the American Top 20 and spawned the Ashford and Simpson-penned single 'I'm Every Woman'. An extremely dynamic slice of hard-edged R&B, the title marked Khan's first British hit, reaching No.11 during January 1979.

In May 1979, as Rufus's *Numbers* album sold poorly, Khan officially left the group, although they insisted, 'Chaka has two more albums to do with us, and we may tour together. People seem to want to believe that there is antagonism between us, but we're very happy with what Chaka's doing and she's happy for us.' Khan in reply told Nathan, 'I learned a lot since I went out on my own . . . I had to be self-sufficient and I had to stand back and take stock. There was a certain nakedness which [I] had to deal with.'

By the new decade, Khan's commitment to Rufus was fulfilled with the *Masterjam* album, from which the single titled 'Do You Love What You Feel?' was lifted. Both were Top 20 American hits.

Khan was now clear to concentrate on her own career, starting with the *Naughty* album, a Top 50 American hit. A year on, she issued a staller in the American Top 60, 'What Cha' Gonna Do For Me?', lifted from the album of the same name. Two further singles in 1981 also bombed, namely 'We Can Work It Out' and 'Any Old Sunday'.

However, the situation was to turn around. In 1983, Khan returned to the American chart with a cover version of Michael Jackson's 1971 debut solo single titled 'Got To Be There', extracted from her *Chaka Khan* album which itself went on to win a 1984 Grammy Award for Best R&B Vocal Performance, Female. Meanwhile, her *Live: Stompin' At The Savoy* album recorded with Rufus during a 1982 reunion concert in New York spawned the Top 30 American hit 'Ain't Nobody', which also went on to win a Grammy Award for the Best R&B Performance by a Duo or Group with Vocal. 'Ain't Nobody' represented the group's first and long-awaited British hit in the Top 10.

Khan further told Nathan, 'In 1982 I moved from Los Angeles to New York City [to live] in Manhattan, and I love it. I'm happier there than I've been in ten years. I think it's because with all the activity that's going on in the city, I'm stimulated.' By now she had two children both under ten years old and lived with Albie, a school-teacher. Together they had as normal a family life as was possible with Khan's unsociable lifestyle.

On the professional front, her career peaked during 1984 when she topped the British chart with the Prince composition 'I Feel For You', originally earmarked for his eponymous album. A heavy yet sharp R&B/funk track, it featured Stevie Wonder on harmonica and Grandmaster Melle Mel's rap introduction, following a recom-mendation from the song's producer Arif Mardin. Khan was at first unaware of Melle Mel's contribution. 'I was embarrassed! When I first heard it I said "oh my God" and turned to Arif and asked him how he could do that to me!' Embarrassed or not, the chart-topper, lifted from the British Top 20 album of the same name, went on to win the songstress another Grammy Award for Best R&B Vocal Performance, Female. According to Khan, 'I didn't think I'd win because Tina Turner looked like she'd make a clean sweep and win everything that she was nominated for . . . so when they announced my name I was a little surprised!' With so much media attention, the singer told an *NME* journalist, 'I'm almost afraid of [fame]. At least I can walk to the grocery store unmolested, or take my children to the doctors. At the moment Michael Jackson and Diana Ross can't show their faces. I would never have bodyguards – I would rather carry a gun myself.'

Into the next year Khan's first single, titled 'This Is My Night', secured a healthy position in the British Top 20, while across the Atlantic it faltered in the Top 60. It was a totally unexpected turn of events, particularly when its follow-up 'Through The Fire' only managed ten positions higher. Happily, the news was better in Britain, where the 'Eye To Eye' single maintained her Top 20 status.

During the next months, the fiery songstress was heard on the titles 'Can't Stop The Street' from the *Krush Groove* dance movie and 'Own The Night' from an episode of television's cult series *Miami Vice*. Into 1986, Khan returned to the British and American charts, albeit the Top 60, with 'Love Of A Lifetime', penned by Scritti Politti, while the mother album *Destiny* stalled in the Top 70 on both sides of the Atlantic in the August. When not recording her own work, Khan contributed to other acts, including Stevie Winwood's 'Higher Love', which soared to the top of the American chart late in 1986, and David Bowie's soundtrack of his *Labyrinth* film.

Prior to the new decade, Khan embarked upon a lengthy European tour, coinciding with the release of the single 'It's My Party' swiped from the *C K* album, issued early in 1989. As the single slowly peaked in the British Top 80, a reworked version of 'I'm Every Woman' soared into the Top 10, followed by a further remixed title, 'I Feel For You', which made the Top 50. Both titles were, incidentally, swiped from an entire reworked album, *Life Is A Dance: The Remix Project.*

Into the '90s, Khan worked with Quincy Jones and guested at various functions including the television gala *Celebrate the Soul of American Music* with icons like Dionne Warwick. Returning to her own career, she issued the 'Love You All My Life' single during April 1992; it was a Top 50 British hit, Top 70 in America. This preceded her *The Woman I Am* album, which she also produced. Regrettably, the title stalled outside the American listing, but she happily scooped a Grammy for the Best R&B Vocal Performance, Female. Following a rare London appearance during the July, Khan performed a series of American dates at the start of her world tour.

With her recording career now on hold, the singer flitted from stage to studio as a session singer until she returned to the British stage to perform the role of Sister Carrie in *Mama, I Want To Sing*, the rousing off-Broadway American Gospel biographical musical based on the life of singer Doris Troy. By now, Khan had relocated to West Hampstead, London. 'What I love the most is . . . I can go about my business and people don't bother me. I don't have the same kind of hassle I have in the States.'

At this point in her career, Khan signed a recording deal with Mercury Records, where her single 'Never Miss The Water' was issued via the Reprise label in 1996. This was followed by an album, *Epiphany: The Best Of Chaka Khan*, a compilation of her best-selling titles plus five new tracks – her first releases in some considerable time. This was also the year when she celebrated 25 years in the music business and confirmed her determination to complete her autobiography, which she claimed was 'like going through major therapy sessions'.

When Warner Brothers lost Khan's last album, it was obvious that the two would part company. In 1998 this happened. Khan refused to sign with another major company; instead she opened her own label, Earth Song International, and hooked up with the Artist formerly known as Prince. His company, NPG Records, distributed Khan's label and released her first album titled *Come 2 My House*, a joint effort by the singer and the Artist.

The Chaka Khan of the '90s is now regarded as a music diva, a term she naturally loathes because of its implications, and is a powerful force on both record and stage. To have survived in the cut-throat world of music is a rare achievement in itself, a feat not overlooked by Khan, who laughed, 'I now span three generations – and that's a surprise to me!'

(Quotes: *Blues and Soul* magazine, 1975, 1979, 1984, 1985, 1996, interviews by David Nathan)

December 1984

BAND AID

Do They Know It's Christmas?

'There are millions dying in agony. How many more children will you let die in your living-rooms before you act? . . . Please buy this record . . . If you have no money, club together and buy one. Even if you hate the song, buy it and throw it away . . . As I'd hoped, everything about this record was proving superlative' – Bob Geldof

During 1984 Bob Geldof, leader of the Boomtown Rats, like most British television viewers watched horrific reports of the most appalling famine in Ethiopia. 'The pictures were of people who were so shrunken by starvation that they looked like beings from another planet.' As the British public cried in disbelief, Geldof took his grief once step further by formulating plans to raise financial help for the famine victims.

Following the television coverage, Geldof contacted Midge Ure from Ultravox and asked him to help compose a song that could be recorded by a group of artists who, he hoped, would give their services free. When certain artists responded to Geldof's request, he and Ure rushed to complete a suitable track. Said Geldof, 'I wanted something which sounded like a football chant or "Give Peace A Chance" . . . It had to be completely direct, simple and to the point.' For some reason, Geldof started singing 'feed the world', which at first he said, was actually reminiscent of a previous track penned by Ure. With a changed melody and lyric amendment, that track was eventually turned into 'Do They Know It's Christmas?'.

On 25 November 1984, 36 artists from all walks of British music met at the SARM Recording Studios in London's Notting Hill: Ure and Geldof, Duran Duran, Bananarama, Phil Collins, Martin Ware and Glenn Gregory (from Heaven 17), Annie Lennox, Frankie Goes To Hollywood, Marilyn, Ultravox, Sting, Rick Parfitt and Francis Rossi (from Status Quo), George Michael, Robin Bell, James Taylor and Dennis Thomas (from Kool and the Gang), Spandau Ballet, Boy George and Jon Moss (from Culture Club), the Boomtown Rats, Paul Young, Jody Watley, Paul Weller and Bono and Adam Clayton (from U2).

With seven television crews from both sides of the Atlantic, the artists recorded 'Do They Know It's Christmas?', a track that chalked up record advance orders, earning it the distinction of becoming the biggest-selling item of 1984. The studio sessions were broadcast during the day, whereupon hundreds of fans turned up at the recording studios to play a part in the significant event. At 6 p.m. BBC TV news revealed that the single was completed. At 2 p.m. the single's topside had been finished, whereupon the B-side, where artists' spoken messages were mixed against the song's backing tape, was recorded.

Geldof designed a logo for the group of singers: a globe of the world, representing a plate, with Africa in black and a knife and fork at the side. The logo was to be stamped on the record labels and subsequent promotional items alongside the group name Band Aid, chosen by a member of Phonogram Records' staff. Next, Geldof contacted the media at large. The *Daily Mirror* took up the challenge by carrying the Band Aid story on its front page; other newspapers followed. Tackling the Musicians' Union followed. The Union's agreement with the BBC companies meant a fee was paid to artists every time their record was played. If the BBC paid to play 'Do They Know It's Christmas?', the Corporation would have to pay 36 artists upon each spin! Eventually, after all contributing artists to Band Aid waived their fees, the Musicians' Union likewise agreed to that waiver.

Phonogram Records played an integral part in the single's birth. The company's staff pressed and packaged the disc rapidly and by working day and night had sufficient copies available for the single to be launched on 7 December 1985 at the Royal Albert Hall, London, during the Save The Children Fund's Ethiopian Benefit concert. Eight days later, and released on Phonogram's Mercury label, 'Do They Know It's Christmas?' was in the record stores. Within one week the single entered the British chart at No.1, a position it would dominate for five weeks. It sold in excess of three million copies, earning it the distinction of becoming the fastest- and biggest-selling single ever in Britain. Columbia Records issued 'Do They Know It's Christmas?' in America, where it enjoyed a Top 20 hit during January 1985. America also had its own plans, and in the January, as the first shipment of Band Aid food was transported to Ethiopia, Geldof joined the recording session for 'We Are The World' by USA For Africa, a gathering of American artists inspired by Band Aid. In this instance, 'USA' didn't stand for the United States of America, rather the United Support of Artists. The single would be followed by a compilation album *We Are The World*. (See 'We Are The World' by USA For Africa, April 1985.)

Hot on the heels of 'Do They Know It's Christmas?', Virgin Video released a 22-track compilation video which Geldof described as 'simply the best collection of pop videos there has ever been', with half of the proceeds earmarked for the Ethiopian Famine Relief fund. Spanning 90 minutes, the videos included Elton John's 'Passengers', Culture Club's 'War Song', Paul McCartney's 'No More Lonely Nights' and a live version of Frankie Goes To Hollywood's 'Relax' and were linked by artists like David Bowie, Mick Jagger and Geldof, who also introduced the compilation.

Among the industry awards won by 'Do They Know It's Christmas?', Geldof and Ure scooped the Ivor Novello Award for the Best-Selling A-Side in March 1985. The presentation was made to both during a ceremony held at the Grosvenor House Hotel in London.

Having gathered artists together to record a single, Geldof realised far more money could be generated if those artists also performed live in concert. However, it wasn't until promoter Harvey Goldsmith contacted Geldof that he realised the project could actually reach fruition. What Geldof failed to grasp, though, was the time, energy and utter stress that would be involved in organising a concert not only in Britain, but also America.

In June 1985, Geldof announced that two Live Aid concerts were to be staged simultaneously in London and Philadelphia, with a possible television viewing audience of over two billion in Britain, Europe, America and the Far East. Plans were in force to enable 72,000 people to attend the show at Wembley Stadium, while British television viewers could watch the 15-hour show beginning at 12 noon on 13 July 1985. From 5 p.m. the show would include live coverage from America. What Geldof called a 'global jukebox' would last until 3 a.m. British time, broadcasting the final stages of the American perform-ances in full. Due to the time difference between the two countries, the American section would kick off five hours after the Wembley event.

Now all Geldof needed was the artists. He needn't have worried, for hundreds offered their services free, including Queen, Elton John, Simple Minds, David Bowie, George Michael, Sting, Dire Straits, Paul McCartney and the Boomtown Rats with Geldof. On the American Live Aid stage the British talent was joined by Lionel Richie, Bob Dylan, Madonna, the Beach Boys, Mick Jagger, Tina Turner, Patti LaBelle and Hall and Oates.

When Geldof finalised Live Aid's performing artists, he attracted criticism for not including reggae, African and Third World groups in the line-up. In retaliation, Geldof claimed he chose the acts he did because more money would be donated by the public to see their performances.

Among the unexpected events throughout the day, one was quite adventurous, to say the least. After performing on the Wembley stage,

Phil Collins flew to Philadelphia to play a second set later in the evening. Collins's 3,000-mile trip made rock-music history and doubtless collected other awards on the way.

The Live Aid concerts will never be forgotten. It was the day that music lived again, thanks to the determination of one young man.

On the Monday following Live Aid, the trust fund was boosted by £4 million from Britain and £5 million from Ireland, adding to the £100 million already raised, with further money promised from countless organisations, merchandise sales and spin-off projects.

There would follow several variations as the theme for charities across the world. One such function resulted from the American farmers' crisis in September 1985 which, many felt, was as devastating as the Great Depression. Country and western artists including Kenny Rogers, Willie Nelson and Loretta Lynn were joined by rock acts like Neil Young and Bob Dylan in the town of Champaign in Illinois for a benefit concert titled Farm Aid. The project, organised to lighten the heavy financial load, raised an initial $10 million in concert tickets, donations and merchandise. Farm Aid II was earmarked for 1986.

Back in Britain, in December 1985, as 'Do They Know It's Christmas?' re-entered the British chart at No.3, Carol Aid, a seasonal event featuring Cliff Richard, Alvin Stardust and Chris De Burgh, among others, was staged in London. 'Do They Know It's Christmas?' showed its face again during future festive seasons and was actually rerecorded in 1989 by Band Aid II, a project instigated by Stock, Aitken and Waterman. (See Band Aid II, 'Do They Know It's Christmas?', December 1989.)

As Band Aid and Live Aid became events of the past, Bob Geldof was honoured for his tireless and selfless work with a knighthood in 1980. Quiet-natured Geldof believed he didn't deserve the honour; happily, the rest of the world disagreed with him. As many people have said, without Bob Geldof, Ethiopia would truly have died in 1984.

(Quotes: *Is That It?* by Bob Geldof)

January 1985

FOREIGNER

I Want To Know What Love Is

It's likely that most people will remember this chart-topper, but how many could name the group?

Mick Jones, born in London on 27 December 1944, worked his way through numerous bands that included Nero and the Gladiators before relocating to Paris. While in France he performed as support singer to Johnny Hallyday and the Beatles, among others, before joining the group called Spooky Tooth, with whom he remained for approximately two years.

From France, Jones moved to America, where he worked as a talent scout before joining the Leslie West Band. Through this outfit, the musician befriended Ian MacDonald, late of King Crimson, and together they recruited drummer Dennis Elliott, born in London on 18 August 1950. With further musicians including Lou Gramm, born in Rochester, New York, on 2 May 1950, and later New York-born Al Greenwood and Ed Gagliardi, the group became Foreigner in 1976.

A year on, Foreigner secured a recording contract with the major company Atlantic Records, whereupon their debut eponymous album was issued during the February. Three months later, the extracted track titled 'Feels Like The First Time' debuted in the British Top 40 and soared into the American Top 4 in June. As the album passed quadruple-platinum sales, the second swiped single 'Cold As Ice' reached No.24 in Britain, No.6 in America. It had been an exceptionally brisk year for the new group, and this would continue.

Throughout 1978 Foreigner's selling power increased, particularly in America, thanks to a handful of singles beginning with the title 'Long Long Way From Home', Top 20, 'Hot Blooded', Top 3, and 'Double Vision', Top 2 at the close of the year. 'Hot Blooded' was the group's solitary 1978 British hit, faltering in the Top 50. These titles were, incidentally, swiped from Foreigner's second album *Double Vision*, itself a five-million-selling item in America, although only reaching the British Top 40. Touring was high on the year's agenda as Foreigner kicked in a six-week trek that included Canada and Britain, where the group's performance at the annual Reading Festival attracted a huge new fan following. Due to this unprecedented public reaction, Foreigner returned the following year as headliners.

In 1979 a trio of singles kept the rock group in the charts on both sides of the Atlantic. 'Blue Morning' peaked in the American Top 20 and British Top 50 early in the year, 'Dirty White Boy' charted in America only at No.12, while 'Head Games' reached the Top 20. The last release was the title track from their Top 5 American album which later passed platinum status twice.

To start the '80s, Foreigner's chart success was restricted to the 'Woman' single, which surprisingly faltered in the Top 50. The group membership was reduced to a quartet, now reading Lou Gramm, Rick Wills (late of the revamped Small Faces unit), Mick Jones and Dennis Elliott.

It took until August 1981 for Foreigner to issue their next musical project, the album *4* – rather an unimaginative title, by anyone's standards! The project topped the American chart, selling in excess of six million copies in that country alone. The first track swiped for single release, 'Urgent', featured the distinctive sax of Jr Walker, Motown's main musician man. It shot to No.4 in America but faltered in the British Top 60. 'Juke Box Hero' followed, once again selling badly in Britain, while the title 'Waiting For A Girl Like You', where Foreigner replaced the rock sound with a ballad, soared to No.2 in America late in 1981. The single peaked at No.8 in the British chart during January 1982, boosting the sales of their album *4* and pushing it into the Top 5. To sustain these chart profiles, Foreigner toured constantly, beginning with an American trek through to Britain, where the group performed at Wembley Arena.

A year's hiatus followed, when the obligatory 'greatest hits' package titled *Records* was issued to ensure that Foreigner's name stayed in the public's mind. The album eventually sold in such vast quantities that it passed platinum sales not once, or twice, but three times! This elevated position was just the right launching pad for a chart-topping title featuring the band, soul stylist Jennifer Holliday ('She was a real inspiration for everybody') and the New Jersey Mass Choir, among others. 'I Want To Know What Love Is', a monumental rock ballad of the highest calibre, flew to the top of the British chart in January 1985; a month later, the title repeated the success in America. Said to be the single of the decade by many respected musicians, 'I Want To Know What Love Is' was the fusing of love and lyric, rock and soul. Jones told *Pulse!* magazine, 'This is our first No.1 single. People seem to think we've had millions of No.1 singles, but we never had. We've had No.1 albums.' He further told *Billboard* magazine, 'People might think we've gone soft or something. I certainly want to retain the rock image. We just put this out because the song was so strong and . . . it had the right kind of mood.'

Hot on the chart-topper's trail, the *Agent Provocateur* album topped the British chart, later peaking in the American Top 5, *en route* to sales of double-platinum status. Before 1985 ended, the group returned to the British and American singles charts with 'That Was Yesterday', Top 30 and Top 20 respectively, before the aforementioned title 'Cold As Ice' faltered around the British Top 70.

Lou Gramm's solo album *Ready Or Not* opened the new year and reached the American Top 10, while the swiped single 'Midnight Blues' later peaked in the Top 5. During July 1987, Foreigner as a group returned to the spotlight with the *Inside Information* album, a poor British seller but a Top 20 American entrant, representing, as wild as it seems, the group's last multi-million seller. 'Say You Will' was the mother album's extracted single and reached the American Top 10 during February 1988, followed three months on by 'I Don't Want To Live Without You', a high-flying American Top 5 title.

In the lead-up to the '90s, Gramm and Mick Jones concentrated on solo projects. This resulted in Foreigner's next album being delayed until mid-1991. Titled *Unusual Heat* and introducing the group's new principal singer Johnny Edwards, the title struggled into the British Top 60. The group then watched helplessly as the album failed to dent the American Top 100 listing. Gramm rejoined Foreigner's membership during 1992, when the first album of the year, *The Very Best Of Foreigner*, peaked in the British Top 20. During the next year, the group toured across America for six months, issuing the *Classic Hits Live* album as they trekked from state to state.

Following a further change of membership and a switch of record company from Atlantic to Arista Records, the group's 'White Lie' single and the album titled *Mr Moonlight* sold poorly. It was disappointing, to say the least, as both reflected the Foreigner sound tagged 'adult rock' previously loved by the record-buying public.

Following this sudden career downturn, Foreigner spent much of their time touring America, and with the Doobie Brothers visited Britain during 1995. It is a real pity that a group capable of producing such seductive material should suddenly lose its way. The lack of public support obviously contributed to the downfall, but maybe Lou Gramm was correct when he said, 'We worried that "I Want To Know What Love Is" might do irreparable damage to our rock image.'

February 1985

DEAD OR ALIVE

You Spin Me Round (Like A Record)

It was a chance release, a cash-in that presented this young group born from new-wave music with the much-desired No.1 position. Dead Or Alive's career was relatively short-lived, but thanks to their extrovert singer they are remembered fondly.

Pete Burns, born in Liverpool on 5 August 1959, passed through local new-wave groups as a singer, including the Mystery Girls and Nightmares In Wax. While in the latter group Burns recorded for the Liverpool-based label Inevitable Records. After a switch in the line-up of Nightmares In Wax, Burns went on to form the nucleus of the future Dead Or Alive with members including Joe Musker and Martin Healey.

During 1982, as a signed act to the Black Eye label, Dead Or Alive issued the EP titled 'It's Been Hours', which peaked in the British Independent chart's Top 20. There was no crossover into the mainstream music listing, but the record had been successful enough to instigate a recording contract with CBS Records' subsidiary Epic. The signing marked another change in the make-up of the group, which now included Mike Percy, born in Liverpool on 11 March 1961.

The switch to the Epic label also saw Dead Or Alive changing musical direction from new wave/rock to the current dance style, as typified by their first single in June 1983 titled 'Misty Circles'. The single bombed but received high-profile nightclub exposure, as did its follow-up 'What I Want'. The recording side of Dead Or Alive's career might have presented problems at this juncture but as a whole the group was gaining hefty support for its music, complemented by Burns's androgynous image. His individualistic approach was in line with that of Boy George, who also confused his loyal audiences under a layer of make-up and frills. Nonetheless, the persona of both artists attracted much media attention, which in turn sold records. Burns admitted clothes were his downfall: 'I go shopping a lot. I spent about £15,000 on clothes in Japan alone.'

Two months on from their second unsuccessful single, Dead Or Alive underwent a further personnel change, this time adding Steve McCoy and Tim Lever. With Burns and Percy, this line-up represented the group's permanent membership.

'That's The Way (I Like It)', previously a Top 4 British hit for the disco act KC and the Sunshine Band in August 1975, was reworked by Dead Or Alive and became their first British hit at No.22 during April 1984. The single's sales helped their album titled *Sophisticated Boom Boom* to peak in the Top 30 one month later.

Enlisting the Midas touch of the hit-making trio Stock, Aitken and Waterman, Dead Or Alive released 'You Spin Me Round (Like A Record)'. The title's mainstream disco style was ideal for the current trend, so much so that, following a lengthy, painful climb up the chart, the single finally heaved itself on to the top spot in February 1985. Dead Or Alive had finally proved themselves to be Britain's premier-selling band, although many fans believed the choice of song was dubious!

Two months on, the chart-topper's follow-up, a diluted clone titled 'Lover Come Back To Me', failed to reach such dizzy heights, faltering in the Top 20. Nonetheless, this success boosted the sales of Dead Or Alive's second album. Titled *Youthquake*, it was another Stock, Aitken and Waterman production and reached the Top 10. Flushed with this unexpected chart success, Dead Or Alive began their first serious tour of Britain. While on the road, the group cracked the American chart with 'You Spin Me Round (Like A Record)' when the single soared into the Top 20 while the following *Youthquake* album peaked in the Top 30. This breakthrough encouraged Dead Or Alive to embark upon a lengthy American tour.

While absent from home ground during 1985, Dead Or Alive issued a further pair of singles, namely 'In Too Deep' and 'My Heart Goes Bang (Get Me To The Doctor)', Top 20 and Top 30 hits respectively. However, the group's next British charting title was during September 1986, when 'Brand New Lover' struggled to No.31. Its follow-up, 'Something In My House', fared much better, peaking at No.12 early in January 1987. A month on, the *Mad, Bad And Dangerous To Know* album peaked in the British Top 30 and Top 60 in America. During the remainder of the year, 'Hooked On Love' and 'I'll Save You All My Kisses' fought for British chart status, while across the Atlantic 'Brand New Lover' and 'Something In My House' sold poorly.

Into 1988, and following a spate of abysmal sales with singles like 'Turn Round And Count 2 Ten' and the album *Nude*, Dead Or Alive practically kissed farewell to their success. Indeed, the next year, when 'Come Home With Me Baby' faltered at No.62, Epic Records had no choice but to drop the act from its artist roster. This in turn led to Dead Or Alive disbanding. While the other members retired gracefully, Pete Burns carved out a solo career for himself, primarily in Japan, where his popularity continued until the '90s.

Dead Or Alive had proved their musical point, but they needed the experienced hand of Stock, Aitken and Waterman to assist in the groove. The track was tailormade for stalwart dance punters.

March 1985

PHIL COLLINS AND PHILIP BAILEY

Easy Lover

'I can't think of myself as a sex symbol. Maybe the attraction is that I'm accessible and I'm a bit cuddly as well . . . more likely it's sympathy' – Phil Collins

During 1984 Phil Collins married his long-term girlfriend Jill Tavelman, purchased a century-old house in Surrey, converting an upstairs room into a small studio, and settled into married life. Professionally speaking, Collins rose higher. His music continued to promote his love for Motown and R&B, confirming his roots were indeed in black music. It was this that inspired him to work with Earth, Wind and Fire's Philip Bailey.

Maurice White, the son of a Memphis preacher, held a passion for music from the age of 11. He played the drums with his school chum Booker T. Jones (who later formed Booker T. and the M.G.'s, the premier soul group). While he was a teenager, White and his family relocated to Chicago, where he attended the Chicago Conservatory of Music with a burning ambition to become a music teacher.

Working as a session musician for Chess Records, White moved through the Ramsey Lewis Trio. During his three-year stay, the Trio toured the Middle East, where White developed an interest in mysticism. His experience led him to form his own group. Guided by his astrological chart, White wanted his band to represent his spiritual vision, signifying his birth sign of air, fire and earth. With a slight alteration, White named his group Earth, Wind and Fire. The line-up comprised meditators and vegetarians, including his brother Verdine, Wade Flemons and Leslie Drayton.

During 1971 the ten-piece group secured a recording contract with Warner Brothers and issued their debut album *Earth, Wind and Fire*, which spawned the single 'Love Is Life'; both bombed. A year on, with the release of the group's second album, titled *The Need Of Love*, the group line-up altered to include Larry Dunn, Ralph Johnson and Philip Bailey, born 8 May 1951 in Denver. Bailey had in actual fact relocated to Los Angeles, where he worked with the gospel group the Stovall Sisters. Meanwhile, also in 1971, Clive Davis, an executive of CBS Records, saw Earth, Wind and Fire perform in New York, wanted the group for the company's Columbia label and bought them out of their Warner Brothers contract. Earth, Wind and Fire released their first album under the new deal in the November, titled *Last Days And Time*.

Into the next year, and following a further change in personnel, the group issued the *Head To The Sky* and *Open Our Eyes* albums. Both titles soared into the American Top 20, while singles like 'Mighty Mighty', 'Kalimba Story' and 'Devotion' sustained their chart presence. During 1975 Earth, Wind and Fire topped the American listings with their sixth album, *That's The Way Of The World*, and the extracted single 'Shining Star'.

And so the success story of Earth, Wind and Fire continued at an alarming rate. To complement their recorded work, the group, under the scrupulous guidance of Maurice White, performed on the touring circuits across America and later Europe. Their dance style and precise musicianship was enhanced by their colourful costumes and high-tech stage props. Indeed, Earth, Wind and Fire was the group their peers looked to for inspiration.

It was in 1983 that Philip Bailey flexed his musical muscle to release his debut solo album titled *Continuation*. Produced by George Duke, the project peaked in the American Top 80. A year on, while Earth, Wind and Fire were 'rested' by White to enable him to concentrate on other production work, Bailey issued his *Chinese Wall* album, recorded in London's Townhouse Studios. Phil Collins was the project's producer.

Prior to 'Easy Lover' being issued, Bailey, a born-again Christian, recorded *The Wonders Of His Love*, a spiritual album, for Myrrh Records, followed by other album titles that included *Family Affair* in 1990. The original intention was for Bailey and Collins to produce an album comprising R&B tracks but that proved unworkable; white and black just didn't mix in this instance.

'Easy Lover', penned by Nathan East with Bailey and Collins in mind, was actually the last track to be recorded. It was also the most difficult to promote, especially in America. Black radio stations refused to play the single because Bailey was duetting with a white singer, while mainstream stations objected because Collins was a white man singing R&B! Nonetheless, 'Easy Lover' soared to No.2 during February 1985, proving that common sense, not racism, prevailed. A month on, the single was sitting at the top of the British chart, where it stayed for four weeks. However, what delighted Collins most was the fact that 'Easy Lover' had cracked the American R&B chart to peak at No.3! Bailey told *USA Today* magazine that Collins had soul: 'He's got feeling, conviction and the ability to sell a song.' The single's success naturally triggered requests from other black acts like Tina Turner for Collins's productions, but he couldn't do it all.

The runaway success of 'Easy Lover', which went on to win the Ivor Novello Award in 1986 for the Most Performed Work, naturally benefited Bailey's *Chinese Wall* album, which went on to peak in the Top 30 on both sides of the Atlantic. His solo career would flourish and would run parallel to that with Earth, Wind and Fire when the group reunited during 1987. In that year, the group with a legacy that included double-platinum albums, gold and silver discs and awards by the hundred issued the *Touch The World* album, featuring both Bailey and White on lead vocals. Into the '90s, Earth, Wind and Fire returned to the international touring routes, switched record companies from CBS Records to return home to Warner Brothers, and enjoyed numerous tributes on vinyl and CD via 'greatest hits' compilations.

Returning to 1985 and Phil Collins, the titles 'One More Night' and 'Take Me Home' followed the British chart-topper, Top 10 and Top 20 hits respectively, while Collins closed 1985 by duetting with Marilyn Martin on the title 'Separate Ways', which went on to be included in the movie *White Nights.* The single marked Collins's fifth American No.1 title, reaching No.4 in Britain. Martin said she had originally felt intimidated at the thought of recording with an artist of Collins's stature, but relaxed when she discovered he had actually requested her as his singing partner.

To start the next year, Collins's star shone even brighter when he collected the Brit Award for Best British Album and a Grammy for Album of the Year for *No Jacket Required.* Before 1986 closed, he performed at the Prince's Trust Rock Gala with Tina Turner and Elton John among others and contributed to Eric Clapton's *August* album. Into the '90s, Collins performed on the Wembley Stadium stage with others in celebration of Nelson Mandela's 70th birthday, while a handful of singles guaranteed his high chart profile.

While Collins had carved out a phenomenal solo career that not even he could have dreamt of, he remained active with Genesis, whose members had likewise embarked upon individual careers. Following a series of high-charting titles, Genesis returned with a vengeance to top the American chart in June 1986 with 'Invisible Touch', the title track from the album of the same name, their first since *Genesis* during 1983 and first since Collins became a multi-million-selling commodity. To celebrate, or rather capitalise upon, this return to fame, Genesis played American dates as part of their sell-out world tour.

Having conquered the music world with Genesis, his own career and with other acts, Collins, ever the workaholic, turned his ambitions to another area of entertainment: movies.

Also see: 'You Can't Hurry Love', January 1983; 'A Groovy Kind Of Love', September 1988

(Quotes: *The Phil Collins Story* by Johnny Waller)

April 1985

USA FOR AFRICA

We Are The World

'It was so wonderful to be involved in an experience in which many artists came together to support each other. It was a special moment in history' – Diana Ross

'I think that "We Are The World" is a very spiritual song, but spiritual in a special sense. I was proud to be a part of that song.' – Michael Jackson

The British projects Band Aid and Live Aid instigated and organised by Bob Geldof inspired American calypso singer Harry Belafonte to think hard about drawing some of the biggest names in black music together to perform on stage in a spectacular concert to help ease the plight of Africa's starving population. His intention was to raise sufficient funds to go towards providing medical relief, emergency food supplies and, perhaps, self-help programmes for the millions of stricken people.

Belafonte contacted Ken Kragen, an entertainment manager with a history of fundraising success, to help his quest. Kragen, whose top clients were Lionel Richie and Kenny Rogers, instantly liked the concert idea but suggested to Belafonte that a record similar to the British release 'Do They Know It's Christmas?' would generate far larger sums. Belafonte agreed, whereupon Kragen promised to discuss the project with his two top clients. In turn, Richie contacted Stevie Wonder to add weight to the proposal and, following his agreement, Richie secured Michael Jackson's support, who not only wanted to sing on the track but offered to co-write a song with him.

A week of nights where Richie and Jackson locked themselves away in the latter's Enico mansion produced the track titled 'We Are The World'. They both agreed that the result had to be catchy, yet instantly memorable, particularly as they intended to utilise several lead vocalists. In other words, they said, they wanted an anthem for the world. While Richie and Jackson conceived the song, Kragen beavered away, finally getting 45 artists to agree to participate in the project, including Diana Ross, Bob Dylan, the Pointer Sisters, the Jacksons, Daryl Hall and John Oates, Kim Carnes, Kenny Loggins, Paul Simon, Tina Turner, Smokey Robinson, Al Jarreau, Ray Charles, Steve Perry, Cindy Lauper, Bruce Springsteen, James Ingram, Dionne Warwick, Huey Lewis and Bette Midler. Another 50 artists were put on hold. Quincy Jones, who at the time was working on the movie soundtrack for *The Color Purple*, agreed to produce the project. And, like the British contingent before them, all were willing to offer their services free of charge.

'We Are The World' was completed the day before the actual recording session on the night of 28 January 1985, the same evening as the American Music Awards ceremony was being held. It was a deliberate ploy, because it meant most of the contributing artists were already under one roof; they could then move on from the ceremony directly to A&M's recording studios. The first thing they saw was a notice pinned to Studio A's door declaring that all egos had to be checked at that point!

Prior to the recording of the song, all key singers had been sent tapes of the music track with Jackson's sketchy vocals added, enabling them to at least have an idea of their intended contribution. With the artists gathered, Kragen explained where the money was to be directed, leaving Bob Geldof to relate his experiences of visiting Africa and two Ethiopian women to personally report their plight.

Chalk marks on the studio floor ensured all the artists were correctly placed for recording around the six main microphones, while video cameras were trained on the singers throughout the session. Michael Jackson's contribution was to be filmed separately when the studio was empty. The all-night session ending at 8 a.m. was intense, tiring and highly charged but personally rewarding, as the future commercial video proved. Not included on this, however, were a couple of light-hearted moments from Wonder, intended to lighten the seriousness of the occasion. He laughed, 'It gave me a chance to see Ray Charles again. We just sort of bumped into each other.' And later, when the session ran into overtime, he quipped that if the song wasn't completed on the next take, he or Ray Charles would drive everyone home!

Released early in March 1985 via CBS Records' Columbia label in America, with an initial shipment of 800,000 copies sold within its first week on sale, 'We Are The World' topped the chart within three weeks of release, selling in excess of three million copies and earning the title of the fastest-rising chart-topper since 1975. While the single dominated the American chart for four weeks, Kragen continued to work, organising the *We Are The World* album featuring tracks from several of the contributing acts with the exception of Prince, who despite saying he wanted to sing on the single failed to attend the recording session. More than two million copies of the *We Are The World* album were rush-released in America during the April; it shot to the top of its chart where it stayed for two weeks, selling over three million copies during its reign. When released in Britain, the title peaked in the Top 40.

On 5 April 1985 at 3.59 p.m. UK time, 5,000 radio stations throughout the world simultaneously broadcast the 'We Are The World' single, whereupon the title shot to the top of the British chart the same month, a position it held for two weeks.

The first royalty cheque was for approximately $6 million, followed a year later by a further reputed $50 million collected from merchandise and record sales that included over seven million singles and four million albums, while the *We Are The World: The Video Event* boosted funds further. The project's contributing artists were also honoured by the American music industry when the single won the Grammy Award for the 1985 Record of the Year.

Money continued to flow into America for the USA For Africa fund from various off-shoot projects, including another instigated by Ken Kragen during 1986. Titled 'Hands Across America', it was a domestic event to help poverty in America. It was intended that ten million Americans would pledge $10 each, raising $100 million in total, to join hands from New York to Los Angeles.

Ten years on from the release of 'We Are The World', the USA For Africa fund had raised $88 million. Not bad for one evening's work!

(Quotes: *Memoirs: Secrets of a Sparrow* by Diana Ross; *Moonwalk* by Michael Jackson)

May 1985

THE CROWD

You'll Never Walk Alone

Written by Richard Rodgers and Oscar Hammerstein, 'You'll Never Walk Alone', produced by Ray Levy and Graham Gouldman, featured over 50 artists, some not associated with the music business, to raise financial support for one of Britain's most horrific of disasters.

During 1985 the British nation mourned the loss of 56 football fans attending the Valley Parade ground, home to Bradford City Football Club. The fans died when a stand caught fire, and countless others were injured. The full horror was screened live on television, as cameras intending to cover the match were witness to the tragedy. As policemen wandered confused and the inevitable mayhem gripped the scene, the viewing public joined television commentators in an open display of grief.

Those touched by the disaster wanted to offer help, support and finance and none more so than Gerry Marsden, who discussed with his manager Derek Franks possible projects which would help the families of the victims. The quickest way to raise cash was to record a single; radio airplay was a certainty and the public, as always, would rise as one in support.

Prior to finalising recording plans, Marsden visited some of the victims in St Lukes Hospital, where he saw little girls aged eleven and twelve who were badly scarred. A later visit to the Valley Parade ground, where he witnessed the charred debris and the shrines of wreaths, crosses and flowers, likewise shocked him deeply.

The original intention was for Marsden to sing 'You'll Never Walk Alone' with the Bradford City team. They declined. As the singer and Franks went on to approach artists keen to participate, Ray Levy, the project's executive producer, and Spartan Records were primed to give their talent and facilities free of charge. Said Marsden, 'The turnout of artists was simply stupendous, right across the range of showbusiness, from light entertainment to heavy rock artists . . . we had Tony Christie and Rick Wakeman . . . John Conteh, the Barron Knights, Jess Conrad, Kiki Dee, Bruce Forsyth, Rolf Harris, Kenny Lynch, Keith Chegwin, Tony Hicks, Colin Blunstone, the Nolans, John Entwistle, Motorhead, Phil Lynott, Smokie, among others.'

As 'You'll Never Walk Alone' was being mixed, Marsden was informed that on advance orders alone the single would top the British chart. Within ten days of being recorded the single was on sale, and it entered the chart at No.4 on its way to the top spot during May 1985, a position it held for two weeks. Selling in excess of 300,000 copies during its chart climb, 'You'll Never Walk Alone' eventually topped sales of one million.

However, there was a downside to the success of the single and the cash generated. Despite the participating artists, producers and record company giving their services free of charge, the music publishers of 'You'll Never Walk Alone' refused to waive their rights to the song's royalties. And there was a further downside, as Marsden wrote in his autobiography. 'Six weeks after our record project [we] contacted the Disaster Appeal to be advised it had closed and they didn't want the money.' As the public had willingly raised the cash to help the victims' families, Marsden now had to find a constructive use for the money. To this end, he sought the advice of surgeon David Sharp, who had attended to the injured burned in the fire. 'A burns research unit was opened in Bradford, and supporting that was totally in keeping with the nature of the tragedy.' Other cash was earmarked for research into a method of support to aid the recovery of broken wrists and arms, a further side effect of injuries sustained during the fire.

As a quick aside, when 'You'll Never Walk Alone' topped the British chart in 1985, Gerry Marsden won the distinction of becoming the first artist to reach No.1 in Britain with two versions of the same song.

Despite the setbacks, Marsden was pleased with the music project; the song he had so casually included in his stage act during his early career with the Pacemakers on the Hamburg club circuit as a diversion to basic rock'n'roll had, through the years, meant so much to millions of people. Not only had 'You'll Never Walk Alone' given him a pair of British chart-toppers, it had also been adopted as a football anthem to unite people in times of tragedy and joy.

'Our efforts were not in vain and I'd do the same thing in the same way tomorrow' – Gerry Marsden
Tragically, four years on, he would do just that.

(Quotes: *You'll Never Walk Alone: An Autobiography* by Gerry Marsden)

June 1985

SISTER SLEDGE

Frankie

This slice of commercial disco earned the American sisters international success. On the other hand, how irritating it was to constantly hear 'Frankie!' blaring from the radio. And how many men named Frank received this single as a gift?

Debra (Debbie), born in 1955, Joan (Joni), born in 1958, Kim, born in 1958, and Kathy, born in 1959 in Philadelphia, were all raised in a musical family environment. Encouraged by their mother, Floorez Sledge, and opera-singing grandmother, Viola Williams, the sisters rehearsed from an early age, building the foundation for a future recording career.

As teenagers, the girls, now calling themselves Sister Sledge, recorded the single titled 'Time Will Tell' during 1971 under an arrangement with Money Back Records, based in Philadelphia. This led to the sisters being hired as session singers for composer/producers Kenny Gamble and Leon Huff, later the instigators of 'the Sound of Philadelphia' via their record labels, TSOP and Philadelphia International, before joining Atlantic Records as artists in 1973.

Within a short time Sister Sledge were recording their own material with producer Thom Bell such as the titles 'The Weatherman' and 'Mama Never Told Me', the group's debut British Top 20 hit, released by Atlantic Records during January 1975. The sisters issued further material under the Atlantic banner, including the American hit 'Love Don't Go Through No Changes', also in 1975, and albums titled *Circle Of Love* and *Together*. By and large, though, the sisters' stay with Atlantic Records was pretty dire.

'Pretty dire' likewise summed up Sister Sledge's British recording career. Further success took four years, when they began a working relationship with Nile Rodgers and Bernard Edwards, the power behind the Chic musical empire. The result was the heavy-selling disco favourite 'He's The Greatest Dancer', a No.6 hit during March 1979. The single also scorched its way through the world's charts, eventually being hailed as the year's best-selling dance track, a title it would, incidentally, carry for several years. Naturally, Sister Sledge admitted 1979 was a year to remember. 'It made up for all the years we lay dormant, when people would tell us that trying to pursue singing careers whilst we were completing our education, we wouldn't do it.'

They did it, and more. In May 1979 the sisters followed 'He's The Greatest Dancer' with 'We Are Family'. Not only did the single peak at No.8 in the British chart, it also swept across the world's listings, selling millions of copies on the way. With this unprecedented success, an album carrying the single's title was hastily shipped into the stores and became a 1979 top-selling item. A further track was subsequently swiped from the *We Are Family* album for single release. Titled 'Lost In Music', the title soared into the British Top 20, proving without doubt that Sister Sledge and Rodgers and Edwards was a money-spinning commercial combination. The girls were now the world's most famous dance act, but as the disco market was extremely fickle, they would be quickly replaced. Nonetheless, let the girls bask in the long-deserved glory. Said Joni, 'Now people know who we are as a group, we've gotten people's attention as Sister Sledge. Now it's about staying there. We're still developing the full potential of the group and we don't feel as if we've even come halfway yet.'

Into the new decade, Sister Sledge struggled for chart placings; indeed, their track record was dreadful considering the great heights they'd reached in the recent past. In 1981 the sisters were dealt a further blow when their relationship with the Chic organisation ended, although one single charted in the British Top 40, namely 'Got To Love Somebody', and a year later the solitary single 'All American Girls' faltered in the Top 50. Album-wise, Sister Sledge issued a trio during the two-year period: *Love Somebody Through Today, All American Girls*, recorded with Narada Michael Walden in San Francisco, and *The Sisters*. The last title bombed; it was a bitter blow, as it was the girls' first attempt at producing themselves. Joni claimed, 'I think we honestly got closer to the real Sister Sledge than we have ever been before . . . it was an experience that was really good for us.' 'My Guy', the group's version of Mary Wells's 1964 American chart-topper, was the first single to be extracted from the album. It was a song the sisters had included in their stage act for some years, but the title was a poor seller. From the self-produced *The Sisters* album, the group turned to George Duke to produce their next album, *Betcha Say That To All The Girls*, due for 1983 release. Sister Sledge were delighted at the liaison, although Joni was concerned. 'I felt he had too many other things on at the same time, then when we got a buzz on the title cut, we couldn't release it as a single because it featured Al Jarreau and his record company wouldn't let us!' When both projects bombed, much to the sisters' obvious dismay, their failure was blamed squarely on record-company reorganisation, as Joni explained. 'They were going through internal changes at the time . . . our label, Cotillion Records, was being phased out, so we moved on to the main Atlantic label.'

Like so many acts before and, of course, after them, Sister Sledge enjoyed far more recorded success outside their own country. Indeed, the group had extensively toured through Europe, Japan, where they won the silver prize in the fourth annual Tokyo Song Festival, and Australasia since their early career. In particular, Britain supported the family group and as if to prove that loyalty gave Sister Sledge their first British chart-topper. Released as the follow-up to 'Thinking Of You' and a remixed version of 'Lost In Music', both Top 10 entrants during 1984, 'Frankie' shot to the top of the British chart in June 1985. An extracted track from the *When The Boys Meet The Girls* album, it was a tiresome single, chirping and bouncing across a simple melody, yet the British public lapped up every irritating lyric. To celebrate their unexpected success, Sister Sledge toured the country for the third time. By comparison, 'Frankie' was a poor American seller. Joni said, 'It's amazing . . . if you don't have a monumental hit [in America] everyone assumes you're not doing anything at all . . . But we've been keeping ourselves really busy overseas, as well as working steadily in places like Las Vegas.'

A further track was swiped from *When The Boys Meet The Girls*, namely 'Dancing On The Jagged Edge', which floundered in the British Top 50. However sluggish sales were, WEA Records, the parent company for Atlantic Records, had no intention of abandoning Sister Sledge. But a sister did. In 1988 Kathy left the group to pursue a solo career. To this end, she signed a recording deal with Epic Records, a subsidiary of the major CBS Records (now Sony), where she debuted with the single titled 'Heart'. Regrettably, Kathy's success was limited. Meanwhile, it took until 1993 for the Sister Sledge story to begin again with a trio of remixed dance singles, 'We Are Family', 'Lost In Music' and 'Thinking Of You', all returning Sister Sledge to the British Top 20. Also during 1993 Sister Sledge celebrated their 20th anniversary as a recording group. A tour of Britain and the release of the top-selling album *The Very Best Of Sister Sledge* marked the occasion.

Following the resurgence in their chart career, Sister Sledge re-established themselves on the touring circuit, but since 1993 their chart presence has been nil. However, the ladies, now married with families, have no complaints. They reunite regularly to perform, usually in Europe and particularly in Britain, where they are a prime attraction on the holiday-camp circuit and on soul programmes where they share the billing with similar acts who made their name during the disco explosion.

(Quotes: *Blues and Soul* magazine, interviews by John Abbey 1979, 1983; by David Nathan 1980, 1985; by Ralph Tee 1984)

July 1985

EURYTHMICS

There Must Be An Angel (Playing With My Heart)

It was the unlikely combination of two opposite talents; she was extrovert, he introvert. When the two gelled, the Eurythmics produced music that shocked, warmed and enthralled the world. Glamour, rock, theatre and melody, the Eurythmics had it all.

Annie Lennox, born in Aberdeen, on 25 December 1954, learned to play the piano and flute as a youngster. She abandoned her studies at the Royal Academy of Music in London to work at the Hampstead restaurant Pippins. It was at this restaurant that Lennox met Dave Stewart.

Dave Stewart, born in Sunderland, Tyne and Wear, on 9 September 1952, was already experienced as a recording artist when he met Lennox. With Brian Harrison he had released the single titled 'Deep December' on the Multicord label, before moving to the group Longdancer, signed to Rocket Records.

Stewart persuaded Lennox to abandon her waitressing to live on benefit, thus enabling her to concentrate fully on their future career together. Within a short time the couple were lovers, rented a flat situated over the Spanish Moon record store in Crouch End, London, and survived blissfully on the state benefit of £11 per week. The owner of Spanish Moon allowed Lennox and Stewart to experiment in his basement studio, which led to the couple recording the single 'Borderline'/'Black Blood' with Catch. The title was released late in 1977 via Logo Records and sold badly.

When Catch increased their membership, their name changed to the Tourists, under which title they enjoyed their first taste of British success with 'Blind Among The Flowers', a Top 60 hit mid-1979. The Tourists went on to sustain their charting career which included an uncool version of Dusty Springfield's first solo outing titled 'I Only Want To Be With You'. Both Springfield's and the Tourists' versions peaked in the British Top 4, the first in 1963, the second in 1979. Also during 1979, the Tourists embarked upon their first serious British tour, with Roxy Music. This was followed by an across-Europe trek, a repeat of their British success. A trio of albums was also released by the Tourists, the biggest-selling being the Top 30 title *Reality Affect*.

Into the '80s, and with an Australian tour to their credit, the Tourists disbanded, although towards the close of 1980 the group charted for the last time with the Top 40 single 'Don't Say I Told You So'. Lennox was tiring of the group restrictions, yet defended their work: 'I'm into quality. Good-quality sounds with a quality message. Not just saying what everybody's said before.' Without Lennox's input, of course, the Tourists had no guiding force. The band's demise and the strain of the past few months led to Stewart being hospitalised with a collapsed lung. One lung was already damaged due to regular drug-taking and the second collapsed following a car accident. Stewart admitted, 'It was a pretty wretched time . . . I'd broken up with Annie, who thought I was completely nuts, and I was alone.'

That said, it was also natural that Lennox and Stewart would go on to record together with support musicians. The combination was a good one. Both were young; Stewart was streetwise, with a business acumen, Lennox was classically trained with a clean attitude towards life. Their relationship thrived on difference. The result of their collaboration was 'Never Gonna Cry Again', earmarked for single release under the name Eurythmics, a name inspired by Lennox's earlier training in Eurythmic dancing which author Lucy O'Brien reported was a discipline adapted by Emil Jacques Dalcroze, a professor of harmony at the Conservatoire of Music in Geneva during the 1890s. 'Never Gonna Cry Again' was issued via a recording deal with RCA Records but stalled in the British Top 70 during July 1981. The duo would then wait a further year before returning to the chart with 'Love Is A Stranger', a Top 60 hit in 1982.

Early in 1983, the *Sweet Dreams (Are Made Of This)* album shot into the British Top 3 and Top 20 in America. The album gave birth to the Lennox/Stewart sound which went on to form the basis of a string of hit singles. The concept was simple: a combination of Stewart's synthesised melodies with Lennox's often complex lyrics, stylishly combined. The album was soon followed by its title track, which soared to No.2 in Britain. When released in America, the 'Sweet Dreams (Are Made Of This)' single catapulted to No.1, selling in excess of one million copies. Not a bad start for a newly formed commercial band!

In the April, the rereleased title 'Love Is A Stranger' fared better by hitting No.6 in Britain, while the official follow-up to 'Sweet Dreams (Are Made Of This)', titled 'Who's That Girl?', returned the Eurythmics to the top section of the British chart. The duo closed 1983 with the Top 10 British hit 'Right By Your Side' and the Top 30 American charter 'Love Is A Stranger'. With Lennox's love of theatre, the single's accompanying video introduced her to the public as the starlet-cum-hooker-cum-pusher. In later videos Lennox would often be dressed in a style to confuse viewers, given freedom to roam through characters, portraying some to the extreme. Obviously, as the Eurythmics' music appealed to so-called impressionable youngsters, Lennox was careful that her later move into cross-dressing wasn't too realistic. Even so, her public was confused as to her sexuality. In defence, the artist said it was something she had chosen to do to portray authority and control, allowing her to hide behind the male disguise: 'Being in a middle place that's neither overtly male nor overtly female makes you threatening, it gives you power,' she said. In time the lesbian fraternity hailed Lennox as an idol, undeterred by the knowledge that she was a heterosexual. She admitted, 'I've had a few gay girls come on to me but, just for the record, I'm not gay. Because I choose to wear practical male dress, though, I'm always being mistaken for a man.' Lennox was clever, it was as simple as that – everyone purchased records!

As 1984 started, so did the Eurythmics' world tour. A month into the trek during February 1984, their single 'Here Comes The Rain Again' shot into the British Top 8 and American Top 4. The album *Touch* fared better, topping the British chart. It made the American Top 10, and went on to be rifled for four tracks to be remixed by Jellybean and François Keverkian for disco purposes, issued under the title *Touch Dance*; it was a Top 40 British hit in the July but a poor seller across the Atlantic. Prior to this release, Lennox married Rahda Raman, a Hare Krishna monk, during the March. To ensure the registry-office wedding ran without a hitch, Stewart announced his engagement to the fiery American soul singer Nona Hendryx. The ploy worked: media attention zoomed in on Stewart's tale of fantasy, while Lennox and her monk quietly married, later honeymooning in Switzerland in an area near her husband's Krishna community. However, the liaison was doomed and in April 1985 Lennox filed for divorce.

On the professional front, Lennox scooped the Brit Award for Best British Female Artist, while Stewart won the Ivor Novello Award for Songwriter of the Year. Across the Atlantic they were both recipients of MTV Video Music Awards for Best New Artists with 'Sweet Dreams

(Are Made Of This)'. Meanwhile, on the singles front, 'Sex Crime (1984)', included in the soundtrack of *1984*, a film version of George Orwell's work directed by Michael Radford, soared to No.4 in Britain, only reaching the Top 90 in America. The Eurythmics were asked to score the music when first choice David Bowie priced himself out of the running. Lennox and Stewart were unaware of Bowie's involvement at the time. When Radford mentioned the fact during a newspaper interview, the Eurythmics furiously issued their own statement, which included, 'Our credibility as artists has been seriously jeopardised by Michael Radford's misleading comments.' Meanwhile, amid the flurry of press statements, the Eurythmics' own album *1984 (For the Love Of Big Brother)* sat at No.23 in the British chart.

Into the new year, a further single, 'Julia', was swiped from *1984 (For The Love Of Big Brother)*, and surprisingly faltered in the British Top 50. With failure, though, came success, as its follow-up, titled 'Would I Lie To You?', soared into the Top 20 in the May and Top 5 in America. The only album of 1985, titled *Be Yourself Tonight*, sold in abundance to peak in the British Top 3, reaching No.9 in America. It was from this album that the Eurythmics enjoyed their first British chart-topper 'There Must Be An Angel (Playing With My Heart)', with Stevie Wonder happily playing harmonica in the background. Like all the Eurythmics' promotional videos, the one accompanying the chart-topper was cleverly and artistically devised and incorporated Lennox's love of costume, showing children and vestal virgins with the artist herself clothed in white and wearing a long golden wig. Stewart, as co-star, was King Louis XIV, adding his air of decadence. Said Lennox, 'I'm amazed by the power of make-up and costume. I see image as a wrapping, something to play with.'

In November 1985, the soul slant that was apparent in the duo's work went one step further when Lennox duetted with Aretha Franklin to release the 'Sisters Are Doing It For Themselves' single, a Top 10 British hit and Top 20 American title. As an aside, Tina Turner was Lennox's first choice as a duettist, but when she was unavailable Lennox considered Franklin. The very thought of the two artists duetting was an exciting prospect; in reality, though, the recording session was fraught with problems. After insisting certain lyrics be amended, Franklin believed Lennox was gay and such was her dislike of gays refused to converse with her. When shooting the single's promotional video, however, the two singers appeared as soul sisters, bound by the spirit of the music. Said Lennox, 'What can I say? Queen of soul, a living legend. I learned so much from her.'

From composing and recording, it was a natural move for Lennox to become a dedicated actress, and when she appeared, albeit briefly, in Hugh Hudson's *Revolution* it came as no surprise to the public.

Starring Al Pacino and Donald Sutherland, the movie bombed. Two years on, in 1987, Lennox appeared in *The Room*, a film based on Harold Pinter's novel; it was another poorly received movie. Meanwhile, on Stewart's personal front, he married Siobhan Fahey from the British female group Bananarama. The marriage was a magnificent and costly affair, with guests flown from London to Normandy. While the couple honeymooned, Lennox met Uri Fruchtman, an Israeli documentary film-maker. They later married in 1988. A year prior to Lennox's marriage, Siobhan Stewart gave birth to a son, Samuel, while Lennox's first child, Daniel, was stillborn. Professionally speaking, Stewart and his wife would collaborate on record as Shakespears Sister.

A trio of British hit singles during 1986 ensured the Eurythmics continued their high selling profile. 'It's Alright (Baby's Coming Back)' was the first, a Top 12 title which went on to falter in the American Top 80. The British Top 30 title 'When Tomorrow Comes' and, quite possibly the most exciting of all, 'Thorn In My Side', a Top 5 British hit and Top 70 American hit, completed the set. In between these releases, the duo's next album, *Revenge*, hit the Top 3, although it made only the Top 30 across the Atlantic. Touring, of course, also played its part in the Eurythmics' career this year, as by now they were in demand across the world.

In the lead-up to the new decade, Lennox and Stewart never failed to delight. Singles like 'Beethoven (I Love To Listen To)' and 'Shame' maintained their chart presence, as did albums including the British chart-topping project *We Too Are One* in 1989. The album reached the American Top 40 and was the duo's first under a newly negotiated recording contract with Arista Records. On the touring front, the Eurythmics performed, with others, at the Wembley gala to celebrate Nelson Mandela's 70th birthday. Then, to celebrate Christmas 1988, Lennox duetted with soul man Al Green on the title 'Put A Little Love In Your Heart'. The Jackie De Shannon original was, by the way, included in the soundtrack to the movie *Scrooged*. The duet reached the British Top 30 before cracking the American Top 10, representing Lennox's first release without her musical partner, who by now was in demand as a composer and producer. Was a split inevitable?

That question was answered in 1990 when Lennox and Stewart announced they would work apart for at least two years, although the couple lived off the *We Too Are One* album for a while longer when a pair of tracks were swiped for single release, namely the innovative 'King And Queen Of America' and 'Angel'. Both peaked in the British Top 30. Behind the scenes, meanwhile, Stewart had formed his new musical vehicle, Spiritual Cowboys, who would debut on the New York stage at the International Music Awards concert and debut on record with the album *Dave Stewart And The Spiritual Cowboys* in September 1990. It was a Top 40 British hit, as the extracted single, 'Jack Talking', floundered in the Top 70. Lennox, on the other hand, prepared herself for a solo career with her first outing 'Ev'rytime We Say Goodbye', her contribution to the Cole Porter compilation titled *Red Hot + Blue*.

Into 1991, Stewart and others recorded John Lennon's immortal anthem 'Give Peace A Chance' under the overall name the Peace Choir, the *Eurythmics Greatest Hits* album entered the chart at No.1, and a pair of rereleased singles – 'Love Is A Stranger' and 'Sweet Dreams (Are Made Of This)' – faltered around the British Top 50. A year on, as the Eurythmics continued to live on through the album *Eurythmics Live 1983–1989*, Stewart worked with Terry Hall, late of the Specials and Fun Boy Three, before recording with the group Vegas to enjoy a handful of minor British charters. He then moved into television to score the theme and music for the BBC TV programme *Jute City* and Gerry Anderson's *GFI* children's series, among other programmes. From Vegas, Stewart moved towards a career as a soloist; to this end he released the *Greetings From The Gutter* album via a recording deal with East West Records.

So what of Lennox? During the early part of 1992, she issued her sombre title 'Why'. The single shot into the British Top 5. It was extracted from her brilliant solo album *Diva*, which entered the British chart at No.1 in the April. To celebrate the album's success in Britain and Europe, BBC2 screened a documentary bearing its title. This was only one of the artist's extremely high-profile television appearances at this time. The follow-ups to 'Why', the equally compelling 'Precious' and the irresistible 'Walking On Broken Glass', likewise lifted from *Diva*, were British and American hits, cementing a lucrative solo career for one of Britain's favourite artists.

Into 1993, when *Diva* returned to the album chart on its way to selling five million copies, Lennox scooped further industry awards in tribute to her talent, including a pair of Brit Awards for Best Album and Best British Female Artist, and the Ivor Novello Award for 'Why' in the Best Song Musically and Lyrically section.

Having thrown herself totally into her career, Lennox's second album was completed in time for 1995 release. Titled *Medusa*, it followed its predecessor's path by entering the British chart at the top, reaching the Top 20 in America. The lifted track 'No More "I Love You"'s' soared to No.2 in Britain during February 1995; when released in America three months on, the title peaked in the Top 30. Further singles – 'A Whiter Shade Of Pale', 'Waiting In Vain' and 'Something So Right' – sustained the artist's selling power in Britain, although that was starting to crack due to her prolonged absences from the public eye. Indeed, 'Something So Right' marked Lennox's final British placing to date. However, the artist's life is still full, campaigning for environmental issues, vegetarianism, animal welfare and other causes she strongly believes in. Following months of deliberation and rumour, Lennox was also reunited with Dave Stewart on stage. When newspaper advertisements declared that the Eurythmics would tour Britain in 1999, fans treated the announcement like the Second Coming.

(Quotes: *Annie Lennox* by Lucy O'Brien)

August 1985

MADONNA

Into The Groove

She's been heralded as the biggest money-making star of the decade. Her private life would make a nun blush and others, well, envious. Yes, folks, here's Madonna!

Born Madonna Louise Veronica Ciccone on 16 August 1958 to Madonna and Tony, in Bay City's Mercy Hospital, she was nicknamed Little Nonni to avoid confusion with her mother. One of six children, Nonni was raised in a devout Catholic household and inherited her love for music from her mother in the short time she knew her. When she was expecting Nonni's sister, Melanie, Madonna was diagnosed with breast cancer and later died in December 1963. She was 30 years old. Young Nonni turned to her father; her dependence on him was an obsession. He was the only important focus in her young life until he remarried during 1966.

Relocating to Rochester, Michigan, in 1970, Madonna studied at the West Junior High School, where in between studies she and her schoolfriends devoured music, particularly Aretha Franklin and those artists signed to Motown Records. However, it was Nancy Sinatra whom Madonna idolised!

Having graduated during 1972, the young girl visited her grandmother in Bay View, where, among other things, Madonna fuelled her music obsession by spending time with her uncle's band. From the West Junior High School Madonna switched to Rochester Junior High for a four-year stay. She was, by all accounts, a model student with an IQ of 140-plus. She joined the Help The Kid programme, was a lifeguard during the summers and participated in humorous student drama productions. On the downside, Madonna embarked upon wild shopping sprees with no money, mostly at the D & C Dime Store. At the age of 14, she attended the Rochester School of Ballet and was later accepted at the University of Michigan's School of Music. In 1978, with a one-way ticket, Madonna headed for New York, with the clothes she wore, a handful of dollars and her ballet shoes. To earn extra bucks she modelled in the nude, and between dance classes and auditions she befriended graffiti artists.

One audition launched her into the music career she craved. European dance star Patrick Hernandez was so impressed with her song/dance routine that he shipped her to Paris during 1979, where apart from being hailed as 'the next Edith Piaf' she joined the Patrick Hernandez Revue and 'dated a lot of French boys' on her way to becoming a European disco act. Following a six-month stay with Hernandez, Madonna moved on to form her own group, the Breakfast Club, named after the all-night sessions which invariably ended early morning in a coffee bar with the exhausted members fumbling over breakfast. The group performed on the local circuit; when the lead vocalist departed, Madonna was promoted from drummer on the backline to frontline vocalist. She told author Christopher Anderson, 'It doesn't help to be the best singer in the world or to have the most talented band if only a few people know it. I wanted the world to notice me.' From the Breakfast Club, the young girl moved to her own unit Emanon ('no name' in reverse) until 1981, when she decided the time was right to concentrate on her own talent by recording demo tapes of her compositions. Of the companies Madonna approached, Gotham Productions' Adam Alter was sufficiently delighted with what he heard to sign her to the company, find her suitable accommodation, pay her $100 a week and open the door to the recording studio. In return, the company received 15 per cent of her gross earnings.

Mid-1981 Madonna appeared with her new act at a biker club, US Blues, on Long Island. Anderson reported that she walked on stage 'wearing a man's tuxedo, shirt and gold beaded sweater with a huge red M across the chest'. Her first recordings, though, were not as a soloist but contributing to other artists' material, notably for Steve Bentazel from the New York-based Mindfield Records. With no released product, Madonna severed her ties with Gotham Productions to team with disco producer Mark Kamins. Impressed with her demo material, Kamins persuaded Sire Records to sign the young girl to a recording contract during 1982. The title 'Ain't No Big Deal' was earmarked for Madonna's debut single but was replaced by 'Everybody', pressed across both sides of a single. It topped the American dance chart. The follow-up, 'Physical

Attraction', likewise soared to No.1. One step further to realising her ambition, Madonna was now a big-selling disco act.

In the spring of 1983 Madonna started recording her first album, while her record company demanded a new single. The singer consulted her current boyfriend, Jellybean Benitez, who gave her his composition 'Holiday'. The track was recorded within days for release during June 1983, when it peaked at No.16 in America before soaring to No.6 in the British chart, following an intensive promotional trip. Three months on, Madonna's eponymous album was finally issued and peaked in the American Top 10 on its way to 4.5 million sales. Hot on the heels of this success, Madonna issued the title 'Lucky Star' in Britain during September 1983; it peaked in the Top 20. When issued in America a month on, the title soared into the Top 5, passing sales of one million, while the 'Borderline' single peaked in the Top 10, Top 60 in Britain.

Before 1984 closed, Madonna switched track into the film world by playing the role of Susan in the *Desperately Seeking Susan* movie. Her music career had been guaranteed with her second album *Like A Virgin*, from which the title track was lifted as a single to top the American chart during the December, a position it dominated for six long weeks. Released early in 1985 in Britain, the title soared into the Top 3. These single sales naturally boosted the *Like A Virgin* album, which topped the American chart before selling in excess of nine million copies in that country. With the Virgin project, the public viewed the singer differently. Not only was the music heavily raunchy, but her image took the theme several steps further. To promote the single Madonna filmed a video in Venice, where, wrote Anderson, a tarted-up Madonna writhed in a gondola wearing a traditional white lace wedding gown. It had taken a while but Madonna had broken free. This image was simply the beginning; as time passed, she practically broke the decency barriers!

At the time of the release of the 'Material Girl' single, which soared into the Top 3 on both sides of the Atlantic and which portrayed her as a reincarnated Marilyn Monroe, Madonna befriended actor Sean Penn and embarked upon her debut American tour using the overall banner 'The Virgin Tour'.

Following the American première of *Desperately Seeking Susan*, the singer's next single, penned by Lind and Bettis and titled 'Crazy For You', topped the American chart in May 1985, reaching No.2 in Britain. In the July, Madonna joined other American acts to appear at the JFK Stadium in Philadelphia for the second leg of the Live Aid cross-Atlantic gala. She was introduced by Bette Midler, who said Madonna was a woman 'who pulled herself up by her bra straps and who has been known to let them down occasionally'. Ouch! A month on, Madonna topped the British chart with 'Into The Groove'/ 'Angel', two tracks swiped from *Desperately Seeking Susan*. For a particular film sequence, the director needed a track with a dance beat. Madonna suggested 'Into The Groove', a track she had penned for black singer Cheyne, which she had on an eight-track demo tape. The song was more than good enough to become a late inclusion into the movie. The singer shot the 'Into The Groove' promotional video, whereupon MTV screened it constantly. The single sold the film. While 'Into The Groove' dominated British sales, her previous release 'Holiday' catapulted into the British Top 2.

On the downside, during the time of her British success, much publicity was given to *Penthouse* magazine's intention to publish pictures of Madonna in the nude, the shots taken from photo sessions during 1979 and 1980. *Playboy* magazine then dropped the bomb-shell that it too planned to publish photographs of the singer in the raw. Indeed, *Playboy* beat its rival to the newsstands by one day. There was nothing Madonna could do; she had signed the rights away at the time of the sessions. Instead she said, 'I'm not ashamed of anything.' Also at the time of 'Into The Groove', Madonna married Sean Penn in a cliff-top Malibu estate owned by property developer Dan Unger. Selected guests attended a ceremony that was supposed to be a well-kept secret but which was open to helicopters flying overhead crammed with photographers, while reporters wearing disguises mingled with guests. By all accounts, Madonna loved the media attention, while Penn loathed it. The marriage would be rocky, to say the least; Madonna said at the start, 'His temperament is . . . similar to mine [but] that doesn't always make for ideal relationships.'

She wasn't wrong!

Also see: 'Papa Don't Preach', July 1986; 'True Blue', October 1986; 'La Isla Bonita', June 1987; 'Like A Prayer', April 1989

(Quotes: *Madonna: Unauthorized* by Christopher Anderson)

September 1985

DAVID BOWIE AND MICK JAGGER

Dancing In The Street

'Calling out around the world, are you ready for a brand new beat?' Well, were we ready for this?

At Bob Geldof's musical extravaganza Live Aid to help the starving population of Ethiopia, it was intended that Mick Jagger and David Bowie would sing their version of Martha Reeves and the Vandellas' Motown classic 'Dancing In The Street' as a transatlantic duet, an idea dreamed up by the two singers following a night out.

'When I first heard "Dancing In The Street" it was sung by Marvin Gaye. He had written it along with Ivy Hunter and Mickey Stevenson,' Martha Reeves wrote in her autobiography. Reeves disliked the song at first as it was conceived in a male register and only when she modified the track's melody did she 'make it her own'. 'Dancing In The Street' soared to No.2 in the American chart during 1964, with *Billboard* magazine declaring it to be 'one of the most consistently played dance records of all time'. The single also represented Martha and the Vandellas' debut British hit at No.28 in October 1964 and, upon reissue in 1969, reached No.4. According to Martha, 'From the very beginning, no matter where it was played, everybody seemed to get up and dance to it. I love the excitement and magic of [the song].'

'Dancing In The Street' also played a small part in saving lives in 1967 during a performance at the Fox, Detroit. Reeves recalled that while the Motown trio was on stage, widespread rioting broke out across the city: 'A local dispute with the police had sparked the riots, and out-of-control mobs roamed the streets, smashing store windows, looting and setting fire to whole blocks of the city.' With microphone in hand, singing 'Dancing In The Street', the singer stood her ground on stage, encouraging audience order, avoiding a possible stampede.

So back to 1985 and the most unlikely of artists to sing a master-piece that only the brave or the foolhardy would attempt. When the transatlantic duet had to be aborted, Jagger and Bowie were filmed singing 'Dancing In The Street' for inclusion in the Live Aid gala. Shot in London's Docklands, the video showed them prancing and dancing, smiling and pouting like possessed characters attempting to exude sexual vibes. In the short space of time it took to prepare, the video served its purpose. After being screened in 5,000 theatres across America, 'Dancing In The Street' shot to No.10 in America and topped the British chart in September 1985, where it stayed for four weeks. It was Jagger and Bowie's only duet.

Following the announcement that he was to appear in the video with Bowie, Jagger said he intended to appear with Tina Turner on the American section of Live Aid at the JFK Stadium in Philadelphia. When Bob Geldof had originally approached the Rolling Stones to join his list of mega-star performers, they had failed to respond, except Jagger. Backed by Daryl Hall and John Oates, Jagger sang as he ripped off Turner's skirt before an attending audience of 90,000 and an estimated worldwide audience of 1.6 billion. The couple sweated and strutted through a splendidly raunchy 'Honky Tonk Woman' and a medley of 'State Of Shock' and 'It's Only Rock'n'Roll'. This outstanding performance was, incidentally, Jagger's first official date without the Stones. As much as Live Aid was a triumph for him, it turned into an embarrassment for Keith Richards and Ron Wood. Many believed it was in a last-ditch attempt to steal Jagger's glory that they agreed to support Bob Dylan for the concert's gala finale. The result was an unprofessional sham.

When all was said and done, 'Dancing In The Street' raised much-needed finances for the Live Aid project, which in turn went to the starving people of Ethiopia. So who are we to knock it?

(Quotes: *Dancing in the Street* by Martha Reeves and Mark Bego)

See *Every Chart-Topper Tells a Story: The Sixties* for further information regarding Mick Jagger and the Rolling Stones; *Every Chart-Topper Tells a Story: The Seventies* for further information regarding David Bowie. Also see the single 'Under Pressure', November 1981, with Queen

October 1985

MIDGE URE

If I Was

He was the voice that launched Ultravox upon a successful recording career, a distinctive vocal against a musical backdrop of the New Romantic era. He also asked if they knew it was Christmas.

Conceived as Tiger Lily by Chris Cross and John Foxx in 1976, and after recruiting a guitarist and drummer Warren Cann, the musicians moved through several group names, including the Innocents, before settling on Ultravox. Under this moniker they secured a recording contract with Island Records late in 1976, whereupon the debut single was released early in 1977. Titled 'Dangerous Rhythm', the track was an introduction to the group's first album, *Ultravox*. Both titles bombed, as did the group's next single, 'Rockwork', and album, *Ha! Ha! Ha!*, issued in 1977.

Into 1978, Robin Smith became a replacement guitarist and Ultravox issued their four-track EP titled 'Retro'. It also bombed. However, this did not deter Island Records from financing Ultravox's third album, titled *Systems Of Romance*. Released in September 1978, it was another failure. In between these recorded mishaps, Ultravox toured Britain and Europe and appeared with others at the 1977 Reading Festival.

With such an appalling track record, it wasn't surprising when Island Records and Ultravox parted company during 1979. This parting of the ways actually snowballed, and the group disbanded. John Foxx went on to open his own record label Metal Beat and enjoyed a relatively successful career as a soloist, including the albums *Metamix* and *The Golden Section*, while Chris Cross embarked upon a composing career, leaving the remaining Ultravox members to decide their fate. Eventually, Ultravox was to continue; all that was needed was a new lead vocalist. In April 1979 Midge Ure, born James Ure in Scotland on 10 October 1953, filled the vacancy. Late of Visage, one-time replacement for Brian Robertson in Thin Lizzy's line-up and member of Slik, who, incidentally, enjoyed the solitary January 1976 British chart-topper 'Forever And Ever', Ure was perfect.

A new recording deal was signed with Chrysalis Records and the new decade saw Ultravox chart for the first time. Their 'Sleepwalk' single peaked in the British Top 30 in the April, soon followed by Island Records' 'cash-in' album titled *Three Into One*. As that item sold poorly, Ultravox's new studio album *Vienna* soared to No.3 in the British chart; the New Romantic group had finally carved its name in British music.

Now with hit material to support, Ultravox hit the touring trail across Britain, playing before capacity-filled venues. However, the group's wildest dreams were realised when the album's title song 'Vienna' was extracted for single release. A remarkable tune, it certainly deserved chart-topping status, but due to immense competition at the time the title peaked at No.2 during January 1981. Considered a classic of the decade, the single was a timeless, haunting slice of magic.

A trio of singles followed during 1981, ensuring Ultravox's high chart profile: 'All Stood Still', 'The Thin Wall' and 'The Voice'. When the group eventually issued its second Chrysalis Records album, titled *Rage In Eden*, they were once again elevated to the upper section of the British chart.

During 1982 Midge Ure flexed his solo muscle to record his version of the Walker Brothers' 1976 British Top 10 single 'No Regrets'. Ure's version soared into the Top 10 in the June, bearing no resemblance to the Walkers' powerhouse performance. Composer Tom Rush must, in all honesty, have wondered how one song could differ so much! Meanwhile, Ultravox issued the *Quartet* album, another Top 10 charter, which spawned a pair of singles, namely 'Reap The Wild Wind' and 'Hymn', both Top 20 British hits.

In 1983, when Ure issued his second solo outing titled 'After A Fashion', a falterer in the Top 40, Ultravox released the 'We Came To Dance' single, which soared into the Top 20. Never mind, Midge, your time will come! Before 1983 closed, Ultravox's album *Monument: The Soundtrack* shot to No.9 in the British chart.

With the new year, the group's popularity peaked once more when 'Dancing With Tears In My Eyes' swept into the British Top 3. Its sales boosted those of the following album, *Lament*, featuring Mae McKenna on vocals, which made the Top 10.

As Ure composed the track 'Do They Know It's Christmas?' with Bob Geldof, later organising the recording of the title by a large number of Britain's finest artists, Ultravox's selling power waned, although the slide was halted temporarily by the No.12 single 'Love's Great Adventure'. Into 1985, as Band Aid's 'Do They Know It's Christmas?' topped the British chart, Ure and Geldof scooped a host of industry awards including the Ivor Novello Award for Best Selling A-Side. The enterprising couple then embarked upon the awesome task of organising the Live Aid gala staged at Wembley Stadium, during which Ure performed with Ultravox. Before the year ended, the group's career was placed on hold, leaving Ure to concentrate on his much-wanted solo career.

Like other contributing artists to the Wembley spectacular, Ure was to enjoy increased record sales. He shot to the top of the British chart with his third solo single, titled 'If I Was', during October 1985. The chart-topper was soon followed by his album *The Gift*, a No.2 British hit, while the one-million-selling single was followed by 'That Certain Smile', a Top 30 entrant. As 1985 closed, the singer embarked upon his first solo tour of Britain, deservedly enjoying recognition for his tireless work for Live Aid and his status as a worthy soloist.

During 1986 Ure issued a pair of sluggish-selling singles, namely 'Wastelands' and 'Call Of The Wild'; as he struggled to dent the singles chart, Ultravox returned in style with the Top 10 album *U-Vox* and lifted tracks 'Same Old Story' and 'All Fall Down' as singles.

For the next two years Ure concentrated on his political and charity activities, toured Europe and, with his career ever forefront in his mind, began planning his next album. During September 1988 that completed album, *Answers To Nothing*, peaked in the British Top 30 as two lifted tracks, the album's title and 'Dear God', floundered in the Top 50. Of Ure's live performances during 1988, the most spectacular was his contribution to Nelson Mandela's 70th birthday tribute gala staged at Wembley Stadium.

Into the '90s, and with a change of record company from Chrysalis to Arista Records, Ure issued his poor-selling *Pure* album, from which the track titled 'Cold Cold Heart' was released, peaking in the Top 20 during August 1991. It took the singer a further five years to chart in Britain once more, with the single 'Breathe'. Unfortunately, that title faltered in the Top 70. On the other hand, Ultravox enjoyed renewed life; 'Vienna' recharted at No.13 during February 1993, prompting the release of a compilation of the group's and Ure's best material.

Despite his lucrative recording career, the name of Midge Ure will obviously be remembered for his association with Bob Geldof – although, of course, Geldof took the lion's share of the glory. However, Ure proved his talent as an individual and his devotion to life- and earth-saving projects is well known. He is indeed a man of our time.

November 1985

WHAM!

I'm Your Man

'Our music is pop music. We're not ashamed of that. If we wanted to be a cult band we'd have gone about things quite differently' – George Michael

George Michael and Andrew Ridgeley would be the first to acknowledge the support of nightclub DJs who remained loyal to the duo's music from the outset, and none more so than Graham 'Fatman' Canter, premier London jock who was working at Le Beat Route in Greek Street at the time of Wham!'s struggle for recognition. Canter's diligence was rewarded by the duo and CBS Records during a lunchtime press reception where the DJ was presented with a silver disc in recognition of his support. Canter went on to work in several high-profile London nightclubs and dabbled with radio before returning to his previous occupation, that of an accountant. He died on 4 November 1996, a short time after the death of his close friend, fellow DJ and journalist James Hamilton.

Hot on the heels of Wham!'s first chart-topper 'Wake Me Up Before You Go Go', Michael issued his solo title 'Careless Whisper', which also topped the British chart. Now hailed as Britain's top singing sensations, Wham! flew to the south of France in September 1984 to record their second album, tentatively titled *Make It Big*, at the Château Minerval, the home of jazz musician Jacques Louissier.

During this time, the duo met Elton John, who became a close friend to Michael, while on the downside Ridgeley's love of alcohol interrupted recording schedules, annoying his partner sufficiently to write in his autobiography, 'That was the time when Andrew was going out and getting pissed out of his head. Doing it very deliberately, placing himself right in front of the cameras . . . he was getting totally wrecked, he was so lazy and he just couldn't be bothered.' It is true to say that Ridgeley's name was frequently headline news. He attracted bad publicity, earning names like 'Vomit Fountain' and 'Randy Andy', and Michael admitted his partner enjoyed the attention. 'He would actually go to places where he knew that he would be smashed out of his brains by the end of the evening and that they would get their pictures . . . I was going out to places where the press wouldn't be.'

Finally deciding to have his nose reshaped by cosmetic surgery, Ridgeley told the media it had been broken by a champagne bucket which had been thrown at him. The story was a sham; Ridgeley had loathed the shape of his nose since he was a youngster. Nonetheless, the media's coverage was such that the nose operation was known as the Hootergate Affair.

It seemed that part of Ridgeley's craving for publicity stemmed from his being considered by the public to be the useless partner in the duo. 'It niggled because people just didn't seem to grasp the whole thing . . . in videos and in the press, we were very much a duo, and people found it a bit galling that it wasn't like that in the musical sense.' What was clear, though, was that the press had divided Wham! into the good guy and the bad guy; Michael basked in the glow until 1998, when he was arrested for lewd behaviour in a Los Angeles public toilet.

During September 1984, Wham! performed at the Royal Festival Hall as part of the benefit concert for the families of the striking coal miners. The audience, though, reacted strongly against the duo's performance by jeering, not because of their music but because of their suntans – not the ideal appearance when performing for families who couldn't afford to eat, let alone take a holiday!

As the *Make It Big* album shot to the top of the British chart, the duo embarked upon a long-awaited world tour. At the same time Michael contributed to Band Aid's 'Do They Know It's Christmas?'. Ridgeley, however, did not contribute, a move many felt indicated a further crack in the Wham! partnership. 'Do They Know It's Christmas?' instantly topped the British chart, preventing the duo's own 'Last Christmas' from claiming the spot.

On Boxing Day, Wham!'s single was flipped to 'Everything She Wants' and, supported by hefty record-company promotion, it eventually sold over a million copies. Royalties from both titles, estimated to be £250,000, were earmarked for the Ethiopian famine fund.

Into 1985 the duo remained locked in the tour that would take them through Australia, Japan and later America, where, Michael recalled, groupies hounded them. 'Men are not used to being hunted. Initially I thought it was absolutely wonderful . . . and I abused the privilege a little bit maybe, although I wasn't getting anything out of a sexual situation that wasn't being returned.'

In March 1985 *Make It Big* became an American chart-topper, selling over five million copies. The same month Michael earned the distinction of becoming the youngest recipient of the Ivor Novello Award for Songwriter of the Year during a gala staged at the Grosvenor House Hotel. In May Wham! performed in China, the first Western pop unit to be invited to do so by the All China Youth Federation. Joining the necessary touring company of stage and road crew, managers and photographers was a 35-strong film crew to preserve the historical performances.

Before 1985 ended, Wham!'s next British single, titled 'I'm Your Man', soared to the top in the November, supported by a black-and-white video filmed not in China but at the Marquee, London! The single dominated British sales but carried a message – Michael wanted to disband the partnership.

However, before Wham! hung up the dancing shoes, smiles and microphones, one further British chart-topper would be achieved.

Also see: 'Wake Me Up Before You Go Go', June 1984; 'The Edge Of Heaven', June 1986

(Quotes: *Bare* by George Michael and Tony Parsons)

December 1985

WHITNEY HOUSTON

Saving All My Love For You

'My mother was my foundation' – Whitney Houston
To carefully nurture a young artist for two years and then have your dreams come true is like a storybook tale' – Clive Davis
Born in Newark, New Jersey, on 9 August 1963, Whitney Elizabeth Houston was more fortunate than most by growing up in a musical

family comprising dedicated performers. She was the youngest of three children, having two brothers, Gary and Michael.

Houston's mother Cissy Drinkard Houston was obviously the youngster's greatest influence, closely followed by her aunts Dionne and Dee Dee Warwick. Whitney would join her mother when she performed in the gospel group the Drinkard Sisters and would watch her in the recording studio singing with Aretha Franklin, among others. With her husband John as manager, Cissy also formed the Sweet Inspirations, a gospel group hugely popular for three decades. In 1967, the Sweet Inspirations debuted as recording artists for Atlantic Records with their eponymous album. The swiped track 'Sweet Inspiration' was the first single, a Top 20 American hit. The group's subsequent recording career transformed them into an in-demand performing outfit. To this end, they supported Aretha Franklin for two years, who once said, 'Cissy Houston and the Sweet Inspirations are the hottest singers in the business.' According to Cissy, 'Nobody in the world could touch us.' She was right: no one could. During 1968 Elvis Presley requested the Sweets open his show at the International Hotel in Las Vegas. The combination was electrifying.

Further group releases included the albums titled *What The World Needs Now Is Love* and *Sweets For My Sweet*. Early in 1970 Houston and the membership parted company: her replacement was Ann Williams, who recorded a solitary album with them named *Sweet Sweet Soul: The Sweet Inspirations*, before working with the group as support vocalists for Elvis Presley during the next eight years. Meanwhile, Cissy Houston signed as a soloist with Janus Records, where in 1971 she issued the *Cissy Houston* album. According to Whitney, 'My mother was ahead of her time.' Six years on, she issued her second *Cissy Houston* album via Private Stock Records. Produced by dance master Michael Zager and featuring Whitney as one of the back-up vocalists, the album represented the clashing of gospel and mainstream dance. Pure magic! While with Zager, Cissy enjoyed a cross-Atlantic disco hit with 'Think It Over'. Yep, the gospel queen was stepping into pop music and the future looked promising. Then, almost overnight, Private Stock Records folded, taking Houston's career with it. She did, however, go on to record with Columbia Records, but the impetus had gone.

While she was a teenager, Whitney's parents divorced. Her father went on to become her manager, while her mother discreetly guided her daughter's career. Whitney's musical career began at the age of eight, when she first sang in public as a member of her mother's New Baptist church choir. By this time, Whitney had often joined her mother on stage as a contributor to her cabaret performances, where, more often than not, she would sing 'The Greatest Love Of All' from the movie *The Greatest*, the life story of Muhammad Ali. Certainly Whitney was more privileged than most, enjoying a musical education that would prove priceless in future years.

At the age of 14, Whitney joined her mother on stage at New York's Town Hall to sing the song 'Tomorrow' from the musical *Annie*, while a year on she was a regular studio session singer for artists like Chaka Khan. Even at this young age, Whitney was living life in the fast lane.

From singing, the young girl was persuaded to join the CLICK model agency, where, at 17 years of age, she was photographed for the covers of magazines like *Cosmopolitan*. This led to a lucrative contract with Revlon. But although her earning power as a model was attractive, she was bored. To vary the routine, Houston took acting classes in New York which, she said, went on to benefit her when she was interpreting a particularly powerful song on stage. Through these New York sessions, and with a heavyweight management team of Seymour Flics and Gene Harvey, Houston was offered bit parts in a handful of American television shows like *Gimme a Break*.

The young girl was becoming a popular figure as both an actress and a singer to the extent that record companies began approaching her, waving contracts to secure her exclusivity. ('People were interested in me from the time I was 15,' she once said.) An obvious interested party was Michael Zager, for whom Houston and her mother sang; his offer was rejected. In stepped Clive Davis, president of Arista Records. After seeing Houston perform at Seventh Avenue South, New York, he was very impressed with the 18-year-old and she became a signed Arista Records artist in April 1983. From this date the two worked closely together on a creative level, choosing material to complement her talent and selecting producers sympathetic to her voice. 'I saw a rare combination of talent and beauty,' Davis glowed.

With a recording budget in the region of $175,000, Houston began work on her first album with the industry's top producers, composers and vocalists, such as Jermaine Jackson (with whom she duetted on two tracks, namely 'Take Good Care Of My Heart' and 'Nobody Loves Me Like You Do'), Kashif, Michael Masser and Narada Michael Walden. Indeed, it was through Jackson, himself an Arista artist, that Houston was launched when she guested at his media party early in 1984 held at the Limelight Disco, New York City, and later on the daytime television programme *As The World Turns*.

Once Houston's album was completed, her record company created an image for both stage performances and promotional videos. *Whitney Houston* was issued during March 1985. The first single, 'You Give Good Love', attracted British dance-floor interest (but only just), while peaking in the American Top 3. The title was issued to establish the singer in the black marketplace but the plan backfired, as it crossed into the American mainstream chart, bypassing its original destination. Despite its clever cross of ballad and dance and varying production skills, *Whitney Houston* sold poorly. To keep the album alive, the singer undertook a series of low-key performances in the Washington DC and Dallas areas before supporting Jeffrey Osborne on a summer tour where the venues were larger and imposing. 'This was the scariest time,' she told author Jeffrey Bowman. 'My life was changing, I was becoming too popular . . . Sometimes I couldn't sleep. I was so nervous . . . But all in all it was a good tour, a growing experience.'

To sustain her climb to stardom, Houston worked day and night. When she wasn't on stage, she gave interviews, filmed videos, recorded new material – in fact, she did anything needed to better her future. The upside, though, was her rise in earnings. Author Bowman remarked that in 1985 a San Diego show netted $11,500. A year on, Houston commanded $100,000 per concert!

During August 1985 Arista Records released the Michael Masser composition 'Saving All My Love For You', accompanied by a seductive video filmed in Britain. Originally recorded by the husband-and-wife team Marilyn McCoo and Billy Davis Jr, Houston's version was altered to suit her vocal range by Masser, who, incidentally, had also produced the original version. His delight at Houston's interpretation led him to boast, 'It's a torch song that's going to be No.1.' He wasn't wrong! 'Saving All My Love For You', with sales in excess of one million copies, shot to the top of the American chart during October 1985 and did likewise in Britain two months on. The ballad was timeless: Houston's voice soared like a bird against a sweeping melody, Masser's delicate trademark. From Britain and America the single went on to chart in many other countries, including Australia and Japan, before Houston won the Grammy Award for the Best Pop Vocal Performance, Female, in February 1986 and a host of other industry awards.

So what now? The music industry had a new singing sensation whose career was destined to blossom. She was beautiful, natural and behaved in a manner that wouldn't upset the vicar. Sure, she was raised in a privileged environment, but perhaps in some ways that meant she had to prove herself even more. Who really knows what she thought? Publicly, though, Whitney Houston rose and fell on her own talent – although, of course, Clive Davis never allowed her to fall too far.

Also see: 'I Wanna Dance With Somebody', July 1987; 'One Moment In Time', November 1988

(Quotes: *Diva: The Totally Unauthorised Biography of Whitney Houston* by Jeffrey Bowman)

PET SHOP BOYS

West End Girls

When the duo released their first single, a New York newspaper insisted their name, the Pet Shop Boys, was slang for 'rent boys who are in to S and M'. And that's not Marks and Spencer in reverse, either! The true origin of the name, however, was boring by comparison.

Born in Gosforth, Tyne and Wear, to Bill and Sheila on 10 July 1954, Neil Francis Tennant joined the folk band Dust before graduating from the Polytechnic of North London. With a degree in history to his credit, he intended to study for a postgraduate degree in Imperial and Commonwealth history. Then Marvel Comics beckoned. He answered an advertisement in the *UK Press Gazette* for a production editor at Marvel. 'I didn't want it really. I felt I'd like to doss around for a while but I said okay.' His wage was £30 a week, from which he paid his apartment rent of £18; the remainder was, of course, frittered away at weekends.

His position at Marvel included transferring colour comics into black-and-white issues for the British market, often covering up the women's bodies with underwear as they were considered too sexy for the less tolerant readership. Another aspect of the job was to write articles – his first was to interview Marc Bolan – and host launch parties, including one for the Marvel Comic's inventor, Stan Lee.

While working with and befriending the characters Conan, Spiderman and his colourful yet often dangerous colleagues, Tennant befriended Tom Watkins, manager of the group named Giggles. Years later, Watkins would manage the Pet Shop Boys.

Born in Blackpool, Lancashire, on 4 October 1959 to Clifford and Vivian, Christopher Sean Lowe joined the seven-man group called One Under The Eight (get it?) as keyboardist while studying theoretical architecture at Liverpool University. 'I decided I wanted to be an architect when I was 11 or 12. I think it was because as a family we'd always moved about a lot. I used to design houses for fun.' To gain practical experience, he transferred to the London-based architect's company Michael Aukett Associates, where he became involved in designing a hi-tech office development in Milton Keynes.

During August 1981, Tennant and Lowe chanced to meet in a

record store in the King's Road, London. Tennant was waiting for a lead to be welded to plug a synthesiser into his hi-fi unit, while Lowe was purchasing a stylus. They started talking about music, discovered they shared a common interest in producing it and decided to work together to see what, if anything, transpired. Composing together, they recorded demo tracks on a pair of cassette recorders in Tennant's flat before transferring them to a Camden studio, where the professional touch could be added. They then hiked around record companies with tapes credited to the group named West End, before adopting the name the Pet Shop Boys, their nickname for a bunch of male friends working in a pet shop based in Ealing, London. Yep, it was nothing more exciting than that, I'm afraid.

Two years on, while visiting New York to interview Bobby 'O' Orlando for *Smash Hits* magazine, for whom Tennant now wrote, he discussed the possibility of working with Orlando. An agreement was reached and the result of their four-hour liaison in the recording studio was the 'West End Girls' single, previously rejected by most major record companies. Released by Bobcat Records in America during mid-1984, it became a turntable hit, but released via a one-off recording deal with CBS Records' subsidiary Epic, the title bombed in Britain. All was not lost, however, as 'West End Girls' soared high into European charts due to its appeal to the Hi-NRG cult following. By the close of 1984, the duo's relationship with Orlando had disintegrated; the resulting legal altercation prevented Tennant and Lowe from recording with another record company for over a year. They need not have worried: a major deal was in the offing.

Thanks to the European success of 'West End Girls', the Pet Shop Boys secured a new recording contract with EMI Records' Parlophone label early in 1985. Their debut single 'Opportunities (Let's Make Lots Of Money)' was issued during the July. Considered by *Smash Hits'* music critic to symbolise Frankie Goes To Hollywood scrapping with Richard Clayderman (what an insult!), the single bombed despite extensive promotional work by Tennant and Lowe.

Now contractually free from Orlando, however, the duo decided to rework the title 'West End Girls' with producer Stephen Hague. It was Tennant's intention to compose a rap track in the Grandmaster Flash mode but with a British accent. '[Artists] always rap in New York accents [but] this song is a contrast between the East End of London, which is kind of a tough area, and the West End, a glamorous night-time area with clubs and cinemas.' The result was exactly how Tennant envisaged it to be and when issued in 1986 'West End Girls' topped the British chart in the January, a position it dominated for two weeks with 750,000 sales to its credit. The title went on to win a Brit Award for the Best Single of the Year and an

Ivor Novello Award for International Hit of the Year, among other honours.

When released in America, the single repeated its British success; it was, however, to be their only cross-Atlantic chart-topper. 'West End Girls' went on to reach the Top 5 in 13 more countries, garnering sales in excess of one million. Considered by most music papers as top pop single of the year, 'West End Girls' was compared to Marc Almond 'overdosing on mean streets and clublands', but most importantly it introduced to the public the Pet Shop Boys' distinctive blend of synthesised music and vocal harmony which was instantly adopted by gay club punters before crossing into mainstream markets. Throughout their career, the Pet Shop Boys continued to enjoy the support of their gay following, and it was probably these sales that sustained them during the leaner periods.

Hot on the heels of the chart-topper, the duo issued the *Please* album, which soared into the British Top 3. The Pet Shop Boys were making serious musical inroads, and there was more excitement to come.

Also see: 'It's A Sin', August 1987; 'Always On My Mind', December 1987; 'Heart', April 1988

(Quotes: *Pet Shop Boys, Annually 1989* by Chris Lowe and Neil Tennant)

February 1986

BILLY OCEAN

When The Going Gets Tough, The Tough Get Going

'It's important to me to set a good example and try not to get caught up in the negative aspects of showbusiness' – Billy Ocean

Born Leslie Sebastian Charles in Trinidad, West Indies, on 21 January 1950, Ocean first became interested in music as a child when a relative gave him a ukulele, of all things! In 1958, his parents and six brothers and sisters moved from Trinidad to the East End of London, where he attended the Stepney Green School. Whilst his parents intended him to progress to college, Ocean had other ideas – music was his ambition. As a compromise, though, he secured an apprenticeship in a tailor's store in Savile Row, while singing with the Shades Of Midnight in local public houses during the evenings. From this group, Ocean moved through others including Dry Ice, and as a soloist he used a variety of names, including Sam Spade, before recording his first single using the name Scorched Earth.

In time he was sacked from Savile Row – his interest in music far outweighed his diligence with the sewing needle – and moved to Ford Motors based in Dagenham to earn regular money. He eventually left Ford's assembly line to work with record producer Ben Findon. The result of this liaison was Ocean's debut single titled 'Whose Little Girl Are You?' late in 1975. The follow-up track hit the heart of disco. Titled 'Love Really Hurts Without You', it catapulted to No.2 in the British chart during April 1976, reaching the Top 30 in America. Four months on, his next single 'LOD (Love On Delivery)' peaked in the British Top 20, and before the year was out, Ocean released his third for GTO Records, titled 'Stop Me (If You've Heard It All Before)', a Top 20 British hit. Incidentally, the singer's name change had occurred when he left Trinidad. 'There was a football team in the village called Ocean II. They in turn got their name from an old film with Frank Sinatra and Sammy Davis Jr . . . I hit on the name Ocean, forgetting that there was a football team or that there was a film.'

To start 1977, Ocean released 'Red Light Spells Danger', a Top 2 British hit. It then took him two years to chart once more with the title 'American Hearts', albeit in the Top 60, followed early in 1980 with his 'Are You Ready?' single in the Top 50. Certainly these positions were a disappointment, but one couldn't help but wonder if record-company support was as diligent as it should have been.

Further into the new decade, the singer recorded the title 'Nights (Feel Like Getting Down)' but it remained unissued, due apparently to his record company's dislike of the song. This, in turn, led to Ocean departing from GTO Records to sign a recording contract with Jive Records, where he worked with Keith Diamond. Despite high hopes, his first single in 1984, titled 'European Queen (No More Love On The Run)', bombed. As this single had obviously been aimed squarely at the disco market, a 12-inch version of the track, with the record label reading 'Caribbean Queen', had been pressed for nightclub promotion. As it was a success with the after-hours punters, the record company decided to remix the track and issue a seven-inch single version. This time the song shot to No.6 in the British chart late in 1984 and reached No.1 in America, a position it held for two weeks. Who would have believed that a change of title would bring Ocean such a change of fortune! Its mother album *Suddenly* quickly followed, of course, reaching the Top 10 on both sides of the Atlantic. In America the album went on to sell in excess of two million copies. Billy Ocean was now a high-profile artist!

To start 1985 the single 'Loverboy' peaked at No.13 in the British chart, No.2 in America. With this title following hot on the heels of the chart-topper, Ocean toured America for the first time during the May. A month on, the album's title track 'Suddenly' was issued and soared into the Top 5 in both Britain and America, while its follow-up titled 'Mystery Lady' stalled in the British Top 50 and American Top 30.

Ocean's career was once again to turn around, this time thanks to *The Jewel of the Nile*, one of the decade's favourite movies starring Michael Douglas, Kathleen Turner and Danny DeVito. Featured in the film's soundtrack was Ocean's next single, the upbeat 'When The Going Gets Tough, The Tough Get Going', which shot to the top of the British chart during February 1986, a position it held for four weeks. In the accompanying promotional video, the singer was joined on stage by the film's trio of stars. It was a novelty indeed – as none could sing! When released in America, the single soared into the Top 2. The whole project was great fun for both film punters and record-buyers, a welcome aside in a decade that was flooded with serious, level-headed music.

Ocean followed his British chart-topper with the slow-paced 'There'll Be Sad Songs (To Make You Cry)', which reached No.12 three months on. The single went on to top the American chart in the July. Hot on the heels of these singles, his *Love Zone* album became a Top 5 hit on both sides of the Atlantic, while its title track struggled into the British Top 50 and American Top 10. One further item was issued in 1987, namely 'Love Is Forever', another big seller.

Into 1988, and following what had by now become known as the Ocean sound of distinctive driving beat against a sharp production, 'Get Outta My Dreams (Get Into My Car)' soared into the British Top 3, while in America it was his third chart-topper in the April. Ocean had composed the track with producer R.J. 'Muff' Lange and recorded it at Jive Records' Battery Studios in north London. He told journalist Roger St Pierre, 'I always tend to write songs with my producers. "Muff" has a great feel for a song, and while he is best known for his work with heavy-metal rock acts like AC/DC, he really understands black music as well.' However, the single ran into problems, as its lyrical content was sexually questionable. When radio airplay was limited, Ocean was forced to rework the song by editing out the 'groans'. '[Certain people] foresaw it could encourage perverts to molest little children, or encourage men to pick up prostitutes . . . I wouldn't do anything intentionally sexually offensive,' said Ocean. Quite possibly this was a case of over-cautiousness.

A month on, Ocean's next album *Tear Down These Walls* was issued to coincide with his major British tour, which in turn heralded the start of a round-world trek. Of the album, Ocean commented, 'I had a part in writing every song on [it]. We actually wrote a lot more than were needed. We were scrapping numbers as late as demo stage.' Of the tour, he said, 'Live work appeals to me most of all but after three or four weeks out on the road you can get your first withdrawal symptoms and be itching to get back into the studio'. Work aside, Ocean married Judy and was by now the father of three children, spending his time between Britain and Barbados.

Into the '90s, Ocean's career nosedived following the release of 'The Colour Of Love' single. It faltered in the British Top 70 but, by comparison, was a big American title, peaking in the Top 20. Early in 1993 Ocean issued his final British charting single, 'Pressure', followed by his last album, *Time To Move On*, both via the Jive Records label.

Nonetheless, due to the regularity with which *The Jewel of the Nile* is screened on British television, the public is still reminded of the very exceptional talent of a singer who now works behind the scenes of the ever-changing music business.

(Quotes: *Blues and Soul* magazine, 1986 and 1988, interviews by Bob Killbourn and Roger St Pierre)

March 1986

DIANA ROSS

Chain Reaction

'Although I am proud of what I have achieved in my life, there is a part of me that remains restless and uneasy, knowing there is still more to be done' – Diana Ross

Two friends from Detroit, Michigan, Florence Ballard and Mary Wilson, sang in their local church and attended the same school. Wilson, one of three children, was born in Greenville, Mississippi, on 6 March 1944 but raised in Detroit by an aunt and uncle. Like other future members of the Supremes, Wilson moved to the Brewster Projects (where low-salary families lived in small but decent houses). Ballard, one of 13 children, was born to Lurlee and Jessee on 30 June 1943. While a teenager at school she wanted to form her own group; Wilson was her first recruit, and another schoolfriend, Betty Travis, was the second.

As quartets were popular, the girls searched for a fourth member.

A young singer, Paul Williams, lived in the same neighbourhood and he suggested Diane Ross be the fourth member. Ross was one of seven children born to Ernestine and Fred on 26 March 1944. She became obsessed with music during her last two years at the Cass Technical High School, where she graduated with fashion-illustration and costume-design awards. Ross jumped at the chance to complete the all-female quartet. Williams sang with the group the Primes (later to become the Temptations), so the four girls decided to become the Primettes, their sister group.

Ernestine Ross was not keen on her daughter wasting time singing and rehearsing, however, and insisted that Diane remain in high school. The mothers of Ballard and Travis were equally anxious about their daughters' education, eventually pulling their offspring from the group. In time the mothers relented and the four Primettes rehearsed in earnest, working their way towards a recording deal. The girls (by now with Barbara Martin replacing Betty Travis) auditioned for Robert West, owner of the newly opened Lu-Pine label. He signed them to work with his in-house writers/producers Richard Morris and Wilmar Davis. The result was two singles, 'Tears Of Sorrow' and 'Pretty Baby'. Both bombed.

Some time later, Motown Records scout Robert Bateman saw the Primettes perform at a talent show in Canada. He recommended them to Berry Gordy, owner of the record company, who insisted they finish their schooling while allowing them to visit the company offices every afternoon, watching, listening and hoping. In time Gordy relented and allowed them into the recording studio to hand-clap for $2 a time and provide vocals for other signed artists.

Robert Bateman and Brian Holland had composed 'I Want A Guy' for Motown's then premier group the Marvelettes. However, when Ross heard it she wanted to record it. The track became their first single after they signed a recording contract with Motown during January 1961. No one liked the name the Primettes, so Ballard was given a list of 15 names; she chose the Supremes. As the girls were still at school, future recording sessions were slotted in between lessons.

At Gordy's suggestion, Ross was promoted to permanent lead vocalist and material was written with her voice in mind. She also changed her name from Diane to Diana, maintaining there was an error on her birth certificate. 'I Want A Guy', issued on Motown's Tamla label in March 1961, heralded the start, albeit a shaky one, of a career that would turn the world inside out. The Supremes went on to become the world's most successful and most famous female trio ever. Their recordings are immortal and their image often imitated, but no one can equal the international magic of Diana Ross and her group.

And this was the group Ross left late in 1969 to embark upon the rocky road to solo stardom, after leading the trio for almost a decade and living the classic rags-to-riches story so loved by the American public. The Supremes' final single, the aptly titled 'Someday We'll Be Together', issued in America during October 1969, soared to No.1. A month later the title was issued in Britain, where it peaked at No.13 in the chart. The track actually featured Ross only, with two session singers, plus the occasional spoken word from its composer, Johnny Bristol. 'Someday We'll Be Together' marked the end of a musical era; public feelings were mixed and, naturally, many blamed Ross's relentless ambitions for the group's demise.

However, all was not lost as the Supremes lived on as a working group with Ross's replacement, Jean Terrell, who had already been groomed as a Supreme. Terrell was later introduced to a star-studded audience during Diana Ross and the Supremes' highly charged and emotional final concert at the Frontier Hotel, Las Vegas, on 14 January 1970.

Within weeks of her departure, and with the words 'Good evening, ladies and gentlemen, welcome to the "let's-see-if-Diana-Ross-can-make-it-alone-show",' the ex-Supreme stepped on to the New York stage at the Waldorf Astoria for the start of a three-week season. It was the most terrifying night of her career so far, yet she stunned her capacity-filled venue by working her way through $60,000 worth of dazzling costumes, various comedy routines and 20 songs. Her expensive wardrobe included eight different costumes ranging from that of an elegant lady to that of a ten-year-old child. However, many believed the show's high spot was the section featuring memories of the Supremes, where Ross sang a medley of their hits while pictures of the group were screened across the back of the stage. For some years, Ross felt obligated to include Supremes material in her act, despite enjoying a successful career as a soloist.

Although Ross was instantly successful as a performer, she struggled with her debut solo single, the drug-related title 'Reach Out And Touch (Somebody's Hand)', written and produced by Nickolas Ashford and Valerie Simpson. Despite the heavyweight backing, the single struggled to No.33 in the British chart, reaching 13 rungs higher in America. This failure to sell discs was not in the game plan devised by Motown founder Berry Gordy. However, the situation reversed when Ashford and Simpson reworked the 1967 Marvin Gaye and Tammi Terrell hit 'Ain't No Mountain High Enough'. Ross's version carried her to the top of the American chart, selling one million copies *en route*; it reached No.6 in Britain.

Following her solo stage debut, Ross celebrated two further major milestones prior to the release of 'I'm Still Waiting' as a single. On a personal level, she married artists' manager Robert Silberstein in relative secrecy on 20 January 1971 at the Silver Bells Chapel, Las Vegas. It had generally been thought she would marry Berry Gordy; they had been a couple for some considerable time and he was the father of her first daughter Rhonda. On the professional front, she starred in *Diana!*, her first television spectacular shown Stateside in April and five months on in Britain. Guest stars included comedians Bill Cosby and Danny Thomas, while additional music was provided by Motown's newest young signing, the Jackson Five. The hour-long special showcased the star's talent as an all-round entertainer, although the most remarkable sequences were her transformation into Hollywood's greatest – Charlie Chaplin, Harpo Marx and W.C. Fields.

It is fair to say that Ross's first British solo chart-topper, 'I'm Still Waiting', was annoyingly unimaginative, particularly when compared to her emotional 'Remember Me' in May 1971 which soared to No.7 in the British chart and No.16 in America, or her second reworking of an established hit, 'Reach Out (I'll Be There')', the single that was so innovative in musical terms that it escalated her fellow Motowners the Four Tops into the international league. Ross's version bypassed Britain, and faltered in the American Top 30. 'I'm Still Waiting' was hidden on the singer's third solo album, titled *Surrender*, due for American release during July 1971. When advance copies of the album arrived at Motown/EMI's London offices, several were circulated to the media, including BBC Radio One. DJ Tony Blackburn, who hosted *The Breakfast Show*, played the album, selecting 'I'm Still Waiting' as a potential single. He played it constantly on air until Motown agreed to release it. Within days, the title raced to the top of the British chart in September 1971, a position it held for four weeks. Needless to say, this runaway success took both record company and artist by surprise. The former retitled her pending American album *Surrender* after the chart-topper, while the latter changed her touring schedule to visit London on a hastily arranged promotional trip. The Americans failed to share the British love of shmaltz; 'I'm Still Waiting' struggled into the Top 60. Incidentally, the single was rereleased during 1976, reaching the Top 50 during the November.

While a member of the Supremes, Ross had wanted to prove herself as a serious actress, but to date her roles had been decidedly flimsy due to the nature of the 'showbiz' vehicles open to her. That was to change in 1972 when she undertook the challenging role of Billie Holiday in the movie *Lady Sings the Blues*. The film was a dramatisation of the life of the legendary jazz/blues singer in both its glory and despair. Ross gave a spectacular performance which earned her a

Grammy Award nomination; she lost to Liza Minnelli for her role in *Cabaret*. However, the singer did receive the Golden Globe Best New Star award, while the film itself was showered with honours, including three NAACP Image Awards. On the record front, the *Lady Sings the Blues* soundtrack earned Ross a gold disc as it topped the American chart for two weeks, becoming Motown's fastest-selling album, estimated at 300,000 copies during its first week of release. The movie itself grossed in excess of $6 million during its opening days. Diana Ross must have been doing something right!

From this gruelling yet rewarding role, the singer switched to a lightweight character of a fashion designer in her next movie, *Mahogany*. Ross wrote in her autobiography, 'I really enjoyed doing that movie because it was all about fashion. I love clothes, everyone knows that, and with *Mahogany* I was given the opportunity to design all the clothes and wardrobe for Tracy Chambers, the character I played.' The singer went on to play Dorothy in a remake of *The Wizard of Oz*, titled *The Wiz*, with Michael Jackson as her co-star. Turning down the lead role in *The Bodyguard*, which catapulted Whitney Houston into movie stardom, Ross intended to star in the life story of Josephine Baker. When plans for the film were shelved, she tackled another serious role, that of a schizophrenic in the highly disturbing movie titled *Out of Darkness*, released during 1995 on commercial video. In 1999 she starred in the film *Double Platinum*. This time Ross played the singer Olivia King, who leaves her daughter, Kayla Harris, to pursue a singing career. Eighteen years later, mother and daughter are reunited.

On the music front, Ross's sixth hit in May 1972 was 'Doobedood'ndoobe Doobedood'ndoobe' – presumably composed during a bout of hiccups! The title peaked at No.12 in the British chart, while America contented itself with the title as an album track.

Following the première of *Lady Sings the Blues*, the title 'Good Morning Heartache' was swiped from the soundtrack for single release during March 1973. It stalled in the American Top 40. In the August, Ross returned to mainstream music with the Michael Masser and Ron Miller composition 'Touch Me In The Morning', a sweeping tale of love lost and found. The single topped the American chart and reached the Top 10 in Britain. Hot on its heels, the album carrying the chart-topper's title cracked the Top 10 on both sides of the Atlantic. Ross was pregnant during the album's recording sessions, which may, she said, have influenced the baby theme throughout the album. One track, titled 'Young Mothers', was edged out and canned, later to be included on her 1983 *Anthology* album.

While this project was being promoted, Ross was in the studio with fellow Motown artist Marvin Gaye. At least that was what the company's publicity department insisted. In actuality, the two singers were rarely in the studio together. According to Gaye, Ross appeared insecure, lacking the confidence she usually exuded, and she was pregnant with her second child. He, on the other hand, admitted to aggravating the recording sessions by smoking dope and drinking alcohol!

Nonetheless, in 1973, the same year as Ross debuted on the British stage as a solo artist, the *Diana and Marvin* album was issued. It peaked in the American Top 30 but reached No.6 in Britain during February 1974. The first track lifted for single release was 'You're A Special Part Of Me', which soared to No.12 in the American chart, while Britain opted for familiarity with the release of 'You Are Everything', their version of the Stylistics' 1971 Top 10 American hit, which flew into the Top 5. The next American single, 'My Mistake (Was To Love You)', released in the May, reached the Top 20. Once again Britain selected a Stylistics cover version, 'Stop, Look Listen (To Your Heart)', a Top 30 hit. As the duet's album was rifled, so was the solo Ross release *Last Time I Saw Him*, notably, the album's title, 'All Of My Life', 'Sleepin"' and 'Love Me'.

Most of 1975 was devoted to filming her second movie, *Mahogany*, with co-stars Billy Dee Williams and Anthony Perkins, although Ross did enjoy a solitary British single hit with 'Sorry Doesn't Always Make It Right' in the May. Following the American première of *Mahogany*, which grossed $7 million during the first two weeks of its release, the soundtrack album shot into the Top 20, while 'Theme From *Mahogany* (Do You Know Where You're Going To?)' topped the American singles chart during January 1976. When issued in Britain, the single, following a hefty promotional push, zoomed into the Top 5. The follow-up single to the American chart-topper, 'I Thought It Took A Little Time (But Today I Fell In Love)', surprisingly faltered in the Top 50. That failure was soon overlooked when a future major marketing ploy was placed in jeopardy. Motown discovered that the Fifth Dimension intended to release their version of the Ross album track 'Love Hangover'. Having placed such importance on their artist's version, Motown rush-released the title as a single. It topped the American chart in the May, reaching the Top 10 in Britain. 'I Thought It Took A Little Time (But Today I Fell In Love)' followed in Britain, struggling into the Top 40 during the July.

Also during 1976, with her movie commitments behind her, Ross was able to plough her energies into her singing career. To this end, she embarked upon an adventurous series of concerts under the banner 'An Evening With Diana Ross'. The first concerts were staged in New York, followed by other American dates and then into Europe, where the tour opened in Britain during March 1976. While touring,

Ross divorced her husband, Robert, citing grounds of irreconcilable differences; she was granted custody of her three daughters, Rhonda, Tracee and Chudney. Her petition also stated that property and financial settlements had been reached between herself and her husband. Following the divorce, Ross and her children relocated to New York. Meanwhile, the double album *An Evening With Diana Ross*, recorded at Los Angeles' Ahmanson Theater, was issued and reached the American Top 30 and British Top 60.

Through to the end of the decade, the singer maintained her chart profile via a pair of albums, namely *Baby It's Me* and *The Boss*; the latter was the more successful, spawning the title track, 'No One Gets The Prize' and 'It's My House' as hit singles. It was also during this period that Ross was involved in the shooting of *The Wiz*, the black version of the Broadway show and the Judy Garland-starring film. According to Ross, 'Even though *The Wiz* was disappointing at the box office, it was a huge success in my life and the lives of many of the other people involved. Making the movie when I did helped me work through a lot of difficult times and make many important decisions. I had to straighten out my life.'

The title 'Ease On Down The Road', her duet with Michael Jackson, was lifted from the film's soundtrack for single release but stalled in the Top 50 on both sides of the Atlantic in November 1978. For the follow-up single, 'Pops We Love You', Ross joined Stevie Wonder, Marvin Gaye and Smokey Robinson in singing a birthday tribute to Berry Gordy's father. It was another staller in the Top 60.

Into the '80s, the singer dumped her 'safe' image to join the unpredictable young, switching the ballad for beat in the hope of revitalising her flagging career. At the time, the top-selling dance outfit Chic were masterminded by Nile Rodgers and Bernard Edwards, and for the first time in her career Ross handed over her next album, *Diana*, to the couple, who wrote, arranged and produced the project. Unfortunately, the result sounded too similar to their own releases; it was difficult to distinguish the Motown vocalist from one of Chic's own. Both Berry Gordy and Ross were unhappy with the finished tapes, whereupon she returned to the studio to remix the album with producer Russ Terrana. She said, 'When I first listened to the tapes they sounded pretty much like Chic or Sister Sledge . . . both Nile and Bernard have only been in the industry for two or three years and in remixing the album I felt I may be able to put a little Diana Ross into [it].' Both Rodgers and Edwards were furious their work had been tampered with and demanded a public disclaimer be given as they disassociated themselves from the project.

The finished album, packaged in a black-and-white gatefold sleeve showing the singer dressed in tattered jeans and T-shirt, relaunched

Ross's career overnight. In America, the first lifted title was 'I'm Coming Out' in August 1980, while Britain opted for 'Upside Down' as its debut single. It was a No.2 hit, earning the singer a silver disc for sales in excess of 400,000 copies. The mother album went on to pass one million sales in Britain alone. 'Upside Down' was the second single to be released in America during June 1980; the title soared to No.1 but was the last to be issued. In Britain, however, the story was very different; her fans devoured the new sound. The next single, 'My Old Piano', issued during the September, soared into the Top 5, while (at last) 'I'm Coming Out' reached No.13 in the November. Ross supported her British success by hosting a press reception at the Inn on the Park Hotel, London, breaking a private holiday with Kiss member Gene Simmons.

The next year, 1981, was one of change. 'It's My Turn' was the first single, the theme from the movie of the same name starring Michael Douglas. The track soared into the American Top 10 and British Top 20. A collection of previously recorded and canned songs, produced and co-written by Michael Masser, was then issued under the album title *To Love Again*. Old material or not, the album was a big seller during the April, spawning a pair of British hits, 'One More Chance' and 'Cryin' My Heart Out For You'. These titles led the way for one of the decade's most significant of ballads, namely 'Endless Love', Ross's duet with Lionel Richie. Once again it was the theme from a movie of the same name and was recorded in a whirlwind. Ross was performing in Atlantic City, Richie in New York. They met in Nevada, recorded the track and went their separate ways. No one would have guessed its hasty birth; 'Endless Love' topped the American chart during August 1981, selling in excess of two million copies and later winning a pair of music awards: Favourite Single – Soul/R&B and Favourite Single – Pop/Rock.

In Britain, the title soared to No.7 two months later, where it also represented the final Motown single to be released under EMI Records' licensing deal with the American company. Following an 18-year association with EMI Records, Motown switched to BMG Records, which, in later years, led to the British demise of Berry Gordy's operation. But, more importantly for the artist's fans, 'Endless Love' signified Ross's final single for Motown; her recording contract was due to be renegotiated and Gordy was unable to meet her financial demand. Subsequently, the singer moved to RCA Records in March 1981, signing a seven-year contract reputedly worth $20 million, for the territories of North America and Canada. Capitol Records, the American subsidiary of EMI Records, signed her for the rest of the world. Naturally, Gordy was devastated by Ross's decision, but she claimed, 'Motown was a profound experience. The truth is that I did not leave Motown because I was upset or angry or hurt. I left because I was growing as a person and it was time for me to move on.' Primarily, Ross wanted to control her own career, and to this end she opened a series of companies to protect her interests, namely Ross Records, Ross Publishing Company, Ross Town, RTC Management Corporation and Anaid (Diana spelt backwards) Films. To house these, she purchased an office building in New York; after nearly three years she sold the building at a profit to rehouse her interests in a smaller, more manageable property. Ross attended night classes in finance before joining the world of money hands-on. She no longer trusted third parties to handle her cash, saying, 'I won't put my name on a contract unless I understand exactly what I am signing. I sign all my own cheques. I find that to be an area of great importance.' She added that when she was finally alone, 'I was pretty vulnerable in the outside world. I had a barrelful of problems, and it took me a long time to get them all sorted out.'

Meanwhile, the music played on. Ross's recording contract with RCA Records afforded her total creative control, from a song's concept to the record packaging. 'It was a magnificent learning experience,' she said. Finally she was ready to release, and in December 1981 her debut RCA Records single was issued, amid great speculation. Titled 'Why Do Fools Fall In Love?', the track was her version of the Frankie Lymon and the Teenagers' original 1956 hit. Lifted from her album bearing the same name, the single soared into the Top 10 on both sides of the Atlantic.

Before 1982 closed, the singer had cemented her decision to move record companies by enjoying a series of hit singles that included the dance-flavoured 'Work That Body' and 'Muscles', written and produced by her long-standing friend Michael Jackson and accompanied by promotional videos that somehow passed television censorship. The latter track was swiped from her second album, titled *Silk Electric*, itself a Top 30 hit in both America and Britain.

During 1983, Ross began an annual concert stint in Las Vegas, with a pay cheque reputed to be $2 million per season. This was also the year of Motown's 25th anniversary, when, during a spectacular May gala featuring company acts past and present, Ross was reunited on stage with Supremes Cindy Birdsong and Mary Wilson. Two months on, Ross dared to perform during a torrential storm that lashed at her during a free concert on New York's Central Park stage. She abandoned the show following a handful of songs, fearing the electrical equipment would blow, and returned the next night when she, the equipment and the audience had sufficiently dried out! Meanwhile, as was expected, various Motown releases capitalised on her recording success with RCA Records.

The next two years allowed Ross to experiment musically by working with a host of different composers and producers. Late in 1984 she duetted with Julio Iglesias on the 'All Of You' ballad, much to the annoyance of her staunch followers, but she then re-established herself in their favour with her *Swept Away* album, the result of her association with soul masters Arthur Baker, Lionel Richie and Bernard Edwards. The album's title track reached the American Top 20 during October 1984, while a further swiped track titled 'Missing You' soared into the American Top 10 in April 1985. The song, composed by Lionel Richie, was a loving tribute to the memory of Marvin Gaye, who had been shot dead by his father on 1 April 1984. Prior to this release, Ross participated in the USA For Africa project to release the single 'We Are The World', which went on to top both the American and British charts, raising in excess of $88 million.

Returning to 1985, Ross took the unprecedented step of working with the Bee Gees to record the *Eaten Alive* album, released during the November. The lifted track 'Chain Reaction' shot to the top of the British chart in March 1986, a position it held for three weeks. It was her first British chart-topper since 'I'm Still Waiting' in 1971. The success of 'Chain Reaction' was aided by an innovative promotional video featuring black-and-white '60s sequences held together by a full-colour singer performing the song. The follow-up single 'Experience' was a failure by comparison, faltering in the British Top 50 during the May.

Prior to the release of 'Chain Reaction', Ross married for the second time. Her husband was Arne Naess, a Norwegian shipping magnate and Everest climber with three children. They had first met in May 1984 while holidaying in the Bahamas, and when Naess was to be knighted in Oslo, he invited Ross to be his guest at the ceremony. He then asked her to marry him. The wedding was held in February 1986 at the Abbey of Romain Motier, Switzerland, before guests including Stevie Wonder and Gregory Peck. Ross said of their relationship, 'We came from completely different worlds. He doesn't know about the showbusiness world . . . I've never had the adventure that he brings into my life.' Before the glamour of their fairytale wedding in Switzerland, the couple were actually married in a civil ceremony in New York City in October 1985.

Through to the end of the decade, Ross's recording career declined. America was showing signs of abandoning her, while Britain frantically tried to support her mediocre material. In May 1987 the *Red Hot Rhythm'n'Blues* album was released to a mixed reception, while her recording of 'If We Hold On Together', the theme to the Steven Spielberg movie *The Land Before Time*, recaptured her smooth ballad era. The title remained unreleased in Britain until 1993.

The singer's worst move at this juncture was the release of the *Workin' Overtime* album during 1989, recorded for her daughters. The first to be issued on her own label, Ross Records, it reunited her with Motown Records in America via a licensing deal. That association would be pointless and, as the years passed, fruitless. To support *Workin' Overtime*, Ross embarked upon a lengthy European tour, appearing at the Brixton Academy in London, with Aswad as support act, to 'road test' her show. As her recording career slumped, her touring commitments heightened. From Europe, she took her show to North America and finally Detroit, Michigan – Motown's birthplace.

Into the '90s, and on the personal front, Ross helped launch her daughter Tracee's music career by co-appearing in the Herb Ritts-lensec Gap advertisements, before opening her world tour in America. During July 1990, she played capacity-filled houses at the Universal Amphitheatre in Universal City, before a series of sell-out dates in Radio City Music Hall, New York. This was also the year when her recording career would spiral once more. Produced by Peter Asher, the album *The Force Behind The Power* was released during September 1990. Two months on, Ross performed a trio of sell-out concerts at Wembley Arena, before headlining the Royal Variety Show staged at the London Palladium. Meanwhile, the first single to be lifted from the strongest album during this part of Ross's career returned her to the big ballad and the world's charts. Titled 'When You Tell Me That You Love Me', the single shot to No.2 in the British chart in December 1991, while *The Force Behind The Power* soared into the Top 20. Ross was in greater demand than ever, particularly in Britain, a fact exemplified when she opened Harrod's annual New Year sale during January 1992. Her reward was a fat cheque and a fried breakfast! A month on, the album's title track reached the British Top 30, the poor showing a mere blip in the game plan. The title 'One Shining Moment' returned her to the British Top 10 in the July, whereupon Ross promoted the title by touring Eire and Scotland and by standing in for BBC Radio One DJ Simon Bates to host one of his shows. Before the year closed, Ross left her mainstream music to perform jazz and blues material in a New York nightclub setting for American cable television under the title *Diana Ross Live . . . The Lady Sings*. (The programme was later released as a commercial video during April 1993 under the title *Live . . . Stolen Moments: The Lady Sings . . . Jazz and Blues*.) The singer then tested her talent further by performing with Placido Domingo and José Carreras in Vienna City Hall for a televised festive programme titled, naturally, *Christmas in Vienna*.

To start 1993, the much-acclaimed movie theme from *The Land Before Time* titled 'If We Hold On Together' was finally issued as a single and reached No.11 in the British chart, while in the March 'Heart (Don't Change My Mind)', lifted from *The Force Behind The Power*, reached the British Top 30. In between these releases, Ross joined others of her ilk to perform in 'A Call for Reunion: A Musical Celebration' before President Clinton at the Lincoln Memorial, Washington. Perhaps her performance was better remembered for the label showing on her jacket than for the song she sang!

Mid-1993, Ross contributed to the opening ceremony of the famed, and now refurbished, Apollo Theater in New York, while on the recording front, following months of preparation, she released her *One Woman: The Ultimate Collection*, an offshoot from the lavish *Forever Diana* six-CD box set released to celebrate her 30th anniversary in the music business. These issues coincided with the publication of her autobiography, *Secrets of a Sparrow*, and in the December she unveiled her star on the pavement outside Radio City Music Hall. Across the ocean in Britain, her next British single, once more lifted from *The Force Behind The Power* and titled 'Your Love', peaked in the Top 20.

For some time, Ross had been searching for suitable movie scripts to continue her acting career. She remained unimpressed until the script of *Out of Darkness* was given to her. It was a hard-hitting story of a schizophrenic mother and the heartache she faced and during the film's early life viewers were hard pushed to realise it was Ross playing the lead role. Following its American screening, and during February 1994, the singer was honoured at the music conference Midem '94, held in France, when she received the Commander in the Order of Arts and Letters from Jacques Toubon, the French Minister of Culture. She was also given the City of Cannes Gold Medal. Two months on, the next British single, 'The Best Years Of My Life', previously previewed on the *Oprah Winfrey Show*, peaked in the Top 30. To close the year, the *A Very Special Season* CD was issued; it was a Top 40 hit.

Into 1995, the only hit single of the year was the title track to her next album *Take Me Higher*, which struggled into the British Top 40. Nonetheless, the singer was active elsewhere. Berry Gordy presented her with the Heritage Award for Career Achievement during the Soul Train Music Awards ceremony; she also performed a pair of concerts in Moscow, before performing in Detroit and at Radio City Music Hall. In between these and other dates, the *Take Me Higher* album was issued during October 1995. It was a poor British seller, as were the lifted singles. To close the year, Ross returned to Britain to headline the Greatest Music Party in the World concert, staged at the NEC in Birmingham and screened on Christmas Day.

Into 1996, Ross paid tribute to her loyal gay following by recording an updated, up-tempoed cover version of Gloria Gaynor's 1979

British chart-topper 'I Will Survive'. Unfortunately, Ross's version did not; nonetheless, the impact was remarkable. Produced by Narada Michael Walden, the track was dedicated, she said, to her girls, her gay public. Said Ross, 'They've always been wonderfully supportive of me, and this is my way of saying thanks for their loyalty. But it isn't just about being gay, it's about being allowed to live your life . . . There's a lot of pain in the world. To me what matters is if you're a good person, that's all that counts. If you're a good person, I'm going to love you, if not, I won't have time for you.' The single's accompanying video was stunning, featuring the famous drag queen Ru Paul, countless Ross lookalikes and 5,000 fans in a recreation of Los Angeles' annual Gay and Lesbian Pride celebration.

This release was followed by the CD compilation titled *Diana Ross: Voice Of Love*, comprising tried and tested material and a trio of new recordings including the powerful track 'In The Ones You Love', the first swiped single. It reached the British Top 40 late in 1996. Within months of the single peaking, Ross announced her 'Voice Of Love' tour, kicking in with British dates during July 1997. Much of 1998 was spent behind closed doors, recording a new album and shooting the *Double Platinum* movie, while rumours persisted that plans were in hand for an extensive American tour.

During September 1999, following a lengthy wait, Ross finally released her new album, *Every Day Is A New Day*, with the title 'Not Over You Yet' extracted for single release. As her career took off once more, so her personal life plummeted, with her husband Arne Naess announcing to the media that their marriage was over.

When Diana Ross celebrated 30 years in the music business, she was listed as the most successful female artist in the British singles chart. This achievement won her a place in the 1994 edition of the *Guinness Book of Records*, under the 'Arts and Entertainment' section. During a lavish ceremony held in London during October 1994, Ross was presented with a *Guinness Book of Records* Lifetime Achievement Award to honour this success. There were no direct competitors for the award, although Madonna and Barbra Streisand both met criteria necessary for consideration.

'Looking back through my life there have been many turning points and peak experiences. I have learned a lot about myself and I know there is so much more' – Diana Ross

(Quotes: *Secrets of a Sparrow: Memoirs* by Diana Ross; *Motown: The History* by Sharon Davis)

See *Every Chart-Topper Tells a Story: The Sixties* for further information regarding Diana Ross and the Supremes

CLIFF RICHARD AND THE YOUNG ONES

Living Doll

During 1985 a gathering of comic writers, comedians and others connected with laughter pooled their talents to raise funds for the population crisis in Africa under the title Comic Relief. Within a year a trio of live Comic Relief shows had been screened by BBC TV and Cliff Richard had joined the Young Ones to record a version of his single 'Living Doll'. These and other projects raised financial help for Oxfam and Save the Children, among other charitable organisations. To placate those who believed charity begins at home, at least 20 per cent of funds raised were designated for British charities via a series of grants for the disabled, drug users and the homeless. Priority was given to those small charities not given access to larger donating bodies. Artists freely contributing to Comic Relief included Cliff Richard and the Young Ones, Mel Smith, Rowan Atkinson, Stephen Fry, Dawn French, Griff Rhys Jones, Lenny Henry, Graham Chapman, Angus Deayton, Michael Palin and Bill Tidy.

One of the most popular alternative-comedy series screened on British television at the time was *The Young Ones*, named after Richard's 1959 chart-topper. One of the main characters, played by Rik Mayall, was an avid Cliff Richard fan, so when the programme's cast decided to record a version of 'Living Doll' for the Comic Relief fund, it was a natural move to request the single's originator to join them.

On 29 January 1986, Richard went into the Master Rock Studios to record a new version of 'Living Doll' with the Young Ones, comprising Mayall, Nigel Planer, Christopher Ryan and Adrian Edmondson, with the Shadows' Hank Marvin recreating his original 1959 guitar solo and Pete Wingfield on keyboards joining the session musicians. Produced by Stuart Coleman, the single was recorded in 20 minutes, while the mixing took up to six weeks to complete. The day after the recording, the contributing artists filmed the 'Living Doll' promotional video, showing an ill-at-ease Richard.

When released by EMI Records, 'Living Doll' became Richard's 97th single and his 11th British chart-topper, 27 years after the title's first No.1 position. With sales passing the one million mark, matching the single's original sales, 'Living Doll' topped the British chart in April 1986 for three weeks before repeating the success in a handful of European countries and Australia. All proceeds from this runaway success were destined for Save the Children and Oxfam. To capture the 1986 Christmas sales, Comic Relief published the *Utterly Utterly Merry Comic Relief Christmas Book*. Within its pages crammed with often unsavoury and wicked humour, a letter was published from Rik of the Young Ones to Lionel Bart, composer of 'Living Doll'. Expressing serious doubts about the sexual politics expressed in the song's lyrics, citing 'Cliff was too young to know the difference in 1959', Rik printed a rewritten version of 'Living Doll', now titled 'Living Person', which fell within the guidelines of the politically correct manual!

It was thanks to all those associated with Comic Relief and Cliff Richard and the Young Ones that the funds of the two main charities were dramatically boosted.

Also see: 'Mistletoe And Wine', December 1988

May 1986

GEORGE MICHAEL

A Different Corner

'I decided to take some time off and reconsider . . . All through the time I took Ecstasy, I never took coke . . . I had a great time for a while and then an absolutely awful time. So I stopped doing it' – George Michael

George Michael has admitted on numerous occasions that he decided to dissolve Wham! during a bout of heavy depression. Be that as it may, the duo's demise was kept an industry secret until early 1986, the period when Michael was preparing to release his second solo single titled 'A Different Corner'.

'A Different Corner' reflected a confused and delicate state of mind that anguished over his future career, his drug and alcohol intake and his sexuality, although few listeners realised it at the time. The single became Michael's second British chart-topper in May 1986, a position it held for three weeks, before soaring into the Top 10 in America. Tony Parsons wrote in *Bare*, '"A Different Corner" was the work of a man whose life had finally had a chance to go wrong, and the sweet power of his voice seemed to be coming from a place that was poisoned with regret.' Even the accompanying promotional video portrayed a sense of despair, shot in black and white in a location resembling an asylum. In later years Michael admitted, 'The pain comes back when I perform [it] or hear [it]. At first I couldn't even listen to it, especially when I was trying to get over the emotions I was singing about.'

Happily for the singer, he was able to pull himself from the blackness to enjoy a solo career that surpassed even his wildest dreams.

Also see: 'Careless Whisper', September 1984; 'I Knew You Were Waiting (For Me)' (with Aretha Franklin), February 1987

(Quotes: *Bare* by George Michael and Tony Parsons)

June 1986

WHAM!

The Edge Of Heaven

'[The single] was deliberately and overtly sexual, especially the first verse . . . I thought nobody is going to care because no one listens to a Wham! lyric' – George Michael

Andrew Ridgeley and George Michael's future together as Wham! was to be short-lived, but they would end with a British chart-topper. In the rundown, the duo scooped a handful of honours at the American Music Awards staged in January 1986 at Los Angeles' Shrine Auditorium. A month on, the single 'I'm Your Man', a previous British chart-topper, hit the American Top 3.

Before Wham! could release their next outing, Michael issued his second solo single and second chart-topper, 'A Different Corner', and officially announced the intention to dissolve the partnership and the management deal with Simon Napier-Bell. Perhaps if Michael's consuming determination to become a mega solo star hadn't been so strong, Wham! would have lasted a few chart-toppers longer. However, that wasn't to be.

Released as a title on a four-track EP, 'The Edge Of Heaven' stormed to the top of the British chart during June 1986, the same month as the singers performed their final concert at Wembley Stadium before an estimated 72,000 fans. Under the banner 'The Final', Wham! could have performed the concert ten times over, such was the demand for tickets. Both aged 23 years old, Ridgeley and Michael were joined on stage by several other acts including Elton

John and Gary Glitter. Said Michael, 'I really did enjoy the day and the concert very much, but looking at pictures of it now I can see that something was very wrong.' According to Ridgeley, 'It wasn't even our best show . . . there were too many other considerations. It was difficult to enjoy the actual doing of the show.'

Following 'The Edge Of Heaven', Wham! issued the *The Final* album, a compilation of their best-selling material. It was a No.2 hit in the British chart. Across the Atlantic, the hits package was retitled *The Edge Of Heaven* and became a platinum seller. In the December the duo and CBS Records cleaned up by repackaging and repromoting *The Final* as a boxed set with stationery items included, while the single 'Last Christmas' was rereleased for the second time and reached the British Top 50.

Into the '90s, Ridgeley and Michael reunited as Wham! to perform at the Rock in Rio festival held in Rio de Janeiro. Ridgeley had in fact branched out as a soloist with the *Son Of Albert* album and the swiped single titled 'Shake', but decided that the private life suited him better. Michael, on the other hand, hit his bleakest period, lost in a haze of Ecstasy and alcohol, not knowing, he said, where his destination lay. He would, of course, make it through this hellish time to emerge as one of Britain's foremost male acts.

But were Wham! forgotten? No such luck. In 1997 the duo reappeared via the compilation titled *If You Were There: The Best Of Wham!* to capitalise on the Christmas period. If nothing else, the tracks reminded the public of the fun time during music's growth through the '80s and how two young men with ambitions to be a part of that growth played such a significant role.

As a final word, Ridgeley believed his partner had lacked the confidence to end Wham! and strike out as a soloist prior to 1986. 'He felt a nagging insecurity . . . the band was always there to exploit his talent and sooner or later he was going to have to do it alone.' Michael replied, 'No way could I have done it without Andrew. I can't think of anybody . . . in my life who would have been so perfect in allowing something which started out as a very naïve, joint ambition to become what was still a huge double act but what was really mine.'

Also see: 'Wake Me Up Before You Go Go', June 1984; 'I'm Your Man', November 1985

(Quotes: *Bare* by George Michael and Tony Parsons)

July 1986

MADONNA

Papa Don't Preach

The single told of a pregnant teenager pleading with her father to allow her to keep her unborn baby. Madonna knew full well she was heading for criticism from some sections of the public and the media. However, the singer's story had a happy ending.

Rounding off 1985 with a couple of British Top 5 sellers, namely 'Gambler' and 'Dress You Up', which by Madonna's standards were remarkably nondescript, the singer settled into married life with Brat Pack member Sean Penn. She also planned her next movie, titled *Shanghai Surprise*. It told the tale of an American missionary leaving the boredom of a marriage to befriend an American vagrant, and the arguments were said by some to be on a par with those experienced within Madonna's own marriage, which were reputed to have forced her to seek psychiatric help. Thankfully she found the solace she craved with her career. With *Shanghai Surprise* secured, Madonna and her husband negotiated to star in the film *Blind Date*. Eventually the roles were given to Bruce Willis and Kim Basinger.

On the recording front, the *True Blue* album entered the British chart at the top during July 1986, while the extracted track 'Papa Don't Preach', composed by the singer and Brian Elliot, became a British chart-topper. The single's accompanying video, shot on Staten Island, was what author Christopher Anderson termed 'a compelling mini-melodrama' of a father coping with his young daughter's pregnancy. The singer switched from T-shirts to black bodysuits during the short film, doubtless confusing the issue further. A month on from the British chart-topper, both single and album topped the American charts.

When Madonna had opted to record 'Papa Don't Preach', she realised she would provoke media outcry, with the public condemning the song's message of her condoning young girls who have become pregnant. 'But then I thought, wait a minute, this song is really about a girl who is making a decision in her life,' Elliot told the *Los Angeles Times*. 'If Madonna has influenced young girls to keep their babies, I don't think that's such a bad deal . . . I just wanted to make this girl a sympathetic character. As a father myself, I'd want to be accessible to my children's problems.'

As Madonna peaked internationally as a vocalist, her career as an actress looked less successful when *Shanghai Surprise* was premièred in the November to scathing reviews and subsequent poor houses. Costing $17 million and earning a mere $2.2 million, the film was destroyed by Madonna and Penn, leaving George Harrison, whose company Handmade Films had persuaded the couple to star in the film, and MGM, its distributor, to placate the media and shrug off the public disinterest. Ever the gentleman, Harrison was forced to admit he 'walked away from that experience hating Madonna'.

Also see: 'Into The Groove', August 1985; 'True Blue', October 1986; 'La Isla Bonita', June 1987; 'Like A Prayer', April 1989

(Quotes: *Madonna: Unauthorised* by Christopher Anderson; *The Billboard Book of Number One Hits* by Fred Bronson)

August 1986

CHRIS DE BURGH

The Lady In Red

Oozing with love and romance – or slush, as some people prefer to call it – and reputedly written for de Burgh's wife, this chart-topper earned the distinction of being one of the most-performed titles of the decade. On the downside, no woman wearing an outfit of red was safe!

Born Christopher John Davidson in Argentina on 15 October 1948, a British diplomat's son, he graduated from Trinity College in Dublin where, among his courses, he had studied the composition of songs. De Burgh's innate expertise led to him touring Eire with the Horslips late in 1973, while a year on he secured a recording contract with A&M Records. This in turn led to him supporting the group Supertramp throughout a British tour. Yes, it was as easy as that!

Now known as Chris de Burgh, early in 1975 the singer issued his debut album titled *Far Beyond These Castle Walls*, from which the track 'Hold On' was extracted for single release. Both titles bombed. De Burgh's second single, 'Flying', likewise disappeared into obscurity, although the following album *Spanish Train And Other Stories* eventually mustered sufficient sales to crack the British Top 80 during August 1985, ten years after the original release.

De Burgh struggled in the run-up to the '80s by performing across the world, notably in Europe and South Africa, while on the recording front he issued a pair of albums, namely *At The End Of A Perfect Day* in 1977 and *Crusader* in 1979. British sales remained low for the singer, yet outside the country he was growing into a high-profile entertainer and concert earner. It's true to say that, at this point in his career, de Burgh began despairing over whether he would enjoy popularity in what he now considered to be his home country. However, his situation was to change.

A flash of inspiration – or perhaps desperation – led to A&M Records issuing a compilation of de Burgh's best tracks under the title *Best Moves*. The marketing ploy worked; the album presented de Burgh with his second British charting title, albeit in the Top 70, during 1981. A year on, his vinyl selling power was low-key once more until he cracked the British Top 50 with the single titled 'Don't Pay The Ferryman', swiped from the Top 30 album *The Getaway*. At last de Burgh's recording career in Britain was shifting. It took a further year for both titles to fracture the American listings; 'Don't Pay The Ferryman' became a Top 40 single hit, *The Getaway* a Top 50 entrant.

During 1984 de Burgh charted once in Britain with the 'High On Emotion' single in the Top 50. His album titled *Man On The Line* soared to No.11, his first to crack the Top 20. When released in America, the titles struggled.

A&M Records believed the climate of the mid-'80s was right for a second compilation. This time the company leased the material to Telstar, one of Britain's leading compilation record companies specialising in television advertising. The album, appropriately titled *The Very Best Of Chris de Burgh*, shot to No.6 in the British chart during February 1985 and went on to spend at least 70 weeks in the top 100 listing. It was a remarkable achievement for a compilation devoted to material few people outside de Burgh's specialist middle-of-the-road market had heard. During his recorded work, de Burgh continued to tour extensively; probably his most prestigious date this year was answering Cliff Richard's call to perform in Carol Aid, staged in London to provide further funds for the Band Aid charities.

However, it was to be 1986 when Chris de Burgh's career turned dramatically upwards. During the August his *Into The Light* album, again comprising middle-of-the-road tracks, was issued to placate the demands of young romance. The track to be issued as a single was titled 'The Lady In Red' and was typical of the easy de Burgh style and a fine example of his flair for sympathetic lyrics. The single worked, reaching all quarters of the buying market as it captured the nation's hearts and pockets. 'The Lady In Red' shot to the top of the British chart during August 1986, a position it held for three weeks. It only took 24 singles before de Burgh captured an artist's most prized position – but he did it! The chart-topper's popularity also sent its mother album into the No.2 slot and reintroduced de Burgh's catalogue items to the public.

The singer's British achievement led to international sales and fortune, earning de Burgh a long-overdue high-profile status. 'The Lady In Red' went on to become his biggest-selling American hit at No.3 in May 1987, on its way to one million sales.

The British follow-up to the chart-topper was titled 'Fatal Hesitation' and was a staller in the Top 50. It's a cruel world; with one hand the public supported the singer, with the other it snatched that support away. Nonetheless, de Burgh sustained his distinctive romantic, melodic styling which still sold in vast quantities, but not sufficiently to chart.

De Burgh's first and only outing in 1987 was 'A Spaceman Came Travelling' and 'The Ballroom Of Romance', a double-top-sided single which was a Top 40 British hit. In 1988 a pair of singles charted in Britain, namely 'The Simple Truth (A Child Is Born)', Top 60, and 'Missing You', a belter of a hit at No.3 during the November. On the album front this year, his title *Flying Colours* soared to the top of the chart.

On to the '90s, de Burgh sold poorly; his singles 'Tender Hands' and 'This Waiting Heart' both faltered in the lower chart regions. Yet his third compilation, *From A Spark To A Flame: The Very Best Of Chris de Burgh*, returned him to the British Top 4. Also issued in 1990 was the Top 20 album *High On Emotion: Live From Dublin*, while on the performing front de Burgh appeared on the Wembley Arena stage during May 1991 following the Gulf War as a contributor to 'The Simple Truth' charity gala, where all proceeds were earmarked for the Kurdish refugees. In the September de Burgh performed at the theme park Alton Towers, among several selected dates throughout Europe. A year on the singer, prior to embarking upon a further European tour through to the December, issued the 'Separate Tables' single, which reached the British Top 30, and the Top 3 album titled *Power Of Ten*.

De Burgh struggled to maintain his chart presence from 1993, but his concerts were packed with enthusiastic audiences who regarded him as the purveyor of mainstream romance in much the same way as soul fans classed Barry White or Luther Vandross.

Always a welcome visitor in South Africa, de Burgh kicked in 1993 with a 20-date concert tour. The singer's purse was in excess of $2 million. Into 1994, his album titled *This Way Up* returned him to the British Top 5, while the extracted single 'Blonde Hair Blue Jeans' struggled.

Throughout his career de Burgh, happily married with children, conducted himself in an exemplary fashion in public; no derogatory words appeared to tarnish his clean image. Why, even Diana, Princess of Wales, hailed him and 'The Lady In Red' as her favourite singer and song, but that image was to be battered slightly when de Burgh hit the tabloids following a reputed brief affair with his children's nanny. Was this the lady in red, the media asked, particularly when de Burgh later admitted that his wife was not, after all, the inspiration behind the track. Whatever, de Burgh's fans ignored the headlines.

On the professional front, de Burgh's *Beautiful Dreams* album, recorded live and featuring material by the Beatles and Elvis Presley among other music icons, faltered in the British Top 40 in 1995, while the swiped single titled 'The Snows Of New York' crawled into the Top 60. Perhaps the newspaper articles had had more of a damaging effect than expected.

As recently as 1998, de Burgh appeared with others at a specially arranged concert on the first anniversary of the death of Diana, Princess of Wales. The gala, organised by the Princess's brother, attracted much criticism, but those participating and attending believed the gala to be a sincere tribute.

Chris de Burgh is one of a handful of artists who has remained true to his art.

September 1986

COMMUNARDS

Don't Leave Me This Way

This chart-topper was the third version to reach the British chart. The other two were recorded by American acts who had for years struggled for recognition outside their country. Did we do it better?

Jimmy Somerville, born in Glasgow on 22 June 1961, Larry Steinbachek, born in London on 6 May 1960, and Steve Bronski, born in Glasgow on 7 February 1960, formed Bronski Beat during 1984. It was this trio which would form the nucleus of the Communards.

The highlight of the Bronski Beat sound was Somerville's distinctive high vocals; indeed, it was this that immediately attracted record-buyers. During June 1984 Bronski Beat recorded the title 'Smalltown Boy', released as a single on the Forbidden Fruit label via a distribution deal with London Records. The single marked the trio's first British hit when it soared to No.3 in the chart. Three months on,

Bronski Beat returned to the British Top 10 with 'Why?', the second single to be extracted from *The Age Of Consent*, the trio's debut album. The album soared into the Top 4.

To all intents and purposes *The Age Of Consent* marked the end of the trio's career, Somerville announcing his pending departure from the group. However, that statement was retracted when, early in 1985, he was persuaded to stay to release 'It Ain't Necessarily So', a reworking of Gershwin's showstopper, previously recorded by countless music icons. The track worked for Bronski Beat, presenting them with a Top 20 British hit. During the May, Somerville duetted with Marc Almond, late of Soft Cell, on a trilogy of tracks, namely Donna Summer's 'I Feel Love' and 'Love To Love You Baby' and John Leyton's 'Johnny Remember Me'. The unusual combination of artists and material attracted buyers by the thousand and pushed the single into the Top 3. It truly marked the final title to be recorded by Bronski Beat featuring Somerville in its line-up.

Bronski Beat went on to enjoy further recorded success with singles like 'Hit That Perfect Beat' in 1985, 'Come On, Come On' in 1986 and, via a recording contract with Arista Records, 'Cha Cha Heels', featuring Eartha Kitt, in 1989.

Meanwhile, Somerville hitched up with Richard Coles, born in Northampton on 23 June 1962, to perform as the Committee, later the Communards. They secured a recording contract with London Records, where their debut single 'You Are My World' reached the British Top 30 during October 1985. As with Bronski Beat, the highlight of the Communards was Somerville's falsetto vocals which many compared favourably to American disco icon Sylvester. Like Sylvester, Somerville became a forerunner in gay dance music.

Into 1986, the Communards maintained a high profile on the concert circuit, including the 'Red Wedge' British tour in support of the Labour Party. Throughout the tour and on television spots, Somerville and Coles were supported by session musicians, bringing visuality to the music. Mid-1986 the group issued their second Top 30 hit titled 'Disenchanted', but it was their version of Thelma Houston's 'Don't Leave Me This Way' that elevated them to the top of the British chart in September 1986. Houston's version, issued during 1977, had been a No.13 British hit and was itself a dance restyling of Harold Melvin and the Blue Notes' mid-paced interpretation, likewise issued in 1977 but a bigger hit in the British Top 5.

Singing with Somerville on the British chart-topper was Sarah Jane Morris and together they sold in excess of 750,000 copies, enabling the Communards to hold the British pole position for four weeks. When released in America during 1987, 'Don't Leave Me This Way' peaked in the Top 40. Meanwhile, the British sales explosion boosted the advance orders of the Communards' eponymous album to push it into the Top 20 before 1986 closed, while the chart-topper's follow-up titled 'So Cold The Night' soared into the Top 10.

During the next year, with the AIDS crisis reaching its peak, the pop world rose to meet the challenge with a series of charity concerts, peaking with a gala staged at Wembley Arena during April 1987. Participating artists included George Michael, Boy George and Elton John. The Communards joined the star-studded line-up, then went on to become heavily involved in a British public-information film regarding the dangers of AIDS and encouraging the use of condoms.

Also in 1987, the Communards issued a further cover version, namely 'Never Can Say Goodbye', which, like 'Don't Leave Me This Way' before it, had been recorded by two hit American acts. Disco diva Gloria Gaynor had enjoyed a British Top 2 hit with the title in 1974, while the Jackson Five had taken their version into the British Top 40 in 1971. With the same styling as 'Don't Leave Me This Way', 'Never Can Say Goodbye' soared into the British Top 5 in November 1987. Prior to this runaway hit, the Communards had issued a pair of Top 20 titles, namely 'You Are My World ('87)' and 'Tomorrow', and all three titles were extracted from their high-selling album *Red*.

The Communards issued two further singles before Somerville left the group to embark upon a solo career. The first title was a tribute to Somerville's deceased chum Mark Ashton, titled 'For A Friend', followed by 'There's More To Love'. Both were Top 30 sellers, whilst Somerville's duet with June Miles-Kingston titled 'Comment Te Dire Adieu' peaked in the Top 20.

Early in the '90s, the compilation *The Singles Collection 1984–1990*, featuring tracks from both the Communards and Bronski Beat, was issued and reached the British Top 5, proving there remained a market for both bands – or was it Somerville's voice? He issued his urgent Sylvester cover 'You Make Me Feel (Mighty Real)' as his debut single of the decade and it soared into the British Top 5 in January 1990. Sylvester's original had reached No.8 in the British chart in 1978, but remained the No.1 disco title for years to come. What was particularly touching about Somerville's version was the single's accompanying video, which included a television flickering Sylvester's own video across the screen.

Read My Lips (Enough Is Enough), Somerville's debut solo album, and the next single soon followed, both reaching the British Top 30. It was a poor showing in view of his recent success. Yet the title 'To Love Somebody' soared to No.8 in the British singles chart in November 1990. All titles were, of course, high in the gay listings and, naturally, were dance-floor fillers.

Before 1990 ended, Somerville relocated to San Francisco, the heart of the gay community and, coincidentally, former home city to Sylvester, who had died from an AIDS-related illness in 1988. Somerville stayed there until 1995. Despite his American base, the singer was a regular performer in Britain and participator in gay functions and benefits throughout the world. Recording-wise, he maintained a relatively high British status with releases like 'Smalltown Boy' and 'Run From Love', both hits in 1991, 'Heartbeat', 'Hurt So Good' and 'By Your Side' during 1995, and the top-selling album *Dare To Love*.

October 1986

MADONNA

True Blue

'"True Blue" [is] an extended sigh over Sean Penn,' one reviewer penned, while the album of the same name was seen as 'Madonna sinking gratefully into a bed of cotton candy'. Whatever that means!

As Madonna's single 'Papa Don't Preach' topped the British chart in July 1986, her album co-produced with Patrick Leonard and Stephen Bray titled *True Blue* entered the British chart at the top. It dominated this position for five long weeks, the same length of time it stayed at the top of the American chart, on its way to passing platinum status several times.

During October 1986 the album's title track 'True Blue' was finally swiped for single release, presenting the singer with another British chart-topper; it was No.3 in America. For the follow-up title Madonna lifted the first song recorded for inclusion in the album, namely 'Open Your Heart'. The title peaked at No.4 in Britain, while in America it shot to No.1 during February 1987, her fifth chart-topper and third from the *True Blue* project. Could this girl do anything wrong? More to the point, what was it about her that prompted the public by the million to support her recorded work?

When not penning articles concerning Madonna's music, the media slashed her marriage into printed shreds, claiming it was deteriorating rapidly, particularly in view of Penn's notorious violent streak. Indeed, certain factions of the press who had been victim to his uncontrolled punches had nicknamed the couple S and M. The more scribes faulted them, the higher Madonna rose in defence: 'I've been dealing with the media since the very beginning of my career and Sean never really had to. I wanted it, and I was . . . ready to deal with it. He wasn't.'

When tensions between the couple erupted in public, reporters naturally refused to turn a blind eye. One incident in particular during 1986 fell within the media glare; Madonna and her husband were engaged in a loud argument outside her film offices on the Universal Studios complex. This verbal exchange stemmed from the singer's growing concern for her gay friends in the wake of the AIDS epidemic. She had already lost several of them to the disease. Penn reputedly refused to understand his wife's feelings and then moved on to Madonna's association with singer-cum-model Nick Kamen, star of the television commercial for Levi's 501 jeans during which he stripped to his shorts in a launderette. Through one means or another, Madonna had expressed interest in producing Kamen on record; indeed, the couple later worked together in the recording studios with the resulting title 'Each Time You Break My Heart'. The single peaked in the British Top 5 late in 1986. Kamen went on to enjoy a relatively successful recording career through to 1990. Meanwhile, Madonna's marriage stumbled on through desperate times.

Also see: 'Into The Groove', August 1985; 'Papa Don't Preach', July 1986; 'La Isla Bonita', June 1987; 'Like A Prayer', April 1989

November 1986

BERLIN

Take My Breath Away

John Crawford was responsible for Berlin. While convalescing after breaking his leg during a basketball game, Crawford learned to play the guitar with the intention of forming a group of musicians. Not keen on the music that was then strangling Los Angeles, Crawford decided his band had to reflect mystery, with a slice of decadence. The name Berlin sprang to mind. Crawford then advertised for a lead vocalist, persuading Terri Nunn, a one-time actress appearing in television shows like Lou Grant to join his group. Nunn had actually auditioned for 25 groups and each one had offered her the lead-vocal position. For some reason she chose Berlin, where she would remain for one year, being replaced by Virginia Macalino.

With Chris Velasco and Dan Van Patten, Berlin secured a recording contract with IRS Records under which they issued one single before disbanding during 1981. Undeterred, Crawford and Nunn went on to steer their enthusiasm into a new act, recruiting Rod Learned, Rick Olsen, Matt Reid and David Diamond.

During 1982 Berlin released their first EP, titled 'Pleasure Victim', via a recording arrangement with Geffen Records. Its single 'Sex (I'm A)' represented the group's first taste of American success; the album *Love Life* followed in 1984. With the release of their American Top 30 single titled 'No More Words', Berlin's membership reduced to a trio, namely Nunn, Crawford and Rob Brill.

Meanwhile, Giorgio Moroder and Tom Whitlock were beavering away composing material for the soundtrack of the film *Top Gun* starring Tom Cruise. Two of the songs, 'Danger Zone' and 'Take My Breath Away' were earmarked for Berlin, but eventually Kenny Loggins recorded 'Danger Zone'. It was the first single swiped from the movie and soared into the American Top 2.

When 'Take My Breath Away' was released, the record-buying public were seriously introduced to Berlin's music for the first time. Nunn told author Fred Bronson, 'We hadn't written anything up to that point that could be played on the [American] adult contemporary stations. It was shocking for me because the first station I heard it on was something my mother listens to.' As if to prove the cliché 'mother's always right', Berlin shot to the top of the American chart during September 1986 with 'Take My Breath Away'. Two months on, that incredible success was repeated in Britain.

Nunn recalled that during the recording of the single Moroder had devised a 'strange' musical arrangement which she had admired. 'But [Giorgio] had both the record company and the movie company asking him to be as normal in arrangement as possible. So he couldn't be as experimental as he would have liked.'

The world didn't just like 'Take My Breath Away', it adored it, so much so that the single charted in most overseas territories, the bulk of its sales boosted by the immense popularity of *Top Gun*. In January 1987, though, Berlin's British follow-up, 'You Don't Know', sold badly, reaching No.39 – not what the band had intended! However, on the upside, the British chart-topper would not curl up and die. The title entered the British singles chart on two further occasions: in 1988, as a Top 60 entrant, and again during 1990, when it was a Top 3 smash. Being the musical backdrop to the television commercial for the new Peugeot 405 obviously helped the track's '90s sales no end! Among the honours bestowed upon the cross-Atlantic chart-topper, the title won an Oscar for the Best Original Song of 1986.

The remainder of Berlin's charting life seemed to be centred around a pair of albums. In 1987 *Count Three And Pray* sold sufficiently to sustain their chart presence, then the inevitable compilation *Best Of Berlin 1979–1988* was issued one year later. Sadly, though, Berlin lived success in the fast lane for only a short while. Indeed, the American chart-topper's follow-up titled 'Like Flames' smouldered in the Top 90, and when issued in Britain in March 1987 crawled into the Top 50.

Perhaps Berlin's then manager Perry Watts-Russell adequately summed up the group's position when he told *Los Angeles Times* journalist Paul Grein that the success of 'Take My Breath Away' had seemed beneficial in the short term but definitely was not useful in terms of the band's career because 'it alienated rock radio stations which considered the song too Top 40'. Watts-Russell then added that Berlin had expressed no regret at recording the track, even though the move meant the group lost its real identity. 'The lesson here is that if you're going to have a big hit, it'd better be with a song that is truly representative of who you are.'

(Quotes: *The Billboard Book of Number One Hits* by Fred Bronson)

December 1986

EUROPE

The Final Countdown

Another Swedish export, although not on such a grand scale as Abba, Europe reached No. 1 with a track that matched Sylvester Stallone for punches.

During 1982 Joey Tempest and John Leven were members of the group called Force based in Stockholm. A year on, the group entered and won a national rock talent contest where the first prize was a recording contract with a Stockholm record company.

Things moved quickly. Force released their eponymous album in 1982, a Top 10 in Sweden. Encouraged by these sales, the band issued a second, titled *Wings Of Tomorrow*, which repeated its predecessor's success. This pair of titles attracted CBS Records' A&R staff, who dangled a recording contract with its subsidiary label Epic in front of the group.

With a new group line-up that included Ian Haughland, Kee Marcello and Mic Michaeli, Force changed its name to Europe and became an Epic recording act. The world now beckoned.

Europe's first success under the new arrangement was the main track for the *Rocky IV* movie starring Sylvester Stallone. Titled 'The Final Countdown' and sung in English because of its inclusion in the blockbusting film, the single shot to the top of the British chart during December 1986. Although as Force the group had pioneered a type of heavy-metal sound in Sweden, the renamed outfit's first outing was that of solid rock with strong melodies. It was a complete change of styling that obviously worked but which, of course, could have been performed by any group at the time. When released in America in March 1987, 'The Final Countdown' soared into the Top 10. Meanwhile, Europe's album, also titled *The Final Countdown*, spawned a second single, 'Carrie', the group's next American hit and third British entrant at No.22. The second British charter had been titled 'Rock The Night', a healthy seller in the Top 20.

In between these releases, Europe toured Britain and America to promote and capitalise on their recent successes. The band also introduced to their audiences tracks from their next album, *Out Of This World*, due for 1988 release. Although the project would sell badly in comparison to the group's past releases, it did spawn the single 'Superstitious', a No.34 British hit which reached the Top 40 in America.

Into the new decade, and with further extensive touring to their credit, Europe issued their third album, titled *Prisoners Of Paradise*. Unfortunately this was another poor seller, although once again it bore two British hits, namely 'I'll Cry For You', at No.28, and 'Halfway To Heaven', a falterer in the Top 50.

With such sluggish sales following a runaway chart-topper which had obviously sold only because of its inclusion in *Rocky IV*, Europe and Epic Records parted company, whereupon the group disbanded. A short career, maybe, but at least the group members can tell their grandchildren that they topped the British chart in 1986.

January 1987

JACKIE WILSON

Reet Petite (The Sweetest Girl In Town)

'"Reet Petite" was a funny record. I loved it at first sight, so that shows how nutty I was. Berry Gordy wrote it in the way I sang it, so if I hadn't come along, God knows who could have recorded it' – Jackie Wilson

'Reet Petite' might have caused its singer some amusement when it was released in 1957, but 29 years later it shot to No.1 in Britain during the January, a position it held for four weeks, selling in excess of 750,000 copies. The reissued track was accompanied by a nauseating promotional video featuring a plasticine-type animated character. Interestingly, on the single's first outing, released on the Coral label in Britain, it spent 14 weeks in the chart, peaking at No.6 during November 1957.

Jackie Wilson was born in Detroit, Michigan, on 9 June 1934. 'My teen years were spent listening to the Mills Brothers, Vaughan Monroe and Mario Lanza and Caruso, just as much as Muddy Waters, who was about the top black name in my youth . . . I used to love the bit where he would go down on one knee.'

Blues vocalist Roy Brown also influenced the youngster, whose school years comprised learning in the classroom, music and boxing. In his teens, Wilson, like many black youngsters of the day, turned to the boxing ring to earn money, and shortly before his 17th birthday he became the Golden Gloves champion, one of several amateur tournaments. It was during this period Wilson met fellow Detroiter Berry Gordy Jr who, like himself, had ambitions set firmly in the music business. Indeed, Gordy would form Motown Records, the most influential black-music company in the history of music.

In time, or rather at his mother's insistence, Wilson left his boxing ring behind and graduated from the Highland Park High School to work on the assembly line in one of Detroit's several car factories. His musical ambitions were confined to evenings and weekends when he performed at local nightspots, usually as a member of the Thrillers. When he participated in a talent show at his local Paradise Theater, Johnny Otis from King Records was in the audience. Through Otis, Wilson was introduced to Billy Ward, lead singer with the doo-wop group the Dominoes. In time, Wilson worked as Ward's back-up vocalist.

In 1953, while on a trip to the Fox Theater in Detroit, Billy Ward and the Dominoes were rehearsing. Ward needed a replacement for the group's lead singer, Clyde McPhatter, who had recently departed. Wilson filled the vacancy and would, years later, acknowledge McPhatter as another major influence in his life. As a member of the group, Wilson recorded numerous singles during their stay at King Records and, later, Federal Records.

Unfortunately, the Dominoes were unable to sustain their high status with Wilson on lead vocals. They moved from Jubilee Records to Decca and recorded the ballad titled 'St Therese Of The Roses', which soared to No.13 in the American chart in September 1956. The group continued to enjoy a lucrative career on the nightclub circuit, until Wilson embarked upon a solo career. Detroit was not short of local talent – acts fought among themselves to secure stage inches in local clubs – but Wilson was luckier than most when Al Green, a nightclub owner and publisher, booked him for a season at the Flame Bar Show and negotiated a recording contract with the Decca Records offshoot Brunswick. It was during one of his performances at the Flame Bar Show that Wilson renewed his friendship with Berry Gordy Jr, hot from the car assembly line and now a struggling composer.

According to Gordy, 'My sister sent me to a publishing company where the owners managed Jackie Wilson. They liked my songs and my ideas, so I got involved. We wrote the first six or seven Wilson hits: "Reet Petite", "To Be Loved", "Lonely Teardrops", "That's Why I Love You So" and two or three others.'

Said Wilson, 'I admired Berry's nerve and will to get on. I had just left the Dominoes, and my manager at that time introduced us, and there was this little guy with a briefcase crammed full of tunes. Must have been at least 50 in that little bag . . . I was the first artist to actually record one of Berry's songs and we must have recorded close on 20 at that first session in New York. Sure, there were some we didn't record at the time.' Indeed, one title Wilson passed on was 'You Got What It Takes', which went on to become a big-selling American hit for Marv Johnson. Wilson continued, 'My opinion at the time of Berry Gordy was that he was a little man with a big dream. I always said he was underrated as a songwriter and even at that time he could foresee what the future held. There was a feeling of magnetism that you immediately sensed.'

The title 'Reet Petite' was Wilson's debut release in September 1957. It sold in excess of 250,000 copies and peaked in the American Top 70. The singles 'To Be Loved' (a Top 30 entrant in both America and Britain), 'We Have Love' (a poor seller) and 'Lonely Teardrops' followed the debut. The last single topped the American R&B chart at the close of 1958; two months on, it crossed over into the mainstream chart and soared into the Top 10, selling in excess of one million copies *en route*. The titles 'That's Why' and 'I'll Be Satisfied' (the last to be co-written by Berry Gordy) and 'You Better Know It' maintained Wilson's standing as an American charting name. The single 'Talk That Talk' started the new year and marked Wilson's expansion into the white nightclubs of New York and Las Vegas.

Wilson was a rising star, not only through his recorded work but also for his racy, energetic stage shows which put many of his contemporaries to shame. Author Gary Herman reported that during his shows, 'Wilson jumped into the willing arms of the women clustered round the edge of the stage and completely disappeared into the turmoil. Shirt shredded, he had to be escorted to safety by the police.' Herman further wrote that in 1960, Wilson was arrested at a New Orleans performance with 5,000 people attending. Police had intended to prevent the singer from launching forth into the audience; instead, they provoked a riot which, in turn, led to the concert being cancelled.

Once Wilson's association with Berry Gordy had ended after the latter opened his own record company based in Detroit, the two never collaborated musically again. According to Wilson, 'The Motown thing was expanding, and he had fallen out with his publisher and decided to go his own way. I have often wondered what would have happened to me if I had gone along with Berry as a recording artist back then.' Wilson need not have worried; in May 1960 he soared into the American Top 5 with the double-A-sided single 'Night' and 'Doggin' Around'. The latter title was released in Britain and bombed. Before the year closed, a handful of further singles became American hits, including 'A Woman, A Lover, A Friend'. In Britain, meanwhile, he enjoyed a pair of charting titles, '(You Were Made For) All My Love' and 'Alone At Last'.

Many people agreed that Wilson's attraction was his voice, best described as a cross between classical opera and semi-heavy, bluesy R&B. He explained it as 'a mix between my natural voice and the training I had over the years. You have to develop a voice to get the very best out of it and I would lay a lot of credit to Billy Ward, who was also my vocal coach when I was just a teenager.' In actual fact, Wilson attempted to emulate the singers who recorded his demo discs, 'but gradually I developed a style and I found that songs were coming to me with singers trying to sound like me! For example, Eddie Holland used to do the vocal on all Berry Gordy's songs, and Eddie even made a hit record that sounded so much like me that at the time people were asking me about my new record. That record was "Jamie".'

Between the late-'50s and mid-'60s, Wilson stood alongside the best America had to offer by way of popular black vocalists. However, his rising star could have come to a sudden halt when, in February 1961, he returned to his New York apartment late at night to discover Juanita Jones, a young black fan, waiting for him. She demanded his favours; he refused, whereupon she drew a .38 pistol, threatening to shoot herself. In the struggle that followed, Wilson was shot in the back and stomach. Jones was arrested for 'felonious assult', claiming, 'I hope I haven't hurt him.' It took the singer two years to recover; during this time Wilson released titles that included 'Baby Workout', 'Shake! Shake! Shake!', 'The Greatest Hurt' and 'I Found Love', a duet with Linda Hopkins. All were semi-hits. Wilson had by now also released a trio of albums, namely *Jackie Wilson Sings The Blues*, *Jackie Wilson At The Copa and Baby Workout*.

Wilson was from a rare breed of artists whose power over an audience was a spectacle in itself, and it was those performances that sustained him until he returned to the American Top 10 in 1966. 'I was the one to record the first Eugene Record [a member of the group the Chi-lites] composition with Barbara Acklin, and that was "Whispers". Gene was still driving a taxi at that time, but I always loved that song from the first time I heard it.' 'Whispers (Getting Louder)' also pushed Wilson into the soul market, where he would later become a leading figure.

Released as the follow-up to 'I Don't Want To Lose You', Wilson's next million-seller and Top 10 entrant was titled '(Your Love Keeps Lifting Me) Higher And Higher'; a hit in America in October 1967, it finally reached No.11 in Britain during June 1969. Also in 1967, Wilson brushed with the police once more. He was arrested in New York State for the possession of firearms, heroin and syringes. Following a further career blip, his next American hit was 'I Get The Sweetest Feeling', a Top 40 hit in 1968. Said Wilson, 'Van McCoy was the man behind that one. He was such an easy guy to work with. I wish we'd done more. He's such an educated man, that's what I admire most about [him].' The single soared to No.9 in the British chart during September 1972.

To all intents and purposes, the early '70s were relatively quiet for the singer recording-wise, while on the concert circuit his schedules were exhausting. Performing sustained him until his concert at the Latin Casino in Cherry Hill, New Jersey, during October 1975. Wilson was touring with Dick Clark's Rock'n'Roll Revue when he suffered a heart attack on stage while singing 'Lonely Teardrops'. Hitting his head while falling, the singer suffered severe brain damage. When he regained consciousness, following four months in a coma, Wilson had lost control of his faculties. To pay for his hospitalisation, Barry White and others performed benefit concerts. Despite having earned a reputed $200 million during his career, Wilson was penniless.

On 21 January 1984, Jackie Wilson's nine-year struggle for life ended in a New Jersey nursing home, a few months before his 50th birthday. His funeral, held at Detroit's Chrysler Drive Baptist Church, was attended by Berry Gordy and Motown acts.

'I Get The Sweetest Feeling' was released (yet again) in March 1987 as the follow-up to the British chart-topping 'Reet Petite' and soared to No.3 in the chart. Four months on, 'Higher And Higher' followed, peaking in the Top 20.

If he had lived, Wilson would doubtless have enjoyed a renewed career in much the same way as Ben E. King or James Brown. However, tasteful repackaging and compilations have kept the music of Jackie Wilson very much alive.

(Quotes: *Blues and Soul* magazine, 1987, interview by Sharon Davis; *Rock'n'Roll Babylon* by Gary Herman)

February 1987

GEORGE MICHAEL AND ARETHA FRANKLIN

I Knew You Were Waiting (For Me)

This single was the meeting of two musical giants from the worlds of soul and pop. The uniqueness of the combination disguised the fact that the song wasn't that inspiring.

During June 1986 George Michael, with two British chart-toppers to his credit ('Careless Whisper' and 'A Different Corner'), prepared for his debut solo album titled *Faith* and began recording in London and Denmark. However, prior to working in earnest, he flew to Detroit, Michigan, to record a duet with the queen of soul, Aretha Franklin.

Born 25 March 1942 in Memphis, Tennessee, Aretha Franklin was one of six children raised by the Reverend C. Franklin and his wife Barbara, who left the household during 1948. Growing up in the gospel environment, Franklin learned to play the piano and was later taught to sing by family friends who included Mahalia Jackson. Through this musical upbringing, 14-year-old Franklin recorded for the Checker label, based in Chicago. The album titled *The Gospel Sound Of Aretha Franklin* featured live versions of hymns sung in her father's New Bethel Church.

In 1960, with her education behind her, Franklin toured America as a gospel singer before switching to the so-called mainstream music of the '60s. Signed to CBS Records, she issued her debut album, *The Great Aretha Franklin*, before appearing for the first time on stage in New York.

Moving on to March 1961, Franklin cracked the American Top 80 chart with the title 'Won't Be Long'. Through the next two years, her name could regularly be spotted in the lower chart regions, while on the album front she released projects that included *The Electrifying*

Aretha Franklin. Late in 1964, her Top 60 single titled 'Runnin' Out Of Fools' paved the way for albums like *Unforgettable: A Tribute To Dinah Washington.* Her career then floundered, and with little guidance from CBS Records, Franklin issued her final album, *Soul Sister,* for that company, switching to Atlantic Records in 1966, where she planned to work with Jerry Wexler.

Recording at the Muscle Shoals Studio in Atlanta and working with music's main men under Wexler's control, Franklin recorded 'I Never Loved A Man (The Way I Love You)', heralding the start of soul's most successful of careers. Released as a single with 'Do Right Woman, Do Right Man' as the flipside and featuring her two sisters, Carolyn and Erma, as prime vocalists, the disc passed the million-sales mark and topped the American R&B chart before the album bearing its name was released and passed gold status. The album, perfection in every note and melody, was hailed as a soul classic; Franklin was subsequently crowned the queen of soul.

By the close of 1967 she had issued two further million-selling singles, namely 'Respect' and 'Baby I Love You', an American chart-topper and No.4 respectively, before releasing the single that epitomised all aspects of soul. '(You Make Me Feel Like A) Natural Woman', composed by Carole King, soared into the American Top 10.

Franklin went from strength to strength in the music business, collecting awards and honours, while on the recording front her name was a regular charter. Early in 1968 the *Aretha: Lady Soul* album passed gold status, while singles like '(Sweet Sweet Baby) Since You've Been Gone', 'Think' and 'I Say A Little Prayer' sustained her selling power within and outside R&B circles.

As personal anguish that included the breakdown of her marriage plagued her life, Franklin's career steered gradually towards main-stream influences, as she recorded versions of the Beatles' 'Eleanor Rigby' and 'Let It Be'. Her single 'Call Me' had a version of Dusty Springfield's 'Son Of A Preacher Man' as its B-side and soared into the American Top 20 in May 1970, and an interpretation of Ben E. King's 'Don't Play That Song' became her first million-selling item since 1968.

Throughout the '70s Franklin's material was varied, and mostly successful. She was revered on an international level and was an inspir-ation to her imitators. Into the new decade, the singer played a waitress, singing 'Think' in *The Blues Brothers* movie also starring Ray Charles and, of course, Dan Akroyd and John Belushi. Ignored by cinema punters at the time, said to be the reason Belushi committed suicide, the film later attracted a huge cult following and later still was the inspiration for the stage show which toured Britain as recently as 1998.

It was also in 1980 that Franklin switched record companies from

Atlantic to Arista, believed by soul pundits to be an unwise decision. The *Aretha* album debuted in the November, the same month as the artist performed at the Royal Variety Show in London. *Love All The Hurt Away* was the solitary album during 1981, while a year on she won the Grammy Award for Best R&B Vocal Performance, Female, for the 'Hold On, I'm Comin'' single. After whipping up a storm with 'Jump To It', a hit in the singles charts on both sides of the Atlantic, much of 1982 was devoted to performing, most notably with others including Gladys Knight at the Jamaica World Music Festival.

During 1983 the *Get It Right* album peaked in the American Top 40; its title track struggled to sell as a single. However, two years on, Franklin issued the dynamic *Who's Zooming Who?* album, re-establishing herself as a saleable item as the album passed the one-million-sales mark. Three singles were extracted for release, namely 'Freeway Of Love', 'Who's Zooming Who?' and her duet with Annie Lennox titled 'Sisters Are Doin' It For Themselves'. All were hit titles. Flushed with success and the subsequent demand for her talent, Franklin scooped more awards before recording 'Jumpin' Jack Flash', the title track to the movie of the same name starring Whoopi Goldberg, whose talent is as impressive as her wonderful wide smile. Keith Richards produced Franklin's version of the Rolling Stones' track which he had previously penned with Mick Jagger, before inducting Franklin into the Rock'n'Roll Hall of Fame early in 1987.

Then Aretha Franklin teamed up with George Michael. Franklin's record company approached Michael with the idea of recording the duet during the time of Wham!'s demise. Written by Dennis Morgan and Simon Climie and produced by Narada Michael Walden, 'I Knew You Were Waiting (For Me)' proved to be the ideal vehicle to bridge black and white, R&B and British pop, although many were sceptical at the union. Michael said, 'We recorded the song together and then did our ad libs separately . . . I was nervous, but vocally, I was getting very confident at the time.'

'I Knew You Were Waiting (For Me)', released by Michael's record company Epic, shot to the top of the British chart in February 1987. In America, the single was issued via Arista, Franklin's company, and reached the top during the April. The accompanying promotional video, likewise filmed in America, appeared to show Michael in awe of Franklin; nonetheless, the film supported the single admirably.

To start 1988 Franklin issued the gospel double album titled *One Lord, One Faith, One Baptism* before collecting further Grammy Awards for *Aretha*, the Best R&B Vocal Performance, Female, and 'I Knew You Were Waiting (For Me)', the Best R&B Performance by a Duo or Group with Vocal. She joined Michael on a Detroit stage to sing the song before the year closed.

Now an experienced hand at duets, Franklin's next was with Elton John on the title 'Through The Storm'; it was a poor-selling item. Next was Whitney Houston on 'It Isn't, It Wasn't, It Ain't Never Gonna Be'. It was a Top 30 British hit, Top 50 in America, and was included on Franklin's *Through The Storm* album, also featuring the Four Tops and James Brown.

Into the '90s, Franklin, constantly an in-demand performer, concentrated on the American touring circuit; her fear of flying prevented her from performing in Europe. She also debuted at Caesar's Palace in Las Vegas before performing at Radio City Music Hall. During 1992, the artist further duetted, this time on stage with Michael McDonald to sing 'Ever Changing Times' at the annual Grammy Awards ceremony, and attended political and record-industry functions until her next significant recordings were issued in 1993 under the title *Queen Of Soul: The Atlantic Recordings*. Two months on, in the April, she hosted the television special *Aretha Franklin: Duets* featuring her singing partners of George Michael and Elton John, together with Smokey Robinson and Rod Stewart, among others.

A highly prominent figure in America's music and political and social issues, Franklin remained one mighty lady. In 1994 the artist re-established herself in British mainstream music with 'A Deeper Love', swiped from Goldberg's *Sister Act* movie, which reached the Top 5; remarkably, the title stalled in the American Top 70. The singles 'Honey' and 'Willing To Forgive' maintained her chart status, while on the album front her *Queen Of Soul: The Very Best Of Aretha Franklin* peaked in the Top 20. She contributed to Whitney Houston's *Waiting To Exhale* movie with the track 'It Hurts Like Hell', which also featured Lionel Richie, among others.

In 1998, the much-awaited new studio album titled *A Rose Is Still A Rose* was issued; critics were mixed in their opinions. Nonetheless, a new Franklin album always gives rise to celebration!

Let's return to 1987 and Mr Michael. While his debut album *Faith* hit the presses, he issued the 'I Want Your Sex' single, his first since Wham! dissolved. The title alone caused controversy, particularly in view of the high profile of AIDS at the time. As expected, BBC Radio One banned airtime play until 9 p.m.; other stations followed suit, afraid of public outcry. Amid the moral protests, the singer cried to anyone who would listen that sex wasn't the enemy, promiscuity was; he was attempting to push the message across to the public that one-partner sex was imperative. He also admitted in 1998 that the single hinted at his homosexuality. Was anyone listening, though? The promotional video featured American make-up artist Kathy Jeung, across whose back he wrote in lipstick the words 'Explore

Monogamy', although the young man who bared all on film wasn't the singer. Michael defended his work. 'American rap music and heavy metal are so aggressively sexual in a completely distasteful way, and I didn't think "I Want Your Sex" was at all.' The single soared into the British Top 3 during June 1987 and reached No.2 in America two months later.

Before the year ended, the long-awaited album *Faith* was issued and topped the British chart. Composed and produced by the singer, its title track, which he said was inspired by a couple of failed relationships when he was on the rebound from Wham! splitting up and prior to his relationship with Jeung, was issued as a taster and soared into the Top 2 a month earlier. When released in America the single shot to the top within days.

'Father Figure' was the title of Michael's first 1988 single, again swiped from *Faith*. As the single peaked at No.11 in Britain, its mother album claimed the top spot in America, where it would eventually pass the one-million-sales mark. To coincide with this success, the singer embarked upon his 'Faith' tour in the February, the same month as 'Father Figure' became an American chart-topper, his sixth.

The image Michael chose for the *Faith* project was one of ripped jeans, leather jacket, dark glasses and an arrogant look. He said this attire represented his everyday clothes. '[It] had a lot of restrained aggression in it. I don't think it's over-the-top aggression . . . Obviously I can't wear the whole outfit all together now because I would just look like a real wanker – a George Michael lookalike.' As the tour plodded on, the 'One More Try' single was issued and reached the British Top 8, making No.1 in America. The track was the third from *Faith*.

Before the 'Faith' tour reached Europe, the singer joined others to perform at the gala staged at Wembley to celebrate Nelson Mandela's 70th birthday. Opting not to promote his own material – 'I wanted to separate myself from any kind of self-promotion' – he sang a trio of soul cover versions, namely Marvin Gaye's 'Sexual Healing', Gladys Knight and the Pips' retitled 'If You Were My Woman' and Stevie Wonder's 'Village Ghetto Land'. From this concert, Michael quickly switched to London's Earls Court to perform his own show.

Midway through his European dates, Michael was diagnosed as suffering from tour fatigue. However, a London specialist confirmed he had a large cyst on his throat which required immediate surgery. Several dates were cancelled as the singer underwent the operation before convalescing for one month in St Tropez. From here, Michael kick-started the 'Faith' trek in America, where he performed 42 consecutive dates without missing a note.

The final single of 1988 was a further track from the *Faith* album titled 'Kissing A Fool'. It reached the Top 20 in Britain and the Top 10 in America, while the *Faith* video, a compilation of clips, sold by the thousand. *Faith* and its spin-off singles, tour and video just could not fail, and naturally the singer scooped a host of awards and honours as a result. These included the Grammy Award for Album of the Year, the Video Vanguard Award, presented during MTV's Music Awards ceremony, and gold and platinum discs for singles sales of 'Faith', 'One More Try' and 'I Want Your Sex'.

In the run-up to the new decade, Michael co-wrote and produced the single titled 'Heaven Help Me' for his Wham! support musician Deon Estus, was featured on ex-Shalamar member Jody Watley's album *Larger Than Life* and won a libel action against *The Sun* newspaper which had printed a story claiming the singer had been drunk and disorderly, gatecrashing a party hosted by Andrew Lloyd Webber.

The '90s dawned with Michael's finances with CBS Records being updated once more, prompting the media to report that the singer's personal fortune was around £65 million. His record company undertook the review because their artist's second album, *Listen Without Prejudice Vol I*, was due. In September 1990, the project's first single was issued. Titled 'Praying For Time', it peaked at No.6 in Britain and when issued across the Atlantic shot to the top. As expected, *Listen Without Prejudice Vol I* became a British chart-topper within days of its release; in America the project peaked at No.2. Released as a follow-up to 'Praying For Time', the single 'Waiting For That Day' faltered in the British Top 30 during the November, followed by 'Freedom 90', which likewise sold poorly. Across the Atlantic, though, the single reached the Top 10, probably due to the country's love of supermodels like Naomi Campbell and Cindy Crawford who featured in the song's promotional video. This shoot also featured the ceremonious burning of the artist's leather jacket associated with the *Faith* project.

During 1991 *Listen Without Prejudice Vol I* scooped the Best British Album category at the Brit Awards ceremony. Michael dedicated the award to an Epic Records marketing man who had died a year previously at the age of 34. The singer then embarked upon another world tour, this time performing at smaller venues with a show comprising a selection of his favourite tracks, hence the tour's name: 'Cover to Cover'. Dates ranged from Birmingham and Wembley Arena through to Oakland, California, and Madison Square Garden, where he performed two sell-out concerts. On the recording front, Michael issued a pair of British singles, namely 'Heal The Pain' and 'Cowboys And Angels'. Neither reached the Top 30.

In December 1991, Michael's live version of 'Don't Let The Sun Go Down On Me' with Elton John became an unexpected British chart-topper within days of its release and prior to being included on John's *Duets* album. Proceeds from the single benefited two children's charities, following Michael's own donation of $500,000 to several AIDS charities in Britain and America. In February 1992, the single also topped the American chart; again proceeds boosted numerous organisations, including those involved with cancer research.

In 1992 and 1993 the singer lent his talent to several high-earning and high-profile charity concerts. First appearing at the Wembley-staged 'A Concert For Life', where he joined other acts to celebrate the life of Queen's Freddie Mercury, an AIDS victim, the singer shifted venue to Madison Square Garden to support Elizabeth Taylor's AIDS Foundation Benefit with others who included Lionel Richie and Elton John. However, Michael's various live appearances were overshadowed by his filing of a $1 million law suit for the reputed slap-happy handling of his pension fund by Chancery Financial Management, followed by a dispute against his record company CBS's Epic Records, Michael questioning its ability to promote his product. Further, when Sony Entertainment, the new parent of Epic Records, was advised by Michael's lawyer that his client was subsequently not bound by his recording contract and therefore owned his masters (original recordings of his material), artist and record company became embroiled in a vicious and lengthy legal case that was heard in the High Court late in 1993. In a public statement, Michael said that since the Sony Corporation had purchased his contract, alongside those of other artists signed to CBS Records, he had witnessed the great American company that he'd so proudly signed to as a teenager be transformed into a production line for a major electronics factory, which had little or no concept of creativity, while adding, 'Sony appears to see artists as little more than software.' Naturally, the action prevented Michael from recording elsewhere, which in turn placed his career on hold.

While the lawyers clashed, the 'Too Funky' single hit both the British and American Top 10, before an EP featuring live tracks from 'A Concert For Life' was issued via Hollywood Records. The tracks included Michael's version of Queen's 'These Are The Days Of Our Lives' and 'Somebody To Love', and under the title 'Five Live EP' Michael entered the British chart at No.1 during May 1993.

In April the courts decided in the Sony Corporation's favour, whereupon Michael, who declared he would never sing again, was ordered to pay the costs for both parties, estimated to be in the region of $3 million. A month on from the ruling, Michael appeared on the ITV programme *A Television Interview with Sir David Frost*, where he was painfully honest regarding his recent court experience but said that he had his career to consider, despite his insistence of never singing again – but should the Sony Corporation offer him his freedom to record elsewhere, he would gladly oblige. In August, still knee deep in legal costs, the singer filed his appeal against the court's decision, once again citing the poor sales of his second album *Listen Without Prejudice Vol II* as a direct result of Sony's lack of promotion.

Meanwhile, the music played on. Michael participated in the MTV European Music Awards ceremony staged in Berlin, where he performed his new title 'Jesus To A Child'. The song's next official airing was during Capital Radio's annual 'Help A London Child' project, when the title raised several thousand pounds for the station's fund. Early in 1996, 'Jesus To A Child' signified Michael's debut release as a free artist and entered the British chart at the top; it made the Top 10 in America. The Sony Corporation had, as Michael wished, agreed to release him from his commitments – in return for approximately $40 million, plus a small percentage of the sales from the singer's next two albums.

'Jesus To A Child' was released by Virgin Records in Britain and everywhere outside America, where Dreamworks SKG handled Michael's material. With the singer now back on track, the title 'Fast Love' was issued as the chart-topper's follow-up; it became another British No.1 seller in May 1996. Both titles were, incidentally, extracted from Michael's self-composed and self-produced new album *Older*, a British chart-topper and No.6 in America.

To stir memories, and to capitalise on the huge Christmas sales generated by television advertising, the compilation titled *If You Were There: The Best Of Wham!* was released late in 1997. The magic that was Wham! returned, if only for a short time. But alongside the fun memories, 1997 was a year of sadness for Michael: his beloved mother Lesley died from cancer, and his friend Diana, Princess of Wales, died in a car crash in Paris. Michael accompanied Elton John to the Princess's funeral, together with other mourners from the worlds of music and entertainment.

In 1998 there was more grief, and this time of the singer's own making. During April, with *The Sun* newspaper's front page glaring 'Zip Me Up Before You Go Go', Michael hit the headlines in a manner not befitting a star of his stature after being arrested for alleged lewd behaviour in a public toilet situated in the Will Rogers Memorial Park, Beverly Hills. Michael was handcuffed before spending two hours in custody and being released on £308 bail. His court date was booked for 5 May 1998. During a CNN television interview, Michael admitted he had put himself in an 'extremely stupid and vulnerable position, especially because I am in a privileged position . . . I won't even say that it was the first time that happened . . . I have put myself in that position before.' He also said the arrest had forced him to publicly admit his homosexuality, while regretting his admission had been associated with the arrest. In the exclusive interview, he further admitted that several of his solo singles had hinted at his gayness, citing 'I Want Your Sex' and 'Fast Love' as examples.

During October 1988, Michael issued the British Top 10 single 'Outside'. This title appeared on the Sony double CD *Best Of George Michael*. Released at the time of the single's success, the project, containing other new material, was part of the singer's settlement with Sony.

Also see: 'Careless Whisper', September 1984; 'A Different Corner', May 1986

(Quotes: *Bare* by George Michael and Tony Parsons)

March 1987

BEN E. KING

Stand By Me

It's still so amazing to me that all those hits of the early '60s have left such a strong impression on people' – Ben E. King

Born Benjamin Earl Belson in Henderson, North Carolina, on 28 September 1938, he was educated at the James Fenimore Cooper Junior High School and in his spare time sang in the church choir and on street corners. As a schoolboy, he joined the Four Bs, later moving to the Moonglows, then the Crowns.

The Crowns' break in the music business came following a performance at the Apollo Theater in Harlem. They released the single titled 'Kiss And Make Up', which became a local hit, before becoming integral members of the Drifters. George Treadwell, manager and owner of the Drifters, dismissed existing members, replacing them with members of the Crowns. In time, Ben E. King was elevated to the Drifters' lead singer and principal composer. King told journalist David Nathan in 1985, 'I'd written some things. "There Goes My Baby" was the first song that had done pretty well for the Drifters. I was fortunate too because I had a good deal with my publishing situation. Back then, a lot of us would sign contracts which were just not fair. But what did we know? We were green in the business and when someone gave us a bottle of champagne to celebrate a hit song, we thought it was a big deal.'

With King in the line-up, the Drifters recorded a series of evergreen singles that included the aforementioned 'There Goes My Baby', a Top 2 American hit in June 1959 and, before the year was out, 'Dance With Me', a Top 20 hit in both America and Britain. During 1960, '(If You Cry) True Love True Love', 'The Magic Moment' and 'Lonely Winds' became American hits, while the classic 'Save The Last Dance For Me' topped the American chart late in 1960. Yet despite healthy record sales and capacity-filled venues, the Drifters' earnings were paltry. King explained: 'I asked for a raise and when I didn't get it I decided to move on and go out on my own. I was still recording with the group but I didn't perform with them.' Midway through 1960, Ben E. King signed a solo recording contract with the Atco label, a subsidiary of Atlantic Records. His debut single 'Spanish Harlem' soared into the American and British charts and would be rerecorded countless times by other acts including Aretha Franklin in 1971. King's next hit, 'Stand By Me', was actually composed by him for the Drifters to record. The group, of course, lost out when King departed. 'I was really looking forward to having them record it. I had actually been inspired to write it by an old gospel song, "Lord Stand By Me" . . . Of course, the lyrics were very different. I wrote the song from a very personal experience. I fell in love.' The single peaked in the British Top 30 and reached No.4 in America in June 1961. In actuality, 'Stand By Me' was the result of surplus minutes in a recording session with producers Mike Stoller and Jerry Leiber. Said King, 'I thought that I might be able to persuade the Drifters to do it at some later date, but I figured, well, why not just go ahead, since we did have some studio time. The whole thing was really unplanned, unrehearsed and, of course, I had no inkling that it would not only give me a hit but become virtually a standard.'

During September 1961, the single 'Amor Amor' soared into the British Top 40 and American Top 20. The title marked King's last British entrant until 'Stand By Me' was reissued in 1987. Before 1961 closed, the 'Young Boy Blues' single peaked in the American Top 70 and King's debut album *Spanish Harlem* was issued. The next year, the singer released a trio of American hits, namely 'Ecstasy', 'Don't Play That Song' – once again, Aretha Franklin went on to rerecord this track in 1970 – and 'Too Bad'. King's next single, titled 'I (Who Have Nothing)', peaked in the Top 30 for him during 1963. The title heralded his last American big-seller.

To start 1964, the singer embarked upon his debut British promotional tour, including an appearance on the Friday night music programme *Ready Steady Go*, his first in a series of appearances. Through to the next decade, Ben E. King established himself as a noted soul artist; certainly in Britain he was revered as such, alongside others including Arthur Conley, Wilson Pickett and Joe Tex. Indeed, he returned to British audiences several times, building a loyal following that remained through to the '90s.

Into the '70s, King switched record companies to Crewe Records and issued the *Rough Edges* album. His next, titled *The Beginning Of It All*, was released two years later via Mandala Records. During 1975, he returned home to Atlantic Records at the request of the company's founder Ahmet Ertegan, where his debut album *Supernatural* spawned the Top 5 American hit 'Supernatural Thing'. Two years on, following the release of his second album at Atlantic, *I Had A Love*, King recorded the *Benny And Us* album with the Average White Band.

Through to the next decade, the singer continued to earn a good living as a performer. He actually returned to the Drifters' line-up early in the '80s, although the original group no longer existed as such. Said King, 'There's been a 20-year argument as to who owns the name but now we have it figured out. There are two "Drifters"; one group does European tours, the other one does US dates. That way we all get to work.'

In 1986, King's career took an unexpected turn with the release of the *Stand By Me* movie. According to King, 'A book written by Stephen King called *The Body* was out and they'd planned doing a movie but decided the title was too heavy for a film. So Rob Reiner, Carl Reiner's son, who directed the film, was playing his old records at home one night and played "Stand By Me". He made the decision then that this would be the title of the movie.'

When rereleased as a single, 'Stand By Me', written by King and produced by Leiber and Stoller, soared into the American Top 10 at the close of 1986. In Britain, meanwhile, the track was also used in a television advertisement for Levi 501 jeans, which helped push it to the top of the British chart during March 1987. Said King, 'It's a great song, from the era when music was music, and there have been some good cover versions over the years from people like Otis Redding, John Lennon, even Muhammad Ali.' Hot on the chart-topper's heels, *Stand By Me (The Ultimate Collection)* was issued, containing tracks by King and the Drifters. The title 'Spanish Harlem' was lifted from the compilation as a follow-up single and reached the British Top 20.

Four months on from the success of 'Stand By Me', King signed a recording contract with EMI Records' Manhattan label. He told journalist Roger St Pierre, 'There was some vague talk of signing a new deal with Atlantic, but I wanted fresh beginnings, so we went for EMI . . . Of course the success of "Stand By Me" helped stimulate the company's interest in me.' The *Save The Last Dance For Me* album was issued as King's debut during 1988, with contributions from luminaries that included Lamont Dozier, Mark Knopfler and Ruby Turner. Produced by John Paul Jones, the album was recorded in New York and San Francisco, but regrettably failed to reach expectations. Any new career King had craved disintegrated with this album.

Into the '90s, Ben E. King remained in demand as a performer on the concert circuit and as a guest artist at soul gala concerts that included an appearance at the Apollo Theater Hall of Fame during 1993. He really was synonymous with the best from America during a decade that was, primarily, not geared for soul music.

'People still want to hear those oldies but goldies. As long as they want to hear them, I'm going to keep singing them' – Ben E. King

(Quotes: *Blues and Soul* magazine, 1985 and 1987, interviews by David Nathan and Roger St Pierre)

April 1987

BOY GEORGE

Everything I Own

Just when the public believed their most colourful of characters would fade into obscurity, drowning in a mire of bad publicity and tragedy, he returned to prove his selling power was as strong as ever.

At the start of 1987, and on a much happier note, George was a guest on Terry Wogan's BBC TV chat show. During the interview the singer told viewers that he was clean and that the Culture Club era was definitely over. A month after the televised announcement, George's version of Bread's 1972 Top 40 hit and the 1974 British chart-topper for Jamaican artist Ken Boothe 'Everything I Own' returned him to the top of the British chart. It was a welcome-back gift for the singer from his loyal following.

The follow-up single, 'Keep Me In Mind', struggled into the British Top 30; nonetheless, the poor showing did not prevent George's debut solo album, titled *Sold*, from being issued. It also reached the Top 30 in June 1987. A month on, the album's title track was swiped for single release and was a further Top 30 hit and before 1987 closed the singer enjoyed a Top 20 British placing with a further album track titled 'To Be Reborn'. It seemed that despite George's tarnished reputation, record-buyers either chose to ignore it or refused to allow it to interfere with his music.

In 1988, the single 'Live My Life', included in the soundtrack of the movie titled *Hiding Out*, crawled into the British Top 70 and American Top 40. Mid-year, amid the furore regarding the government's banning of local-government promotion of gay people, George released 'No Clause 28', a Top 50 hit. His next, 'Don't Cry', sold fewer copies, crawling into the British Top 60.

With the '90s looming, a pair of singles – 'Don't Take My Mind On A Trip' and 'After The Love' – struggled into the British Top 70. The latter title, under the name 'Jesus Loves You', was issued on George's newly opened record label, More Protein. In between these releases, the *High Hat* album bombed.

Into the new decade, the singer openly promoted his newly discovered Hare Krishna faith by releasing the 'Bow Down Mister' single. It was another poor seller, while the Jesus Loves You album, titled *The Martyr Mantras*, peaked in the Top 60 during April 1991. A further cover version in 1992 boosted George's flagging career by returning him to the British Top 30. This time the singer reworked Dave Berry's 1964 British Top 5 single 'The Crying Game', the theme from the movie of the same name. When released in America the single peaked in the Top 20. The future appeared secure once more.

Exchanging the musical note for the written word, George settled down to pen his top-selling autobiography *Take It Like A Man*. With writer Spencer Bright, George wrote one of the most forthright life stories published in this country – it certainly ruffled a few feathers. Extremely entertaining, this compulsive book was a sheer delight.

With his recording career temporarily on hold, performances sustained George's popularity in both Britain and America. The most notable were the 'Commitment To Life VIII', a charity gala in Elton John's honour, with the proceeds destined for various AIDS organisations, and his participation in the annual Gay Pride Festival held in Victoria Park, London. George did return to his music to release 'Funtime' and 'Same Thing In Reverse'; regrettably, both titles floundered in the British Top 60.

George then returned to the turntables as DJ and mixer of tracks, embarking upon a club tour as guest DJ, working in packed night-clubs. More recently, the singer was spotted mingling with guests on Channel 4's *Coming Out Party*. The occasion in April 1998 was in honour of Ellen DeGeneres telling the American viewing public that she was gay during her sitcom series *Ellen*. The singer then re-formed

Culture Club to hit the British touring circuit, bringing the magic alive once more.

With a career that dodged from the recording studios and public stage to the courts where he was hauled to face drugs charges, this talented man will hopefully remain a contributor to British music for some time to come. Indeed, he and Culture Club returned to the British Top 10 in 1998 with the single 'I Just Wanna Be Loved'. Remarkably, his competitors in the chart were George Michael and Cher, who held the pole position. In a decade that seemed to thrive on so-called young talent, it was a pleasure to see a trio of old friends at the top once more.

Also see: 'Do You Really Want To Hurt Me?', October 1982; 'Karma Chameleon', October 1983

May 1987

STARSHIP

Nothing's Gonna Stop Us Now

'Being part of a band is recognising that all of us are going to be assholes at some time or other' – Paul Kantner

Jefferson Airplane, Jefferson Starship, then Starship. There were numerous changes in personnel and group offshoots, but in the end the disruptions paid off with three American chart-toppers.

In 1965 Paul Kantner and Marty Balin met in San Francisco, whereupon they recruited Bob Harvey, Jorma Kaukonen, Skip Spence and Signe Anderson to form the group known as Jefferson Airplane. According to Kantner, 'We took drugs and ran away from authority and the institutions that didn't necessarily deserve our respect. I suppose it was that our generation didn't grow up, didn't accept the world as it was.'

Within a year, and with extensive touring experience to their credit, Jefferson Airplane secured a recording deal with RCA Records. As their recording career took hold during 1966, Anderson left the group to have a baby; her replacement was Grace Slick from the Great Society group. Spence then left Jefferson Airplane to form the outfit Moby Grape; his replacement was Spencer Dryden. The line-up then remained untouched for a while and enjoyed considerable American success with singles like 'Somebody To Love' and 'White Rabbit', until 1970 when Dryden and Slick departed, leaving the remaining membership to flounder. Said Kantner, 'In the early '70s we started breaking apart . . . And Janis Joplin's death, that was probably the final "whew!".'

A great deal of action occurred with past and present group members embarking upon solo careers or hitching up with other groups. While this confusion reigned, Jefferson Starship was created, releasing their first single in 1974 titled 'Ride The Tiger', followed by their biggest-selling items 'Miracles' and 'Count On Me' during 1978. Grace Slick then returned to the group as a permanent member and Kantner departed in the throes of disagreement – which led to him taking the group's name with him. The remaining members, including Mickey Thomas, therefore decided to be known as Starship and recorded their debut album under this name, titled *Knee Deep In The Hoopla*. It was also as Starship that the group enjoyed its first American chart-topper in 1985 with 'We Built This City'. The single, released by RCA Records, also marked Starship's debut British hit at No.12. Prior to this, Jefferson Starship had placed 'Jane' in the British Top 30 during 1980.

Four months on from their American chart-topper, Starship returned to the No.1 position for one week with the 'Sara' single, composed by Peter and Ina Wolf, who had previously recorded under the name Wolf and Wolf for Motown Records and as Vienna for Warner Brothers. Peter Wolf had worked on material for Jefferson Starship, particularly their 1984 album *Nuclear Furniture*.

Starship's third and final American chart-topper saw a change of composers to Albert Hammond and Diane Warren. With the single 'Nothing's Gonna Stop Us Now', Starship topped their homeland's chart for two weeks in April 1987, before repeating that success in Britain a month on. Remarkably, though, 'Nothing's Gonna Stop Us Now' would represent the group's last British success.

When Hammond and Warren were approached to score the music for the *Mannequin* movie, they decided to compose a track that was both meaty and uptempo. The song was apparently completed in one day and then presented to Starship's producer Peter Wolf. He rejected Hammond and Warren's interpretation, preferring the group to work with Narada Michael Walden, known for his splendid work with Diana Ross and Whitney Houston, among other celebrated artists. Walden was eager to experiment with the track, feeling it was a hit record. As Starship were ensconced in an American tour at the time, Walden recorded the musical background; it was heavy on drums, emulating the Phil Spector Hall of Sound on modern-day equipment. Once Starship had finished their trek, Slick recorded her vocals first, with Thomas adding his at a later date to complete the duet. Once done, the booming Spector atmosphere and production were added thanks to a recording studio crammed with musicians and people who rattled things and blew whistles! Walden's instinct was spot on: the single was an instant international chart-topper, selling in excess of one million copies in America alone.

Said Kantner, 'In the end we did what we did for the ride . . . for the thrill of the energy . . . That's the way it was with us.'

(Quotes: *Off the Record: An Oral History of Popular Music* by Joe Smith)

June 1987

MADONNA

La Isla Bonita

'Although there will be times that your moods may falter, and you'll question each other's motives, the faith and love that you share will help to show that your inconsistency is only for a moment' – extracted from the wedding vows exchanged by Madonna and Sean Penn

When the *Shanghai Surprise* movie bombed, Madonna vowed never to appear on film with her husband again. To this end she turned down several roles, including one in *Dead End Street*, directed by his father. In any event, the singer had her sights set higher: on the role of Eva Perón in the movie version of *Evita*. To prove her seriousness, she dressed in a 1940s evening gown with her hair styled in a Perón twist to meet the film's producer Robert Stigwood.

While Madonna continued to plough her energies into her singing career, she also publicly admitted that her marriage was high on violence with her husband's love of guns and his growing jealousy of the men his wife worked with, including her dancers. He also objected to her work for AIDS charities – several of Madonna's friends suffered from the killer disease – via performances or the donation of personal items for auction. With their often tempestuous marriage now public knowledge, it came as no surprise when Madonna instructed her lawyers to prepare divorce papers. When Penn then declared his undying love, the divorce was put on hold.

In January 1987 Madonna was the recipient of the American Music Award for Favourite Female Video Artist and in the May she topped the British chart for the fourth time with 'La Isla Bonita'. Penned by Patrick Leonard for Michael Jackson, who rejected the title, Madonna reworked the song's lyrics to record it herself. When released in America, 'La Isla Bonita' earned the distinction of becoming the fifth Top 5 single from the *True Blue* album.

By June 1987, Madonna was heavily involved with her role of Nikki Finn in her third movie, originally titled *Slammer*. Working once again with Leonard and Stephen Bray (composers of *True Blue*), she completed the song 'Who's That Girl?', which she considered to be a more suitable film title than *Slammer*. She was granted her wish and went on to pen with Leonard 'The Look Of Love' and with Bray 'Can't Stop' and 'Causing A Commotion'. Said Madonna, 'There's a spirit to this music that captures both what the film and the character [I play] are about.' When the movie, with co-stars Sir John Mills and Griffin Dunn, was premièred, however, critics were less than kind. Madonna had bombed once again.

When 'Who's That Girl?' was released as a single, the title topped both the British and American charts. While the film's soundtrack peaked at No.4 and No.7 respectively, Madonna toured Britain for the first time, using 'Who's That Girl?' as the tour's banner. Perhaps 'tour' isn't the right word here, as she performed only four concerts: one in Leeds and three at Wembley Stadium. When she stepped on the Wembley stage before a 75,000-strong audience, dressed in a black corselet, the crowd surged forward and fighting ensued, forcing water hoses to be used by frantic security guards. Fainting fans were carried over barriers to safety, while order was restored to a degree. Madonna had arrived in Britain!

Meanwhile, Penn faced a jail sentence following his second probation violation, a reckless-driving charge. Madonna learned about her husband's arrest by reading newspaper headlines. Her ignorance of her husband's activities was due to her career commitments, and the same was true the other way around. On the eve of her European trip, *Penthouse* magazine carried the singer on its cover, while within were eight pages of nude photographs shot during her modelling days, over which she had no control. Penn saw the pictures when he received the magazine through the mail while incarcerated in the Mono County Jail. He was due to be released in September 1987. With her touring commitments completed, Madonna awaited his release in their Malibu home, whereupon Penn accused her of having affairs in his absence, began drinking heavily and generally treated her badly.

In December 1987 Madonna filed a second divorce petition in the Superior Court, Los Angeles, stating that her prenuptial agreement stood and that her maiden name Ciccone be restored. The petition was withdrawn as Madonna was reunited with Penn in Los Angeles, staying at the Hotel Shangri La. Within two weeks, the marriage was in full bloom once more. So was her acting career, as Madonna appeared in the television production *Bloodhounds on Broadway* with co-stars Matt Dillon and Jennifer Grey. The singer agreed to appear in the movie because the director Howard Brookner, who had been diagnosed with AIDS, was a close friend. In November 1989 *Bloodhounds on Broadway* was screened, nine months after the director's death. From the television screen Madonna switched to the Broadway stage and *Speed The Plow*, playing an office clerk working for two Hollywood high fliers. Madonna admitted, 'It was a real mind-fuck of a script . . . Little did I know that . . . everybody else involved saw me as a dark, evil spirit.' Critics generally agreed: 'No, she can't act.' Madonna responded, 'I expected it. There are people who are violently opposed to the fact that I exist on this earth, so I was just thankful that there were people who liked it.' When *Speed The Plow* opened during May 1988, Penn was filming *Casualties of War* in South-East Asia. Following an eight-month stint, the singer left the show's cast, whereupon ticket demand decreased drastically.

Meanwhile, Madonna's music continued. In Britain the single 'Causin' A Commotion' soared into the Top 4, while in America it peaked two positions higher. The *You Can Dance* album comprising dance-mixed tracks hit the British Top 5 but faltered in the American Top 20 early in 1988. The project nonetheless passed platinum status. During March 1988, as her *The Virgin Tour* video passed sales of 100,000 copies, Madonna's personal life once more hit the tabloids when she attended one of her husband's performances in the stage show *Hurlyburly*, in Los Angeles. On the singer's arm was Sandra Bernhard, with whom she was reputedly having a lesbian affair.

Again the big screen beckoned, or rather Warren Beatty did. He was casting the role of Breathless Mahoney against his Dick Tracy. His first choice was Kathleen Turner, but when Madonna offered to take a minimal salary in place of a several-million-dollar pay packet, Beatty was able to complete the movie within his $30 million budget. Penn was livid at the deal struck by his wife; this in turn led to drinking binges, culminating in him physically injuring Madonna, whom he'd strapped to a chair in their Malibu home. He left the property with his helpless wife within, only to return, whereupon she was able to persuade him to release her. She headed straight for the Malibu sheriff's office to swear a complaint against Penn, and Christopher Anderson reported, 'There, bruised and bleeding, she told the horrifying story of her nine-hour ordeal to dumbstruck officers.' Penn was arrested as his wife once more filed for divorce. She later dropped her complaint, with no criminal charges pressed.

On the professional front, the media reported that Meryl Streep had been wooed to play Eva Perón in *Evita*, but Madonna eventually secured the role for herself. Like her life so far, nothing remained static for long. She was the media's dream: always good copy, with revealing pictures. However, she also had a great talent – and there's much more to come.

Also see: 'Into The Groove', August 1985; 'Papa Don't Preach', July 1986; 'True Blue', October 1986; 'Like A Prayer', April 1989

(Quotes: *Madonna: Unauthorized* by Christopher Anderson)

July 1987

WHITNEY HOUSTON

I Wanna Dance With Somebody (Who Loves Me)

'I don't pretend to be anything other than what I am, nor do I want to be' – Whitney Houston

As life continued in the fast lane, Whitney Houston issued the follow-up to her international chart-topper 'Saving All My Love For You' titled 'How Will I Know?', a track reportedly rejected by Janet Jackson. Whereas the chart-topper had been seductively smoochy, this release struck the dance chord. Lifted from her debut album *Whitney Houston*, the single, composed by George Merrill and produced by Narada Michael Walden, peaked in the British Top 5 in February 1986, reaching No.1 in America. The album also shot to the top of the American listing.

Now said to be a millionaire at 22 years old, Houston spent all her time promoting her career, whether it was on stage, in a television studio or in another country. Her private life became a non-entity overnight; her family rarely saw her and she awoke each day in states and countries she didn't easily recognise. Some fans obsessively tracked her, while her mail was a cross between the sincere and the sinister. Houston admitted, 'The fact is that some of these fans are downright scary . . . it's a big issue. I think it should be taken seriously.' She was easy prey: a young, beautiful singing sensation – and single. In an attempt to whip up a romance for her, the media reported she was dating actor Eddie Murphy. The two did in fact date, but any chance of the relationship succeeding was ended by the demands of their respective careers.

For her next single, Houston returned to the ballad. Titled 'The

Greatest Love Of All', it was a cover version of George Benson's blinding original, included in the movie *The Greatest*, the life story of Muhammad Ali. When Houston first recorded it, Arista Records hid it away as the B-side to her 1985 single 'You Give Good Love', never intending it for top-side release, but radio airplay and subsequent public pressure forced her record company to release it. It was a wise decision: 'The Greatest Love Of All' gave the singer her third consecutive American chart-topper and reached the British Top 10 during May 1986.

A further track from the *Whitney Houston* album was considered as follow-up, titled 'All At Once', but Clive Davis resisted the temptation, believing that issuing the track at this time would over-expose his artist.

During 1986 Houston announced her plans to headline her first major American tour, while in the November she performed in Britain for the first time as part of a European trek. Her perform-ances surprised her audiences, to say the least. Not only did she move little on stage, with negligible contact with the audiences, but she altered the presentation of her material, particularly that featured on her album. It left fans who expected to hear live versions of her recorded work disappointed and annoyed, believing they had been conned. Despite these feelings, however, the singer was warmly welcomed.

By the time *Whitney Houston* passed sales of 13 million worldwide, earning a handful of multi-platinum albums *en route*, plans were afoot for her second. A month prior to the pending album's release, Arista Records extracted the track 'I Wanna Dance With Somebody (Who Loves Me)', amid an expensive promotional campaign. Arista, or rather Clive Davis, was leaving nothing to chance; Houston was too valuable a commodity. Aimed at the dance floor, 'I Wanna Dance With Somebody (Who Loves Me)', penned by George Merrill and Shannon Rubicam and produced by Narada Michael Walden, was actually not a reference to dancing at all. Rubicam explained, 'I pictured somebody single wishing that they could find that special person for themselves . . . "I wanna do that dance of life with somebody", that was the thought behind the song.' On the other hand, Walden felt the track was too country-and-western orientated: 'It reminded me of a rodeo song with Olivia Newton-John.' He changed his mind, of course, when he heard Houston's funky version.

American radio stations were issued with a directive from Arista Records forbidding the single to be played until early morning on 29 April 1987, thus guaranteeing simultaneous airplay across American states. While her home country fawned, however, British critics were mixed in their views. Many believed Houston's magic was faultless and the track was perfection, while others believed she was boring and oh-so-predictable.

The single easily shot up the American and British charts to the top during July 1987, making it Houston's fourth consecutive American chart-topper. Her second album was then launched, titled *Whitney*. Once again the release was a musical pot-pourri, thanks to a list of producers that included Kashif, Jellybean Benitez and Walden, and it was more confidently presented than her first. The duet with her mother, Cissy Houston, titled 'I Know Him So Well' was particularly inspiring. *Whitney* entered the British and American charts at the top, earning the singer the distinction of being the first female vocalist ever to enjoy an album debut at No.1. The American position was, incidentally, held for a staggering 11 weeks.

To close 1987, the musical treadmill ground on. Houston issued a further two singles, both swiped from *Whitney*. The first, the ballad 'Didn't We Almost Have It All?', stormed to the top of the American chart, while in Britain it stalled in the Top 20. The second, titled 'So Emotional', represented the final single to be lifted from the album and would eventually present Houston with her sixth consecutive American No.1 single. This time British record-buyers sent the single into the Top 5 during November 1987.

Financially speaking, Houston was now reputedly worth a cool $44 million, but she still did not, author Jeffrey Bowman reported, enjoy a steady relationship. She admitted, 'I have felt the feeling of being in love, but I've also turned away from it.' While her picture appeared on countless magazine covers, her music was criticised for being too white. Houston was black yet she sang mainstream pop. Sure, the material was undeniably commercial, but what the critics failed to recognise was that she probably didn't have the final choice – and the fact that her mother was the mistress of gospel didn't automatically mean that her daughter had inherited that talent. Houston claimed, 'I was accused of selling out, of being a black singer doing pop for white audiences . . . there's no way I would attempt to make myself less black, whatever that entails, to be more commercial.'

Also see: 'Saving All My Love For You', December 1985; 'One Moment In Time', November 1988

(Quotes: *Diva: The Totally Unauthorised Biography of Whitney Houston* by Jeffrey Bowman)

August 1987

PET SHOP BOYS

It's A Sin

'"It's A Sin" was . . . meant to be a little outrageous and we liked the idea of it being about sin because there aren't many songs about sin' – Neil Tennant

In April 1986 the single 'Love Comes Quickly' was issued as the follow-up title to the Pet Shop Boys' first British chart-topper 'West End Girls'. Unfortunately, it failed to follow in its predecessor's footsteps and stalled in the British Top 20. A month on, the reworked 'Opportunities (Let's Make Lots Of Money)' peaked at No.11 in the chart. When released in America during the August, the single peaked in the Top 10.

Back on home turf, the duo's 'Suburbia' single soared into the Top 10, bringing the total number of singles swiped from their *Please* debut album to four. 'Suburbia' was inspired by the movie of the same name. Having seen the film several times, Tennant and Lowe planned to compose a track based on its theme. Lowe already had an untitled melody drafted, so Tennant adapted this. Said Lowe, 'I wrote the tune on the piano at home in Blackpool. The chorus simply came out exactly as I played it . . . What I especially liked about "Suburbia" was that the verse was in a minor key and the chorus in a major key. That's why it sounds quite happy.'

Towards the close of 1986, a six-track dance album titled *Disco* peaked in the British Top 20. Within a month of its release in January 1987, the *Television* video topped the British video chart. Featuring clips from their singles to date, the package highlighted the Pet Shop Boys' flair for visual imagination, albeit through Eric Watson's eyes; this talent would surpass many of their contemporaries' attempts in future years.

Midway through 1987, the Pet Shop Boys issued a track originally penned during 1982 when they had first begun experimenting with recording in the Camden Studio. Initially, the duo had intended the song to be for a third party, perhaps the transvestite dance star Divine, who had previously impressed them with the dance hit 'You Think You're A Man', produced by Stock, Aitken and Waterman. When that plan was rejected, Tennant and Lowe believed the song to be ideal for disco songstress Miquel Brown and her producer Ian Levine. However, as Brown had recently recorded a track with similar lyrics, Levine likewise rejected the duo's track. It appeared the only path open to the Pet Shop Boys was to record and release 'It's A Sin' themselves. How Divine and Brown must have cringed when the title – with its lyrics dripping with the Catholic attitude towards sex – shot to the top of the British chart in August 1987. 'European disco drama' was how one reviewer summed up the single. 'It's A Sin' went on to become a chart-topper in 11 countries, including Spain, Israel, Finland and Switzerland.

The astonishing sales of the single were boosted by its promotional video partner. The original intention had been to portray the burning of St Joan of Arc at the stake but this idea was quickly abandoned and replaced by a story telling of a jury of monks deliberating on the fate of Tennant, playing a prisoner following an undisclosed crime. Filmed at London's Millennium Wharf, the video was darkly atmospheric in a medieval style, with actors like Ron Moody as support cast.

It was obvious to the public that promotional visuals were now as important as their music to the Pet Shop Boys. The videos were also a necessity because of the very nature of their stage act. A pair of static artists, one at a keyboard and the other 'talking' lyrics, hardly makes compulsive viewing!

The Pet Shop Boys were growing into a highly profitable business, although they were yet to step on a British concert stage.

Also see: 'West End Girls', January 1986; 'Always On My Mind', December 1987; 'Heart', April 1988

(Quotes: *Pet Shop Boys, Annually 1989* by Chris Lowe and Neil Tennant)

September 1987

MICHAEL JACKSON AND SIEDAH GARRETT

I Just Can't Stop Loving You

'Never believe the tabloid garbage. If you hear it from my lips, then you can believe it' – Michael Jackson

As 1986 closed, leaving behind bizarre tales of an oxygen chamber and Captain Eno, Jackson's next year looked set to become even 'badder'. Indeed, 1987 saw the release of Jackson's follow-up album to *Thriller*, titled *Bad*, which took two years to record. The singer had deliberately taken his time recording this project because he was desperate to outsell *Thriller*. That failed to happen, simply because there was no comparison between the two – the first was sincere, the second egotistical.

Prior to the release of the *Bad* project, though, in August 1987, Jackson was asked to leave the Jehovah's Witnesses membership, a move probably instigated by the *Thriller* video's theme and the singer's lifestyle. Also before the album release, as part of the hype to ensure the singer a high public profile, he declared his intention to purchase the remains of John Merrick, the Elephant Man, held in London's Medical College. To support his intention, Jackson viewed the remains and offered $1 million, while a press release stated he was 'a dedicated and devoted collector of art and antiques.' His offer was naturally rejected, the media coverage exhaustive – and CBS Records hadn't spent a dime from its promotional budget!

As a taster of the forthcoming music project, the title 'I Just Can't Stop Loving You' was lifted for single release, although it failed to represent the overall feel of the album. Intended by Jackson as a duet with Barbra Streisand or Diana Ross, he settled for songwriter Siedah Garrett, an unknown name in Britain. Garrett first came to his attention with her composition titled 'Man In The Mirror', which he recorded for inclusion in the *Bad* album. 'I Just Can't Stop Loving You' shot to the top of the British chart during September 1987, also reaching the No.1 position in America and several European countries. The media believed Garrett looked similar to Jackson and attempted to instigate a romance between them. That rumour was quickly quashed once the publicity blitz was exhausted.

With a hastily switched packaging – Jackson clad in black leather replaced his portrait – and an industry hype of alarming proportions under way including television specials, videos, media packs and so on, the *Bad* album was eventually released. It shot to the top of both the British and American charts on its way to multi-platinum sales. Yet amid the media celebrations and public hysteria, the readers of the American magazine *Rolling Stone* voted *Bad* the Worst Album, likewise the spin-off single and video, before dealing the biggest blow to the singer himself as the Most Unwelcome Comeback!

Within weeks of the album's release, the singer began the first leg of his one-and-a-half-year 'Bad' tour in Japan. The trek went on to gross an estimated $125 million through its 15-country journey. Each performance cost in excess of $500,000 to stage, with hi-tech sound and light shows to portray his material in a manner audiences flocked to share. Jackson's act also introduced his new gimmick – sticking plasters on three of his fingers. No, he'd not cut himself, but wanted to follow Howard Hughes's obsession of not touching what he considered to be germ-contaminated surfaces and objects.

Before 1987 ended, two further singles were swiped from *Bad*, namely the album's title track and 'The Way You Make Me Feel'. Both were Top 3 British hits and chart-toppers in America. In 1988 the first single was Garrett's composition 'Man In The Mirror', with support vocals from her and the Winans, among others. The title surprisingly flopped in the British Top 30, but, once again, gave Jackson an American chart-topper.

The 'Bad' tour rolled on. From Japan it moved to Australia, but during the trek Jackson returned to California on several occasions. On one such visit during 1988 he purchased a Santa Ynez Valley property which he later called Neverland (previously known as Sycamore Ranch) for an estimated $17 million.

In July 1988 Jackson hit London, where he performed seven concerts at Wembley Arena before an estimated 73,000 people. Prior to one performance the singer presented Prince Charles and Princess Diana with a cheque for £300,000 made payable to the Prince's Trust, while during the show he sang a *Bad* track titled 'Dirty Diana' for the Princess, with whom he enjoyed a friendship until her death in 1997. When issued as a single, 'Dirty Diana' peaked at No.4 in Britain and reached the top in America during July 1988.

Turning briefly from musical notes to the written word, Jackson's autobiography *Moonwalk* was published by Doubleday. Ghostwritten by Shaye Areheart, one of the publishing house's editors, the book contained an introduction by the late Jackie Onassis which many believed was more interesting than the singer's actual rags-to-riches story.

Back to the music, a further pair of singles lifted from *Bad* were issued before the close of 1988, namely 'Another Part Of Me' and 'Smooth Criminal'. Both were huge sellers. Awards and honours were inevitably showered upon the singer, including the Brit Award for Best International Solo Artist and a NAACP Image Award.

Early in 1989, whilst Jackson was completing his tour, the *Moonwalker* video was issued, spanning his career to date. Within two weeks of its release, the video had sold in excess of 500,000 copies, surpassing the *Thriller* video. Not surprisingly, it became the top-selling home video of all time, grossing more than $30 million. Throughout 1989 the singer was a virtual recluse, yet he was never far from the headlines. Such was the ludicrous nature of some stories that the British press tagged him 'Wacko Jacko', much to the singer's disgust. To be fair, though, he only had himself to blame. His music career also caused him concern; he was angry because *Bad* had failed to top the sales of *Thriller* and laid much of the blame on his manager, Frank Dileo, whom he later sacked. Dileo's replacement was Sandy Gallin.

On the professional front, two singles sustained Jackson's British chart profile, namely 'Leave Me Alone' and 'Liberian Girl'. The first shot to No.2, while the second faltered in the Top 15.

Into the new decade, and among further honours, Jackson received the American Cinema Award for Entertainer of the Year, before being honoured at the White House by President Bush, who before a huge media presence likewise proclaimed him Entertainer of the Year. Also in 1990, Jackson was rushed to Saint John's Hospital, Santa Monica, after collapsing at his home during a strenuous dance routine. He was later diagnosed as suffering from cartilage inflammation between his ribs and sternum. Jackson's health was always considered fragile but his emergency trips to hospital were, rightly or wrongly, sometimes considered as possible publicity stunts.

Before CBS Records, now known as Sony, could issue its megastar's next album, *Dangerous*, executives had to renegotiate his recording contract. The company paid the singer a reputed $18 million advance and agreed to him receiving 25 per cent of the retail price of each record sold and an additional $5 million per album by way of an advance-sales guarantee. Jackson's own label, Nation, later to become MJ Records, would also be distributed by Sony as part of the new deal.

Shortly before the release of *Dangerous*, the promotional video for the first lifted single, titled 'Black And White', was premièred across several American networks and over 20 overseas countries before an estimated 510 million viewers. Now publicly known as the King of Pop (a name said to have been conceived by the singer himself), Jackson was heavily criticised for grabbing his crotch several times throughout the video, which was, after all, aimed at the children's market. ('I'm a slave to the rhythm,' he told Oprah Winfrey by way of explanation.) 'Black And White' entered the British chart at the top during November 1991, and did the same in America a month on. The date 20 November 1991 was the official launch date of *Dangerous* and within days the album had jumped to the top of the British and American charts. Jackson announced that Pepsi would sponsor his forthcoming world tour, under the 'Dangerous' banner, and the opening of his Heal The World Foundation, whose aim was to benefit worldwide children's charities and selected ecology projects. Actually, a percentage of his earnings had for some years been earmarked for numerous charities, usually those devoted to children's welfare.

At this juncture in his career, Jackson was said to be regretting the surgery he had undergone. Author Christopher Anderson listed the operations performed on the singer, in addition to the reported six nose jobs, as: 'the cleft inserted in his chin . . . tattooed permanent eyeliner . . . several face lifts, fat suctioned from his cheeks, his upper lip thinned, bone grafts on his cheeks and jaws . . . a 'forehead lift' . . . eye jobs to remove bags and crow's feet . . . supposed skin peels and the bleaching creams he used to lighten his complexion'. Jackson, on the other hand, strenuously denied having any surgery whatsoever. Who knows? Certainly Michael looks different these days, doesn't he? Actually, the *Daily Mirror* attempted to clarify the position by printing a front-page picture of the singer in July 1992. To say the pose was dire was an understatement; Jackson agreed and sued the newspaper.

The second track to be swiped from *Dangerous* as a single was 'Remember The Time', a Top 3 British and American hit. The accompanying video was delightful. With its Egyptian theme, it starred Eddie Murphy as the Pharaoh, Iman as his Queen Nefertiti and Magic Johnson. Jackson played an entertainer, opting not to dress up in Egyptian gear save a shawl draped around his waist over his trousers. The title 'In The Closet' followed, with his video co-star this time Naomi Campbell in a Palm Springs desert setting. The title peaked in the Top 10 on both sides of the Atlantic during May 1992. A month on, the 'Dangerous' tour started in Munich, Germany, while the British leg kicked in at the end of June. While on the road, Jackson was a regular British chart name with singles like 'Who Is It?', Top 10; 'Jam', Top 20; and 'Heal The World', Top 2. And for the second time he turned to the printed word, publishing a collection of poems and photographs under the title *Dancing the Dream*.

Into 1993, as the tour lumbered on, Jackson took time out to be interviewed by the overpaid but powerful talk-show host Oprah Winfrey. Filmed at Neverland, the exclusive televised conversation was his first in approximately 14 years and was recognised as the most candid interview ever. Winfrey was invited to view the attractions and facilities for visiting children, including the terminally ill, which the singer had installed at his home. To close the programme, Jackson premièred the track 'Give In To Me'. Viewers and media alike discussed and dissected the programme for days, with a large percentage concluding it was a sham. While the comments lingered, however, one incident not widely reported was the singer's message of condolence sent to the heartbroken parents of two-year-old James Bulger, savagely murdered by two youngsters.

As the American music industry bestowed all manner of honours upon the megastar, including music awards for the Best-Selling American Artist of the Year and lifetime achievement awards from various industry sections, Jackson's world collapsed amidst the growing speculation surrounding his friendship with young Jordy Chandler which resulted in him being reported to the Californian police authorities. The charge was alleged child abuse. In July 1993, while visiting his dentist father, young Chandler spoke while under anaesthetic of a relationship with the singer. His father demanded to meet Jackson, and after doing so believed the singer had indeed molested his son. Jackson hired Anthony Pellicano, a private investigator specialising in celebrity cases, to look into Chandler's serious allegations. Pellicano later told the media that Jordy's father had attempted to extort $20 million from the singer and when that failed had brought forward the child-abuse charges.

Within days various stories had been leaked to the American press; the tabloids grabbed what they could with damning headlines and implied that further investigations were afoot regarding other young boys who had been welcomed at Jackson's home. Then, in September 1993, Mark and Faye Quindoy, former Jackson employees, hosted a press conference where they read extracts from their diaries before an eager flock of media personnel. The Quindoys claimed they had seen the singer molest youngsters; their statement was subsequently questioned because the singer was in arrears with their salary. The Michael Jackson nightmare was beginning.

The police accelerated their investigations; while Jackson was in Bangkok, they raided his American properties, lifting videos, photographs and other items. His fans rushed protectively to his defence while his record company remained optimistically tight-lipped. With these charges coming at him from several quarters, Jackson broke down, unable to perform, and cancelled dates in Singapore, sending for close friend Elizabeth Taylor to comfort him. She flew to Singapore, where she hosted a party to celebrate Jackson's 35th birthday. Although on the verge of a nervous breakdown, Jackson appeared better for Taylor's presence and agreed to fulfil the Singapore dates. However, instead of stepping on stage, Jackson collapsed beside it. A brain scan and other tests revealed no serious problems other than severe migraines and an addiction to painkillers like Demerol and Valium.

And still the nightmare rolled on. While Jordy Chandler's attorney filed charges of a sexual nature in a Santa Monica court, the singer performed in Russia. The multi-paged document detailed specific acts that Christopher Anderson described 'were for the sole purpose of satisfying his "lust and sexual desires"'. The Santa Monica court in turn demanded Jackson's deposition in reply to this civil case during January 1994, citing the date for trial as two months on. Actions for and against Jackson ensured lawyers and associates for both parties piled on the expenses, while the subject of this expanding business was in Switzerland in the company of members of the Cascio family while Jordy Chandler relied on therapists for sanity and survival.

From the information being fed to Jackson, he believed if he returned to America he would be arrested immediately. This, coupled with his pill intake and escalating tour problems, led to his suicide attempt. Elizabeth Taylor decided he required immediate medical treatment and flew with Jackson to Britain, where, after several diversions to confuse and avoid the ever-vigilant media, he entered the Charter Nightingale Clinic in London. A press release from Jackson's office then stated the 'Dangerous' tour was cancelled as the singer was being treated for painkiller dependency, whereupon the tour's sponsor Pepsi cancelled its financial injection, leaving Sony Records to increase its support of its biggest money-spinner. They were troubled times indeed.

Despite his incapacity, Jackson's business ploughed on. During November 1993 he signed a $150 million deal with the recording giant EMI to administer ATV's Music Publishing catalogues. The deal spanned five years and represented the biggest ever music-publishing agreement known to the industry. A month on, the singer returned to America to face his accusers.

He didn't have to wait long. On 20 December 1993 two policemen, a photographer, a doctor and others visited Jackson at Neverland to photograph his genitalia and examine him. Two days on, the shaken singer broke his silence to appear in a four-minute broadcast, transmitted live by CNN from Neverland and subsequently reshown across the world. Wearing a bright red shirt and matching lipstick, Jackson declared his innocence to all charges – 'Don't treat me like a criminal because I am innocent' – before detailing the humiliating body search by police which allowed them, he said, 'to view and photograph my body, including my penis, my buttocks, my lower torso, my thighs and any other areas that they wanted'. Once again, media, public and stalwart fans dissected his speech, with the result that no one could agree or disagree with his heartfelt statement.

While his lawyers beavered away, Jackson attempted to live as normal a life as possible. He flew to Las Vegas on 30 December, where he stayed at the Luxor Hotel and watched Barbra Streisand's performance at the MGM Grand, and early in 1994 he appeared at a gala ceremony staged in Pasadena to present Debbie Allen with a NAACP Image Award for Best Choreographer. During his short speech there he once again insisted his innocence, prompting the audience to honour him with a standing ovation. 'Together we will see this thing through. The truth will be my salvation,' he told them.

Also early in 1994, representatives for both the singer and Jordy Chandler reportedly reached a financial settlement, reputed to involve several million dollars. The settlement exonerated Jordy's father from the extortion claim, while the subsequent press release included, 'The civil suit will be dismissed to allow the parties to get on with their lives.' Despite this agreement, the Santa Barbara prosecutors maintained their stand and continued their investigations.

With the nightmare continuing to haunt Jackson as further child-abuse claims sprang from nowhere, leaving his personal and professional life in tatters, his family rallied around him and showed their support by presenting *The Jackson Family Honours* television show from the MGM Grand in Las Vegas. The show included the entire family, with the promise that Michael would appear. He did but refused to perform, prompting many of the 11,000 audience to demand a refund on a ticket that had already been reduced to $50 from $1,000 each.

While the world reeled in confusion and disbelief, Michael Jackson stunned his public once again. He married Elvis Presley's only daughter Lisa Marie on 26 May 1994 in La Vega, in the Dominican Republic. He was 35 years old, she 26, and both signed a prenuptial agreement ensuring their personal fortunes remained just that. Three months on, Lisa Marie placated disbelievers by issuing a statement confirming her marriage: 'I understand and support him. We both look forward to raising a family and living a happy, healthy life together.' It was generally felt that the marriage would quash all the charges against Jackson as he would now be considered as an upstanding husband and step-father to Lisa Marie's five-year-old child from her marriage to Danny Keough.

To end 1994, Santa Barbara and Los Angeles District Attorneys confirmed child-abuse charges had been dropped, the accuser having been paid a substantial amount of money by Jackson. Christopher Anderson, though, further reported, 'Jackson was not exonerated and prosecutors said they would leave the case open for five years to allow for the possibility the boys might change their minds.'

Into 1995, Jackson's career needed rejuvenation. His music was to be repackaged for public consumption under the title *'HIStory: Past, Present And Future Book I*, earmarked for June release. Of the handful of new tracks included, the title 'Scream', his public statement against his recurring nightmare, a duet with his sister Janet, was issued to test public reaction. The single peaked in the British Top 3, selling in excess of 280,000 copies during the first week of release; it reached No.5 in America.

The chart positions were a disappointment and the media were quick to recognise this, claiming the singer's popularity had crumbled not because of his music but because of his adverse publicity of late. The single's $6 million promotional video, which, inexplicably, was not available on the single's release date, also featuring Janet, was largely shot in black and white and was considered by some to be extremely boring – like the single itself!

To further promote the over-budgeted *HIStory* project, a 30-foot-high fibre-glass statue was hauled along the Thames for all to see before being transported overseas to be exhibited along European waterways. Naturally, the media covered the spectacle of the giant Jackson's Thames maiden voyage, which, in all honesty, was awesome.

Days before the release of *HIStory* in Britain, BBC TV screened the American programme *Primetime Live*, featuring Jackson and Lisa Marie and hosted by Diane Sawyer. During the interview, Sawyer asked whether the child-abuse allegations were true. Jackson replied, 'It's not in my heart, it's not who I am.' When she argued the point, he was angered but answered, 'Nobody wonders when kids sleep at my house. It's all on the level of purity and innocence and love.' Lisa Marie said little and appeared disinterested. An estimated 60 million viewers worldwide watched the programme.

The double album *HIStory*, with accompanying 52-page booklet, entered both the British and American charts at the top during July 1995 and, incidentally, broke the American record for first-week sales previously held by Pink Floyd. The next lifted single, titled 'You Are Not Alone', likewise became a chart-topper in both countries during the September, with its accompanying video featuring shots of a half-nude Jackson and a totally nude Lisa Marie. Two months on, Jackson merged his ATV publishing catalogue, which included many of the Beatles' compositions, with Sony and received from the record company a reputed $100 advance. 'It's not about money, it's about growth,' he said at the time.

As the year ended, Jackson worked on the forthcoming House Box Office special *Michael Jackson: One Night Only*. However, rehearsals suddenly ended when the singer collapsed and was rushed to the intensive-care unit of the Beth Israel Medical Center, where he was diagnosed as suffering from a viral infection.

Meanwhile, on the singles front, 'Earth Song' topped the British chart. During February 1996 Jackson performed the song at the Brit Awards ceremony staged at Earls Court, London, after being presented with the Artist of a Generation award by an embarrassingly gushing Bob Geldof. During his performance Jackson was joined on stage by several children against a backdrop of a hi-tech set, but many objected when Jackson stripped off his clothes to reveal a white shirt, T-shirt and pants before adopting the pose of Jesus at his crucifixion and movements indicating he had the power to heal. Pulp's Jarvis Cocker made his objection public when he walked on stage, causing an 'unearthly' disruption during which some children were reputedly hurt. Cocker was arrested but not charged and the incident was edited from the televised version of the awards ceremony; Pulp sold 40,000 albums following the incident and the Independent Television Commission received a handful of viewer complaints. No action was taken against Jackson, as no programme code had been violated.

As Jackson was once more being hauled before the media in London, one track on *HIStory* titled 'They Don't Care About Us' had attracted more than a healthy interest. In America, several television stations, tabloid newspapers and representatives of the Jewish faith claimed Jackson's lyrics in the song were anti-Semitic and racist, containing words like 'Jew' and 'kike' during highly charged verses. However, while America reeled, other countries didn't bat an eyelid. Naturally, Jackson was devastated at the reaction, claiming, 'I could never be anti-Semitic [and] I'm not a racist person . . . I'm talking about myself as the victim.' Nonetheless, he respected public power and rerecorded the track, ensuring an apology was printed on the single's packaging.

At this juncture, Jackson publicly admitted that he had no intention of touring America during 1996, emphasising that plans were progressing for an extensive European tour instead. Had he turned his back on his home country, the media asked. Who could have blamed him? Then, further shockwaves occurred when Lisa Marie filed for divorce, citing irreconcilable differences. The parting was seemingly amicable.

In March, the stage musical *Sisterella*, a play based on the fairytale *Cinderella* best known to the British as a pantomime, opened at the Pasadena Theater. This musical was Jackson's first major venture into the music hall; such was its success that *Sisterella* went on to scoop eight NAACP Theater Awards. A month on, the much-criticised title 'They Don't Care About Us' was the fourth track to be swiped from *HIStory*. The video was banned in America, portraying as it did racism in the country by showing actual news footage of rioting. A No.4 British hit, 'They Don't Care About Us' crawled into the American Top 30 due to poor promotion following the video's ban. No further singles were lifted from HIStory Stateside.

Into April 1996, Jackson diversified once again by turning to the big screen to start shooting *Ghosts*, based on society's outcasts and featuring the track titled '2 Bad'. Jackson himself played several characters. *Ghosts* would be premièred in London during 1997. A month later he was honoured at the 1996 World Music Awards gala held in Monaco, receiving five awards, including the Best-Selling R&B Male Recording Artist and Overall Best-Selling Male Recording Artist. Jackson then confirmed his 'HIStory World Tour', which would start in Prague during September 1996. Fresh from his appearance in Monaco, the singer performed a free concert at the JerudongTheme Park, Brunei, to celebrate the birthday of the Sultan of Brunei before visiting South Africa to wish Nelson Mandela a happy birthday.

From Prague, the 'HIStory' tour trundled through 26 cities during 17 weeks, ending in January 1997 in Hawaii.While touring, Jackson's personal life once more became headline news with rumours that Debbie Rowe, a nurse who had cared for his vitiligo for several years, was carrying his child. Jackson went on to confirm the rumour, then insisted, 'The reports speculating that Ms Rowe was artificially inseminated and that there is any economic relationship are completely false and irresponsible . . . I am thrilled that I will soon be a father.' Days following this press release, Jackson and Rowe married in Sydney.

On 13 February 1997, Prince Michael Junior was born. The rights to pictures of the baby and his parents were purchased by *OK!* magazine, although, of course, a handful escaped for tabloid exclusives. The undisclosed sum was paid into the singer's Heal The World Foundation. The publishing of the pictures in March coincided with the announcement that Jackson's next musical project was due. Titled *Blood On The Dance Floor: HIStory In The Mix*, the CD contained five new tracks plus eight remixed titles from *HIStory*. The first lifted for single release, 'Blood On The Dance Floor', was issued during April 1997.

On the personal front, Debbie Rowe gave birth to a daughter named Paris Katherine in April 1998; she will be raised with her brother by their father in Europe. Their mother remains in Los Angeles, visiting her family regularly, an arrangement the couple made prior to their marriage. In actual fact, since their marriage, Rowe has spent much of her time moving from one American location to another in an attempt to confuse the ever-hungry media. Meanwhile, Jackson, who lives in rented accommodation in Britain and France, has placed his fantasy Californian home Neverland up for sale.

In February 1998, Jackson completed a tour of South Africa and released a new video titled *Ghosts*, a 40-minute blend of dance and drama which included the tracks 'Ghost', '2 Bad', swiped from his *HIStory* set, and 'Is It Scary?', his latest outing extracted from the *Blood On The Dancefloor* CD. The video, based on Jackson and Stephen King's concept and featuring state-of-the-art special effects, was premièred at the 1997 Cannes Film Festival.

With the comment 'It's been a long time coming and we're all excited', Jackie Jackson confirmed that Michael had been reunited with his brothers to record an album tentatively titled *J5*. The announcement, however, was premature – the project was reputedly abandoned in 1998.

Even so, the Jackson dynasty continues. 'To me, nothing is more important than making people happy, giving them a release from their problems and worries, helping to lighten their load' – Michael Jackson

Also see: 'One Day In Your Life', July 1981; 'Billie Jean', March 1983

(Quotes: *Moonwalk* by Michael Jackson)

October 1987

RICK ASTLEY

Never Gonna Give You Up

'I think I'll last for a good few years . . . You can't expect to get No.1s forever. I'll still be around, though' – Rick Astley

Born in Great Sankey, Warrington, on 6 February 1966, Rick Astley grew up in Newton-le-Willows. 'I was five when my dad was left to bring me up, along with my brothers [Mike and John] and sister [Jayne]. It was tough for Dad but good for me because it taught me to stand on my own feet from an early age.'

He was educated at the Selwyn Jones High School, where, at the age of 15, he realised his only ambition was music. 'Muddling through school', he sold his leather jacket to purchase a drum kit, which he played relentlessly as support to two schoolfriends playing guitars. Together they were called Give Way. The group auditioned for a school concert, with Astley singing for the first time from behind the security of his drum kit; their reward was an enthusiastic response.

Give Way eventually did just that when Astley, without a qualification to his credit, finished school. He joined FBI, a group so named because the lead guitarist was a Shadows fan. Using working-men's clubs to perform, FBI sang the Beatles' material and played versions of the Shadows' instrumentals. In time, Astley left his drum kit to stand as lead singer, with a preference for Northern Soul material recorded by élite American R&B artists.

While performing with FBI at Warrington's Monks Sports and Social Club, Astley was spotted by Pete Waterman, one third of the Stock, Aitken and Waterman team who were composing and producing artists under the 'Hit Factory' banner. Their Midas touch transformed artists like Sinitta, Kylie Minogue, Hazell Dean, Mel and

Kim and Jason Donovan into international sellers, while established artists including Donna Summer and Cliff Richard requested their material. Waterman, impressed by the youngster's voice and presentation, expressed a wish to work with him. However, the offer did not include FBI as a whole. Astley admitted, 'I liked the idea of being with a top producer . . .what unknown singer in their right mind wouldn't? But we'd always had this ambition to succeed as a band.' It took all of two weeks for the ambitious young man to make his move, which, he said, caused considerable bitterness within the group.

Between leaving FBI and embarking upon a solo career, Astley recorded a duet titled 'When You Gonna' under the name Rick And Lisa. The single bombed in Britain but apparently peaked in the American dance chart. He also recorded a single during 1984 titled 'Car Jam' as a member of a group called Bonk.

Joining ranks with Pete Waterman did not automatically guarantee access to the recording studio. Instead, Astley was the company's office boy for at least two years,. 'I used to do all the running around and make the tea, and they promised me one day they would make me a star.' It was not an idle promise.

The transformation from shy northern boy into a quietly confident recording artist began when Astley recorded a duet with O'Chi Brown titled 'Learning To Live Without Your Love' in 1986. This led to his debut album, *Whenever You Need Somebody*, from which the first lifted single was 'Never Gonna Give You Up', written and produced by Stock, Aitken and Waterman. Astley's vocals were reminiscent of those of the R&B acts he admired so much. 'Because of my voice, people expected to see a six-foot-four bloke from Philadelphia or something. They were quite surprised when they saw this small guy with ginger hair, a pale face and a northern accent.' Most certainly he possessed a 'black' voice with no trace of an accent, so it was a forgivable error by the public. What wasn't forgivable though, were the allegations that his voice had been overdubbed by a more powerful vocalist during recording sessions. To curb the rumours, critics were invited to attend a live studio date. Astley admitted that the music he loved was obviously an influence on the way he sang, but stressed, 'I'm not actually consciously trying to kid people I'm a black American. It's just something I do naturally when I'm singing because it makes the words blend together better.'

'Never Gonna Give You Up', released by RCA Records, soared to the top of the British chart in October 1987, a position it held for five weeks, earning the title the distinction of becoming Britain's biggest-selling single of the year. It also won the Brit Award for the Best British Single. Astley's home success was repeated in 16 countries including America, where the title likewise topped the chart for two weeks during March 1988. During this period, it was estimated that Astley performed 'Never Gonna Give You Up' 50 times in ten different countries, travelling over 9,000 miles to do so. He said, 'I don't ever expect to follow [the single] in the same way. It was a nice sound which came together well and it had five weeks at No.1 – how often does that happen?'

The follow-up, 'Whenever You Need Somebody', soared into the British Top 3 during November 1987. Astley's debut album, *Whenever You Need Somebody*, was also released, topping the British chart during its first week of sale and going on to sell in excess of one million copies. His final single of the year was a cover version of Nat 'King' Cole's 1957 classic 'When I Fall In Love', which narrowly missed the British top spot. Aimed at the Christmas market, the accompanying video was a festive one with reindeers and snow, filmed at a Swedish resort.

During this chart-topping year, Astley promoted his career with British personal appearances for six months. Young fans welcomed him as the new singing sensation, a side of his career that would later worry him. 'I can't relate to it. I was never like that as a youngster. When they see me they actually find that I do have spots and I'm not the coolest person in jeans.' That aside, with his professional appearance of boyish, clean looks and sharp dress, the singer appealed to both youngsters and adults; the former devoured him, while the latter approved from a distance.

Into 1988, following his first visit to Australia and the Far East, Astley issued his first single of the year. Titled 'Together Forever' and originally earmarked as the follow-up to 'Never Gonna Give You Up', the title soared to No.2 in the British chart during the March, while American sales sent it to No.1 three months on. It was his second chart-topper and his last. 'It Would Take A Strong Man' followed, peaking in the American Top 10, while a different title was chosen for British release, namely 'She Wants To Dance With Me', a Top 10 entrant in the October. Before the year ended, Astley had performed at the Royal Variety Show and issued 'Take Me To Your Heart', another Top 10 single in Britain. Hot on its heels came the second album, *Hold Me In Your Arms*; as the title peaked in the British Top 10, the singer embarked upon a world tour spanning 16 countries in total.

In February 1989 the album's title track was extracted for single release and became a Top 10 British hit, while 'She Wants To Dance With Me' soared into the American Top 6. Touring America mid-1989 boosted the sales of a further pair of singles, namely 'Giving Up On Love' and 'Ain't Too Proud To Beg', his version of the Temptations' 1966 hit. There seemed no way Rick Astley's star would fail to shine, but then he hadn't reckoned on the new decade. The

'90s heralded change and the subsequent end of a career that should easily have lived through to the next decade. Astley's insistence on independent creative control which led to the end of his hit-making association with Stock, Aitken and Waterman was a foolish move.

It took a year for the singer to re-enter the British and American Top 10 with the full-blooded single 'Cry For Help', produced by Gary Stevenson, a lavishly gospel-flavoured title so superior to the pop-slanted material of the previous decade. Following soon after was the aptly titled *Free* album, comprising material from contributing artists including members of Level 42. The album soared into the British Top 10 and American Top 40. Incredible as it seems, it represented the final Astley album to chart across the Atlantic. By the close of 1991, his only stab at the singles chart with 'Move Right Out' struggled into the Top 90. His profitable American career was all but over.

Back on home soil, the situation was marginally better but it was obvious his star was fading. A rethink was vital. Turning his back on the public spotlight for a year, Astley returned with the blinding *Body and Soul* album, co-penned and produced by third parties including Lisa Stansfield. Despite the brilliance of the project and a lot of media hype, the album bombed on both sides of the Atlantic during 1993. Two singles were swiped for British release during the year, namely 'The Ones You Love' and 'Hopelessly', Top 50 and Top 40 stallers respectively. These poor sales did nothing to shift the album either. Nothing worked and by 1994 the young, good-looking singer with a squeaky-clean image was no longer a chart name. In the space of six years, Rick Astley's status had fallen as quickly as it had risen.

'I can't stand the so-called glamorous scene . . . I'm not flamboyant and good at being a pop star . . . I'm more of a musician really' – Rick Astley

(Quotes: *Rick Astley Special, 1988* by Jayne Lanigan and Robin MacKintosh)

November 1987

BEE GEES

You Win Again

'People tend to get this image of us with the hairy chests and with medallions and white trousers and all that sort of rubbish' – Maurice Gibb

Barry Gibb was born on 1 September 1947 and his twin brothers Maurice and Robin were born on 22 December two years later, all in Douglas, Isle of Man. Their mother, Barbara, was a singer, while their father, Hughie, was the leader of his own orchestra, performing on the Mecca circuit. The family relocated to Lancashire before emigrating to Australia, where Andy, their fourth son, was born. Before leaving Britain, though, the brothers had already performed before an audience, usually at the Manchester Gaumont's Saturday picture shows where, known as the Rattlesnakes, they sang the then current songs. Said Maurice, 'The three of us knew what we wanted to do from day one. I can remember us walking down the street in Manchester and we were all saying we wanted to be appreciated for what we do in music.'

Once settled in Australia, the brothers, still using the name the Rattlesnakes, befriended Bill Good, organiser of the Speedway Circus in Brisbane, where they performed between races, and 4KQ Radio's Bill Gates, who played their taped material on air. In fact, the Gibb brothers took their name from Bill Gates' and Bill Good's initials to become the BGs, although years later Maurice denied this, saying, 'It stands for "Brothers Gibb". That's where the Bee Gees came from. We never knew if Andy was going to join us or not.'

The group's first television appearance on *Anything Goes* during 1960 led to further spot performances before they secured a residency at Brisbane's Beachcomber Hotel. Two years on they moved to Sydney, where one of their first performances was as support act to Chubby Checker at the city's stadium. The brothers also began flexing their composing hand to write the title 'Let Me Love You' and 'Starlight Of Love'; the latter title was actually recorded by the Australian vocalist Col Joye. Most of 1963 was devoted to a residency at a Queensland nightclub, which in turn led to the BGs signing a recording contract with Festival Records, where their debut release was 'Three Kisses Of Love'. Two years on the single 'Wine And Woman' became the brothers' first hit. Switching to Spin Records, they recorded a series of minor Australian hits until 'Spicks And Specks', released late in 1966, presented them with their first Australian chart-topper.

Early in 1967 the BGs returned to Britain. According to Maurice, 'We went as far as we could go in Australia. We were sort of like a dirty version of the Osmonds.' He further admitted the brothers were in awe of the Beatles and wanted to be 'where all the action was', particularly as *Sgt Pepper's Lonely Hearts Club Band* had just broken worldwide. Despite their parents' initial disappointment at their sons' relocation, Hughie Gibb posted copies of their current Australian album to countless British management companies, including

NEMS Enterprises, originally owned by Brian Epstein, before being purchased by Robert Stigwood. Stigwood agreed to audition the BGs, who would from now on be called the Bee Gees, upon their arrival in Britain, which in turn led to a recording contract with Polydor Records.

The title 'New York Mining Disaster 1941' was the Bee Gees' debut Beatles-soundalike British single and the first to be recorded outside Australia, released during May 1967. The song also marked two additions to the line-up, namely guitarist Vince Melouney and drummer Colin Peterson, both Australians. The three-part vocalising on 'New York Mining Disaster 1941' helped push the single to No.12 in the British chart, No.14 in America. The single sold in excess of one million copies, an amazing achievement for a new group. Interestingly, when the initial copies of the single were circulated to the media, the label bore no artist credit. The thinking was to confuse radio DJs into believing this was a Beatles disc in order to receive maximum airplay. When the truth was revealed, many still believed it was the Beatles, recording under another name! In actual fact, two members of the Fab Four were at the recording session, so the disbelievers may have had a point.

While the Bee Gees were in America midway through 1967 to promote 'New York Mining Disaster 1941', they composed a track for Otis Redding. However, despite good intentions, the Bee Gees then opted to record the song themselves. Titled 'To Love Somebody', it peaked in the Top 50 in Britain and Top 20 in America but, more importantly, became one of the most rerecorded Bee Gees compositions. Nina Simone in particular released a blinding version in 1969, while Janis Joplin, Jimmy Somerville and Michael Bolton released their own versions.

A further track penned during their first American trip was 'Massachusetts'; when issued as a single in 1967 the title became the Bee Gees' first British chart-topper in the November, reaching the Top 20 in America. Once more, it was the superb three-way harmonising that made the song so compelling, and it's fair to say it was this that sustained the trio's popularity for years to come. Mind you, the harmonising was often the point of ridicule by impressionists – but who laughed all the way to the bank? Before 1967 closed, the Bee Gees' fourth single, titled 'World', soared into the British Top 10, establishing the brothers among the biggest-selling acts of the year.

The trio's first live appearance in 1968 was at the Convention Center in California, while their first single was 'Words', a Top 10 hit in Britain during the February, Top 20 in America a month later. This charting coincided with the brothers' first appearance on *The Ed*

Sullivan Show. Upon their return to Britain, the Bee Gees hit the road for a lengthy tour with Dave Dee, Dozy, Beaky, Mick and Tich.

Without doubt, the Bee Gees' '60s success spiralled them into the top league within months, but as often happens with instant over-whelming success, the pressures that followed took over. The brothers fell foul of this during 1968 when minor disagreements became major ones, Barry finally announcing his intention to leave the group to concentrate upon a movie career. When Robin collapsed from exhaustion during a British tour and was admitted into a London nursing home, the brothers realised their lifestyle needed to be modified. Robin's illness caused their pending American tour to be postponed for one month until August 1968, which in turn meant they could not adequately promote their next British single, 'I've Gotta Get A Message To You'. The title told a chilling tale of a man on Death Row whose only future was the electric chair. The public loved it and pushed it to the top of the British chart in September 1968; it reached the Top 10 in America. The title was to have been Barry's final outing, but events changed things somewhat.

During the November, midway through a German and Australian tour, Robin and Barry were taken ill and ordered to rest, whereupon the trio's remaining dates were cancelled. Their musicians Melouney and Petersen handed in their notice but agreed to remain with the brothers until May 1969. The disagreements between the brothers worsened, being heightened by their alcohol binges, until it was a miracle they could record at all. But thankfully they did!

'It Started As A Joke' was the trio's first single of 1969, a No.6 American hit, and was the last to feature Melouney and Peterson. The title also marked the final single for Robin, who, tired of the constant arguments with Maurice, left the trio. He did, however, forget his differences to be best man at Maurice's wedding to Scottish singer Lulu in April 1969. Maurice said the marriage was 'good fun for about five years'. No wonder Lulu shouted so much! As a duo, Maurice and Barry became involved in the *Cucumber Castle* movie starring Frankie Howerd, Spike Milligan and Lulu, among others. The title 'Don't Forget To Remember' was lifted from the soundtrack during September 1969 and soared into the British Top 2.

Following a period during which each brother was involved in his own projects, the Bee Gees re-formed late in 1970 at Robin's instiga-tion. However, success wasn't as instant second time around. The British were slow in supporting them and their first single, titled 'Lonely Days', struggled into the Top 40; it made the Top 3 in America. The situation in Britain would, of course, change dramat-ically.

From 1971 through to 1974, the Bee Gees toured the world and released Top 20 singles on both sides of the Atlantic, but music was changing. The public wanted to dance. The '70s were slowly being strangled by disco music, and artists not previously associated with the dance beat were capitalising on the trend, losing credibility on the way. Nonetheless, disco was booming and new acts were becoming big-selling items. The Bee Gees would be responsible for changing – or, as many believed at the time, destroying – the good of the dance with *Saturday Night Fever*.

Prior to the *Saturday Night Fever* phenomenon, in August 1975 the brothers released the single 'Jive Talkin'', a fiery dance track. The single soared into the British Top 5 and topped the American chart. The track was swiped from the recently completed *Main Course* album, as was its follow-up, titled 'Nights On Broadway'. A year on 'You Should Be Dancing', extracted from the *Children Of The World* album, smashed into the world's charts, peaking at No.5 in Britain and at No.1 in America, presenting the Bee Gees with their third chart-topper there. Indeed, the brothers had returned to the music business with a compulsive new sound that they tagged 'New York R&B' but which others called 'disco'.

Early in 1977 Robert Stigwood, now owner of his own RSO Records, became interested in producing a movie based on an article by Nik Cohn published in *The New Yorker*. Cohn had headlined his work 'Tribal Rites of the New Saturday Night', highlighting the disco explosion that compelled dancers to 'dress in their best and to strut their stuff' on the nightclub dance floor. Stigwood approached John Travolta to play the starring role and the Bee Gees for material. At the time the trio were planning tracks for a new album. According to Maurice, 'We wrote "How Deep Is Your Love?", "If I Can't Have You" and "Stayin' Alive" and Robert Stigwood . . . said he needed five songs for this film he was doing . . . When someone offers you the chance to have your music in a motion picture, it really freaks you.' The brothers had earmarked 'How Deep Is Your Love?' for American vocalist Yvonne Elliman, but when Stigwood insisted the Bee Gees sing it on the soundtrack, they gave her 'If I Can't Have You' (the title went on to become the fourth American chart-topper from the movie soundtrack). Incidentally, a further title, 'More Than A Woman', was recorded by both the Bee Gees and the group Tavares; both versions were featured in the film and both were released as singles.

The movie was conceived as *Saturday Night* but when the Bee Gees told Stigwood they had already composed the title 'Night Fever' he agreed on a compromise. *Saturday Night Fever* was world premièred in New York during December 1977; John Travolta's starring role as Tony Manero, whose life was centred around Saturday nights at his local nightspot, was perfectly portrayed. And thanks to the Bee Gees' contributions, disco music would never be the same again. Twenty years on, *Saturday Night Fever* was reborn on the London stage as part of a strong '70s revival that included reissued material, nostalgic tours and the opening of Biba clothes stores nationwide.

'How Deep Is Your Love?' was the first single to be lifted from the movie soundtrack in 1977. The title peaked at No.3 in the British chart during the December and reached No.1 in America, where it went on to sell one million copies. The song also won the 1978 Grammy for the Best Pop Vocal Performance by a Duo, Group or Chorus, and an Ivor Novello Award for Best Pop Song and Best Film Music or Song.

Early in 1978 the *Saturday Night Fever* double-album soundtrack was issued and immediately topped the American listing, while during the February 'Stayin' Alive' was swiped as a single and likewise topped the American chart. A month on the title soared into the British Top 4. The follow-up, 'Night Fever', likewise shot to the top in America during March 1978, a position it held for a staggering eight weeks. When released in Britain, 'Night Fever' also became the country's top seller, but only for a short two weeks. The soundtrack album, also a British chart-topper, went on to sell in excess of 30 million copies worldwide, topping the chart in most countries.

According to Maurice, 'The "Fever" thing was a phenomenon that just happened. All the world wanted to dance . . . All we did was just write these songs for our new album. "Disco" to us was Donna Summer.' Once the excitement had died down, the Bee Gees were blamed for killing disco music. However, the film was also a curse on them, and they carried it like a millstone around their necks into the next decade and beyond. Said Maurice, 'We don't like being labelled as something because our music was put to a motion picture, and everybody was labelling us with the "John Travolta" look.'

Let's backtrack here. Prior to becoming involved with the movie, the trio were actually working on their own film. Titled *Sgt Pepper's Lonely Hearts Club Band*, it was based on the Beatles' mind-bending recording project and featured the Gibb brothers as composers and actors. Due to their commitment to Stigwood, this film was put on hold to follow *Saturday Night Fever* and was premièred in America in July 1978. The *Sgt Pepper's Lonely Hearts Club Band* soundtrack peaked in the British Top 40 the same month, before soaring into the American Top 5 during the August. Compared to the Travolta blockbusting dance film, this one bombed. So devastating was the public response that it contributed to the downfall of RSO Records, the Bee Gees' record company, owned by Stigwood.

However, instead of bemoaning their failure, the Bee Gees returned to recording, working on their first studio album since 1976. Locked within the walls of the Criteria Studios in Miami for nearly a year, the brothers appeared to have an awesome task. How could they hope to follow the biggest-selling album of all time?

They nearly did it with the magnificent *Spirits (Having Flown)* project, from which 'Too Much Heaven' was swiped as the debut single. Released in 1978, the title soared to No.3 in the British chart and early in 1979 became an American No.1. While the single dominated the top spot, the Bee Gees performed at the Music For UNICEF gala concert, celebrating the International Year of the Child, staged in New York. The American company NBC TV went on to broadcast the performance, while the brothers donated all the royalties from 'Too Much Heaven' to UNICEF.

During March a further track was lifted from the mother album, titled 'Tragedy'. A piercing slice of Bee Gees magic, the single romped to the British top, where it stayed for two weeks. This success was repeated across the Atlantic. An impassioned, complex track, 'Tragedy' stretched Barry's lead falsetto voice to the limit – and quite probably beyond.

Remarkable as it seems, 'Tragedy' was just that, marking the trio's final British Top 10 hit, although America would continue to support them with multi-million sales. A good example of Stateside support was 'Love You Inside Out', a No.1 title which became the Bee Gees' sixth consecutive chart-topping single, tying them with their musical heroes the Beatles. 'Love You Inside Out' was, by the way, the third consecutive chart-topper to be lifted from *Spirits (Having Flown)*. The story in Britain was, of course, an unhappy one by comparison. 'Love You Inside Out' managed only a Top 20 placing late in 1979, marking the end of a career for one of the most successful groups of the decade.

But this wasn't the end of the brothers, rather a rejuvenation, as they went on to work as composers and producers for other artists. Using the vocals of Barbra Streisand, the Bee Gees wrote and produced the *Guilty* album, from which the track 'Woman In Love' was swiped; it became an American and British chart-topper during October 1980. The album likewise topped both countries' charts. A further single, 'Guilty', soared to No.3 in America, reaching the Top 40 in Britain.

Late in 1981, the Bee Gees issued a taster from their own next album, *Living Eyes*. Titled 'He's A Liar', the single stalled in the American Top 30. Maurice believed the project had been an error on their part because, at the time, they were experiencing personal traumas. 'Robert Stigwood was trying to sue us and we were suing him . . . We never went to court. It was just blown all out of proportion, especially by the rubbish press.' The finances involved in the legal action were, however, far from 'rubbish' – the trio filed the biggest lawsuit in the history of the music business. Accusing Stigwood of misrepresentation of their financial affairs, the brothers filed a suit for $75 million against their record company, Polygram, and a staggering $125 million against Stigwood himself and his family of companies. Stigwood called their action 'a cheap stunt', before the rift was healed with an out-of-court settlement of $200 million. The action also meant, of course, that the Bee Gees were without a record company.

During 1982, after composing 'Heart (Stop Beating In Time)' for British singer Leo Sayer (a Top 30 hit), Barry produced the *Heartbreaker* album for Dionne Warwick, from which the hit singles 'Heartbreaker' and 'All The Love In The World' were lifted. The next year the brothers composed material for the *Staying Alive* movie, produced by Sylvester Stallone and the sequel to *Saturday Night Fever*. The film paled by comparison. According to Maurice, 'Halfway through the movie we wanted to pull out because Stallone unfortunately knew nothing about music. They edited all our music to pieces.' The trio also believed the film was actually a vehicle for Stallone's brother Frank, who enjoyed an American Top 10 hit with 'Far From Over'.

With the Bee Gees' own career still somewhat undecided, Robin embarked upon a solo career as a Polydor International artist. He was relatively successful: 'Another Lonely Night In New York' was a minor British hit in June 1983. Later that year Barry produced the *Eyes That See In The Dark* album for Kenny Rogers, before releasing his own debut solo album, *New Voyager*. During 1985 he then turned his talent towards a further female star, Diana Ross. The result, her *Eaten Alive* album, spawned 'Chain Reaction' as a single. The title was Ross's second solo British chart-topper in March 1986.

However, the Bee Gees were destined to return with a vengeance. In 1987, with a new recording contract with Warner Bros Records, they issued their strongest album for some time titled *E.S.P.* The lifted single, the superb 'You Win Again', returned the brothers to the top spot in Britain during November 1987, while in America the title struggled into the Top 80. My, how the tables had turned!

On the personal front, tragedy hit the Gibb family when the youngest brother, Andy, died from an inflammatory heart virus in the John Radcliffe Hospital, Oxford, on 10 March 1988. He had, like his brothers, enjoyed a colourful American career that had included two chart-toppers, namely '(Love Is) Thicker Than Water' and 'Shadow Dancing', both in 1978. Married to actress Victoria Principal, he had succumbed to the attraction of drug taking.

On a happier note, through to the '90s the Bee Gees continued to make their presence felt via prestigious live performances and British hits that included the titles 'How Can You Mend A Broken Heart?' in 1990, 'Secret Love' in 1991 and 'Paying The Price Of Love' and 'For Whom The Bell Tolls' during 1993. Their secret in longevity was the ability to record catchy, spontaneous chorus lines, although by now, of course, their hairlines were higher than their vocals!

The Bee Gees are now celebrating their third decade in the music business. Without doubt they were the international leaders of the '70s, whose strength lay in their willingness to experiment with music that ranged from sultry ballads to vital disco and slices of soul/R&B. Their constant demand for perfection is something others could learn from. Indeed, that perfection was honoured in 1997 when Elton John presented them with a Brit Award for their Outstanding Contribution to the Music Industry. The presentation, incidentally, coincided with their new single titled 'Alone', which went on to peak in the British Top 10.

At the end of the '90s, the Bee Gees are still planning several projects, with talk of live performances before the decade ends. Retire? No, never!

(Quotes: *We Had Joy We Had Fun* by Barry Scott)

December 1987

PET SHOP BOYS

Always On My Mind

During 1987, following their British chart-topper 'It's A Sin', the Pet Shop Boys fulfilled a personal ambition by working with Dusty Springfield. The two acts collaborated on the 'What Have I Done To Deserve This?' single, which soared to No.2 in Britain in the August and in America during February 1988. According to Tennant, 'We always wanted Dusty to sing it but for ages we couldn't get her to agree . . . EMI [the duo's record company] were trying to get us to use Tina Turner but we thought Dusty was more interesting.' At this point in her career, Springfield was living in America, so she flew to London to record the track.

Six months on, the audience attending the Brit Awards ceremony at London's Grosvenor House saw the Pet Shop Boys perform 'What Have I Done To Deserve This?' on stage with the unannounced guest appearance of Springfield. She went on to sign a short-lived recording contract with EMI Records, while Tennant and Lowe issued their next album, titled *Actually*, completed during the summer of 1987. This title followed the duo's Top 10 British single 'Rent', composed during 1984 when Tennant was still engaged in penning his 'Bitz' column for *Smash Hits* magazine. *Actually* shot into the British Top 2, reaching the Top 30 in America. Tennant believed writing a follow-up to the *Please* album would be a challenge but later said, 'Now *Please* looks quite weak next to *Actually*.' The album's front cover showed Lowe and Tennant dressed in dinner jackets and bow ties. Tennant was yawning – 'I was tired,' he said.

An approach from Central TV pointed the dance duo towards the Elvis Presley camp. The television company intended to commemorate the tenth anniversary of the King's death with a music programme titled *Love Me Tender* featuring various artists singing his material. Tennant and Lowe had up to this point in their career avoided recording cover versions, and had preferred Presley during his Las Vegas era to his rock'n'roll period. Nonetheless, they agreed to contribute to the programme. Their choice was the 1985 single 'Always On My Mind', which had faltered in the British Top 60. Although the Pet Shop Boys' version bore little resemblance to the original, it prompted *Melody Maker*'s music critic to write that it was 'the lousiest, most ham-fisted idea that the Pet Shop Boys will ever have'. Tennant was unfazed, saying, 'We added an extra chord to it. There's a Bb at the end of each chorus that wasn't in the original. It makes it far more like a pop song.'

'Always On My Mind' was not intended for single release; at the very most it was to be considered as a future B-side. However, following record-company and management pressure, the duo relented. It was a wise move, as within days of its release during December 1987 the title shot to the top of the British chart, marking the first cover version from the Pet Shop Boys and their first Christmas chart-topper. When released across the Atlantic, 'Always On My Mind' soared into the Top 5 in mid-1988.

And still the Pet Shop Boys hadn't embarked upon a British tour.

Also see: 'West End Girls', January 1986; 'It's A Sin', August 1987; 'Heart', April 1988

(Quotes: *Pet Shop Boys, Annually 1989* by Chris Lowe and Neil Tennant)

January 1988

BELINDA CARLISLE

Heaven Is A Place On Earth

From dressing in black bin liners and living on a punk commune to drifting through the all-female punk band the Go-Gos, the young singer eventually found her vocation – being recognised as a respected singer.

Born in Hollywood, California, on 17 August 1958, the eldest of seven children, as a high school cheerleader Carlisle joined the female novelty group the Go-Gos. She told author Fred Bronson that despite the group having serious intentions, they were treated as a joke. 'We didn't know how to play. We didn't know how to write songs. As time went on we realised there was some natural talent in the band.' In desperate need of assistance, the Go-Gos turned to Charlotte Caffey for her musical expertise, whereupon Carlisle was, very much against her wishes, elevated to lead vocalist. 'I wanted to play bass . . . They said drums or singing [was left]. I certainly didn't want to play drums because I'm much too lazy.'

The group's career moved onwards, particularly on the American touring circuit. As punk music spread its aggression across Britain, the Go-Gos toured as support act to Madness and recorded 'We Got The Beat', released via Stiff Records, punk's premier label. Back in America the girls enjoyed two hit singles, namely 'Our Lips Are Sealed' in 1981 and, of course, 'We Got The Beat' during 1982. When the Go-Gos had notched up seven big-selling American singles and a trio of albums issued via IRS Records, Carlisle departed from the line-up to pursue a solo career midway through 1985. She told a packed press conference, 'When you stop growing artistically it's time to try something else.'

A year on, Carlisle was sufficiently confident to perform as a soloist for the first time and mid-1986 issued her debut album titled *Belinda*, from which the track 'Mad About You' was swiped for single release. Much to the amazement of the singer, the title soared into the American Top 3, while its mother album, spurred on by the success, peaked in the Top 20, eventually passing gold status. During the October a second title was extracted as a single, namely 'I Feel The Magic'; this time the title stalled in the American Top 100. Nonetheless, the poor showing did not prevent Carlisle from performing selected American dates as support act to Robert Palmer before headlining her own club tour. By the close of 1987, Carlisle switched record companies to Virgin Records in Britain and MCA Records in America, whereupon her career took an unexpected turn.

With her new associations keen to promote her talent, Carlisle issued her first album, *Heaven On Earth*, featuring a collection of mainstream contributors like Rick Nowels and Ellen Shipley, aiming the project towards the pop market. Composed by Nowels and Shipley, the lifted track titled 'Heaven Is A Place On Earth' catapulted to the top of the American chart during December 1987. A month on the title represented Carlisle's first (and only) British chart-topper, a position it held for two weeks. Said Nowels, 'All along I knew [the song] had a great chorus, but I was always a little uncomfortable with the verse.' He therefore rewrote the track with Shipley, then was nervous at Carlisle's reaction because 'I put her through a lot of changes to get her to sing the other vocal.' Helping Carlisle on the second version were composer often session singer Diane Warren and Mamas and Papas member Michelle Phillips. The runaway success of the single boosted the sales of the *Heaven On Earth* album past platinum status. In Britain, the album would eventually peak in the Top 4.

As a follow-up single Carlisle swiped a second album track, namely 'I Get Weak'. It was a Top 10 British hit and reached No.2 in America. She also toured America for the first time as a solo artist. In June 1988, her third lifted single, 'Circle In The Sand', became her third British hit at No.4, making the Top 10 in America. The support shown by Britain prompted the singer to embark upon her debut British tour, where the trio of dates at the Hammersmith Odeon in London were sold out, while Virgin Records issued the 'World Without You' single to coincide with the concerts. Carlisle was hot property, yet the title's sales were poor. It faltered in the British Top 40, while the next, 'Love Never Dies', floundered in the Top 60.

Next Carlisle recorded and released the Nowels and Shipley composition 'Leave A Light On', featuring George Harrison. The single returned the singer to the British Top 4 during October 1989, reaching No.11 in America. Within a month of the single's success, its mother album *Runaway Horses*, which reunited Carlisle with members of the Go-Gos and rock singer Bryan Adams, likewise soared into the Top 4, making the Top 40 in America.

The '90s loomed. Carlisle's first contribution to the new decade was the 'Summer Rain' single, which peaked in the American Top 30 during March 1990, leaving Britain to enjoy the title track from her *Runaway Horses* album, a Top 40 hit.

Enthusiastically involved with Greenpeace and animal-rights organisations, the singer once more stood by her convictions by pulling out of a Cheyenne rodeo, citing her abhorrence of the inhumane treatment of the performing livestock at so-called fun functions.

Meanwhile, on the singles front, Carlisle charted twice in Britain during 1990 with 'Vision Of You' and '(We Want) The Same Thing', Top 50 and Top 10 hits respectively. In America the singer and the Go-Gos reunited on American television to promote their forthcoming tour together.

After the 1990 American hit 'Summer Rain' was finally issued in Britain, reaching the Top 30 in January 1991, the singer released two further singles, namely 'Live Your Life Be Free' and 'Do You Feel Like

I Feel?', Top 20 and Top 30 hits respectively. The year also saw the release of her *Live Your Life Be Free* album, her fourth as a soloist. During 1992 Carlisle reached the Top 40 in Britain with the title 'Half The World', followed in the October by 'Little Black Book', a No.28 hit. Carlisle's career had been a bit of a rollercoaster ride; happily her personal life was more stable and, following her marriage to Morgan Mason, son of actor James, she gave birth to a son, James.

If she was to survive professionally, Carlisle once again needed a rethink. Sure, she was enjoying hit material, but most of it was struggling for life. One way to instantly boost morale is to release a 'greatest hits' package, and this is exactly what she did. In September 1992, the compilation titled *The Best Of Belinda Carlisle Volume I* shot to the top of the British chart. The ensuing high British profile guaranteed her presence on several major television shows and in many magazines. The ploy had worked, and Carlisle rode on the success.

Into 1993 she issued her next album, titled *Real*, from which the track 'Big Scary Animal' was swiped as the first single. As that peaked in the British Top 12, the album soared into the Top 10. 'Lay Down Your Arms' was the final single of the year, a Top 30 British entrant.

Carlisle returned to the Go-Gos' line-up a year later for a lengthy American tour to promote their *Return To The Valley Of The Go-Gos*, before turning her back on her career altogether until 1996. Switching record companies to Chrysalis, Carlisle worked once more for her animal-rights and humanitarian causes with the album titled *A Woman And A Man*, on which she was joined by like-minded artists including the Beach Boys' main man Brian Wilson and the Bangles' prime vocalist Susannah Hoffs. The project was regrettably Carlisle's last.

(Quotes: *The Billboard Book of Number One Hits* by Fred Bronson)

February 1988

KYLIE MINOGUE

I Should Be So Lucky

Love her or hate her, Kylie Minogue worked her way through *Neighbours* into a singing career that earned her the title of Britain's top-selling female artist. It was a terrific achievement for one so young, but did her singles have to be so damned irritating?

Born on 28 May 1968 in Melbourne, Australia, Kylie was the first child to Ron and Carol, who went on to have another daughter, Danielle, and a son, Brendan. From an early age Kylie loved music and in particular was influenced by Abba. 'I wanted to be Agnetha when I grew up, but that's as far as my pop-singing aspirations went,' she said.

As an 11-year-old Kylie showed signs of following in her mother's footsteps as an entertainer, and this encouraged Carol to contact Crawford Productions, responsible for the popular Australian soap *The Sullivans*. She persuaded the producers to audition Kylie, whereupon she won the role of a Dutch orphan, Carla, her first of several child characters. Her roles included a part in *Skyways*, where she met Jason Donovan for the first time. Moving on, she played a young rebel in *The Henderson Kids*, claiming this role would be her final juvenile character.

In an attempt to recapture her lost school days, Minogue studied for her Higher School Certificate, the Australian equivalent to GCSEs. After her studying culminated in a pass, the youngster returned to the small screen during 1985 to appear in two series, *Fame And Fortune* and *The Zoo Family*, before joining a cast that included Jason Donovan in a new soap called *Neighbours* in 1986. During the October, *Neighbours* was screened for the first time in Britain and became one of the nation's most popular of soaps.

Initially Minogue was signed to play Charlene Mitchell for just one week. Then it was 13 weeks, until her contract was extended until 1988. Charlene was such a popular character that Minogue became the youngest actress to win the Australian Silver Logie Award for Most Popular Actress. Not content with that, she went on to win four more, signifying beyond doubt that she was Australia's most popular television actress. She was asked, along with other members of the cast, to sing at an Australian Rules football match held in Sydney. She sang 'The Locomotion' (first recorded by Little Eva during 1962) because no one else knew the lyrics, which in turn led to her signing a recording contract with Mushroom Records, an Australian-based company. 'The Locomotion' was issued during August 1987 and soared to the top of her home chart, a position it held for seven weeks.

A month after the single's release, Minogue came to the attention of Pete Waterman, whose music company had been formed in 1983 before he joined forces with Mike Stock and Matt Aitken to form the innovative Stock, Aitken and Waterman partnership. He invited her to record in London, whereupon the result was the featherweight dance track 'I Should Be So Lucky'. Waterman told the *Daily Express* in June 1996, 'She was the best artist I had ever had in my studio from day one . . . She recorded "I Should Be So Lucky" and left to go back to Australia within two hours.' Many believed Waterman was trying to exploit her soap-star status but he defended his action. 'I had never heard of her and had never watched *Neighbours*. I couldn't get a record label to take her so I set up my own record company, PWL Records, and it proved an enormous success.'

'I Should Be So Lucky' soared to the top of the British chart during February 1988, selling in excess of 750,000 copies. That success was repeated in Australia, before the single topped charts in a further 12 countries. Interestingly, her homeland success had little to do with radio promotion. Two of Sydney's major stations refused to air the single, citing the reasons as 'a high irritant factor' and 'adverse audience reaction'. Irrespective of these and other comments, the Australian nation purchased 500,000 copies, earning Minogue a platinum disc.

The British follow-up single looked set to return the singer to the top. Titled 'Got To Be Certain', it fell short at No.2 in May despite being supported by countless personal appearances across Britain. This trek also helped her debut album, *Kylie*, on its way to No.1 and was later responsible for the singer being listed in *The Guinness Book of Records* for being the youngest female soloist to reach No.1 with her first album and have Top 5 hits with her first ten singles.

With a pair of hit singles behind her, Minogue was now at the crossroads of her career – acting or singing? At the pace demanded, there was no way she could combine both – 'I started a musical career only so I would have an extra string to my bow in case anything went wrong with my acting,' she admitted. Eventually she chose music and in 1988 departed from the cast of *Neighbours*. 'The producers told me that the door's open anytime I want to climb into Charlene's clothes again. But I've been Charlene Mitchell for long enough. I'm enormously fond of her, but she's not me.'

During August 1988, a reworked version of 'The Locomotion' was released in Britain and soared to No.2, enraging music critic/artist Jonathan King sufficiently to accuse Waterman of 'bunging together an electronic, soulless version with Kylie bleating blandly'.

Having secured a recording contract with Geffen Records in America, Minogue undertook a promotional tour there, where 'The Locomotion' had peaked in the Top 3. While this single refused to lie down, 'Je Ne Sais Pas Pourquoi' was released in Britain, reaching No.2 in October 1988. Following her contribution to the Royal Variety Performance and after issuing *Kylie: The Videos*, the singer announced earnings of £1,500,000, grossing more in a single week than the entire cast of *Neighbours* did performing in five episodes of the show. Minogue was one of the top-selling artists of the year, yet this astonishing success had its downside. She suffered her first nervous breakdown; the second followed within months. This time with help from her family she pulled through, but the pressures of whirlwind fame had taken their toll. 'Everyone just thought of me as a product . . . I got to the point where I couldn't make sense of it any more,' she said.

In 1989, Minogue teamed up with her fellow *Neighbours* actor Jason Donovan on record. The combination of two teen idols was far too much to resist; predictably, their duet 'Especially For You' topped the British chart. (See Kylie Minogue and Jason Donovan, 'Especially For You', January 1989.) Their vinyl love affair prompted the media to dig further; in fact, they relentlessly hounded the youngsters. Minogue said at the time, 'Jason is not my boyfriend . . . we're friendly and nothing else. I don't have time for any man in my life. All I ever do is work, work, work.' Donovan said, 'I know the press have got a job to do . . . so in a way I can understand why all these stories about Kylie and me keep appearing. They can say what they want, though, because I know the truth and that's what's important. I'm still looking for the ideal female.' What a load of rubbish! The media for once was correct. The two were lovers, but for some reason their management decided it should remain a secret from the public. The rumours, however, persisted and Donovan also enjoyed an exceptionally successful recording career as a soloist.

As Minogue became increasingly high-profile, critics were quick with the poisonous pens. Once they had dissected her music, they became obsessed with her as a person. Sure, she stood a petite five foot one, but accusations of her being anorexic demanded response at the time. She claimed, 'I survive on fruit, prawns and water. That's enough for me. I am just skinny. I would prefer to be taller, but certainly not curvier.' In actual fact the story was quite different. 'In desperation to make sure I kept my looks, I gave up eating. It was turning into a very serious problem,' she later admitted.

Music-wise, 'Hand On Your Heart', the follow-up to the Donovan duet, returned Minogue to the top of the British chart. It was another extremely transparent dance number from Britain's most successful singer – the perfect combination. Shortly prior to the release of her second album, *Enjoy Yourself*, the single 'Wouldn't Change A Thing' soared into the Top 2. The album shot to the top during October 1989.

Minogue's run of No.2 singles was finally broken when 'Never Too Late' stalled at No.4 in November 1989, while her final title of the year was with other artists singing 'Do They Know It's Christmas?' under the name Band Aid II, a second version of Bob Geldof's Band Aid original. Like its predecessor, the new version shot to the top of the British chart, although sales were nowhere near as high.

After the release of Minogue's first single of the new decade, titled 'Tears On My Pillow', her fourth British chart-topper, she set forth on her first Australian tour, followed by a British trek, closing at a sell-out concert at Wembley Arena. The tours promoted a pair of singles, namely 'Better The Devil You Know' and 'Step Back In Time'. The former was a wilder version of the dance tempo that had established her and was included in the *If Looks Could Kill* movie. Guess what position it reached in the British chart? Yes, No.2! The latter title made the Top 5.

The single's accompanying video astounded viewers. Gone was the twee Minogue image and in its place was a half-naked singer cavorting with an equally revealing black dancer. This 'exposé' was thanks to her boyfriend, Michael Hutchence, known for his excessive appetite for alcohol, drugs and sex and who, apart from changing her appearance, introduced her to his often dangerous lifestyle in the fast lane. The youngster's lifestyle was turned inside out by Hutchence; she partied at night and slept in daylight hours. 'He expanded my world a little further,' she once told friends. The couple would also disappear for days, much to Minogue's minders' annoyance, and she'd miss deadlines for interviews and recording sessions. Of her drug taking, Minogue later confessed, 'It can be fun and it can be dangerous . . . you have to experience something to have a view on it.'

During 1990, with their romance at its height, Minogue purchased a £200,000 villa in the south of France as their love nest. But by 1991 the affair had finished, Minogue having discovered Hutchence had been unfaithful during an American tour with his group INXS. 'I was very much in love with him . . . I was so hurt when we broke up,' she said. Hutchence went on to date model Helena Christensen, then Paula Yates, while Minogue moved on to her next big romance. In November 1997, however, Hutchence was found hanged in a Sydney hotel room on the eve of INXS's 20th anniversary tour.

Before 1990 ended, Kylie issued the Top 10 album *Rhythm Of Love* amidst rumours of her imminent departure from Stock, Aitken and Waterman. Remarkable as it seems, she was voted the worst singer by readers of a BBC music publication, while *Smash Hits* magazine readers voted her Worst Singer and Worst Dressed Person.

During the next two years, the young Australian shrugged off competition to continue as a chart name, the biggest sellers being 'What Do I Have To Do?', 'If You Were With Me Now' and 'Give Me Just A Little More Time', her version of the Chairmen of the Board's 1970 Top 3 hit. By 1992 Minogue, now tired of singing banal lyrics with an image befitting a clean-living teenager, had honoured her SAW recording commitment of five albums and, as neither party was keen to renegotiate a new deal, looked elsewhere. 'At 18 you don't really know what suits you . . . I was a little naïve and I took what people gave me. I have now discovered my own style,' she insisted at the time.

In 1993 she made the switch to the Deconstruction label owned by BMG Records. A year on, the 'Confide In Me' single reached the Top 2, soon followed by her Top 4 eponymous album. The album represented a total change of style in contrast to her transparent dance tracks. The move was too late, though, and Minogue's selling power began to slide. Following the release of 'Put Yourself In My Place' at the end of 1994, she hosted BBC TVs music programme *Top of the Pops* and issued the Top 20 staller 'Where Is The Feeling?' during July 1995.

With her singing career faltering, the artist returned to the screen, and this time movies. Following a rigorous martial-arts training programme, she starred in *Street Fighter* with Jean Claude van Damme, then as a scientist in *Bio Dome* with Stephen Baldwin, a short-lived cinema movie which can now be rented from video stores. However, as a money-spinner, nothing beat her role in *The Delinquents* back in 1990. In one of her British small-screen appearances she joined Dawn French in an episode of *The Vicar of Dibley*.

As Minogue's sister Dannii secured a lucrative recording contract with Warner Brothers in 1996, Kylie moved in the opposite direction, almost into obscurity. Now concentrating more on her private life with French video producer Stephane Sednaoui than on her career as an actress and singer, Minogue's name continues to crop up in the newspapers, with people curious to learn of her whereabouts. Certainly the heady days of fan hysteria are long gone. Indeed, she was quoted as rubbishing her recordings that had helped her achieve millionaire status – I wonder how her fans felt about that. Nonetheless, the singer left her mark, selling in excess of 2.8 million records in Britain alone – not a figure to be sneezed at, whether she actually liked the material or not!

Originally earmarked for release during autumn 1997, Minogue's sixth album, titled *Impossible Princess*, was withheld following the sudden death of Diana, Princess of Wales, in a Paris car crash. Rescheduled for March 1998, the album, retitled *Kylie Minogue*, met with indifferent reviews. Adrian Thrills wrote in the *Daily Mail*, 'Most erstwhile bubblegum stars make the mistake of taking themselves far too seriously as they strive for musical depth.' By attempting this, he believed, they forgot what made them popular in the first instance. Minogue fell into this category. *Kylie Minogue* certainly was heavyweight with contributors that included members from the Grid, Manic Street Preachers and Brothers In Rhythm, together with a pair of tracks, 'I Don't Need Anyone' and 'Some Kind Of Bliss', co-penned by the songstress. It is now over ten years since the singer dominated the British chart with 'I Should Be So Lucky', so perhaps it's time for her triumphant return.

Also see: 'Especially For You' (with Jason Donovan), January 1989

(Quotes: *Kylie Minogue Special 1989* by Robin Mackintosh)

March 1988

ASWAD

Don't Turn Around

Rastafarianism meets mainstream – almost. The group certainly changed the public's opinion of undiluted reggae, earning them the distinction of being Britain's most successful reggae outfit of the decade.

Brinsley Forde and Angus Zeb formed Aswad during 1975 with musicians that included Courtney Hemmings and Donald Benjamin. Having built a staunch following in London's Notting Hill district, the group secured a recording contract with Island Records in 1976. During Aswad's stay with the company, the most significant release, 'Back To Africa', topped the British reggae chart. This single was extracted from Aswad's debut eponymous album, also a good-selling item.

With no further hit material, Aswad, named after the Arabic word for 'black', switched record companies from Island to Grove Muzik in 1978, the same year they embarked upon a lengthy British tour. This trek came after Aswad became the first group to perform in Senegal, the concert being staged as part of their West African visit.

A year on, as the group's line-up was reduced to Forde, Zeb and guitarist Tony Gad, Aswad issued their second album, titled *Hulet*. It was a poor-selling item. The group then switched from music to movies; while Forde starred in the British film *Babylon*, Aswad were featured on the soundtrack, spreading the music to a wider audience.

One year into the '80s, Aswad moved record companies once more to join CBS Records, where their first album was titled *New Chapter*. However, it took until 1982 for Aswad to dent the British chart with their next album, *Not Satisfied*. This Top 50 hit was isolated, with no hit singles to boost its sales.

A further year marked another record-company change – a return to Island Records! There, Aswad's first album *Live And Direct* floundered in the Top 60 late in 1983, while in 1984, following their headlining performance in Brixton supporting the London Against Racism project, their first charting single, titled 'Chasing The Breeze', faltered in the Top 60. Its follow-up single '54-46 (Was My Number)' fared worse, reaching No.70 during October 1984. Towards the close of the year, Aswad issued the album *Rebel Souls* and kicked in a British tour.

Throughout 1985 touring was still high on the group's schedule, with their first significant album for two years issued mid-1986. Titled *To The Top*, the project, released via their own label Simba, suffered the fate of its predecessors, faltering in the Top 70. Before 1986 ended, Aswad did what they did regularly – they switched record companies to Mango Records, distributed by Island Records.

Following two years of having a relatively low profile, Aswad returned triumphantly to release the Hammond and Warren composition 'Don't Turn Around'. The single, soft reggae at its finest, shot to the top of the British chart in March 1988, a position it held for two weeks. Aswad's years of struggle and disappointment had finally paid off. To capitalise on the chart-topper's sales, the group hastily released their *Distant Thunder* album, which peaked in the British Top 10. When issued in America during the September, the album faltered outside the Top 100 listing. Back on home ground, though, Aswad returned to the chart with 'Give A Little Love', a No.11 hit, while its follow-up, titled 'Set Them Free', failed dismally in the lower regions of the Top 70.

In the run-up to the '90s, the reggae group's sixth album, *Renaissance*, was issued, this time via a new recording deal with Stylus Records. In April 1989 Aswad's cover version of the Temptations' 1966 Top 20 British hit 'Beauty's Only Skin Deep' reached the Top 30. A further reworking followed. Titled 'On And On', the song was first recorded by Stephen Bishop, but Aswad could only push it into the Top 30.

A pair of singles charted in Britain during 1990, namely 'Next To You' and 'Smile', Top 30 and Top 60 hits respectively. The solitary album *Too Wicked* re-established Aswad as Top 60 sellers, but passing through the barriers of the chart's lower regions seemed almost impossible for the reggae band at this point, although they would enjoy further Top 10 success in 1994.

Of Aswad's concerts across the world in 1990, probably the most prestigious were their contribution to Nelson Mandela's 'An International Tribute to a Free South Africa', staged at Wembley Stadium, and their appearance at the Glastonbury Festival in the June.

During the next three years, which included Aswad's chart

presence in the Top 70 with 'The Best Of My Love', a version of the Eagles' 1975 American chart-topper and a track extracted from the 'Too Wicked' EP, the group hit the American touring trail. The highlight of this trek was their participation in the Reggae Sunsplash American tour, with dates in Los Angeles followed by others across the world.

Into 1993, Aswad recorded and released their version of Ace's 1974 Top 20 hit titled 'How Long?', released by Polydor Records. The single, featuring both Aswad and Yazz, sold fewer copies than the original, reaching No.31 in the British chart during the August. Aswad once more did what they were good at – they moved! Their recording association with Island Records ended with the release of the Top 50 'Dance Hall Mood' single and the *Rise And Shine* album on the Bubblin' Records label. 'Shine', extracted as a further single, soared into the British Top 5 in 1994, while 'Warriors' faltered in the Top 40.

Yet another thirty-something hit opened 1995. Titled 'You're No Good', it was the first of two to chart during the year. The second was 'If I Was', a staller in the Top 60, and Aswad's final charting title to date.

Many felt that Aswad had abandoned their reggae roots in favour of commercial music. That wasn't strictly true. What the group did, through varying line-ups, was bring an easier-listening form of reggae to the public's attention, thus encouraging those interested to delve further into the pure reggae movement.

April 1988

PET SHOP BOYS

Heart

Still refusing to tour, the Pet Shop Boys continued to rely on media interviews, radio airplay and videos to promote their recorded work. And it was on the visual front that they decided to take their career one step further.

Tennant and Lowe opened negotiations with scriptwriter Jack Bond to work on a movie featuring the best of their recordings. However, the duo realised that while behind the scenes teams collated and experimented, they would need to sustain their recording career. To this end they released their fourth British chart-topper in April 1988. Titled 'Heart', it was a combination of corn and mainstream pop. In fact the single, born as 'Heartbeat', had been recorded during jamming sessions for their *Please* album. So insignificant was the track that Lowe forgot about it, and Tennant intended to rework the chords at a later date. Like much of their material, 'Heart' when completed was intended for the disco artist Hazell Dean. However, when the duo finally completed it with producer Andy Richards, it was decided to release it as a new Pet Shop Boys single. The accompanying video told the story of Dracula via an atmospheric and powerful backdrop. The duo called it another in a series of costume dramas, and said it was probably the last in this style.

Two months on from the chart-topper, the Pet Shop Boys were persuaded to perform, with other acts, at a charity concert staged at London's Piccadilly Theatre. Meanwhile, their movie, now titled *It Couldn't Happen Here*, had been completed and hit the big screen in the July. Said Tennant, 'The story is basically us playing our songs as we drive to London in this car and meet phantom-like figures.' It was a strange concept, yet the story took the duo across Britain, with the support stars joining in the journey. These included Barbara Windsor playing a landlady, Gareth Hunt as a salesman and kiosk keeper and Joss Ackland as a priest. The script was cluttered yet creative, entertaining and musical, yet critics slated it. Not so the duo's fans, who loved every frame.

Back on the recording front, 'Domino Dancing' faltered in the Top 10 singles chart, while *Introspective*, a six-tracked album, fared much better by peaking at No.2. And before 1988 closed, they pulled another cracker by issuing 'Left To My Own Devices', which re-established them as Top 5 recording artists.

Into the new year, Tennant and Lowe worked for a second time with Dusty Springfield. This time they produced 'Nothing Has Been Proved', a track featured in the movie *Scandal*, which told the story of the Profumo affair. The single peaked at No.16 during February 1989, re-establishing Springfield as a major selling force.

This was also the year of change: the Pet Shop Boys announced they would embark upon their long-awaited debut British tour. They played before standing-room-only audiences, winning further accolades for the imaginative use of visual projections and costume changes which accompanied their music. The trek spanned Britain before going across to Japan.

Also during 1989, the duo collaborated on disc with their second female vocalist. This time they turned 'showbiz' by working with Liza Minnelli to present her with her first British hit single. Titled 'Losing My Mind', it was a remarkable track. This title was swiped from her excellent *Results* album, which went on to spawn 'Don't Drop Bombs' and 'So Sorry I Said', Top 50 and Top 70 British hits respectively.

To start the '90s, Tennant formed the group Electronic along with Johnny Marr and Bernard Sumner. Together they issued the 'Getting Away With It' single, which became a Top 20 British hit. Two months on, in the July, four Pet Shop Boys productions were included on Dusty Springfield's *Reputation* album, and the duo released their own album titled *Behaviour*, a Top 2 hit. The album had already spawned the single 'So Hard', also a Top 2 charter. Both releases faltered in the American Top 50. Then the unthinkable happened: for the first time since 1986, the Pet Shop Boys failed to hit the British Top 10 when they issued 'Being Boring' late in 1990. Perhaps the single's title was an omen! It was, however, a minor setback in the game plan.

Into 1991, and having cracked the British touring circuit, the twosome embarked upon a fully fledged tour stretching from Florida through to Canada. This adventurous haul coincided with the release of two cover versions released as one track – 'Where The Streets Have No Name'/'Can't Take My Eyes Off You', borrowed from U2 and Frankie Valli respectively. These titles were coupled with 'How Can You Expect To Be Taken Seriously?' The single soared to No.4 in Britain and reached two positions higher in America.

Following a further British tour, a pair of singles, namely 'Jealousy' and 'DJ Culture', both hit the British Top 20, while the final title of the year, 'Was It Worth It?', faltered in the Top 30. In between releases the Pet Shop Boys maintained their album selling power with *Discography*, a Top 3 hit.

It was, however, becoming apparent that Tennant and Lowe were losing their musical punch; perhaps the enthusiasm had worn thin. Whatever the reason, their music was becoming predictable, although Tennant denied this at the time. Indeed, Electronic's single titled 'Disappointed', issued mid-1992, seemed appropriate. However, when it soared into the Top 10, the duo returned to the recording studio with renewed vigour. The result was exciting; the pair of 1993 singles titled 'Can You Forgive Her?' and 'Go West', their version of the Village People's 1979 hit, confidently returned the Pet Shop Boys to the Top 10. On the album front, the title *Very* re-established them as a chart-topping act.

Into 1994, 'I Wouldn't Normally Do This Kind Of Thing' was followed in the British Top 20 singles chart by 'Liberation' in the April, while 'Yesterday When I Was Mad' hit the Top 20 at the close of the year. Alongside their recording commitments, the duo had continued to tour, albeit sporadically, during the last three years. 'Stonewall Equality' staged at London's Royal Albert Hall was probably the most significant date, while television spots included being featured on ITV's prestigious *South Bank Show*. A year on, the twosome still reigned as a chart act, notably with the *Alternative* album and the single 'Paninaro', Top 2 and Top 20 hits respectively, and during 1996 the singles 'Before', 'Se A Vide E (That's The Way Life Is)' and 'Single' continued their high-selling success.

Throughout their career to date, the Pet Shop Boys' material has been issued via the EMI Records subsidiary Parlophone, and there's no reason to suppose that will now change. However, the duo did release a solitary single on the Spaghetti outlet titled 'Absolutely Fabulous', recorded with the performers of the BBC TV programme of the same name starring Jennifer Saunders and Joanna Lumley.

The title of this one-off single pretty much sums up the extra-ordinary career of the Pet Shop Boys, who, most people believe, are as musically innovative in the '90s as they were a decade earlier when they were experimenting on their cassette recorder. Only the equipment has changed.

Also see: 'West End Girls', January 1986; 'It's A Sin', August 1987; 'Always On My Mind', December 1987

(Quotes: *Pet Shop Boys, Annually 1989* by Chris Lowe and Neil Tennant)

May 1988

S EXPRESS

Theme From S Express

The title was born from dance and raised on rhythm. It also represented the only chart-topper for S Express, who deserved better success than was achieved.

Mark Moore, born of Korean extract in London on 12 January 1965, became a self-contained musical unit within the industry, putting several of his contemporaries to shame. As a child he was taken into care and as a youngster became a follower of punk music. With rhythm in his blood, Moore soon made his mark as a nightclub DJ, notably in the Mud Club.

Influenced by different musical styles, Moore eventually chose to concentrate on the growing funk theme, influenced by the American dance explosion at the time. As his popularity grew, the quietly spoken Moore opened his own Splish label, distributed through Rhythm King Records. Under this arrangement, Moore issued his first hit under the name Mark Moore presents S Express. The single, titled 'Theme From S Express', took everyone by surprise as it danced itself up to the top of the British chart during May 1988, boosted by sales from the loyal nightclub punters. It was an excellent slice of dance/funk that undoubtedly turned heads and moved feet. Actually, so hypnotic was the track that it lived on into 1996, when, as a reworked title, it charted once more at No.14.

Three months on from the British chart-topper, S Express issued its follow-up titled 'Superfly Guy', a Top 5 British hit. Into the next year, two singles sustained Moore's selling power, namely the No.6 hit 'Hey Music Lover' and the Top 20 title 'Mantra For A State Of Mind'. Meanwhile, the title *Original Soundtrack* ensured S Express's high presence in the album chart.

Into the '90s, Moore struggled to keep S Express afloat, creeping into the British Top 40 with the 'Nothing To Lose' single. It then took a further two years to return with the title 'Find 'Em, Fool 'Em, Forget 'Em', but that faltered in the Top 50. The *Intercourse* album followed during 1992, but although welcomed by dance fans, it failed to sustain S Express's mainstream selling appeal. Subsequently, Moore turned his attention to other artists, promising to resurrect S Express when he felt the time was right.

We're waiting, Mark!

June 1988

WET WET WET

With A Little Help From My Friends

Sweet, blue-eyed soul Scottish-style, and a career that swung like a pendulum before peaking with a 15-week-long chart-topper.

Tom Cunningham, born in Glasgow on 22 June 1965, Graeme Clark, also born in Glasgow on 15 April 1966, and Neil Mitchell, born in Strathclyde on 8 June 1967, were educated at Glasgow's Clydebank High School. Outside their study periods the trio formed a music unit but later decided a lead vocalist was required. Marti Pellow, born Mark McLoughlin in Strathclyde on 13 March 1966, took on the challenge, leading the group, now calling itself Vortex Motion, along the 1982 local club circuit, building up a solid following as they went. In time, Vortex Motion became Wet Wet Wet, a name swiped from a Scritti Politti track.

During 1984 Wet Wet Wet were sufficiently confident to record material, featuring examples of their best work, and to form their own record label, titled the Precious Organisation, with their manager Elliot Davis. A year on, several record companies showed interest in the young group, but it was Phonogram Records who offered the best financial deal. With Wet Wet Wet's love of American R&B and sweet soul music, it was difficult for the record company to decide which musical avenue they should pursue. The group desperately wanted to work with veteran producer Willie Mitchell, who had worked with Al Green. That wish was granted.

Following selected British concerts, Wet Wet Wet flew to Memphis, Tennessee, to record with Mitchell. Phonogram Records' A&R staff were disappointed with the result and canned the tracks, much to the dismay of the group. However, in 1987 Wet Wet Wet decided to push once more for the material to be released. To this end the group reworked one title, namely 'Wishing I Was Lucky', which Phonogram Records agreed to release. The single proved Wet Wet Wet were a group to be heard; 'Wishing I Was Lucky' soared to No.6 in the British chart, while Phonogram choked on their vinyl, knowing that in future Wet Wet Wet would be the controllers of their recording career.

In June, two months on from the success of 'Wishing I Was Lucky', Wet Wet Wet supported Lionel Richie during his British tour. Regrettably, few in the audiences realised the group's true potential and headed for the nearest bar.

The single 'Sweet Little Mystery' followed, soaring into the British Top 5 during August 1987, and was a taster for the group's debut album *Popped In Souled Out*. The project was an impressive release, thoughtfully produced and conceived under American guidance, and it certainly deserved its British chart-topping achievement.

Wet Wet Wet's first 1988 outing returned them to the Top 5. 'Angel Eyes (Home And Away)', heavily promoted by the group, convinced the public that they were destined for a lengthy career. Indeed, Wet Wet Wet scooped the Brit Award for Best British Newcomer. And the music continued. In March 1988 the single 'Temptation' peaked at No.12, but it was to be a track recorded as an album item that first elevated Wet Wet Wet to the top of the British chart. The group was asked to contribute to the *Sgt Pepper Knew My Father* compilation being recorded to benefit Childwatch. Wet Wet Wet chose the Beatles' song 'With A Little Help From My Friends', which, with Billy Bragg's version of 'She's Leaving Home', was issued as a single. It topped the British chart in June 1988.

While flushed with this unexpected success, Wet Wet Wet were naturally in demand as a performing unit. They performed with others at the annual Prince's Trust Rock Gala staged at London's Royal Albert Hall and from this high-profile appearance switched to the Wembley stage to celebrate, again with others, Nelson Mandela's 70th birthday. Wet Wet Wet then toured Britain in their own right, as 'Wishing I Was Lucky' made the American Top 60 and *Popped In Souled Out* recorded modest sales Stateside. After much ado, the material recorded with Willie Mitchell was finally issued under the title *The Memphis Sessions* and became a Top 3 British album.

In the run-up to the '90s, Wet Wet Wet enjoyed two further British hits, namely 'Sweet Surrender', Top 10, and 'Broke Away', Top 20. On the album front, sales were stronger as their third, titled *Holding Back The River*, narrowly missed the top spot, peaking at the No.2 position.

The poor-selling single 'Hold Back The River' opened 1990, and 'Stay With Me Heartache', backed with 'I Feel Fine', closed the year. All in all it was a dismal year for Wet Wet Wet, as was the next, when the group crawled around the British chart, unable to cross that barrier into the Top 10. But they would be back!

During January 1992 Wet Wet Wet topped the British chart for a second time with 'Goodnight Girl'. The title dominated the chart for four weeks, promoting the pending *High On The Happy Side* album, which likewise shot to No.1. Its sales were also helped by the eight-track freebie 'Cloak And Dagger', featuring Wet Wet Wet's most performed cover versions. Meanwhile, the single chart-topper was followed by 'More Than Love' and 'Lip Service', both Top 20 hits.

On the touring front, Wet Wet Wet embarked upon a high-profile British trek using 'Lip Service' as its banner. Included were performances at Edinburgh Castle and at the Royal Albert Hall. In 1993 the group kicked in their 'Greatest Hits' British tour and released a pair of Top 30 singles – 'Blue For You', extracted from the recent album *Wet Wet Wet Live At The Royal Albert Hall*, and 'Shed A Tear'. Once more the slow-selling titles paved the way for another chart-topper.

Wet Wet Wet's version of the Troggs' 1967 Top 5 British hit 'Love Is All Around' was included in the soundtrack of the movie *Four Weddings And A Funeral*. The group's reworking of the brash original captured the public's imagination; as the movie soared to blockbusting proportions, so did Wet Wet Wet's single. It topped the British chart in May 1994, a position it held for an unprecedented 15 weeks. As Wet Wet Wet tired of performing the title, the music industry became angry that no single could match, let alone top the sales of 'Love Is All Around'. American record-buyers failed to follow the British enthusiasm, however, and the single peaked in the Top 50 Stateside.

Wet Wet Wet returned to the higher section of the British chart during April 1995 when the chart-topper's follow-up, 'Julia Says', soared to No.3. The same month the group's *Picture This* album entered the chart at No.1. Although the group have yet to make the top spot again, they have enjoyed two further Top 10 singles, namely 'Don't Want To Forgive Me Now' and 'Somewhere Somehow'. To close 1995, the title 'She's All On My Mind' peaked in the Top 20, as did the 1996 outing 'Morning'.

Overall, Wet Wet Wet have enjoyed a successful career. Their music is uncomplicated, they never fail to please and all ages support their talent.

July 1988

BROS

I Owe You Nothing

The Bros, twins were the answer to many a young girl's dream. The boys' squeaky-clean image was approved of by parents – until stories of their unquenchable thirst for spending money were splashed across the tabloids. Nonetheless, they made a name for themselves in the '80s, but for the shortest of time.

Matt and Luke Goss were born within 20 minutes of each other on 29 September 1968 in Lewisham, London, to their cabaret-singing mother Carol and father Alan, a London policeman. When the twins were six years old their father left the family home, leaving Carol to raise them. Young life was hard, with little money available, and this would be remembered by the boys in later life.

While at school, Matt and Luke befriended Craig Logan, born on 22 April 1969 in Fife, Scotland, and invited him to join their group named Caviar. Whilst at school, they were driven by their ambition to become a successful recording group and to this end rehearsed, performed and composed, perfecting their music. During 1984, with schooldays finished and now known as Gloss, the group performed in earnest across south London's clubland. A year on they met Nicky Graham, who in turn arranged an introduction to Tom Watkins, then manager of Hi NRG's foremost duo the Pet Shop Boys. Gloss moved on quickly. By 1987, thanks to Watkins, they had secured a recording contract with CBS Records, who were confident they could be presented to the public as the newest teen idols. The record company was right, but it was to be an extraordinary rise to and fall from fame.

Beavering away behind the scenes, the record company set about manufacturing the trio's image until executives were confident the boys could promote their debut single. Titled 'I Owe You Nothing' and issued under the name Bros, it bombed. Not even the hyped slick, clean image of three good-looking young men could save the single. This was certainly not part of CBS Record's masterplan.

Early in 1988 Bros released their second single, 'When Will I Be Famous?', an appropriate enough title! Following a sluggish start, the single soared into the British Top 4. 'When Will I Be Famous?' went on to chart in the American Top 90 five months later. Hot on its heels in Britain, however, their next single, titled 'Drop The Boy', with vocal padding from Dee Lewis, shot to No.2 in March 1988, thanks to the sustained industry hype. Teenage magazines crammed their pages with photos of and articles about the boys. The media rose to the occasion as Brosmania simmered. By the time the hysteria peaked, even the tabloids carried column inches.

A month on from 'Drop The Boy', Bros issued their much-awaited album *Push*, containing tracks composed by Matt and Luke. The title narrowly missed the top spot. Following their televised performance at the Montreux Rock Festival in Switzerland, and with no suitable single available, 'I Owe You Nothing' was reworked and rereleased. Boosted by Bros's appearance at the festival, the single topped the British chart during July 1988. It was a timely achievement as the brothers were scheduled to tour Britain, their first lengthy trek. The tour was one big riot from start to finish, with audience hysteria surpassing the boys' music.

Before 1988 ended, Bros managed two releases, namely 'I Quit' and 'Cat Among The Pigeons'; both singles shot into the British Top 4. With such unprecedented successes achieved within the space of a year, Bros began spending wildly. In total contrast to their upbringing, when money had been so limited, the twins were uncontrollable in their spending, buying clothes, cars, property and so on. Such was their reputation that the media referred to them as 'offensively rich'.

With the band having the whole world at their feet, and after winning the Brit award for Best British Newcomer, Craig Logan surprised the media by leaving the group early in 1989 amid rumours of behind-the-scenes discontent. One of the provisos of Logan leaving was that the money he had earned with Matt and Luke, estimated to be £5.2 million, remain untouched. The twins agreed and the dispute with Logan was settled midway through the year. Logan went on to work with Kim Appleby, who later forged a successful career as a duettist with her sister Mel.

On a personal level, at this juncture in 1989, unbeknown to the media and, of course, Bros fans, Luke had met and was dating Shirley, back-up singer for several contemporary artists including

George Michael. Against great odds, Shirley and Luke maintained a relationship, as he told journalist Lester Middlehurst in 1997. 'As much as I . . . didn't want a steady relationship, I couldn't imagine being without Shirley. But I paid the price for it.' He cited being hauled before CBS Records executives to be told he should drop Shirley. In retaliation, Luke told them his career took second place to his personal life. A compromise was hastily reached.

Meanwhile, Bros kept their momentum going with a trio of singles, namely 'Too Much', 'Chocolate Box' and 'Sister'. All were Top 10 hits, yet when details of Bros's concert at Wembley Arena were announced, the promoters feared they would suffer a huge financial loss. On the night of the concert, touts outside the venue were forced to reduce ticket prices, selling some at £1 to get rid of them. A Wembley representative told the *NME*, 'Things could have been a lot worse. If you believed everything written in the papers, you would have been expecting a half-full arena.' The performance wasn't sold out, by any means, but remarkably promoters made a profit. During the show, Matt shouted to the audience that he and Luke had proved the world wrong – 'We've played the arena and we're here to stay!' Such optimism . . .

While their second album, *The Time*, rounded off 1989 by reaching the Top 5, Bros were voted Britain's Worst Group by readers of a popular music magazine. It was a far cry from the start of the year, when they could do no wrong.

Following the high profile enjoyed by the brothers during 1989, it really was unthinkable that their decline was about to begin in earnest. The downside started with media support slacking off and a surprise drop in sales of their next single, titled 'Madly In Love', which crawled into the British Top 20. Bros's career needed a rethink. To this end they switched managers to team up with John Reid, then responsible for Elton John's business affairs. Meanwhile, their spending sprees had left them with virtually zero bank balances. Instead of facing the public, and despite Matt's outburst during the Wembley show, Bros relocated to America to work with Qwest Records.

Into 1991, a pair of singles – 'Are You Mine?' and 'Try' – reached the Top 20 and Top 30 respectively, while the album *Changing Faces* sold so badly that it entered and fell from the chart within three weeks. Their hopes of breaking into the American market also failed. The Bros era had ended, and Luke, particularly, took it to heart, as he told Middlehurst. 'I allowed my negativity and bitterness to take over. I let myself go.' Thankfully Shirley, whom he married in 1995, helped him through the hard times. He regained sufficient confidence to form the group Luke Goss and the Band of Thieves, who recorded the poor-selling single 'Sweeter Than The Midnight Rain', released during 1993.

Two years on Logan had carved out a successful marketing career with EMI Records, while in 1996 Matt returned as a soloist to release 'If You Were Here Tonight', before disappearing once again. Luke, on the other hand, beavered away for a second chance. From a performance in a low-key repertory production of *Plan 9 from Outer Space*, he joined London's West End cast of *Grease* in 1997, playing the role of Danny. So successful was *Grease* that Luke headed the cast through a British tour, where theatres were packed to bursting.

The Bros story was a conversation piece for some time; no one could adequately explain why the rise and fall had been so sudden. However, the pitfalls that befell Bros were avoided when managers and record-company personnel planned future artists' careers.

August 1988

YAZZ AND THE PLASTIC POPULATION

The Only Way Is Up

Yasmin Evans, born in London on 19 May 1960, first entered the music business in the Biz. Unfortunately, the group achieved little success – not a good start for a girl determined to carve her name in music's history books. For a time Evans turned to modelling, then she became a make-up artist and stylist for other artists and models before she was given the opportunity to join the line-up of Coldcut, a production duo, to record 'Doctorin' The House', a Top 6 British hit in February 1988. (See Black Box, 'Ride On Time', August/ September 1989)

Following the success of Coldcut, the newly formed Yazz and the Plastic Population recorded the title 'The Only Way Is Up', a monstrously hip sound that roared and belted its way to the top of the British chart during August 1988, much to the delight of club punters.

Happily, Yazz and the gang weren't one-hit wonders. The chart-topper's follow-up, 'Stand Up For Your Love Rights', was another in the same heavy mould, again credited to Yazz and the Plastic Population. It narrowly missed the No.1 spot but soared to No.2 in the October. The album *Wanted* was issued in between the singles and notched up healthy sales.

During 1989, a pair of singles returned Yazz to the Top 20, namely

403

'Fine Time' and 'Where Has All The Love Gone?', while the next year she enjoyed only one hit title, 'Treat Me Good', another Top 20 entrant.

Switching from the Big Life label to Polydor Records, Yazz issued a solitary single in 1992 titled 'One True Woman'. Surprisingly, it floundered around the British Top 60. A year on, she teamed up with the reggae outfit Aswad to record the 'Have Mercy' single, but it was another slow seller, this time in the Top 50.

'Everybody's Got To Learn Sometime' peaked at No.56 in the singles chart during 1994. The title was Yazz's final chart entrant for two years, before she struggled and reached the Top 60 with 'Good Thing Going', an East West label release.

September 1988

PHIL COLLINS

A Groovy Kind Of Love

Toni Wine, composer of 'A Groovy Kind Of Love' with Carole Bayer Sager, admitted that when Stephen Bishop recorded the title, they hoped Phil Collins would produce it. However, when Collins heard Bishop's demo tape, he insisted on recording the track himself for inclusion in the *Buster* movie soundtrack. One wonders what Bishop felt about this!

With his stage debut as the Artful Dodger in *Oliver* a faded memory, and one which he vowed never to repeat, it came as a surprise when Collins accepted the role of Buster Edwards in the film *Buster*, the story of the 1963 Great Train Robbery. The singer was approached to play the role following his performance as Phil the Shill in the American detective series *Miami Vice*, and the challenge was too hard to resist. Collins was also responsible for the soundtrack, which included not only his next British chart-topper in September 1988 but also his next American No.1 a month on. Titled 'A Groovy Kind Of Love', it was a cover version of the Mindbenders' 1966 British hit, and when Toni Wine first heard Collins's version she was delighted: '[It's] very intimate, and maybe that's why it does make me swallow hard . . . when I hear it . . . it's a very touching record.' On the other hand, the singer was convinced that the single had 'trivialised' his talent; he intended to change his music and stamp out a new identity. Nonetheless, the public loved it!

Before the year closed, the follow-up, titled 'Two Hearts', the second release to be swiped from the *Buster* soundtrack, peaked at No.6 in Britain, while across the Atlantic the title presented Collins with his seventh No.1. The single was, incidentally, the result of a working relationship with Lamont Dozier, one of Collins's Motown musical heroes. Indeed, a pair of Dozier and Collins compositions appeared in *Buster*. One was 'Loco In Acapulco', recorded by Dozier's fellow Motown artists the Four Tops, for whom he had written and produced countless million-selling titles with his partners Eddie and Brian Holland. The second was 'Big Noise', recorded by Collins.

Following his immensely popular portrayal of Buster Edwards, the singer accepted the role of dancer when he joined HRH Queen Elizabeth on the floor at Prince Charles's 40th birthday celebrations! In between collecting awards for *Buster* and its associated music, Collins also played Uncle Ernie in the Who's *Tommy*, staged at the Universal Amphitheater in California with a star-studded cast that included the mighty Patti LaBelle and Elton John, before returning to his music to release his finest album since *Face Value*. Titled . . . *But Seriously*, the album, composed following Collins's involvement in *Buster*, represented the fun element returning to his music.

The first track swiped for single release, 'Another Day In Paradise' (originally conceived under the title 'Homeless'), soared to No.2 in Britain during November 1989, while a month on the title returned Collins to the top of the American chart. Meanwhile, . . . *But Seriously* topped both countries' charts.

Collins greeted the new decade with a world tour under the banner 'The Serious Tour', a crazy, sell-out experience. Following the British release of 'Something Happened (On The Way To Heaven)', a Top 20 hit, Collins embarked upon the American leg of the tour, promoting on the way the 'Do You Remember?' single, which reached No.4. He then transferred to British soul to join Genesis at a gala concert staged at Knebworth Park in Hertfordshire, where all the proceeds were earmarked for the Nordoff Robbins Music Therapy Centre. Joining the group were Cliff Richard, Elton John and the Shadows, among a host of top names. Collins then returned to America to continue the world tour and collect a vast collection of music-industry awards for his most recent recorded work. In October 1990 the tour ended. As an exhausted singer headed for home, the *Serious Hits Live* album and *Seriously Live* video were released, selling by the million. This came as no surprise, as by now most of Collins's work reached the six-figure level.

Travelling across the Atlantic with increasing regularity, the singer filled time between charting titles with personal appearances and the occasional concert. He returned to acting to appear in the *Frauds* movie, filmed in Australia, where he swapped his previous criminal role for that of an insurance claims inspector. The next significant appearance was during 1993 as manager of a San Francisco bath house in *And the Band Played On*, screened on American television. Also during 1993, Collins issued his *Both Sides* album, which, not surprisingly, entered the British chart at the top. The lifted single 'Both Sides Of The Story' peaked in the Top 10, making the Top 30 in America. The slow singles sales didn't bother Collins; as long as he made chart-topping albums, his career would survive.

Early in 1994, Collins returned to the concert circuit once more, first through Europe, then across America, before returning to Britain to receive the honour of Lieutenant of the Royal Victorian Order for his concentrated work for the Prince's Trust. The road beckoned again. Into the next year, the singer toured South Africa, then the Latin American countries, closing in Hong Kong. He was hardly in the same country long enough to change his socks, and certainly was not resident in his British home for months at a time. Perhaps to avoid the constant Atlantic crossings, Collins purchased a Beverly Hills mansion in addition to the house held in trust for his children situated in Vancouver, Canada.

Following 'Both Sides Of The Story', in 1994 Collins had four singles in the British Top 50: 'Everyday', 'We Wait And We Wonder', 'Dance Into The Light' and 'It's In Your Eyes'. On the personal front, with two marriages having ended in divorce, he moved to Geneva to live with his girlfriend, Swiss heiress Orianne Cevey. His children from his first marriage, Simon and Joely, lived in Canada, while his daughter from his marriage to Jill, Lily, lived with her mother in Britain. Relocating to Switzerland was not as traumatic a move as he thought. In fact, Collins claimed in a *Q* magazine interview with Danny Eccleston that there was nothing he missed about Britain – 'And it surprises me, 'cos I never thought I'd live in another country, let alone one with another language.'

During 1996, when Collins and Genesis finally parted company, Walt Disney commissioned him to compose the soundtrack for its animated movie *Tarzan*, scheduled for release in 1998. Meanwhile, Collins issued what he believed to be his strongest album to date, titled *Dance Into The Light* and recorded in a castle located in the French Alps, a short journey from his Geneva mansion. He said he had mixed humour against an update of the Collins sound with lyrics that reflected his most recent past.

Early in 1998, during a visit to Britain, Collins announced his intention to marry his girlfriend before the end of the millennium. During his interview with *The Sun* newspaper, the singer also criticised the ticket price of £40 for the planned Princess Diana tribute concert in the summer, saying he would not be appearing, wanting no part in 'feeding the frenzy'. He had his own sadness to deal with, he said, which would remain private.

In 1998 Collins released his long-overdue *Hits* CD which, due to extensive television advertising, peaked in the British Top 10. A year later, in July 1999, 48-year-old Collins married 27-year-old Orianne Cevey in a civil ceremony at the Beau-Rivage Palace Hotel, by Lake Geneva.

For all his international megastar status and the hundreds of accolades, awards and honours showered upon him, Phil Collins remains a remarkably modest man. His vast talent has been recognised by the various music quarters, from pop through to R&B, while his personal life has been publicly scrutinised as he searched for the total happiness he wrote about in his songs.

Also see: 'You Can't Hurry Love', January 1983; 'Easy Lover' (with Philip Bailey), March 1985

(Quotes: *The Phil Collins Story* by Johnny Waller; *The Billboard Book of Number One Hits* by Fred Bronson)

October 1988

THE HOLLIES

He Ain't Heavy, He's My Brother

Often overshadowed by the groups responsible for the Liverpool explosion, the Hollies were in fact one of Britain's most successful acts to rise in the '60s. The sharp-edged vocals of Allan Clarke against tight group harmonies launched 32 British hits, at the last count.

Graham Nash, born in Blackpool on 2 February 1942, and Allan Clarke, born in Salford on 5 April 1942, performed on the local circuit using the name the Two Teens. In time the duo recruited Don Rathbone and Eric Haydock, born in Stockport on 3 February 1943, and became known as the Fourtones, later the Deltas. During one of their performances at the Cavern Club, Liverpool, the group was spotted by Ron Richards, producer for EMI Records, who offered them an audition in London. At this juncture, Tony Hicks, born in Nelson, Lancashire, on 16 December 1943, joined the group now known as the Hollies.

In 1963 the Hollies were signed as a recording act to EMI Records, the company which represented the cream of the Liverpool acts including Cilla Black, Billy J. Kramer and the Beatles. In June 1963 they were presented to the public on vinyl via their debut single titled '(Ain't That) Just Like Me', a cover version of the Coasters' classic. The single gave the group its first British hit at No.25 in the chart. A month on, Bobby Elliott, born in Burnley on 8 December 1942, replaced Rathbone on drums as the Hollies toured Britain. Before 1963 closed, the Coasters' material was rifled once more as the Hollies revamped the group's title 'Searchin''. This time the single soared to No.12 in the British chart, its sales boosted by the lengthy tour and several television spots.

A further cover version returned the Hollies to the British chart and to their highest position to date at No.8. The title was 'Stay', an American chart-topper for the Zodiacs during 1960 which had come to the group's attention when Hicks found the original tucked away in a Scottish second-hand record store. Hot on the heels of this Top 10 hit, the group finally issued their first album, *Stay With The Hollies*, a Top 2 British hit in March 1964. Next, soulster Doris Troy's classic 'Just One Look' received the group's treatment, giving them a No.2 British hit. Ironically, the Hollies' version cracked the American chart, albeit only in the Top 90, the group's first taste of success American-style.

Throughout 1964 a pair of Top 10 British hits – 'Here I Go Again' and 'We're Through', their first composition to be a single – sustained the group's profile. Then, to close the year, the Hollies joined Gerry and the Pacemakers and others to celebrate the festive season on a Liverpool stage in 'Gerry's Christmas Cracker'. The Hollies were having fun, as Nash said, 'We were five guys who escaped from Manchester . . . We escaped from the cycle of doing what our fathers did and what their fathers before them did.'

For the first outing of 1965 the Hollies recorded The Monkees' track 'Yes I Will', a Top 10 British hit, before joining a mouthwatering line-up that included the Rolling Stones and Goldie and the Gingerbreads to tour Britain. Then, before the Hollies could unpack their travel bags, they switched to the American touring circuit to perform in New York with a host of acts including Little Richard.

Once back on home turf, the Hollies' 'I'm Alive' single shot to the top of the British chart in July 1965. After several attempts, the group had finally achieved a No.1. 'Look Through Any Window', the chart-topper's follow-up, failed to repeat its predecessor's success, securing the No.4 position. In between these releases, the *The Hollies* album peaked in the British Top 10. As this was, of course, the decade of mega concerts featuring several high-profile acts, the Hollies once more joined others of their ilk, together with American soul star

Wilson Pickett, to perform at Wembley Arena in the Glad Rag Ball. All in all it had been a remarkable year for the Hollies.

The group's first single in 1966 was a further cover version, not swiped from the Americans this time, but from the Beatles! The Hollies bravely recorded the *Rubber Soul* album track 'If I Needed Someone', which reached the British Top 20. 'I Can't Let Go', 'Bus Stop' and 'Stop Stop Stop' all sustained their chart popularity during the year, while across the Atlantic the band held their own, although the chart placings were considerably lower. Mid-year Haydock left the group, whereupon Bernie Calvert stepped in. He learned on the job during an extensive British tour with co-stars like Paul Jones and the Small Faces. From Britain, the Hollies' next major trek crossed into Germany, followed by a further British tour kicking in during March 1967, with the Spencer Davis Group, among others, for company.

Ill health hit the Hollies' members during 1967. Elliott was hospitalised with an inflamed appendix and Hicks underwent an operation for a recurring nose problem. On the recording front, meanwhile, the group rarely hit a bum note. In March 1967 the single 'On A Carousel' shot into the Top 4, 'Carrie-Anne' made the Top 3 and 'King Midas In Reverse' reached the Top 20. By now the Hollies appeared to rely on their own compositions, usually penned by Clarke, Hicks and Nash. It was an extremely wise move: the group earned royalties not only for performing the material but also for composing it. As the singles notched up high positions, a trio of albums was issued, namely *Stop Stop Stop, Evolution* and the much-needed *The Hollies' Greatest Hits* compilation. All were healthy-selling items.

In the run-up to the '70s, the Hollies, now Britain's most consistent of hit-makers, spent the bulk of their time touring Britain, Europe and America. And it would be America, or rather one of the country's top artists, who would instigate the Hollies losing one of its most valued members. Nash befriended David Crosby, late of the Byrds, and Mama Cass, who among other things introduced him to grass. He admits, 'I started smoking a lot. I started to get more intro-spective, which was one of the reasons I was attracted to Crosby.' It was through Crosby's influence that Nash decided to leave the Hollies in December 1968. 'I began to realise there was much more to music than creating a three-minute song, which the Hollies were brilliant at.' Early in 1969 Terry Sylvester replaced the departing Nash and the group recorded the 'Sorry Suzanne' single; it made the British Top 3 and American Top 60. The final single of the decade was 'He Ain't Heavy, He's My Brother', composed by Bobby Russell and Bobby Scott and featuring Elton John on piano. The single shot to

No.3 in the British chart and No.7 in America, eventually accumulating sales of several million. Meanwhile, two albums rounded off the '60s, namely *Hollies Sing Dylan*, a Top 3 hit, and *Hollies Sing Hollies*, which, remarkable as it seems, bombed.

Into the '70s, the single 'I Can't Tell The Bottom From The Top', again with John's musical input, peaked in the British Top 10 and the Top 90 in America. The last charter of the year in Britain, 'Gasoline Alley Bred', hit the Top 20, as the album *Confessions Of The Mind* peaked in the Top 30. As the Hollies continued to inspire record-buyers, it seemed a natural move for lead vocalist Clarke to venture into a solo career. His vacancy was instantly filled by Mikael Rickfors. With an RCA Records recording contract signed, Clarke issued his *My Real Name Is 'Arold*, yet despite obvious high hopes, he was unable to repeat as a soloist his group success. He returned to the line-up in 1973 with the concession that he could also record as a soloist.

With the return of their distinctive lead vocalist, the Hollies continued their chart profile through to 1974, when they released yet another immortal masterpiece. Titled 'The Air That I Breathe', the single re-established the group as No.2 sellers, reaching the Top 6 in America. A wonderful slice of crisp harmonising, relaxed melodies presented in a commercial package, 'The Air That I Breathe' was the Hollies' last British charter until 1980. Compilation releases and occasional tours sustained them through to the next decade, and in 1980 the title 'Soldier's Song' returned them to the Top 60, their third hit under a new recording deal with Polydor Records. A year on, the group line-up suffered a battering, leaving Hicks, Clarke and Elliott as a trio. They worked with numerous musicians and singers, but their hit status was nil. On the upside, though, in 1981 EMI Records – the parent company of the Parlophone label to which the Hollies had been signed – issued *Holliedaze (A Medley)*, capitalising on the growing popularity of segued track singles. The title reached the British Top 30. It was this success that inspired Nash and Haydock to perform with the remaining trio on British television.

With this unexpected return to selling power, the Hollies, with Nash, flew to America to record an album for Atlantic Records. Prior to the project being completed, the group released 'Stop! In The Name Of Love', a reworking of the Supremes' 1965 British Top 10 hit and American chart-topper. The Hollies' 1983 version peaked in the American Top 30, introducing the album *What Goes Around* to the public.

As Nash returned to his own career, the Hollies rejoined their first record company, EMI, to sign to its Columbia subsidiary. A series of non-charting material followed, until 'He Ain't Heavy, He's My

Brother' was used in a television commercial for Miller Lite. Not to have cashed in on this extensive free publicity would have been criminal, so EMI Records reissued the track composed by Albert Hammond and Mike Hazelwood. What a clever move, EMI! 'He Ain't Heavy, He's My Brother' topped the British chart in October 1988, a position it held for two weeks. It was the Hollies' second single to do so, following 'I'm Alive' during 1965.

Naturally, the Hollies were once more in demand, and to maintain public interest the group embarked upon a lengthy British tour. This trek coincided with the release of *All The Hits And More: The Definitive Collection* and the chart-topper's follow-up, the further reissue and obvious choice of 'The Air That I Breathe'. Ironically, the title stalled in the Top 60. The next time the Hollies charted in Britain was during March 1993, when 'The Woman I Love' struggled into the Top 50. It was the group's final hit to date. Two years on from the single, Nash and the group were reunited once more, this time to record the title 'Peggy Sue Got Married', a track destined for inclusion on a Buddy Holly tribute album.

With their recording career on hold for the time being, the Hollies have hit the holiday-camp and nostalgia touring circuit, where people of a certain age can see and sing along with the group. The line-up may now be mature, but their music most certainly isn't!

(Quotes: *Off the Record: An Oral History of Popular Music* by Joe Smith)

November 1988

WHITNEY HOUSTON

One Moment In Time

'I was knocked out by Whitney's talent on stage . . . she has the necessary grace, charm and dignity to play Rachel . . . It took me a whole year to get her to actually say "yes" to taking the role . . . I promised her . . . she wouldn't be bad because I refuse to let anyone fail' – Kevin Costner

Whitney Houston's career continued to rise; she was the talk of America, the country's most popular star. She maintained a pure, clean image. Indeed, that image, coupled with her religious upbringing and her level-headed approach towards her success, meant that she was often viewed as perfect in every regard. Sure, Houston was criticised, and more often than not she'd speak out, sometimes in defence, other times in direct attack. However, there was one subject that plagued her, and probably does to this day: that of her relationship with Robyn Crawford, a close friend since their schooldays. My, how the media dissected that friendship, and, of course, rumours began that the two were lovers. Nothing Houston said or did could convince the media otherwise. Journalists' questions became more pointed, and the constant probing into her personal life must have driven her to sleepless nights. Finally she told a *Rolling Stone* magazine reporter that journalists lied about her and Crawford: 'I'm really sick of it . . . Our relationship is that we are friends. We've been friends since we were kids . . . I have denied [being lovers] over and over again and nobody's accepted it. Or the media hasn't.' As publications either trashed or supported her, Houston concentrated on her career.

In 1988 the singer returned to the top of the American chart during the April with the slow yet dramatic 'Where Do Broken Hearts Go?'. The British failed to share the enthusiasm, pushing the single into the Top 20. During the June she returned to Britain, headlining the concert celebrating Nelson Mandela's 70th birthday staged at Wembley Stadium as part of her world tour, with the title 'Love Will Save The Day' issued to coincide. The result was a Top 10 British hit and a No.9 success in America.

While touring, Houston enjoyed her next British No.1 single titled 'One Moment In Time', a position it dominated for two weeks during November 1988. This powerful slice of vocalism surprisingly stalled in the American Top 5.

In 1989 Houston received a handful of American Music Awards before releasing a duet with her Arista label-mate Aretha Franklin. Titled 'It Isn't, It Wasn't, It Ain't Ever Gonna Be', the title should have vaulted into the million-seller category. Instead the single bubbled around the British Top 30 and American Top 50.

With the music world conquered, Houston's attention was moving towards films. For some time she had been itching to secure a significant acting role. She had, of course, been given scripts by the ton, including that of the starring role in the life story of Diana Ross. However, before she could seriously consider any script, her recording commitments beckoned. She was required to release her third album, her biggest challenge. As a taster, Arista Records swiped the track 'I'm Your Baby Tonight', a Top 5 British hit and American chart-topper, before using the single's title for the album, released during November 1990. It entered the album chart at No.6 in Britain, No.3 across the Atlantic.

Although the *I'm Your Baby Tonight* album distinctly carried the singer's beloved hallmark in vocal styling, the material was too

412

distracting as pop clashed with ballad and soul. However, most of the criticism was directed at her producers like L.A. Reid and Babyface, a ploy to ensure the singer airplay on the black radio stations across America and, ultimately, the support of her fellow black people. Houston was quick to retaliate during an interview with *USA Today*: 'I would think that black people would be proud. I don't sing music thinking this is black, or this is white. I just sing songs that I think and hope everybody is going to like.'

Into 1991 Houston notched up her ninth American chart-topper with a 1981 composition previously recorded by Linda Clifford and Sister Sledge titled 'All The Man That I Need'. When issued in Britain, despite heavy promotion the title stalled in the Top 20. The singer then followed in her peers' footsteps and performed 'The Star-Spangled Banner' during the Super Bowl XXV at the Joe Robbie Stadium in Miami. Although she was far from being at her best, two performances – part live, part recorded – were later gelled to provide a recording suitable for single release. Intended to rally the American nation in the wake of the Gulf War, the single sold in excess of 800,000 copies within two weeks of its release, with the proceeds earmarked for the Gulf Crisis Fund. Whitney Houston on the same level as Vera Lynn, the UK forces' sweetheart? No, not quite; nonetheless, Houston's profile soared to an all-time high as she went on to perform for the American troops, cancelling her trip across the Atlantic to perform before British audiences. Houston's British trip was, of course, rescheduled for September 1991, with a series of concerts at Wembley Arena and a guest spot at an AIDS charity gala staged in London's Hyde Park.

Music aside, rumours had circulated for some time about Houston's romantic involvement with rap artist Bobby Brown, six years her junior. No confirmation was given until May 1992, when the couple's engagement was announced. Meanwhile, Houston had finally taken steps into the movie world by agreeing to co-star with Kevin Costner in the film titled *The Bodyguard*. Written 20 years previously by Lawrence Kasdan, the romantic thriller centred around Houston's character Rachel Marron, a spoilt singer at the peak of her career. With regular death threats from an unknown yet later obvious fanatic, Marron hires a personal bodyguard, Frank Farmer, played by Costner, and the tale twists and turns, interrupted only by the occasional song. Diana Ross, incidentally, had rejected the role, which went on to launch Houston as a bankable actress.

Shooting was interrupted when, despite lengthy rest periods, Houston miscarried Brown's baby. Nonetheless, she fulfilled her filming commitments, and after the shoot came to an end early in 1992, Houston and Brown married on 18 July during a ceremony held at Houston's $2.8 million New Jersey mansion. Guests were asked to contribute to the Whitney Houston Foundation for Children instead of giving wedding gifts. The couple's daughter, Bobbi Kristina, was born during March 1993.

The Bodyguard was premièred in America during November 1992 and met with mixed reviews. No matter what the critics spat out, however, nobody could dismiss the film's music, particularly its highlight titled 'I Will Always Love You'. Originally composed and recorded by Dolly Parton in 1982, the title was lifted from the soundtrack album and topped the American chart, a position it held for a remarkable 14 weeks. With sales passing the one-million mark, 'I Will Always Love You' went on to become a British chart-topper *en route* to earning the distinction of becoming the best-selling single of all time on an international basis.

While the single sold, its follow-up, a reworking of Chaka Khan's 'I'm Every Woman', was issued. Featuring Khan and the song's composers Nickolas Ashford and Valerie Simpson on disc and video, the single soared into the British and American Top 4. Meanwhile, *The Bodyguard* soundtrack album remained a chart-topper on both sides of the Atlantic. Before 1993 closed, the movie was further milked with a trio of singles, namely 'I Have Nothing', 'Run To You' and 'Queen Of The Night'. The most successful title was the last, which scraped into the British Top 15. Houston's power was shaky on foreign land, but most people believed this was due to an overdose of *The Bodyguard*. In retrospect, they were probably right.

As was predicted, the film's singles scooped numerous awards during 1994, including American Music Awards for 'I Will Always Love You', the Sammy Davis Jr Award and a trio of Grammy Awards, while the soundtrack, which went on to sell a staggering 33 million copies, was named as the Best-Selling Album of the Year by various industry bodies. To date, *The Bodyguard* has grossed in excess of $400 million internationally, while the soundtrack album has passed platinum status seven times, beating *Saturday Night Fever* by several thousand sales.

As the flurry of movie excitement wore off, the singer embarked upon a South American tour before announcing her intention to appear in Rodgers and Hammerstein's *Cinderella*, an American television production, and September dates in New York. At the close of 1994, she performed in the Rose Garden at the White House, following a state dinner in honour of Nelson Mandela.

Now an accredited actress, Houston commanded $10 million for her starring role as Julia in the remake of the 1947 film starring Cary Grant titled *The Preacher's Wife*. Her co-stars were Denzel Washington and Courtney Vance. *The Preacher's Wife* was lacklustre and was poorly received by the public, while the soundtrack, due to the very nature of the film, was knee-deep in gospel cuts and, subsequently, not as successful as Houston's mainstream music projects. However, this soundtrack did, she said, fulfil the deal secured with Clive Davis when agreeing to join Arista Records. She told *Blues and Soul* journalist Jeff Lorez, 'Now I have a gospel album, which I was dying to do because it relates to my faith and my belief in God, so I'm not worried about whether it's going to come in at No.1 or whatever.'

With her career taking on a further successful slant, Houston's personal life was a shambles. Life was not kind to the married couple. The Internal Revenue Service served Brown with a writ claiming he owed $3 million in back tax. In turn, Brown sued his former business-management company for an estimated $10 million. To delay foreclosure on his Atlanta mansion, Houston, via her company, Nippy Inc, arranged a second mortgage for him totalling $850,000. Newspapers reported that their relationship was stormy and rumours were rife, including one about Brown's reputed affair with a dancer. The couple separated and got back together at least three times, amid media speculation of a final break-up. During one reconciliation Houston fell pregnant, and she told her husband the news during an American performance. She went on to miscarry the child. In fact, it was reported the singer suffered three miscarriages in as many years.

In September 1995 Houston and Brown separated once again; in November they got back together in Miami. It was during this period that Brown admitted himself to the Betty Ford Clinic in California for drug- and alcohol-dependency treatment. Houston braved media provocation and her husband's 'cheap shots', including one which said it was her gay affairs that had, according to Brown, driven him over the edge. In a 1996 interview with Gill Pringle in *Here!* magazine, Brown was quoted as saying, 'I was out to prove I was a man because Whitney made me feel so low . . . every time she went off with a woman. I know I've been a lousy husband. I've lied, I've played around. Despite everything, I still love my wife.'

Meanwhile, on the professional front, Houston's single 'Exhale (Shoop Shoop)', composed and produced by Babyface, soared to No.1 in America in November, reaching the Top 20 in Britain. The track was extracted from the soundtrack of *Waiting To Exhale*, in which the singer also starred. Premièred in Britain during 1996 and based on Terry McMillan's novel *To Exhale*, the film starred Loretta Devine and Angela Bassett. A further single from the soundtrack, – which, incidentally, also contained tracks by Aretha Franklin and Patti Labelle, among others – was issued. Titled 'Count On Me', it was a duet between Houston and Ce Ce Winans. It was a Top 20 British hit and Top 10 American hit during February and May respectively.

Celebrating their fourth wedding anniversary on the sumptuous Caribbean island of St Barts, Houston admitted to Pringle that she had damaged her ovary two years previous and was worried she would be unable to give birth again. The singer also said, 'We've been through hell and back over the past year, but despite everything, there is an undeniable electricity which works between us.'

Into 1997, it was rumoured Houston's next major project was to be the starring role in a remake of *Mary Poppins* (Julie Andrews beware!), while a year on she returned to Europe for an across-country tour, including Britain, where she performed a solitary concert at Manchester's Nynex centre during July. Ticket prices were high at £30 each, with a limited number of premium seats priced £45 each. This tour was scheduled between recording sessions for her fourth studio album. Then, in August 1998, when the singer celebrated her 35th birthday, it was confirmed that she and Mariah Carey had recorded the duet titled 'When You Believe', the theme to the Dream Works animated feature *Prince of Egypt*. The track was earmarked for Houston's CD titled *My Love Is Your Love*, scheduled for late-1998 release and which presented a younger, more soulful and contemporary sound, solidifying her place in musical history.

Houston now believes she has covered most areas of entertainment, and has little idea how her future will span out. 'I've seen it all at this point. It would have to be something in life as opposed to music, the industry . . . there ain't nothin' new, baby.'

Also see: 'Saving All My Love For You', December 1985; 'I Wanna Dance With Somebody (Who Loves Me)', July 1987

(Quotes: *One Moment in Time* by Richard Seal; *Blues and Soul* magazine, 1997, interview by Jeff Lorez; *Here!*, 1996, interview by Gill Pringle)

December 1988

CLIFF RICHARD

Mistletoe And Wine

'I've done everything I could possibly want to do and possibly everything anybody could want to do . . . So if it all ended for me, the one thing I could say is that I've lived a fuller life than most people will ever do' – Cliff Richard

Cliff Richard was born Harry Roger Webb in Lucknow, India, on 14 October 1940 to Roger and Dorothy. His first sister, Donella, was born three years later and his second, Jacqueline, in 1948. That same year the family boarded the troopship SS *Ranghi* and emigrated to Britain with £5 between them. They moved into a room in Carshalton, Surrey, where Webb attended the Stanley Park Road Primary School. At this point his father was unemployed, so times were hard. In 1950, however, Roger Webb's luck changed when he was hired by Ferguson's Radio in Enfield, Middlesex, while his wife found factory work in Broxbourne. This meant the family had to relocate to Waltham Cross, Hertfordshire, switching Harry Webb to the King's Road Primary School in 1950, the same year as his third sister, Joan, was born.

When Webb failed his 11-plus examination, he was forced to attend the Cheshunt Secondary Modern School and for the third time the family moved home, this time into a council house in Cheshunt. Webb's school life was consumed with amateur dramatics and rock'n'roll music; in fact, the youngster often played truant to watch touring shows by American artists.

In 1957, Webb left school with one GCE 'O' Level in English and a skiffle group called the Quintones, formed with schoolfriends. However, this disbanded when the three female members moved on to secretarial college on a full-time basis.

For his first job, Webb worked at Atlas Lamps, Enfield, as a credit-control clerk. During his spare time, he joined Terry Smart and others in the Dick Teague Skiffle Group. Eventually, Webb and Teague left to form the rock'n'roll group named the Drifters, whereupon they came to the attention of John Foster, who offered to manage them. The first problem to overcome was the name – Harry Webb and the Drifters held little magic for prospective booking agents. After much discussion, John Foster chose the name Cliff Richard.

In the summer of 1958, with money loaned by Foster's parents, Cliff Richard recorded his first demo record at HMV Records Store, Oxford Street, London. He chose two cover versions – Jerry Lee Lewis's 'Breathless' and Lloyd Price's 'Lawdy Miss Clawdy', which entrepreneur George Ganjou took to Norrie Paramor, A&R manager for the Columbia record label, owned by EMI Records.

Suitably impressed, Paramor took Richard and the Drifters into Abbey Road Studios to record a handful of tracks. The first single was intended to be a version of Bobby Helms's 'Schoolboy Crush' but the public supported the B-side titled 'Move It', penned by Ian Samwell, sending it to No.2 in the British chart during September 1958. The record label on the initial pressings read Cliff Richards, and this misspelling of his surname by EMI Records (a company who should really have known better) has dogged him ever since.

In September, the group, with Richard dressed in a pink jacket and black tapered trousers, debuted on national television on Jack Good's popular *Oh Boy* music show. Then, with the line-up of Bruce Welch, born Bruce Cripps in Bognor Regis, Sussex, on 2 November 1941, Hank Marvin, born Brian Rankin in Newcastle, Tyne and Wear, on 28 October 1941, Ian Samwell and Terry Stuart, they toured Britain during October with the Most Brothers and the Kalin Twins. During this tour Richard met bass guitarist Jet Harris, born Terence Harris in Kingsbury, London, on 6 July 1939, and before it ended Harris had replaced Samwell (who was becoming more involved in composing and production), while his friend, Tony Meehan, born Daniel Meehan in London on 2 March 1943, replaced Terry Stuart.

In December 1958, Richard's second single, another Samwell composition titled 'High Class Baby', was issued. It peaked at No.7 in the British chart. Early the next year, with two hit singles to his credit, Richard and the Drifters embarked upon their first headlining British tour, with Jimmy Tarbuck and Wee Willie Harris as support acts. Part-way through the tour Richard lost his voice, so Wee Willie Harris sang from backstage while Richard lipsynched on stage!

'Livin' Lovin' Doll', featuring Jet Harris, Hank Marvin and Bruce Welch for the first time on record, was the third single. The title climbed to No.20 in January 1959, while the Drifters issued their debut album titled *Feelin' Fine*. A month on, Richard won the Best New Singer section in the annual NME readers' poll. To support the release of their first album and next single 'Mean Streak', which became a Top 20 hit, Cliff Richard and the Drifters toured Britain once more, this time with the Dallas Boys and Des O'Connor, among others.

During the May, cinemagoers saw Cliff Richard in his first full-length movie, *Serious Charge*, also starring Anthony Quayle and Sarah Churchill. Richard was cast as a young amateur rock'n'roll singer, Curly Thompson. For the role, Richard curled his hair with hot tongs each morning before shooting began and sang three tracks, namely 'No Turning Back', 'Mad About You' and 'Living Doll', while the Drifters performed 'Chinchilla'. 'Living Doll' was swiped from the movie soundtrack as a single during July 1959. Written by Lionel Bart, the title sold in excess of 500,000 copies to top the British chart for five weeks, earning Richard his first gold disc. Said Richard, 'It wasn't an out-and-out rocker. But by then I was coming to see that rock wasn't a tempo but a musical culture, and that a song like "Living Doll" fitted into it.' It was also at this juncture that the Drifters became the Shadows to avoid confusion with the American soul group who had been using the name considerably longer than Richard's backing band.

Filming started on Richard's second movie in September 1959. Titled *Expresso Bongo*, he played 18-year-old 'Bongo' Herbert, a rock'n'roll artist waiting for stardom. Laurence Harvey played his manager whose interest lay more in his percentage than his protégé. Sylvia Sims was Harvey's girlfriend, who lent a sympathetic ear in the inevitable lovers' triangle. *Expresso Bongo* was premièred at London's Carlton Cinema on 20 December 1959.

Meanwhile, Sid Tepper and Roy C. Bennett's composition 'Travellin' Light' – reputedly written for the Elvis Presley movie *King Creole* – and its flipside 'Dynamite' began its upward chart climb. The latter stalled at No.16, while the former topped the British chart in October 1959, where it stayed for five weeks. It also became a Top 30 American hit, prompting Richard and the Shadows to undertake a five-week tour there early in 1960. In their absence, the track 'Voice In The Wilderness' (the last to be issued in the 78rpm format) was lifted from the *Expresso Bongo* movie soundtrack and soared to No.2 in the British chart during January 1960, while the 'Expresso Bongo' EP peaked in the Top 20.

Cliff Richard's rise to fame was remarkable. His career appeared to follow that of his idol, Elvis Presley, inasmuch as both turned from singer to actor, both combined ballad and rock in their material and both had the support of effective management. Richard was quick to credit Presley as his inspiration, from the curling of the lip to the sexual gyrations on stage. Indeed, such was the similarity that Richard was to be dubbed 'The British Presley'. Alongside the stardom came the fans. Uncontrollable and hysterical, they were whipped to a frenzy at capacity-filled concerts.

By the close of the decade, Richard had won most of the prestigious industry awards ranging from silver and gold discs to Ivor Novello Awards. He had been voted Best British Male Vocalist on countless occasions, and had appeared regularly on stage and television. He was now as popular on the small screen as he was on the cinema circuit, and in the singing stakes he could do little wrong.

The Cliff Richard dynasty was to grow during the '60s. In the early part of the decade, he topped the bill on television's prime entertainment show *Sunday Night at the London Palladium* before an estimated 19 million viewers, then the biggest audience in British television's history.

As the single 'Fall In Love With You'/'Willie And The Hand Jive' soared to No.2 in the British chart during March 1960, Richard relocated himself and his family to a semi-detached house in Winchmore Hill. In the May he joined a star-studded cast that included Diana Dors, Adam Faith and Max Bygraves at the Royal Variety Performance before the Queen at the Victoria Theatre, London.

Recording sessions, British tours and media spots continued, ensuring Richard and his Shadows worked non-stop. In mid-1960 they opened a season titled *Stars In Your Eyes* at the London Palladium, and a month on they starred in a Sunday-night series for Radio Luxembourg titled *Me And My Shadows*. The 15-minute show ran for 13 consecutive weeks.

At this juncture, Richard's management made the unorthodox move of asking the singer's fan-club members to choose his next single. Eighty youngsters were asked to vote on twenty songs recorded a month earlier. The title 'Please Don't Tease', penned by Bruce Welch, was chosen – a wise decision! The single soared to the top of the British chart during August 1960, a position it held for four weeks – before being displaced by the Shadows' 'Apache'!

The fan-club members' runner-up title, 'Nine Times Out Of Ten', quickly followed the chart-topper. Indeed, while 'Please Don't Tease' descended the chart, the new single catapulted into the Top 10, peaking at No.3 during the September. This was Cliff Richard's tenth single and broke the industry's record for advance sales with an estimated 180,000 orders. In the first two years of his career, Cliff Richard had sold a staggering 5.5 million singles. But the best was yet to come.

During May 1961, the singer announced he planned to star in his third movie, *The Young Ones*. His co-stars were Carole Grey, Robert Morley, Melvyn Hayes, Richard O'Sullivan and, of course, the Shadows. Richard played Nickie, leader of a youth club situated in a rundown area of London. His father, a property owner, intended to purchase the land for redevelopment and the storyline was centred around the arguments between the two. The finale was a concert which raised £2,000 to save the youth club. Produced by Kenneth Harper and directed by Sidney J. Furie, it was a musical for the family to enjoy and certainly the finest teenage entertainment to emerge from Britain in a long time.

'When The Girl In Your Arms Is The Girl In Your Heart'/'I Got A Funny Feeling' were the first tracks swiped from the movie soundtrack. The titles comprised Richard's 15th single and it peaked in the British Top 3 during October 1961. Two months on, *The Young Ones* was premièred at the Warner Theatre, London, whereupon the soundtrack album was issued. It replaced Elvis Presley's soundtrack of *Blue Hawaii* from the top of the album chart.

During January 1962, *The Young Ones* opened in various cinemas around Britain and eventually became the second-highest box-office hit of the year behind the war epic *The Guns Of Navarone*. And with advance orders in excess of one million, 'The Young Ones' single, written by the 'Living Doll' composers Sid Tepper and Roy Bennett, was issued. Norrie Paramor, who produced it, said, 'Some people said that when I dubbed on the strings it "made" the record. I don't agree. They added to the effect, by all means, and they probably made it sound much nicer.' The single entered the British chart at No.1, earning the singer a gold disc. It was Richard's biggest-selling single to date.

As Richard and the Shadows were touring Britain, Richard was voted the Top British Male Singer in the *NME* readers' poll for the second year running, received the Showbusiness Personality of the Year Award from the Variety Club of Great Britain and was the recipient of a special award at the annual Ivor Novello Awards ceremony held at the BBC Television Centre, London.

Before 1962 closed, two further singles were issued, namely a version of Peggy Lee's 'I'm Looking Out The Window'/'Do You Wanna Dance?', originally recorded by Bobby Freeman, and Jerry Lee Lewis's 'It'll Be Me'. Both were hits. Richard and the Shadows also appeared on *The Ed Sullivan Show* as part of the short promotional visit to America, but he was never able to crack the country as a popular singer, unlike most British acts during the 'invasion' era.

Upon his return, Richard did what he was best at – performing before British audiences, a craft he had perfected during the early stages of his career. 'When you are standing on the stage before a vast audience, to the majority of the people out front you are a comparatively tiny figure on a large stage. This means you've got to work darned hard to project yourself to everyone,' he said. And as his popularity grew, so did the size of the venues he played, and that, he said, meant exaggerated stage movements. 'From the microphone amplification of the voice to broader facial expressions to body movements . . . the artist's technique has to take the place of binoculars to make the audience feel it's much nearer to them than it actually is.'

Always in demand as a performer, Richard now spent much of his career on stage, a useful vehicle for testing out future releases. And this is what he did when, following a series of concerts at the London Palladium, he embarked upon a fully fledged tour to discover audience reaction to his next single, the double-A-sided 'The Next Time'/ 'Bachelor Boy', due to be his first release of 1963. The combination of the ballad 'The Next Time' and the semi-paced 'Bachelor Boy', was a winning formula. The single sold in excess of 900,000 copies and soared to the top of the British chart during January 1963.

Although Elvis Presley's influence on Richard's public image was by now well known, Richard did not fall into the trap of starring in movies that had a similar theme, with lightweight storylines and music. Instead, he concentrated on quality and his next was a perfect example.

Midway through 1962, Richard started shooting *Summer Holiday* with a supporting cast of Una Stubbs, Ron Moody, David Kossof, Melvyn Hayes, Laurie Peters and the Shadows. The plot this time centred around a group of mechanics who updated a London Transport double-decker bus to drive through five European countries. Naturally, plans went astray. The group met a young girl whose car had broken down on the way to Athens, while a young boy who stowed away on their bus turned out to be a girl. It transpired that she was a starlet on the run from her overpowering mother. The adventures the group subsequently encountered made the movie extremely enjoyable, with the inevitable ending of Richard falling in love with his co-star. 'I wouldn't have believed that such a first-class musical could have been made in this country,' one critic gushed.

The movie was premièred simultaneously in London and South Africa during January 1963, whereupon Richard and the Shadows embarked upon a South African tour that included dates in Durban and Johannesburg. Shortly before the release of the 'Summer Holiday' single, Richard had three other singles in the chart, namely 'Bachelor Boy', 'The Next Time' and 'Dancing Shoes'. When 'Summer Holiday' charted, he became the first artist to secure four songs from one movie in the chart. Said Richard, 'My last couple of singles were ready-made. In a sense they more or less selected themselves, since they came straight from the film. We would never have released "Summer Holiday" as a single if it hadn't been featured in the film. Frankly, we didn't think it was good enough to stand up on its own.'

'Summer Holiday', Richard's 20th single, did not stand at all; it raced to the top of the British chart during 1963, a position it held for two weeks. The soundtrack, meanwhile, dominated the album chart for an incredible 14 weeks. The movie then went on to win the Ivor Novello Award for the Year's Most Outstanding Score of a Musical.

'Lucky Lips' was the next single, peaking in the British Top 4 in May 1963 and also becoming Richard's first American hit (in the Top 70) since 'Living Doll'. The title 'It's All In The Game', a cover version of Tommy Edwards's 1958 British chart-topper, followed, becoming a Top 2 single, and following Richard's appearance on *The Ed Sullivan Show*, the title became his biggest American hit, peaking in the Top 30.

In December 1963, Richard and the Shadows began shooting their next film, titled *Wonderful Life*, in the Canary Islands. Co-starring with the singer this time were Susan Hampshire, Walter Slezak, Richard O'Sullivan, Una Stubbs and Melvyn Hayes. Cliff and the Shadows were the ship's entertainment on a luxury Mediterranean cruise, but they lost their jobs. The ship's captain put them to sea on a raft, whereupon they drifted to the Canary Islands, where they became a distraction in the shooting of the *Daughter of a Sheik* movie. Hardly Academy Award-winning material!

Wonderful Life was premièred in July 1964 at London's Leicester Square Empire Theatre. 'No one will be able to say they haven't had their money's worth – there's everything in it except the kitchen sink,' one critic wrote.

The title 'On The Beach' was swiped from the film's soundtrack for single release; it became a No. 7 British hit during August 1964. It was the follow-up single to 'Constantly', a Top 5 hit. The last two singles of the year were 'The Twelfth Of Never' (previously recorded by Johnny Mathis, among others) and 'I Could Easily Fall (In Love With You)'; both were Top 10 British hits. The latter track, incidentally, was taken from Richard's pantomime *Aladdin and his Lamp* staged at the London Palladium, where advance ticket bookings topped the £100,000 figure.

The first single of 1965, titled 'The Minute You're Gone', topped the British chart; 'On My Word' followed in the July and reached the top 12. 'The Time In Between' then faltered in the Top 30, while 'Wind Me Up (Let Me Go)' re-established Richard in the Top 2. In between releases, Richard and the Shadows toured Britain and Europe. However, behind the scenes the singer was in turmoil. He complained that he was out of touch with the real world and that his life was passing him by in a whirlwind of recordings and tours. He told *Disc*, the weekly music newspaper, 'Sometimes I'd love to have a job where I could work regular office hours and have weekends off.' One of the main reasons Richard craved normality was his discovery of Christianity by joining a group of north London schoolteachers who did the 'simple things' – 'I had been rejuvenated and my career seemed uninteresting. At the same time, the success of the Beatles and the Stones had shelved me and the Shadows. We were now the oldsters.' In time, though, Richard used his faith to help his career, and through that, others.

Following their debut at the premier cabaret nightspot Talk of the Town in London during February 1966, Richard recorded and released the Mick Jagger/Keith Richards track 'Blue Turns To Grey'. The title reached No. 15 in the British chart. Richard and the Shadows then went on to perform with Dusty Springfield and the

Rolling Stones, among others, at the annual NME Poll-Winners' Concert staged at Wembley. A month on, he returned to that stage to join evangelist Billy Graham to talk of his new-found Christian faith, before being confirmed into the Church of England at St Paul's Church in Finchley, London, in December 1967.

On the movie front, Richard had already completed *Two a Penny*, due to be premièred in London during June 1968. He played the role of a young pedlar, Jamie Hopkins, who encountered the Christian faith through his girlfriend, Carol. Co-stars this time included Dora Bryan, Billy Graham (who also produced the film) and Ann Holloway. And lurking in the wings was another. Titled *Finder's Keepers*, it was a musical comedy about a nuclear bomb lost off the coast of Spain!

Richard's most significant release of 1968 was the Bill Martin/Phil Coulter composition 'Congratulations', the title he performed as Britain's entry in the Eurovision Song Contest held at London's Royal Albert Hall. It was runner-up to 'La La La', Spain's entry. Nonetheless, the track soared to the top of the British chart in the April, where it stayed for two weeks. It was the singer's first chart-topper for three years and his last for seven. He had recorded the single in numerous languages, helping it to sell in excess of one million copies in Europe. Germany alone had advance orders of 150,000. The single went on to become a universal song, and even Charles and Diana swayed to it on their wedding day.

Before the close of 1968, Richard and the Shadows celebrated their tenth anniversary in the music business by releasing the *Established 1958* album, from which 'Don't Forget To Catch Me' was swiped as a single to reach the Top 30 in January 1969. During this year, Richard issued a further four singles, namely 'Good Times (Better Times)', 'Big Ship', 'Throw Down A Line' (a duet with Hank Marvin) and 'With The Eyes Of A Child'. All were Top 20 hits.

To start the new decade, the singer hosted his own BBC TV series and issued a second duet with Hank Marvin, the theme of the television shows titled *The Joy Of Living*. The single peaked at No.25 in the March.

In between the release of two singles, 'Goodbye Sam, Hello Samantha' (his 50th single in Britain) and 'I Ain't Got Time Anymore', Richard debuted in a straight stage role in *Five Finger Exercise*, presented in Kent, and issued a trio of albums titled *Cliff Live At The Talk Of The Town*, *About That Man* and *Tracks'N'Grooves*.

Into the new decade came a further BBC TV series titled *It's Cliff Richard*; this time his resident guests were Una Stubbs and Hank Marvin. Following the release of 'Sunny Honey Girl', a Top 20 hit single in February 1971, Richard recorded the Hank Marvin composition 'Silvery Rain', a Top 30 hit. A further pair of singles were also issued in 1971, namely 'Flying Machine' and 'Sing A Song Of Freedom', Top 40 and Top 20 hits respectively. Along with his recorded work, Richard returned to tread the boards at Sadlers Wells Theatre, London, appearing in *The Potting Shed*, before contributing to the gala concert in tribute to the late Dickie Valentine at the London Palladium. To add to his ever-expanding collection of awards, honours and trophies, Richard also received the prestigious Ivor Novello Award for Outstanding Services to British Music in a ceremony staged in Juan Les Pins.

In similar fashion to the previous two years, 1972 began with a series of *It's Cliff Richard*, with resident guests the Flirtations and Olivia Newton-John, with whom Richard was reputedly romantically involved. A trio of singles was also issued during the year, including 'A Brand New Song', his first title not to reach the Top 50. It was a minor hiccup which no one heeded that much, particularly when Richard once again represented Britain in the 1973 Eurovision Song Contest. The title chosen this time was 'Power To All Our Friends'; it lost to the Luxembourg entry 'Wonderful Dream' by Anne Marie David. Nonetheless, Richard's title soared to No.4 in the British chart during the March.

During the following two years, Richard's star continued to shine brightly as an actor and singer. He first starred in the movie *Take Me High* along with George Cole and Debbie Watling, before playing the role of Bottom in his old-school production of *A Midsummer Night's Dream*. A series of singles and albums ensured his chart presence, although he experienced one scare with the 1975 release '(There's A) Honky Tonk Angel (Who Will Take Me Back In)'. When Richard discovered the lyrics glorified the virtues of prostitution, he withdrew the title from sale.

However, it was a year on that his most significant album of the decade was issued. The material was vital and current due primarily to Bruce Welch producing the recording sessions. Titled *I'm Nearly Famous*, released in June 1976 and supported by a massive promotional campaign by his record company EMI Records, the album soared to No.5 in the chart, spawning a handful of hit singles *en route*, namely 'Miss You Nights', 'Devil Woman' and 'I Can't Ask For Anymore Than You'. The album was also issued in Russia, alongside *The Best Of Cliff Richard*, earning the singer the distinction of being one of the few British acts to release material in that country. In the September, Richard capitalised on that fact by touring Russia, starting with a sell-out concert in the then-named Leningrad, followed by a reception at the British Embassy in Moscow.

The next year, Richard continued with his fresh musical direction and image, releasing the *Every Face Tells A Story* album, another Top 10 seller. Once more, a run of singles, including 'My Kinda Life', sustained his chart presence. It was also a year of prestigious awards: the British Phonographic Institute presented him with the Britannia Award for the Best British Male Solo Artist of the Last 25 Years, and the Song-Writers' Guild of Great Britain honoured him with a Gold Badge Award. It's anyone's guess where he stored them all! Before 1977 closed, he received a gold disc for the double-album package titled *40 Golden Greats*, one of several in EMI Records' 'greatest hits' series. Thanks to maximum television advertising, *40 Golden Greats* shot to the top of the album chart in the November, his first chart-topper since *Summer Holiday* in 1963.

Twentieth-anniversary celebrations started with a two-week stint at the London Palladium at the beginning of 1978 and ended at the Royal Albert Hall in the December. Richard was reunited on tour with the Shadows, while in the March he issued the religious album titled *Small Corners* from which the poor-selling single 'Yes, He Lives' was extracted. Two months on, he received the Silver Clef Award for Outstanding Services to British Music during a ceremony hosted by HRH the Duchess of Gloucester. In the October he released his next secular album, *Green Light*, a Top 30 hit.

It was often the case for Richard that when a particular single attracted poor sales, the follow-up re-established him in the chart. This was indeed the case in 1979. 'Green Light' bombed by his standards, yet the Alan Tarney composition 'We Don't Talk Anymore' which followed shot to the top of the British chart in the September, a position it held for four weeks. The title, produced by Bruce Welch, was Richard's first British chart-topper since 'Congratulations' in 1968 and became 1979's biggest-selling disc with sales in excess of five million copies. Released the same month was his *Rock'n'Roll Juvenile* album, a Top 3 seller. Then, true to form, the chart-topper's follow-up, 'Hot Shot', swiped from the album, struggled into the Top 50! To complete the successful year, Richard led more than 30,000 people in a carol concert staged outside Buckingham Palace in aid of the International Year of the Child.

Into the '80s, Cliff Richard, now a major contributor to British entertainment for more than two decades, a dedicated charity worker and, whether he liked it or not, a significant part of the British Establishment, was included in the Queen's New Year Honours list, receiving an OBE, which he collected at Buckingham Palace during July 1980. Recording-wise, he carried on relentlessly. During the early part of the new decade, he issued top-selling albums that included the chart-topping compilations *Love Songs*, and *Wired For Sound, Now You See Me . . . Now You Don't, Dressed For The Occasion* and *Silver*. The last title represented 25 years as a recording artist. A series of singles were extracted from these titles, including 'Daddy's Home', 'The Only Way Out', 'She Means Nothing To Me' (a duet with Phil Everly) and his first dance track to be pressed on a 12-inch single, 'Never Say Die (Give A Little Bit More)'.

Following the release in 1984 of a trio of poor-selling singles, 'Baby You're Dynamite', 'Two To The Power' (a duet with Janet Jackson) and 'Shooting From The Heart', Richard announced his intention to star in the Dave Clark stage musical *Time*. The musical opened at the Dominion Theatre, London, in April 1986. Richard's year-long stay attracted capacity audiences, while two singles in particular became charting titles. The first, 'She's So Beautiful', featured Richard on vocals and Stevie Wonder as producer and solitary musician; the second, 'It's In Every One Of Us', was composed by David Pomeranz. When Richard left the musical to resume his recording career, David Cassidy stepped into his role.

While Richard played the London stage, he enjoyed his second British chart-topper in seven years with a spoof version of 'Living Doll'. Accompanying him on the 1986 version were the Young Ones, then leaders of British alternative comedy, and Hank Marvin as guitarist. 'Living Doll' topped the British chart, with all proceeds destined for the Comic Relief charity. (See 'Living Doll' by Cliff Richard and the Young Ones, April 1986.)

Before 1986 ended, the *Time* soundtrack album was issued, featuring Dionne Warwick and Freddie Mercury, among others, along with two Richard duets – 'All I Ask Of You' with Sarah Brightman, taken from Andrew Lloyd Webber's musical *The Phantom Of the Opera*, and 'Slow Rivers' with Elton John. The first title soared into the Top 3; the second title didn't!

As Richard re-signed a further lucrative recording contract with EMI Records in 1987, with special provision for his charitable contributions, his next album, *Always Guaranteed*, was issued. The Alan Tarney-produced release shot to No.3 in the chart and passed platinum status, becoming Richard's best-selling album to date. Two singles of note were swiped for release, namely 'Some People' and 'Remember Me'; the first catapulted into the Top 3, whilst the second struggled in the Top 40.

The year 1988 was extra special, as it celebrated the 30th anniversary of Richard's debut hit, 'Move It', and marked his next British chart-topper. In June 1988 he went into the studio to record the Chris Eaton title 'Mistletoe And Wine', a track Eaton also produced. Issued in the November, during Richard's 30th anniversary British tour, the song was tailor-made for the festive market. The record-buying public agreed; 'Mistletoe And Wine' easily shot to the top of the British chart in December 1988. The title represented Richard's 99th single and dominated sales for four weeks, earning the distinction of becoming Britain's biggest-selling single of the year.

Richard's success continued. The double album *Private Collection* passed quadruple-platinum status, with sales in excess of one million. Then, the next year, Richard was honoured at the Brit Awards ceremony staged at the Royal Albert Hall for his Outstanding Contribution to British Music; released his 100th British single titled 'The Best Of Me', which entered the chart at No.2 but could go no higher; staged 'Cliff Richard: The Event' at Wembley Stadium before 72,000 people; recorded his first Stock, Aitken and Waterman composition 'I Just Don't Have The Heart'; and duetted with Van Morrison on 'Whenever God Shines His Light', a Top 20 hit in December 1989.

The new decade saw Cliff Richard the recording artist, entertainer and all-round celebrity rise to even greater heights, if that was possible. He was in demand in all sectors of the entertainment business, and his 'Access All Areas '92' tour spanned a staggering 13 sell-out dates at Birmingham's NEC, a series of concerts at the Sheffield Arena and the Glasgow SECC, plus an unprecedented 16 dates at Wembley Arena!

During October 1995, Richard visited Buckingham Palace for the second time. Accompanied by sisters Jacqui, Donna and Joan, the singer received a knighthood from the Queen for his tireless charity work and his contribution to the entertainment business. Already the recipient of an OBE, Richard was advised he was to be honoured with a knighthood during his involvement in the VE Day anniversary celebrations in London. Richard insisted that being a rock star was a career he loved – 'It's no great shakes' – but told *Today* newspaper in the October that receiving the knighthood was totally different. 'The award has a charitable status because it lifts it above what I do for a living. What I am proud of is that I have received this for nothing to do with politics, commerce, or even rock'n'roll.'

In 1962, while Richard was filming *Summer Holiday*, he had told a journalist his acting ambition was to play Heathcliff in *Wuthering Heights*. Thirty-four years on, that ambition was realised. He joined the cast of the Tim Rice/John Farrar musical adaptation of the Emily Brontë novel, which had been in the pipeline for at least five years. With a $2 million investment from Richard, capacity-filled theatres watched the musical during a six-month tour of Britain. Richard spent much time studying the role of Heathcliff, including visiting Brontë country, particularly Top Withers, the building said to have inspired the author. Said Richard, 'All that's left are the four walls and a couple of doorways, but the ruin stands on the crest of a hill which rolls into moorland. The isolation and bleakness sums up the story of the unhappy hero Heathcliff and his doomed romance with Catherine Earnshaw, whose father had taken him in as an orphan from the streets of Liverpool.'

Richard also took guidance from Steve Green, a fitness trainer who worked with the singer for a year, ensuring a healthy body weight of 11st 8lb with a noticeable half-stone of muscle added to the singer's legs, chest and biceps. Richard told the *Daily Mail* in October 1996, 'I've no doubt it's done me good. I'm feeling stronger and fitter, mentally as well as physically.'

Playing opposite Helen Hobson's Catherine, Richard was the perfect Heathcliff, and the more the critics belittled his performance, the more the public flocked to see him. The character of Heathcliff was the total opposite to Richard's pure-white image, and the singer was keen to discard such an image to adopt the role. 'In one scene I beat my stage wife, Isabella, and I'll be doing it with great pleasure. The fact that in many people's eyes I am Mr Goody-Two-Shoes will make it seem so much more disgusting, and I think that will work in my favour.' It did. One newspaper headline glared, 'Mean and moody, snarling and stubbly. Yes, this really is Sir Cliff!'

And a further celebratory year loomed. In 1998 Sir Cliff celebrated 40 years in the music business and to mark the occasion issued the single 'Can't Keep This Feeling In', swiped from the *Real As I Wanna Be* CD. However, as the singer had, for some considerable time, been unofficially banned from radio airplay, the single was first released under the name 'Blacknight'. This version was a dance-floor styling of the commercial release and was played regularly by unsuspecting radio stations. The result was Sir Cliff enjoyed a Top 10 hit during October 1998.

Cliff Richard is as much a part of Britain's heritage as the royal family. He's always been there; it's as if he's a friend of the family. People talk of him as if they know him personally. That's the way it is with our Cliff.

Also see: 'Living Doll', April 1986

(Quotes: *The Biography: Cliff Richard* by Steve Turner; *The Complete Chronicle: Cliff Richard* by Mike Read, Nigel Goodall and Peter Lewry)

See *Every Chart-Topper Tells a Story: The Sixties* and *Every Chart-Topper Tells a Story: The Seventies* for further information regarding Cliff Richard

KYLIE MINOGUE AND JASON DONOVAN

Especially For You

'There were so many people asking in the shops for the duet before we'd even decided to record it. We thought we'd better cater for the public's demand' – Jason Donovan

Born on 1 June 1968 at the Franciz Xavier Cabrini Hospital in Malvern, Australia, to Sue McIntosh, a television personality, and Terry, one of the country's top actors, Donovan saw his parents divorce when he was four years old. In time, though, his mother remarried and had three more children, while Donovan was raised by his father. From primary school, the young boy moved to Malvern's Spring Road School before switching to De La Salle, a Catholic boys' school where he joined the Australian Boys' Choir. 'You had to work your way up through various probationary sections until you got to the actual choir itself. I can't remember how far I got but I remember I really liked singing.'

Living within a showbusiness environment meant Donovan spent a lot of time in television studios. He was, he said, intrigued by this often crazy world, particularly when his father would sign him as an extra, usually in a crowd scene. But school plays were as far as any acting ambitions went; Donovan had set his sights on becoming a pilot.

Donovan's father was involved with Crawford Productions, a company then producing the television series *Cop Shop*. Through this company, Donovan auditioned and won a role in the soap series titled *Skyways*, where he first befriended Kylie Minogue. From *Skyways* he moved through several television programmes before joining the cast of a new series called *Neighbours*, playing the future screen idol Scott Robinson.

Said Donovan, 'When [Kylie and I] started on *Neighbours* we had a lot of dialogue and storylines and we were working together maybe 12 hours a day. It was very hard work.' The chemistry between them grew as their storyline threw the couple together. They became the sweethearts of the series, finally marrying.

During 1987, young, blond-haired Donovan's popularity had risen sharply. He scooped the Logia Award for Best New Talent, among other honours showered upon him thanks to his connection with *Neighbours*. The soap also instigated the move into music when

Donovan signed a recording contract in 1988 with the Australian-based Mushroom Records. Naturally, the media made much of the switch from screen to recording studio, claiming he was simply following in Minogue's footsteps. However, had the hacks dug deeper they would have unearthed the fact that Donovan had actually studied at the Melbourne Conservatoire of Music and later mastered the piano, among other instruments. In actual fact, Mushroom Records had approached Donovan three years previously but he had declined, stating he needed to establish himself as an actor before moving into other areas.

He next recorded a handful of demos for Mushroom Records before travelling to Britain to record for PWL Records. Donovan recalled, 'We did two songs, a Noiseworks [an Australian group] song and one other. Pete Waterman heard those and that's where it all started.' Being associated with PWL Records and, of course, the company's owners Stock, Aitken and Waterman was exciting yet nerve-racking for the young Australian; so much was expected from him. However, with guidance he nurtured his voice, improving his singing talent dramatically.

While preparing to launch himself as a singer, Donovan continued in his role of Scott Robinson and accepted the role of 'Happy' Hutson in the television movie titled *The Heroes*, the true story of 14 Australian youngsters travelling in a Japanese ship to Singapore during World War II.

With seven songs recorded in London to his credit, Donovan returned to Australia to record 'Sealed With A Kiss' with Mike Stock. That title wasn't, however, destined to begin Donovan's recording career. The track 'Nothing Can Divide Us' was issued instead during 1988 and soared into the British Top 5. 'I was amazed at the reaction. It really launched my singing career, which I'm obviously grateful for . . . I think it's a good song,' said Donovan.

In 1989 came Donovan's first British chart-topper, with Kylie Minogue. Originally the couple were reluctant to share the recording credit on the label but eventually decided to prove to themselves that their individual success wasn't totally due to *Neighbours*. Under the control of Pete Waterman and Matt Aitken, 'Especially For You' was recorded in ten hours in Sydney's Rhinoceros Studios. According to Donovan, 'We didn't actually sing the duet together, just recorded our parts separately . . . we had to learn the song very quickly.' The accompanying video was shot while Donovan was involved in filming *The Heroes*, using several Sydney locations and maintaining a romantic ambience for viewers. Donovan admitted the video was fun to do because 'it just kept people wondering and guessing as to what was going on between us'. As if we didn't already know!

The recording package worked; 'Especially For You' topped the British chart in January 1989 before stretching across Europe into Japan, where it peaked in the Top 10. Young fans idolised the couple from *Neighbours*; every magazine carried photos and interviews, while the soap attracted unbelievable viewing figures.

The duet was the one and only but both artists went on to enjoy remarkably successful careers.

Also see: 'Too Many Broken Hearts', March 1989

(Quotes: *The Official Book: Jason* by Lesley O'Toole)

February 1989

SIMPLE MINDS

Belfast Child

Born from punk in the '70s, Simple Minds got the media searching for another category in which to place the young bunch of musicians; 'futurist' and 'electo-disco' were contenders. Irrespective of the category, however, Simple Minds remained true to their upbringing.

Jim Kerr, born in Glasgow on 9 July 1959, Charlie Burchill, likewise born in Glasgow on 27 November 1959, and ex-members of the Scottish punk outfit Johnny and the Self Abusers, Brian McGee and Tony Donald, formed the nucleus of the group that would become Simple Minds.

As time passed, further group members were recruited, including Mick McNeil, born in Glasgow on 20 July 1958, and Derek Forbes, who replaced Tony Donald, while Duncan Barnwell drifted through. However, it was the line-up of Kerr, Burchill, McNeil and Forbes which slowly established a staunch following on the Scottish circuit, and this in turn prompted them to start recording their first album in Amersham's Farmyard Studios. Released by the Edinburgh-based record label Zoom during April 1979, its title track, 'Life In A Day', had been extracted as a single in the March.

With the major company Arista marketing the Zoom label, Simple Minds enjoyed their first taste of British success, albeit in the Top 70, with the single, while the album received mixed reviews. Nonetheless, *Life In A Day* made the Top 30 album chart. To capitalise on their success, Simple Minds embarked upon a British and European trek with Magazine, appearing on a handful of television spots and participating in recording sessions in between dates. At the close of this lengthy stint, Simple Minds commanded £300 a performance, a step up from their original £75 fee but still insufficient to cover their touring costs. The fact that media attention was by now slowly increasing encouraged them to persevere.

Into the '80s, as Simple Minds toured Europe, their second album for the Zoom label titled *Real To Real Cacophony* bombed. It was a bitter blow, because the group loved it. According to McNeil, 'It's all really good . . . it's just a load of wee ideas and we got it all on tape, and it's all on record.' Said Kerr, '*Real To Real* was laughing at ourselves, which I think is healthy, particularly with our sort of music where we're leaving ourselves open maybe to accusations of having pretensions beyond our station.' The downturn continued: the Zoom label closed, whereupon Simple Minds became Arista Records artists proper by default. Adam Sweeting reported, 'The group found themselves bound to a company which simply had no comprehension of how best to market and develop their abilities, despite MD Charles Levison's genuine enthusiasm for them.'

Determined to make the best of a bad situation, Simple Minds issued their third album, a milestone in their career, titled *Empires And Dance*. It was a Top 40 hit. Critics compared the project to Gary Numan's material, a comparison Simple Minds detested. Yet it was Peter Gabriel who requested the group accompany him on an across-Europe tour. As *Empires And Dance* rose, so the extracted single 'I Travel' plummeted, finally prompting Simple Minds to drop Arista Records in December 1980. The final straw was the record company's handling of the album and single, when stocks failed to meet demand. Indeed, so incensed were the group that they issued a press release blaming Arista for the low sales of both items.

In 1981, when Virgin Records offered Simple Minds a recording deal, the company took on the group's debts, while the group itself admitted the attraction for signing was Richard Branson. Kerr said at the time, 'Now we feel we're one of the best-liked bands, not in terms of money, just in terms of people and respect, because we work and we get things done and if we argue, it's good.' The first single of the year, 'The American', peaked in the British Top 60, while the next, 'Love Song', issued as a taster for the pending double album *Sons And Fascinations/Sister Feelings Call*, achieved healthier sales, reaching the Top 50 during the August. The album itself soared to No.11, although in time the albums would be sold separately. With the single 'Sweat In Bullet' closing 1981 at No.52, Simple Minds were destined for greater heights, but without member McGee, who departed through ill health. Kenny Hyslop filled the vacancy.

Touring Europe was Simple Minds' first commitment of 1982,

while Arista Records could not resist cashing in on the group's recent success by issuing a compilation of older tracks under the title *Celebration*:; the album became a Top 50 hit. Meanwhile, with a new album ready for release, Simple Minds issued an insight titled 'Promised You A Miracle', a top 13 British hit. As the single soared, Hyslop left the line-up, whereupon a previous session musician, Mel Gaynor, born in Glasgow on 29 May 1959, joined.

With Pete Walsh in the producer's chair, Simple Minds released the *New Gold Album (81, 82, 83, 84)* album. It shot into the Top 3 late in 1982, and when issued in America in 1983 the title peaked in the Top 70, the group's first healthy showing there. Two further singles were lifted, namely 'Glittering Prize' and 'Someone Somewhere (In Summertime)', Top 20 and Top 40 hits respectively.

For the next four years, 1983 to 1986, Simple Minds sustained their selling power with singles like 'Speed Your Love To Me' featuring Kirsty MacColl, 'Up On The Catwalk' and 'Don't You (Forget About Me)', which raced to the top of the American chart during May 1985. The title was also the second the group did not compose (Lou Reed's 'Street Hassle' was the first), and its sales were boosted because it was included in *The Breakfast Club*, the ultimate brat-pack movie. A month on, the single soared into the British Top 10. Naturally, Simple Minds capitalised on their American success with selected live dates, including a performance at the JFK Stadium in Philadelphia as part of Bob Geldof's Live Aid spectacular.

On the personal front, in May 1984 Kerr married the Pretenders' mentor and vocalist Chrissie Hynde, whereupon the two groups toured America together. The couple went on to have two children, Natalie and Jasmin, who would tour with their mother, assisted by two nannies.

In 1986 the single 'Sanctify Yourself' was the first to chart at No.10 in Britain, reaching the top 15 in America, while the last of the year to become a British entrant, 'Ghostdancing', peaked in the Top 20. On the album front, *Sparkle In The Rain* shot up the chart to No.1 during 1984, while its follow-up titled *Once Upon A Time* crashed into the chart at the top, passing platinum sales. In between these runaway successes, Simple Minds toured the world, a trip that spanned 12 months.

In the lead-up to the '90s, Simple Minds' career peaked in Britain – a long-overdue achievement, of course. Inspired by the folk song 'She Moved Through The Fair', the single 'Belfast Child' topped the chart in February 1989, a position it dominated for two weeks. The sales of the chart-topper's follow-up 'This Is Your Land' were poor by comparison, as the single struggled to No.13 in the April.

Street Fighting Years, issued in the May, hit the album chart at the top. An ambitious, politically themed project, its title was a dedication to the murdered political prisoner Victor Jara. Initial sales pushed the album through the platinum barrier, yet as a catalogue item it later struggled for regular sales. Outside recording activities, Simple Minds were well known for their active support of various charities and political movements. Indeed, in 1988 the group joined others to celebrate Nelson Mandela's 70th birthday, and they performed again two years on in a second Wembley-staged benefit for Mandela, under the banner 'An International Tribute for a Free South Africa'.

Most of 1989 was taken up touring the world, the British leg kicking off in Leeds during the July and closing in London. While on the road, a pair of singles were released, namely 'Kick It In' and 'The Amsterdam' EP. Both peaked in the Top 20. The latter was ideally named, as Simple Minds' next album was recorded in the Dutch city.

Into the new decade, the group's line-up altered once more. Burchell and Kerr had been the only permanent members for some time, as McGee and Forbes departed to join the unit Propaganda. Malcolm Foster and Peter Vetesse were among the replacement musicians.

Following Virgin Records' release of *Themes: Volume 1, Volume 2, Volume 3* and *Volume 4*, featuring Simple Minds' best material in release-date order, the group's *Real Life* album, issued in March 1991, was preceded by the 'Let There Be Love' single. The album rose to No.2, whilst the single peaked at No.6. As *Real Life* struggled into the American Top 80, Simple Minds embarked upon their world tour, including concerts in Britain and Canada. A series of swiped album tracks ensured their presence in the British chart, including 'Stand By Love' and the album's title song.

As Simple Minds' professional life sustained its high-selling profile, Kerr divorced Chrissie Hynde, marrying Patsy Kensit early in 1992. Two further albums were issued through to 1995, with the group's career now a little less frantic. The first, *Glittering Prize '81/'92*, a 'greatest hits' compilation, was a British chart-topper, whilst *Good News From The Next World* was a Top 10 entrant, reaching the Top 90 in America. Touring Europe and issuing a pair of hit singles, 'She's A River' and 'Hypnotised', rounded off the year. In fact, the latter single also rounded off Simple Minds' British chart career.

From a profitable career with Virgin Records, the group switched to Chrysalis Records, owned by EMI Records, during 1996. To date, Simple Minds have yet to repeat their previous selling power; nonetheless, their presence is still felt on compilations and via radio airplay.

(Quotes: *Simple Minds* by Adam Sweeting)

JASON DONOVAN

Too Many Broken Hearts

By now both Jason Donovan and Kylie Minogue were teen idols, pin-up stars and, of course, British chart-toppers with 'Especially For You' in January 1989. The hype had gone according to management plan, the pair exploding from the television cast of *Neighbours* into the international charts. With their healthy, fresh, ultra-clean young images, how could they fail?

Prior to the release of the 'Too Many Broken Hearts' single, Donovan had his doubts as to the suitability of the track. He explained that the title was recorded in typical Stock, Aitken and Waterman fashion – they went into the studio and listened to the song, and while Donovan was recording certain sections, the trio polished the verses and hooklines. The process, although extremely unusual, obviously worked. Said Donovan, 'I think [the song] shows in my voice that I'm comfortable with the style of writing and that I'm starting to relax.'

'Too Many Broken Hearts' sold in excess of 510,000 copies to top the British chart during March 1989. A month on, the singer filmed his final scenes in *Neighbours*, although his character Scott Robinson would be seen in the daily soap for a further year in Britain. During the May, Donovan's first album, *Ten Good Reasons*, was issued. It topped the British chart, with sales of over a million.

For his next single, Donovan chose 'Sealed With A Kiss', originally recorded by Brian Hyland in 1962 when it peaked in the British Top 3. Donovan's interpretation rose higher, giving him his second consecutive British No.1 title during June 1989. To ensure maximum promotion was afforded, its follow-up, 'Every Day (I Love You More)', was issued within three months of the chart-topper, but the title broke the No.1 run by peaking at No.2. Before the year closed, the Australian recorded the Christmas single 'When You Come Back To Me', another Top 2 British hit.

Jason Donovan-mania was now rife. He was hounded by both adoring fans and hard-nosed media, and was constantly under the public spotlight. Although he passionately protected his privacy, he refused to live as a recluse, yet during his rare trips travelling alone his only disguise was wearing glasses. However, like few in his position, Donovan respected the media, despite clashing with them on several occasions. 'I've had people follow me to get to my house and there's been high-speed car chases. In London they follow you on motorbikes from the airport to find out where you're staying.' It was during one of these breakneck chases that Donovan's bodyguard stopped the car in which they were travelling, grabbed the photographer's motorbike handlebars and threw the keys across the motorway. One magazine editor also crossed the line. *The Face* published a picture of the singer wearing a T-shirt that cast doubt on his heterosexuality. Donovan sued and won libel damages in the region of £200,000.

To start the new decade, 'Hang On To Your Love', again from the Stock, Aitken and Waterman partnership, failed to elevate Donovan into the higher chart positions, faltering in the British Top 10. Happily, his second album, *Between The Lines*, returned him to the Top 2. Prior to embarking upon a short British tour culminating with a sell-out concert staged at Wembley Arena, Donovan issued a pair of singles, namely 'Another Night', a Top 20 hit, and 'Rhythm Of The Rain', a Top 10 success. The latter track was a reworking of the Cascades' 1963 classic; it was an odd choice by the singer.

Aside from recording, and like Kylie Minogue, Donovan turned to acting when he played Private Talbot in the *Blood Oath* movie and later, during mid-1991, appeared on the London stage in *Joseph and the Amazing Technicolour Dreamcoat*. He played the lead role for 11 months before television personality Philip Schofield replaced him. 'Any Dream Will Do', swiped from the stage show and issued on the Really Useful label, re-established the singer as a chart-topping artist in June 1991, as did the show's soundtrack album. Donovan returned to the show late in 1993 for another stint.

It was then time for a further cover version. Donovan's interpretation of the Turtles' 1967 Top 20 hit titled 'Happy Together' stormed into the British Top 10 and represented his last hit for Stock, Aitken and Waterman, who by now must have tired of his desire to record other people's material, denying them composers' royalties.

From the hit-making trio, the singer switched to Polydor Records, where, amid a massive marketing campaign, his debut single titled 'Mission Of Love' stalled at No.26 in the British chart in July 1992. Donovan's selling power had sharply decreased, indicating that, like other teen idols before him, he had been replaced, record-buyers having moved on. Nonetheless, Donovan tried again with his version of the standard 'As Time Goes By'; the title stalled in the Top 30 during the November. In between releases Donovan returned to the small screen to play a farmer in the Australian series *Shadows of the Heart*, later transmitted by BBC TV. He then returned to the British concert trail, only to find that the previous fan hysteria had been reduced to a ripple. The party was over.

As a final shot, the 'All Around The World' single and album followed the same fate as its predecessors, crawling into the Top 50 and Top 30 respectively during 1993. They were Donovan's last charting titles. Throughout the following years the singer's name occasionally hit the headlines once more, and as recently as March 1998 theatregoers saw him return to the stage to play the role of the transvestite in *The New Rocky Horror Show*, which opened in Birmingham.

Also see: 'Especially For You' (with Kylie Minogue), January 1989

(Quotes: *The Official Book: Jason* by Lesley O'Toole)

April 1989

MADONNA

Like A Prayer

When she first recorded this track, Madonna played it over and over in an attempt to conjure up a visual sense of what fantasy it would evoke in her. As she was a Catholic, many believed 'Like A Prayer' would be steeped in religion. Not quite!

Pepsi Cola and Madonna had joined forces in a sponsorship deal worth $5 million. To promote the soft drink, the singer composed the track 'Like A Prayer' with Patrick Leonard. It would be advertising history in the making: Pepsi Cola would sponsor the debut of a new single, the lead track on Madonna's pending album. Like Michael Jackson, Madonna refused to actually drink Pepsi during the advertisement, and held a can of the drink only twice. Madonna told *Rolling Stone* magazine that she liked the challenge of merging commerce and art. 'Making a video is also a commercial. The Pepsi spot is a great and different way to expose the record. Record companies just don't have the money to finance that kind of publicity.'

At this stage, Pepsi were unaware of the singer's promotional video for the single. Directed by Mary Lambert, who had worked with Madonna on the 'Like A Virgin' promotional film, the video's intention was debatable: to promote the single or to promote religious provocation? The storyline saw Madonna witnessing a girl being raped by a white gang, with a black man rushing to her aid. The police arrived on the scene and arrested the black man. Madonna took refuge in a nearby church, not wanting to become involved as a witness. Inside the church she saw a statue of a black saint resembling the man accused of being the girl's rapist. The saint then became human and made love to the singer in the church. When over, Madonna headed to the police station and confessed what she had seen and the black man was freed. While the gospel choir belted forth, Madonna, with bleeding hands, skipped through large burning crosses. Said the singer, 'I kept imagining this story about a girl who was madly in love with a black man, set in the south, with this forbidden interracial love affair . . . he sings in a choir, she's obsessed with him . . . then it turned into a bigger story, which was about racism and bigotry.'

On 2 March 1989, the two-minute Pepsi commercial was screened on prime-time television in 40 countries before an estimated 250 million viewers. The video promoting the single 'Like A Prayer' followed within hours. Reaction was immediate, from Catholic organisations to the American Family Association through to fundamentalist organisations. The video was accused of being blasphemous, and boycotts of Pepsi products were threatened as letters and telephone calls swamped the company. Initially Pepsi stood its ground, before deciding to withdraw their association with Madonna, citing 'consumer confusion' as the reason. The singer pocketed her $5 million fee, Pepsi swallowed the additional $5 million spent on production and other promotional activities, while the offending commercial was replaced by one featuring Robert Palmer.

In the light of all this, how could the single fail? It didn't. In April 1989 'Like A Prayer' topped the British and American charts, a position it held for three weeks. The album carrying the single's title likewise soared to No.1 on both sides of the Atlantic. Madonna had shocked the world, and had reaped the rewards tenfold!

To close 1989, a trio of tamer singles sustained the singer's extremely high chart profile, namely the Motown-infused 'Express Yourself', 'Cherish' and 'Dear Jessie'.

The autobiographical single titled 'Oh Father' opened the new decade in America and became a Top 20 hit, while in Britain Madonna's first, 'Vogue', soared to the top. Before the *Vogue* album could hit the record-store shelves, Madonna opened the first leg of her 'Blonde Ambition' tour in Japan before an estimated 35,000-strong audience. From Japan, the singer switched to America and into Canada, where she was threatened with arrest for public indecency that included her simulating masturbation to 'Like A Virgin' on stage. The tour went on to span 55 dates across the world. Madonna's performances weren't without their critics – some considered her to be tasteless in her stage antics – but others praised her for sheer originality. Needless to say, each venue was sold out as screaming fans paid homage to their heroine.

While she toured, Madonna's next movie was secured, namely *Dick Tracy*. Warren Beatty had purchased the film's rights and would play the lead role; Madonna was to play his co-star Breathless Mahoney. Before shooting began, the two became lovers. The movie, incidentally, was Beatty's first as director since *Reds* and would be Madonna's first acting success since *Desperately Seeking Susan*.

Meanwhile, the world tour trudged on. In June 1990 she introduced her show to Europe but her Italian performances were banned. A month on, the singer was bound for Britain for perform-ances that included a riotous welcome at Wembley Arena. An *NME* reviewer commented that with no new album to promote, Madonna's show reminded him of a pantomime. 'She cast herself as Barbarella in a brothel for "Like A Virgin", switched to black mass cassock gear for a frenzied gospel rave through "Like A Prayer", while the songs from her *Dick Tracy* movie had her stretched out atop a grand piano doing the sequin 'n' sleaze nightclub chanteuse bit.' While in Britain, Madonna clashed with the media and fought the flak when *Dick Tracy* was premièred in London. Musically speaking, her single 'Hanky Panky' was issued to coincide with the visit, soaring into the Top 2 and Top 10 in America, while the album *I'm Breathless*, carrying the message 'Music from and Inspired by the Film *Dick Tracy*', became a surprise runaway success worldwide.

Next was her long-awaited 'greatest hits' compilation titled *The Immaculate Collection*, issued to capture the Christmas market. Naturally, the project topped the British chart, a position it dominated for nine long weeks. In America the package peaked at No.2, selling in excess of six million copies. On the singles front, Madonna narrowly missed a British chart-topper with 'Justify My Love' late in 1990, a year when her albums reputedly sold in excess of 48 million copies. 'Justify My Love' went on to top the American chart in January 1991, sales said to be encouraged by the black-and-white promotional video of steamy hotel sessions with Tony Ward, who had replaced Beatty in Madonna's personal life and who had first been seen as a 'merman' in the singer's 'Cherish' video. With the release of 'Justify My Love', Madonna managed to upset both the Arabs and American Jews by calling the remixed single 'The Beast Within' mix after Saddam Hussein and including an anti-Semitic quote lifted from the Book of Revelations that stated 'the slanders of those who say they are Jews but they are not, they are a synagogue of Satan.' In defence of her work, the singer told the media, 'I had no anti-Semitic intent and the message, if any, is pro-tolerance. The song is about love.' Remaining with the subject of love, while Madonna switched partners, her ex-husband Sean Penn dated Robin Wright, with whom he would have a daughter.

And the hits continued. During March 1991 'Rescue Me' entered the American chart in the Top 20 and it reached the Top 3 in Britain a month later. On the film front, and following the unprecedented success of the *Madonna: Four Clips* video, the singer starred in the revealing *Truth or Dare: On the Road, Behind the Scenes and in Bed with Madonna*, premièred in America and at the Cannes International Film Festival during May 1991 and in July at London's Marble Arch Odeon. Audiences reeled in delight and disbelief.

In between movie premières, the singer, wearing $20 million worth of loaned diamonds against a white Bob Mackie gown and ermine wrap, attended the Academy Awards ceremony in Los Angeles with Michael Jackson, before performing Stephen Sondheim's Oscar nomination 'Sooner Or Later (I Always Get My Man)'. Prior to attending the awards gala, Madonna and Jackson dined at the Ivy, also in Los Angeles. She took off his glasses, wanting to see his eyes; he placed his hand on her breast. It's unclear whether this was before, during or after eating!

From the awards ceremony, the couple switched to the annual Oscar party held at Spago; once inside, she flirted with Warren Beatty, he with Diana Ross. Madonna and Jackson met again to discuss the possibility of recording a duet on Jackson's pending album titled *Dangerous*, but when asked what they had to chat about, Madonna replied, 'We exchange powder puffs, powder our noses and compare bank accounts.'

Into 1992, Madonna took care of business and launched into soft pornography. During April her record company, Warner Bros, negotiated a seven-year contract with her and her various companies, a deal reputed to pass the $60 million mark. In the October, as part of her deal, the singer issued her *Sex* book and album. You didn't need a crystal ball to guess the book's content! On the singles front, meanwhile, 'This Used To Be My Playground', 'Erotica', the title track from her new album, and 'Deeper And Deeper' guaranteed the singer's chart presence across the world. Throughout 1993 and 1994, further singles – 'Bad Girl', 'Fever' and 'Rain' and, later, 'I'll Remember', 'Secret' and 'Take A Bow' – sustained her sales power.

In 1995, Madonna performed at the Brit Awards ceremony staged at Alexandra Palace, London, while 'Bedtime Story' peaked in the British Top 4. In her home country the title 'Take A Bow' topped the chart, her 11th chart-topper, but 'Bedtime Story' later struggled, peaking in the Top 50, as did its follow-up single, 'Human Nature', in the July. Happily, though, British sales sent the title into the Top 10 a month later. Before the year closed, the singer joined others to contribute the title 'I Want You' to the Marvin Gaye tribute project *The Music Of Marvin Gaye* and released the *Something To Remember* album and extracted single 'You'll See', a sweet ballad representing the mood of its mother album, which, like the single before it, peaked in the Top 5 on both sides of the Atlantic.

The film industry also beckoned during 1996 in a way that was destined to alter Madonna's career in a way she could never have envisaged. At a media conference early in the year, she announced her intention to star as Eva Perón in the film adaptation of Sir Andrew Lloyd Webber's musical *Evita*. Produced by Cinergi Pictures and distributed by Walt Disney's Hollywood Pictures, the film also starred Antonio Banderas and Jonathan Pryce, who played the role of General Juan Perón. The singer surprised the critics by playing an extremely convincing wife of the dictator, who rose from poverty to become one of the world's most powerful women. Perón died from cancer in 1952 at the age of 33.

Following the film's première at the Shrine Auditorium in Los Angeles, the *Evita* promotional ball started rolling. Madonna attended the première and received a standing ovation for her performance. From Los Angeles, the star attended premières throughout Europe, kicking in in London, where the film was premièred on Boxing Day 1996. Madonna said more than once that she easily identified with Eva Perón, felt compassion and admired her courage in transforming herself from a small-town girl into a city name held in awe.

From movies to music and finally motherhood. Madonna had never made a secret of her desire to have a baby; indeed, she claimed finding the right father was the problem. So, with her marriage to Sean Penn finally dissolved in 1989, the singer admitted to having numerous lovers, until she met Carlos Manuel Leon jogging through Central Park, New York, in 1994. A fitness trainer and competitive race cyclist, Leon fathered Madonna's daughter Lourdes Marie Ciccone Leon, conceived during the shooting of *Evita* and born in October 1996. Said Madonna, 'I had a very easy pregnancy. I didn't really ever have morning sickness. I was pregnant during the entire filming, but I didn't know until halfway through.'

While beginning the process of raising her daughter, Madonna recorded her first studio album in four years. Titled *Ray Of Light*, it dominated British and American album sales during March 1998. Interestingly, the album's title track was 27 years old, composed by David Curtiss and Clive Maldoon, who recorded it on their debut album in 1971, which bombed. Curtiss and Maldoon never tasted the big time, retiring from showbusiness shortly after their album's demise. Madonna discovered the track via Maldoon's niece, a singer with the Baby Fox dance group, and restyled it to make it the prime track on her album. A month prior to *Ray Of Light* peaking in the charts, and following her first live performance in 15 years on the peak-time National Lottery draw, Madonna's album track 'Frozen' was issued as a single. With prime-time promotion, 'Frozen' shot to the top of the British chart and was followed by the album's title track in April 1998, which shot into the Top 10, selling approximately 300,000 units. Sadly, Maldoon didn't live to benefit from the song's royalties; he had choked to death in 1976 following a drugs binge.

From music Madonna returned to movies, and in May 1998 she announced her intention to appear in *The Next Best Thing*, a comedy co-starring Rupert Everett. She then planned to hit the touring circuit once more. And so the Madonna world continues to revolve. Love her or hate her, she is one of the foremost artists of the past decade, and there's no reason to suppose that with maturity she'll change.

Also see: 'Into The Groove', August 1985; 'Papa Don't Preach', July 1986; 'True Blue', October 1986; 'La Isla Bonita', June 1987

(Quotes: *Madonna: Unauthorized* by Christopher Anderson)

May 1989

BANGLES

Eternal Flame

With Susanna Hoffs as lead vocalist, this British chart-topper was totally alien to the Bangles' sound. It was a commercial ballad that held none of the '60s musical styles that the girls had always encompassed in their material.

Vicki Peterson, born in Los Angeles on 11 January 1958, and her sister Debbi, also born in Los Angeles on 22 August 1961, had performed together in groups like the Fans during 1979. With an ambition to emulate their '60s music heroes like the Hollies and the Beatles, the girls created their own musical unit, recruiting Susanna Hoffs, born in Newport Beach, California, on 17 January 1957, and became known as the Supersonic Bangs, later reduced to the Bangs.

In time, bass player Annette Zalinskas joined the group, and it was this line-up that recorded and released the single 'Getting Out Of Hand' on the group's own Down Kiddie label during 1981. The title bombed. Author Fred Bronson reported that the girls played 'at smaller clubs in Los Angeles [and] they became part of the "Paisley Underground", a loose-knit collection of psychedelic and folk-rock influenced groups.'

In 1982 the Bangs were renamed the Bangles because an East-coast group already bore the name. They came to the attention of radio DJ Rodney Bingenheimer, who went on to include one of the girls' tracks, titled 'Bitchin' Summer', on his compilation *Rodney On The ROQ*. This exposure led to a management deal with Miles Copeland, who began touring the girls in earnest, now minus Zalinskas, who left the line-up during 1983. Zalinskas had intended becoming the Bangles' lead vocalist; the others had different ideas. Micki Steele, born 2 June 1954 and late of the Runaways, replaced the departing Bangle, joining the group as they secured a recording contract with CBS Records.

During August 1984 the Bangles charted in America for the first time, albeit in the Top 80, with their album *All Over The Place*. No extracted singles charted. A year on, the album floundered in the British Top 90, despite being promoted by the group's first tour in the country. The start of 1986 saw the girls embarking upon a world tour; these dates included further concerts in Britain, primarily to promote their next album, titled *Different Light*, from which the track 'Manic Monday' was swiped for single release. The title soared to No.2 in the American and British charts, marking the Bangles' first hit in the latter, while the album soared into the British Top 3 during March 1986. 'Manic Monday' was followed by 'If She Knew What She Wants', a Top 40 British hit, Top 30 in America, and 'Going Down To Liverpool', a reissued track from their first album, which faltered in the British Top 60. Despite the single's low placing, the Bangles toured Britain once more during July 1986. Before the year closed, 'Walk Like An Egyptian', a further track swiped from *Different Light*, shot to No.3 in Britain. The title fared even better in the girls' home country, representing their first American chart-topper, a position it held for four weeks.

The Bangles kicked in the new year with the Top 20 British hit 'Walking Down Your Street', the fourth title to be taken from *Different Light*, before they scooped the Best International Group award at the Brit Awards ceremony held in London. Several notable appearances saw the Bangles into 1988, while singles like 'Hazy Shade Of Winter' and 'In Your Room' maintained the girls' chart status. Album-wise, *Everything* raced into the American chart at No.15 during the December.

The next single, 'Eternal Flame', composed by Hoffs, Billy Steinberg and Tom Kelly, shot to No.1 in America during April 1989. Two months on, it crashed into the British chart to peak again at

No.1, representing the Bangles' first and only chart-topping title. Composer Kelly told author Fred Bronson, 'It was different than everything else on the album. They were trying very hard at that time to make an album that reflected their song-writing skills and musicianship, and all of a sudden here was this ballad that required some different production values.'

To enjoy the buzz of a No.1 single, CBS Records rereleased the 'Walk Like An Egyptian' single. It sold poorly in the June, the same month as the compilation titled *Bangles' Greatest Hits* shot into the British Top 4. Remarkable as it seems, American sales of this compilation were sluggish, the album stalling in the Top 100 listing.

In the remainder of 1989 the Bangles returned to the British singles chart twice with 'Being With You' and 'I'll Set You Free', while their public waited for news of the next tour. That wasn't to be; the only announcement made was of the Bangles' decision to disband. The story had originally leaked that the group intended to take a short break after nine long years together. Hoffs told the *Los Angeles Times* that the girls had worked hard and had enjoyed each other's company, 'But it got to a point where everyone in the band . . . was feeling compromised. Each person had a certain vision of what they wanted to do artistically and it seemed like none of us were being satisfied.'

Into the '90s, the individual members embarked upon solo careers, starting with Hoffs, who issued her *When You're A Boy* album and 'My Side Of The Bed' single, both hits in Britain and America. Hoffs went on to enjoy a renewed career for several years. Vicki Peterson formed the group Kindred Spirit before branching out as a soloist. The remaining Bangles gradually disappeared from the spotlight.

(Quotes: *The Billboard Book of Number One Hits* by Fred Bronson)

June 1989

THE CHRISTIANS

Ferry 'Cross The Mersey

'The idea for a Hillsborough fundraising record struck an immediate chord in the hearts of the three Liverpool artists [I] quickly approached to join me' – Gerry Marsden

The Christians were among the three.

Henry Priestman, born in Liverpool on 21 July 1958, befriended the three Christian brothers Roger, born in Liverpool on 13 February 1950, Garry, born in Liverpool on 27 February 1955, and Russell, also born in Liverpool on 8 July 1956, to form the Christians. Priestman had moved through a handful of musical units including It's Material before heading the Christians as their composer. The Christian brothers also possessed a musical heritage as an a cappella trio known as Natural High, among other names. Indeed, it was as Natural High that the brothers performed on the television talent programme *Opportunity Knocks* hosted by Hughie Green during the mid-'70s.

The young quartet began working together in a Liverpool studio in 1985, concentrating on Priestman's compositions, before performing selected local dates. The studio sessions laid the musical foundation for the Christians' future releases.

Early in 1986 the group signed a recording contract with Island Records, where they were teamed with producer Laurie Latham. Several tracks were completed, ready for release. However, before the music could hit the stores, discontent within the group arose when Roger objected to the growing popularity of his brother Garry. The family feud bothered Priestman sufficiently to threaten departure from the outfit.

Minus Roger, the Christians performed selected television spots to promote their debut single 'Forgotten Town' during March 1987. As the title peaked at No.22 in the British chart, the Christians, as a trio, kicked into the touring circuit, promoting their two future singles 'Hooverville (They Promised Us The World)' and 'When The Fingers Point', both Top 30 hits. Hot on the heels of this moderate success, the group issued their first album, titled *The Christians*, which soared to No.2 in the October. The buying public had fallen in love with the group's silky rock/soul styling and easy melodies, although the love affair would end as quickly as it began.

Into the next year, the title 'Ideal World' once more proved the selling power of the Christians by shooting into the Top 15, while a further track from *The Christians*, 'Born Again', faltered in the Top 30. Before 1988 closed, the group rerecorded a version of the Isley Brothers' 1976 Top 10 British hit titled 'Harvest For The World'. The Christians' version likewise peaked in the Top 10.

'The dreadful crush at Hillsborough football ground, where Nottingham Forest were playing Liverpool, was a bitter experience for anyone living on Merseyside,' Gerry Marsden wrote in his autobiography. The tragedy at the stadium claimed 96 lives. The enormity of the disaster was spread across newspapers and television, while Britain mourned the further loss of innocent lives at a football match. Said Marsden, 'It was like wartime all over again. The sheer horror of people who knew someone who'd just gone to a football match and then got crushed to death couldn't fail to chill us.'

Once again Marsden had to be active in the only way he could. Originally a rerecording of the Crowd's 'You'll Never Walk Alone' was considered, but the idea was dismissed. That track had been recorded and released to raise funds for the Bradford football disaster and it was felt that to reissue the track would reopen dreadful wounds and be disrespectful for the Bradford victims. Whatever song was selected, though, it had to have a Liverpool flavour.

Marsden contacted Pete Waterman, with whom he'd been working, for advice. As Marsden had originally composed 'Ferry 'Cross The Mersey' for Liverpudlians, the pair believed it to be the most appropriate song to raise funds.

A trio of Liverpool artists was contacted immediately: the Christians, Holly Johnson from Frankie Goes To Hollywood and Paul McCartney. It was hoped, by the way, that the two remaining Beatles, Ringo Starr and George Harrison, would also join them, but that wasn't to be. Other artists also offered their services, including Cliff Richard. They were turned down because, Waterman told *NME*, 'The gesture has to come from people who know the city. So I asked them to make a donation.'

First Gerry Marsden recorded 'Ferry 'Cross The Mersey' in its entirety, leaving McCartney, Johnson and the Christians to record their vocals together. The vocals were then duplicated and interwoven for the best result. Within two weeks the track was completed, whereupon it was agreed by Britain's network of radio stations that the first airplay would be on Waterman's *Saturday Show* on Liverpool's Radio City station.

'Ferry 'Cross The Mersey' entered the British chart at No. 1 in June 1989, selling in excess of 800,000 copies. Future sales were generated by the track's inclusion on compilation albums. During this year the Hillsborough Fund raised approximately £13 million, of which half was generated by the chart-topper's sales. All proceeds were directed to the victims' families via the newly formed Mersey Aid.

Understandably, no act could hope to follow such a poignant reminder of tragedy; the Christians did not try. Instead, the group waited until the close of 1989 before releasing their next single, 'Words', a Top 20 British hit, although in the October Roger had issued his first solo album, titled *Checkmate*, from which the Top 70 single 'Take It From Home' was lifted.

The Christians' album *Colour* greeted the new decade, topping the British chart; three months on, the single 'I Found Out' broke the run of hits by floundering in the Top 60, followed by the further poor seller titled 'Greenback Drive'. Through to the end of 1990, the

Christians toured Britain, before concentrating on their next album, *Happy In Hell*, due for release in October 1992. While locked in the recording studio, the Christians issued a pair of singles, namely 'What's In A Word?' and 'Father', Top 40 and Top 60 British hits respectively.

With a 'greatest hits' package titled *The Best Of The Christians* which included two new tracks and the 1993 single 'The Bottle', a Top 40 British hit, the group's success petered out, although they continued to perform throughout Britain and Europe.

As a footnote, eight years on, during May 1997, approximately 34,000 fans celebrated 96 lives by filling Anfield to attend the Hillsborough Justice Concert. Participating acts included the Lightning Seeds, the Beautiful South and the Manic Street Preachers. The concert raised in the region of £500,000 for Mersey Aid and forced the authorities to open a fresh inquiry into the disaster.

(Quotes: *I'll Never Walk Alone: An Autobiography* by Gerry Marsden)

July 1989

SOUL II SOUL FEATURING CARON WHEELER

Back To Life (However Do You Want Me)

With Jazzie B at the helm, Soul II Soul changed British dance music beyond recognition. Fusing the elements of R&B, soul and reggae, their raw, bold interpretations guaranteed dance floors were packed. And how the British music industry glowed with pride when Soul II Soul spread the homegrown word across the world!

Jazzie B, born Beresford Romeo in London on 26 January 1963, and Philip Harvey, also born in London on 28 February 1964, started their career in the music business during 1982 as DJs, hiring out their services and equipment on the flourishing club circuit. When not travelling from venue to venue, the duo hosted their own rave nights under London's King's Cross arches. In time, the pair earned the reputation of being master dance organisers, or 'the main men'. Yep, Soul II Soul were Britain's most wanted purveyors of street music.

Within two years of spreading the musical word, Soul II Soul had recruited Nellee Hooper, late of Massive Attack and the Wild Bunch Crew, while other members drifted through until the final line-up secured a residency in London's Covent Garden.

Into 1987, Jazzie B and Hooper completed a demo tape to send to record-company A&R staff. The tape included the title 'Fairplay'; it was this track that secured Soul II Soul a recording contact with 10 Records, an offshoot of Virgin Records. Meanwhile, the Soul II Soul operation as a whole expanded across local radio stations, notably via the pirated airways until Kiss FM was legally born and into clothes shops in Camden and Tottenham Court Road, while Jazzie B oversaw the music interests for Soul II Soul and other acts.

The single 'Fairplay', with Rose Windross as lead vocalist, was issued, peaking in the British Top 70 during May 1988, and before the year closed its follow-up title 'Feel Free', with Do-reen on vocals, fared no better in the chart stakes. However, with a growing interest being shown in Soul II Soul's various activities, Jazzie B told journalist Vie Marshall that the struggle had been tough. 'No one expected us to get this far . . . For years people have been trying to block our path . . . it took years to get people to believe in us . . . I couldn't breathe when I heard the news about us getting into the chart.' And this was just the start.

The group's first single of 1989 featured Caron Wheeler's vocals and heralded the start of Soul II Soul's true sound, which one journalist called 'a dance shuffle rhythm'. Titled 'Keep On Movin'', the single did just that, dancing into the Top 5 during the April. When released in America, the single soared into the Top 20, later becoming that country's top 12-inch dance track of 1989. To capitalise on this runaway success, Soul II Soul's debut album was released, *Club Classics Volume One*, a remarkable album spanning all quarters of dance music from the very nucleus of Jazzie B's expanding empire. This project rightly topped the British album chart before spreading the innovative Jazzie B word across Europe.

'Back To Life (However Do You Want Me)' was next out, issued in June 1989. Swiped from the debut album, the track was remixed for single release, once again featuring vocalist Caron Wheeler, whose name was also listed in the composer credits. Public support was such that 'Back To Life (However Do You Want Me)' leapfrogged up the British chart to the top in the July, while across the Atlantic the title soared into the American Top 4 during December 1989. This single was, incidentally, the last to feature Wheeler's vocals, as she went on to embark upon a solo career with RCA Records. As the Americans danced to the British chart-topper, its follow-up 'Get A Life' peaked in the British Top 3. 'I think I've proved something for the talent that's here in the UK,' Jazzie B told *Blues and Soul* magazine, also confirming that following the success of his work in America he was in demand there as a producer, notably for Teena Marie and Barry White. While working elsewhere, Jazzie B had already prepared Soul II Soul's next album, *Club Classics Volume II: 1990 – The New Decade*, which, he explained, was a musical progression from the debut, utilising many instrumentals. 'There's a lot of diversity and just basically some really good music, as opposed to just synthesised empty dance grooves.'

Into the new decade, Jazzie B and Hooper's names cropped up on numerous third-party recordings, including those by the Chimes, Neneh Cherry and, the most successful, 'Nothing Compares 2 U', a No.1 British hit for Sinead O'Connor. Soul II Soul were also honoured with countless American awards, primarily for the singles 'Keep On Movin'' and 'Back To Life (However Do You Want Me)'. These honours included a pair of Grammy Awards, Soul Train trophies and music-magazine nominations. 'I think it's good for the States to have a fresh face with a fresh approach,' Jazzie B commented. 'Make them start to think about what they're doing.'

Back on home ground, as *Club Classics Volume II: 1990 – The New Decade* entered the British chart at the top, Soul II Soul's single 'A Dream's A Dream', with Victoria Wilson-James as the lead vocalist, peaked in the British Top 10, reaching the Top 90 in America during July.

Aside from his music, Jazzie B continued to cast his watchful eye over the Soul II Soul empire, the stores and the handful of artists signed to his Silent Productions film, video and talent companies. 'We're concentrating on business ethics and that's what will ensure the continuous longevity of what we're doing.'

With international acclaim now within Soul II Soul's grasp, they experienced a near tragedy. During August 1990, as the group was part-way through an American tour, while travelling to Chicago from Detroit a car swerved in front of the leading tour coach, causing the rear coach and four other nearby vehicles to collide. A total of 31 people were transferred to a local hospital. Jazzie B and several of his musicians and dancers were among those held for treatment. Thankfully nobody was seriously injured, although Jazzie B's back injuries were such that the American tour was cancelled. Four months on, a recovered Soul II Soul embarked upon a British haul, kicking off at Wembley Arena under the banner 'The Further Adventures of Soul II Soul' and closing at the end of September in Brixton, the home of their company headquarters. It was at this juncture that Jazzie B announced that Soul II Soul would abandon all live performances, much to the dismay of their public. 'Missing You', with Kym Mazelle on lead vocals, was the title of the group's last single of the year, a Top 20 British hit. What an incredible 12 months it had been for this group of young, talented people who shared one goal: to revolutionise British dance music.

With the new year came another venture. Jazzie B opened his own record label, Funki Dred, with financial and marketing support from Motown Records. The act Kofi was among the first to be secured to the new set-up, which initially maintained too low a profile for its own good, although Jazzie B insisted, 'It's basically a development label. We're nurturing what we've got . . . It's about careers and acts we can relate to.' While his label ticked over, Soul II Soul's next single 'Joy', featuring Richie Stephens on vocals, soared to No.4 in Britain during April 1992, the same month as the *Volume III – Just Right* album raced into the British Top 3. Before 1992 ended, Soul II Soul charted twice more in Britain, albeit in the Top 40, with 'Move Me No Mountain' and 'Just Right', both swiped from the album.

A British Top 30 single titled 'Wish' and the Top 10 album *Volume IV: The Classic Singles '88–'93* represented Soul II Soul's only hits of 1993, while two years on the group's selling power waned once more with 'Love Enuff' and 'I Care', both peaking in the British Top 20 singles chart. In between these hits, the *Believe: Volume V* album featuring Caron Wheeler, Penny Ford and Melissa Bell, among others, climbed into the Top 30 chart. Jazzie B said the album's title indicated, 'Believe it or not, it's finished,' and that it represented a more understanding relationship with Virgin Records. 'There was no real pressure from them this time round . . . so now that things seem to have come full circle, we are celebrating the fact that we are still in there.'

As his group suffered poor sales, Jazzie B spread his talent to work with American artists like James Brown, and it is this involvement that sustains the talented music innovator today. However, his brush with American acts hasn't encouraged him to move from Britain. The strong belief that British black music, particularly new, untapped talent, remains extremely healthy fuels his determination to give these acts a chance.

Soul II Soul's next release of note, their sixth album, titled *Time For Change*, was issued during 1997. The project represented ten years of recording and saw an unexpected switch from Virgin Records to Island Records. The first track swiped for single release, 'Represent', was targeted for enthusiastic promotional campaigns.

Jazzie B, Jazzi Q, Daddae Harvey and Aitch B, better known as Soul II Soul, once more proved to the public that they remain worthy of the title 'pioneers of British black music'. Long may they groove!

(Quotes: *Blues and Soul* magazine, 1989–92, interviews by Jeff Lorez and David Nathan)

BLACK BOX

Ride On Time

They accepted the glory and the accolades, knowing that the chart-topper wasn't what it should have been. Yep, it was one of music's many swindles which may have conned the public for a while but not the original vocalist.

Italian studio session musicians Valerio Simplici, Mirko Limoni and Daniele Davoli comprised the membership of Groove Groove Melody. This trio regularly used vocalist Katrine, born Catherine Quinol in Paris, for their sessions. Located in northern Italy, Simplici had been a member of the La Scala Classical Music Orchestra, Limoni was a keyboard expert and Davoli was a DJ well-known in Italian clubs.

With their fingers on the computerised dance pulse, Groove Groove Melody were in demand as producers for third-party acts. Their reputation grew as their Midas touch transformed dance music into industry awards. One of Limoni's biggest triumphs was the Italian act Spagna, who had first discovered Katrine singing on the nightclub circuit.

It was Katrine's rampant gospel vocals that were highlighted on the single 'Ride On Time', credited to Black Box, the first in a series of Italian house sounds to win international recognition and support. A thoroughly irresistible house track, 'Ride On Time' danced to the top of the British chart in September 1989, a position it dominated for six long weeks. Released by Deconstruction Records, 'Ride On Time' went on to sell in excess of 800,000 copies in Britain alone. It was a remarkable coup for the record company, and a truly unexpected hit for Black Box.

However, the more the single was played and listened to, the more familiar it sounded – until it was discovered that Black Box had sampled the vocals on Loleatta Holloway's 'Love Sensation' single, itself a dance hit. American soul artist Holloway, Salsoul Records' major disco diva, was no newcomer to having her recording work plagiarised. This time, though, she said, Black Box had gone too far, as she told journalist David Nathan in a *Blues and Soul* interview: 'I was practically singing the whole song. We settled on that one but I still don't think I got the right royalties.' The songstress with a string of hits to her credit including 'Cry To Me' believed Black Box had 'messed me up for a little while mentally'. Then, during subsequent trips to Europe, the public recognised her music but not her. At one point, Holloway stressed, Black Box insisted her vocals weren't used at all – the final insult!

The title 'I Don't Know Anybody Else' was the chart-topper's follow-up for Black Box and soared into the British Top 4 during February 1990. 'Everybody Everybody', signifying the end of the Black Box 'sound', so to speak, was next, faltering at No.16 in the chart during the June. Before 1990 ended, the group tried a different tack and released their version of the Earth Wind and Fire single titled 'Fantasy'; it was a Top 5 hit, with 'The Total Mix' following. This title comprised club mixes of their work – 'Ride On Time', 'I Don't Know Anybody Else', 'Everybody Everybody' – remixed by Graeme Park and backed by 'I Don't Know Anybody Else', a Steve Hurley rework. 'The Total Mix' peaked at No.12 in Britain, while a restyled 'Strike It Up'/'Ride On Time' peaked in the Top 20 in April 1991.

'Open Your Eyes', the title of Black Box's final 1991 outing, a Top 50 staller, led the way for their second album, *Remixed Reboxed Black Box/Mixed Up*, follow-up to *Dreamland*, a year earlier.

In 1993 Black Box enjoyed the solitary Top 40 British hit 'Rockin' To The Music', their last under their recording arrangement with Deconstruction Records. Switching to Mercury Records, Black Box enjoyed chart success with 'Not Anyone' in 1995, while Manifesto Records were responsible for their 1996 hit 'I Got The Vibration'/'A Positive Vibration', which represented their final British hit to date.

October 1989

LISA STANSFIELD

All Around The World

She's down to earth, with a bubbly personality, and has a passion for hats. She's also one of Britain's few soul singers to crash into and rule the world's markets.

Born on 11 April 1966 in Rochdale, Stansfield entered more local talent contests as a child than she cares to remember. At the age of 14 she performed in a Manchester club, where she was spotted by a producer working for Granada Television. She began working in television, which, she said, was a weird feeling because she had to dress up as a 40-year-old woman! She presented the music show

Razzmatazz for one year, before realising her ambitions were in music, not as a television presenter.

Switching to singing meant the young girl needed to convince others of her talent. Her determined spirit didn't fail her; partying one night, she met Ian Devaney and Andy Morris, friends from school. Stansfield told her tale to two patient listeners. Devaney in particular felt Stansfield possessed the quality to make a success of her life and encouraged her to start songwriting in earnest. Morris was later persuaded to join them, whereupon the music team Blue Zone that was to play a vital role in Stansfield's future was born. The singer told journalist Jeff Lorez, 'We wrote three songs, did a demo and trudged around the record companies.' The trek was, she added, demeaning, as her self-esteem was crushed by A&R staff trashing her material.

One record company, however, felt differently. Working under the title Rockin' Horse, the company was a small, independent outfit and secured the trio to a recording contract. One year on, Rockin' Horse was purchased by Arista Records, whereupon Stansfield and the team became a major company's act by default. As Blue Zone, the unit recorded their debut album titled *Big Thing*, from which a trio of tracks featuring Stansfield on vocals were issued. All titles bombed. Said Stansfield, 'By the time we'd done the album, we'd spent so long messing about that our direction had totally changed.' Basing their music on soul/funk influences, Stansfield had compromised her art to record an album groove-deep in mainstream tracks. However, one of Blue Zone's released singles featured the soul-tinged flipside titled 'Big Thing', a track the team had composed in 30 minutes. The song, having attracted public interest, prompted Stansfield and Morris to stick to their soul roots for future compositions.

By 1989 Devaney and Morris had worked with third-party acts – including Matt Black and Jonathan Moore's hit 'Stop This Crazy Thing', featuring Junior Reid and the Ahead of Our Time Orchestra, released on the Ahead of Our Time label – when they asked Stansfield to vocalise on their Coldcut dance single titled 'People Hold On'; it was a Top 20 British hit. This single and the aforementioned 'Big Thing' interested Jazz Summers of Big Life Records and Management sufficiently to sign Stansfield to a recording contract during 1989. Morris and Devaney would continue in their capacity of composers and producers.

In the September, the songstress and her pair of backroom music men worked on the 'This Is The Right Time' track, Stansfield's debut solo single and another Top 20 British hit via the Big Life label, distributed by Arista Records. A mere month later, Stansfield sat at the top of the British singles chart with 'All Around The World', which she called an 'archetypical '70s disco record'. The title held the top position for two weeks. Her soul-laden vocals inspired record-buyers in 12 counties to repeat her remarkable British success, while her debut album *Affection*, written and produced by Morris and Devaney, closed the year as a Top 2 British hit. Hailed as a masterpiece of its era, the album convinced doubters that Stansfield was indeed worthy of the title of British soul singer. *Affection* went on to sell over four million copies, launching Stansfield's career across Europe. Her elevated position was recognised at the Brit Awards ceremony when she was named the Best British Newcomer and when she was named Recording Artist of 1989 by the Variety Club of Great Britain. 'All Around The World' went on to win the Ivor Novello Award for International Hit of the Year during a gala held in London, while its singer later won the 1991 Brit Award for Best British Female Artist.

Leaving these honours and awards at home, Stansfield flew to America to host a press reception in Beverly Hills, California, in February 1990. While there the singer performed with the Four Tops, Dionne Warwick and others of their status at the benefit gala 'That's What Friends Are For' in celebration of Arista Records' 15th anniversary. A month after her performance in April 1990, the 'All Around The World' single soared into the American Top 3, before topping the R&B listing, earning Stansfield the honour of becoming only the second white female act ever to achieve this. Like Dusty Springfield two decades earlier, before Stansfield personally promoted her work in America, the record-buying public believed she was black. 'Most people over there [were] pretty surprised when they saw me and what I looked like!' America led to Europe and ultimately a world tour, kicking in at the Soul Weekender in Prestatyn during 1990. Despite initial nerves, Stansfield and her band played to a packed, enthusiastic venue, a trait that continued throughout Europe. However, audiences in the different countries worried the singer, as she explained to Lorez. 'It's weird when you do concerts in places that have never had many pop concerts before and the crowd are really quiet because they think they shouldn't clap, like they're at an opera or something.' Stansfield soon changed that by demanding the audiences participate from the show's commencement.

High-profile performances were similarly rife during 1991, including an AIDS gala benefit staged in Brixton and Amnesty International's Big 30 concert for television. In between live dates, Stansfield began recording her second album due for British release early in 1992. Titled *Real Love*, produced and co-composed with Morris and Devaney, the title soared into the British Top 3, reaching the Top 50 in America. Several of the tracks had been composed while touring, and the album was recorded in much the same fashion as its precedessor – 'We just dossed around and when we had an inspiration we went in the studio and did it.' From *Real Love*, the title 'All Woman' was swiped for single release as follow-up to the Top 10 British hit titled 'Change'. It peaked in the British Top 20 and Top 60 in America.

Through to the end of 1992, a further pair of singles, namely 'Time To Make You Mine' and 'Set Your Loving Free', sustained Stansfield's name in the British chart. To promote these titles she embarked upon a further British tour during the June, followed by a short American visit, where she played before a capacity-filled audience at Radio City Music Hall in New York. While basking in her American success, Stansfield confirmed her concern that when marketing music in that country, the industry tended to make artists look alike. By way of explanation, she said, 'My impression of a soul-ballad video is a guy in a shiny suit with a glass of champagne. It's so tacky.'

The first outing of 1993 was a song featured in the movie *The Bodyguard* starring Kevin Costner and Whitney Houston. Titled 'Someday (I'm Coming Back)', the single peaked in the British Top 10. Three further hit singles followed, namely 'In All The Right Places', 'So Natural' and 'Little Bit Of Heaven', while Stansfield's album *So Natural* crashed into the chart at No.6 during the November. There really was no way this young singer could be held back, although her career would hit rocky times within a few months. Of the prestigious concerts in 1993, the most high profile was the Freddie Mercury tribute gala 'A Concert For Life', staged at Wembley Stadium. Among a host of contributing acts, Stansfield duetted with George Michael on the Queen track 'These Are The Days Of Our Lives', which, when released on the 'Five Alive EP', shot to No.1 in the British chart in May 1993.

Since 1993 Lisa Stansfield has been a stranger to the British charts. Her presence is missed, because her talent is rare.

'When a dance artist gets in the national Top 20, the dance market drops them, and what's really amazed me is the fact that so far I've managed to bridge both markets' – Lisa Stansfield

(Quotes: *Blues and Soul* magazine, 1989–91, interviews by Jeff Lorez)

November 1989

NEW KIDS ON THE BLOCK

You Got It (The Right Stuff)

'We ain't no saints. The press have given us this wholesome image. We are all very positive people' – Donald Wahlberg

Donald Wahlberg, born 17 August 1969 in Dorchester, Massachusetts, was responsible for recruiting his classmates to the membership of the group that would become known as New Kids On The Block. The line-up comprised Danny Wood Jr, born 14 May 1970 in Boston, Massachusetts, Jordan Knight, born 17 May 1971 in Worcester, Massachusetts, Jonathan Knight, born 29 November 1968, also in Worcester, and Joseph McIntyre, born 31 December 1972 in Needham, Massachusetts, who apparently replaced original group member Jamie Kelley.

They formed the group following a request from composer/producer Maurice Starr, late of the Johnson Brothers. With his brother Michael, Maurice had recorded a pair of noteworthy albums, namely *Flaming Starr* and *Spicey Lady*, released by RCA Records. When their recording career ended, Maurice moved into management, primarily promoting and overseeing the career of New Edition, an extremely successful young R&B group that included Bobby Brown in the line-up and which was modelled on Motown's Jackson Five.

Following the release of their first album, New Edition were enticed to sign a recording deal with RCA Records and Maurice Starr was excluded from the arrangement. 'After my down period,' he said, 'I went to work. I got in my car and said, "I'm going to find these five young white kids and put this group together."' Where better to search than at the Department of Education in Massachusetts, where, with assistance from the personnel boss, they contacted the William M. Trotter Elementary School in Roxbury and Wahlberg.

Using the group name Nynuk, Starr nurtured and groomed his young white protégés until they were sufficiently proficient to perform before a paying audience. During March 1984 the group did just that at the Joseph Lee School in Dorchester. Unhappy with the group name, the youngsters swiped their new title from one of the backing tracks they lipsynched to on stage, namely New Kids On The Block.

With Starr's industry colleague Larkin Arnold, who was responsible for Marvin Gaye's 'Sexual Healing' project, New Kids On The Block signed a lucrative recording deal with the black division of CBS Records during January 1986. Wheels turned quickly, and three months after the signing the group's first single, titled 'Be My Girl', was issued. Hyped by heavy promotion including a record-company launch ceremony, the single floundered, then bombed. Said McIntyre, 'Maybe our first record not doing too well was good for us. We tasted failure and perhaps learned how to avoid it.'

New Kids On The Block then embarked upon an American tour as

support act to the Four Tops before promoting their debut eponymous album via personal appearances that ranged from nightclubs to
record stores. The exposure failed; the album bombed. Nothing
seemed to work.

An American radio station came to the rescue. WRBQ in Tampa,
Florida, devoted regular airtime to the group's 'Please Don't Go Girl'
single, a cover version of Irving and the Twins' original, also a Starr
act. The unexpected interest in this title was sufficient to secure New
Kids On The Block as the support group to songstress Tiffany during
an across-America tour. This in turn led to the group's own trek,
which, at the tail end of 1988, included a trip to Japan. Said
McIntyre, 'It's real tough being on the road all the time but it's such
a positive experience meeting all our fans.'

Into 1989 New Kids On The Block were still hitting the tour trail
despite negligible chart presence. That, however, was to change in
March, when the title 'You Got It (The Right Stuff)', swiped from the
Hangin' Tough album, soared to No.3 in America. The mother album,
meanwhile, peaked at No.4, although it would stay on the listing for
at least two further years, passing platinum status eight times!

In June 1989 a track titled 'I'll Be Loving You (Forever)' which
Starr had composed for Smokey Robinson elevated his young
protégés to the top of the American chart. Said Starr, 'I was sitting
down at the piano and could not think of a song . . . It came together
subconsciously and I said, "This would be great for Smokey".' The
Motown star never heard the song; Starr's priority was New Kids On
The Block. To capitalise on the American chart-topper, the group's
first album was repromoted. Boosted by their popularity, it went on
to sell in excess of three million copies.

Flushed with success, New Kids On The Block returned to the top
of the respective American charts in the September with the 'Hangin'
Tough' single and album; indeed, the latter went on to sell more than
eight million units. According to Starr, 'We needed a song that
symbolised what we were going through. So we talked, and I said I
had an idea for a song called "Hangin' Tough".' Meanwhile, these
impressive chart positions encouraged CBS Records in Britain to
invite the youngsters for a promotional visit to coincide with the
release of the 'Hangin' Tough' project. The result was a Top 60 British
single.

While New Kids On The Block were in Britain, the fifth single from
the *Hangin' Tough* album, titled 'Cover Girl', was issued, reaching the
American Top 2 in the November. A month on, thanks to the intense
promotion, the group topped the British chart with 'You Got It (The
Right Stuff)', where it stayed for three weeks. The *Hangin' Tough*
album peaked at No.2. The promotional trip had finally paid off.

Back in America, and to close the year, the group issued the *Merry, Merry Christmas* album, which reached the Top 10, selling two million copies *en route*, had notched up a trio of top album titles and had toured for approximately 300 nights. Not bad! By the new decade, when New Kids On The Block mania exploded across the world, the group's stage act had been reworked to include highly intricate choreographed dance routines.

Their first outing of the '90s was the sentimental title 'This One's For The Children', a Top 10 American hit, the group's sixth. All profits from this title, by the way, were donated to the United Cerebral Palsy charity. In Britain the 'Hangin' Tough' single was eventually issued, presenting New Kids On The Block with their second chart-topper in January 1990.

Mid-1990 the youngsters' popularity reached boiling point; the world had gone New-Kids crazy! This was also the year when the industry honoured them by presenting them with a pair of American Music Awards in the Pop/Rock category for Best Album and Favourite Band, Duo or Group. The industry may have fêted the youngsters, but *Rolling Stone* magazine readers voted them the worst band, album, single and tour!

Touring also dominated 1990, starting with a frenzied American trek. According to Knight, 'When the kids come to our concerts there are no drinks or drugs. Everyone comes just to have a real good time.' Said Wahlberg, 'Some of our fans are real young, so their folks bring them to our concerts and they too seem to have a good time.' On the downside, though, Wahlberg admitted some more adventurous fans were a nuisance. 'We've had them get on to the floor where we're staying dressed up as hotel maids. It's weird. Sometimes we don't even know where we're staying and still they turn up.'

Their first European tour followed the across-America stint, and Wood injured his ankle on a stuffed toy thrown by a fan on to a Manchester stage. The injury necessitated the youngster returning to Boston for treatment. To coincide with the British tour, the 'Cover Girl' single was issued, peaking at No.4 during May 1990, followed a month later by 'Step By Step', a No.2 hit originally recorded by the Dynamic Superiors. Said Starr, 'The company thought it was a dud. Even some radio stations said it's not a hit record.' That was indeed true for the Dynamic Superiors, but not so for New Kids On The Block. The *Step By Step* album followed, entering the British listing at the top, a position repeated in America in the June.

Most of the young group's touring schedules and money-spinners were, of course, across America. The fortune earned from playing before full houses was phenomenal. However, a percentage of that fortune was stolen when, during a Canadian concert, armed thieves stole group merchandise estimated to be worth $250,000. Other adverse publicity at this time included Knight's bodyguard reputedly injuring two fans, while Wahlberg was accused of assaulting a magazine editor aboard a flight from Salt Lake City to Atlanta. Certainly this was the period of high-profile publicity, and all guaranteed maximum sales for the singles 'Tonight' and 'Let's Try It Again'/'Didn't I (Blow Your Mind?)', and a trio of music videos titled *Hangin' Tough*, *Step By Step* and *Hangin' Tough Live*, which sold in excess of three million copies. The total income earned by New Kids On The Block at this point was approximately $860 million!

By comparison, 1991 was marginally calmer on the recording front. The first single out, titled 'Games', faltered in the British Top 20, as did 'Call It What You Want' during the May, while in December the title 'If You Go Away' returned the youngsters to the Top 10 in Britain. The singles were promoted through another year crammed with tours on the seemingly never-ending American trail, earning New Kids On The Block the title of highest-paid entertainers in the country, beating Michael Jackson and Madonna.

Crossing the Atlantic during May 1991, New Kids On The Block performed at Wembley Arena, contributing to a benefit gala for Kurdish refugees. This performance was the first of eight nights at Wembley which earned the group over £1 million. Alongside the glowing British and American headlines, however, the group once again fell foul of the law. This time Gregory McPherson, a music teacher from a Massachusetts University, filed charges, claiming that Starr himself recorded the group's vocals, leaving them to lipsynch during their concerts. In response, New Kids On The Block interrupted their Australian tour to perform live in Los Angeles before filing a civil suit against McPherson for defamation. The music teacher subsequently dropped the charges, while Wahlberg quietly conceded that the group did use recorded backing vocals and Starr's harmonising during live performances!

Life was much quieter during 1993, when New Kids On The Block officially shortened their name to NKOTB (typesetters roared in appreciation!) and then broke free from Starr's production control to record their first album in three years. While locked in the recording sessions, the group's only significant release was 'Keep On Smiling'. Early 1994 marked the release of the *Face The Music* album, with tracks produced by Narada Michael Walden and others. NKOTB missed Starr's personal Midas touch, the project struggling into the British and American Top 40, while two extracted singles, 'Dirty Dawg' and 'Never Let You Go', also faltered.

The American dream was over. New Kids On The Block, or NKOTB, had finally out-danced and out-lipsynched their young adoring audiences, who had by now switched their allegiance elsewhere. The individual group members relocated with their personal fortunes into other musical avenues, but the phenomenon that had been created, originally said to be on a par with that of Beatlemania two decades earlier, was gone. Unlike the Fab Four, though, who can remember the New Kids On The Block songs that sold by the million?

'Music has given us something to aim for. Being in a group is like belonging to a basketball team. It keeps you off the streets' – Donald Wahlberg

(Quotes: *New Kids On The Block Official Annual 1991*)

December 1989

BAND AID II

Do They Know It's Christmas?

'I once said that we would be more powerful in memory than in reality. Now we are that memory' – Bob Geldof

The Band Aid single and subsequent related projects – including, of course, the spectacular Live Aid concert – remained in the public's memory for several months. One man persuading a host of British and American acts to give their time for free to raise funds for the starving people of Ethiopia was a feat nobody expected anyone to achieve. That the same man also persuaded record companies and other industries to likewise offer their facilities free of charge was another remarkable achievement.

Following the projects during 1985, the Live Aid idea was continued in Ireland during April 1986. Masterminded by the Irish end of the Live Aid fundraiser, the biggest music event known in the country was staged to encourage the public to pledge a job or money for an urgently required work-creation programme. Under the banner Self Aid, participating acts included Van Morrison, Clannad, the Boomtown Rats and Rory Gallagher.

From Ireland to London and British disco. During August 1986, over a hundred artists in the dance-music business recorded the track 'Give Give Give', penned by the Cool Notes member Steve MacIntosh and produced by Paul Hardcastle. Organised by DJ Steve Walsh – also owner of Total Control Records, responsible for issuing the single in October 1986 – participating artists included Beggar and

Co, Jaki Graham, Phil Fearon, Galaxy, Lenny Henry, Odyssey, Mel and Kim, Ruby Turner, Edwin Starr, Sheila Ferguson, Jean Carne, Hazell Dean and Boris Gardiner. 'Give Give Give' was launched on 1 November 1986, named as Disco Aid Day, when nightclubs and discos across Britain, Europe and America pledged to donate a percentage of their takings to the fund, while artists performed five-minute personal appearances in the club of their choice. All proceeds raised were earmarked for the Band Aid fund.

Two years on, the dream was still alive. In October 1988 more than 20 million people ran in 117 countries to help the world's starving people. Under the title 'Sport Aid's Race Against Time', it was the largest mass-participation event in history. To coincide with the event, a gala concert, 'Sport Aid '88', was staged in Sheffield, with artists like Heaven 17, Womack and Womack and Mica Paris participating. The concert kicked in with the words 'Every minute we spend here today, 29 kids will die in Africa.'

The public responded generously to all the Live Aid projects, although by now many believed more should be done to help those people in Britain whose lives were tormented by illness or homelessness. And, of course, with high-profile fundraising activities by the Aid functions, other less-publicised charities were feeling the financial pinch.

However, there was one more significant commercial contribution to Geldof's cause – Band Aid II, with a reworking of the track 'Do They Know It's Christmas?' It was felt the time was right for the single to be restyled, and to this end Cliff Richard, Kylie Minogue, Chris Rea, Jason Donovan, Lisa Stansfield, Sonia, Matt Goss and Marti Pellow recorded a second version under the production control of Stock, Aitken and Waterman. Like its predecessor, 'Do They Know It's Christmas?' by Band Aid II entered the British chart at No.1 in December 1989.

By 1992 the Ethiopian fund was closed, having raised in excess of $144,000,000. Geldof stated that 49 per cent of the money was earmarked for development projects, 49 per cent for relief work and 2 per cent for administration costs. In admitting he never expected to raise such a staggering amount in seven years, Geldof said he did not want Band Aid to die altogether. 'Our idea was to open the avenues of possibility. The possibilities of ending hunger in Africa are there. There can be other Band Aids; there must be others, in new times, in different ways.'